Cultural Typologies of Love

Victor Karandashev

Cultural Typologies of Love

Springer

Victor Karandashev
Department of Psychology and Counselor Education
Aquinas College
Grand Rapids, MI, USA

ISBN 978-3-031-05345-0 ISBN 978-3-031-05343-6 (eBook)
https://doi.org/10.1007/978-3-031-05343-6

This Springer imprint is published by the registered company Springer Nature Switzerland AG
The registered company address is: Gewerbestrasse 11, 6330 Cham, Switzerland

*To my international friends and colleagues
who shaped my multicultural mind and
supported my cultural exploration of love*

Abstract for the Book

Cultural Typologies of Love offers an *integrative approach* and provides a general framework for the construction of *personal* and *cultural typologies of love models.* Chapter 1 of the book presents the culturally diverse conceptions, experiences, expressions, actions, and relationships, which constitute the multi-faced, multi-level, and multi-cultural constructs of love. Chapter 2 outlines and elaborates methodologies and methods for categorization of love into cultural typologies of various kind. Chapters 3 through 8 present several most common cultural models of love, along with their typologies. Among those are evolutionary socio-biological models, sexual models, passionate and affectionate models, romantic models, rational models of love, and the models of love as social connections. Each chapter describes several other models and typologies, which come under their broad categories. Each chapter integrates multiple publications reporting cultural and cross-cultural studies and findings from across the world, presenting relatively comprehensive reviews and systematic descriptions of the *typologies* and *cultural models of love*. The book sets up the background and perspectives for further typological exploration of love in a cross-cultural perspective.

The key features of the book are as follows:

- A comprehensive review of the love conceptualization, strategies, and methods of categorization for construction of cultural models of love
- A comprehensive review of multiple research perspectives in the studies of conceptualizations, models, and typologies of love across world cultures
- A comprehensive review of the cultural models and typologies in international perspective
- A comprehensive review of the cultural models and typologies from interdisciplinary scientific perspective

The book *Cultural Typologies of Love* offers an *integrative approach* and provides a general picture of how the cultural diversity of love conceptions, experiences, and expression builds *individual* and *cultural typologies of models of love* that have been present in societies across the world. The book makes an integration of cultural and cross-cultural studies on how culture affects our experiences and expressions of love into systematic description of *types* and *cultural models of love*. The comprehensive reviews of methodology and findings, which are presented in the book, set up the background and perspectives for further cross-cultural exploration of love.

Keywords Across the Book (not Chapter Specific)

Love across cultures, Models of love, typologies of love, Personal models of love, Scientific models of love, Evolutionary models of love, Ecological models of love, Social models of love, cultural models of love, Individualistic models of love, Collectivistic models of love, Western models of love, North American models of love, Western European models of love, East European models of love, Eastern models of love, East-Asian models of love, American models of love, Puritan model of love, Mormon models of love, Victorian model of love, Chinese models of love, Japanese models of love, Indian models of love, African models of love, Ancient Greek models of love

The names of countries and cultures can also be among the keywords.

Acknowledgments

I am lucky and appreciative to meet so many international friends and colleagues in my life. These short-term cross-cultural encounters and long-term intercultural relationships have shaped my multicultural mind, which is open to various individual and cultural views of relationships and transnational perspectives. I am also grateful for their friendly and collegial continuous support of my cross-cultural explorations of love.

Other words of appreciation are to Sharon Panulla and her Springer editorial and production team. They have been supportive of my cross-cultural plans, responsive and responsible, patiently understanding, and gently encouraging to complete the book before too long.

Introduction

The Historical Origins of Love Categorization

For centuries, philosophers, theologists, historians, writers, poets, artists, and musicians in many societies have been contemplating about love in its abstract and concrete sense. The others have not been thinking about love, they just have been feeling, expressing, and doing something what the thinkers would call love. The abstract concept of love was discovered and explored by scholars quite late and only in some advanced cultures, such as Ancient Egyptian, Greek, Roman, and Chinese. Many other people in many other cultures understood love very concretely, practically, contextually, situationally, and externally, rather than internally (see for review, Karandashev, 2017). Love—the same way as other emotions—was actional and interactional, rather than experiential. *What you do* was more important than *what you feel*. Real behaviors and actions of love were more important than love attitudes, desires, and intentions. People shied away from thinking, talking, and sharing their emotions. Internal experience and expression of emotions were less worthwhile for social life than external behavior and actions (see for review, Karandashev, 2021a, 2021b). Relationships were practical and interactional, rather than introspective and emotional. Partners discussed *what they did*, rather than what *they felt*. Bonds were practical, rather than emotional. Emotions were just the concomitants.

Majority of people have been busy and preoccupied with their survival, day-to-day tasks, duties, and chores. They did love, rather than thought or talked about it. They liked sex, cared for their children, respected elders, revered seniors, enjoyed entertainments, appreciated beauty, and worshipped their Gods. They planted, harvested, hunted, domesticated animals, cooked food, and cleaned their dwellings. Doing all these specific things was their love for each other. The love was imbedded and imbodied in daily life and relationships. They *lived through love*, rather than reflected it. They just did not have much leisure time for that, and therefore, maybe not much interest to do this.

Theoretical contemplation about love was a luxury of wealthy and noble people who were free from daily concerns for survival. They had time available for education. They had time for meditation, thinking, painting, sculpting, and writing. Since social connections and relationships are the essential parts of the life, they were the topics of special scholarly, theological, and artistic attention. Scholars, philosophers, theologists, artists, and writers explored various positive connections between people in various social and relationship contexts. They dared to call some of these connections "love" or other similar words conveying this meaning (see for review, Karandashev, 2019).

The Scientific Puzzle of Love

Love scholarship has had an abundance of publications throughout centuries and especially in the twentieth century. Empirical researchers in several scientific disciplines have actively engaged in the exploration of love and relationship in recent decades. This area of study seems proliferating in the number and diversity of topics. The construction of the huge love puzzle is in progress. Qualitative and quantitative methods explore from different perspectives the various concepts, emotional experiences, expressions, and relationships, which we can call love. Researchers from many countries across the world have been engaging in love studies. They provide their valuable knowledge in a multifaceted and colorful picture of what love is. The love puzzle has been becoming more cross- and multi-cultural (see for review, Hill, 2019; Karandashev, 2017, 2019; Mayer & Vanderheiden, 2021).

The main point is that *love is a multifaceted and multidimensional construct*—the moto that I elucidated in *Cross-Cultural Perspectives on the Experiences and Expressions of Love* (Karandashev, 2019). Love is also multi-conceptual and multi-layered construction.

The allegory of the "The Elephant in the Dark" is very suitable in this case. It has been enduring throughout the centuries as an illustration of limitations that our perception and cognition have in understanding a whole object. In the tale, an elephant was exhibited in a dark room. Several men touched and felt the elephant in the dark. Depending upon where they touched it, they believed the elephant should be like a waterspout (trunk), a fan (ear), a pillar (leg), and a throne (back). The versions of the story have been known across times and cultures in Hinduism, Jainism, Buddhism, and Sufism as an example of the limits of individual cognition. The American poet John Godfrey Saxe (1816–1887) introduced the story to the Western people retelling the Indian parable "The Blind Men and the Elephant" (Saxe, 1884). Each man was partly in the right and all were in the wrong.

The metaphor served as a methodological and substantive analogy in several disciplines, such as physics and biology. I believe the studies of love also resemble the research approach wisely described in that metaphor.

The researchers have gained an abundance of knowledge about what love is. Numerous scholarly viewpoints, theories, professional observations, and empirical findings are available in publications and unpublished manuscripts. However, many researchers are not aware of this huge amount of knowledge, being bound by their school of thought, and the need to "fit in theory" and "fill in gap." Sometimes, being overwhelmed with their current research projects, they even don't have time to read each other works beyond the publications of their pressing needs. Therefore, these multiple pieces of discoveries and findings still do not come together in the beautiful and coherent puzzle of love.

Despite the centuries of scholarly contemplations and recent century of empirical research, the science of love is still piecemeal and patchy. Many new theories and empirical findings are available. They add new pieces in the puzzle of love. They, however, still do not come together in a relatively comprehensive picture of what love is. It is normal. Love, as we'll see in the following chapters, is so multifaceted and manifold construct that can be rather a set of related constructs, not one. New theories open new horizons, angles of view, and perspectives.

Personal Evolution in Understanding of Love

This book—the same way as my previous books (Karandashev, 2017, 2019, 2021a, 2021b)—is a tribute to the diversity of love. It strives to build a *comprehensive multicultural compilation and representation* of the *complex science of love*, with a strong belief that *culture matters* in adequate understanding of love.

The *Cultural Typologies of Love* aims to integrate the findings from various disciplines in comprehensive interdisciplinary representations of their varieties. It naturally and logically evolves from my previous scholarly explorations of love as biological, individual, and cultural construct presented in my earlier books on these topics.

The book *Romantic Love in Cultural Contexts* (Karandashev, 2017) presented a historical review and recent anthropological explorations of how love functions in specific cultural contexts. That book is characterized by an emic, rather than an etic approach. This means that the concept of love was described in terms of its cultural aspects and functioning, rather than in terms of any theoretical and comparative scheme (as in an etic approach). It presented the *holistic approach* to the concept of romantic love from the perspective of the culture under review, rather than from the perspective of an outsider.

That book defined a narrative framework for the love research *within* cultures. It is evidently *descriptive* showing the extensive anthropological, historical, journalistic, and sociological representations of the *love* (largely romantic) within specific historical and cultural contexts. It has demonstrated that having a lot in common, the cultural conceptions of love vary across time and societies bearing culturally specific connotations, associations, and interpretations.

Different from that holistic and multifaceted perspective, my recent book *Cross-cultural perspectives on the experience and expression of love* (Karandashev, 2019) presented an *analytic cross-cultural approach*. The book has further elaborated conceptualization of love constructs across various cultures in a *comparative perspective.* It reviewed and summarized the multiple studies in philosophy, sociology, journalism, linguistics, psychology, and anthropology, published over the recent 70 years, which investigated a cross-cultural diversity of love experiences and expressions. That book provided an analytical view of cross-cultural findings on the topic. It was intentionally descriptive and comparative to illuminate and highlight the cross-cultural diversity of love. It demonstrated that people across the world developed their culturally specific understandings of love that was suitable to communicate within their societies. The experiences and expressions of love evolved accordingly. The book presented a *systematic* review of love experiences and expressions in various societies across the world. It provided a *comprehensive reviews* and *analytical comparisons* of multiple studies which have investigated love in cross-cultural perspectives.

The Main Highlights and Structure of This Book

While previous books were mostly *descriptive, comparative, and analytic*, this book *Cultural Typologies of Love* is rather *integrative.* It attempts to present a *systemic view* on *love concepts, categories, and typologies* on both *individual and cultural levels.* The *interdisciplinary* and *multi-methodological approaches* are still at work presenting multifaceted and multilayered categories of love.

Chapters 1 and 2 are introductory and methodological in their contents. They set a background for the remaining, more content-specific chapters, in which the diverse scope of cultural typologies and models of love is presented.

Chapter 1 "*Love concepts, their diverse contents, and definitions*" analyzes the complex conceptual reality and phenomenology of *many things*, which we call love and other closely related constructs. Among those are the basic and complex units of subjective internal experience of love, such as sensations, appraisals, emotions, moods, attitudes, traits, and values, which represent a multilevel structure of love experience. Among those are the units of objective external reality of love, such as expressions, actions, interactions, behaviors, relationships, and love as evolving process. The chapter also highlights the need for theoretical clarity in conceptual and operational definitions of what love is in a particular study. Various types of scientific definitions are possible. The distinctions between individual and relationship levels of love, as well as between personal and cultural models of love are important to include.

Chapter 2 "*Models and typologies of love*" suggests the integrative typological approach to the studies of love. It defines the concepts of models and types and specified their varieties. Among those are *scientific, personal, cultural models of love*, the *ideal models of love*—what people think about love, and *real models of love*—how they really experience love. This chapter proposes methodological strategies and specific methods of categorization for the construction of individual and cultural typologies. Methods of *categorization* include the selection of specific representations of categories, implementation of the data transformation, and techniques of statistical analyses. Personal, cultural models, and typologies of love are presented as illustrative examples.

The remaining Chaps. 3 through 8 present the varieties of individual and cultural typologies of love, which are grouped around the general umbrella types. These classifications of typologies are based largely on the salient features, which the typologies within a chapter have in common. These classifications are contingent upon these criteria, not strictly defined. Some specific models and typologies can be flexibly classified into other groups based on other features. Some models and typologies are complex in terms of defining characteristics and, therefore, can be attributed to several groups. The models and typologies in the chapters are not necessarily exclusive from each other in their group memberships, but they can be rather overlapping. They also can be in subordinate and superordinate relations with each other, being more general or more specific categories. Their *topological membership representations* can be of different configurations.

Chapters 3 through 8 look at some traditional conceptualizations of love, such as passionate, romantic, and companionate love, consolidating the constructs, attributes, and findings, partly presented earlier (Karandashev, 2019), in a more integrative picture. These chapters also present other conceptualizations of love, which are less scholarly established, less conventional, and less frequently considered in a general comprehensive puzzle of love. All these models of love have been reviewed in these chapters based on extensive scholarship and empirical research.

Chapter 3 "*Socio-biological models of love*" describes the basic principles, levels, and processes which are pertinent to evolutionary models of love. It shows how the evolution of biological, genetic, ecological, technological, and cultural parameters characterizing human species and societies shape corresponding models of love. The chapter reviews the sexual reproduction, social-bonding, and pair-bonding models of love.

Chapter 4 "*Sexual models of love*" presents *sexual love*, *sensual*, and *erotic* models of love. The arguments have made that *sex* and these forms of love are psychologically different realities of sexual life. The chapter shows the cultural differences in understanding the relations between *sex, love,* and *sexual love*. The freedom of sexual relationships, including premarital sex, is considered in a cross-cultural perspective across times and societies. The chapter also presents evidence that *sensual and erotic models of love* are special and distinct types of love closely intertwined with *sexual love*.

Chapter 5 "*Models of passionate and affectionate love*" describes these two models comprehensively, in a consolidated way. Basic components of *passionate model* are considered in a cross-cultural perspective, demonstrating its ubiquitous nature and cultural variety. The chapter also highlights *affectionate and muted models of love*, which are less visible in modern scholarship, yet widely present in the older centuries and in many modern societies.

Chapter 6 "*Models of romantic love*" describes one of the most scholarly visible forms of love, yet frequently misunderstood in its content and features. Some of its characteristics are shared with other models, while the others are unique. Several salient attributes of romantic love, such as its sexual and passionate nature, are reviewed in comprehensive cross-cultural perspectives. The *specific romantic beliefs and perceptions*, especially *idealization*, which make *romantic* love "*romantic,*" received special emphasis in the chapter. *Parasocial and narcissistic models of love* are elucidated in light of the *romantic features*.

Chapter 7 "*Models of love as social connections*" characterizes several models, which come under this umbrella feature. Among those are *community-bonding and pair-bonding* models of love, the models of love as *attachment, commitment,* and *union, companionate and friendship* models, *altruistic and benevolent* models.

Chapter 8 "*Models of rational love*" presents *realistic and pragmatic models* of love, which are opposites of romantic models. They have been common *in real life* of people throughout centuries. The modern scholarship has elaborated several specific rational models, which consider love in light of such characteristics as *investment, social,* and *economic exchange*. The *communal and equitable models of love* are juxtaposed here—they are rational, yet different from others in the group. This chapter also describes such psychologically disengaged love, which can be labeled as *role-play, gamified,* and *ludus* models of love. They came under the umbrella term of *performing models* because they are the exhibiting and demonstrative ways of love, rather than really experiencing ones. Their joy is the joy of an actor and gambler.

I shall acknowledge that many important and interesting models and typologies are not included, mostly due to the limited volume of the book. For example, parental love—maternal and paternal—is important, however, it is very complex and multifunctional, so it can fit to many different categories. Actually, it is represented in the suitable chapters and sections, just not separately and not on its own. In the same vein, religious models of love are also presented in the contexts of appropriate sections, yet not as a whole model on its own. Among other models not included in the book are the modern virtual models of love in social media, hook-up cultural model, and others.

The book *Cultural Typologies of Love* offers an *integrative approach* and provides a general picture of how the cultural diversity of love conceptions, experiences, and expression builds *individual* and *cultural typologies of models of love* that have been present in societies across the world. The book makes an integration of cultural and cross-cultural studies on how culture affects our experiences and expressions of love into systematic description of *types* and *cultural models of love*. The comprehensive reviews of methodology and findings, which are presented in the book, set up the background and perspectives for the further cross-cultural exploration of love.

The book *Cultural Typologies of Love* may have practical importance as well. Recent decades witnessed the increased cultural migration and higher frequency of blended cultural communities. The rate of intercultural romantic relationships and marriages has increased. Therefore, the book provides cross-cultural knowledge for a better understanding of partners in intercultural couples and, therefore, can be helpful for practitioners in relationship, marriage, and family counseling. They will be able to understand better that their clients have in their minds the explicit or implicit *cultural model of love*, which they grew up with, as well as the *typological models of love*, which they develop for themselves based on their individual and cultural experiences.

References Hill, C. T. (2019). *Intimate relationships across cultures: A comparative study*. Cambridge University Press.

Karandashev, V. (2017). *Romantic love in cultural contexts*. Springer.
Karandashev, V. (2019). *Cross-cultural perspectives on the experience and expression of love*. Springer.
Karandashev, V. (2021a). *Cultural models of emotions*. Springer.
Karandashev, V. (2021b). Cultural diversity of romantic love experience. In C. Mayer & E. Vanderheiden (Eds.), *International handbook of love* (pp. 59–79). Springer.
Mayer, C. H., & Vanderheiden, E. (Eds.). (2021). *International handbook of love: Transcultural and transdisciplinary perspectives*. Springer.
Saxe, J. G. (1884). *The poems of John Godfrey Saxe*. Houghton.

Contents

About the Author

Victor Karandashev is Professor of Psychology at Aquinas College, Grand Rapids, Michigan. He is a scholar with extensive international and cross-cultural experience and interests. He has conducted research on international psychology in several European countries, including universities in Germany, Norway, Russia, Sweden, Switzerland, and the UK. He was a visiting professor and a Fulbright Scholar in the USA. He has presented his work related to international and cross-cultural psychology at many conferences. He co-edited three volumes of *Teaching Psychology around the World* (2007, 2009, 2012). His major area of research interests is the studies of love and culture, a topic about which he has published several articles, chapters, and monographs. His recent books *Romantic Love in Cultural Contexts* (2017), *Cross-Cultural Perspectives on the Experience and Expression of Love* (2019), and *Cultural Models of Emotions* (2021) are among the most distinguished interdisciplinary contributions to the field.

Chapter 1
Love Concepts, Their Diverse Contents, and Definitions

1.1 Multifaceted Concepts of Love

1.1.1 Variety of the Meanings of Love

Love as an Elusive Concept

Everybody knows what love is. However, while individuals are talking about love, they may keep in mind different things. This can be passion of love as a *highly aroused emotion*, which a young lover experiences in presence of a beloved. This can be a *loving relationship* between loving partners. This can be *adoration* and *respect to God*. This can be *maternal love*. This can be *aesthetic admiration of a thing*, of *an activity*, of *a food*, etc., as in frequently said expression "I love it." Laypeople frequently use the verb of *love* in place of *liking*.

Love is a widely used word, at least in modern English. It is used in many different contexts and in different meanings, and people generally understand each other. Communicators know what they are talking about – just from the context of situation, conversation, and relationship. They usually understand without extended explanations what kind of love they mean.

Nevertheless, misunderstanding happens between laypeople, as well as between scholars. *People do not always mean what they say*. Our daily discourse tends to use many double meanings, hidden messages, and vague statements to avoid straight, yet awkward responses. "Yes" does not always mean "yes"; "no" does not always mean "no." The context of communication means a lot for adequate comprehension. It is true for people in some *low-context* West-European *cultures* and the USA. It is even more true for the *high-context* Japanese and Chinese *cultures* (see for review Karandashev, 2021a, 2021b). Scholars of love are also quite prone to such imprecision and biases in their academic communication, especially in the topic of love and relationships.

V. Karandashev, *Cultural Typologies of Love*,
https://doi.org/10.1007/978-3-031-05343-6_1

Love is a concept that appeared in the lexicon of people quite late in their historical evolution. Many other words have been used to denote various experiences, relationships, and types of love. Apparently, they were sufficient for many daily situations of their life. The word "love" itself became a result of high abstraction of thinking which some people in some cultures reached in their cultural evolution. It must be really challenging to find *one very general word* for so many diverse experiences, situations, and relationships. The word *love* evolved yet used for many different things. *Polysemy* occurs in many languages: a word can convey multiple meanings and have contiguity of meanings in a semantic field. Some cultures did not need such an abstract word as love; other words meet their communication needs (see for review Karandashev, 2017, 2019).

Love in Its Diversity of Kinds, Constructs, Meanings, and Types

Love is quite subjective and multifaceted reality to define it objectively and precisely.

Scholars strive to explore love objectively, yet they inevitably succumb to subjective understanding and interpretation. Some consider *love* as *sex*; others as *passion*; others as *intimacy*, *commitment*, or *compassion*; yet others as *attachment*. These words are frequently used as synonymous to each other. All their similarities are true, at least metaphorically or metonymically, but only partially true. Love can be the sex in one or another sense – you may recall the expression "making love." The onset of love is frequently passionate. Evolving love is accompanied by increasing psychological intimacy. Love admits some personal commitment to a partner for a short or long time. And occasionally, love is on need for a compassionate attitude. Thus, the concept of love can embrace any of these meanings or all together.

Different Planes of Love

The word *love* can stand for the reality of an individual internal experience or the reality of an interpersonal relationship. Therefore, it would be worthwhile to keep in mind that many debates and disagreements occur because people discuss different things, although they think they are discussing the same subject. Or vice versa, they discuss the same thing, even though they think they are discussing different subjects. Definitions are useful in many cases to avoid such confusions.

The word *love* is used to denote many *different things – planes, realms, areas, or spheres of reality*, which people call *love*. These can be the different kinds of love, depending on its objects and actors/subjects: child, parent, God, friend, dating partners, spouse, stranger, and "everyone." These can be any specific feeling or attitude, in which love embodies its meaning: passion, affection, compassion, intimacy, attachment, or commitment. These can be different emotional, cognitive, and behavioral processes and states of love. These can be different types of relationships. They are reviewed in the following sections.

The Varieties of Love

Love differs in *its kinds,* or *varieties,* depending on an object and subject/actor of love. These are maternal love, paternal love, love for God, romantic love, the love of children to parents, etc. For individuals, these kinds of love may be separate in their meaning and function or intertwine. They can transfer their energy from one to another. My young friend once shared her concern with uncle asking him: how to know that you genuinely love a man. Her uncle told: you truly love a man when you want to have a child with him. This example shows that romantic love can be closely intertwined and transferred into parental love.

Love in Its Salient Meanings

Love differs in the *salient meaning*, *value*, and prevalent *attitudes*. The *defining construct* of love may differ across individuals and cultures. Some equate love with *passion*; others with *compassion*, *sex, intimacy,* or *commitment*; yet others with *attachment*. Some may associate love with several of these constructs and with some others as well. *Love* is *a social construct*, and individuals construct their own *models of love* from various building blocks (e.g., emotions, attitudes), which can be associated with love in accord with cultural and personal conceptions of love. Theoretically, it is likely that the only *own construct of love* is *liking*, as a positive emotion or attitude toward another thing, person, or situation. All other constituents of love (constructs) might be just the concomitants of love which people tend to include in the extended, elaborated, and embellished concept of love. Thus, love can be understood in a narrow meaning or a broader sense.

The English *word love* is good and lovely, yet not perfect for adequate understanding of each other, for scholarship, and for research. It is contextual, multi-meaningful, and sometimes ambiguous. The word *love* has come in the modern English as a result of high abstraction and generalization of many things, which they presumably have in common. It is frequently used among scholars and educated people in many modern cultures inclined to abstract thinking. Yet, for many lay-people the *word love* may be not frequent in their lexicon. When they use it, they use it in specific meanings, like *sex*, *care*, *affair*, and so on.

Many historical cultures, as well as the cultures of nowadays across the world, do not have the *word love* (see review Karandashev, 2017, 2019). You know, for instance, that ancient Greeks used several words to denote different meanings of love. In the history of other cultures, the *word love* was also not in their regular lexicon. Anthropological studies of nineteenth–twentieth centuries have shown that *love* in the lexicon of many nowadays societies is expressed in several words denoting various specific meanings, rather than an abstract idea like in English.

We shall not shy away from many good *love words*, which scholars have been using for a long time. They may still be adequate. The overuse in scholarship and research of the vague words like *love and romantic*, instead of others, which denote more concrete and specific meanings, can obscure our scientific understanding.

Anyway, the *love* and *relationship words* shall be defined, not just assumed, in the context of scholarly communication.

Psychological Complexity of Love Phenomena

The meaning of *love* differs in the empirical reality of emotional, cognitive, and behavioral processes, states, dispositions, and relationships, which researchers investigate. The word *love* can stand for the *basic emotion, complex emotion, personal disposition of an individual,* subjective realities of mental and behavioral experiences and processes, or for the *relationship between individuals, their actions, and interactions,* objective realities.

Love as individual experience engages three sorts of processes and states: *emotional, cognitive, and behavioral.* They can be (1) situational, short-term, mid-term, or long-term, (2) be aware by a person in more or less degree, and (3) be more concrete or general in their effect on an individual.

Subjective emotional components of love involve *sensory experiences, basic emotions, complex emotions, moods, attitudes, traits,* and *values.*

Subjective cognitive components of love involve *personal models of love*; adopted *cultural models of love*; *other expectations*, which a person has; *appraisals* of situation; current *perceptions and interpretations* of partners and their actions; and *retrospective reflections* of all these experiences and relationships.

Behavioral emotional components of love involve *motives, action tendencies, expressions, actions/reactions, habits, intentions, deeds, typical behaviors,* and the plots and stories, which people live through.

These emotional, cognitive, and behavioral processes and states work together in parallel and in interaction with each other. Systematization and investigation of their interactions and integrations are worthwhile for the construction of the future complex and beautiful science of love.

Love as relationship is an interactive process which involves two or more persons with their motivations, actions, and reactions, with their appraisals, experiences, and expressions. Love is a sequence of events, episodes, scripts, and stories. The actions and interactions can be mental and behavioral. A beloved one may not even know that someone loves him/her. One, *an actor of love*, loves another one, *an object of love.* In case of partnership love, both partners are actors and objects of love at the same time.

It is worthwhile to distinguish all these various aspects of love and integrate in the future complex conception of love, which will be constructed someday.

Love Emotions and Love Dispositions

Love engages a constellation of emotions and dispositions. Love can be situational, episodic emotions, or mood. Today you love, tomorrow don't. Sounds familiar? Is it love? Yes, it is. Love is fluctuating emotions and moods. When it consistently and persistently penetrates emotional life of a person, it become a disposition, or love attitude. Thus, love is an interplay of emotions, moods, and attitudes.

It looks like people are capable of differentiating *love* as a *state-like* experience from love as *attitude-like* experience. Empirical evidence has been obtained at least in the samples of English and German students (Lamm & Wiesmann, 1997; Meyers & Berscheid, 1997).

In English (Meyers & Berscheid, 1997), the term *being in love* stands for a *state-like category* characterizing an emotionally charged state of excitement, infatuation, longing, and yearning for someone. It is a relatively short-lived emotional experience. Different from this, the *love* term is a higher-order generic and larger *category of attitude-like. Loving someone* is a long-term positive emotional disposition, a deeper affection, despite temporary fluctuation of episodic emotions. The feeling can be of moderate or low intensity.

In German (Lamm & Wiesmann, 1997), these terms have similar differences in meanings: "verliebt sein" versus "lieben." German students largely characterize the first one as *state-like* experiences of *liking someone as desire for interaction with other* and *being in love with someone* as *arousal*, while the second one as the *attitude-like* experience of *loving someone* as *trust in the other.*

Thus, the wording makes a difference in the meaning referring to the *being in love* (with somebody) as a *state* (emotion and mood) and *love* (somebody) as a *disposition* (attitude and trait). The similarity in English and German with regard to the meanings of "love" versus "be in love" and "lieben" versus "verliebt sein" is possibly related to the common Germanic origin of both languages. However, such lexical differentiation of these two verbs is present not only in English and German languages but also in French "être amoureux" versus "aimer," in Portuguese "estar apaixonado" versus "amar," in Russian "быть влюбленным" versus "любить," in Finnish "olla rakastunut" versus "rakastaa," and in Persian "Aaghegh Boodan (عاشق بودن)" versus "Eshgh Varzidan (عشق ورزیدن). It is worth noting that in many of these expressions, the verb "be in love" characterizes the passive or descriptive nature of a situational emotional experience of love, while the verb "love" characterizes the active or dispositional nature of an attitudinal action tendency of love.

Love as a Relationship

Love can also denote the *love relationship* between an actor of love (lover) and an object of love (loved one). The word *love* in this case is a shortcut for the word *love relationship*. The relationship, emotions, and dispositions between actor and object of love can be unidirectional, when actor loves object, yet not vice versa (as in case of unrequited love), or bidirectional, when an actor loves object, while object in turn is an actor of love and loves another actor of love as an object (as in case of mutual love). *Love relationships* of youngsters with sexual interest in each other are often called *romantic relationship*. The word *romantic relationship* is frequently used as a euphemism for sexual, or sexually related relationships. Yet, its meaning is still vague.

Many modern laypeople and scholars tend to shy away from the word *love* in this relationship meaning, replacing it with the word *romantic relationship, or just relationship*. They believe that the word *love*, and especially *romantic love*, is too idealistic, too lovey-dovey, and elevated from everyday reality of relationship.

The word *romantic relationship* is frequently used as simply conventional indication on sexually saturated early stage of relationship before marriage or breakup. Even though it is not quite adequate, it seems the word *romantic relationship* might be inevitable in modern public discourse and scholarship. The English lexicon is quite ambiguous in this regard. The words can mean something different depending on the context and instead of something else. The *boyfriends* and *girlfriends* are usually just *lovers*, or *dating* and *mating persons*, not the male and female friends. The *lovers* are frequently the *sexually engaged partners*, not admirers of a beloved. The same way, the word *romantic relationship* attempts to replace the meaning of dating or mating relationships, in other cases – the meaning of a relationship with sexual intensions or sexual relations. All these are not necessarily *romantic* ones. The word *romantic* has had a special meaning in scholarship for a long time (see for review Karandashev, 2017, 2019).

The early stages of relationship are not always *romantic* and can be purely sexual, realistic, or practical instead. The word *romantic* means idealized and beautiful (Karandashev, 2017, 2019). The words *early stage of relationship*, *dating*, or *mating* might be more adequate and specific in this meaning than *romantic relationship.* It should be also noted that the relationships of people in older ages and in *later stages of the relationship* might be also *romantic*. Alternatively, the world *love relationship* would be more adequate admitting its general and diverse meaning. Researchers shall use more specific words to denote the specific type of relationships, which they study.

Diverse Scholarship on Emotions and Love

Scholarship of love is interdisciplinary endeavor that involves history, literary studies, anthropology, sociology, psychology, and communication studies. These disciplinary approaches tend to favor their own theories and methodologies of emotions (see for review Karandashev, 2021a, 2021b; Roberts, 2013).

Researchers explore cultural ideas of love, as well as the reality of love experience and expression. They delve into the study of love on the *level of relationship* and on the *level of individuals*. In first case, love is an objective relationship construct (how it is observed by others), while in second case, love is an internal psychological construct (how it is observed by an individual).

On the level of relationship, they investigate actions and interactions between individuals. In this case, love commonly means positive connections between people in distant or close relationship. The love relationship is characterized by frequency of interactions, the means of contacts, reciprocity, compatibility, etc. Love as the relationship is an objective reality observable by others. It is a characteristic of two (or more) individuals and their relations. Love *on relationship level* assumes that individuals experience emotional processes, states of love, and dispositions *on individual level.*

On the *level of individual*, researchers explore internal emotional experiences and external expressions. They investigate *emotional appraisals* of events and *emotions of love and liking*, which can be mixed with other emotions. In this case, love is a momentary state, or surge. It is a short-term process, which arises as an emotional response to an event. It is short-lasting emotion. Love can also be an *attitude* or *emotional disposition of love*. On the *level of individual*, researchers can also explore the actions and interactions between individuals how they are perceived by an individual.

The *word love* can stand for a cultural idea, feeling, emotion, action, attitude, and relationship. These conceptual realities, which are equally labeled with a beautiful word *love*, are important things to distinguish in scholarship to avoid confusion and misunderstanding.

1.1.2 Love as Emotion and Emotional Process

Love as Emotional Process

An individual can experience love as an emotion – a short-lived emotional feeling that last for seconds or minutes. These are the moments or upsurges of love. Even during such short time, love unfolds as a complex bio-psycho-social emotional process, which engages the antecedent events eliciting love emotions, appraisals of the events, patterns of physiological reactions, subjective experiences, bodily sensations, expressive behaviors, emotional regulation, and action tendencies.

Emotions fulfill *adaptive functions* of an individual. In a *survival-related function*, emotions trigger prompt adaptive responses to typical situations. In a *communicative function*, emotions signal others about internal state of the individual (Plutchik, 1982). In this sense, *emotions* are *stereotypical adaptations* and *responses to typical challenges* of the life. Behavioral reactions usually involve visceral components, such as elevated blood pressure and increased heart rate, and somatic components, such as typical posture and increased muscle tone. Emotions typically evolve in the sequence of three groups of processes: (1) primary evaluations as appraisals, (2) feelings as subjective experiences, and (3) responses, such as visceral and motor responses (Köteles, 2021).

From componential-dynamic approach, emotions evolve over time while an individual interacts with environment and other people (e.g., Ekman & Davidson, 1994; Frijda, 1986; Gross, 2002; Lazarus, 1991; Matsumoto & Hwang, 2012; Scherer, 1984; see for detailed review Karandashev, 2021a, 2021b). The studies throughout recent decades have found cultural similarities and variations in various domains and components of emotional process (see for detailed review Matsumoto & Hwang, 2012; Mesquita & Frijda, 1992; Mesquita & Leu, 2007). Likewise, love can be investigated as an emotional process from componential-dynamic approach.

Love can be a basic emotion when it is experienced as a single unit of emotional experience, like joy, excitement, happiness, anger, and sadness (Lazarus..., Shaver ...). Love can also be a complex emotion when it is comprised of several basic emotions. Love emotion is complex in conjunction with sadness when a loved one is leaving, in conjunction with empathy/compassion emotion when the loved is suffering, or in conjunction with anger when a loved has betrayed.

Primary evaluation of an object, person, situation, or event is called *appraisal* (Arnold, 1960; Reisenzein, 2006) and consists of primary, mostly automatic, and secondary components (Lazarus, 1991). Cognitive *appraisal*, as an evaluation and interpretation of a situation, is linked to the possible emotions, which the situation triggers (Ellsworth & Scherer, 2003; Frijda, 1993; Moors, Ellsworth, Scherer, & Frijda, 2013; Scherer & Fontaine, 2019; Siemer, Mauss, & Gross, 2007).

Certain characteristics of the future, present, and past situations, which elicit emotions, and the ways how individuals appraise those, determine the quality and intensity of emotions (Roseman & Smith, 2001; Scherer, Schorr, & Johnstone, 2001). Being appraised differently, the same situations can cause different emotions. Being appraised similarly, different situations can cause similar emotions.

Scholars have proposed a variety of *dimensions of appraisal*. Among the major themes of appraisal are *goal conduciveness* and *goal achievement*, *certainty* and *control*, *attentional activity*, *coping ability*, *anticipated effort*, *responsibility*, *legitimacy*, *compatibility with norm or self*, *blaming other*, *self-blame*, *danger and threat*, *irrevocable loss*, *and helplessness* (Mauro, Sato, & Tucker, 1992; Smith & Lazarus, 1993).

The *love experiences*, *expressions*, *and actions* have received little attention in research from such a dynamic and componential perspective. The *dynamics and appraisals* of emotions involved in *love* have been rarely the subject matter in the science of love so far.

Appraisals and Relationship Emotions

Appraisal in love frequently occurs unconsciously, without deliberate and careful analysis of the love object. This often causes a sudden *surge of love* that arises naturally without intention – beyond a person's will. Falling in love at first sight is an example. An individual experiences instant, intense, and irresistible romantic attraction to another person at the first meeting. Something unknown in that person triggers the rapid unfolding of emotional process engaging love.

Appraisal in the occurrence of basic emotions has the core *relational themes* that describe (1) the relations between self, object, and environment and (2) an appraisal of event and an action or action tendency. According to Lazarus (1991), the major *theme of love* is characterized as affection, whereas the theme of *romantic love* includes "viewing the partner at a given moment in a highly positive way, probably but not necessarily with desire or passion, and the seeking of and yearning for sexual intimacy, which may have already been attained" (p. 276).

Several dimensions of appraisal are especially important for positive connection of one person to another which determine *relationship emotions*. These are (1) *pleasantness* vs. *unpleasantness* of the event; (2) *desirability* vs. *undesirability* of the event to the relationship; (3) *importance* vs. *irrelevance* of the event; (4) the *perceived globality vs. specificity* of the cause; (5) *what were the direct causes* of the event, *partner, self, or circumstances*; (6) *who can take credit*, or *who is to blame*, for the eliciting event; (7) the *perceived degree of control* of the situation by self and partner; (8) *responsibility of self and partner* for the event; (9) *typicality* of event (10) *uncertainty* vs. *certainty* in understanding the event; (11) *unpredictability vs. predictability* of the event; (12) *a number of perceived obstacles*; and (13) *anticipated efforts in coping* with the event (Fitness & Fletcher, 1993).

Two major objects of appraisal determine quality of emotions: a partner and relationship (Karandashev & Evans, 2019). Appraisal of partner can induce such emotions as attraction, affection, compassion, and admiration. Appraisal of relationship can induce such emotions as anxiety, joy, intimacy, and happiness.

Studies have shown that these appraisal themes and dimensions are linked to the experience of certain emotions (Lazarus, 1991; Oatley & Duncan, 1994; Smith & Lazarus, 1993). In particular, the appraisals of *other-blame* provoke *anger*, *self-blame* triggers *guilt*, *threat* and *danger* prompt *fear*, *irrevocable loss* and *helplessness* cause *sadness*, *goal conduciveness* and *goal achievement* activate *joy*, and *positive interpersonal encounter* excites *love* and other *positive interpersonal emotions*.

When Nezlek, Vansteelandt, Van Mechelen, and Kuppens (2008) examined the relations between these appraisals and emotions in natural situations of daily life using *experience sampling*, they found more complex relationships than expected. Some relationships between appraisals and emotions were stronger than others. The appraisal of *other-blame* was strongly associated with experience of anger. The appraisal of *self-blame* was strongly associated with experience of *guilt*; the appraisal of *threat*, with experience of *fear*; the appraisal of *loss*, with *sadness*; and the appraisal of *positive encounter*, with experience of *love*. Some emotions are linked with more than one appraisal. For example, the experience of *joy* was equally associated not only with *appraisal of success* but also with appraisal of situations as *positive encounters* and negatively correlated with *other-blame*.

As authors found (Nezlek et al., 2008), the links between emotions and appraisals vary across individuals depending on their sensitivity to situational cues, discriminative facility, and emotional reactivity to certain appraisals. The emotion-appraisal links, which authors found, may also be culturally specific – participants were from The Netherland (a western nation).

Other studies have shown that the relations between emotions and appraisals can vary across cultures (e.g., Mesquita & Ellsworth, 2001; Nezlek et al., 2008; Smith & Lazarus, 1993, see for review Karandashev, 2021a, 2021b). However, no sufficient cross-cultural data are available so far about appraisals associated with love emotions.

The studies conducted in Australia have demonstrated (Fitness & Fletcher, 1993) that *emotions* involved in *relationship* – such as love, hate, anger, and jealousy – have more complex, yet distinctive profiles of appraisal patterns in terms of the appraisal dimensions. For example, the profile of love is described in this summary description:

> Subjects feeling love for their spouses felt warm and relaxed and were thinking positively; they wanted to be close to their spouses and usually expressed their feelings to them, both
>
> verbally and nonverbally. In addition, love-eliciting events were appraised as pleasant, good for the relationship, and involving little effort. The cause of love was appraised as being global
>
> rather than specific. Subjects felt calm and relaxed before the eliciting event, and their partners' reactions were overwhelmingly positive. (p. 948)

Other appraisals of other life conditions and circumstances can generate passionate feelings of love. For example, appraising the *events as transformative*, a person is aware of them as moving "between greatly motive-inconsistent and greatly motive-consistent outcomes." Such appraisals generate mixed emotions, in which the affective states opposite in valence and of high intensity co-occur at the same time. This experience sparks passionate emotions (Roseman, 2017, p. 133).

Love as a Basic Emotion

Love can be a *situational experience* and in this sense be considered as an *emotion* among others, such as joy, happiness, sadness, fear, and anger. For people in many languages and cultures, *love* is among the most prototypical emotions (e.g., Fehr & Russell, 1984, 1991; Shaver, Schwartz, Kirson, & O'Connor, 1987).

Some scholars have placed *love* in the list of basic emotions (e.g., Lazarus, 1991; Shaver, Morgan, & Wu, 1996). The same way as happiness, joy, sadness, fear, and anger, they reasonably include *love* in the list of basic emotions. I believe it is correct considering the basic meaning of love in the sense of liking.

Other researchers have not included love as a basic emotion in their theories (e.g., Ekman, 1992a, 1992b; Frijda, 1986; Frijda, Mesquita, Sonnemans, & van Goozen, 1991; Izard, 1991; Oatley & Johnson-Laird, 1987). Instead, they considered love as a complex emotion, an emotionally charged attitude, and a disposition to respond emotionally to an object or person. I will review these conceptual approaches in the following sections.

The answer to the question whether love is a basic or not basic emotion depends on the criteria included in the definition of basic emotions. These criteria differ across scholars and may include distinctive universal signals, facial expressions, distinctive physiology and patterns of ANS and CNS responses, distinctive universals in antecedent events, brief duration, major themes of emotions, and distinctive subjective experience (Ekman, 1992a, 1992b, 1999; Ekman & Cordaro, 2011; Shaver et al., 1996).

One more challenge in this regard is ambiguity of interpretation of the word *love* when it is used as a stimulus. Presenting this stimulus word, researchers often do not know for sure which meaning participants – as laypersons – have in mind. This can be the simple basic meaning of *liking* – "I love it"; "I like her." In this case, *love/liking* can be considered as a basic emotion – the primary, unidimensional, indivisible emotional unit. The meaning of love can also be more complex when the emotion of *liking* is tightly intertwined with other emotions and attitudes involved in relationships. In the latter case, it may be *love/liking* as *affection*, or *passion*, or *intimacy*, or *attachment* – as a more complex emotion. In this sense, *love* is more complex emotional experience.

Thus, the views that consider love as a *basic emotion* or as a *complex emotion* may be compatible with each other. Yet, the specific meaning of the *concept of love* must be assured in conceptual and operational definition (see more about this in the following section). For me, the *basic* means the simplest, indivisible, categorical, unidimensional unit, while the *complex* means the united multidimensional structure of several basic emotions.

Love as a Complex Emotion

Love is a simple and basic emotion only in the meaning of liking. Otherwise, love is a complex emotion evolving as an intricate structure in the context of an emotional episode and its appraisal. This process engages other emotions, such as joy, happiness, jealousy, sadness, compassion, affection, and commitment as situational emotional experience. Although love is a core emotion of the episode, yet it manifests itself in the *joy of being together*, *happiness of love being reciprocated*, *sadness before separation*, etc. In case of such interpretation of the construct, *love* does not have its own emotional content; it is rather represented in combination of other emotions, which evolve in emotional episode depending on antecedent event and appraisal.

Love is a complex emotion changing its subjective internal appearance over time. Ekman (1992a, 1992b) viewed love as a mixture of basic emotions, rather than a pure emotion. Love is typically experienced not as a single emotion; instead it involves rather a blend of basic emotions. In the same vein, Izard (1991) considered love as an emotional phenomenon different from such discrete emotions as joy, anger, or sadness. Love can elicit the arousal of a variety of strong emotions. A lover can experience joy when encountering a beloved, sadness when separated from them, and anger when frustrated by unfair treatment. In their combinations they comprise complex emotions. Love can be a complex and fuzzy emotion, yet unlikely basic one.

Love as an emotional complex can engage a variety of emotions: joy and happiness of being together with loved one, fear of rejection, nostalgia of former happy times, anger toward people which hurt the beloved, etc. Therefore, love is not one emotion or feeling, but rather a constellation of various feelings that arise in different life circumstances and situations. They can be experienced as short-term or long-term. They are also culturally dependent.

Emotions are frequently grouped according to their major themes, such as *prosocial emotions* (McCullough, Bono, & Root, 2007; Stürmer, Snyder, & Omoto,

2005), *self-conscious emotions* (Lewis, 2008; Tangney & Fischer, 1995; Tracy & Robins, 2004), and *moral emotions* (Haidt, 2003; Tangney, Stuewig, & Mashek, 2007). These groups of emotions overlap with each other, and the emotions within these categories are complex, rather than basic ones. Which of these groups does the *emotion of love* belong to? We can theoretically contemplate about this.

It is likely a *prosocial emotion*; one study came in support of this assertion (Sugawara, Muto, & Sugie, 2018). As a positive emotion, love can be classified in the *other-oriented* category, versus *self-oriented* one. This categorization has been identified at the high level of abstraction in semantic organization of 132 positive-emotion words among students in Japan. At the basic level, *love* (*aijo*), along with *wonder* (*kantan*) and *awe/respect* (*ikei/sonkei*), was categorized within *other-oriented positive emotions*, whereas *peacefulness/joy* (*nagomi/yorokobi*), *enthusiasm* (*ikigomi*), and *pride* (*hokori*) were within *self-oriented positive emotions* (Sugawara et al., 2018). It is important to note that these two higher-order categories were revealed empirically in the hierarchical cluster analysis of the 132 terms sorted by students.

Generally, *love as a complex emotion* can include several basic or complex emotions which arise in *emotional episode* contingent on antecedent event and its appraisal. These can be joy, affection, or gratitude; passion, happiness, or pride; empathy, sympathy, or compassion; sadness, embarrassment, or anger; or regret, guilt, or shame.

Anyway, being basic or complex, *love* can be *situational*, *episodic*, or *state-like* experiences that resemble all characteristics of emotion. These are the phenomena, which Shaver et al. (1996) named as "momentary surges of love" (p. 86) that is characterized by a quick onset, a sudden rush of intense feelings, and brief duration – the rush may come and go.

It is important to note that the concepts of *love as emotion* and *love as disposition* (attitude) may not contradict to each other (Lazarus, 1991; Shaver et al., 1996). It is possible that emotional disposition is another form of emotion. Emotions can be experienced as *momentary surges*, *short-lived emotional episodes*, and *long-standing dispositions*. Love can be present as the *surge of love-moment* during a short period when a person feels *being in love* or *loving*. In such fleeting moments, the person may experience a quick onset and increasing intensity of love.

The Dimensions Describing Love Emotion

As any emotion, love consists of *pleasure* and *activation* as elemental individual processes, which a person can be consciously aware. From this position of a *core affect* (Russell & Barrett, 1999), love can be experienced as a (1) pleasant, unpleasant, or mixed emotion of (2) high or low intensity.

Other dimensions of emotional experience, which can be applicable to the studies of love, are *evaluation/pleasantness*, *potency-control*, *activation-arousal*, and *unpredictability* (e.g., (Alonso-Arbiol et al., 2006; Fontaine, Scherer, Roesch, & Ellsworth, 2007; MacKinnon & Keating, 1989; Osgood, May, & Mirron, 1975;

Shaver et al., 1987, 1996; Shaver, Murdaya, & Fraley, 2001; Shaver, Wu, & Schwartz, 1992), and they are cross-culturally applicable.

The dimensions of love emotions can also be categorized as self-centered, other-centered, and relationship-centered (e.g., Karandashev & Evans, 2019; Londero-Santos, Natividade, & Féres-Carneiro, 2020). Other possible dimensions of love as emotions are reviewed elsewhere (Karandashev, 2021a, 2021b).

Feelings associated with love, as any other emotion, unfold naturally and unconsciously during individual's engagement with social environment. It is not easy to produce such feelings intentionally. People cannot fall or stop falling in love because they want to (Cromby, 2007). Certain stimuli, circumstances, biological conditions, cultural ideas, affordances, and appraisals shall intertwine to trigger the process of growing or fading love sensations – in a short or long run.

Emotions Embodied in Sensations

Love, as any emotion, can be a fleeting subjective experience with a certain pattern (or patterns) of feelings, body sensations, and physiological processes. Among those are *warm rush* or *feeling hot*, *racing heart*, *fast breathing*, *blushing*, the *flushed face*, sweating, and *butterflies in stomach*.

Body sensations are the *conscious experiences* which an individual feels from internal perspective. Body feelings are conscious body-related experiences. They are usually localized in specific parts of the body, wherever their sensory origins are. On another side, affective feelings are non-isomorphic evaluative representation (Feinberg & Mallatt, 2016; Köteles, 2021).

Emotions have distinct *patterns of body sensations*, even though their relations can be bidirectional. Body sensations can be the causes generating emotional experiences, such as affective feelings, be just concomitants, or be the consequences of the processes. Body sensations can cause affective feelings, while at the same time, body percepts and their affective evaluations can alter body sensations.

Body feelings and affective feelings are vague experiences and, therefore, difficult to verbalize. Their overlap in self-reports of people can be the consequence of their ineffability since they cannot be described in words. The embodied experiences and sensations of love are widely reflected in bodily metaphors being a common verbal expression of emotion (see, e.g., Kövecses, 1988, 2003).

Researchers have investigated the bodily sensations associated with several emotions, including love (e.g., Breugelmans et al., 2005; Cromby, 2007; Nummenmaa, Glerean, Hari, & Hietanen, 2014).

The sensation patterns related to the experience of different emotions are discernible and coincide with physiological functioning. Body sensations of many basic emotions are experienced as elevated activity in the upper chest area, increased heart rate and breathing, the changes of sensations in the head area (such as facial musculature activation, skin temperature, and lacrimation), and changes in activity and sensations in the limbs, the digestive system, and around the throat region. It is worth noting that happiness sensations are experienced all over the body. The pattern of body sensations associated with *love* is topologically closer to the patterns of *happiness* and *pride* among other emotions (Nummenmaa et al., 2014). The bodily sensation maps, which researchers discovered, were concordant across East Asian (Taiwan) and West European (Finland) cultures.

Overall, the scientific knowledge of the embodied sensations associated with love is still limited. While bodily sensations experienced in *sexual love* and *passionate love* have been explored (e.g., Bosman, Spronk, & Kuipers, 2019; Hatfield & Rapson, 2009; Liebowitz, 1983; Spronk, 2014), the knowledge about body sensations associated with other types of love, such as romantic love, companionate love, and maternal love, is not available. Based on neurobiological research of maternal, romantic, and sexual love (e.g., Acevedo, Aron, Fisher, & Brown, 2012; Bartels & Zeki, 2004; Esch & Stefano, 2005), we can expect many similarities in embodied sensations for these types of love.

Methodological Issues in the Study of Love as Emotion

The question is how love can be studied empirically as *emotion*, *surge of love*, rather than as *disposition*. Two perspectives in such studies are possible: internal, *self-reflective*, and external, *observational*. These methodological innovations were used by Shaver and his colleagues (Shaver et al., 1987). They instructed participants (1) to write about the moments when they personally felt in *love* or *loving*, self-reflection, and (2) to describe what person typically feels when she or he feels in *love* or *loving*, external reflection. Authors found that the antecedents and experiences of *surges of love* were similar in both the self and typical conditions. Participants described *finding the other attractive*, *communicating easily and openly with the other*, and *feeling loved or appreciated by the other*, as the common antecedent circumstances for emotions of love. As the frequent experiences of love emotions, they described *wanting to spend time with the other*, *wanting physical closeness with the other*, *being obsessed with the other*, *daydreaming about the other*, *being forgetful or distracted*, and *feeling self-confident and energetic because of the other*.

That study methodology inspires two important methodological contemplations, important for future cross-cultural love research. First, love can be a *situational emotion*, like a surge of love; an *emotional episode*, short-term emotional process; or a *disposition*, long-term recurring emotion. Therefore, the instructions to participants must refer to a specific temporal perspective. Love is not a static emotional state or characteristic, as dispositional theories admit. It is dynamic in short-term as well as in long-term perspectives. Love is like waves of emotions – it has the high and low tides; it come and go; it is in constant flux. General statements and questions, like in many love questionnaires, are possible yet should still refer to a specific period.

Second important methodological point is the distinguishing of self-report view and observer view. In the first case, asking how participants feel certain emotions in situations, researchers explore how individuals experience love in a culture. In the second case, asking how other people behave and what they do being in love in those situations, researchers explore external objective culturally typical actions and expressions of love in the culture. While the first approach proliferates in cross-cultural love research, the second approach is still less frequently used.

Emotional Complexity of Love

Cultural models of love frequently refer to the *typical patterns of emotional experiences and expressions* among people in different cultures. Such models present so-called "*profiles*" *of love* describing differences and similarities in prevalent certain love emotions, love styles, emotional complexity, etc.

Studies also discovered cultural differences in complexity of emotional experience between East Asians and Westerners, when they are in love (Shiota et al., 2010). Interaction with a romantic partner may involve the experience of both positive and negative emotions together. In the study of Shiota et al. (2010), couples (98 individuals in 49 monogamous, heterosexual romantic relationships) participated in four semi-structured conversations with their romantic partner which generally resembled everyday relationship experience. The conversations in Asian American and European American couples were similar in content: partners did not express more negative or complex messages. During these conversations participants reported and rated their experience of love and relationship-focused negative emotions.

For each of the four conversations, researchers examined the correlations between experience of love and the target negative emotion (e.g., anger, contempt, or shame). Analysis was conducted separately for Asian American and European American women and men. It is important to note that all participants in the sample resided in the same geographical region of the USA, attended the same university, spoke the same language, and rated their emotions using the same scales. Only cultural background was different.

The results of the study showed that during these conversational interactions Asian American participants more likely reported both love and negative emotion, while European American participants usually reported their experience of either love or the target negative emotion. For example, when hearing a partner talk about a current non-relationship concern, Asian Americans who reported more love toward their partner might also report some contempt as well; European Americans reported either love or contempt, but not both. This suggests that among the European American participants, feelings of anger, contempt, or shame during interaction with a romantic partner were thought to preclude feelings of love, whereas Asian American participants were more likely to report feeling both types of emotion (Shiota et al., 2010, p.795).

Thus, these findings brought evidence that East Asian culture admits fewer barriers than Western culture for a person' experience of both positive and negative emotion in love, either at the same time or in near sequence.

1.1.3 Dispositional Conception of Love

Emotions and Dispositions

Love can be a basic emotion in its basic forms, as defined in previous sections. Love can also be a complex emotion, consisting of several other emotions, which are evoked depending on several factors. These can be anger, hate, sadness, and other emotions, in which love embodies conveying the meaning of love. All these emotional experiences are contingent of the context, situation, and personal love dispositions.

Disposition is a personal tendency to think, feel, and act in a specific way in typical conditions and contexts. It is possible to distinguish cognitive, emotional, and behavioral dispositions; however, many dispositions express all three components in a certain proportion. Emotional dispositions are in focus of this chapter. Generally, emotional disposition is an individual tendency to experience certain types of affective experience across some typical situations and contexts. These can be, for example, positive or negative affective states.

Emotional disposition predisposes a person to feel a specific emotion toward an object, person, situation, or idea (Krams, 2016). For example, emotional disposition may prompt to experience and express emotions of anger, anxiety, sadness, joy, or love. A person with an emotional disposition to love does not always feel the emotions of love, but only in applicable occasions.

There are several types of emotional dispositions, moods, attitudes, and traits, which differ from emotions and each other in their time perspective. They interact with each other and with emotions in emotional process. The concept of love can also be considered in these short-term and long-term perspectives. Emotions are temporary affective states which in their cumulative effect can transform into such dispositions as mood, attitudes, and traits.

Emotions and emotional dispositions are connected to each other in two ways. On the one hand, an appraisal being biased by situational, contextual, individual, and cultural factors activates more frequent and intense experience of specific emotions. As a result, an emotion disposition emerges. On the other hand, due to that emotional disposition, people experience specific emotions more likely and more readily than others.

Emotion disposition is a stable individual tendency to experience some emotions more (or less) frequently and intensely than other people in similar kinds of events and situations (Scherer, 2020). These tendencies of dispositional negativity or positivity can be quite typical for some people. High levels of dispositional negativity and positivity can cause prevalent daily emotions and feelings of satisfaction and happiness in relationship.

The individuals, who are more negative in their dispositions, frequently experience tonically heightened and indiscriminate negative affect in their daily life. They also have more frequent exposure to stressors and experience intense reactivity to stressors, which may be uncertain, diffuse, or remote. Studies (Shackman et al.,

2016) have also shown that some personality traits and brain activities in some regions (e.g., the amygdala and prefrontal cortex) predict such individual differences in indiscriminate negative affect.

Prevalent *negative disposition* of some people is due to their *appraisal bias* – biased evaluation of situations. They show the tendency toward external versus internal causal attribution of events. As Scherer (2020) suggested, many appraisal dimensions, such as pleasantness versus unpleasantness, goal conduciveness versus obstruction, novelty versus expectedness, control, power, causation, and compliance to norms, can exhibit such biases. Due to these biases in appraisals, individuals have a disposition to experience certain emotions more frequently than others. For instance, people can have dispositional negativity or positivity (e.g., Puccetti et al., 2020; Shackman et al., 2016). Those who hold negative dispositions appraise many situations, even ambiguous ones, more negatively than those with positive dispositions. They experience less positive and more negative emotions, as well as on average lower positive and higher negative affect in their daily life (Puccetti et al., 2020).

And culture mediates all these processes. Values and beliefs reward certain cultural biases in appraisal. Encouraging these biases, societies shape some cultural emotional dispositions (Scherer & Brosch, 2009).

Thus, from the sections above, one can see the close connections of emotions, as short-term affective states, with moods, attitudes, and traits, as long-term dispositions which vary in their duration.

Love Dispositions

It is reasonable to theorize that love is not only emotions but may also include such love dispositions as moods, love attitudes, and love traits. Love can also be an interpersonal disposition. In this case, love is the long-lasting quality of emotions, rather than short-term emotional state. Enduring affection, trust, commitment, concern, and care for security and well-being of the loved one are the examples of such emotional attitudes. Many scholars of emotions and love are proponents of such dispositional approach (e.g., Ekman, 1992a, 1992b; Frijda et al., 1991; Naar, 2013; Pismenny & Prinz, 2017; Scherer, 2020).

For example, Ekman (1992a, 1992b) believed that love is an *emotional attitude* since the duration of its experience is longer than the short-term duration of emotion. In the same vein, Frijda et al. (1991) considered love as emotionally charged attitude, as a disposition to respond emotionally to an object or person (they called it *sentiment*).

Love – the same way as anger, sadness, and other emotions – can be a complex attitude consisting of several emotions as the dimensions, which appear subjectively simultaneously and successively over time. If researchers consider the duration of emotional experience in the short or long period of time as the criteria distinguishing emotions and attitudes, then any emotion can take both forms. For example, an individual can experience a short-term surge of anger and can be angry for a very long time. The same way, the individual can experience happiness as an emotion for a short time – due to a particular event – or be happy for an extended period. As Shaver et al. (1996) suggested, many basic and non-basic emotions can have both situational form (as emotion) and long-term form (as disposition): "there are momentary surges of every emotion as well as more long-standing, dispositional forms" (p. 86).

Therefore, the concept of love as an emotion may not contradict with the concept of love as an attitude. Love can take both forms: dispositional and state-like (Lazarus, 1991; Shaver et al., 1996).

Moods, Attitudes, and Traits as Disposition of Love

Furthermore, there are several kinds of dispositions depending on their relative short- and long-term perspective: *moods, attitudes, and traits*. Love in all these dispositional forms is considered in the following sections. Love is a complex concept that is represented not only in different emotions and dispositional forms but also in different categories and multiplexes of their groupings. Love is a set of emotions, moods, attitudes, and traits embodied in passion, affection, compassion, care, and so on. Passion can be emotion as a situational experience, mood as a short-term disposition, attitude as a long-term disposition, and trait as a personality disposition. All these experiences are intertwined in love.

The biased appraisals of another person' appearance, expressions, actions, behaviors, relationship, and own sensations shape not only one's emotions and moods but also attitudes in love. Due to such individual differences and biases, some people are more romantic, more practical, more companionate, more caring, or more obsessive and possessive than others.

Studies have shown not only individual and typological but also cultural differences in these emotional dispositions (see for review Karandashev, 2021a, 2021b).

1.1.4 Love as Moods and Habits

The Love Mood

While *emotions* are short-term transient, situation-focused, and object-specific experience, *moods* are long-term, diffuse, and global emotional experience. Joy, surprise, sadness, anger, and other emotional phenomena discussed in previous section are emotions. Elation, boredom, irritability, anxiety, and depression are the examples of moods. Despite distinction between emotions and moods, a *dispositional theory of moods* (Siemer, 2009) maintains that moods tend to elicit certain types of situational appraisals and, consequently, trigger specific emotions of one sort or another.

Moods are the temporary dispositions to make specific kinds of emotion-relevant appraisals and, therefore, experience certain emotions: depression is a disposition for sadness, irritability is a disposition for anger, and romantic mood is a disposition to perceive another person idealistically generating love emotions. Furthermore, despite distinction between moods and dispositions, the moods can be viewed as temporary dispositions that can shape long-term dispositions, attitudes, and traits (Izard, Libero, Putnam, & Haynes, 1993; Nowlis, 1970; Siemer, 2009).

The Dynamics of Love Mood

The conception of love as a mood can explain the dynamic of love emotions throughout time. Besides momentary surges of love emotions, which occur during a very short time of seconds and minutes, there are also relatively longer short-term surges of love and feelings, which occur during a short time of hours and days. Love is not constant and static, but rather dynamic and fluctuating experience.

For instance, individuals do not feel love on the same level of intensity all the time. Levels of testosterone, serotonin, and dopamine, as well as external environmental factors, can increase or decrease the mood disposition for love. Love temporarily goes down with a good chance to surge up once again later. Emotional experience of love is intertwined with mood fluctuation. Some mood may be more conducive for love than other.

Psychophysiology of Love Mood

The love moods are physiologically and neurologically grounded. For instance, women experience stronger sexual interest, more sensitive to sexual cues, and are more inclined to sexual encounters during their ovulatory phase. Evolutionary, this mood makes woman more receptive to love because she is more likely to conceive a child during this period. The increased level of *estrogen* sets a woman in the mood for love (Dölen, 2017). Culturally, romantic music, candle lights, wine, and dinner also enhance her mood for love. However, the fear of undesired pregnancy – culturally reasonable for woman in some societies – can inhibit her motivation and mood for a sexual encounter.

For many people, especially young men and women, spring is the season when they are in the mood prone to fall in love. It is true at least for the geographical locations with four seasons. Why does spring so conducive for love? March and April bring more sun giving people more vitamin D and, thus, boosting their mood *and* libido. *Dopamine* is a neurotransmitter that is involved in the feeling of pleasure. It increases positive affective state and puts a person in the mood for love (Aron et al., 2005; Fisher, 2004, 2006; Nicholson, 2007; Takahashi et al., 2015).

Novel experiences of spring season – singing birds, blooming flower, more color, new smells – trigger the increased production of dopamine. These new stimuli trigger the brain and drive up dopamine, thus making people euphoric and more receptive to new feelings, sensations, and love.

Studies have shown that the changes in love status among Swiss and Iranian adolescents are closely intertwined with such mood states as anxiety, depression, and hypomania (Bajoghli et al., 2013, 2017; Brand, Luethi, von Planta, Hatzinger, & Holsboer-Trachsler, 2007). It is not always clear whether falling in love triggers alteration of mood or, vice versa, the mood precipitates growing love. These experiences are so tangled that can be called as love moods.

The feelings of boosted arousal, overwhelming joy, recurrent thoughts of the loved person, and desire to maintain proximity to the beloved one are the symptoms of passionate romantic love, which are similar to a *hypomanic state.* Swiss adolescents at the early stage of romantic love (Brand et al., 2007) experienced heightened positive moods in the mornings and in the evenings. Although they slept fewer hours, they had higher subjective sleep quality and experienced increased concentration during the day. A longitudinal study (Bajoghli et al., 2017) assessing love status and mood of Iranian adolescents in 8 months has shown that those who were still stably in love over this period had higher state anxiety. They also felt lower hypomania, probably indicating fading of passion. However, those who were newly in love experienced high anxiety, and high hypomania, but low depression. Thus, experience of love as mood is similar between Swiss and Iranian adolescents.

Romantic Mood Induction

Experiments with *romantic mood induction* brought even more convincing evidence of power of love mood. The men who were exposed to the romantic mood manipulation experienced greater attraction to a woman which was dissimilar from them in attitudes, compared to the men, which were not exposed to such mood induction. Furthermore, the men in *romantic mood induction* condition perceived the dissimilar woman as more similar to themselves, compared to the men in control group (Gold, Ryckman, & Mosley, 1984).

The mood of love is emerged and maintained due to recurrent and frequent occurrence of related emotions, such as joy, happiness, affection, compassion, and others. All these emotional experiences can appear in an individual's life as situational emotions or as short-term moods. And they are intertwined affecting each other producing an emotional state when a person is in mood for love.

1.1.5 Love as Attitudes

Love Attitudes as Personal Dispositions

The concept of attitudes characterizes enduring internal affective predispositions toward things, ideas, persons, situations, and events. These are the attitude objects (Albarracin, Johnson, & Zanna, 2014; Wood, 2000). Although the terms *attitudes* and *psychological dispositions* are frequently used interchangeably, some scholars distinguish them (Stokvis, 1953).

Attitude is evaluation of an object expressing preference against or for the object. While appraisals determine qualities, affective tones, and intensity of emotions, evaluations determine corresponding characteristics of attitudes. Individual attitudes have strong roots in psychosomatics and emotions (Stokvis, 1953). The attitudes engage affective, cognitive, and behavioral mechanisms and communicate endorsements of attitude objects in such words as like/dislike, agree/disagree, prefer, and alike (Lalljee, Brown, & Ginsburg, 1984). Some attitudes are more emotionally loaded than others.

The attitudes serve the variety of social, personal, and interpersonal functions (Lalljee et al., 1984). Interpersonal attitudes and dispositions play important roles in close relationships (Huston & Rempel, 1989). In many cases, however, the research on love attitudes does not make the explicit references to a specific time frame, while implicitly assumes the attitudes as permanent dispositions for the time being. Questions and statements are phrased in a general timeless manner: "Do you love, or you don't"? Such an approach tends to ignore situational and circumstantial nature of emotional attitudes, which can be expressed or not, which can fluctuate and change depending on interpersonal, social, and cultural context.

Many researchers have treated love as an attitude or as a set of attitudes (e.g., Hendrick & Hendrick, 1986, 1989, 1990; Hendrick, Hendrick, & Dicke, 1998; Rubin, 1970). For example, Rubin (1970) considered love as an attitude of a loving person toward a loved one that predisposes the lover to feel, think, and behave toward the beloved in certain ways. Hendrick and Hendrick (1986, 1989, 1990) did not define the *love attitudes* conceptually. Borrowing the idea of six love styles from Lee (1973, 1976), authors converted these into love attitudes and used the terms *attitudes* and *styles* interchangeably, without their conceptual distinction. According to the wording of items, the Love Attitudes Scale (Hendrick et al., 1998; Hendrick & Hendrick, 1986, 1989, 1990) measured *love attitudes*.

Throughout recent decades, the *love attitudes* have been widely explored in love research, yet not many measurement instruments were available. The Love Attitudes Scale has been overwhelmingly popular and largely used on love research arena. The results of these studies, which are relevant to the cultural and cross-cultural models of love, will be presented in the following chapters.

Sternberg's (1986, 1997) Love Theory and Triangular Love Scale have been also popular in love research. However, author used the very general and vague term *components* for the dimensions of the scale. The term *components* can be interpreted variably, so it is conceptually not evident which emotional reality the scale measures. Nevertheless, from the context of the work and the wording of items, it looks like the scale measures *intimate*, *passionate*, and *committed love attitudes*. There were several attempts to use the scale in different cultures (see for details in the next chapters).

Love Attitudes and Love Experience

Individual attitudes affect how individuals experience positive and negative emotional events Fuochi & Voci, 2020). For instance, a longitudinal study across 12-week periods conducted in Italy has demonstrated that individuals' reactions to events and their experience of negative affect, positive affect, and life satisfaction vary depending on their dispositions. Positive dispositions of hedonism, self-compassion, mindfulness, gratitude, and eudaimonism help cope with negative emotions and build positive emotions and well-being (Fuochi & Voci, 2020).

Love dispositions determine how people experience love relationships at the stages of their initiation, maintenance, and dissolution (Hammock & Richardson, 2011). The individuals with *pragma love attitudes* strive to select an appropriate partner when initiating a relationship. The individuals with *ludus* attitude typically have short and uncommitted relationships and do not concern for partner loyalty. Different from this, those with *agape* and *mania* attitudes are highly loyal and involved in maintenance of relationships. The experience dissolution of relationship for those with *ludus* is associated with positive emotions whereas for the individuals with *eros, agape, and mania* attitudes, with negative emotions.

Person-Focused and Relationship-Focused Love Attitudes

Relationship attitudes rely on perception and evaluation of the two kinds of information – about individuals and about their relations with each other (Baldwin, 1992; Fletcher, Simpson, & Thomas, 2000; Karandashev & Evans, 2019). Although both attitudes are closely intertwined, yet the scripts of some "love stories" emphasize more the characteristics of beloved while in the other the nature of love relationships (Sternberg, 1995, 1996; Sternberg, 1999). Analyzing participants' reports of positive aspects of their partner and relationship, Londero-Santos et al. (2020) identified 19 concepts referring to the relationship and 21 concepts referring to the partner (presumably in Brazilian Portuguese). They found that the categories of *trust* and *companionship* most frequently describe positive aspects *of relationship*, while *affectionate* and *caring* most frequently characterize positive aspects *of the partner*.

Thus, the study of love attitudes should distinguish (1) the attitude toward a partner and (2) the attitudes of a relationship (Karandashev & Evans, 2019). They differ in the objects of attitudes: a partner or a relationship with the partner. These two kinds of love attitudes are *person-focused* and *relationship-focused*. Forty concepts characterizing love, which have been explored throughout recent 60 years in America, are grouped into two umbrella categories: affection and compassion, as *person-focused* attitudes, and closeness and commitment, as *relationship-focused* attitudes.

Appraisal of a person (attractiveness and suitability), appraisal of relationship (actions and interactions), and individual differences in emotion disposition (positivity and negativity) determine experience of emotional attitudes toward another person.

Emotional attitudes are socially rooted, shaped by culture, and grounded in group memberships and social identities. Attitudes generally reflect normative influence of social groups which individuals belong to (Smith & Hogg, 2008).

Love as a set of attitudes can be embodied in such attitudes as affection, compassion, commitment, intimacy, and others. Largely, compassion can be emotion as a situational experience, mood as a short-term disposition, or an attitude as a long-term disposition to an object, person, situation, norm, or idea.

Self-Report and Indirect Assessments of Love as Attitudes

Emotional attitudes can be assessed directly as *evaluations of attitudes objects* (person, situation, social norms, and so on) using *self-report measures*. Indirectly, attitudes can be assessed with several measures of facial expressions, implicit cognition, arousal, and neuroimaging of the prefrontal cortex and amygdala (Banaji & Heiphetz, 2010; Cunningham, Raye, & Johnson, 2004; Cunningham & Zelazo, 2007; Mendes, 2008). When individuals have stronger attitudes toward objects, persons, relationships, and attributes, they *rate* them *higher* and *endorse* statements *stronger*.

The attitude strength can also be assessed by cognitive accessibility measured with response time: *how quickly it comes to mind* (Fazio, 1995; Fazio, Powell, & Herr, 1983; Krosnick & Petty, 1995). The stronger attitudes are, the easier they come to mind. The stronger attitudes activate a faster reaction when a person recognizes the *attitude object* (Handy, Smilek, Geiger, Liu, & Schooler, 2010). The response to a stronger attitude needs less time, while the response to a weaker attitude needs more time to think about it (see for review Fazio, 1995; Karandashev & Evans, 2017).

1.1.6 Love as Traits

From Emotions to Emotional Traits

Occurrence of positive or negative emotions as affective states can become recurrent throughout a certain period, thus transforming into prevalent positive or negative moods as temporary dispositions. In turn, these emotional processes regularly repeating can form positive or negative affectivity as traits.

For example, experiences of enjoyment, interest, and general positive emotionality predict extraversion traits. On the other hand, experience of negative emotions and negative emotionality predict neuroticism trait (Izard et al., 1993). Frequent occurrence of positive or negative emotions and mood can form extroversion or neuroticism traits. On the other hand, these traits can predispose individual experience positive or negative affective states. Thus, *emotional phenomena can be conceptualized* not only as situational emotions, dispositional moods, or emotional attitudes *but also as emotional traits*.

Societies promote certain kinds of *affective personality traits* when cultural values and norms reward culturally specific biases of appraisals. These biased appraisals prompt experience of specific emotions, while frequently and intensely experienced, they form culture-specific modal personality traits (Scherer & Brosch, 2009).

Positive and Negative Affectivity

Dispositional affect can be an example of such a personality trait (Huelsman, Furr, & Nemanick Jr, 2003; Watson, Clark, & Tellegen, 1988). It is a global predisposition to perceive situations in a positive or negative way and act and react in stable positive or negative ways.

Positive or negative dispositional affectivity influences sensations and behaviors instantly, often unconsciously, and has a prolonged effect during several weeks, sometimes months.

Positive affectivity trait is characterized by prevalence of positive, pleasurable engagement, high energy, and enthusiasm in life of a person. Individuals with *high positive affectivity* are more sensitive to positive facets of life and perceive events and people through rose-tinted glasses. They are cheerful and energetic. They more frequently feel excited and experience positive moods across many situations. Different from this, individuals with *low positive affectivity* typically experience melancholy and low energy. They frequently feel sad, sluggish, or weary.

Negative affectivity trait is characterized by prevalence of negative, unpleasurable engagement, nervousness, and distress in life of a person. Individuals with high negative affectivity are more sensitive to negative aspects of life and perceive people and events through jade-colored glasses. They have a negative view of situations and circumstances over time and across contexts. They tend to feel nervous, irritable, and angry, or fearful, upset, and distressed. Different from this, individuals with *low negative affectivity* typically are relaxed, calm, and tranquil (Barsade & Gibson, 2007; Huelsman et al., 2003; Watson et al., 1988).

It is also reasonable to expect that individuals with *positive affectivity* would have more idealistic and romantic love attitudes compared with those with *negative affectivity*. *Neuroticism trait* might be considered as a component of the *mania love* attitudes. Individuals with anxiety trait would have *low attachment love* attitude.

Loving Traits

The same way, frequent occurrence and prevalence of some sensations, perceptions, emotions, moods, and positive attitudes can form long-term predispositions to love, such as habits of love, or personality loving traits. Love is consciously or unconsciously created and cultivated (Davis, 2020). Love traits play motivational function.

On the other hand, *love as a personal and cultural value* may guide loving traits, attitudes, moods, and emotions. For example, Mother Teresa (1910–1997), Roman Catholic nun and missionary, is honored in the Catholic Church as Saint for her amazing loving personality and deeds. She had distinctive traits of love, such as being of *kind, tender, loving*, and *caring* which were remarkable (Allegri, 2011; Greene, 2004; Scott, 2009).

Personal dispositions as *personality traits* greatly determine individual's attitudes and behaviors. In this sense, love can be conceptualized as a constellation of love traits. Some people are more loving or more lovable than others. Passionate, affectionate, compassionate, and caring individuals are more capable to love compared to those who are low in these traits. Those who strive to do good things to others and who express gratitude for what others do for them are more lovable.

Experience of love in everyday life, feelings of intimacy, passion, and commitment are closely associated with personality traits and fundamental motives. People high in *extroversion* and *conscientiousness* and low in *neuroticism* feel higher levels of love (Engel, Olson, & Patrick, 2002; Oravecz, Dirsmith, Heshmati, Vandekerckhove, & Brick, 2020). Traits also characterize certain love attitudes. Disinhibition and limited detachment are attributes of the *eros* love attitudes. Pathological personality traits accompany *mania* and *ludus* love attitudes (Jonason, Lowder, & Zeigler-Hill, 2020).

1.1.7 Love as Actions and Interactions

Behavioral Aspects of Love

In parallel and in interaction with *subjective emotional realities*, love also involves several behavioral manifestations. While the *subjective emotional realities* are sensory experiences, emotions (basic and complex), moods, attitudes, dispositions/attitudes, traits, and values, the *behavioral emotional realities* are motivations, action tendencies, expressions, actions/reactions, habits, behaviors, styles/types of behavior, the plots, and stories, which people live through.

Love is *the actions of love*. Three types of actions are evidently plausible when a person loves another: (1) do something what is good for himself/herself, (2) do something what is good for the loved one, and (3) react to what the loved one did for the loving person. All these actions bring a joy of love. However, they are driven by different motivational orientations and, consequently, form different models and types of love. The first type can be called *hedonistic model of love*, with a possible version of *masochistic model* and variations in between. The second type can be called *benevolent model of love*, with a possible version of *altruistic model* and variations in between. The third type can be called the *grateful model of love*, with a possible version of *unappreciative model* and variations. As we'll see in the following chapters, the individual and cross-cultural prevalence and variation of these models can be observed in real emotional experiences and relationships.

In some respects, the *actions of love are more valuable* for the *loved one* than the lover's subjective emotions and attitudes. Many believe that the true *love* is the *doing of something good for another* – in a short-term or long-term perspective. The common acts of love are the protecting or caring, making meal or doing laundry, giving gifts and quality time, helping and doing other acts of service, hugging, touching, and saying words of affirmation to the loved partner, spouse, child, parent, and stranger. Their importance and meaning can vary across individuals and cultures (e.g., Arman & Rehnsfeldt, 2006; Dowrick, 1997; Michael, 2016; Reis, Maniaci, & Rogge, 2014; Watson, 2012).

Equivocal Actions of Love

Understanding *tolerance*, *violence*, *forbearance*, *forgiveness*, and *assisted dying* as the acts of love can be more controversial (e.g., Bonino, 2018; Dowrick, 1997; Frieze, 2005; Jamison, 1995; Maurer, 2020) because interpretations of *what is good* and *what is bad* in love can vary.

Some parents, for instance, believe that punishment – *doing bad for their child* – is *out of their love* for him/her. Every parent believes that he/she loves their child and does this out of their good intentions and love. Presumably, *it is bad* in a short-term perspective, yet *it is good* for the long-term perspective of their child. Cultures and individuals vary in their interpretations of these multifaceted aspects of love.

The violence of one spouse toward another can also be deemed as an act of love motivated by good intentions. Such interpretations of love are acceptable in some families and cultural contexts (e.g., Bonino, 2018; Borochowitz & Eisikovits, 2002; Frieze, 2005; Steinmetz, 1977; Wolf-Light, 1999; Wood, 2001). In these cases, *love* and *violence* are deemed as *mutually functional*, while in others they are incompatible.

A qualitative study has shown that in some couples, the feelings of love can exist between spouses, even in their violent environment. This is a viable option because a battered woman and her partner ascribe similar meanings to the love and violence (Borochowitz & Eisikovits, 2002).

Actions of Love as Habits

The *actions of love* can become the *good habits of behavior* in daily life of people (e.g., Bacon, 2012; Bellah, Madien, Sullivan, Swidler, & Tipton, 1985; Davis, 2020). This is, for example, what often occurs in the *companionate love model*. Partners may not notice what they do and what their partners do. The *acts of love can be implicit*, not explicit, in everyday behaviors and relationships. They can be a part of daily routine – the habits of love, which are, nevertheless, not less valuable.

Love in Motivational Tendencies

Appraisals of objects, individuals, situations, and contexts evoke specific emotional responses that fulfill signaling function and make a person ready for action. The common types of *motivation*, *action tendencies*, and *actions* are to *approach* or *avoid* the objects and individuals or situations and contexts. This general framework and other motivational characteristics of actions in various cultural contexts (e.g., Boiger & Mesquita, 2014; Elliot, Eder, & Harmon-Jones, 2013; Mesquita, 2003; Mesquita & Ellsworth, 2001) can serve for theoretical interpretation of the relations between emotions and behaviors, which activate *approach and avoidance motivations*, *action tendencies*, and *actions* in love.

The Approach and Avoidance Motivation in Love

The *approach motivation* in relationships is manifested in *interpersonal attraction* as psychological and physical *gravitation toward another*, with associated emotional experiences. *Love* is a special kind of *attraction* that is motivated by specific needs, drives, and motives, which pull a person toward another. The *avoidance motivation* in relationships is manifested in *interpersonal repulsion* as psychological and physical *gravitation away from another*, with associated emotional experiences. *Hate* is a special kind of *repulsion* that is motivated by specific needs, drives, and motives, which push a person away from another. Some sorts of love may engage both approach and avoid motivations – with corresponding emotions, which are triggered by meeting or not meeting different needs, drives, and motives in a relationship with a partner.

The *approach motivations, action tendencies, and actions* are rewarding and entail positive implications. The *avoidance motivations, action tendencies, and actions* are punitive and aversive and entail negative implications. When a person is experiencing specific emotions of positive or negative valence, of high or low arousal, either approach or avoidance motivations and action tendencies emerge. Positivity of emotions motivates approach tendencies, while negativity of emotions motivates avoidance tendencies (Peeters, 1971).

Love as a *positive emotion* drives attraction as an *approach tendency*. Positive emotion of love for another evokes a person's approach motivation and action tendency to lean or move closer to her/him increasing interpersonal proximity. In other cases, negative emotion of fear may compel a person to avoid another one by moving away from him/her. The ambivalent complex emotion of love experienced as *elation of attraction* and *fear of rejection* engenders controversial action tendencies causing emotional tension.

Love is not only emotional and expressive but also motivational and actional process. Emotions of love generate corresponding behavioral motivation, action tendencies, readiness for action, actions, and interactions. Actions of love can be active or passive, active or reactive, initiative, supportive, or counteracting. Actions of love can be individual actions or interactions and unfold according to implied love scenario. Interactions can be synchronal or asynchronous. The same actions may have different personal meanings, admit various appraisals, and be interpreted corresponding with individual and cultural scripts of relationships.

Love in Action Tendencies

Frijda (1986, 2010; Mesquita & Frijda, 1992) included *action tendencies* and states of *action readiness* as the important components of emotion process that fulfill the adaptive function of emotions. Emotions cause and determine actions. The events, being *appraised* by an individual, elicit *emotions* and then prompt certain *states of action readiness*, which in turn may motivate and cause actions, or may not. The *actions*, elicited by this process, can be *impulsive* (automatic, without prior intention), or *intentional* (deliberate, with prior intention). Perception of (a) the physical, biological, and social affordances, available in an appraised event eliciting emotions, (b) the repertoire of actions available for an individual, and (c) the qualities of action readiness, all these components determine the course of action(s). The actions shall presumably fit the *perceived affordances* and meet the motivation of the *state of action readiness* (Frijda, 2010).

Love as *action tendencies* involves a *desire to be closer, longing to touch the beloved* person – a child or a romantic partner (Shaver et al., 1996). *Affection* of love is an urge toward proximity seeking, while *tenderness* is an impulse toward tender, a caregiving tendency and act.

Children experiencing love exhibit their loving emotions in kissing, hugging, scuffling, sitting close to each other, confessing their love to each other, seeking each other out and excluding others, feeling jealous, giving the gifts, and making sacrifices for each other (Bell, 1902, p. 330).

Action tendencies for various emotions, including care and love, can be studied in self-report measures, asking what people could do or did during certain emotional experiences (e.g., (De Hooge, Breugelmans, & Zeelenberg, 2008; Fontaine et al., 2007; Tiedens, Ellsworth, & Mesquita, 2000). The action tendencies of various emotions, including care and love, can be studied experimentally in speeded response time tasks providing valid behavioral measures of emotional experience (e.g., Badhwar, 2014; Markman & Brendl, 2005; Proctor & Zhang, 2010; van Dantzig et al., 2008).

Love in Actions and Interactions

Different from the scholarly tradition to look at *love as a person's subjective feelings, drives, and thoughts*, love is also conveyed in *actions and interactions* between two persons. Many theories and research on love highlight this interactive nature of love experience and expression. Several conceptions of sexual love focus on sexual interaction postulating that love is a frustrated desire (Freud, 1922/1951), erogenous stimulation (Watson, 1924), or rewarding interactions between partners (Centers, 1975).

Love can be interpreted as the *love actions* of one person toward another, rather than the person's internal loving experience. Love in this case is *doing something good* to a beloved. It may be *sexually intimate intercourse*, which brings pleasure to the beloved. Swensen (1972) defined love in terms of interactions and behaviors of loving partners such as shared activities, disclosing intimacies, and gifts. For example, love can be expressed in the gifts given to a beloved as the material things intended to make the beloved recipient happy (Katz, 1976; Swensen, 1972). Love can be expressed in acts of service and care for the beloved. For example, a loving person may show their love in good cooking and serving a meal, or cleaning, doing laundry, and earning money for a family. In many cultures, these practical ways of validating love are considered as more important than other expressions of love.

For example, Buss proposed that love is the *acts of love* with their tangible consequences. The key consequences of *love acts* are to *achieve reproductive success* (Buss, 1988; Wade, Auer, & Roth, 2009). Among the *primary goals* of *love acts* are sexual intimacy, reproduction, commitment, exclusivity, resource display, resource sharing, and parental investment.

Structure of Love Interactions

The structures of *actions* and *interactions* include – in a basic form – two individuals: one, *who loves*, and another, *who is loved*. In some cases, they cannot be called the *partners* since they may not have *bidirectional interactions*, as in *admiration love* of an admirer to a pop singer.

In case of unrequited and mutual love, which engages an *interaction*, both persons play the roles of *a lover* and *a loved one* – they are partners. A person who loves, the *lover*, is *an actor of love* since she/he is in an *acting position* of experiencing and expressing emotions. Another person, the *loved one*, or the *partner*, is *an object of love* since he/she is in a receiving position of being loved. *An actor of love* is a lover who loves something or somebody. On another side, there is *an object of love* – a loved thing, activity, or a beloved person. *An object of love* can be passive or reactive. She or he may even do not know that they are loved by someone, as in case of adoration of singers and performing actors. Reaction of the *object of love* can be experienced and expressed as *unrequited* or *mutual love*. In case of mutual love, the functions of actor and object of love converge in a person. Having the roles of an object of love and an actor of love makes a person a partner.

In the positions of *actor* and *object* of love, individuals experience and express love differently. A person as *an actor of love* feels *attraction*, *compassion*, and *commitment*, active emotions and attitudes, and expresses these in *lovely words*, *cares*, and *promises* – active actions. A person as *an object of love* feels *being loved*, *nurtured*, and *supported*, reactive emotions, and expresses gratitude, mutual interest, and the joy of being loved – reactive actions.

When two persons initiate a relationship, they become partners. Studies have shown that love partners are very good in the synchrony of their actions, interactions, and some vocal qualities, the "ahs and oohs"; in the tendency to mimic a partner's expressive behavior; and in their sensitivity to a partner's feelings. They are also predisposed for emotional contagion (Carlson & Hatfield, 1992; Hatfield, Cacioppo, & Rapson, 1994).

Actions of Compassion and Caring

C*ompassionate love* is not just the experiences and expressions of altruistic feelings, concern, and caring for other. It is also expressed in behavioral manifestations and acts of compassion (Reis et al., 2014).

Experience and expression of love typically include caregiving tendencies and caregiving behavior toward the loved one (Frijda, 1986; Lazarus, 1991) that are exhibited in increasing physical closeness, in caring touching and hug, in soft and muted smile, and in soft and high voice.

The Dimensions of Agency and Communion in Relationships

Interpersonal behavior in relationships consists of individual actions and interactions that are described by *agency* and *communion* (McAdams, Hoffman, Day, & Mansfield, 1996; Wiggins, 1991). *Agency* characterizes a person as a differentiated individual striving for mastery, success, achievement, and status, with strong power motivation and feeling of responsibility. *Communion* characterizes the person as a member of social group striving for dialogue, union, community, care, friendship, and love, with strong needs for affiliation, nurturance, intimacy, and close relationships.

These qualities of a person are two conceptual coordinates measuring interpersonal behavior in relationships. Behaviors manifesting control and dominance (versus submissiveness) are actorsic actions, while affiliation, agreeableness (versus quarrelsomeness), and warmth (versus hostility) are communal actions (Moskowitz, Suh, & Desaulniers, 1994). This theoretical framework has been successfully applied to analyze couple relationships (e.g., Hagemeyer & Neyer, 2012; Smith et al., 2009). Motivations of these tendencies are rooted in social biochemistry (Locke, 2015, 2018). Testosterone and oxytocin hormones regulate agentic and communal motives of people contributing to their individual differences. "Testosterone appears to amplify agentic motives to enhance and defend one's social rank. Oxytocin appears to amplify communal motives to nurture and protect one's social bonds and significant others" (Locke, 2018, p. 71). The qualities of another person as an object of love play definitely important role. Some people are more adorable and easily lovable than others because of their physical appearance, pleasing disposition, and similarities to a loving individual.

Expressions of Love

Love as emotion is expressed nonverbally and verbally. Love is evident in blushing and flushing which a loving individual exhibits in the presence of the loved person. Eyes look glistening, soft, and tender displaying sideway glances. The pupils of the eyes are dilating. Facial muscles are relaxed displaying a gentle and joyful smile (Bloch, Orthous, & Santibañez-H, 1987; Morris, 1971). Intensity of love is reflected in more time that partners spend gazing at each other (Bolmont, Cacioppo, & Cacioppo, 2014; Kellerman, Lewis, & Laird, 1989; Rubin, 1973). On the other hand, mutual gazing can increase momentarily attraction between strangers. In an experimental condition (Kellerman et al., 1989) when strangers of opposite sex were gazing into each other's eyes to gain rapport – like lovers' natural gazing – participants experienced attraction to, interest in, and warmth feelings of love for their partner.

Studies have shown that people are able to distinguish faces of individuals experiencing love from those experiencing other emotions, such as joy, sadness, anger, and fear (Bloch et al., 1987; Hatfield & Rapson, 1993). Both erotic love and tender love are distinct in their facial expression from joy and from each other. *Erotic love* is displayed in semi-closed eyes while *tender love* in a slight head tilt and a slight smile (Bloch et al., 1987). The smile of love is recognizable in both rewarding and affiliative functions (Rychlowska et al., 2017).

Young romantic lovers exhibit their behaviors and expression that may look childish. They walk holding hand in hand, their bodies come closer, the frontal embrace becomes intimate with gentle caresses, the heads touch, and they kiss each other. The hands fondle the face, the hair, and the private parts of the bodies of the loved one. The words, which they speak, become less important than the soft tone of their voice, and the phrases may sound infantile (Morris, 1971, pp. 98–99)

1.1.8 Love as a Relationship

The Concept of Love as Relationship

Love can be the attributes/characteristics/qualities of *subjective individual emotional experience and expression*, as well as the attributes/characteristics/qualities of *objective relationship between two (or more) individuals*. These *two realities of love* are certainly intertwined. The *subjective individual experience of love* reflects the qualities of relationship, while the *objective characteristics of relationship* reflect *individual subjective experiences*. Yet methodologically, it is worthwhile to distinguish these two sides of love because they embrace different objects of study.

While the *concept of love* as *emotional experiences* focuses on the study of sensations, emotions, moods, attitudes, and traits, the *concept of love* as *relationships* focuses on the study of actions (e.g., help, care, hugging, expression of love), reactions (e.g., gratitude), and quality and quantity of relationship (e.g., mutual, unrequited, equitable, caring, respectful) between *agent* and *object of love*, partners – in case of interactional relationship.

It is common in scholarship that one and the same word *love* is often used for two different things: (1) emotional experience of love and (2) love relationship. Authors just imply different meanings in the term. This usage may cause a confusion in reading. So, I would suggest reserving the word *love* for the emotional experiences of love (and their expressions), whereas the word *love relationship* for the relationships. This would be useful, at least, in the scholarship of love. In German, for instance, there are two different words for these two meanings: "Liebe" and "Liebesbeziehung."

Diversity of Love Relationships

Love may characterize certain types of relationships between peoples. These are sexual relationships, romantic relationship, companionate relationship, conjugal relationships, filial relationships, friendship, parent-child relationships, relationships between people and God, and other possible relationships. Some scholars consider some of these relationships (e.g., romantic love, love by God) as loves while others not. However, a variety of relationships can be called love. It depends on how one defines love.

Sometimes love is characterized even in very general and all overarching meaning – as social connections (The Love Consortium, n.d.). It seems that love is ubiquitous and penetrates many fields of human relationships. I would, however, highlight that *love* is a *positive connection*.

Love Relationships and Romantic Relationships

It is worth noting that the word *romantic relationship* has been overused in scholarship and frequently used in the very broad and vague meaning, which does not necessarily stand for the *romantic* relationships, especially in cases of dark or violent sides of such relations. There are several other appropriate terms, which are more accurate, definite, and characteristic of such relationships. For general use, the concept of *love relationship* is well suitable. The specific kinds of love relationships can be called, for instance, mating relationships, dating relationships, premarital relationships, sexual relationships, and others, depending on the focus and subject of a study.

Scholars shall be aware that the word *romantic* in the scholarship of *romantic love* and *romantic relationship* has been traditionally utilized in other, more specific meaning. It is love associated with *idealization* of a beloved, the relationship, and its context (see details in Chap. 6 of this book).

Characteristics of Love as Relationship

Definitions and studies of love as relationship include descriptors, characteristics, and measurements of relations, rather than emotions or attitudes. It is important to distinguish these aspects of love in conceptualizations and operationalizations of variables in studies, even though in real life they obviously interact and closely entangle. Therefore, many studies apparently include the variables of both emotional *experiences* and *relationships*.

Love as *love relationship* is described by the characteristics, different from those describing *love* as *internal experience*, even though they may sound like similar. They can be *short- and long-term* relations. They can be *caring* and *careless*, *responsible* and *irresponsible*, *respectful* and *disrespectful*, *mutual and unrequited*, *equitable and unfair*, and so on.

Researchers have identified the four major dimensions characterizing the prototype of relationship quality: *independence*, *agreement*, *intimacy*, and *sexuality* (Hassebrauck & Fehr, 2002). This four-factorial structure has been replicated in American, Canadian, and German cultural samples. All four parameters of relationship affect partners' satisfaction with their relationship. Intimacy has the highest impact, while sexuality has the least impact on overall relationship satisfaction.

Dyadic Love Relationship

Relationship has two (or more) persons involved. Expressions, actions, and interactions and their typical patterns in the short- or long-term scripts and stories are the major focuses of studying love as relationship. The relationships can be affectionate, committed, caring, fair, beneficial, equitable, and mutual, if they are characterized from the objective standpoint or perception of an individual. Subjective variables of love, such as attitudes, can certainly be included in such relationship studies. The attitudes can be affection, commitment, and care.

Interdependence in Love Relationships

Love is a series of *actions* and *interactions* between partners, which in their sequence and general context can be characterized as a *relationship*. *Love* as a *relationship* between individuals makes them interdependent from each other. The degree of their interdependency, however, can vary depending on their personalities, relationships, and cultural contexts.

The ideas of *interdependence theory* and *theory of social interaction* have been on arena of the behavioral and social sciences for several decades (Johnson & Johnson, 2005; Kelley et al., 2003; Kelley & Thibaut, 1978; Thibaut & Kelley, 1959). They are based on the analysis of relationship situation (its characteristics and goals), interaction, transformation, and adaptation to it by interacting people. The theories maintain that the ways how goals are structured influence the ways how people interact with each other. These interactions involve such social and psychological phenomena as self-presentation, information seeking, attribution, stereotyping, dependence, trust (or distrust), power, conflict, and cooperation (Van Lange & Balliet, 2015).

The *theory of interdependence* has been widely employed in research of close relationships (e.g., Arriaga, 2013; Rusbult & Arriaga, 1997; Rusbult & Van Lange, 2003, 2008; Rusbult, Verette, Whitney, Slovik, & Lipkus, 1991; Sels et al., 2020). According to the interdependence theory, interactions and relationships between individuals entail certain structures of interdependence (Rusbult & Arriaga, 1997). The variations of mutuality of dependence, degree of dependence, correspondence of outcomes, and basis for dependence in relationships form a taxonomy of interdependence patterns. Several factors play their role in the interaction of partners. Among those are transformation of motivation (e.g., transformational activity), habitual transformational tendencies (e.g., relationship-specific motives, dispositions, and social norms), as well as self-presentation, affect, and cognition.

The *actor–partner interdependence model* (APIM) allows researchers to apply and test various aspects of relationships in terms of *interdependence theory* (e.g., Campbell et al., 2001, b; Kashy & Kenny, 2000; Kenny, 1995; Kenny & Ledermann, 2010; Wickham & Knee, 2012).

The interdependence theory was applied as the *investment model* of relationships (Macher, 2013; Rusbult, 1983; Rusbult, Drigotas, & Verette, 1994; Rusbult & Martz, 1995; Rusbult, Martz, & Agnew, 1998, which explains why and how some relationships fade and fall into decay or crisis, while others endure and thrive. These processes of interactions involve characteristics of a specific situation and a partner's traits that determine how they perceive the situation and behave during interaction. Their personality traits affect the selective perception and attribution of each other's behaviors. These subjective perceptions determine how their interaction evolves, the situation changes over, and adaptive processes occur. A person may recalibrate one's own characteristics pertinent to the relationship, reevaluate the relationship, and manage future similar situations with a partner (Arriaga, 2013).

1.1.9 Love in the Temporal Evolving Perspectives

Dynamic Concept of Love Experience and Relationship

Love is a dynamic process that is embodied in physiological sensations, subjective experiences, and various emotions, such as surprise, joy, love, happiness, sadness, jealousy, and others, which appear sequentially or in concurrent mixtures. Appraisals and re-appraisals of situations, circumstances, verbal and nonverbal expressions, as well as implicit meanings determine the course of emotional experience of love during a short period of several days or weeks.

In the 1960s–1970s, several early conceptions and studies considered love in the context of gradual progression from dating to marital relationships (e.g., Berscheid

& Walster, 1974; Bolton, 1959; Borland, 1975; Lewis, 1973; Reiss, 1960). For example, Lewis (1973) proposed a developmental framework to explore premarital dyadic formation, which included such processes as the achieving of similarity perception, pair rapport, self-disclosure, role-taking, and role-fit. The longitudinal test of premarital dyadic formation over a period of 2 years supported validity of this developmental framework predicting the continuance and the dissolution of dyads.

Love as Evolving Emotional Process

Love as any emotional and relational process is a complex of internal experiences, external behaviors, and interactions that evolve over time and includes a sequence of events, appraisals, emotions, actions of one person, and reactions of another one, which are causally related to each other. The component-processing theories of emotional life (e.g., Barrett, Mesquita, Ochsner, & Gross, 2007; Frijda, 1986; Lazarus, 1991; Matsumoto & Hwang, 2012; Mesquita, 2003; Roseman, Dhawan, Rettek, Naidu, & Thapa, 1995; Scherer, 1984) can provide the productive conceptual and methodological framework for the study of love as an evolving process. Emotions of love are the complex bio-psycho-social processes that involve several components, such as body sensations, physiological reactions, appraisals, feelings, emotions, their expressions, action tendencies, actions, reactions, and interactions, which evolve as events, behavior, episodes, and stories of love (Barrett et al., 2007; Lazarus, 1991; Matsumoto, Kudoh, Scherer, & Wallbott, 1988; Mesquita & Frijda, 1992; Perunovic, Heller, & Rafaeli, 2007; Roseman, 2017).

An antecedent event activates appraisal, physiological, cognitive, affective, and behavioral responses. The dynamic structure of the process involves various emotions, such as love, joy, jealousy, sadness, shame, fear, and anger. Some of them represent a core affect, while the others are peripheral components of an emotional episode. Vertically, they are organized in a fuzzy hierarchy. Horizontally, they are organized in a circumplex structure (Russell & Barrett, 1999).

Love as Episodic Process

Love evolves in temporal sequence depending on the events occurring in relationship, actions, reactions of partners, and their appraisals. *Episodic construct of love* is a series of episodes illustrating love. Some of them can be more prototypical than others. *Prototypical emotional episodes* constitute love as a story and unfold according to social scripts and schemas represented in *personal* and *cultural models of love*.

In the short terms, love is an episode of social life saturated by emotions. *An emotional episode* begins as a response to an event and unfolds over time as a complex process that includes appraisal, physiological, cognitive, affective, and behavioral changes. Some emotional episodes can occur more recurrently and look more prototypically for a person than others (Russell & Barrett, 1999).

Many elements of the narrative approach in the description of love as a dynamic and episodic process have been use in the Lee's typology of love styles (Lee, 1973, 1976). This theory presents *love styles* as a set of typical events, experiences, expression, actions, reactions, attitudes, and other temporary episodes in love relations of people (see more details in the next chapter).

The *Love Ways Theory* and studies investigated the typology of individual subjective experience of love and the ways in which people communicate love (Hecht, Marston, & Larkey, 1994; Marston, Hecht, & Robers, 1987). Initially, researchers analyzed the data of face-to-face interviews. Cluster analysis discovered six "*ways of love*": *secure love*, *intuitive love*, *committed love*, *traditional romantic love*, *active love*, and *collaborative love.* Subsequent questionnaire-type research and factor analysis of data categorized the "love ways" in the five groups, which were largely the same in the first four types; yet, instead of the last two, they revealed *companionate love.*

Love as relationship is also present in its story. In this case, researchers explore how a relationship between individuals evolves over time. Love as a story approach focuses attention to the sequence and the whole scripts of evolving events, which one can call *love.*

The theory of love *as a story* (Sternberg, 1995, 1996, 1999; Sternberg, Hojjat, & Barnes, 2001) conceptualizes love and loving relationships as a set of typical plots. In these narrative stories, men and women depict the contents and sequences of partners' actions, interactions, and relationship roles in short-term and long-term perspectives. The stories are labeled according to their major themes, such as *travel*, *mystery*, *police*, *addiction*, and so on. This typology will be reviewed in more detail in the next chapter.

A State of Uncertainty in the Beginning of Love

The *beginning of love* naturally encounters various *uncertainties* about another person and the relationship with him/her. Partners may feel unconfident in their perception of each other, interaction, and relationship. *The Uncertainty Reduction Theory* explains the processes of initial interactions between strangers, as well as the beginning of other types of interpersonal relations (Berger & Bradac, 1982; Berger & Calabrese, 1975; Knobloch, 2008; Knobloch & Solomon, 1999; Livingston, 1980). Validity of this theory was demonstrated in different cultures (Gudykunst, 1985; Gudykunst, Yang, & Nishida, 1985).

The theory was also reconceptualized and applied to the evolvement of romantic and close relationships (Knobloch & Solomon, 2002a; Knobloch & Solomon, 2002b; Livingston, 1980). *Relational uncertainty* is the *ambiguity* that a person experiences concerning *partner*, *self*, and *relationship* in some respects (Knobloch & Solomon, 1999)

In the context of *emerging love* and *initial relationship*, one may have uncertainty about other's and one's own feelings, emotions, attitudes, desire for this relationship, their goals, and values. Do I truly love him/her? A person is wondering whether their feelings are mutual or not and what their relationship in future can be. Can my love be reciprocated or destined to be unrequited? Partners can experience *uncertainty* about relationship and partner's expectation and the ambiguity about appropriate behaviors and acceptable norms.

Relational Uncertainty in the Beginning of Love

Relational uncertainty may occur on an *attitudinal level*, the general ambiguity a person has about a relationship, and on an *episodic level* – the doubts the person has about specific events. Relationship attitudes and emotions concerning events interact increasing or decreasing partners' uncertainty (Knobloch & Solomon, 2002b; Planalp, Rutherford, & Honeycutt, 1988).

The *feelings of relational uncertainty* can have *negative* and *positive consequences*. Appraisals of unexpected events can provoke face threat and anxious waiting of the responses. In such conditions of ambiguity, partners tend to refrain from discussion of unexpected events, are less likely to express jealousy, and prefer to avoid certain topics. They prefer the less open and explicit conversations with less affiliative topics (Knobloch, 2007; Knobloch & Solomon, 2005).

Relational uncertainty can bring not only *obstacles* but also *opportunities* (Knobloch, 2007). It depends on individual appraisals. The people appraising a partner's appearance, communication, and actions as annoying will experience their ambiguity in more negative emotional tones. They usually perceive and appraise unexpected events in a pessimistic perspective. As a result, the relational uncertainty may be disappointing. However, in case of positive appraisal of uncertainty, the new perceptual impressions and unusual behavioral and expressive manners of the partner can incite curiosity, elation, and interpersonal attraction (Knobloch & Solomon, 2002a; Livingston, 1980).

The *sources* of relational uncertainty can be further distinguished by content areas. The boundaries and conditions that make *relational uncertainty* beneficial or detrimental to intimate relations, whether they suppress or inflame love feelings, need more research.

In terms of visual perceptions, the novel and unknown people attract us unless they irritate and frighten us. The less we know a person, the more we are attracted, probably in the hope of a wonderful opportunity. For example, the lack of information in perception of face consistently and strongly ignites the subjective attraction to a person (Sadr & Krowicki, 2019). A reduced visual input – with images of faces, which are blurred, reduced in contrast, and half-occluded – increases the impression of face attractiveness. Perception of left or right half faces makes them more attractive compared to bilaterally symmetric whole faces. These tendencies had no gender differences.

Tolerance of Ambiguity in Love

Love is a complex of emotions and feelings, and a lover encounters many ambiguous situations. He/she wants to know whether the beloved one loves him/her reciprocally or not in circumstances of uncertainty. He/she tries to guess looking in the eyes, gesture, accidentally dropped words, and other behaviors. He/she wants to decide when it would be better time to say "I love you."

In love, the *ambiguity intolerance* may lead to an emotional conflict between glorification and hostility and expectation of joy and pain in the attitudes toward love and a beloved one. People with *ambiguity intolerance* are anguished lovers. Love for them is suffering (The Sorrows of Young Werther, Goethe).

Ambiguity tolerance in love allows avoiding an emotional conflict, accepting reality as it is – with its joy and pain. People with *ambiguity tolerance* embrace love as it is.

Therefore, the study of effect of *ambiguity tolerance* on love experience might be an interesting topic. However, there have not been studies of this kind so far. In cross-cultural context, the topic might be interesting in light of cultural differences in emotional complexity, which are described above.

Cultural norms of attitudes toward emotional complexity of love, which are described above, should correlate with *ambiguity tolerance*, as a cultural pattern. *Ambiguity tolerance* is also a personality trait, which characterizes how a person perceives ambiguous situations with unfamiliar and incongruent cues and emotionally experiences them (Furnham & Ribchester, 1995). Some men and women are willing to encounter such situations and feel emotional ambivalence, others can tolerate them, yet others are intolerant of ambiguity in relationships and emotions.

Love as the Short-Term and Long-Term Dynamic Emotional Experience

Love fluctuates in a short-term as well as transforms in a long-term perspective. External factors can facilitate or inhibit experience and expression of love. One may experience intense love for a partner today, yet may not experience it tomorrow and the day after tomorrow. It is normal – love emotions come and go, yet positive emotions prevailing throughout many days maintain the disposition of love alive.

Love is a dynamic process also in a long-term period of several months or years. In this case, love attitudes and general appraisals of relationship quality undergo alterations and transformation. For example, passionate attitude modifies into affectionate attitude. The emotions prevailing during many days throughout months and years gradually change love attitudes.

As Berscheid (2010) discussed in her review article, relationship science needs to develop the temporal models of love suggesting that the *romantic*, *companionate*, *compassionate*, and *attachment types of love* can be present or absent. Being related to different causal conditions, they may follow different temporal courses as a relationship progresses through time. Several cross-sectional and longitudinal studies (see for review Berscheid, 2010) have brought some findings about possible paths, which these types of love may take. The hypotheses regarding temporal trajectories of love were proposed.

Nonetheless, the long-term perspectives on how love evolves throughout years of individual life and relationship have received limited investigation so far. The longitudinal research design is still rare. Developmental approach to the culturally specific typologies of love has received little attention.

The Stages of Ongoing Development in Love

The *Wheel Theory of Love* considered love as an ongoing development from courtship to relationship development and further to mate selection (Reiss, 1960). The theory describes this evolving process as the sequential and circular progression through four stages: *rapport*, *self-revelation*, *mutual dependency*, and *intimacy need fulfillment*. The *spokes of a wheel* represent these four integrated psychological processes. How primary social relationship develops over time was represented in a visual graphic conception (Reiss, 1960), while later, an alternative dynamic graphic model of that concept was proposed (Borland, 1975).

Each of these processes engages variety of biological, psychological, social, and cultural factors. A love relationship starts with establishing a rapport, which includes sharing likes and preferences and discovering common interests. On the next stage, partners disclose more personal information and reveal their deeper aspects of self. Opening herself/himself, a person expects that the partner would also share more personal information. Thus, both take some risk relying on building trust. On this stage, partners may engage in sexual intimacy that also affects their relationship. With time, partners may disclose even more personal facts or thoughts revealing themselves with the hope this information will be adequately understood, accepted, and supported by the partner. This way, they gradually evolve into the relationship of mutual dependency. Slowly or fast, partners begin to rely on each other to fulfill their needs. The conceptions of social roles and cultural models of love determine the expectations, perceptions, experiences, expressions, and interactions in a loving relationship.

The lasting love relationship continues to be processed through this wheel of love. To maintain rapport, the partners discuss the recent and current events; express their desires, beliefs, and hopes; and talk about plans and goals. They communicate trust and rely on each another to fulfill their certain needs.

In case when the wheel of love happens to turn backward, the partners start to talk with one other less and less, less likely to disclose their thoughts and wishes, and rely less on one another in their pursuits and fulfillment of their needs (Martin & Luke, 1991).

Episodic Nature of Emotional Experience and Love

Emotions as psychological experiences involve different interconnected levels and modes, which function with or without awareness. Emotional experiences flow in *continuous format*, which are represented in *discrete format* as images or words symbolizing emotions. These emotional experiences include sensory impressions and bodily sensations associated with particular situations, specific contexts, and people. *Emotion schemas* organize these continuous experiences into *emotional episodes* using *referential process* as bidirectional connections between "multiple sensory channels and the discrete single channel verbal code" (Bucci, 2021a, 2021b). The process of a*rousal* activates an *emotion schema.* Then, the process of s*ymbolizing* describes an event associated with the activated schema. And then, the process of *reflection* explores, elaborates, and reorganizes the emotional meaning of an event (Bucci, 2021a, 2021b; Bucci, Maskit, & Murphy, 2016).

1.1.10 Love as a Cultural Idea

The Idea of Love and Reality of Love

Love is an enduring cultural idea that people and cultures have entertained throughout centuries in their fantasies, literary traditions, art, and music. *Love* in this sense is an emotionally saturated *mental representation of love relationships and love emotions of others*. Individuals may likely transfer these representations into their possible experience. Yet, this love is objectified and observed, rather than personally experienced in real life.

Despite empathic identification with a character, these feelings do not refer to the actual personal relationships or emotions of an individual with others. The idea of love is a subject of exploration in such disciplines as philosophy, literary and linguistic studies, fine arts, and music. Scholars, artists, and musicians show what love can be at its best and worst, at various dramatic, tragic, or comedian scenarios.

Scholars of various social disciplines (e.g., De Munck, Korotayev, & Khaltourina, 2009; De Munck, Korotayev, de Munck, & Khaltourina, 2011; Jankowiak, & Fischer, 1992, Jankowiak, 1995, 2008; Karandashev, 2017, 2019) have studied the cultural ideas, beliefs, and mental representations of love in many cultural contexts and found that the cultural idea of love is present in majority of cultures around the world.

The Idea of Love Reflected in Languages Across Cultures

Universality of love lexicon across cultures can also provide evidence of cross-cultural universality of love. Problem, however, is that the word *love* is not universal across languages in historical and modern cross-cultural perspectives. Wierzbicka (1992, 1999) showed the diversity of love concepts across languages. Although a variety of words conveying the meaning of *love* are available in all languages, yet they may be not precisely equivalent to the word *love* in other languages.

Some languages do not have the exact word corresponding to the English *love* (Kövecses, 2003, 2005; Wierzbicka, 1992, 1999), yet this does not mean that the emotion and disposition of love are missing in those societies. Several other words corresponding to different kinds and aspects of love are still present in those languages (see for detailed review Karandashev, 2019).

Love in many cultures exists in specific forms (e.g., love to God, familial love, brotherhood love, sexual love, romantic love), not as an abstract idea. Only some cultures have developed and coined in words *love* as a general concept.

Despite diversity of the cultural ideas about love and variety of its types, forms, and features, the extraction of some basic features is still possible. The most general and essential idea of any love is *bringing and doing something good to another person* (Wierzbicka, 1992, 1999), or in other words, *investment in the well-being of the other for their own sake* (Hegi & Bergner, 2010).

Thus, generally, to love someone is to will their good and do what is best for the person. This and other emotional concepts of love, however, can be expressed in a variety of verbal and nonverbal ways across cultures.

Religious Conceptions of Love

The love of God and the love for God are among the ancient ideas of love in the major religious traditions (e.g., Abdin, 2004; Armstrong, 2011; Aronson, 1996; Lindberg, 2008; Starr, 2012; Williams, 1968). However, the conceptions of love and its interpretations vary not only between religions but also within a religion. Agape love is probably the most common across religions. It means the caring love of God for humans and the devotional love of a human for God (Templeton, 1999). This love also encourages people to love each other. This kind of love is characterized by empathy, the unselfish desire of good to other(s) and willingness to self-sacrifice for their well-being. In Buddhist cultural tradition, it is described as loving kindness and compassion.

1.2 The Contents and Definitions of Love Concepts

1.2.1 Conceptual Definitions of Love

Importance of Conceptual Definition of Love

Love is a general, abstract, and fussy concept that people use in various meanings depending on a context. Many scholars speak about love with an implicit and unspoken assumption that others understand love in the same way. However, the word *love* stands for so many things that it is easy to confuse. These can be, for instance, emotions (Bell, 1902; Shaver et al., 1996), attitudes (Hendrick & Hendrick, 1986; Karandashev & Evans, 2019; Sternberg, 1986, 1997), scripts (Sternberg, 1995, 1996, 1999), actions (Buss, 1988; Wade et al., 2009), behavioral systems (Hazan & Shaver, 1987; Shaver & Mikulincer, 2006), and relationships (Berscheid, 2010; Davis & Todd, 1982).

Unfortunately, in many cases, scholars do not define love or define it in vague and abstract terms, such as components or dimensions, without explanation of the nature of these words. On some occasions, they use the words *emotions* and *attitudes* interchangeably throughout their text as synonyms, without distinction. This ambiguity makes it difficult or impossible to identify which part of reality of emotional life they mean.

Due to multiplicity of meanings and constructs, which scholars have in mind when they write about love, it would be a good manner, may be a requirement, to define the concept of love in every publication for better understanding between scholars. It is also important to define the components and attributes characterizing love since they can have various meanings.

Conceptual and operational definitions are important for adequate and meaningful data collection in empirical research. When the word *love* is used as a stimulus presented to a participant, a researcher should make sure that all participants understand the word the same way, as the researcher intended. Participants may have different kinds of love in their mind, different situations, etc. This might be love to a child, love to a parent, love to a romantic partner, love to a companionate partner, and love to God.

A Possibility of a Common Conceptual System of Love

Love is a concept with the lack of clarity, and it is a contested concept (Hamilton, 2006). Theorists and researchers of love are usually the authors or strong proponents of one theory or another. It is normal and understandable unless they view their own as the best one, or as the truest one, or the one which deserves attention, discarding, or neglecting others. They tend to openly or quietly disagree with the concepts and theories of love that other authors propose, thus neglecting multifaceted and contestable nature of the love concept. Researchers of love often do consider scientific legitimacy of such disagreement, but, nevertheless, regularly slip into prescriptive mode. Some philosophers (e.g., Hamilton, 2006) argue for the need of scholarly modesty and willingness of researchers to think about disagreements honestly.

As Lee reasonably noted (Lee, 1977, p. 173), the scholarly publications on love throughout times, especially in the twentieth century, have scattered many various definitions of love, which are quite divergent. Authors commonly acknowledge and describe different kinds of love. However, when they try to define love, they are obviously and carelessly biased. They tend to narrow love to their favorite and culturally ethnocentric constructs while neglecting the others. The *cultural biases* in *love definitions* are often noticeable in theories and research. Some scholars attempt to define what the *true love* is and what is not. As Berscheid noted (Berscheid, 2010), the major problems to advance the systematic study of love phenomena are the challenges to explicate the love constructs.

Scholars recognize the presence of the love theories, other than their own. Yet, they usually do not have interest and do not make attempts to put various theories and models of love in a cohesive system. It seems they study different psychological, behavioral, and relationship realities. It is partially understandable and may be reasonable. Love is a collection of so diverse philosophical and cultural ideas and beliefs, an assortment of so various individual and typological experiences and expressions, that a *universal conception of love* seems impossible.

This book, along with my previous books (Karandashev, 2017, 2019), strives to bring closer the possibility to see the *wood of love*, not just the *trees of love*. I hope that systematization and integration of the conceptions and research findings on love obtained in different cultural contexts, which are compiled in the book, allow to imagine a *constellation of love*, not just a *scatter plot of love* theories and research.

An Array of Things We Can Conceptualize as Love

There are several levels of conceptualization and abstraction in descriptions and definitions of love. They can be organized in a hierarchical structure: from concrete and tangible sensations, emotions, moods, and actions of love through more abstract attitudes, traits, values, relationships, and ideological models of love. It is worthwhile to understand love as a complex and hierarchical construct.

Love can be defined as a *basic* or *complex emotion*. In the latter case, love is a more complex concept: it is a group of other emotions which are experienced in specific situations of interpersonal encounters. Love can be defined as a basic disposition, such as mood, attitude, and trait, or as a set of dispositions, such as moods associated with love emotions, love attitudes, or loving traits. As we saw in previous sections, a variety of such conceptions of love are possible depending on the thing(s) which researcher call *love*. When researchers include in their model of love several of those love phenomena, they develop more complex conceptions of love.

Logical Definitions of Love

Conceptual definitions of love – according to the principles of logics – include notification of group of objects to which the concept belongs. Therefore, love should be defined as (1) an emotion, (2) a disposition, (3) a relationship between people, or another scientific category, which author has in mind talking about love.

Then, definition includes the description of attributes, which characterize various objects within the framework of this concept, yet apart from other concepts belonging to the same category.

Descriptive Definition of Love

This type of definitions just describes the concept characterizing its phenomenology or listing the objects belonging to this concept. Comparative definitions of love are similar. They define the concept of love in terms of other most characteristic constructs. Consequently, they reduce a complexity of the love concept to a particular construct, such as *passion*, *attachment*, *intimacy*, and *commitment*, thus defining the concept by some of its important qualities.

Prototypical Definitions

In the prototype approach to the concept of *love*, a definition may be not necessary because participants themselves define love through the words which they associate with love.

Following this prototypical methodology, researchers (Fehr & Russell, 1991) presented the participants with the *concept of love* and asked them to make a list of the examples of *subtypes of love*, which come to their mind. Then, authors asked participants to order various examples of love and rank them as the better or poorer examples of love.

Such a prototypical approach is an admirable and promising methodology to study laypeople definitions of love. It demonstrates the range of various types and subtypes of love and how they are represented in their salience (prototypicality) in the network of a person's semantic associations. The results showed (Fehr, 1988, 1994; Fehr & Russell, 1991) that laypeople consider *familial love* and *friendship love* as the kinds of love, which are closer to their prototypical views of love than *passionate* and *romantic love*.

Using *prototype methodologies*, researchers were able to understand how laypeople conceptualize the semantics of sex, love, and romantic love. The findings (De Munck, Kronenfeld, & Manoharan, 2021; Manoharan & De Munck, 2017) have shown that *American cultural model of romantic love* represents a merger of *love as bonding* and *sex*.

The same way as any emotion, love can be defined as a set of scripts of an event, or emotional episodes, which include motivational impulses, behavioral expression, proactive actions, and partner reactions. These scripts and episodes can be more or less prototypical (Russell, 1991; Russell & Barrett, 1999).

The typology of their ranking – the degree of their prototypicality in people's minds – can serve as an important basis for the typology of cultural models of love, which individuals have in mind.

The problem, however, is that general *concept of love* is too general, too abstract, and too overarching to define. Due to a personal network of association, participants have in mind its different types, like familial love, maternal love, romantic love, and love for God, which seems not well comparable and meaningful to average and generalize. Besides, participants mentioned not only the types of love, such as *parental love*, *sisterly love*, and *friendship*, but also the mixture of various words, which are in one or another way associated with love. Among those were some characteristics of love, such as *affection*, *commitment*, and *infatuation*. Thus, different concepts of love – types and dimensions – were mixed. I believe that a prototypical study of the narrower and more specific concepts of love would be more revealing.

The further research (Fehr, 1994) has made this next advancement exploring the more specific types of love. The studies have developed a new methodology to study the laypeople's understandings of various kinds of love, while prototype-based instruments and measures have demonstrated their validity and reliability for assessing people's conceptions of several emotions, including love (e.g., Fehr, 1994, 1999; Fehr & Sprecher, 2009; Le et al., 2008; Regan, Kocan, & Whitlock, 1998).

Cultural Universality and Variety of Definitions

Theoretical contemplations, conceptualization, and philosophical reasoning are the productive ways to better understand love in its omnipresent nature and diverse forms. They may proclaim what the true love is. However, the theoretical and general assertions of this kind should be grounded in the reality of life being backed by some evidence. Such evidence is usually embodied in indicators and needs operational definitions.

Definitions of love constructs – components, dimensions, factors, clusters, models, and types – encounter the issues of terminology. How shall one label the love constructs – types, styles, and models? These are conventional terms, yet there might be some preferences.

For example, talking about love styles, Lee (1977) preferred the colloquial words, such as obsessive love, dutiful love, and playful love, in general conversations and popular publications, while preferred to use the Greek and Latin terminology, such as *mania*, *pragma*, and *ludus*, in his scientific taxonomy of love.

1.2.2 The Multifaceted and Multilevel Conceptual Structure of Love

Tapping Complexity of Love

This book does not propose a new theory of love. It rather proposes a new conceptual framework to theorize and explore love as a multifaceted, multi-componential, and multilayered concept, or better as a conceptual structure. These can be a few conceptual structures, as in case of the personal models of love, typologies of personal types of love, and cultural models of love.

I believe it is time for the *science of love* to move toward more complex, multifaceted, and hierarchical models of love, consisting of the emotional experiences, expressions, and actions of various levels outlined in the section above. The hierarchical models of other human processes present the good examples in this regard. They show, for example, the importance of hierarchical structure of motivational processes (Vallerand, 2000; Vallerand & Ratelle, 2002).

Let us draft several possibilities for the hierarchical models of love.

Multilevel Structure of Love

Love is *a multilevel structure* that includes, at least, two levels: (1) *individual level* and (2) *relationship level*. On the individual level, the concept of love represents an *individual structure* of how individuals experience, express, and act when they are in love or love another. On the relationship level, the concept of love represents a *relationship structure* of how individuals interact and relate to each other when someone (any or both of them, or an external observer) may call this relationship as love. These two levels of love are in constant interaction and influence on each other. Emotions, moods, and attitudes determine interaction, relations between loving individuals, and events, which can happen in their life. And conversely, the events, interactions, and relations can change individuals' emotional experiences. The multilevel study of love in this regard is a quite interesting direction of love research.

Love on the Individual Level

On individual level, love is a hierarchical conceptual structure that includes several planes of existence. These are individual experiences, expressions, and behavioral tendencies of *sensations*, *emotions*, *moods*, *attitudes*, and *traits*. Sensations and emotions are situational, state-like experiences of love, which affect the moods, attitudes, and traits as dispositional experiences of love. And the other way around, dispositional experiences affect situational experiences of love. Each plane of individual love in the hierarchy of these concepts– sensations, emotions, moods, attitudes, traits – describes experiences of different temporal perspective. The plane of each level affects and is affected by others. Sensations determine emotions and moods, while the latter can alter the sensations. Emotions determine attitudes and traits, while the latter predispose to experience certain emotions.

Each plane of the emotional experience can engage (c) cognitive, (e) emotional, and (b) behavioral processes. For example, in case of love emotions, these are (c) cognitive appraisals, (e) subjective experience of emotions, and (b) action tendencies and expressions of emotions. In case of love attitudes, these are (c) cognitive, (e) emotional, and (b) behavioral attitudes. The sensations, moods, and traits can also include these three components. How and in what extent these components are represented in each of these emotional experiences can vary. For example, individuals frequently experience mood with a hidden cognitive component – they are not aware of the origins of their mood.

Personal and Cultural Models of Love

In addition to the *real experience of love*, as described above, individuals also have in their mind *personal* and *cultural models of love* – as regulatory components of love.

The *personal models of love* represent what they think and imagine on how love shall be and can be. These are their expectations and aspirations about love in their lives – their expected feelings, emotions, attitudes, traits, roles, and relationships.

The *cultural models of love* represent what societies and cultures prescribe on how love shall be and can be. These are the cultural expectations about what love shall be and can be experienced and expressed and what kind of behaviors and relationships are ideal, acceptable, permissible, and forbidden.

Love on the Relationship Level

On the relationship level, love is a hierarchical conceptual structure that includes several planes of interaction. These are *situational actions* and *reactions* of partners, their episodic *dyadic interactions*, the short-term and long-term *patterns of interaction*, the *scripts of interactions* related to certain events, and the general *trait-like qualities* of their actions and interactions as the characteristics of their love relationship. These *planes of interactions* can be considered in a certain concordance with individual experiences, expressions, and behavioral tendencies (*sensations*, *emotions*, *moods*, *attitudes*, and *traits*), at least in terms of their temporal perspectives.

References

Abdin, A. S. (2004). Love in Islam. *European Judaism, 37*(1), 92–102.

Acevedo, B. P., Aron, A., Fisher, H. E., & Brown, L. L. (2012). Neural correlates of long-term intense romantic love. *Social Cognitive and Affective Neuroscience, 7*(2), 145–159. https://doi.org/10.1093/scan/nsq092

Albarracin, D., Johnson, B. T., & Zanna, M. P. (Eds.). (2014). *The handbook of attitudes*. Psychology Press.

Allegri, R. (2011). *Conversations with Mother Teresa: A personal portrait of the saint, her mission, and her great love for God*. The Word Among Us Press.

Alonso-Arbiol, I., Shaver, P. R., Fraley, R. C., Oronoz, B., Unzurrunzaga, E., & Urizar, R. (2006). Structure of the Basque emotion lexicon. *Cognition and Emotion, 20*(6), 836–865.

Arman, M., & Rehnsfeldt, A. (2006, January). The presence of love in ethical caring. *Nursing forum, 41*(1), 4–12. Blackwell Publishing Inc.

Armstrong, K. (2011). *A history of God: The 4,000-year quest of Judaism, Christianity and Islam*. Ballantine Books.

Arnold, M. B. (1960). *Emotion and personality* (Vol. 2). Columbia University Press.

Aron, A., Fisher, H., Mashek, D. J., Strong, G., Li, H., & Brown, L. L. (2005). Reward, motivation, and emotion systems associated with early-stage intense romantic love. *Journal of Neurophysiology, 94*(*1*), 327–337. https://doi.org/10.1152/jn.00838.2004

Aronson, H. B. (1996). *Love and sympathy in Theravāda Buddhism*. Motilal Banarsidass Publishing House.
Arriaga, X. B. (2013). An interdependence theory analysis of close relationships. In J. A. Simpson & L. Campbell (Eds.), *Oxford library of psychology. The Oxford handbook of close relationships* (pp. 39–65). Oxford University Press.
Bacon, R. E. (2012). *8 habits of love: Overcome fear and transform your life*. Grand Central Life & Style.
Badhwar, A. (2014). *Measuring prosocial action tendencies for caretaking emotions* (Doctoral dissertation, University of Michigan).
Bajoghli, H., Joshaghani, N., Gerber, M., Mohammadi, M. R., Holsboer-Trachsler, E., & Brand, S. (2013). In Iranian female and male adolescents, romantic love is related to hypomania and low depressive symptoms, but also to higher state anxiety. *International Journal of Psychiatry in Clinical Practice, 17*(2), 98–109.
Bajoghli, H., Farnia, V., Joshaghani, N., Haghighi, M., Jahangard, L., Ahmadpanah, M., … Brand, S. (2017). "I love you forever (more or less)" – Stability and change in adolescents' romantic love status and associations with mood states. *Brazilian Journal of Psychiatry, 39*(4), 323–329.
Baldwin, M. (1992). Relational schemas and the processing of social information. *Psychological Bulletin, 112*(3), 461–484. https://doi.org/10.1037/0033-2909.112.3.461
Banaji, M. R., & Heiphetz, L. (2010). Attitudes. In S. T. Fiske, D. T. Gilbert, & G. Lindzey (Eds.), *Handbook of social psychology* (Vol. 1, 5th ed., pp. 353–393). Wiley.
Barrett, L. F., Mesquita, B., Ochsner, K. N., & Gross, J. J. (2007). The experience of emotion. *Annual Review of Psychology, 58*, 373–403.
Barsade, S. G., & Gibson, D. E. (2007). Why does affect matter in organizations? *Academy of management perspectives, 21*(1), 36–59.
Bartels, A., & Zeki, S. (2004). The neural correlates of maternal and romantic love. *NeuroImage, 21*(3), 1155–1166. https://doi.org/10.1016/j.neuroimage.2003.11.003
Bell, S. (1902). A preliminary study of the emotion of love between the sexes. *The American Journal of Psychology, 13*(3), 325–354.
Bellah, R. N., Madien, R., Sullivan, W. M., Swidler, A., & Tipton, S. M. (1985). *Habits of the heart: Individualism and commitment in American life*. University of California Press.
Berger, C. R., & Bradac, J. J. (1982). *Language and social knowledge: Uncertainty in interpersonal relationships*. Edward Arnold.
Berger, C. R., & Calabrese, R. J. (1975). Some explorations in initial interaction and beyond: Toward a developmental theory of interpersonal communication. *Human Communication Research, 1*, 99–112.
Berscheid, E. (2010). Love in the fourth dimension. *Annual Review of Psychology, 61*(1), 1–25. https://doi.org/10.1146/annurev.psych.093008.100318
Berscheid, E., & Walster, E. (1974). A little bit about love. In T. L. Huston (Ed.), *Foundations of interpersonal attraction* (pp. 355–381). Academic.
Bloch, S., Orthous, P., & Santibañez-H, G. (1987). Effector patterns of basic emotions: A psychophysiological method for training actors. *Journal of Social and Biological Structures, 10*(1), 1–19.
Boiger, M., & Mesquita, B. (2014). A socio-dynamic perspective on the construction of emotion. In L. F. Barrett & J. A. Russell (Eds.), *The psychological construction of emotion* (pp. 377–398). Guilford Press.
Bolmont, M., Cacioppo, J. T., & Cacioppo, S. (2014). Love is in the gaze: An eye-tracking study of love and sexual desire. *Psychological Science, 25*(9), 1748–1756.
Bolton, C. D. (1959). *The development process in love relationships* (Doctoral dissertation, University of Chicago, Department of Sociology).
Bonino, S. (2018). *Nature and culture in intimate partner violence: Sex, love and equality*. Routledge.
Borland, D. (1975). An alternative model of the wheel theory. *The Family Coordinator, 24*(3), 289–292. https://doi.org/10.2307/583179

Borochowitz, D. Y., & Eisikovits, Z. (2002). To love violently: Strategies for reconciling love and violence. *Violence Against Women, 8*(4), 476–494.

Bosman, M., Spronk, R., & Kuipers, G. (2019). Verbalizing sensations: Making sense of embodied sexual experiences. *Qualitative Sociology, 42*(3), 411–430.

Brand, S., Luethi, M., von Planta, A., Hatzinger, M., & Holsboer-Trachsler, E. (2007). Romantic love, hypomania, and sleep pattern in adolescents. *Journal of Adolescent Health, 41*(1), 69–76.

Breugelmans, S. M., Ambadar, Z., Vaca, J. B., Poortinga, Y. H., Setiadi, B., Widiyanto, P., & Philippot, P. (2005). Body sensations associated with emotions in Rarámuri Indians, rural Javanese, and three student samples. *Emotion, 5*(2), 166–175.

Bucci, W. (2021a). Overview of the referential process: The operation of language within and between people. *Journal of Psycholinguistic Research, 50*(1), 3–15. https://doi.org/10.1007/s10936-021-09759-2

Bucci, W. (2021b). Development and validation of measures of referential activity. *Journal of Psycholinguistic Research, 50*, 17–27. https://doi.org/10.1007/s10936-021-09760-9

Bucci, W., Maskit, B., & Murphy, S. (2016). Connecting emotions and words: The referential process. *Phenomenology and the Cognitive Sciences, 15*(3), 359–383. https://doi.org/10.1007/s11097-015-9417-z

Buss, D. M. (1988). Love acts: The evolutionary biology of love. In R. J. Sternberg & M. L. Barnes (Eds.), *The psychology of love* (pp. 100–118). Yale University Press.

Campbell, L., Simpson, J., Kashy, D., & Fletcher, G. (2001). Ideal standards, the self, and flexibility of ideals in close relationships. *Personality and Social Psychology Bulletin, 27*, 447–462.

Campbell, L., Simpson, J. A., Kashy, D. A., & Rholes, W. S. (2001). Attachment orientations, dependence, and behavior in a stressful situation: An application of the actor-partner interdependence model. *Journal of Social and Personal Relationships, 18*(6), 821–843.

Carlson, J. G., & Hatfield, E. (1992). *Psychology of emotion*. Harcourt Brace Jovanovich.

Centers, R. (1975). *Sexual attraction and love: An instrumental theory*. Charles. C. Thomas.

Cromby, J. (2007). Toward a psychology of feeling. *International Journal of Critical Psychology, 21*(94), 94–118.

Cunningham, W. A., & Zelazo, P. D. (2007). Attitudes and evaluations: A social cognitive neuroscience perspective. *Trends in Cognitive Sciences, 11*(3), 97–104.

Cunningham, W. A., Raye, C. L., & Johnson, M. K. (2004). Implicit and explicit evaluation: fMRI correlates of valence, emotional intensity, and control in the processing of attitudes. *Journal of Cognitive Neuroscience, 16*(10), 1717–1729.

Davis, L. A. (2020). *Love habits: Easy strategies for a stronger, happier relationship*. Rockridge Press.

Davis, K. E., & Todd, M. J. (1982). Friendship and love relationships. In K. E. Davis & T. D. Mitchell (Eds.), *Advances in descriptive psychology* (Vol. 2, pp. 79–122). JAI Press.

De Hooge, I. E., Breugelmans, S. M., & Zeelenberg, M. (2008). Not so ugly after all: When shame acts as a commitment device. *Journal of Personality and Social Psychology, 95*(4), 933–943. https://doi.org/10.1037/a0011991

De Munck, V., Korotayev, A., & Khaltourina, D. (2009). A comparative study of the structure of love in the US and Russia: Finding a common core of characteristics and national and gender differences. *Ethnology: An International Journal of Cultural and Social Anthropology, 48*(4), 337–357.

De Munck, V. C., Korotayev, A., de Munck, J., & Khaltourina, D. (2011). Cross-cultural analysis of models of romantic love among US residents, Russians, and Lithuanians. *Cross-Cultural Research, 45*(2), 128–154.

De Munck, V. C., Kronenfeld, D. B., & Manoharan, C. (2021). A prototype analysis of the cultural and evolutionary construction of romantic love as a synthesis of love and sex. *Journal of Cognition and Culture, 21*(1–2), 25–48.

Dölen, G. (2017). Setting the mood for love. *Nature Neuroscience, 20*(3), 379–380.

Dowrick, S. (1997). *Forgiveness and other acts of love*. W. W. Norton & Company.

Ekman, P. (1992a). Are there basic emotions? *Psychological Review, 99*(3), 550–553. https://doi.org/10.1037/0033-295X.99.3.550

Ekman, P. (1992b). An argument for basic emotions. *Cognition & Emotion, 6*, 169–200.
Ekman, P. (1999). Basic emotions. In T. Dalgleish & T. Power (Eds.), *The handbook of cognition and emotion* (pp. 45–60). Wiley.
Ekman, P., & Cordaro, D. (2011). What is meant by calling emotions basic. *Emotion Review, 3*(4), 364–370.
Ekman, P., & Davidson, R. (Eds.). (1994). *The nature of emotion: Fundamental questions*. Oxford University Press.
Elliot, A. J., Eder, A. B., & Harmon-Jones, E. (2013). Approach-avoidance motivation and emotion: Convergence and divergence. *Emotion Review, 5*(*3*), 308–311. https://doi.org/10.1177/1754073913477517
Ellsworth, P. C., & Scherer, K. R. (2003). Appraisal processes in emotion. In R. J. Davidson, H. Goldsmith, & K. R. Scherer (Eds.), *Handbook of the affective sciences* (pp. 572–595). Oxford University Press.
Engel, G., Olson, K. R., & Patrick, C. (2002). The personality of love: Fundamental motives and traits related to components of love. *Personality and Individual Differences, 32*(5), 839–853.
Esch, T., & Stefano, G. B. (2005). The neurobiology of love. *Neuroendocrinology Letters, 26*(3), 175–192.
Fazio, R. H. (1995). Attitudes as object-evaluation associations: Determinants, consequences, and correlates of attitude accessibility. In R. E. Petty & J. A. Krosnick (Eds.), *Attitude strength: Antecedents and consequences* (pp. 247–282). Lawrence Erlbaum.
Fazio, R. H., Powell, M. C., & Herr, P. M. (1983). Toward a process model of the attitude-behavior relation: Accessing one's attitude upon mere observation of the attitude object. *Journal of Personality and Social Psychology, 44*(4), 723–735.
Fehr, B. (1988). Prototype analysis of the concepts of love and commitment. *Journal of Personality and Social Psychology, 55*, 557–579.
Fehr, B. (1994). Prototype-based assessment of Laypeople's views of love. *Personal Relationships, 1*(4), 309–331.
Fehr, B. (1999). Laypeople's conceptions of commitment. *Journal of Personality and Social Psychology, 76*(1), 90–103. https://doi.org/10.1037/0022-3514.76.1.90
Fehr, B., & Russell, J. A. (1984). The concept of emotion viewed from a prototype perspective. *Journal of Experimental Psychology: General, 113*(3), 464–486.
Fehr, B., & Russell, J. A. (1991). The concept of love viewed from a prototype perspective. *Journal of Personality and Social Psychology, 60*(3), 425–438. https://doi.org/10.1037/0022-3514.60.3.425
Fehr, B., & Sprecher, S. (2009). Prototype analysis of the concept of compassionate love. *Personal Relationships, 16*(3), 343–364.
Feinberg, T. E., & Mallatt, J. (2016). The nature of primary consciousness. A new synthesis. *Consciousness and Cognition, 43*, 113–127.
Fisher, H. E. (2004). *Why we love: The nature and the chemistry of romantic love*. Henry Holt.
Fisher, H. E. (2006). The drive to love: The neural mechanism for mate selection. In R. J. Sternberg & K. Weis (Eds.), *The new psychology of love* (pp. 87–115). Yale University Press.
Fitness, J., & Fletcher, G. J. O. (1993). Love, hate, anger, and jealousy in close relationships: A prototype and cognitive appraisal analysis. *Journal of Personality and Social Psychology, 65*(5), 942–958. https://doi.org/10.1037/0022-3514.65.5.942
Fletcher, G. J., Simpson, J. A., & Thomas, G. (2000). Ideals, perceptions, and evaluations in early relationship development. *Journal of Personality and Social Psychology, 79*, 933–940. https://doi.org/10.1037/0022-3514.79.6.933
Fontaine, J. R. J., Scherer, K. R., Roesch, E. B., & Ellsworth, P. C. (2007). The world of emotions is not two-dimensional. *Psychological Science, 18*(12), 1050–1057. https://doi.org/10.1111/j.1467-9280.2007.02024.x
Freud, S. (1951). *Group psychology and the analysis of the ego* (J. Strachey, Ed. and Trans.). Liveright (Originally work published 1922).
Frieze, I. H. (2005). *Hurting the one you love: Violence in relationships*. Thomson Learning.

Frijda, N. H. (1986). *The emotions*. Cambridge University Press.

Frijda, N. H. (1993). The place of appraisal in emotion. *Cognition and Emotion, 7*, 357–387.

Frijda, N. H. (2010). Impulsive action and motivation. *Biological Psychology, 84*, 570–579. https://doi.org/10.1016/j.biopsycho.2010.01.005

Frijda, N. H., Mesquita, B., Sonnemans, J., & van Goozen, S. (1991). The duration of affective phenomena or emotions, sentiments and passions. In K. T. Strongman (Ed.), *International review of studies on emotion* (Vol. 1, pp. 187–225). Wiley.

Fuochi, G., & Voci, A. (2020). Dealing with the ups and downs of life: Positive dispositions in coping with negative and positive events and their relationships with well-being indicators. *Journal of Happiness Studies*, 1–22. https://doi.org/10.1007/s10902-020-00329-2

Furnham, A., & Ribchester, T. (1995). Tolerance of ambiguity: A review of the concept, its measurement and applications. *Current Psychology, 14*(3), 179–199.

Gold, J. A., Ryckman, R. M., & Mosley, N. R. (1984). Romantic mood induction and attraction to a dissimilar other: Is love blind? *Personality and Social Psychology Bulletin, 10*(3), 358–368.

Greene, M. (2004). *Mother Teresa: A biography*. Greenwood Press.

Gross, J. J. (2002). Emotion regulation: Affective, cognitive, and social consequences. *Psychophysiology, 39*, 281–291.

Gudykunst, W. B. (1985). A model of uncertainty reduction in intercultural encounters. *Journal of Language and Social Psychology, 4*(2), 79–98.

Gudykunst, W. B., Yang, S. M., & Nishida, T. (1985). A cross-cultural test of uncertainty reduction theory: Comparisons of acquaintances, friends, and dating relationships in Japan, Korea, and the United States. *Human Communication Research, 11*(3), 407–454.

Hagemeyer, B., & Neyer, F. J. (2012). Assessing implicit motivational orientations in couple relationships: The Partner-Related Agency and Communion Test (PACT). *Psychological Assessment, 24*(1), 114–128. https://doi.org/10.1037/a0024822

Haidt, J. (2003). The moral emotions. In R. J. Davidson, K. R. Scherer, & H. H. Goldsmith (Eds.), *Series in affective science. Handbook of affective sciences* (pp. 852–870). Oxford University Press.

Hamilton, R. P. (2006). Love as a contested concept. *Journal for the Theory of Social Behaviour, 36*(3), 239–254.

Hammock, G., & Richardson, D. S. (2011). Love attitudes and relationship experience. *The Journal of Social Psychology, 151*(5), 608–624. https://doi.org/10.1080/00224545.2010.522618

Handy, T. C., Smilek, D., Geiger, L., Liu, C., & Schooler, J. W. (2010). ERP evidence for rapid hedonic evaluation of logos. *Journal of Cognitive Neuroscience, 22*(1), 124–138. https://doi.org/10.1162/jocn.2008.21180

Hassebrauck, M., & Fehr, B. (2002). Dimensions of relationship quality. *Personal Relationships, 9*(3), 253–270.

Hatfield, E., & Rapson, R. L. (1993). *Love, sex, and intimacy: Their psychology, biology, and history*. HarperCollins.

Hatfield, E., & Rapson, R. L. (2009). The neuropsychology of passionate love and sexual desire. In E. Cuyler & M. Ackhart (Eds.), *Psychology of social relationships*. Hauppauge, NY.

Hatfield, E., Cacioppo, J., & Rapson, R. (1994). *Emotional contagion*. Cambridge University Press.

Hazan, C., & Shaver, P. (1987). Romantic love conceptualized as an attachment process. *Journal of Personality and Social Psychology, 52*(3), 511–524. https://doi.org/10.1037/0022-3514.52.3.511

Hecht, M. L., Marston, P. J., & Larkey, L. K. (1994). Love ways and relationship quality in heterosexual relationships. *Journal of Social and Personal Relationships, 11*(1), 25–43.

Hegi, K. E., & Bergner, R. M. (2010). What is love? An empirically-based essentialist account. *Journal of Social and Personal Relationships, 27*(5), 620–636.

Hendrick, C., & Hendrick, S. S. (1986). A theory and method of love. *Journal of Personality and Social Psychology, 50*, 392–402.

Hendrick, C., & Hendrick, S. S. (1989). Research on love: Does it measure up? *Journal of Personality and Social Psychology, 56*(5), 784–794. https://doi.org/10.1037/0022-3514.56.5.784

Hendrick, C., & Hendrick, S. S. (1990). A relationship specific version of the love attitudes scale. *Journal of Social Behavior and Personality, 5*, 239–254.

Hendrick, C., Hendrick, S. S., & Dicke, A. (1998). The love attitudes scale: Short form. *Journal of Social and Personal Relationships, 15*(2), 147–159.

Huelsman, T. J., Furr, R. M., & Nemanick, R. C., Jr. (2003). Measurement of dispositional affect: Construct validity and convergence with a circumplex model of affect. *Educational and Psychological Measurement, 63*(4), 655–673.

Huston, T. L., & Rempel, J. K. (1989). Interpersonal attitudes, dispositions, and behavior in family and other close relationships. *Journal of Family Psychology, 3*(2), 177–198. https://doi.org/10.1037/h0080537

Izard, C. E. (1991). *The psychology of emotions*. Plenum.

Izard, C. E., Libero, D. Z., Putnam, P., & Haynes, O. M. (1993). Stability of emotion experiences and their relations to traits of personality. *Journal of Personality and Social Psychology, 64*(5), 847–860. https://doi.org/10.1037/0022-3514.64.5.847

Jamison, S. (1995). *Final acts of love: Families, friends, and assisted dying*. Tarcher/Putnam.

Jankowiak, W. (Ed.). (1995). *Romantic passion: A universal experience?* Columbia University Press.

Jankowiak, W. (Ed.). (2008). *Intimacies: Love and sex across cultures*. Columbia University Press.

Jankowiak, W., & Fischer, E. (1992). A cross-cultural perspective on romantic love. *Ethnology, 31*(2), 149–155.

Johnson, D. W., & Johnson, R. T. (2005). New developments in social interdependence theory. *Genetic, Social, and General Psychology Monographs, 131*(4), 285–358.

Jonason, P. K., Lowder, A. H., & Zeigler-Hill, V. (2020). The mania and ludus love styles are central to pathological personality traits. *Personality and Individual Differences, 165*, 110159.

Karandashev, V. (2017). *Romantic love in cultural contexts*. Springer.

Karandashev, V. (2019). *Cross-cultural perspectives on the experience and expression of love*. Springer.

Karandashev, V. (2021a). *Cultural models of emotions*. Springer.

Karandashev, V. (2021b). Cultural diversity of romantic love experience. In C. Mayer & E. Vanderheiden (Eds.), *International handbook of love* (pp. 59–79). Springer.

Karandashev, V., & Evans, N. D. (2017). *Test of implicit associations in relationship attitudes (TIARA): Manual for a new method*. Springer.

Karandashev, V., & Evans, N. D. (2019). Quadrangular love theory and scale: Validation and psychometric investigation. *Journal of Methods and Measurement in the Social Sciences, 10*(1), 1–35.

Kashy, D. A., & Kenny, D. A. (2000). The analysis of data from dyads and groups. In H. Reis & C. M. Judd (Eds.), *Handbook of research methods in social and personality psychology* (pp. 451–477). Cambridge University Press.

Katz, J. M. (1976). How do you love me? Let me count the ways (the phenomenology of being loved). *Sociological Inquiry, 46*(1), 17–22.

Kellerman, J., Lewis, J., & Laird, J. D. (1989). Looking and loving: The effects of mutual gaze on feelings of romantic love. *Journal of Research in Personality, 23*(2), 145–161.

Kelley, H. H., & Thibaut, J. W. (1978). *Interpersonal relations: A theory of interdependence*. Wiley.

Kelley, H. H., Holmes, J. G., Kerr, N. L., Reis, H. T., Rusbult, C. E., & Van Lange, P. A. M. (2003). *An atlas of interpersonal situations*. Cambridge University Press.

Kenny, D. A. (1995). The effect of nonindependence on significance testing in dyadic research. *Personal relationships, 2*(1), 67–75.

Kenny, D. A., & Ledermann, T. (2010). Detecting, measuring, and testing dyadic patterns in the actor-partner interdependence model. *Journal of Family Psychology, 24*, 359–366. https://doi.org/10.1037/a0019651

Knobloch, L. K. (2007). The dark side of relational uncertainty: Obstacle or opportunity? In B. Spitzberg & W. Cupach (Eds.), *The dark side of interpersonal communication* (2nd ed., pp. 31–59). Lawrence Erlbaum.

Knobloch, L. K. (2008). Uncertainty reduction theory. In L. A. Baxter & D. O. Braithwaite (Eds.), *Engaging theories in interpersonal communication* (pp. 133–144). Sage.

Knobloch, L. K., & Solomon, D. H. (1999). Measuring the sources and content of relational uncertainty. *Communication Studies, 50*(4), 261–278.

Knobloch, L. K., & Solomon, D. H. (2002a). Information seeking beyond initial interaction: Negotiating relational uncertainty within close relationships. *Human Communication Research, 28*(2), 243–257.

Knobloch, L. K., & Solomon, D. H. (2002b). Intimacy and the magnitude and experience of episodic relational uncertainty within romantic relationships. *Personal Relationships, 9*, 457–478.

Knobloch, L. K., & Solomon, D. H. (2005). Relational uncertainty and relational information processing: Questions without answers? *Communication Research, 32*(3), 349–388.

Köteles, F. (2021). *Body sensations: The conscious aspects of interoception*. Springer Nature.

Kövecses, Z. (1988). *The language of love: The semantics of passion in conversational English*. Bucknell University Press.

Kövecses, Z. (2003). *Metaphor and emotion: Language, culture, and body in human feeling*. Cambridge University Press.

Kövecses, Z. (2005). *Metaphor in culture: Universality and variation*. Cambridge University Press.

Krams, I. (2016). Emotional disposition. In V. Weekes-Shackelford, T. Shackelford, & V. Weekes-Shackelford (Eds.), *Encyclopedia of evolutionary psychological science*. Springer. https://doi.org/10.1007/978-3-319-16999-6_3052-1

Krosnick, J. A., & Petty, R. E. (1995). Attitude strength: An overview. In R. E. Petty & J. A. Krosnick (Eds.), *Attitude strength: Antecedents and consequences* (pp. 1–24). Lawrence Erlbaum.

Lalljee, M., Brown, L. B., & Ginsburg, G. P. (1984). Attitudes: Disposition, behaviour or evaluation? *British Journal of Social Psychology, 23*(3), 233–244.

Lamm, H., & Wiesmann, U. (1997). Subjective attributes of attraction: How people characterize their liking, their love, and their being in love. *Personal Relationships, 4*(3), 271–284.

Lazarus, R. S. (1991). *Emotion and adaptation*. Oxford University Press.

Le, B., Loving, T. J., Lewandowski, G. W., Jr., Feinberg, E. G., Johnson, K. C., Fiorentino, R., & Ing, J. (2008). Missing a romantic partner: A prototype analysis. *Personal Relationships, 15*(4), 511–532.

Lee, J. L. (1973). *The colors of love: The exploration of the ways of loving*. New Press.

Lee, J. A. (1976). *The colors of love*. Prentice-Hall.

Lee, J. A. (1977). A typology of styles of loving. *Personality and Social Psychology Bulletin, 3*(2), 173–182.

Lewis, R. A. (1973). A longitudinal test of a developmental framework for premarital dyadic formation. *Journal of Marriage and the Family, 35*, 16–25.

Lewis, M. (2008). Self-conscious emotions: Embarrassment, pride, shame, and guilt. In M. Lewis, J. M. Haviland-Jones, & L. F. Barrett (Eds.), *Handbook of emotions* (pp. 742–756). The Guilford Press.

Liebowitz, M. R. (1983). *The chemistry of love*. Little, Brown, and Co..

Lindberg, C. (2008). *Love: A brief history through Western Christianity*. Wiley.

Livingston, K. R. (1980). Love as a process of reducing uncertainty. In K. S. Pope (Ed.), *On love and loving* (pp. 133–151). Jossey-Bass.

Locke, K. D. (2015). Agentic and communal social motives. *Social and Personality Psychology Compass, 9*(10), 525–538.

Locke, K. D. (2018). Agentic and communal social motives. In A. Abele & B. Wojciszke (Eds.), *Agency and communion in social psychology* (pp. 65–78). Routledge.

Londero-Santos, A., Natividade, J. C., & Féres-Carneiro, T. (2020). Romantic relationship and partner schemas: Concepts associated with a positive valence. *Trends in Psychology, 28*, 511–528.

Macher, S. (2013). Social interdependence in close relationships: The actor–partner-interdependence–investment model (API-IM). *European Journal of Social Psychology, 43*(1), 84–96.

MacKinnon, N. J., & Keating, L. J. (1989). The structure of emotions: Canada-United States comparisons. *Social Psychology Quarterly, 52*, 70–83.

Manoharan, C., & De Munck, V. (2017). The conceptual relationship between love, romantic love, and sex: A free list and prototype study of semantic association. *Journal of Mixed Methods Research, 11*(2), 248–265.

Markman, A. B., & Brendl, C. M. (2005). Constraining theories of embodied cognition. *Psychological Science, 16*(1), 6–10. https://doi.org/10.1111/j.0956-7976.2005.00772.x

Marston, P. J., Hecht, M. L., & Robers, T. (1987). True love ways': The subjective experience and communication of romantic love. *Journal of Social and Personal Relationships, 4*(4), 387–407.

Martin, P., & Luke, L. (1991). Divorce and the wheel theory of love. *Journal of Divorce & Remarriage, 15*(1–2), 3–22.

Matsumoto, D., & Hwang, H. S. (2012). Culture and emotion: The integration of biological and cultural contributions. *Journal of Cross-Cultural Psychology, 43*(1), 91–118.

Matsumoto, D., Kudoh, T., Scherer, K. R., & Wallbott, H. (1988). Antecedents of and reactions to emotions in the United States and Japan. *Journal of Cross-Cultural Psychology, 19*(3), 267–286.

Maurer, C. (2020). Tolerance, love, and justice. In R. Fedock, M. Kühler, & R. Rosenhagen (Eds.), *Love, justice, and autonomy: Philosophical perspectives* (pp. 150–166). Routledge.

Mauro, R., Sato, K., & Tucker, J. (1992). The role of appraisal in human emotions: A cross-cultural study. *Journal of Personality and Social Psychology, 62*(2), 301–317.

McAdams, D. P., Hoffman, B. J., Day, R., & Mansfield, E. D. (1996). Themes of agency and communion in significant autobiographical scenes. *Journal of Personality, 64*(2), 339–377.

McCullough, M. E., Bono, G., & Root, L. M. (2007). Rumination, emotion, and forgiveness: Three longitudinal studies. *Journal of Personality and Social Psychology, 92*(3), 490–505.

Mendes, W. B. (2008). Assessing autonomic nervous system reactivity. In E. Harmon-Jones & J. Beer (Eds.), *Methods in the neurobiology of social and personality psychology* (pp. 118–147). Guilford Press.

Mesquita, B. (2003). Emotions as dynamic cultural phenomena. In R. Davidson, H. Goldsmith, & K. R. Scherer (Eds.), *The handbook of affective sciences* (pp. 871–890). Oxford University Press.

Mesquita, B., & Ellsworth, P. C. (2001). The role of culture in appraisal. In K. R. Scherer, A. Schorr, & T. Johnstone (Eds.), *Appraisal processes in emotion. Theory, methods, research* (pp. 233–248). Oxford University Press.

Mesquita, B., & Frijda, N. H. (1992). Cultural variations in emotions: A review. *Psychological Bulletin, 112*(2), 179–204. https://doi.org/10.1037/0033-2909.112.2.179

Mesquita, B., & Leu, J. (2007). The cultural psychology of emotion. In S. Kitayama & D. Cohen (Eds.), *Handbook of cultural psychology* (pp. 734–759). Guilford Press.

Meyers, S. A., & Berscheid, E. (1997). The language of love: The difference a preposition makes. *Personality and Social Psychology Bulletin, 23*(4), 347–362.

Michael, J. (2016). *Acts of love*. Simon and Schuster.

Moors, A., Ellsworth, P. C., Scherer, K. R., & Frijda, N. H. (2013). Appraisal theories of emotion: State of the art and future development. *Emotion Review, 5*(2), 119–124.

Morris, D. (1971). *Intimate behavior*. Random House.

Moskowitz, D. S., Suh, E. J., & Desaulniers, J. (1994). Situational influences on gender differences in agency and communion. *Journal of Personality and Social Psychology, 66*(4), 753–761. https://doi.org/10.1037/0022-3514.66.4.753

Naar, H. (2013). A dispositional theory of love. *Pacific Philosophical Quarterly, 94*(3), 342–357.

Nezlek, J. B., Vansteelandt, K., Van Mechelen, I., & Kuppens, P. (2008). Appraisal-emotion relationships in daily life. *Emotion, 8*(1), 145–150. https://doi.org/10.1037/1528-3542.8.1.145

Nicholson, C. (2007). Fact or fiction? "Spring fever" is a real phenomenon. *Scientific American,* posted on March 22, 2007 at https://www.scientificamerican.com/article/fact-or-fiction-spring-fever-is-a-real-phenomenon/

Nowlis, V. (1970). Mood: Behavior and experience. In M. B. Arnold (Ed.), *Feelings and emotions: The Loyola Symposium* (pp. 261–277). Academic.

Nummenmaa, L., Glerean, E., Hari, R., & Hietanen, J. K. (2014). Bodily maps of emotions. *Proceedings of the National Academy of Sciences, 111*(2), 646–651.

Oatley, K., & Duncan, E. (1994). The experience of emotions in everyday life. *Cognition and Emotion, 8*, 369–381.

Oatley, K., & Johnson-Laird, P. N. (1987). Toward a cognitive theory of emotions. *Cognition & Emotion, 1*, 29–50.

Oravecz, Z., Dirsmith, J., Heshmati, S., Vandekerckhove, J., & Brick, T. R. (2020). Psychological well-being and personality traits are associated with experiencing love in everyday life. *Personality and Individual Differences, 153*, 109620.

Osgood, C. E., May, W. H., & Mirron, M. S. (1975). *Cross-cultural universals of affective meanings*. University of Illinois Press.

Peeters, G. (1971). The positive-negative asymmetry: On cognitive consistency and positivity bias. *European Journal of Social Psychology, 1*(4), 455–474.

Perunovic, W. Q. E., Heller, D., & Rafaeli, E. (2007). Within-person changes in the structure of emotion: The role of cultural identification and language. *Psychological Science, 18*(7), 607–613.

Pismenny, A., & Prinz, J. (2017). Is love an emotion? In *The oxford handbook of philosophy of love* [online ahead of print]. Oxford University Press. https://www.oxfordhandbooks.com/view/10.1093/oxfordhb/9780199395729.001,1

Planalp, S., Rutherford, D. K., & Honeycutt, J. M. (1988). Events that increase uncertainty in personal relationships II: Replication and extension. *Human Communication Research, 14*(4), 516–547.

Plutchik, R. (1982). A psychoevolutionary theory of emotions. *Social Science Information, 21*(4–5), 529–553. https://doi.org/10.1177/053901882021004003

Proctor, R. W., & Zhang, Y. (2010). "Mother nature doesn't have a bullet with your name on it": Coding with reference to one's name or object location? *Journal of Experimental Social Psychology, 46*, 336–343. https://doi.org/10.1016/j.jesp.2009.10.010

Puccetti, N., Villano, W., Stamatis, C. A., Torrez, V. F., Neta, M., Timpano, K., & Heller, A. S. (2020, December 28). Daily emotion links task-based negativity bias and variability in depressive symptoms. https://doi.org/10.31234/osf.io/gdszp

Regan, P. C., Kocan, E. R., & Whitlock, T. (1998). Ain't love grand! A prototype analysis of the concept of romantic love. *Journal of Social and Personal Relationships, 15*(3), 411–420.

Reis, H. T., Maniaci, M. R., & Rogge, R. D. (2014). The expression of compassionate love in everyday compassionate acts. *Journal of Social and Personal Relationships, 31*(5), 651–676.

Reisenzein, R. (2006). Arnold's theory of emotion in historical perspective. *Cognition and Emotion, 20*(7), 920–951.

Reiss, I. L. (1960). Toward a sociology of the heterosexual love relationship. *Marriage and Family Living, 22*(2), 139–145.

Roberts, R. C. (2013). Emotion. In H. Lafollette (Ed.), *International encyclopedia of ethics*. https://doi.org/10.1002/9781444367072.wbiee290

Roseman, I. J. (2017). Transformative events: Appraisal bases of passion and mixed emotions. *Emotion Review, 9*(2), 133–139.

Roseman, I. J., & Smith, C. A. (2001). Appraisal theory: Overview, assumptions, varieties, controversies. In K. R. Scherer, A. Schorr, & T. Johnstone (Eds.), *Appraisal processes in emotion* (pp. 3–19). Oxford University Press.

Roseman, I. J., Dhawan, N., Rettek, S. L., Naidu, R. K., & Thapa, K. (1995). Cultural differences and cross-cultural similarities in appraisals and emotional responses. *Journal of Cross-Cultural Psychology, 26*, 23–48.

Rubin, Z. (1970). Measurement of romantic love. *Journal of Personality and Social Psychology, 16*, 265–273.

Rubin, Z. (1973). *Liking and loving: An invitation to social psychology*. Holt.

Rusbult, C. E. (1983). A longitudinal test of the investment model: The development (and deterioration) of satisfaction and commitment in heterosexual involvements. *Journal of Personality and Social Psychology, 45*(1), 101–117. https://doi.org/10.1037/0022-3514.45.1.101

Rusbult, C. E., & Arriaga, X. B. (1997). Interdependence theory. In S. Duck (Ed.), *Handbook of personal relationships: Theory, research and interventions* (pp. 221–250). Wiley.
Rusbult, C. E., & Martz, J. M. (1995). Remaining in an abusive relationship: An investment model analysis of nonvoluntary commitment. *Personality and Social Psychology Bulletin, 21*, 558–571. https://doi.org/10.1177/0146167295216002
Rusbult, C. E., & Van Lange, P. A. M. (2003). Interdependence, interaction, and relationships. *Annual Review of Psychology, 54*, 351–375. https://doi.org/10.1146/annurev.psych.54.101601.145059
Rusbult, C. E., & Van Lange, P. A. (2008). Why we need interdependence theory. *Social and Personality Psychology Compass, 2*(5), 2049–2070.
Rusbult, C. E., Verette, J., Whitney, G. A., Slovik, L. F., & Lipkus, I. (1991). Accommodation processes in close relationships: Theory and preliminary empirical evidence. *Journal of Personality and Social Psychology, 60*, 53–78. https://doi.org/10.1037/0022-3514.60.1.53
Rusbult, C. E., Drigotas, S. M., & Verette, J. (1994). The investment model: An interdependence analysis of commitment processes and relationship maintenance phenomena. In D. J. Canary & L. Stafford (Eds.), *Communication and relational maintenance* (pp. 115–139). Academic.
Rusbult, C. E., Martz, J. M., & Agnew, C. R. (1998). The investment model scale: Measuring commitment level, satisfaction level, quality of alternatives, and investment size. *Personal Relationships, 5*, 357–391. https://doi.org/10.1111/j.1475-6811.1998.tb00177.x
Russell, J. A. (1991). Culture and the categorization of emotions. *Psychological Bulletin, 110*, 426–450.
Russell, J. A., & Barrett, L. F. (1999). Core affect, prototypical emotional episodes, and other things called emotion: Dissecting the elephant. *Journal of Personality and Social Psychology, 76*(5), 805–819. https://doi.org/10.1037/0022-3514.76.5.805
Rychlowska, M., Jack, R. E., Garrod, O. G., Schyns, P. G., Martin, J. D., & Niedenthal, P. M. (2017). Functional smiles: Tools for love, sympathy, and war. *Psychological Science, 28*(9), 1259–1270.
Sadr, J., & Krowicki, L. (2019). Face perception loves a challenge: Less information sparks more attraction. *Vision Research, 157*, 61–83.
Scherer, K. R. (1984). Emotion as a multicomponent process: A model and some cross-cultural data. In P. Shaver (Ed.), *Review of personality and social psychology* (Vol. 5, pp. 37–63). Sage.
Scherer, K. R. (2020). Evidence for the existence of emotion dispositions and the effects of appraisal bias. *Emotion*. https://doi.org/10.1037/emo0000861
Scherer, K. R., & Brosch, T. (2009). Culture-specific appraisal biases contribute to emotion dispositions. *European Journal of Personality, 23*(3), 265–288.
Scherer, K. R., & Fontaine, J. R. (2019). The semantic structure of emotion words across languages is consistent with componential appraisal models of emotion. *Cognition and Emotion, 33*(4), 673–682.
Scherer, K. R., Schorr, A., & Johnstone, T. (Eds.). (2001). *Appraisal processes in emotion: Theory, methods, research*. Oxford University Press.
Scott, D. (2009). *A revolution of love: The meaning of Mother Teresa*. Loyola Press.
Sels, L., Cabrieto, J., Butler, E., Reis, H., Ceulemans, E., & Kuppens, P. (2020). The occurrence and correlates of emotional interdependence in romantic relationships. *Journal of Personality and Social Psychology, 119*(1), 136–158.
Shackman, A. J., Tromp, D. P. M., Stockbridge, M. D., Kaplan, C. M., Tillman, R. M., & Fox, A. S. (2016). Dispositional negativity: An integrative psychological and neurobiological perspective. *Psychological Bulletin, 142*(12), 1275–1314. https://doi.org/10.1037/bul0000073
Shaver, P. R., & Mikulincer, M. (2006). A behavioral system approach to romantic love relationships: Attachment, caregiving, and sex. In R. J. Sternberg & K. Weis (Eds.), *The new psychology of love* (pp. 35–64). Yale University Press.
Shaver, P. R., Schwartz, J., Kirson, D., & O'Connor, C. (1987). Emotion knowledge: Further explorations of a prototype approach. *Journal of Personality and Social Psychology, 52*, 1061–1086.
Shaver, P. R., Wu, S., & Schwartz, J. C. (1992). Cross-cultural similarities and differences in emotion and its representation: A prototype approach. In M. S. Clark (Ed.), *Review of personality and social psychology* (pp. 175–212). Sage.

Shaver, P. R., Morgan, H. J., & Wu, S. (1996). Is love a "basic" emotion? *Personal Relationships, 3*, 81–96. https://doi.org/10.1111/j.1475-6811.1996.tb00105.x

Shaver, P. R., Murdaya, U., & Fraley, R. C. (2001). Structure of the Indonesian emotion lexicon. *Asian Journal of Social Psychology, 4*, 201–224.

Shiota, M. N., Campos, B., Gonzaga, G. C., Keltner, D., & Peng, K. (2010). I love you but…: Cultural differences in complexity of emotional experience during interaction with a romantic partner. *Cognition and Emotion, 24*(5), 786–799.

Siemer, M. (2009). Mood experience: Implications of a dispositional theory of moods. *Emotion Review, 1*(3), 256–263.

Siemer, M., Mauss, I., & Gross, J. J. (2007). Same situation – Different emotions: How appraisals shape our emotions. *Emotion, 7*(3), 592–600. https://doi.org/10.1037/1528-3542.7.3.592

Smith, J. R., & Hogg, M. A. (2008). Social identity and attitudes. In W. D. Crano & R. Prislin (Eds.), *Frontiers of social psychology. Attitudes and attitude change* (pp. 337–360). Psychology Press.

Smith, C. A., & Lazarus, R. S. (1993). Appraisal components, core relational themes, and the emotions. *Cognition and Emotion, 7*, 233–269.

Smith, T. W., Berg, C. A., Florsheim, P., Uchino, B. N., Pearce, G., Hawkins, M., Henry, N. J. M., Beveridge, R. M., Skinner, M. A., & Olsen-Cerny, C. (2009). Conflict and collaboration in middle-aged and older couples: I. Age differences in agency and communion during marital interaction. *Psychology and Aging, 24*(2), 259–273. https://doi.org/10.1037/a0015609

Spronk, R. (2014). Sexuality and subjectivity: Erotic practices and the question of bodily sensations. *Social Anthropology, 22*(1), 3–21.

Starr, M. (2012). *God of love: A guide to the heart of Judaism, Christianity and Islam*. Monkfish Book Publishing.

Steinmetz, S. (1977). The battered husband syndrome. *Victimology, 2*(3–4), 499–509.

Sternberg, R. J. (1986). A triangular theory of love. *Psychological Review, 93*(2), 119–135.

Sternberg, R. J. (1995). Love as a story. *Journal of Social and Personal Relationships, 12*(4), 541–546.

Sternberg, R. J. (1996). Love stories. *Personal Relationships, 3*(1), 59–79.

Sternberg, R. J. (1997). Construct validation of a triangular love scale. *European Journal of Social Psychology, 27*(3), 313–335.

Sternberg, R. J. (1999). *Love is a story: A new theory of relationships*. Oxford University Press.

Sternberg, R. J., Hojjat, M., & Barnes, M. L. (2001). Empirical tests of aspects of a theory of love as a story. *European Journal of Personality, 15*(3), 199–218. https://doi.org/10.1002/per.405

Stokvis, B. (1953). Disposition and attitude as psychosomatic conceptions. *Acta Psychotherapeutica, Psychosomatica et Orthopaedagogica, 1*, 65–73.

Stürmer, S., Snyder, M., & Omoto, A. M. (2005). Prosocial emotions and helping: The moderating role of group membership. *Journal of Personality and Social Psychology, 88*(3), 532–546. https://doi.org/10.1037/0022-3514.88.3.532

Sugawara, D., Muto, S., & Sugie, M. (2018). The conceptual structure of positive emotions in Japanese university and graduate students. *Japanese Journal of Psychology, 89*(5), 479–489. https://doi.org/10.4992/jjpsy.89.17049

Swensen, C. H. (1972). The behavior of love. In H. A. Otto (Ed.), *Love today: A new exploration* (pp. 86–101). Association Press.

Takahashi, K., Mizuno, K., Sasaki, A. T., Wada, Y., Tanaka, M., Ishii, A., … Watanabe, Y. (2015). Imaging the passionate stage of romantic love by dopamine dynamics. *Frontiers in Human Neuroscience, 9*, 191.

Tangney, J. P., & Fischer, K. (Eds.). (1995). *Self-conscious emotions: The psychology of shame, guilt, embarrassment, and pride*. Guilford Press.

Tangney, J. P., Stuewig, J., & Mashek, D. J. (2007). Moral emotions and moral behavior. *Annual Review of Psychology, 58*, 345–372. https://doi.org/10.1146/annurev.psych.56.091103.070145

Templeton, J. (1999). *Agape love: Tradition in eight world religions*. Templeton Foundation Press.

The Love Consortium. (n.d.). Retrieved March 12, 2021, from https://www.theloveconsortium.org

Thibaut, J. W., & Kelley, H. H. (1959). *The social psychology of groups*. Wiley.

Tiedens, L. Z., Ellsworth, P. C., & Mesquita, B. (2000). Sentimental stereotypes: Emotional expectations for high-and- low-status group members. *Personality and Social Psychology Bulletin, 26*(5), 560–575. https://doi.org/10.1177/0146167200267004

Tracy, J. L., & Robins, R. W. (2004). Putting the self into self-conscious emotions: A theoretical model. *Psychological Inquiry, 15*(2), 103–125.

Vallerand, R. J. (2000). Deci and Ryan's self-determination theory: A view from the hierarchical model of intrinsic and extrinsic motivation. *Psychological Inquiry, 11*(4), 312–318.

Vallerand, R. J., & Ratelle, C. F. (2002). Intrinsic and extrinsic motivation: A hierarchical model. In E. L. Deci & R. M. Ryan (Eds.), *Handbook of self-determination research* (pp. 37–63). University of Rochester Press.

van Dantzig, S., Pecher, D., & Zwaan, R. A. (2008). Approach and avoidance as action effects. *The Quarterly Journal of Experimental Psychology, 61*(9), 1298–1306. https://doi.org/10.1080/17470210802027987

Van Lange, P. A. M., & Balliet, D. (2015). Interdependence theory. In M. Mikulincer, P. R. Shaver, J. A. Simpson, & J. F. Dovidio (Eds.), *APA handbooks in psychology®. APA handbook of personality and social psychology, Vol. 3. Interpersonal relations* (pp. 65–92). American Psychological Association. https://doi.org/10.1037/14344-003

Wade, T. J., Auer, G., & Roth, T. M. (2009). What is love: Further investigation of love acts. *Journal of Social, Evolutionary, and Cultural Psychology, 3*(4), 290–304. https://doi.org/10.1037/h0099315

Watson, J. B. (1924). Hereditary modes of response: Emotion. In *Psychology from the standpoint of a behaviorist* (2nd ed., pp. 194–230). Lippincott.

Watson, G. (2012). Pragmatic acts of love. *Language and Literature, 21*(2), 150–169.

Watson, D., Clark, L. A., & Tellegen, A. (1988). Development and validation of brief measures of positive and negative affect: The PANAS scales. *Journal of Personality and Social Psychology, 54*(6), 1063–1070.

Wickham, R. E., & Knee, C. R. (2012). Interdependence theory and the actor–partner interdependence model: Where theory and method converge. *Personality and Social Psychology Review, 16*(4), 375–393.

Wierzbicka, A. (1992). *Semantics, culture and cognition: Universal human concepts in culture-specific configurations*. Oxford University Press.

Wierzbicka, A. (1999). *Emotions across languages and cultures: Diversity and universals*. Cambridge University Press.

Wiggins, J. S. (1991). Agency and communion as conceptual coordinates for the understanding and measurement of interpersonal behavior. In D. Cicchetti & W. M. Grove (Eds.), *Thinking clearly about psychology: Essays in honor of Paul E. Meehl, Vol. 1. Matters of public interest; Vol. 2. Personality and psychopathology* (pp. 89–113). University of Minnesota Press.

Williams, D. D. (1968). *The spirit and the forms of love*. Harper & Row.

Wolf-Light, P. (1999). Men, violence and love. In J. Wild (Ed.), *Working with men for change* (pp. 133–152). UCL Press.

Wood, W. (2000). Attitude change: Persuasion and social influence. *Annual Review of Psychology, 51*, 539–570. https://doi.org/10.1146/annurev.psych.51.1.539

Wood, J. T. (2001). The normalization of violence in heterosexual romantic relationships: Women's narratives of love and violence. *Journal of Social and Personal Relationships, 18*(2), 239–261.

Chapter 2
Models and Typologies of Love

2.1 Construction of Models and Typologies in Social Sciences

2.1.1 The Concepts of Models and Types of Love

Scientific Models of Love

In sciences, the word "*models*" stands for *scientific models* – the ways how researchers represent the objects of their studies – components, dimensions, relations, structures, and functional mechanisms. The *model* means a *representation of a scientific construct* in the composition of units connected with each other and structured in various relations. Objects, individuals, their attributes, and other characteristic variables are the units, which are linked to each other in associative, temporal, causational, or other relations. There are different ways of how these models can be constructed.

These models constitute the core representation of scientific theories. For example, the model of love proposed by Hatfield, Schmitz, Cornelius, and Rapson (1988) consists of the two types of love – *passionate and companionate love*, which are characterized by different qualities. This dichotomous model of love turned out to be also a typology of love. *Sternberg's Triangular Theory of Love* (Sternberg, 1986, 1997) considers a model of love containing the three components of love – *intimacy, passion, and commitment* – which can be related producing a variety of love experience. Even though the theory claims that combinations of these components explain other complex states of love, however, this typology of (higher order) states remained largely accepted theoretically and never investigated empirically. Lee's *inductive theory* (1973, 1976, 1977) and Hendrick and Hendrick's *deductive theory* of love styles (Hendrick & Hendrick, 1986, 1989) suggested the model including six love styles which characterize how people approach love relationships. Berscheid (2010) proposed four major types of love, which have distinct causal conditions: romantic love, companionate love, compassionate love, and adult attachment love.

V. Karandashev, *Cultural Typologies of Love*,
https://doi.org/10.1007/978-3-031-05343-6_2

All these *models* propose different *components of love* and *their relations* since they consider love from different angles of view (see more details in the following chapters). They present the *internal constructions of components and their structures* in more or less elaborated details.

Hierarchical Models of Love

The studies of cultural models of emotions (see for review Karandashev, 2021a, 2021b) have presented several interesting examples of hierarchical models of emotional life. For instance, analyzing a nomological network for such factors of expressivity as *negative expressivity*, *positive expressivity*, *impulse intensity*, *masking*, and *expressive confidence*, authors (Gross & John, 1998) developed a *hierarchical model of individual differences in emotional expressivity*.

Up to now, a few complex models of love have been developed. They are mostly limited to dispositional conceptions of love. More complex hierarchical models of love, which include both short-term and long-term, situational (emotions) and dispositional (moods, attitudes, traits) concepts of love would be productive advancement.

For example, Lee (1973, 1976) constructed a hierarchical model, consisting of two levels of love types, in which

- *Eros*, *ludus*, and *storge* are *primary love types.*
- *Mania*, *pragma*, and *agape* are *secondary love types*.

Lee also hypothesized existence of *tertiary love types*, such as *maniac eros*, *maniac ludus*, *maniac storge*, *agapic eros*, *agapic ludus*, *agapic storge*, *pragmatic eros*, *pragmatic ludus*, and pragmatic storge. However, this level was not elaborated empirically.

Karandashev and Evans (2019) proposed a hierarchical model of love, which include attitudes of three levels: 40 *attitudes of basic level*, 4 of *first-order attitudes* (*affection*, *compassion*, *closeness*, and *commitment*), and 2 groups of *second-order attitudes* (the *attitudes toward a partner* and *attitudes regarding a relationship*). In a cross-cultural perspective, this hierarchical structure of love constructs was recently explored and validated across several cultural samples (Karandashev et al., 2022).

The Concept of Type

The *concept of type* characterizes a group/class/category of things, elements, objects, individuals, attributes, or sets and patterns of attributes, which they have in common. A type is a typical combination of its attributes, while a typology is the classification of things in several types, based on general criteria and rules. The types are the groups of the things/elements/objects, constructed in such a way that they have common attributes, specific constellations of those, empirical regularities, and meaningful relationships. In a typology, the elements *within a type* are *internally homogeneous*, similar as much as possible, while between the types, they are externally heterogeneous – differ as much as possible (Kluge, 2000).

The categories of personal models, individual types, relationship types, cultural models, and cultural types are just different planes of love existence. The same types of love can be in these different planes of existence: sexual, passionate, romantic, companionate, and others.

Construction of Typologies

Methods of typification and methodological problems of typology construction and utilization have been an area of interest in social and psychological sciences for quite a long time (e.g., Berger & Luckmann, 1966; Gergen, 1992; Kluge, 2000, January; McKinney, 1966, 1969).

Typologies and the process of typology construction are important in both quantitative and qualitative social research, in which various concepts of types are employed, such as real types, ideal types, extreme types, prototypes, and types of structure.

Several methodologies have been in use to construct typologies in social sciences.

For example, Kluge (2000) suggested the rules for the four stages of empirically grounded construction of types:

- Development of relevant analyzing dimensions
- Grouping the cases and analysis of empirical regularities
- Analysis of meaningful relationships and type construction
- Characterization of the constructed types

Specific methodologies, however, depend on the purpose for which typologies are constructed, available descriptors, variables and their variability, and the degree of familiarity with phenomena and individuals (McKinney, 1966). The exemplar-based and abstraction-based methodologies have been popular for representation of categories in typologies (Park, Judd, & Ryan, 1991). Cluster analysis was proposed for constructing typologies (Ahlquist & Breunig, 2012; Bailey, 1989). Constructive typologies (McKinney, 1966) can represent types in continuums rather than in discrete categories.

Several examples of categorization in love research are presented in the following sections.

Varieties of Models and Types of Love

Based on such *general scientific models of love*, which are listed in previous section, researchers can develop the *single case*, *personal*, *typological*, and *cultural models of love*. In this context, *scientific models* also include the principles, rules, and procedures how researchers put the love phenomena into categories.

The categories of personal models, individual types, relationship types, cultural models, and cultural types are just different planes of love existence. The same types of love can work in these different functions: *sexual*, *passionate*, *romantic*, *companionate*, and others.

The typologies, types, and models of love have been traditional objects of love studies. Their research heavily relies on the methods of categorization, which are typically based on extraction of *essential features* or *prototypes* – see more details in the following sections. The studies of *models* and *types* employ, or at least, shall employ different methodologies. How *models of love* are *different from types*?

Models are the *representations of love* on how *love should be*, *what it is*, or *how it was* in the past. *Models* are the products of our *cognition*– thinking, imagination, dreams, and goals, which play motivational and regulatory roles in our behavior. Generally, *models* are the *mental representations of love* that *individuals*, *scholars*, or *cultures* have in their minds. Consequently, three kinds of models are considered below – *personal models*, *scientific models*, and *cultural models of love*.

Types are the *realities of love* experiences, expressions, actions, and other manifestations of love. The *concept of type* is about what love is in real life of certain group of individuals, similar in some regards. *Description of types* reflects how people live and behave in particular circumstances. Scholars create typologies extracting the types of love based on categorization of real emotional experiences (e.g., emotions, associated with love, love attitudes), emotional expressions, and behaviors. The defining features and prototypes can serve as the criteria for such categorization.

The *concept of style* is similar to the *concept of type*, yet it is different. The *type* is more general term, while the *style* is a *specific kind of type*, which focuses on *behavioral characteristics of a person* – a manner of doing something, cognition, learning, speaking, or expression, a way of arranging appearance. The style is also a *complex characteristic of behavior*, rather than emotions, dispositions, and attitudes of an individual.

Personal and cultural models of love develop due to *individual* and *social categorizations* of emotional experiences, expressions, actions, and relationships – sensations, emotions, moods, attitudes, traits, and values, which *people call love*. Laypeople live with these implicit conceptions.

In love research, multiple indicators, descriptors, and variables such as physiological symptoms, patterns of brain activity, subjective sensations, emotions, moods, attitudes, traits, attributes and features, expressions, actions, reactions, and qualities of relationships can be treated as objects and categories. Individuals experiencing, expressing, and doing these things, as well as relationships between them, can also be categorized.

For instance, VanLear, Koerner, and Allen (2006) have analyzed the major approaches and issues to the categorization of personal relationships into types. The principles for construction of typologies depend on the theoretical orientation of a researcher. Various potential typologies can be constructed at the general, as well as at the specific level.

The Bottom-Up Approach to the Typologies of Love

The two major approaches to the construction of typologies and models of love are possible in terms of generalization and level of abstraction, *bottom-up* and *top-down*, while some researchers use a bidirectional mixture of these approaches. In the *bottom-up approach*, researchers begin with personal scientific and systematic empirical observations, describing events, emotions, attitudes, actions, and relationships, associated presumably with the concept of love. This approach is frequently called as the *data-driven research*; it employs *inductive inferential methodology*. The resulting scientific models are *data-based typologies*. No a priori theoretical conception guides such observations. The recorded narratives are qualitative and descriptive, yet may include some general quantitative measures, which are easily understandable for people in their daily life. This methodology can also be called *laypeople's approach*.

Such primarily descriptive and exemplar knowledge of love has been dispersed in historical and literary studies, in fictional and nonfictional literature, in journalistic and anthropological reports from their field trips, in clinical and counseling observations of practitioners, and in the journey notes of travelers. Authors attempt to take a broad view on their observations creating a general picture and typologies using remarkable or salient characteristics of love relationships and emotional experiences and expressions as the distinctive features of types. The typical relations between emotional phenomena characterize the distinctive picture of a unique cultural type or can become a basic pattern of love construction that is compared with other similar or different cases and cultures. This approach usually adheres to *emic methodology* in research, which focuses on culturally specific features of societies. Such methodology generates the typologies, which are evidence-based and vivid, concrete, and practical, even though they may lack theoretical grounding, conceptualization, and justification. Among the examples of these typologies are Sternberg's (1995, 1996, 1999) *love as a story theory* and de Munck's (2019) anthropological theory. We'll see more examples in the following sections.

The Top-Down Approach to the Typologies of Love

In the *top-down approach*, researchers first rely on their personal contemplations and observations and on previous scholarship, theories, and early studies when they define their theory and conceptual structure. The theoretical conception of love is defined a priori and guides the research design for data collection and analysis. This approach is frequently called as the *theory-driven research.* The empirical data can be qualitatively and quantitatively descriptive. The research design employs *deductive inferential methodology*. Inferences are based on rigor methodologies of analysis. The resulting scientific models are *expert-based typologies.*

Such inferential knowledge of love has been collected in sociological and communication studies; in anthropological, psychological, and biological research; and in clinical and counseling case studies. Authors apply their theoretical conceptualization of typology in an attempt to verify it and identify their theoretically defined types in real cases and individuals. The typical attributes of love relationships, emotional experiences, and expressions or the patterns of relations between emotional phenomena are used as the distinctive features of types. These typical attributes and patterns are used for categorization and comparison with other similar or different cases and individuals. This approach usually adheres to *etic methodology* in research, which focuses on cross-culturally universal typologies; see more in the following sections. Such methodology generates the typologies, which are theory-based and systematic, abstract, and well-structured, even though they may be less illustrative and not vivid, less concrete and limited in practical applications. Among the examples of these typologies are the *Triangular love theory* of Sternberg (1986, 1997) and *Quadrangular love theory* of Karandashev and Evans (2019).

Some scholars combine these *bottom-up* and *top-down approaches* enriching their theories and typologies of love. Lee's (1973) *love styles theory* is a very good example of this bidirectional method. Various instances of the love typologies illustrating all these methodologies are presented in the following sections.

2.1.2 Categorization for Construction of Models and Typologies

What Is Categorization?

Categorization is identification of similar things/objects – qualities, characteristics, attributes, things, events, individuals, and ideas – and the placement of those into a group, a *category*. The *categorization* is the major methodology that researchers need to construct typologies and models.

Categorization is the sorting, classifying, grouping, or categorizing of *somethings* into the sorts, classes, groups, or categories. In terms of research methodology, these *somethings* are of *two kinds*:

1. *Cases*, which may include various objects, individuals, actions, events, scripts, and other things – the *entities* of material and not-material reality. In tables of data, they are usually located in rows.
2. *Indicators*, descriptors, variables, attributes – the characteristics of those *cases* (objects, individuals, and other things). The *indicators* are the observable and measurable *entities* that *characterize concepts in empirically evident ways*. The

indicators are *operationalizations of the concepts*. These are *descriptors* in qualitative research and *variables* in quantitative research. In tables of data, they are usually located in columns.

Researchers can categorize both kinds of *somethings* – the *cases* and *indicators* – for different purposes. First, they explore and establish the guiding principles for categorization. And second, they apply these principles to recognize and practically group things. The first stage is *exploration and investigation* of the possible and suitable ways of categorization, while the second stage is *evaluation and assessment* of the new cases, objects, descriptors, and variables.

The Role of Categorization in Construction of Models and Typologies

Categorization and classifications are the foundations for constructing models and typologies. Generally saying, they set the systems, approaches, and principles of the grouping of objects, ideas, and individuals into different groups based on their characteristics and attributes.

Social categorization puts individuals into groups based on socially ascribed criteria (e.g., age, country of residence, race, ethnicity, religious affiliation), other people's attributions (e.g., social and economic status, social roles, physical traits, introvert or extravert personality), or self-attributions (e.g., sexual or gender identity, self-esteem, cultural identity, religious identity). *Psychological categorization* is usually based on various psychological indicators, such as personality traits, cognitive abilities, emotional experiences, expressions, and individual behaviors.

I omit here a huge and extensive literature on how people categorize individuals in social psychology of groups and intergroup relations in the context of ingroup and outgroup stereotypes, attitudes, and relations. The focus here is rather on methodologies of categorizations of social and psychological phenomena. Such *social* and *psychological categorizations* are especially pertinent to the topic of love in the context of this book.

The Basics of Typologies

Typologies are helpful for researchers to capture variability of love in how people experience, express, and act when they are in love or love others. The typologies provide larger, more comprehensive, and systemic representations of knowledge than the sets of descriptors, variables, measures of central tendencies, correlations, and mediation statistical criteria. Categorizations that compress data sorting and group them are the main methodologies to construct typologies. They allow to see the forest, not just the trees.

In this section, I present the key points of methodologies, a general guide to typology construction, suggestions on useful methods, opportunities, and pitfalls.

To construct a typology, researchers obtain the expert knowledge or laypeople opinions from the interviews, observations, experimentation, surveys, and other methods of data collection.

Typologies can be *theory-driven* or *data-driven*. In the first case, a hypothetical typology is theoretically grounded, preset, and tested with the following data collection and analysis. A theory can be verified, corrected, or adjusted during this process based on statistical analysis of the data obtained. Confirmatory factor analysis can be suitable in such case.

In the second case, when researchers do not have theoretical propositions, the typology construction takes participatory approach. Experts' observations or laypeople's opinions bring appropriate valid and reliable qualitative or quantitative data. The prototype study of love can be an example of this approach. Multidimensional scaling, discriminant analysis, exploratory factor analysis, cluster analysis, or latent class analysis can be suitable for statistical analysis in this case. The prototype approach to the concept of love was a great pioneering perspective (Fehr, 1993, 2006; Fehr & Russell, 1991), yet it was not perfect for the construction of typology because the instruction did not direct what kind of *love things* participants should generate. Therefore, the participants came to the overly diverse *words of love*, which came to their minds. Among those words were the kinds of love, love attitudes, emotions, and anything else, which do not have adequate indicators for categorization. Instead of such free-floating generation, the directed generations of things are the more suitable approach for categorization of love.

Many typologies come from the combination and interplay of these two opposite approaches. Lee's typology of love styles, as we saw above, was constructed this way.

There can be typologies of different classes depending on their purposes and objects. S*tructural typologies* classify variables into (1) the factors of related parameters or (2) dimensions measuring certain parameters. In this class of typologies, descriptors, variables, and factors or dimensions (as the resulting types) describe their diversity. Their sets and structures are at the primary interest. *Functional typologies* classify variables and cases based on their functional roles in love experiences, expressions, and behaviors. In this class of typologies, descriptors or variables explain their diversity of type. The same way, the s*tructural and functional typologies* can classify cases, which represent individuals, cultures, love episodes, and scripts.

Methods of Categorization

Categorization is the way of how researchers differentiate, classify, and identify objects, individuals, ideas, their attributes, and relations. There are several methods of categorization which scientists use in their work.

The simplest *categorization* is *binary*: whether a particular object belongs to the category, or not. Do you love, or you don't? Shall I stay or shall I go? In this case, categorization distinguishes the members of category from nonmembers. The examples of such *binary categorization* are whether a person is in romantic relationship, or not.

More frequently, categorization identifies which one of several categories – based on the criterial indicators – a given object belongs to. This looks like, and is often considered, as classification. Classes or categories are the distinct collections of category members (instances) that researchers consider as equivalent or similar enough. Any units of internal and external experience can be the objects of categorization. They can be related to more abstract and higher-order groups, such as category, class, type, and model.

Methods of *categorization* differentiate between varieties focusing on the grouping of distinctive qualities. Nevertheless, it usually permits overlapping between distinguished varieties. The patterns of indicators are more important to distinguish model and type – they cannot overlap, while the values of single indicators can overlap in different types.

Categorization can be a multilevel and hierarchical system. Many taxonomies of categories have three levels of generality and abstraction: *superordinate*, *basic*, and *subordinate*.

Categorization of the *love* can be on *individual*, *relationship*, *and cultural levels*, depending on the types of *love things*, which researchers select as the love constructs in their study. These can be, for instance, (a) categorization and typologies of personal models of love, (b) categorization and typologies of individual ways to love, (c) categorization and typologies of love relationships, (d) categorization and typologies of cultural models of love, and (e) categorization and typologies of real prevalence of certain cultural models of love in a society.

Methodologies for the Construction of Models and Types of Love

The two approaches in categorization of *cases* and *indicators* are possible: *prototype classification* and *logical classification* (Rosch, 1983), each with its advantages and disadvantages. Both types of categorizations can be used in the construction of typologies and models of love. The structures of models and types being based on categorization depend on the specific object representation(s) and their transformations.

Exemplar and *prototype methods* are the natural ways of categorization that many laypeople and scholars utilize in their everyday encounters with new objects, people, phenomena, and situations. These are the methods of *inductive reasoning*, which are generally based on analogies and similarities between *cases*. In this type of investigation, researchers come to their theories from the recording of indicators and analysis.

Analytical categorization, clustering methods, and fuzzy set approach are based on rather *abstract logical thinking* and *deductive reasoning*. Scientists largely rely on these typical methodologies inspired by Western scholarly traditions. In this methodology, researchers begin with their theories, which guide them to what indicators to record and what kind of analysis to perform.

What Indicators of Love Can Be Categorized?

Constructing typologies of love, researchers can categorize several things, as reviewed in the previous – general – section on categorization methodologies. First, researchers can categorize the *indicators of love*: *descriptors* and *variables*. In the data analysis methodology, these things are usually represented in the columns of a table. In love typologies, such things as *descriptors* and *variables* of sensations, emotions, moods, attitudes, traits, values, actions, interactions, relationships, and cultural ideas, associated with love, can be categorized. If they are qualitatively different in different cases (e.g., individuals, cultures), they are descriptors. If they are comparable quantitatively in different cases, they are variables.

For example, some cultures and individuals believe that *sensations of love* are *in the heart*, while others believe they are *in stomach*. These descriptors categorize the cultures (or individuals) as belonging to qualitatively different types in their cultural ideas and sensations of love.

Another example is the dimensions of love as a constellation of emotions. Categorization of emotions associated with love is the construction of qualitative (descriptive) typology: the two different types may have different combination of emotions experienced as love. And these *qualitatively different indicators of emotions* and their combinations are the *descriptors of love*.

The emotions of love can also be of positive or negative emotional tone, of high or low intensity. These emotional indicators of love are the variables because they vary quantitatively from case to case – from one situation to another, from one individual to another. These *quantitatively different indicators of emotions* are the *variables of love* (embodied in emotions). Categorization of these variables can construct (1) positive, negative, or ambivalent types of love and (2) passionate or dispassionate types of love (Karandashev, 2021a, 2021b).

The same way, researchers can categorize the love attitudes and other love phenomena (see Chap. 1): qualitatively, as descriptors, and quantitatively, as variables. *Qualitative comparison of their descriptors* and *quantitative comparison of the variables* are the main approaches to their categorization. They are realized in several scholarly disciplines. We will see the examples of such typologies in the following chapters.

What Cases of Love Can Be Categorized?

Researchers can also categorize the *cases of love*. They also can be represented in qualitative *descriptions* and quantitative *measures*, characterizing the narratives of love, scripts or love stories, individuals, groups, cultures, and societies – the cases for typological categorization. If the cases differ from each other qualitatively in terms of descriptors (e.g., emotions, attitudes), they are compared and categorized qualitatively – as in many literary, history, and anthropology studies. Researchers employ exemplar and prototypical methodology (see in previous sections).

If the cases are comparable quantitatively, with variables of love (e.g., emotions, attitudes), the cases are categorized quantitatively. In the data analysis methodology, these things are commonly displayed in the rows of a table. In the love typologies, these cases (e.g., individuals, cultures) can be categorized based on the *magnitude of the variables* characterizing sensations, emotions, moods, attitudes, traits, values, actions, interactions, relationships, and cultural ideas, associated with love. The *frequencies*, *means*, *medians*, *modes*, and *standard deviations* of those values or their *typical patterns* and *combinations* can be the criteria for categorization. Several analytical methods can be applied to these measures.

Analysis of variance (e.g., ANOVA) can reveal the typical patterns of central measures (means, medians, modes, standard variations) for variables of love (e.g., emotions, attitudes as indicators of love) that allow to categorize the cases based on one, two, or more variables, as well as on their typical patterns of magnitudes.

Correlation analysis and factor and confirmatory analyses can reveal the typical patterns of relations between variables of love that allow to categorize the cases based on directions, magnitude, and other criteria of their relations. More complex methods, such as bifactor analysis, fuzzy set analysis, and cluster analysis, can also be applied to obtain more complex typologies of love.

2.2 Personal Models of Love

2.2.1 What the Personal Models of Love Represent

What the Personal Models of Love Are

Personal models of love are the *individual mental representations of persons* about *what love is* and *how it should be.* These models represent the *laypersons' conceptions of love*, which they use in their behavior and lives. The *personal models of love* may describe the relationships, feelings, emotions, and attitudes, associated with love, and their causational relations. They can depict how people shall experience, express, and act when they are in love.

Individuals may be aware or not aware of them and can verbalize them or not. Nevertheless, their personal beliefs may guide them in their feelings of love, behavior, and relationships. Such personal laypeople's thinking of love can be *explicitly* expressed in a declarative form in cohesive narrative or abstract manner, with firmer or softer certainty and confidence. A person may look like a "theorist of love." However, more frequently, such personal understandings of love are *implicit* – people are not clearly aware of them and may have difficulty to verbalize their ideas and beliefs.

Personal models of love include individual understanding and plausible explanations of

- *What love is – descriptive representations* of real love relationships, emotions, attitudes, and actions
- *What love is supposed to be – prescriptive representations* of ideal love relationships, emotions, attitudes, and actions

Thus, these models describe both real and ideal representations of affective processes in love.

Personal Models of Love as Implicit Theories

Personal models of love are the *implicit theories of love*, which individuals have about love. In particular, the implicit theories of relationships are the beliefs, social perceptions, and attributions that individuals have about how relationships form, change, and develop throughout time. The implicit theories also represent the predictions of people's social perception, thinking, emotions, attributions, attitudes, and behaviors in romantic relationships. They can be oriented toward the evaluation and cultivation of relationships, destiny, and growth beliefs (Knee, Patrick, & Lonsbary, 2003; Knee & Petty, 2013).

Personal models of love are represented in qualitative descriptions, readily available exemplars, and personal prototypes, which characterize how people believe love should be. *Personal models of love* develop based on individual experience of a person, observations of family relationships, interactions with peers, as well as acquisition of societal and cultural scripts.

Many studies attempt to make the *implicit theories*, which individuals have about love, *explicit* and readily available for rigor scientific analysis with qualitative or quantitative methods. For example, the *self-report assessments* permit participants to project their *personal models* on scientific measures of love, which can be represented in the scores, indices, measures of central tendency, deviation, and other statistics.

Researchers make efforts to assess these *personal* and *social representations* making them explicit with scientific methods. Love researchers explore these implicit categorizations to understand varieties of love and taxonomies of love concepts.

In line with these ideas, social categorical approach to love employs such methods as autobiographical reports, direct questioning, the prototype approach, and inferential studies. In the social categorical method (Berscheid & Meyers, 1996), "respondents place persons in their actual social worlds into social categories, and the associations among the memberships of those categories are examined" (p. 19).

One typical approach is the free listing and pile sorting of the words for love scripts, categories, types, attributes, and so on. It is frequently employed in anthropological studies (see for review de Munck, 2019; Jankowiak & Nelson, 2021). Such methodology has been also used in the repertory grid techniques (e.g., Fransella, Bell, & Bannister, 2004; Kelly, 1955).

Another typical approach is the quantitative assessment of previously identified constructs: qualities, emotions, attitudes, and others. For example, multiple studies of mate preferences (see more details in the following chapter on evolutionary model of love) have investigated *personal models* of participants concerning the importance of various qualities for mating. The *personal models* – influenced by evolutionary, ecological, cultural, and individual factors – as mental representations of desired qualities of potential mates, rather than the attracting qualities of real mates, were the subject matter of those studies.

Personal Models of Love as Schemas

Cognitive schemas play their important role in *personal models of reality* affecting people's typical cognitions, emotions, and behaviors. The early studies conceptualized *schemas* as cognitive structures, plans, or programs that guide individuals in how they interpret information and act (Fiske & Taylor, 1984).

Love schemas are the core components of *personal models of love*, which guide individuals in their judgment of what they consider as appropriate for them, for a person they love, and for their relationships. These are *representations of love* that may include the subjective sensations, emotions, images, events, scripts, attitudes, motivation, behaviors, and concepts of what love is.

For example, in line with the *model of love as attachment* (Shaver & Hazan, 1988), Hatfield and Rapson (1996) suggested that some individuals may be more interested in romantic relationships, while others can be interested only in casual relationships, which are free from problems, and the others are not interested in relationships at all.

The *love schemas* of those who are interested in relationships are characterized by such dimensions as how comfortable they are (1) with closeness and/or (2) with independence. Authors (Hatfield & Rapson, 1996) classify four types of persons:

- The "secure" (who are comfortable with both closeness and independence)
- The "clingy" (who are comfortable with closeness but fearful of too much independence)
- The "skittish" (who are fearful of too much closeness but comfortable with independence)
- The "fickle" (who are uneasy with either closeness or independence)

The *love schemas* serve as the templates (schema) for individuals to identify whether their own emotional experience, other's personal experience, or observed behavior and relationships are love or not. Once I was talking with colleagues about John Lee's (1977) love styles. When I mentioned the *pragma* love style, colleagues of mine asked whether it is really love. They reflected on the common *cultural schema of love* as *romantic love* and, therefore, did not identify *practical love* (pragma) as *real love*.

Personal Ideals of Love

Personal models of love also include the *ideals* which people expect to have in their partner and romantic relationship. Studies (Fletcher, Simpson, Thomas, & Giles, 1999) found that three groups of personality traits: "attractiveness-vitality", "trustworthiness-warmth", and "resources-status" are the expected qualities of an ideal partner, while two groups of qualities: "relationship intimacy–loyalty" and "passion" are expected in an ideal relationship.

Further studies (Fletcher et al., 1999; Fletcher & Simpson, 2000) confirmed these factor structures, yet the dimensions characterizing *partner* and *relationship* overlapped. The Ideals Standards Model proposed three categories of partner ideals (warmth-loyalty, vitality-attractiveness, and status-resources).

The ideals serve such functions as evaluation, explanation, and regulation (Fletcher & Simpson, 2000). The more positive evaluation of the current relationship is associated with the higher consistency that a person perceives between their ideals and the qualities of the current partner and relationship. The discrepancies between the love ideals and real perception of a partner or relationship can create a contradictory experience for a person. The consequences of such condition depend on which motivating forces – the *need to see the partner or relationship positively* or the *need to be accurate* – are activated (Fletcher et al., 1999; Fletcher & Simpson, 2000).

The studies have shown (Campbell, Simpson, Kashy, & Fletcher, 2001) that romantic ideal standards and their flexibility are predictive of relationship quality. When people believe they have high level of such personal traits as *warmth/trustworthiness*, *vitality/attractiveness*, and *status/resources*, they also have *high ideal standards*; however, these standards are less flexible. When their partners match their ideals, they are happier and more satisfied with their relationship quality. Some of these correlations are mediated by other factors, such as flexibility of standards (Campbell, Simpson, Kashy, & Fletcher, 2001).

Personal models of love also include the people's expectations of what qualities they desire in prospective romantic relationships. For example, the studies (Regan, Levin, Sprecher, Christopher, & Gate, 2000) revealed that women and men (561 American college students) expressed preferences for such *internal qualities*, as personality and intelligence, more than such *external qualities* as physical attractiveness and wealth. Regarding a "short-term sexual" partner, both women and men were interested in such qualities of sexual desirability as attractiveness, sex drive, athleticism, and health. As for a "long-term romantic" relationship partner, they expressed more preferences for such socially appealing qualities of personality as honesty, warmth, and intelligence, placing high value on similarity.

The value of a good look can also vary in men's and women's *personal models of love* for short-term and long-term relationships. Physical attractiveness is considered more important for short-term than for long-term relationships (Buss & Schmitt, 1993). And attractiveness of woman for a long-term relationship was only of moderate importance for men, compared to other such highly valued traits.

2.2.2 *The Factors Forming Personal Models of Love*

Evolutionary, Social, and Personal Functions of Love

Why do people love? Can they live without love? Motivation is a complex set of internal needs motives that energize and direct behavior according to multiple motivating factors. Among those are evolutionary, social, and personal motives which implicitly or explicitly trigger our feelings, emotions, and attitudes of love. Love plays certain functions in people's life. These functions determine their motivation seeking for love. Motivation depends on the biology, society, and culture of individual life.

Historical, literary, anthropological, sociological, and psychological studies have explored the personal and societal functionality of love across cultures in three major groups of functions:

1. Evolutionary functions imply that love serves the purposes of natural selection of human species.
2. Social functions imply that love serves the purposes of optimal functioning of a society, families, and other small social groups.
3. Personal functions imply that love serves the purposes of an individual's satisfaction, well-being, happiness, and personal fulfillment.

Biological Evolutionary Roots Are in the Personal Models of Love

The *individual models of love* reflect the reality that humans are biological species influenced by many physiological and neural mechanisms, which determine their drives in love, associated emotions, and love acts. The modern Homo sapiens evolved from their mammalian ancestors – due to biological evolution – throughout thousands of years (e.g., Buss, 2006; Eastwick, 2009; Esch & Stefano, 2005; Fisher, Aron, & Brown, 2006; Fletcher, Simpson, Campbell, & Overall, 2015; Gonzaga & Haselton, 2008; Lampert, 1997; Zeki, 2007; see more detailed review in the following chapters). Human natural selection shaped people's sexual motivations, love preferences, perceptions, actions, and tendency to bond and care for one another. Human natural also shaped parental love and family support of children.

The biology and evolution determine many *universal qualities of love* – the neurological mechanisms, emotional experiences, expressions, and actions, which are common and similar across all individuals, all females, all males, or other biologically homogeneous types of people. Thus, the biologically and evolutionary-based qualities of *personal models of love* are largely universal, yet they can be the sources of *typological variations* being mediated by individual life experiences and personal events, social relations, and cultural models.

Neurobiological Roots Are in the Personal Models of Love

For example, passionate emotions, such as love, have their biological roots in neural and hormonal processes. *Generalized arousal of* the *central nervous system* (CNS) is a basic and non-specific neuronal "force" which activates a set of ascending and descending parts of nervous system facilitating any motivational, emotional, cognitive, and behavioral processes. Such *generalized arousal* is a fundamental property of the *CNS* and is related to motivational states of hunger, thirst, fear, and other needs. The *states of arousal* can change across minutes, hours, days, weeks, months, seasons, and years. General and current *arousal intensity* can increase or decrease being modulated by homeostatic, circadian, emotional, cognitive, and behavioral processes. Along with environmental pressures, these factors merge triggering internal drives and motives. These variations are associated with behavioral characteristics such as mood, feelings, temperament, and overall cognition (Calderon, Kilinc, Maritan, Banavar, & Pfaff, 2016; Kilinc, Calderon, Tabansky, Martin, & Pfaff, 2016; Pfaff & Banavar, 2007; Pfaff, Westberg, & Kow, 2005).

Personality Traits Are in the Personal Models of Love

Individuals with different temperament and personality traits may have higher or lower *arousability* as a *personality trait* (e.g., Derryberry & Rothbart, 1988; Larsen & Ketelaar, 1989; Strelau, 1994; Zuckerman, 1987) that can predispose a person to fall in passionate love. However, there are few studies available so far to support the latter assertion. According to the study of passionate experience of adolescents for 1 week (Moeller, Dietrich, Eccles, & Schneider, 2017), their personality traits accounted for 20% of variance in passion, while 80% were due to situational factors. Thus, a prospective partner and circumstances of interpersonal encounter may be more important factors of passionate love experience. Experiences of *high arousal* due to various situational dynamics, other people, and contexts trigger *passionate feelings* and can explain the passion of love (e.g., Aron, Norman, & Aron, 2001; Cotton, 1981; Deloyski, 2007; Dutton & Aron, 1974; White, Fishbein, & Rutsein, 1981).

The studies suggest (MacDonald, Marshall, Gere, Shimotomai, & Lies, 2012) that persons with *lower self-esteem* refrain from initiating romantic relationships. Having their low personal self-confidence, they are less confident in positive regard from prospective partners, due to their pessimistic reflected appraisals. Therefore, they just depreciate the value of romantic relationships.

The Role of Imprinting in Personal Models of Love

Individual experiences of childhood and later years also substantially affect formation of personal love models. For instance, the effects of early childhood impressions and connections like priming, the history of child abuse or caring relations, styles of parenting, and opportunities or problems with attachment are on the surface of many anecdotal stories and cases. There is also scientific evidence. Researchers have shown the role of early imprinting in sexual attraction among animals (see for review, e.g., Immelmann, 1972, 1975; Irwin & Price, 1999; Moltz, 1960; Ten Cate & Vos, 1999), as well as in people (see for review, e.g., Belsky, 1997; Belsky, Steinberg, & Draper, 1991; Bereczkei, Gyuris, Koves, & Bernath, 2002; Bereczkei, Gyuris, & Weisfeld, 2004; Vicedo, 2013) suggesting that childhood experience can shape personal models of sexual attraction and love in adulthood.

The positive sexual imprinting occurs by stamping the phenotype of the opposite-sex caregiver, with whom a child spent earlier years, as a prototype in *personal model of attraction*. A parent, stepparent, or other person with whom a child spent much of time in the early years can become such a prototype. For example, it was found that women tend to choose the spouses that resemble their adoptive fathers (Bereczkei et al., 2004). The latter excludes the possible factor of genetic similarity in favor of imprinting.

Despite the incest taboo, the early childhood attraction to a parent or peer of opposite sex can form – via imprinting – the type of partner which boys and girls seek in their adulthood. As Fraley and Marks (2010) proposed, the early experiences with kin can increase sexual attraction when a person is unaware of the incest taboo and decrease sexual attraction when the person is aware of this culturally imposed taboo.

Familiarity can have the opposite effect of negative imprinting in case when a child develops a sexual aversion to the phenotype of other, with whom the child spent much time closely in infancy and early childhood. Animals and humans may not feel sexually attracted to those with whom they spent the early years in childhood because they are negatively imprinted (see for review Lampert, 1997, p. 15). The historical instances from two different cultures – in Israel and Taiwan – present the examples.

In the kibbutz of the past in Israel, children spent most of time in a communal house for children, thus being extensively exposed to their peers, much more than to their family. The kibbutz youngsters who grew up together in early childhood tended to avoid their peers in their mate choice and usually did not marry (Shepher, 1971, 1983).

In Taiwan in the past, parents of a boy adopted baby girl for later matchmaking purposes Due to this custom, the girl's parents saved her upbringing costs, while the boy's parents saved the high bride price. Therefore, the girl and boy grew up as siblings. However, when they were expected to marry, they tried to avoid such a relationship. If they were obedient and married, their marital life was unpleasant and sex life is not satisfying (Wolf, 1995). These two customs of the past go beyond the normal cases, yet they illustrate how negative imprinting affects sexual attraction.

Despite these anecdotal histories, the studies on positive and negative imprinting have shown a limited effect on the formation of personal models of sexual attraction. The evidence for both types of imprinting is present, yet relatively weak in humans (Rantala & Marcinkowska, 2011). Individuals have a lower tendency to fall in love with those with whom they were close in infancy and early childhood, yet they do not feel a strong aversion and can experience sexual desire.

Effect of Daily Experiences on the Personal Models of Love

Individual sources of *personal models of love* are also in people's daily experiences, which they have reflected, and in anecdotal stories and rumors, which they have heard. Their occasional observations, impressions, thoughts, emotions, and events stamp in their minds. Explicitly or implicitly, associated actions, reactions, and emotional expressions are construed in causational ways. Over time, all these factors of individual experience determine formation of piecemeal, sketchy, and patchy representation of what love relationship is, what love emotional experience is, and what they are supposed to be.

Love Is a Rewarding Motivation

Love is rewarding. Sexual pleasure is rewarding. The boost of positive emotions is rewarding. The combination of joy of love and suffering is a thrilling arousal. This is a motivational power of passionate love. Seeing the joy of another is rewarding. The joy of giving, the joy of caring, and the joy of gifting – these boost self-esteem. Being accepted by someone who is valuable boosts my self-esteem.

Personal models of love determine the functions which love fulfills in individual life of people. And these functions depend on the needs and motives which guide a person in love. Various kinds of motivations can activate love feelings: sexual desire, the need for bonding, inspirations for romantic ideals, motives to care, and pragmatic purposes.

The Role of Motivations in Personal Models

A type of *preferred model of love* depends on personal motivations of individuals. The stronger certain kind of motivation, the more prevalent certain type of love. For instance, a person with high testosterone and easily sexually arousable believes that love is sex. Sexually obsessive men or women may perceive *love as a sex* everywhere and attribute to everyone. A person with high need to belong believes that love is bonding. A person with tendency to idealization of life and relationships believes that love is romantic. A person with a strong drive to care or be cared believes that love is care. Some individuals are inclined to deal with life and relationships in a rational manner. They believe that practical ways are the best to treat personal and interpersonal challenges. They believe it is the best way to love. Different individuals experience all these various motivations and corresponding emotions and attitudes in their love life. *Personal models of love* may include some of them as dominant or balanced motivators.

The *motivations to love* adjust according to *social* and *cultural affordances*, such as family kinship, social ties, and cultural norms. Some of these motivations and affordances can be prevalent in their motivating power for individuals' love. *Cultural models of love* determine *social* and *cultural affordances* of a society. They act as the other set of motivators, which shape, sculpt, and polish motivational aspects of *personal models of love*. These models, along with cultural models of love, determine a typology of individual love.

The Role of Cultural Experience in Personal Models

People build their *personal models of love* based on their individual life experience and traits, as well as on the models of love available in society. *Cultural models of love* are the *representations of love* which are accepted by cultural groups in society. The *cultural representations* may include values of love, norms of relationship, permissible and impermissible behaviors between individuals in love, acceptable and not acceptable attitudes, events, and scripts of what love is. These models are embodied in various cultural artifacts and expressed in several genres of oral and written cultural communication.

Love as Aspiration

Personal and cultural models of love aspire individuals to fulfill or avoid these models in their lives. These models of love function like dreams exciting and inspiring people. Dreams about prince or princess are like fairy tales, which people live by. Dreaming and imagining of something beautiful and joyful, they enjoy it like in real life. They have an opportunity to self-express.

Existential Function of Love

Love is also capable to fulfill existential motivation, which individuals may have. Love has a deep existential structure and actualizes two fundamental and opposite existential positions – the extremes of activity and passivity. On a *passive side*, a person *is drawn* toward a loved one in immediacy exceeding their control. Love can be a noncontrollable force. On an *active side*, the person can be responsible for their actions and how love proceeds to the future. Thus, the experience of love involves a periodical swinging from one pole to another – the process that is closely bound to subjectivity. The dialectic of subjective experience of love is the swings between *what is given* and *acting on it*. This is an arena where we most profoundly "*become who we are*" (Sköld & Roald, 2020).

Love can also serve as a protective mechanism to cope with a basic existential concern – dreadful awareness of personal death. This can be among other sociocultural and personal functions of close relationships. According to the *terror management theory* and studies (Hoppe, Fritsche, & Koranyi, 2018; Mikulincer, Florian, & Hirschberger, 2003, 2004):

> First, death reminders heighten the motivation to form and maintain close relationships.
> Second, the maintenance of close relationships provides a symbolic shield against the terror of death, whereas the breaking of close relationships results in an upsurge of death awareness. (Mikulincer et al., 2003, p. 20)

2.3 The Examples of Typological Models of Love

2.3.1 Lee's Typology of Six Love Styles

The Theoretical Descriptions of Love Styles

In the 1970s, scholars and practitioners of North America developed the *typologies of love styles* (Lasswell & Lasswell, 1976; Lasswell & Lobsenz, 1980; Lee, 1973, 1976). These studies were the substantial advancements in scholarly understanding of individual typological differences in the ways how people love.

Lee's (1973) *categorization of love styles* became popular among love researchers. The theory represents the typology of individuals as they function in love relationships across several phenomenological planes, such as love ideas, beliefs, attitudes, personal identity in love, and love behavior. It is worth noting that author found "a puzzling contradiction between the opinions which subjects said they held about true love and the behaviour they reported enacting when actually in a love relationship" (Lee, 1977, p. 176).

Conceptually, the *six love styles* in the typology have the distinct clusters of characteristics related to each other and empirically distinguishable. They are the styles of experiences, expressions, attitudes, actions, and relationships. Their labels are conventional, approximately expressing the meanings of corresponding Greek and Latin words. The summaries of the conceptual descriptions of the love style, as Lee presented them, are below:

1. Individuals with *eros* love style are very interested in and fascinated by physical appearance of a potential partner. The lovers perceive in a beloved the physical type concordant with their ideal image of the beautiful. Physical romantic attraction is a central tenet of their love.
2. Individuals with *ludus* love style are playful and game-loving in their expressions and behaviors. They are pluralistic and permissive in their choices and actions. They often engage in multiple and relatively short-lived relationships. They tend to control their involvement in relationship in attempt to avoid the feeling of jealousy.
3. Individuals with *storge* love style tend to avoid self-conscious passion, slowly disclosing their selves and gradually building up affection and companionship, with expectation of long-term commitment.

4. Individuals with *mania* love style are emotionally intense, very obsessive and preoccupied with the beloved, and therefore frequently jealous. They crave for repeated reassurance of being loved.
5. Individuals with *agape* love style feel their duty to love another with no expectation of reciprocity. Reasons, rather than emotions, guide their feelings and actions. They are caring, altruistic, and gentle.
6. Individuals with *pragma* love style deliberately consider how suitable a potential beloved is for their prospective relationship. They look for a compatible match taking into account the age, religion, education, vocation, and other demographic characteristics of a prospective partner.

Lee (1973, 1976) depicted this *love typology* in the system of colors to provide an illustrative analogy that would be meaningful to represent love styles as a vivid taxonomical structure. The colors themselves do not bear any special meanings, yet the principle of their possibility to mix illustrates their overlapping.

The Structure of Love Styles

Conceptually, the relationship between primary, secondary, and tertiary colors resembles the relationship between the love styles (Lee, 1977). Like secondary and tertiary colors are formed by mixing other colors, the secondary and tertiary love styles are constructed out of a mixture of primaries – the basic ones. *Storge*, *ludus*, and *eros* are primaries, while *pragma*, *mania*, and *agape* are the simplest secondaries. For instance, the secondary styles:

- The *pragma* is a combination of the features of the *storge* and *ludus* as the primary styles.
- The *mania* is a combination of the features of the *eros* and *ludus* as the primary styles.
- The *agape* is a combination of the features of *storge* and eros as the primary styles.

The other secondaries are *storgic eros*, *storgic ludus*, and *ludic eros*. The examples of tertiaries are *manic eros*, *manic storge*, and *manic ludus* (Lee, 1973, 1977). As one can see, typologically, the secondary love styles are the combinations of features salient for pairs of primaries. The structure, however, becomes very complex to outline and illustrate.

The Method to Assess Love Styles

Lee's (1973, 1976) typification of the love styles was based on an initial extensive analysis of literature, which was followed by extensive content analysis and a series of pilot studies. The author, with the aid of judges, verified and described the sets of reliable, mutually exclusive, sufficiently exhaustive, and salient characteristics of six different love styles. The descriptors – indicators – included "physical symptoms involved in the lover's experience of love (e.g., loss of appetite, sleep), sexual attraction, emotional pain, compulsive attention to the beloved, willingness to abase or alter the self to please the beloved, jealousy, self-disclosure, consciously manipulative behavior, the need for reciprocity, and others (Lee, 1973, p. 232).

The main phase of the study utilized the "Love Story Card Sort" – the interview procedure for the sensitive and systematically coded investigation of the love experience. The procedure used 1500 cards (arranged in 170 sets), on which a researcher exposed the brief descriptions of an idea, event, or emotion, which could occur in a love relationship.

The descriptors on the cards refereed to the various aspects of love: the experience and expression of feelings, the expectation of the beloved's feelings and reciprocity, preoccupation with the beloved, the feelings of anxieties, anticipated troubles, the frequency and ways of contact with the beloved, the expectations about a love relationship, the frequency and matters of conflicts with the beloved, and so on. So, "the whole sort comprises an omnibus love story, from which a respondent can select the relevant cards to tell his or her own story" (Lee, 1977, p. 176).

Thus, although one may believe that an individual's experience of love is unique, it involves an assortment of certain ideas, norms, and behavioral patterns that a culture encourages a person to follow. The modules of love experience can be in various combinations, yet the spectrum of these modules and the ways how they can be connected in a love story are limited.

In the interview procedure of the *card sort*, a participant answered a question having a set of cards with possible answers available. For example:

> On our first date, the closest we got to being intimate was

a) just being together, we never actually touched,
b) holding hands,
c) one good-night, or parting kiss,
d) kissing several times,
e) cuddling, holding each other close, embracing while clothed,
(f) close body contact unclothed, without sexual intercourse,
(g) we spent the night in the same bed but did not make love,
(h) making love all the way,

> other (specify). (Lee, 1977, p. 176)

The cards are exposed in consecutive sets. Participants select the suitable cards to report the points in their stories. The method enables a participant to disclose the emotional details of experiences breaking their complex experience into discrete and recordable units. The interviewer has an opportunity to record and code the data. Participants frequently experience their re-invoked emotions. They may cry, laugh, feel nostalgia, or regret the events. Based on the selections of the cards, researchers constructed, or reconstructed, a participant's love relationship, which could be blissful, relaxed, hectic, or tragic.

The *love story card sort* is more flexible method than a survey using a Likert-type scale. On the other hand, it is more systematic, compared with a depth interview, and allows to obtain the distinctive patterns of love styles. An independent study with a large sample (Lasswell & Lasswell, 1976), using a Guttman-Lingoes Smallest Space Analysis, has confirmed that these six love styles are mutually exclusive.

The Empirically Identified Typology of Love Styles

The in-depth interviews with 120 participants employed this *love story card sort* and gathered about 100,000 items of data. The Guttman type scales were constructed. The simple form of factor analysis identified 32 factors that allowed to distinguish the six clearly identifiable love styles with their most salient features.

Eros Love Style

Participants with *eros style* usually have had a happy childhood and a warm relationship with siblings and parents. They feel content with their life and work. They are ready for love, yet do not look anxiously for it. The *erotic lovers* typically clearly know which physical type is attractive to them. They can express it verbally, or by quickly selecting that type among a set of photographs (Lee, 1973, p. 248). Participants with the *eros love style* are quite demanding and specific in their expectations that a beloved must conform to their ideal image. They openly and promptly communicate their recognition and appreciation to the beloved which fulfill their ideal expectation of a physical type.

The *lovers* of *eros style* are inclined to quickly disclose themselves and expect the disclosure of the beloved. They frequently discuss the topics of involvement with a partner to magnify these feelings. From the beginning of a relationship, they are willing to meet the beloved as frequently as possible. They are looking forward to building up an extensive and deep understanding. They are yearning for sexual intimacy. They enjoy experiencing intensive sensations and emotions. They are self-confident in love, and therefore, neither anxious and demanding, nor obsessively possessive.

Ludus Love Style

Participants with *ludus style* recall their childhood as average. They consider their present life satisfactory, yet do not often feel enthusiastic about it. They like the broader range of physical types in potential partners, not much selective, and can easily change their preferences. They do not fall in love in a typical sense. They continue the regular activities as usual and wish the love relationships would adapt to their existing schedule of life. They are not willing to commit themselves and settle down, thoroughly avoiding future commitment to the partner and relationship. They do not like to plan far ahead any events.

The *ludus lovers* make the efforts to prevent too much involvement and intimacy in relationships avoiding to seeing the beloved too often and preventing over-involvement on either side. They may often discuss the problems of involvement with a partner to minimize the feelings of involvement.

A lover of the *ludus style* can play openly, honestly telling the truth to the partner, or can deceive and lead the partner on. The lover, who plays a fair love game, tends to go on and enjoy the ludus style of relationship with current and the next partner. The cheating lover may accumulate the feeling of guilt that sooner or later spoils the joy of game.

The *ludus style lovers* enjoy sexual intimacies as pleasant feelings, entertaining plays, and fun games, rather than as genuine passionate connections. Generally, the ludic lovers are not prone to experience jealousy or feel rivalry. They expect that the partner also does not feel and does not show jealousy.

When the relationship is not enjoyable anymore, the *ludus lovers* think they have a reason to end it. They easily find an alternative partner. To avoid being bored, they like to have two or three partners for different activities and at different nights of the week. The partners are usually not ignorant of each other's existence. This knowledge prevents them from becoming overly engaged.

Storge Love Style

Participants with *storge style* typically experienced secure family environments in their childhood and usually had several siblings. They feel that their life is good, and they can rely on their friends. They believe that their love gradually extends their deep friendship to sexual intimacy and commitment. They are not aware of their favorite physical type for a potential partner. For them, being with the beloved who is affectionate, is companionable, has common interests, and shares activities is more important than attraction to each other.

They experience low mental preoccupation with their partner. They easy tolerate temporary absence of the beloved and do not worry about the security of the relationship. A person with *storge* style does not like to engage in discussions about feelings of involvement. They tend to avoid extreme emotions and conscious deliberation about each other's feelings. They gradually self-disclose themselves sexually. They feel engaged in sexual activities later, when their *storge* relationships evolve. It occurs usually when a lover and their partners feel mutual commitment.

Mania Love Style

Participants with *mania style* generally recall their childhood as unhappy. They often do not enjoy their work, have few friends, and feel lonely. They are anxious to fall in love, yet they are not aware for sure which physical type of a potential partner they perceive as attractive. They frequently fall in love for someone who they initially dislike.

The *mania style lovers* typically experience intense emotion of attraction and preoccupation with a loved one. These feelings of the intense attraction resemble the erotic lover; however, their desires to restrain their feelings and manipulate a relationship resemble the ludic lover. Therefore, they experience contradictory emotions of ambivalence and tension, love and hate, closely intertwined. They are torn in two. The lovers of mania style are obsessively preoccupied with the beloved and experience and express jealousy. They can imagine various rivals and disasters; however, they tend to ignore the warning signs of relationship difficulties until it is too late.

Pragma Love Style

Participants with *pragma style* are controlling, manipulative as *ludus*, and companionate as *storge*. They have not been lucky to find a friend with similar interests or a loved one with whom the relationships can grow in love. Therefore, they decide – more or less consciously – to find someone who might be their companion and suitable partner. They do not wait an appeal of nature; they build a relationship.

Having in mind the desired qualities of a prospective mate, they look for an opportunity to meet a partner of their choice. In case of arranged marriages, the parents, rather than an individual, practice the pragmatic love style. In modern time, the matchmaking in the Internet web does the same work.

Agape Love Style

Participants with *agape style* experience love as a sense of duty. Their emotional will and commitment, rather than attraction and feelings, govern their love. The agapic lovers are generally more emotionally mature than individuals with other styles. In its best form, this love style is an ideal selflessness in affiliative connections. It is an ideal aspiration for doing good to another person. The *agape style lovers* believe that anyone is worthy of love. They love not because of appearance, qualities, or merits of other person, but because they are due their love to that person. To be loved, a person should not earn or deserve it. Love is a gift of a lover to a loved one. Love is an ability of a loving person to love.

Cultural Ideologies and Love Styles

According to Lee (1975, 1977), the preferred patterns of behavior corresponding to these *love styles* could evolve as the socially endorsed system of ideas – *cultural ideology* – due to particular social institutions and philosophies. The social conditions and cultural ideology of life could lead to the widespread prevalence of a specific *love ideology* in historical periods (Lee, 1975).

For example, the Roman historical era was open to sex and love and entertained the art of love and seduction. Cultural ideology supported love as the playful adventure and game (*ludus*), rather than sincere love feelings (Meister, 1963; Ovid, 1939). Love experience and expression followed the principles of entertainment, play, and game.

The Christian ideology of the early centuries of Christian era (cf. Nygren, 1952) opposed that *ludus* love ideology. Instead, religious teachings promoted the *philosophy of agape love*, which was in foundation of Christian conceptions of religious beliefs, practices, and marriages. Love followed the principle of giving, caring, and altruism.

The pragmatic love ideology (pragma love style) emerged in very structured feudal societies with high power distance and followed the *reality principle*. It justified the foundation of arranged marriages.

The cultural ideology of courtly love emerged in the twelfth century. It suited well to the social conditions of the knights' way of life. It further evolved in the following centuries into romantic love (*mania* love). The *pleasure principle* of this love style challenged the Christian conception of *duty love* (*agape-caritas*) and love in arranged marriage (*pragma* love).

All love styles have been present among individuals throughout history and across cultures. However, the social and intellectual climate of some epochs has been more conducive to one of them or another. Different love ideologies were endorsed by cultures as desired ones.

Within-Cultural Variation of Love Styles

A person's love style and associated features may depend on the lover's character, partner's personality, and specific relationships. The person can exhibit the relationships characteristic of different love styles at different times, periods of their life, and stages of relationship evolvement. For instance, mania and eros styles are more typical for the young men and women, while storge style appears later in a relationship.

Lee (1975) suggested that the researchers could use the same method in other cultures. However, to the best of my knowledge, no other cultural studies of the same kind have been conducted so far. For years, the cross-cultural research, which has investigated *presumably love styles* in other countries (see for review Karandashev, 2019), in fact, investigated the *love attitudes* and their cultural differences. The concept of *love attitudes* is not the same as the concept of *love styles* in the meaning of Lee's theory (Lee, 1973, 1976, 1977). The love attitude is the only one component of the love style. Characteristics of the love style are more multifaceted and complex in terms of experience, expression, actions, and relationship (see details in previous paragraphs).

Advantages, Drawbacks, and Pitfalls of Lee's Study of Love Styles

First, the typology categorizes the *love styles of individuals* as the *cases of love*. Types of individuals are the objects of categorization. The factors of variables describing love experience were used for categorization of cases. The variables of love experience were categorized into 32 factors with the simple form of factor analysis on the Guttman type scales. However, these categories of factors were not described, but they seem to be distinct from each other. These factors also were not categorized further into groups.

Second, categorization was *data driven* being based on the narratives depicted in the fictional and nonfictional writings on love ranging throughout centuries. The reliable descriptors of six love styles, which were mutually exclusive and sufficiently exhaustive, were purposefully selected with assistance of judges. At the same time, it appears that this categorization was *imposed by the theory* because researchers collected the descriptors for previously defined six love style.

Justification that these six styles are necessary and sufficient is not evidently presented.

Third, the combination of *feature and exemplar approach* to categorization was successfully employed in the case of this typology. The descriptors, which were considered in this categorization, portrayed several areas of love phenomenology: ideas, values, attitudes, opinions, identities, attraction, physical sensations, emotions, cognitions, and behaviors (see more details above). In the "Love Story Card Sort" interview procedure, participants sorted the cards (organized in sets) with concrete and vivid, yet brief descriptions of a love idea, event, emotion, expression, action, and relationship, which could characterize their personal story. This methodology allowed to embrace and represent the *wide range of what the love has been for them*, not just the love ideas and attitudes. Thus, the *qualitative descriptors* of love were the criteria variables used for categorization of individuals.

Fourth, the author (Lee, 1977) stated that the categories of love styles are overlapping, and some styles were the mixtures of others. However, the procedures of the "Love Story Card Sort" interview assume dichotomous selection. Besides, the two studies (Lasswell & Lasswell, 1976; Lee, 1977) have demonstrated that the six love styles are mutually exclusive.

2.3.2 C. Hendrick and S. Hendrick's Typology of Love Attitudes

Transformation of Love Styles into Love Attitudes

Lee's (1973, 1976) theory and method of *love styles* received reincarnation in the theory and method of *love attitudes* (Hendrick & Hendrick, 1986; Hendrick, Hendrick, & Dicke, 1998). The new theory and survey-based method borrowed the same conceptual ideas and typological labels: *eros*, *storge*, *pragma*, *agape*, *mania*, and *ludus*. However, the *Love Attitude Scale* took another methodological course to explore the *love styles* by converting them into *love attitudes*. Thus, instead of *typology of love styles*, their method assessed the *typology of love attitudes*.

Lee's method (see previous sections) was a comprehensive and deep investigation of many aspects of love experiences, expressions, and behaviors on different stages of relationships. It was based on the detailed descriptions and analyses of the participants' self-reports about their events, feelings, cognitions, and actions, which researchers obtained in their structured interviews. The *love styles* in such format were the complex, multifaceted, comprehensive typological representations of the ways how people love. The method of data collection in the structured interview and their content analysis brought rich depiction of real love, yet it was time-consuming.

The Theory and Method of Love Attitudes

In line with Lee's theoretical ideas of *six love styles*, C. Hendrick and S. Hendrick (Hendrick et al., 1998; Hendrick & Hendrick, 1986) developed the theory and method of *love attitudes*. They proposed the *Love Attitude Scale* (LAS) to measure *six love attitudes*, which represent the important part of love experience that Lee explored more comprehensively in his depth interviews. Authors transformed the notion of *love style as a holistic characteristic of love* into the *variables of love attitudes*. Therefore, the variables, which researchers obtain with *Love Attitude Scale*, shall be more adequately called the *love attitudes*, rather than *love styles*. While in Lee's (1973, 1976) method, individuals are classified in one of six love styles based on the complex match to a set of descriptors, in C. Hendrick and S. Hendrick's method (Hendrick et al., 1998; Hendrick & Hendrick, 1986), individuals are classified in one of the *love styles* – actually *love attitudes* – depending on how high the scores the variables of their salient love attitudes have. This theory and method identify individuals with singular *all or nothing styles*. Nevertheless, authors acknowledge and recognize that individuals may have mixtures of the styles, or love attitudes. The "profile" of their love is defined by the proportions of love attitude variables, which may vary depending on a partner and context. A plot of the six scores corresponding to the love attitude variables can depict the individual profile of love attitudes:

> The "amount" of each love style that an individual manifests can literally be plotted on a graph. The shape of the profile, its change over time, and its relationship to other variables become potential empirical questions to be answered by research guided by hypotheses. To date, our research has not dealt with profiles per se, but with each of the six dimensions individually. (Hendrick & Hendrick, 2006, p. 151)

As in many other typologies, which have been developed in love research so far, authors did not propose the criteria for categorization into each type of love. The exploration of such categorization is still awaiting its researchers.

The Fate of Secondary and Tertiary Love Styles

Lee's theoretical idea of *secondary and tertiary love styles* – a color analogy of love styles – received a limited empirical support in the original studies. In the *theory and method of love attitudes*, this idea was also abandoned and replaced with a variable approach, in which the six love attitudes (presumably styles) were measured as the variables independent from each other. The idea of love as a complex and hierarchical conceptual structure was forgotten. Therefore, the speaking about Lee's theory as a *color wheel theory of love* does not make much sense, until their complex hierarchical structure is empirically confirmed. I believe that an advanced statistical analysis, which is more suitable for categorization, can be more productive in generation of typologies.

Popularity of the Love Attitudes in Research

The *Love Attitude Scale* (C. Hendrick and S. Hendrick) picked and brought further the fascinating ideas of the six love styles, which attracted attention of the researchers in many countries. In the long (Hendrick & Hendrick, 1986) or short version (Hendrick et al., 1998), the scale has been widely translated in other languages and used in different cultural samples. Throughout years, many cultural or cross-cultural studies have been conducted (see for detailed review Karandashev, 2019). However, they have not delivered the sufficiently valid and reliable data to create comprehensive cultural typologies and models of love. Despite providing satisfactory traditional psychometric analysis, those studies have missed the questionable content validity of some subscales (e.g., *eros*, see for detailed analysis Karandashev, 2019) and missed to report *cross-cultural invariance* of the scales.

2.3.3 Sternberg's Categorization of Love Stories

Personal Models of Love Stories

The *personal models of love*, which individuals create in their minds, also include the scripts of perceptions, emotions, and interactions with partners, parents, friends, and other acquaintances. Local environment, society, social situations, personal history of life, experience of interpersonal interaction, and cultural contexts form *personal models as the scripts of love*. Being connected in sequences, these scripts generate the love stories, which individuals live by. *Love* is an *evolving process of interaction* between partners. Fairy tales, novels, and movies, personal observations, and anecdotes of others shape *individual love stories*.

These individual stories, as the *personal models of love*, are the stories of *what people believe love is* and *what the loving relationships should be*. These models guide people in their emotions, attitudes, actions, and relationships. According to Sternberg's *theory of love as a story* (Sternberg, 1996, 1999; Sternberg, Hojjat, & Barnes, 2001), people seek to fulfill these stories in their lives. The theory and method describe the narrative scripts and plots of how people conceptualize love and loving relationships. The stories describe the partners' complementary roles and scripts of their interactions.

The Value of Narrative Approach in Love Categorization

In his research, Sternberg (1995, 1996, 1999) collected the narratives of participants' love stories and categorized these in a taxonomy. The categories' labels of such stories are *mystery*, *addiction*, *police*, *travel stories*, and others. People feel more attracted and fall in love with potential partners who better match to the roles in these stories.

Empirical tests of the theory (Sternberg et al., 2001) have shown that partners in loving relationships likely have similar profiles of their love stories. They also feel more satisfied in a relationship when a partner's story corresponds with their own story and when a partner fulfills expectations of an ideal story.

2.3.4 *Quadrangular Categorization of Love*

Basic Components in Quadrangular Love Theory

A comprehensive definition of love in the *Quadrangular Love Theory* (QLS) considers the concept as a multifaceted construct consisting of the 40 constructs, which have been especially prominent and overarching in the love studies since the 1960s (see for review Karandashev & Evans, 2019). These 40 constructs are presumably the basic dimensions, characterizing individual love experiences. The corresponding descriptive statements expressing the meaning of these attitudes and feelings have been composed, selected, and revised, when it necessary, from multiple publications on these topics throughout recent 60 years. The content analysis of these attitudes/feelings and their equivalent descriptors attributed them into four groups with general overarching themes.

Operational Definition of the Love Constructs

- *Empathy*, *Acceptance*, *Concern*, *Protection*, *Giving Advice*, *Consolation*, *Care*, *Support*, *Nonjudgment*, and *Tolerance*, in their higher-order meaning, are well covered by the umbrella of *Compassion*. The examples of descriptive statements are (1) "I would console this person in times of need" for Consolation and (2) "I accept this person for whom he/she is" for Acceptance.
- *Physical Attraction*, *Personality Attraction*, *Physical Embrace*, *Admiration*, *Respect*, *Considerate*, *Tenderness*, *Elation*, *Appreciation*, and *Compliment*, in their higher-order meaning, are well covered by the umbrella of *Affection*. The examples of descriptive statements are (1) "The appearance of this person is attractive to me" for Physical Attraction and (2) "I have tender feelings toward this person" for Tenderness.
- *Affiliation*, *Attachment*, *Openness*, *Feeling Understood*, *Compatibility*, *Feeling Accepted*, *Reliance*, *Seeking Help*, *Trust*, and *Emotional Comfort*, in their higher-order meaning, are well covered by the umbrella of *Closeness*. The examples of descriptive statements are (1) "I feel that this person and I have a lot in common" for Affiliation and (2) "I can count on this person in this relationship" for Reliance.
- *Desire for Relationship*, *Exclusiveness*, *Devotion*, *Stability*, *Long-Term Orientation*, *Cooperation*, *Investment*, *Forgiveness*, *Coping*, and *Sacrifice*, in

their higher-order meaning, are well covered by the umbrella of *Commitment*. The examples of descriptive statements are (1) I can forgive this person's transgressions" for Forgiveness and (2) "I can set aside my interests for this relationship" for Sacrifice.

One can see that the descriptive statements express long-term or regularly occurring general dispositions (attitude-like or feeling-like) toward a person or relationship with him/her.

Hierarchical Structure of Love Constructs in QLT and QLS

The 40 items of statements in the *Quadrangular Love Scale* can be treated as *basic love constructs* (feelings, attitudes) in analysis of love typologies. They can also be categorized into the higher-order constructs (dimensions) of love.

The Quadrangular Love Theory (QLT) has proposed two levels of hierarchical categorization (Karandashev & Evans, 2019). The four first-order constructs are structured into two second-order constructs:

- *The attitudes toward the partner – compassion* and *affection*
- *The attitudes of the relationship – closeness* and *commitment*

This structure is supported by extensive psychometric investigation in the UK and US samples using exploratory and confirmatory factor analysis (Karandashev & Evans, 2019). At the same time, authors acknowledge that the scope and specifics of basic love constructs and their associations with higher-order constructs may vary contingent on their personal and cultural interpretations. The extensive cross-cultural studies have shown that some of these 40 attitudes are invariant in their meaning across samples and fit into the same first- and second-order umbrella love constructs, while the others vary in their cultural meaning (Karandashev et al., 2022).

Typologies of Love Experience

The love experiences of people in terms of these basic attitudes are individual due to different contextual, situational, and cultural factors. Categorization of these personal cases produces the typology of individual emotional experiences. The two approaches to construction of typologies are possible when researchers categorize cases, individuals, and groups.

In the first approach, researchers create typologies including one or more love variables, which are treated as unrelated to each other. The variables are the single and separate units for categorization across a sample of cases. In the QLS, the objects for categorization are the strength of each *basic*, *first-order*, and *second-order love attitude*. The *t*-test or ANOVA determines how the strength of love attitudes differs in their central tendencies in presumably different categories of participants. The value of external variables (e.g., age categories, gender identities, cultural groups, and social classes) is the descriptive indicators available to label the categories.

In the second approach, researchers create typologies containing multiple love variables, which are represented as the parts of a complex pattern. The objects for categorization are the structures of variables and the patterns of their value across the sample of cases. In the QLS, the objects for categorization are the patterns of relations between *basic love attitudes*, as well as between four *first-order love attitudes*, and between two *second-order love attitudes*. The cluster analysis of cases or latent class analysis allows to identify such patterns of strength of love attitudes in several categories of participants. These categories may be identified as a result of statistical analysis with subsequent search for explanatory variable of categorization. Other methods of cluster analysis or latent class analysis can also run.

The examples of the diagrams representing typical clusters of dimensions of QLS are depicted in the Figs. 2.1, 2.2, 2.3, and 2.4. Figures 2.1, 2.2, and 2.3 depict the three kinds of diagrams which represent three most typical clusters of dimensions of QLS, while Fig. 2.4 shows how the *friendship-type love* can be represented by quantitative and qualitative characteristics with a quadrangular depiction of love attitudes.

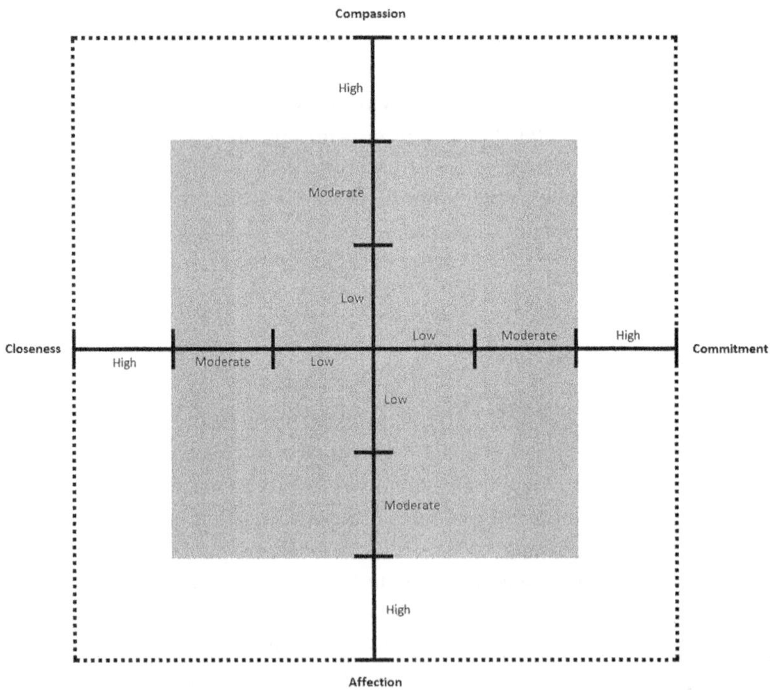

Fig. 2.1 Cluster 1: moderate in compassion, affection, closeness, and commitment

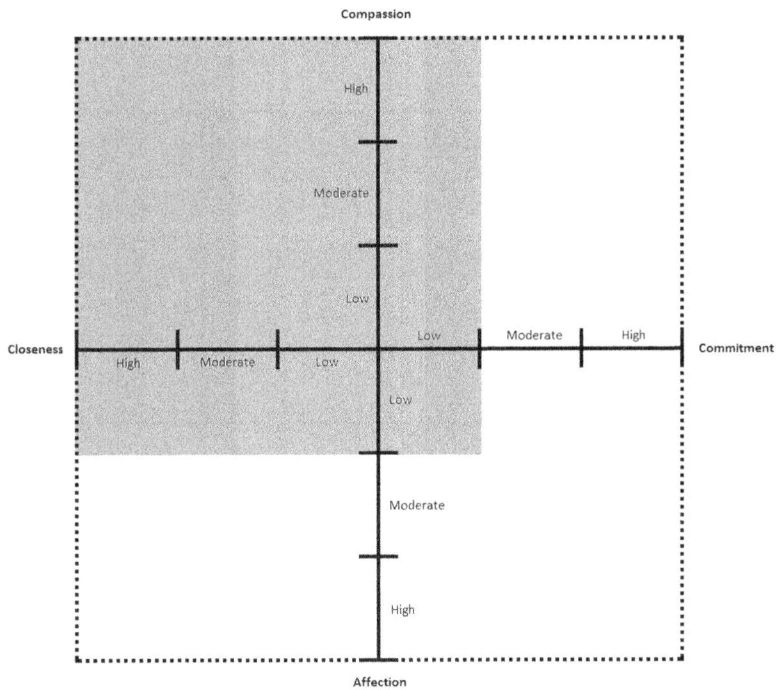

Fig. 2.2 Cluster 2: high in compassion and closeness, and low in affection and commitment

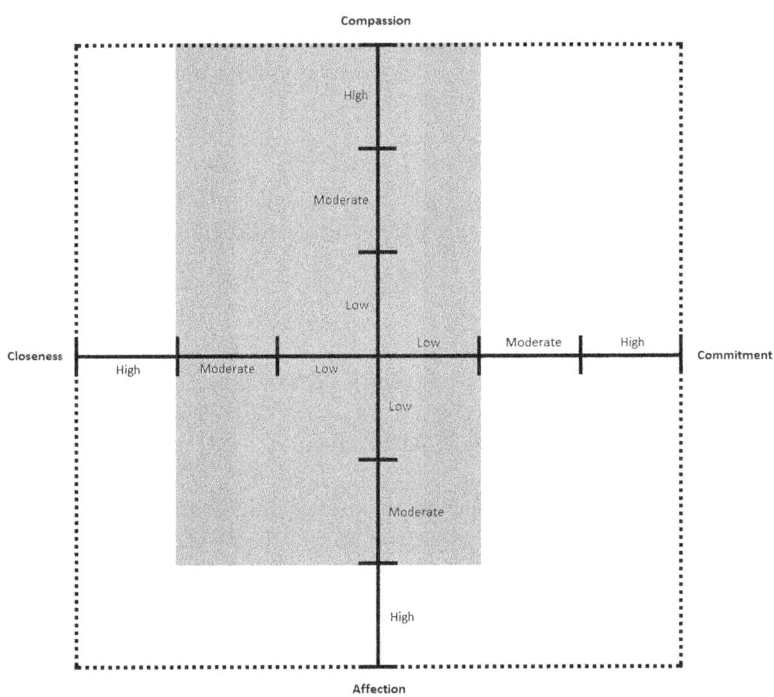

Fig. 2.3 Cluster 3: high in compassion, moderate in affection and closeness, and low in commitment

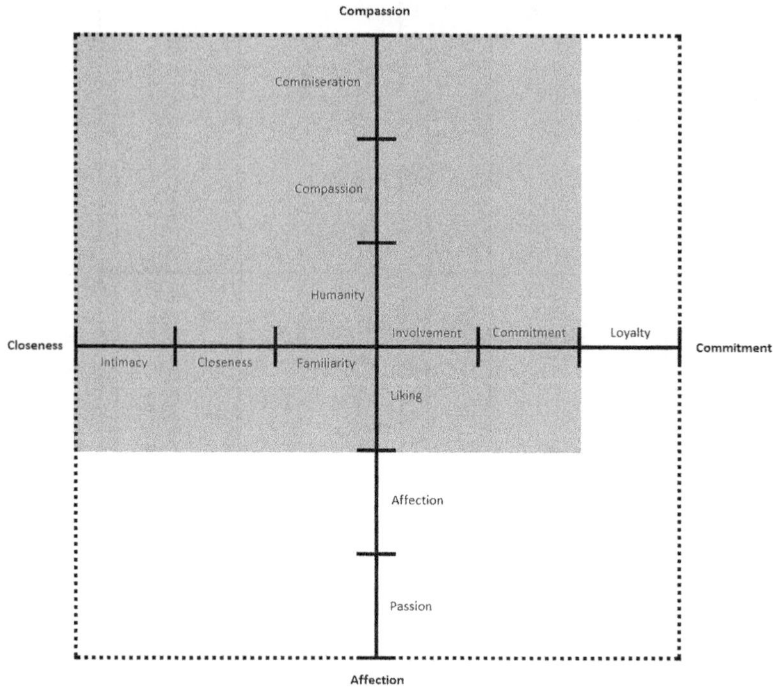

Fig. 2.4 Friendship-type love: A person in this type of love relationship experiences low affection (liking) and high compassion (commiseration) *toward a partner*, while the person experiences high closeness (intimacy) with the partner and moderate commitment (commitment) to the partner *within this relationship*

The same way as the typology of love in the Triangular Theory of Love, this typology of quadrangular love is still a theoretical construction, which has not been empirically validated.

2.3.5 *The Typology of Love as Attachment*

Typology of Behavioral Patterns of Attachment

The *typologies of attachment*, which were developed throughout years, have originated from Bowlby's (1969, 1973, 1980) pioneering theory and his extensive exploration of the attachment in the behavior of infant and child. Attachment develops from a child's bonding with a caregiver. It is experienced in the emotions of attachment, separation, and loss in certain situations.

Ainsworth (1989) and her colleagues (Ainsworth, Blehar, Waters, & Wall, 1978) developed the first *typology of children's attachment* to mothers based on observations of their behavior and emotional reactions in a *strange situation*. The patterns of attachment behavior, which children displayed in safe and frightening contexts, were indicative of the *types of attachment*.

Ainsworth and her colleagues designed a laboratory method, which they called the *strange situation*, for the study of *infant-parent attachment*. In this experimental situation, after their initial staying in the room together, an infant is temporarily separated from a parent. The parent leaves the room where they were together with the child, and in a while, the parent returns reuniting with the infant. Researchers observe the emotional reactions and behaviors of the infants, and their *typical patterns* are classified as the *types of attachment*.

The first type, the "normative" one, is revealed in the pattern of *secure attachment* (about 60% of infants exhibited it). The children with this pattern of emotion and behavior become upset when the parent leaves the room. However, when the parent returns, children actively seek the contact with parent and are easily calm down when the parent comforts them.

The second type is revealed in the pattern of *anxious-resistant attachment* (about 20% of infants exhibited it). The children with this pattern of emotion and behavior look initially uncomfortable. When the parent leaves the room, they become very distressed. When the parent reunites with them, they are difficult to be soothed. Their conflicting behaviors indicate that they wish to be comforted; however, they also wish to "punish" the parent for their separation.

The third type is revealed in the pattern of *avoidant attachment* (about 20% of infants exhibited it). The children with this pattern of emotion and behavior do not look like being too distressed when the parent leaves the room. When the parent returns reuniting with them, they actively avoid communicating with their parent. They may turn their attention to play objects on the floor.

Multiple studies have explored the *parent-child attachment typology* since its early inception in the 1970s, largely in the American, British, and other Western cultures and later in non-Western cultures (see for review Bowlby, 1988/Bowlby, 2008; Bretherton, 1992; Cassidy & Shaver, 1999; Keller, 2013, 2018; Shaver & Mikulincer, 2006). The typology has been popular among many researchers investigating healthy human development in different preschool and school contexts.

The Typology of Styles as Categorical Types of Adult Attachment

The theory and typology of attachment have been extended to the adult romantic relationships between partners (Hazan & Shaver, 1987; Shaver & Mikulincer, 2006). Authors suggested that romantic love emerges in the context of attachment behavioral system. They followed the similar classification, as with the infant-caregiver attachment, and called the corresponding patterns of relations as *attachment styles*.

While Ainsworth and her colleagues classified the *typical patterns of objective behavior*, Hazan and Shaver classified the *typical self-reported identification* of individual experiences. This self-assessment is based on the subjective categorical attribution of personal experience to one of the three narrative descriptions. A simple questionnaire evaluates these typological differences. Participants read the three descriptive paragraphs:

A. I am somewhat uncomfortable being close to others; I find it difficult to trust them completely, difficult to allow myself to depend on them. I am nervous when anyone gets too close, and often, others want me to be more intimate than I feel comfortable being.
B. I find it relatively easy to get close to others and am comfortable depending on them and having them depend on me. I don't worry about being abandoned or about someone getting too close to me.
C. I find that others are reluctant to get as close as I would like. I often worry that my partner doesn't really love me or won't want to stay with me. I want to get very close to my partner, and this sometimes scares people away.

Then, participants select the paragraph, which the most accurately describe the way how they feel, think, and behave in a love relationship. Researcher used this subjective self-reported description to attribute participants to one of the three categories of attachment. Those adults who selected the paragraph A are classified as *avoidant attachment type*, those who selected the paragraph B as *secure attachment type*, and those who selected the paragraph C as *anxious-resistant attachment type.*

The Typology of Adult Attachment as Dimensional Types

Another approach (Brennan, Clark, & Shaver, 1998; Fraley & Waller, 1998) treated attachment as a dimensional, rather than categorical construct. The questionnaire consisting of the statements, such as "I believe that others will be there for me when I need them," assessed the two basic dimensions of adult attachment patterns. *Attachment-related anxiety* characterizes how much respondents worry whether their partner is available, attentive, and responsive or feels secure in a relationship. *Attachment-related avoidance* characterizes how much respondents prefer not to rely on others and how they feel comfortable and secure being in intimate and mutually dependent relationship with others.

The *typology of attachment* is formed as a set of patterns including these two dimensions – *anxiety* and *avoidance*. As a result, the four types of attachment are (1) *secure attachment*, (2), *anxious-avoidant attachment* (3), *anxious-ambivalent attachment*, and (4) *disorganized attachment* (e.g., Bartholomew & Horowitz, 1991; Belsky & Fearon, 2008; Brennan et al., 1998; Keller, 2018).

Secure adult attachment type is characterized by low scores on these two dimensions. *Preoccupied adult attachment type* is characterized by low avoidance and high anxiety. *Fearful-avoidant adult attachment type* is characterized by high avoidance and high anxiety. *Dismissing-avoidant adult attachment type* is characterized by high avoidance and low anxiety.

This taxometric typology assesses the *types of love attachment* dimensionally rather than categorically. The attachment types vary in the extent of dimension rather than in categorical sorts.

2.4 Cultural Models, Typologies of Love, and Cultural Factors Affecting Them

2.4.1 *The Conception of Cultural Models*

Cultural Models in Human Sciences

The studies of various phenomena in behavioral and social sciences from the position of *cultural models* have become popular as an interpretative framework (see for review Karandashev, 2021a, 2021b). The concept of *cultural model* defines a *mental model* or *cognitive schema* which members of a cultural group collectively understand in a relatively similar way. Such collectively shared *mental models* represent cultural knowledge about the world of nature and society, natural and social events, and natural and social phenomena in the *systems of meaningful mental units.*

Cultural models are the mental repositories of normative intellectual and pragmatic knowledge which motivates people to think, feel, and behave in certain ways (e.g., D'Andrade & Strauss, 1992; De Munck, 2019; Holland & Quinn, 1987; Kronenfeld, 2008). The *locus of cultural models* is in the *minds of individuals* comprising a cultural community (Bennardo, 2018; Bennardo & de Munck, 2014, 2020). This means that social individuals are the holders and keepers of cultural models, which they can express externally in various artifacts of a culture.

In the context of this book, *cultural models* are "the *typical patterns of behaviors, beliefs, thoughts, and emotions*, which many people in a culture share with each other due to common cultural background..." (Karandashev, 2021a, 2021b, p. 95). They are reflected in both *cultural models*, objects of culture listed above, and personal models – subjective representation of these *cultural models*. The examples of the *cultural models of emotions* and other *associated cultural models* from this methodological position were presented in my earlier book (Karandashev, 2021a, 2021b).

Structures of Cultural Models

These units and structures of collective knowledge can be simple or complex. They can represent cultural concepts, their features, their relations, culturally important events, and other things. The structure of a *cultural model* can consist of the core and peripheral components. The units of such model can be organized in the system of descriptive, evaluative, propositional, procedural, logical, causal, or part-whole relations (see also de Munck, 2019, p. 23).

The models can be descriptive, comparative, or structural. Their constructions can be unidimensional or multidimensional. They can be simple or complex, categorical, dimensional, or structural, narrative, or conceptual (Karandashev, 2021a, 2021b).

Internal and External Planes of Cultural Models

Cultural models can exist in the two planes: *internal and external*. They are *internal* when they are embodied in the percepts, memories, thoughts, feelings, emotions, attitudes, and values of individuals. Individuals are the *agents* and *subjects* of socially constructed and imposed reality (Holland, Lachicotte Jr., Skinner, & Cain, 1998).

Cultural models are *external* when they are externalized verbally or nonverbally in folk stories, myths, novels, poems, fine arts, music, cinema, people's stereotypes, sayings, proverbs, aphorisms, traditions, and rules, which normatively regulate cultural life of a cultural group. Thus, internal-personal and external-cultural planes of cultural models exist in bidirectional dialectics.

Consequently, *personal* and *cultural models* intertwine bidirectionally. Individuals – leaders or commoners – as the *agents of culture* generate cultural ideas (listed above) as they objectively yet subjectively reflect social life in a society. They transform their internal *personal models of social wisdom* into external *cultural models*. When they are objectified in the cultural artifacts (aforementioned), they become *cultural models*. Then, they in turn determine *personal models of individuals* as the subjects of cultural reality via enculturation, social regulation, unspoken normative influence, and interpersonal contagion. Although a cultural model represents the collectively shared knowledge, the individual members of a cultural group construct their personal representations of this collective knowledge. The cultural ideas of individuals as the agents and subjects of culture subjectively reflect their personal and individual characteristics; therefore, they can deviate from culturally normative models of a society. Therefore, the content of *cultural models* can be similar to *cultural types* in many respects.

Typologies of Cultural Models

Several typologies of cultural models are possible. They can establish certain basic criteria for categorization, such as externality versus internality, cultural ideology versus reality, desirability versus undesirability, and their functional role.

One typology can distinguish the *external and internal cultural models*. I briefly commented on these two above. The *external models* are presented in myths, folk stories, drawings, novels, movies, scholarly writing, traditional practices, institutionalized rules, and other cultural artifacts. They are *the externalized cultural ideas* of outstanding individuals or groups of people in a society. When they are still in the minds and dreams of individuals, they are *personal models of cultural ideas* – the internal versions of cultural models. When they are perceived by other individuals – observers, readers, listeners – the *external cultural models* are internalized into personal models, being transformed by individual traits of the perceiving person and contextualized. These two types of *cultural love models*, for instance, have been extensively explored throughout centuries by writers, poets, philosophers, artists, composers, and folk wisdom.

Another typology can distinguish the *cultural models of cultural ideas* and *the cultural models of real life*. The first type of models is like the external models described above. They describe the various possibilities, which life and love can or could have – in its bright and dark sides. The second type of models – *cultural models of reality* – describes how life and love are and how they really occur in short-term or long-term mental processes, behaviors, and relationships. Both types shall be explored with different methods. Do we study what people think about love? Or do we study how people experience and express love in their real life.

Another typology can distinguish the (1) *cultural models of* which thoughts, feelings, and behaviors are *culturally desirable and encouraged* in love, the *cultural ideals*, and (2) *which are not desirable in love*, or even condemned, the *cultural anti-ideals*.

Like social and cultural norms (Morris, Hong, Chiu, & Liu, 2015), the cultural models can be represented as an *objective normative reality* of *cultural environment* as institutionalized rules and practices, as the patterns of sanctioning and behavioral regularities. On the other hand, cultural models can be represented in the *subjective cultural reality* of *perceived descriptive*, *injunctive*, or *personal norms*. This distinction is like the one described above as *external and internal cultural models*.

Here is the typology of internal cultural models (Morris, Hong, Chiu, & Liu, 2015). In this *internal subjective cultural reality*, the *perceived descriptive norms* are the individual perceptions, expectations, and assumptions that work as interpretive frames shaping how people perceive their society's norms. The *perceived injunctive norms* are certain patterns of expressions and behaviors which elicit social approval or disapproval, while *personal norms* are self-expectations.

There can be other varieties of typologies of cultural models. For instance, they can be more or less prescriptive. Some sound like the declarative imperatives to do or not to do; others, the explicit recommendations, suggestions, or condemnations; yet the others, implicit encouragements/discouragement. They can be more or less flexible: some are rigid and strictly imposed; others are variable and adjustable to a context (Karandashev, 2021a, 2021b).

Methodology of Cultural Models

Methodologically, the distinction of these types of cultural models means that the same *models of cognitions, meanings, emotions, behaviors, and practices* can function as the *personal, as well as cultural models*. Thus, *cultural models* can be studied both on the *cultural* and *individual levels*.

Cultural models provide scientific merits and advantages for social and behavioral sciences because they advance research methodology shifting the basic units of analysis to more complex, systemic, and integrative representations of knowledge. The *cultural model approach* encourages researchers to go beyond componential, dimensional, and correlational analyses toward more complex structural analysis.

The more detailed description of the methods that can be used in the construction of cultural models and corresponding statistical analyses was presented elsewhere (Karandashev, 2021a, 2021b). The book presents several examples illustrating the construction of cultural models of emotions. Researchers can employ these methods in their construction of cultural models of love.

2.4.2 Cultural Models of Love

Conceptualization of the Cultural Models of Love

Cultural models of love exist as the cultural representations of love in drawings, paintings, sculptures, fairy tales, legends, myths, stories, dramatic plays, and movies, as well as in cultural conceptualizations and scripts of love transmitted orally as the words of mouth from people of one generation to the people of other generation.

Cultural models of love are the "properties of collectivities" and imply their "collective awareness." They are acquired, are internalized, and primarily exist as individual representations of them, yet are shared with other people (de Munck & Kronenfeld, 2016).

Cultural models of love, as any categories (see the previous sections), can be represented in concepts; their conceptual relations, actions, reactions, and events; and their correlations or causations. The *conceptual cultural models*, as categorizations, describe, for example, what love is and what is not, how love and marriage are compatible, what the relations between love and sex are, and which love feelings are appropriate and which are not. In cultural anthropology, the free listing and pile sorting of words are the typical inductive methods to discover such models (see for review de Munck, 2019; Jankowiak & Nelson, 2021). *Categorization of culturally normative narratives*, as the cultural models, describes, for example, emotions, expressions, actions, reactions, scenarios, events, and their possible causational relations.

Such events, episodes, scripts, and stories are the *if-then entailments* of cultural models (de Munck & Kronenfeld, 2016). The same methods of free listing and pile sorting can be used to explore such *narrative cultural models of love*. For example, de Munck and Kronenfeld (2016) delved into the cultural model of romantic love in the USA. Their cultural model of romantic love consisted of normative scenarios, which included the following sequence of events and feelings:

> a person would feel excited about meeting their beloved; make passionate and intimate love as opposed to only physical love; feel comfortable with the beloved, behaving in a compan-

ionable, friendly way with one's partner; listen to the other's concerns, offering to help out in various ways if necessary; and, all the while, keeping a mental ledger of the degree to which altruism and passion are mutual.

It is evident that the model of love combines *passion* with *comfort* and *friendship* as the salient qualities of *romantic love*. The two extended case studies have supported this *dynamic cultural model*. It appears as a plausible general representation of American relationships and converges with other knowledge of American culture obtained from other data and sources (see for review Karandashev, 2017, 2019). This study of *American cultural model of successful love* (de Munck & Kronenfeld, 2016) is novel, yet it has a limited cultural scope. The small number of informants, exclusively recruited in upstate New York and in New York City, represents rather North-East American model of love – predominantly of European descent – and can conceal the typological and cultural assortment of a vast and culturally diverse American population.

Relations Between Different Cultural Models of Love

Cultural models of romantic love present in different cultures are not exclusive from each other. In the same way, the cultural models of different emotional concepts are not exclusive from each other. For example, there is substantial overlapping between sensual love, passionate love, and romantic love. Passion – due to high excitation – makes people romantic. In another example, there is overlapping pragmatic love and companionate love, pragmatic and rational.

Cultural models of different emotional (e.g., love, hate, etc.) concepts might be separate from each other, overlap, or include one in another. They can have diversity of topological structures.

For example, free listing and pile sorting methods applied to the concepts of love and sex demonstrated that they are independent prototypes (de Munck, 2019). Although romantic love is a type of love, yet it is not a type of sex. Romantic love shares more core features with love than with sex. Love and romantic love share more core features with each other than with sex.

The data shows that three target domains have both overlapping and distinctive features. Romantic love shares 43% of its characteristics with love and only 10% with sex. Sex and love share only one feature in common – *intimacy*. *Passion* was listed as the third most cited term in the love category and the second in romantic love and was absent from the top 30 terms for sex. Worthwhile to note, however, that the top term for both love and romantic love was sex. De Munck (2019) concludes that the default idea of love and romantic love for many people in their studies is not familial but romantic love. Different from this, the results of Fehr's study showed that sexual or passionate love is a peripheral type of love.

According to De Munck (2019), romantic love is the synthesis of love and sex and includes features that have high prototypicality ratings for both of the other categories. The terms, which have low prototypicality in sex and love, do not have high prototypicality ratings in romantic love. Romantic love also has the fewest unique terms.

How Cultural Models of Love Affect Personal Models of Love

One of the intriguing research questions is how individual personal models of love are affected by prevalent and other cultural models of society. Cultural models through the mass media can mold personal models via social cognition and socialization. However, the personality traits of an individual can be receptive to some ideas presented in cultural models than to other. Several studies have presented interesting examples of this kind of research (e.g., Brommer, 2016; Wells & Hakanen, 1991).

2.5 Cultural Factors Shaping Cultural Models of Love

2.5.1 Ecological, Societal, and Cultural Factors Affecting Love

Interplay of Biological, Ecological, Societal, and Cultural Factors Affecting Love

Throughout centuries, *biological* and *cultural evolution* in societies has developed several models of love. Some of them were specific for certain historical periods of humankind, while others were persistent across time. Nevertheless, they were transformed and modified adapting to ecological conditions in which people lived, changes in societal structures of relations, technological and medical advancements, as well as persistent patterns of cultures.

Competitive, Collectivistic, and Individualistic Societies

Lindholm (1998) proposed the three basic types of societies with distinctive cultural configurations. Their social structures determine prevalent types of relationships and corresponding models of love.

In hierarchical and competitive societies, marriage serves political functions establishing the alliances of power and social dominance and the coalitions for the conflicts and crusades. The role of romantic love is limited to adulterous and often nonsexual relationship. The case of courtly love is an example.

In the traditional collectivistic and hierarchical societies, which are highly structured, the interpersonal relationships are frequently disharmonic. Love is embedded in the system of arranged marriages. The romantic ties between young men and women and their personal preferences are not considered.

In individualistic societies, the social connections are fragmented and fluid. They tend to be more egalitarian and conducive to the free independent choice of relationships and responsibility. Romantic love and marriage become more compatible and go along.

The Main Cultural Types in the Historical Evolution of Societies

Despite the diversity of societies, *three basic types* have been distinctive in their influence on evolution of love: (a) *subsistence-based isolated tribal communities*, (b) *traditional collectivistic societies, and* (c) *modern individualistic societies*. These cultures differ in (1) the conceptions of individuality, in-groups, and out-groups; (2) the low or high geographical, social, and relational mobility; (3) hierarchical versus egalitarian social structures; (4) social power distance versus social equality; (5) rigidity versus flexibility of gender roles; and (6) the values of survival or self-expression. These ecological and social factors establish the *cultural affordances*, which people have in their life and love. The changes in these cultural parameters determine the evolution of the *three big groups of societies* (Karandashev, in press). The evolution from *traditional* to *modern* societies, *modernization* (Inglehart, 1997; Inglehart & Baker, 2000; Inglehart & Welzel, 2005), can explain economic, social, and cultural differences between these two groups of societies and others, which are in cultural transition.

The Cultures of Subsistence-Based Societies

Subsistence-based societies of foragers are the low-technology social groups of a small-scale dwelling in the geographic locations relatively remote from mainstream civilizations. They can survive by *pastoralism*, *foraging*, *horticulture*, and *agriculture* as the modes of subsistence. Their livelihood is centered on basic subsistence economy rather than on market economy. They typically have tribal social organization, living in physical proximity and having limited social mobility. Being *subsistence-based*, these cultural groups have the immediate *survival needs* as their priorities. The *rights of property* are limited because they rarely have excess of resources. The *subsistence* societies largely have *collective tribal* and *personal properties*, but not *private property*. The local ecological and social conditions set many boundaries in their life and relationships. Such limited affordances make people to adapt their expectations, personal preferences, and practices accordingly. They often have loose social structures and nuclear family systems. Their cultures are socially egalitarian, characterized by gender equality (Boehm, 1999, 2012).

The social and gender equality, along with nuclear structure of family organization of early foragers, is conducive for the *bonds of love* between men and women in mating and marital relationships (see for review De Munck, Korotayev, & McGreevey, 2016). The cultural norms and practices are supportive for the value of love. The case of *Hadza* – a tribal cultural group of gatherers and hunters in East

Africa – provides an example of such culture (Scelza et al., 2020). Their social organization in more details is described in further sections.

The Cultures of Traditional Collectivistic Societies

Intensive farming, surplus of resources, the advent of ownership, private and family property, inheritance, and market economy were the major impetuses for the development of *traditional collectivistic societies* and other civilizations (e.g., Bowles & Choi, 2013; Fortes, 2017; Morgan, 1877/2013). Expansion of *these societies* coincided with evolution of traditional religious values, which encouraged social and gender inequality, hierarchical structures of societies, and extended families. The so-called collectivistic cultures fostered *interdependent self-construal* of persons embedded in the *kinship*, *extended families*, and *extended circles of acquaintances*, which were considered as favorable in-groups. People *rely* on these *in-groups* and *feel a responsibility* for these *in-groups*. All these factors determine the restricted social and relationship affordances, which people have in traditional societies. These cultures are characterized by prevalence of *survival and security values* (in a broad sense) over the values of self-expression and tolerance of minorities. The *survival values* put emphasis on physical, economic, and social security.

For example, in the late 1980s (Buss et al., 1990), the cultures of China, India, Iran, and Nigeria placed high value on the provision of resources, domestic skills, chastity, and others – typical for traditional societies. On the other hand, the UK, the Netherlands, Sweden, and Finland had the low value of these traditional values (Karandashev, 2021a, 2021b; Karandashev, in press).

The Cultures of Modern Individualistic Societies

The *modern individualistic societies* encouraged the values of autonomy, social equality, and freedom from social and relationship dependency. They fostered *independent self-construal* of persons. People tend to rely on themselves and close others. They feel responsible for themselves and close others. These cultures have prevalence of *self-expression values and tolerance of minorities* over *survival and security values*. The *self-expression values* emphasize the quality of life, personal well-being, and aspiration to thrive. Individualistic societies vary in their values and real cultural practices; some of them are in transition to modernization. Nevertheless, their modern cultural ideas extend the *social and relationship affordances* providing for persons more freedom of love in mating and marital relationships (Karandashev, 2021a, 2021b; Karandashev, in press).

For example, in the USA, the *new American model* of love has been on rise since the 1960s – the *self-expressive model of love*. For many modern Americans of this new era (Finkel, 2018), love and marriage have become a sphere for exploration of self, validation of self-esteem, personal discovery, fulfillment, and growth. The function of marriage has changed – it became less essential as a formal social institution, for some individuals rather elective.

The Role of Family Structures in the Value of Love

Romantic love appeared later in the human and social history, not in early evolutionary history of a human species (Karandashev, 2017). It is more likely that evolution and society interplayed producing experience of romantic love. For instance, the differences in family structures prevalent in societies determine emergence of romantic love, which is typically associated with nuclear types of family and individualistic structure of societies.

As de Munck and colleagues (2019, p. 19) demonstrated, romantic love plays a different role in societies with different family structures. In the extended family situation, it is not necessary for the care of pregnant females or childrearing. Any members of the family can perform these roles. In an extended arranged marriage, romantic love can be an obstacle and ruin the "wise" marriage plans of senior adults. Therefore, cultural norms suppress youthful ideals of romantic love. Anthropological studies (de Munck, 2019) showed that the presence of the extended family is a predictor of less importance of romantic love for marriage, or even absence of romantic love in a society.

However, in the nuclear family, biological parental roles are more important since it is less likely that "extended" kin reside in the nuclear household. In modern age, urbanization and social mobility detached the individual from place and family. Therefore, romantic love became the primary channel for satisfaction of our desire to be loved. Predisposition toward romantic love holds an important evolutionary function to provide a woman with a secure man during pregnancy and after the birth of a baby only in certain types of societies. As De Munck et al. (2016) explain, "this is likely to be a serious problem just within a neolocal (rather than nonneolocal) contexts where there could be no relatives around and there is a real risk that a female will be left with nobody to look after her and her newborn baby" (p. 9). In the social conditions, where a nuclear family is the norm, a woman can allow to expect love as a premise for a sexual relation with a man.

Modernization of Societies

The modern societies are characterized by ecological and technological mobility, urbanization, social mobility, and evolving independence of the individual from traditional anchors of connection and security, such as stationary location and family ties. Many contemporary traditional societies are in transition and vary in the degree of modernization.

Cultural modernization of societies is typically associated with economic developments, which expand social and economic affordances of the new generations of peoples. Modern generations of young men and women in many countries have more opportunities and possibilities for relationship mobility. Many women do not need to consider a partner for marriage with resources and status to ensure their future economic and social security.

The modern economic and social liberal reforms precipitate cultural transformation and modernization. The higher socioeconomic and relationship freedom first appears in the middle-income, highly educated social classes. Being open-minded, young men and women attempt to realize their new – modern – cultural personal identity, which is free from the old rigid cultural traditions of a society. Such cultural transformation, however, occurs concomitant with controversial feelings of anxiety.

For example, due to neoliberal reforms in Vietnam, and especially in such metropolitan residence as Ho Chi Minh City, the individuals in growing population of middle class tend to accept the role of emotions in their daily life and relationships more than before (Tran, 2018). They recognize the value of personal communication, compatibility, emotional intimacy, and romantic ideals in their life. However, such emotional self-reflexivity often causes anxiety about selfhood, personal cultural identity, and romantic love. Therefore, they reconstruct their discourse of romantic love adjusting to their versions of a *modern cultural identity*.

2.5.2 *Individualistic Versus Collectivistic Values and Models of Love*

The Concepts of Individualism, Collectivism, and Self

In scholarly literature, Western vs. Eastern patterns of emotions are frequently contrasted with each other. The Western cultural pattern, associated with *individualistic values*, appreciates self-seeking, self-sufficiency, personal identity, and intrinsic desire. On the other hand, the Eastern cultural pattern, associated with *collectivistic values*, emphasizes group harmony and cohesion and considers priority of the group over personal.

Although these cultural parameters are societal, they reflect on various personal variables: self-concept, motivation, personal relationships, etc. For example, Roland (1988) compared the *familial self* in India and Japan with the North American *individualized self*. The *Indian and Japanese conception of self* develops in hierarchical relationships within the extended family. It is more relational than autonomous and encourages such qualities as emotional interdependence, a high degree of empathy, mutual caring, reciprocal demands for intimacy and support, and sensitivity to another's needs within the family structure. When Indians and Japanese encounter Western culture, the emotional problems may occur. The successful integration creates a new pattern – the *expanding self*.

The studies in recent decades have revealed the complex and multifaceted nature of *individualism and collectivism*. Research has also shown that current societies are changing over time and are in constant flux. So, the dichotomy of individualism and collectivism with simplistic division is no viable conceptualization of these cultural dimensions (see for detailed review Karandashev, 2019, 2021a, 2021b).

How Individualistic and Collectivistic Values Can Affect Love

The researchers of love and culture *s* usually claim that idea of romantic love better fits in individualistic cultural norms, than in collectivistic ones. In individualistic societies, romantic love is an individual matter and personal experience; a lover pursues personal desires and strives for personal fulfillment, which often does not take into account the interests and well-being of family and relatives (Adams, Anderson, & Adonu, 2004; Lieberman & Hatfield, 2006). On the other hand, in collectivistic societies a person in love is expected to consider not only his or her own personal feelings but also the expectations and interests of parents and family, their group obligations (Hatfield & Rapson, 2005; Smith et al., 2009).

Early cross-cultural research suggested that romantic love should be less valued in traditional collectivistic cultures with strong, extended family ties, while in modern individualistic cultures, the beliefs in romantic love and its valorization should be more common (Goode, 1959; Rosenblatt, 1967; Simmons, Vom Kolke, & Shimizu, 1986).

However, later research revealed more complex findings and interpretation. Although individualistic cultures consider love-based marriage as ideal, yet the individual characteristics of collectivism and individualism may be variable. Therefore, K.K. Dion and K.L. Dion (Dion & Dion, 1988, 1991, Dion & Dion, 1993, 1996) proposed to use the terms *psychological collectivism* and *psychological individualism* referring to these constructs at the individual level and extensively studied the effect of these variables on romantic and marital relationship across cultures. The effect of individualism on subjective perception of love relationship might be controversial.

The recent study has revealed that greater collectivism in Indian cultures, compared to individualism in America, is associated with stronger romantic beliefs (Bejanyan, Marshall, & Ferenczi, 2014). These results look opposite and contradicting to the earlier findings, cited above. The effect of influential Indian Bollywood romantic movies can play its role in this Indian cultural sample.

Love Attitudes in Individualistic Cultures

In *individualistic cultures*, a person with a typical desire to be self-sufficient still perceives the dependency on other people (and another person) ambivalently. The need for the person's unity with a romantic partner can conflict with his or her culturally determined motivation to be independent. This way an individualistic value can affect love for a partner in a negative way and interfere with a love relationship.

A study found (Dion & Dion, 1991) that people with higher degree of individualistic values were less likely of ever having been in love. They also tended to be more likely to endorse the *ludus love style* and be *less intimate* in their love relationships. They perceived their relationships as less deep and as less rewarding. Generally, they had the lower quality of experience of love in a relationship. Dion and Dion (2005) analyzed the data from the General Social Survey for the year 1993 and discovered that individualistic people had the lower satisfaction with their friends and family life as well as experienced less happiness in their marriages.

Another study also showed (Le, 2005) that *individualism* in its *vertical dimension*, considering individuals as autonomous individuals and accepting inequality (Singelis, Triandis, Bhawuk, & Gelfand, 1995), *predisposes* them to *narcissistic traits* and *ludus love* (of game-playing type). Due to corresponding *independent self-construal*, those individuals are *excessively self-focused* and perceive another person as an object of their wishful fulfillment. Nevertheless, *independent self-construal* of participants tends to decrease the ludus love attitudes. Thus, individualism at the individual level shapes people's preferences for the ludus love attitudes (Le, 2005).

Love Attitudes in Collectivistic Cultures

In collectivistic cultures, a person perceives the dependency of being embedded in multiple relationships with their family and close friends as normal. Due to this, when making decisions in a romantic relationship, a person naturally takes into account not only what is best for him/her but also how this can affect other relationships. People with collectivistic values perceive love from pragmatic perspective, having in mind altruistic goals and friendship (Dion & Dion, 2005). Women in collectivistic cultures more commonly than women in individualistic cultures endorse an altruistic view of love. They emphasize the importance of a broader network of close friendships (Dion & Dion, 1993).

Cultures and people with individualistic and collectivistic values conceptualize themselves differently. From the individualistic perspective, an individual is a separate entity, while from the *collectivistic perspective*, the individual is a part of more extended relationships. Consequently, these differences affect how they love and what they experience in love. When an individualistic person is aware of himself/herself as an individual being separate from others and having social boundaries, then his/her love becomes the bridge connecting to another one. This is an opportunity to escape the loneliness of being a separate individual. This is why people in individualistic cultures especially value romantic love. Such a connection, however, should still allow a person's freedom. If a relationship does meet partners' expectations, they have an option to leave the relationship.

From the collectivistic perspective, people perceive the bonds, which they already have, as valuable and consider themselves as a part of these relationships. Therefore, they do not believe that it is necessary to verbally announce their love to someone else or ask another one to confirm those relationship bonds. They express their love in what they do, rather than in what they say (Dion & Dion, 2006). While for people with individualistic values love is the way of feeling and self-expression, for people with collectivistic values, love is the way of doing.

2.5.3 Conservative Versus Liberal Values and Love

Conservative Nature of Romanticism in American Culture

Romantic love beliefs can also be affected by such geographical and cultural parameters as climate of a region and political orientation of conservatism or liberalism of population. The research of these correlations was conducted in the early 1960s–1980s.

Among American scholars, Reiss (1960) suggested that romanticism is a conservative element in American culture. She conducted her study of sexual behavior and beliefs using two major samples: (1) a random adult sample of age 21 and older from across the nation and (2) a sample of 903 school and college students ages 16–22 from 2 high schools and 2 colleges in Virginia and 1 college in New York State. These five schools represented a widespread distribution of the conservative-liberal dimension of permissive attitudes toward premarital sexual relations. Besides several scales measuring sexual behavior, author also used the eight-item scale of romantic love conceptualized as "belief in only one real love, that love leads to perfect happiness, is known at once, and so forth" (p. 693).

The author theorized that since romantic love is an idealistic and conservative characteristic of American culture, then the low adherence to this belief would be associated with more permissive behavior. Therefore, she hypothesized that those who are low in their romantic love beliefs would be more permissive.

The results were different for two cultural subgroups. In the sample of White students, the significant negative correlation has shown that low romantic love beliefs were associated with more permissive, while in the Black sample, the relations between these variables were opposite. In both subgroups, these correlations were stronger for women than for men. Men were more permissive than women, and romantic love does not affect men as much as it does women. However, the weak positive correlation between romantic love and permissiveness among Black women may indicate that for them romantic love includes a more sexual and emotional interpretation. As Reiss (1960) noted, although Black women in the sample were relatively permissive, they were not generally promiscuous. They required affectionate relations as a basis for sexual behavior. Those who are high in their romantic love beliefs are willing to accept *permissiveness with affection* and prefer some form of stable affectionate relationship. Their view of romantic love was probably influenced by the tradition of sexual permissiveness. White women, on the other side, interpret romantic love in more idealistic and less sensual overtones. The White women who were high in romantic love beliefs were most likely to accept abstinence.

Based on this research, she also reported modest associations between romanticism and being Black rather than White, a high school student rather than a college student, and a female rather than a male. She also reported (Reiss, 1967) that the students from New York colleges were less romantic than those from colleges in Virginia. These studies demonstrated that education makes people less optimistic about the power of love.

In the study of the late 1960s, Spaulding (1970) obtained the data in support of association of romantic love beliefs with conservatism in the USA. Spaulding (1970) administered several questionnaires among American freshman college students ($N = 500$, largely of White, middle-class young people, with minority of Blacks or Mexican Americans in the sample) at the University of California, Santa Barbara, in 1967. The author was interested in the relationships of romanticism, measured by the romantic love complex, with values and with dispositions. The results revealed that for both men and women, conservative values had the strongest positive association with romanticism. Americans with conservative cultural values are more likely to accept the romantic love complex. Single, White, middle-class, college men are somewhat more inclined to accept the romantic love beliefs than young women are. Selected personality dispositions were less associated with romanticism in love than conservative cultural values.

Effect of Conservatism on Romantic Beliefs in Australia

In Australia similar research was conducted by Ray (1982, 1985, 1987). He commented on America's Deep South and Australia's Deep North of that time as warm and conservative regions. He also believed that people in those regions are more romantic in love and tested this hypothesis in two Australian states.

The questionnaire contained the scales of conservatism (e.g., statements for and against greater government involvement in the economy, more equal distribution of wealth, greater permissiveness or restraint in matters of sexual morality) as well as *Munro-Adams Attitude to Love Scale* (with three subscales of Romantic Love, Romantic Power, and Conjugal Love).

The survey was sent out to 700 randomly chosen addresses in Queensland and 500 addresses in New South Wales, controlling for urban/rural differences. For each State, the proportion of completed and returned questionnaires was relatively small – 31%. The age range was diverse (in the Queensland sample, 42.9 years, $SD + 17.07$, while in N.S.W. sample, 41.58, $SD = 16.77$). The gender distribution was approximately equal (in Queensland, 108 females and 111 males, while in N.S.W. sample, 79 males and 79 females).

In this study Ray (1982) found interesting, even though relatively small, correlations between moral strictness and more loving attitudes. The respondents from Queensland were more conservative on moral and social issues, yet not more economically conservative or authoritarian. They also showed stronger belief in the transforming and overcoming power of love. The difference between means, as well as correlations, revealed the association between more love-oriented attitudes and moral conservatism. Ray (1982) commented that the pattern of the American South was rather strikingly similar in his study. Queensland was warmer, more conservative, more morally impermissive, and even more romantic.

This conclusion might seem questionable from the theory proposed by Eisler and Loye (1983) that asserts that soft, linking attitudes characterize liberalism whereas hierarchical, aggressive attitudes characterize conservatism. Ray (1982, 1987) tested this theory with a question: Who are the most love-oriented, liberals, or conservatives? Presumably, *soft and linking attitude* should favor love as a value.

The results showed that moral conservatism was the strongest predictor of attitude to love. The impermissive conservatives believed in the power of love more than did the permissive, progressive liberals. The measures of general and social conservatism had correlation of similar kind. Correlations of the love variables (Romantic Love, Romantic Power, and Conjugal Love) with the scales of conservatism in the sample of 377 Australians were in the range from 0.3 to 0.40 for moral conservatism and from 0.2 to 0.3 for other scales of conservatism (correlations were statistically significant, $p < 0.05$). No big differences in the strength of correlations with Romantic and Conjugal Love, yet bigger for Romantic Power. Correlation of conservatism variable with overall score of the romantic love attitude was 0.432, which means that this ideological position substantially influences love attitudes. Naturally, both conservative and liberal people believed in romantic love, but the conservatives believed in it more. Nevertheless, empirical evidence brought the conclusion opposite to the earlier theory: conservatives rather than liberals are more love-oriented. Does permissiveness go along with cynicism about love?

It sounds in the spirit of Victorian age: that "happiness is to be found in self-control rather than self-indulgence" Ray (1985, p. 39). If one would consider conservatism as a cultural parameter, then Australian state of Queensland was particularly conservative in the early 1980s, definitely more than New South Wales. The data showed (Ray, 1985) that Queenslanders were more conservative on moral issues. And they were also more love-oriented and believed more in the power of love.

Unfortunately, no further studies of the effect of these cultural and geographical parameters on love have been conducted. So, one cannot confirm the validity of those findings and their broader cross-cultural generalization.

2.5.4 Gender Equality Versus Inequality in Society and Love

The Cultural Traditions of Gender Equality

The idea of equality in relationships between men and women is not a recent societal development. Anthropological studies demonstrated that loose, yet mainly nuclear families with gender equality were widespread in most nomadic foragers (Boehm, 1999, 2012). Many anthropologists and evolutionary psychologists agree (see for review De Munck et al., 2016) that the nucleated family conditions of early foragers were conducive for romantic love to appear. It kept males and females bonded. "Social conditions of gender equality, the intimacy of daily living, activities such as eating and sleeping together, and distributing the labor for meeting daily subsistence needs then produce cultural values, norms, and practices supportive of romantic love" (De Munck et al., 2016, p. 11). The authors conclude that gender equality is an important condition for romantic love to thrive.

For example, the *Hadza* – the East African tribal society of hunters and gatherers in Northern Tanzania – is an egalitarian society which follow the tradition of bilateral descent and do not recognize clans. Their practice of family lineage considers the relatives on the father's side and mother's side as equal in transfer of property and wealth, as well as in emotional ties. The descent is bilateral, and inheritance is passed equally to both parents. This cultural value of equality coincides with their endorsement of love matches. Serial monogamous marital relationships are typical, with rare occasion of polygynous relationships. Freedom of divorce is culturally acceptable; infidelity is a main cause for separation in marriage (Scelza et al., 2020).

The Modern Rise of Gender Equality and Its Effect on Love

Cross-cultural research demonstrated that the rise of female status and gender equality is an important condition for romantic love and love marriage (de Munck & Korotayev, 1999, 2007). Equality was frequently mentioned as an important feature of romantic love in the free lists in the study of De Munck, Korotayev, de Munck, and Khaltourina (2011). As it was shown in the study of de Munck et al. (2011), Lithuanians, Russians, and Americans believe that a lover should perceive and be perceived by the beloved as an equal. The equality, however, may be seen as symmetrical or as complementary.

Sexual equality was also considered as an important cultural parameter affecting the experience of romantic love. De Munck and Korotayev (1999) suggested that social indicators of sexual equality and sexual permissiveness should be the good predictors of the importance of romantic love. They hypothesized that in the societies which allow both males and females to give or not give love freely and which allow premarital or extramarital sex for both sexes, people consider romantic love as a more important basis for marriage. The authors used Rosenblatt's (1967) 11-point rating scale of romantic love and ratings of extramarital sex and premarital sex in 75 societies to test their hypothesis.

The authors found that in societies in which cultural norms allow premarital and extramarital sex for both males and females, people rate romantic love much higher than in societies which have strong sanctions against female sexuality out of wedlock or have double standards on this issue. They concluded that "it is not just a blanket prohibition against extramarital sex but specifically a prohibition against females and not against males that inhibits the development of romantic love" (de Munck & Korotayev, 1999, p. 272). In addition, the authors concluded that in the societies with sexual inequality, where premarital sex and/or adultery is permitted for only one sex (in their study, males), romantic love is rated of low importance as a basis for marriage. Meanwhile, in the societies with sexual equality, where premarital sex and/or adultery is prohibited for both sexes, people rate romantic love higher than societies where sexual inequality exists. Then, de Munck and Korotayev (1999) suggest that in addition to the nonmarital sexual freedom of women, society should recognize sexual equality as an important factor of romantic love.

Gender Equality and Romantic Love

De Munck and Korotayev (1999, 2007) further investigated this problem proposing that *gender equality* is a conducive condition for romantic love. Man and woman shall view each other as being of equal worth. An empirical study (de Munck & Korotayev, 1999) revealed that the measures of gender equality strongly correlate with high ranking of romantic love. Social attitudes endorse romantic love as a criterion for marriage.

Another important finding (de Munck & Korotayev, 2007) is that the high status of women correlates with intimacy as a measure of romantic love. Such variables as "sleeping together" and "eating together" were the indicators of intimacy in relationships, while cross-cultural variables of women's power in traditional societies were the indicators of their status. The study (de Munck & Korotayev, 2007) showed that intimacy is higher in the societies with high status of women because experience of romantic love and intimacy implies that a lover views a beloved partner as exceptional and not comparable to others.

2.5.5 Social Affordances and Freedom of Love

Arranged Marriages and Love

Throughout history parents frequently controlled the mating behavior of their children. The *arranged marriages* are usually agreed and planned by parents or other persons of kinship, with limited opportunity for groom and bride. These cultural practices have been widely acceptable in many societies of the world throughout centuries. The families of kings, queens, dukes, duchesses, and other nobility could not afford a free choice of their spouses having limited choices of specially designated and arranged partners. Their arranged marriages were a matter of social, legal, and economic relations, rather than the matter of love.

Therefore, traditional arranged marriages strived to avoid the risks associated with freedom of choice. A common assumption is that romantic love is not a priority value in such traditional collectivistic societies. The arranged marriages of commoners considered rather practical grounds such as person's strength and health, food-getting and food-preparation skills, personality traits, status, and interests of alliances created by the marriage at the highest importance. Poor people also used arranged marriages for the uplifting of their social and economic status.

The cultural values of arranged marriage *and/or* free love in the relationship depend on the balance versus disbalance between social affordances and freedom (Karandashev, in press). The available social, cultural, contextual, and situational affordances afford individuals a certain range of options to choose from. In some societies, people have more while in other societies less affordances to choose one or another model of love.

The Systems of Kin Relations and Extended Family Structures

Analysis of the large anthropological data set across many cultural groups (see for review de Munck, 2019) has shown that the importance of romantic love for marriage varies depending on social organization of societies. Traditional arranged marriages are typical in the societies with social organization, which is characterized by the high importance of *community interpersonal relations*, *kinship*, and *normative system of extended family*.

The value of romantic love for a woman and her children is reduced. In such community, kin, and family system, other members of family can take over as the providers, caregivers, and caretakers alternative to a passionate man. A woman does not really need a loving partner as a breadwinner or helper in raising children. There is no real need for commitment, intimacy, and affection for both a man and a woman. Alternative providers and caretakers are available and accessible among kin of extended family. Romantic love in family relations can convert to disadvantages (de Munck, 2019; De Munck et al., 2016).

The practices of arranged marriages are still present in India, China, and Muslim countries and produce corresponding cultural models of love (e.g., Allendorf & Pandian, 2016; De Munck, 1998; Epstein, Pandit, & Thakar, 2013; Jaiswal, 2014; see for review Karandashev, in press).

Arranged marriages are commonly associated with cultures of traditional societies with extended family structures while love marriages with modern societies. The need for romantic love emerges only in the societies with nuclear family systems (Munck, 2019).

Parental Influence in Love: The Romeo and Juliet Effect

A common belief is, especially among proponents of freedom of romantic choice, that parental influence on youngsters' choice of mating and dating is detrimental to romantic love. Driscoll, Davis, and Lipetz (1972) dared this assumption; the analysis of classical literature and small group dynamics allowed them to hypothesize that parental interference in a love relationship actually intensifies the feelings of romantic love. Their psychological study among 140 couples supported this hypothesis using both cross-sectional and longitudinal change score correlations. Referring to the classical example of English poet and playwright Shakespeare, authors named this phenomenon as the Romeo and Juliet effect. They explained it in terms of the motivating effect of frustration and reactance and commented on possible relationship dynamics that might be associated with parental interference and trust. It seemed that findings are applicable to cross-cultural variations in the occurrence of romantic love.

For many years this finding on the Romeo and Juliet effect was cited in popular culture and textbooks; however, none of the follow-up studies used the original scales. The follow-up studies also used different operational definitions of social network opinions (see for review Sinclair, Hood, & Wright, 2014).

Twenty years later, Sprecher and Felmlee (1992) studied the influence of parents and friends on the quality and stability of romantic relationships. Data were gathered in three waves of longitudinal investigation over 2 years (1988–1990) from romantic couples at a large Mid-Western university in the USA (101 dating couples at Time 1). Most of the sample was Caucasian (97.5%) and of the middle or upper-middle class (86.6%). The mean age of the participants at Time 1 was 20 years old. The relations between love variables (*love, general satisfaction in the relationship, and commitment)* and such social network variables as (1) *social reactions from significant others*, (2) *social network overlap*, and (3) *liking for partner's networks* were analyzed.

The authors' hypothesis that "social network approval and support for the romantic relationship have a positive effect on relationship quality (love, satisfaction, and commitment)" (p. 897) was supported in the cross-sectional analyses at each of the three waves of study. "Perceived support from one's own family and friends had a larger influence on satisfaction, love, and commitment than perceived support from partner's family and friends" (Sprecher & Felmlee, 1992, p. 897).

The analysis of longitudinal data also supported this conclusion. Among majority of couples, social network support at one point in time allowed to predict subsequent perceptions of relationship quality (even up to 18 months later): "increases/decreases over time in social network support were consistently, and strongly, associated with increases/decreases over time in the levels of love, satisfaction, and commitment" (p. 897). The results were similar for women and men.

Authors believes that

> this positive effect of social support from networks on relationship quality may occur because there is greater cognitive balance (due to the transitive relationship between the network, dyad, and individual), a reduction in uncertainty concerning the partner (through the information acquired from the network), a stronger sense of identity with the dyad (due to being treated as a "unit" or couple), and/or a perception of network barriers to a breakup (for example, through anticipated social losses and disapproval) (p. 897).

Researchers (Sprecher & Felmlee, 1992) found no evidence for the *Romeo and Juliet effect*, which seems to contradict the study by Driscoll et al. (1972). However, authors admitted that their study was not directly comparable to theirs in several aspects of research design.

Social Networks and Freedom of Love

Further research discovered more *complex system of social network influence* (Felmlee, 2001). Researchers administered questionnaires measuring individuals' intimate relationship and friendship ties among students (169 male, 277 female, average age 20) at a large western university. The ethnic proportion in the American sample was largely Caucasian American (around 50%) and Asian American (around 30%), with a substantially smaller proportion other ethnicities.

The results suggest that perception of approval from an individual's friends and approval from a partner's family members increases relationship stability. Explaining this fact, author believes that friends and relatives are able to predict relationship longevity better than a person himself/herself. They are less likely affected by "rose-colored glasses" and more realistic in evaluating a romantic partner than an involved person.

The findings demonstrated that a close friend can directly affect a person's romantic behavior and his/her actual approval from a close friend predicts relationship longevity, when the friend is familiar with the person's partner. The perception of such an approval is more important for relationship stability than actual approval.

On a more general level, these findings highlight the significance of examining the negative side of social networks by challenging the myth that social connections are uniformly benevolent in their effects on a dyad.

On the other hand, the findings challenged the myth that social connections are uniformly benevolent and highlighted the negative side of social networks: social networks can have not only and not always a direct and positive effect on a romantic relationship. The results of this study revealed that the perception of approval from a person's own family and the perception of overall encouragement from others are related with a higher, not a lower, rate of breakup over time. As author commented, this finding supported the *Romeo and Juliet effect* (Driscoll et al. 1972) that "parental opposition (and maybe opposition from others) drives couples closer together" (p. 1280). As it was earlier suggested, resistance can enhance stability because it induces psychological reactance. However, alternative explanation is also possible (Felmlee, 2001):

Confronting family opposition, partners may positively interact to resolve potential relationship problems raised by family members, and this interaction just strengthens their relationship. Different from the earlier study (Driscoll et al. 1972), findings demonstrate that the family resistance effect has influence only when the opinions and closeness of friends are taken into account. Only being combined with affirming and close friends, family opposition can help keep a love relationship. A little opposition may keep partners together, but only when it is combined with some support. These effects are not gender specific.

Reexamination of Romeo and Juliet Effect
Later, Sinclair et al. (2014) reexamined the *Romeo and Juliet effect* in terms of the relations between social network opinions and romantic relationship outcomes. Researchers used the original scales employed by Driscoll and colleagues as well as contemporary measures with 396 participants who were followed over a 3–4-month period. The participants reported their feelings of love, commitment, and trust, as well as rated the levels of perceived interference from family and friends. Repeating the same analyses as Driscoll et al. (1972), authors found no evidence for the Romeo and Juliet effect. The results of their study demonstrated the opposite: the greater approval (and lower interference or disapproval) was positively associated with better relationship qualities in such a way that the perceived increase in social network support was related to the increase in love, commitment, and trust. It was rather consistent with the social network effect (Felmlee, 2001). This finding was also revealed in a meta-analysis of the literature.

Among 396 participants in the study of Sinclair et al. (2014), there were around 80% of American Caucasians and much smaller percentage of other ethnicities. However, no cross-cultural differences in finding were reported in this study.

The Romeo and Juliet Effect in a Cross-Cultural Perspective

Surprisingly, the studies of the *Romeo and Juliet effect* have been conducted in modern individualistic countries with presumable freedom of choice in love. The responses to parental influence can be mediated by individualistic versus collectivistic cultures. It seems that an *autonomous independent self* in individualistic society shall be resistant and rebellious to family influence, while a *relational interdependent self* in collectivistic society shall be compliant with family influence.

Furthermore, the recent research convincingly demonstrated (Buunk, Park, & Duncan, 2010) that cultural parameter of *parental influence* on the choice in love is more prevalent in the cultures with higher *degree of collectivism*. The participants were largely the immigrants from collectivistic countries. Parental influence is less likely in individualistic societies.

In traditional cultures of nowadays, parental influence on mating choice is still substantial. However, no cross-cultural research of the *Romeo and Juliet phenomenon* was conducted in traditional collectivistic societies. Cross-cultural studies have shown (MacDonald et al., 2012; MacDonald & Jessica, 2006) that individuals in collectivistic cultures (e.g., Indonesia, Japan) are more in favor of the prospective partners and relationships, which would expectedly receive their family approval. Their low self-esteem and the doubts concerning family approval of the partner and relationship decrease their personal value of a romantic relationship. Self-reflected biased appraisal may play its role. As a result, they don't feel constrained by family; they rather adjust their appraisal to make their personal choice, which then goes along with family affordance.

Effect of Social Network on Individual Love Experience

The deeper understanding of effect of social network on love experience came from other three studies (Sinclair, 2015) that investigated the effect of social network reactions on feelings toward a romantic partner.

Consistent with previous findings, results brought an extensive support for the social network effect: "relationship approval from family and friends leads individuals to feel more love, more committed, and more positive about a partner" (p. 77). However, researchers demonstrated how psychological reactance moderated social network influence. It appears that *independent reactance* (a desire to make free and independent decisions), rather than *defiant reactance* (doing the opposite of that urged by others), interacts with effects of social network and buffers the effects of social adversity. Independent persons were capable of ignoring disapproving network opinions.

Across three studies (of the survey and experimental design), reactance moderated perceptions of liking, love, commitment, and positive partner characteristics. As researchers summarized:

> we found extensive evidence that people who experience network opposition maintain rather than magnify their own evaluations of their romantic partner despite the opinions of others when they are high in independent reactance. We also found that the perception of peril to one's autonomy in romantic decisions can modify reactions to both parental and friend disapproval with regard to a wide range of partner evaluations, including perceptions of love, commitment, likeability, and positive partner characteristics. Moreover, reactance becomes particularly relevant when the odds are stacked against a couple. When both parents and friends disapprove, highly reactant individuals stand firm in their feelings, as do those with at least one source of network support. In contrast, those low in reactance report significantly less positive evaluations when their network disapproves. (pp. 95–96)

It is interesting to note that the research of this topic has been mostly conducted in modern countries, where parental influence on dating choice occurs less frequently than in traditional societies. This might limit variation of this *parental influence* variable. It seems also unknown so far how *psychological reactance* moderates the effect of social network in different types of cultural contexts.

Freedom of Mating Choice and Love

Freedom to choose a spouse is an important factor encouraging romantic love in heterosexual relationships, especially as a basis for marriage. A cross-cultural study of Rosenblatt and Cozby (1972) revealed that the more contacts between men and women allow more freedom of mating choice. Therefore, in societies, where people have more freedom when choosing a spouse, sex and feelings of affection are perceived as an important source of attraction and romantic love is considered as an important basis for marriage (Rosenblatt & Cozby, 1972).

Do we choose to love, or love chooses us to love? Freedom of choice and affordances balance our explicit or implicit choice.

Heidegger (1982/Heidegger, 2002) asserted that freedom of choice, which individuals have in their life, is essentially a *situated freedom*. They are free in their choices, yet not absolutely free: the environmental and social conditions of their lives limit the range of their choice.

References

Adams, G., Anderson, S. L., & Adonu, J. K. (2004). The cultural grounding of closeness and intimacy. In D. J. Mashek & A. P. Aron (Eds.), *Handbook of closeness and intimacy* (pp. 321–339). Lawrence Erlbaum Associates Publishers.

Ahlquist, J. S., & Breunig, C. (2012). Model-based clustering and typologies in the social sciences. *Political Analysis, 20*, 92–112.

Ainsworth, M. D. S. (1989). Attachments beyond infancy. *American Psychologist, 44*, 709–716.

Ainsworth, M. D. S., Blehar, M. C., Waters, E., & Wall, S. (1978). *Patterns of attachment: A psychological study of the strange situation*. Erlbaum.

Allendorf, K., & Pandian, R. K. (2016). The decline of arranged marriage? Marital change and continuity in India. *Population and Development Review, 42*(3), 435–464.

Aron, A., Norman, C. C., & Aron, E. N. (2001). Shared self-expanding activities as a means of maintaining and enhancing close romantic relationships. In J. H. Harvey & A. Wenzel (Eds.), *Close romantic relationships: Maintenance and enhancement* (pp. 47–66). Erlbaum.

Bailey, K. D. (1989). Constructing typologies through cluster analysis. *Bulletin of Sociological Methodology/Bulletin de Méthodologie Sociologique, 25*(1), 17–28.

Bartholomew, K., & Horowitz, L. M. (1991). Attachment styles among young adults: A test of a four-category model. *Journal of Personality and Social Psychology, 61*, 226–244.

Bejanyan, K., Marshall, T. C., & Ferenczi, N. (2014). Romantic ideals, mate preferences, and anticipation of future difficulties in marital life: A comparative study of young adults in India and America. *Frontiers in Psychology, 5*, 1355.

Belsky, J. (1997). Attachment, mating, and parenting: An evolutionary interpretation. *Human Nature, 8*, 361–381.

Belsky, J., & Fearon, R. M. P. (2008). Precursors of attachment security. In J. Cassidy & P. R. Shaver (Eds.), *Handbook of attachment: Theory, research, and clinical applications* (pp. 295–316). The Guilford Press.

Belsky, J., Steinberg, L., & Draper, P. (1991). Childhood experience, interpersonal development, and reproductive strategy: An evolutionary theory of socialization. *Child Development, 62*, 647–670.

Bennardo, G. (2018). Cultural models theory. *Anthropology Newsletter, 59*(4), e139–e142.

Bennardo, G., & de Munck, V. C. D. (2014). *Cultural models: Genesis, methods, and experiences*. Oxford University Press.

Bennardo, G., & de Munck, V. (2020). Cultural model theory in cognitive anthropology: Recent developments and applications. *Journal of Cultural Cognitive Science, 4*, 1–2. https://doi.org/10.1007/s41809-020-00055-4

Bereczkei, T., Gyuris, P., Koves, P., & Bernath, L. (2002). Homogamy, genetic similarity, and imprinting; parental influence on mate choice preferences. *Personality and Individual Differences, 33*, 677–690.

Bereczkei, T., Gyuris, P., & Weisfeld, G. E. (2004). Sexual imprinting in human mate choice. *Proceedings of the Royal Society of London B, 271*, 1129–1134.

Berger, P., & Luckmann, T. (1966). *The social construction of reality*. Doubleday.

Berscheid, E. (2010). Love in the fourth dimension. *Annual Review of Psychology, 61*(1), 1–25. https://doi.org/10.1146/annurev.psych.093008.100318

Berscheid, E., & Meyers, S. A. (1996). A social categorical approach to a question about love. *Personal Relationships, 3*(1), 19–43.

Boehm, C. (1999). *Hierarchy in the forest: The evolution of egalitarian behavior*. Harvard University Press.

Boehm, C. (2012). *Moral origins: The evolution of virtue, altruism, and shame*. Basic Books.

Bowlby, J. (1969). *Attachment and loss: Vol. 1. Attachment*. Basic Books.

Bowlby, J. (1973). *Attachment and loss: Vol. 2. Separation: Anxiety and anger*. Basic Books.

Bowlby, J. (1980). *Attachment and loss: Vol. 3. Loss*. Basic Books.

Bowlby, J. (1988/2008). *A secure base: Parent-child attachment and healthy human development*. Basic books (Originally published in 1988).

Bowles, S., & Choi, J. K. (2013). Coevolution of farming and private property during the early Holocene. *Proceedings of the National Academy of Sciences, 110*(22), 8830–8835.

Brennan, K. A., Clark, C. L., & Shaver, P. R. (1998). Self-report measurement of adult attachment: An integrative overview. In J. A. Simpson & W. S. Rholes (Eds.), *Attachment theory and close relationships* (pp. 46–76). Guilford.

Bretherton, I. (1992). The origins of attachment theory: John Bowlby and Mary Ainsworth. *Developmental Psychology, 28*(5), 759–775. https://doi.org/10.1037/0012-1649.28.5.759

Brommer, S. J. (2016). Love and fire: The role of passion in representations of intimate partner violence. In M. Husso, T. Virkki, M. Notko, H. Hirvonen, & J. Eilola (Eds.), *Interpersonal violence: Differences and connections* (pp. 221–232). Routledge.

Buss, D. M. (2006). The evolution of love. In R. Sternberg & K. Weis (Eds.), *The new psychology of love* (pp. 65–86). Yale University Press.

Buss, D. M., & Schmitt, D. P. (1993). Sexual strategies theory: An evolutionary perspective on human mating. *Psychological Review, 100*, 204–232.

Buss, D. M., et al. (1990). International preferences in selecting mates: A study of 37 cultures. *Journal of Cross-Cultural Psychology, 21*, 5–47.

Buunk, A. P., Park, J. H., & Duncan, L. A. (2010). Cultural variation in parental influence on mate choice. *Cross-Cultural Research, 44*(1), 23–40.

Calderon, D. P., Kilinc, M., Maritan, A., Banavar, J. R., & Pfaff, D. (2016). Generalized CNS arousal: An elementary force within the vertebrate nervous system. *Neuroscience & Biobehavioral Reviews, 68*, 167–176.

Campbell, L., Simpson, J., Kashy, D., & Fletcher, G. (2001). Ideal standards, the self, and flexibility of ideals in close relationships. *Personality and Social Psychology Bulletin, 27*, 447–462.

Cassidy, J., & Shaver, P. R. (Eds.). (1999). *Handbook of attachment: Theory, research, and clinical applications*. Rough Guides.

Cotton, J. L. (1981). A review of research on Schachter's theory of emotion and the misattribution of arousal. *European Journal of Social Psychology, 11*(4), 365–397.

D'Andrade, R. G., & Strauss, C. (Eds.). (1992). *Human motives and cultural models*. Cambridge University Press.

De Munck, V. (2019). *Romantic love in America: Cultural models of gay, straight and polyamorous relationship*. Lexington Press.

De Munck, V. C. (Ed.). (1998). *Romantic love and sexual behavior: Perspectives from social sciences*. Praeger.

De Munck, V. C., & Korotayev, A. (1999). Sexual equality and romantic love: A reanalysis of Rosenblatt's study on the function of romantic love. *Cross-Cultural Research, 33*, 265–277.

De Munck, V. C., & Korotayev, A. V. (2007). Wife–husband intimacy and female status in cross-cultural perspective. *Cross-Cultural Research, 41*(4), 307–335.

De Munck, V. C., & Kronenfeld, D. B. (2016). Romantic love in the United States: Applying cultural models theory and methods. *Sage Open, 6*(1). https://doi.org/10.1177/2158244015622797

De Munck, V. C., Korotayev, A., de Munck, J., & Khaltourina, D. (2011). Cross-cultural analysis of models of romantic love among US residents, Russians, and Lithuanians. *Cross-Cultural Research, 45*(2), 128–154.

De Munck, V., Korotayev, A., & McGreevey, J. (2016). Romantic love and family organization: A case for romantic love as a biosocial universal. *Evolutionary Psychology, 14*(4), 1–13. https://doi.org/10.1177/1474704916674211

Deloyski, A. (2007). *Novelty, arousal, and love: The mediating role of self-expansion.* Indiana State University.

Derryberry, D., & Rothbart, M. K. (1988). Arousal, affect, and attention as components of temperament. *Journal of Personality and Social Psychology, 55*(6), 958–966. https://doi.org/10.1037/0022-3514.55.6.958

Dion, K. L., & Dion, K. K. (1988). Romantic love: Individual and cultural perspectives. In R. J. Sternberg & M. L. Barnes (Eds.), *The psychology of love* (pp. 264–289). Yale University Press.

Dion, K. K., & Dion, K. L. (1991). Psychological individualism and romantic love. *Journal of Social Behavior and Personality, 6*(1), 17–33.

Dion, K. K., & Dion, K. L. (1993). Individualistic and collectivistic perspectives on gender and the cultural context of love and intimacy. *Journal of Social Issues, 49*(3), 53–69. https://doi.org/10.1111/j.1540-4560.1993.tb01168.x

Dion, K. K., & Dion, K. L. (1996). Cultural perspectives on romantic love. *Personal Relationships, 3*(1), 5–17.

Dion, K. K., & Dion, K. L. (2006). Individualism, collectivism, and the psychology of love. In R. J. Sternberg & K. Weis (Eds.), *The new psychology of love* (pp. 298–312). Yale University Press.

Driscoll, R., Davis, K. E., & Lipetz, M. E. (1972). Parental interference and romantic love: The Romeo and Juliet effect. *Journal of Personality and Social Psychology, 24*(1), 1–10.

Dutton, D. G., & Aron, A. P. (1974). Some evidence for heightened sexual attraction under conditions of high anxiety. *Journal of Personality and Social Psychology, 30*(4), 510–517. https://doi.org/10.1037/h0037031

Eastwick, P. W. (2009). Beyond the pleistocene: Using phylogeny and constraint to inform the evolutionary psychology of human mating. *Psychological Bulletin, 135*(5), 794–821. https://doi.org/10.1037/a0016845

Eisler, R., & Loye, D. (1983). The "failure" of Liberalism: A reassessment of ideology from a new feminine-masculine perspective. *Political Psychology, 4*, 375–392.

Epstein, R., Pandit, M., & Thakar, M. (2013). How love emerges in arranged marriages: Two cross-cultural studies. *Journal of Comparative Family Studies, 44*(3), 341–360.

Esch, T., & Stefano, G. B. (2005). The neurobiology of love. *Neuroendocrinology Letters, 26*(3), 175–192.

Fehr, B. (1993). How do I love thee? Let me consult my prototype. In S. Duck (Ed.), *Understanding personal relationships: Vol. 1: Individuals in relationships* (pp. 87–120). Sage.

Fehr, B. (2006). The prototype approach to studying love. In R. J. Sternberg & K. Weis (Eds.), *The new psychology of love* (pp. 225–248). Yale University Press.

Fehr, B., & Russell, J. A. (1991). The concept of love viewed from a prototype perspective. *Journal of Personality and Social Psychology, 60*(3), 425–438. https://doi.org/10.1037/0022-3514.60.3.425

Felmlee, D. H. (2001). No couple is an island: A social network perspective on dyadic stability. *Social Forces, 79*(4), 1259–1287.

Finkel, E. J. (2018). *The all-or-nothing marriage: How the best marriages work.* Dutton.

Fisher, H. E., Aron, A., & Brown, L. L. (2006). Romantic love: A mammalian brain system for mate choice. *Philosophical Transactions of the Royal Society B: Biological Sciences, 361*(1476), 2173–2186.

Fiske, S. T., & Taylor, S. E. (1984). *Social cognition.* Addison-Wesley.

Fletcher, G., & Simpson, J. (2000). Ideal standards in close relationships. *Current Directions in Psychological Science, 9*, 102–105.

Fletcher, G. J. O., Simpson, J. A., Thomas, G., & Giles, L. (1999). Ideals in intimate relationships. *Journal of Personality and Social Psychology, 67*, 72–89. https://doi.org/10.1037/0022-3514.76.1.72

Fletcher, G. J., Simpson, J. A., Campbell, L., & Overall, N. C. (2015). Pair-bonding, romantic love, and evolution: The curious case of Homo sapiens. *Perspectives on Psychological Science, 10*(1), 20–36.

Fortes, M. (2017). *Kinship and the social order: The legacy of Lewis Henry Morgan*. Routledge.

Fraley, R. C., & Marks, M. J. (2010). Westermarck, Freud, and the incest taboo: Does familial resemblance activate sexual attraction? *Personality and Social Psychology Bulletin, 36*(9), 1202–1212.

Fraley, R. C., & Waller, N. G. (1998). Adult attachment patterns: A test of the typological model. In J. A. Simpson & W. S. Rholes (Eds.), *Attachment theory and close relationships* (pp. 77–114). The Guilford Press.

Fransella, F., Bell, R., & Bannister, D. (2004). *A manual for repertory grid technique*. Wiley.

Gergen, K. J. (1992). The social constructionist movement in modern psychology. In R. B. Miller (Ed.), *The restoration of dialogue: Readings in the philosophy of clinical psychology* (pp. 556–569). American Psychological Association. https://doi.org/10.1037/10112-044

Goode, W. J. (1959). The theoretical importance of love. *American Sociological Review, 24*, 38–47.

Gonzaga, G., & Haselton, M. G. (2008). The evolution of love and long-term bonds. In J. P. Forgas & J. Fitness (Eds.), *Social relationships: Cognitive, affective, and motivational processes* (pp. 39–53). Psychology Press.

Gross, J. J., & John, O. P. (1998). Mapping the domain of expressivity: Multimethod evidence for a hierarchical model. *Journal of Personality and Social Psychology, 74*, 170–191.

Hatfield, E., & Rapson, R. L. (1996). *Love and sex: Cross-cultural perspectives*. Allyn & Bacon.

Hatfield, E., & Rapson, R. L. (2005). *Love and sex: Cross-cultural perspectives* (2nd ed.). University Press of America.

Hatfield, E., Schmitz, E., Cornelius, J., & Rapson, R. L. (1988). Passionate love: How early does it begin? *Journal of Psychology and Human Sexuality, 1*, 35–52.

Hazan, C., & Shaver, P. (1987). Romantic love conceptualized as an attachment process. *Journal of Personality and Social Psychology, 52*(3), 511–524. https://doi.org/10.1037/0022-3514.52.3.511

Heidegger, M. (1982/2002). *The essence of human freedom: An introduction to philosophy*. A&C Black.

Hendrick, C., & Hendrick, S. S. (1986). A theory and method of love. *Journal of Personality and Social Psychology, 50*, 392–402.

Hendrick, C., & Hendrick, S. S. (1989). Research on love: Does it measure up? *Journal of Personality and Social Psychology, 56*(5), 784–794. https://doi.org/10.1037/0022-3514.56.5.784

Hendrick, C., & Hendrick, S. (2006). Styles of romantic love. In R. J. Sternberg & K. Weis (Eds.), *The new psychology of love* (pp. 149–170). Yale University Press.

Hendrick, C., Hendrick, S. S., & Dicke, A. (1998). The love attitudes scale: Short form. *Journal of Social and Personal Relationships, 15*(2), 147–159.

Holland, D., & Quinn, N. (Eds.). (1987). *Cultural models in language and thought*. Cambridge University Press.

Holland, D., Lachicotte, W., Jr., Skinner, D., & Cain, C. (1998). *Identity and agency in cultural worlds*. Harvard University Press.

Hoppe, A., Fritsche, I., & Koranyi, N. (2018). Romantic love versus reproduction opportunities: Disentangling the contributions of different anxiety buffers under conditions of existential threat. *European Journal of Social Psychology, 48*(3), 269–284.

Immelmann, K. (1972). Sexual and other long-term aspects of imprinting in birds and other species. *Advances in the Study of Behavior, 4*, 147–174.

Immelmann, K. (1975). Ecological significance of imprinting and early learning. *Annual Review of Ecology and Systematics, 6*(1), 15–37.

Inglehart, R. (1997). *Modernization and postmodernization: Cultural, economic, and political change in 43 societies*. Princeton University Press.
Inglehart, R., & Baker, W. E. (2000). Modernization, cultural change, and the persistence of traditional values. *American Sociological Review, 65*(1), 19–51. https://doi.org/10.2307/2657288
Inglehart, R., & Welzel, C. (2005). *Modernization, cultural change, and democracy: The human development sequence*. Cambridge University Press.
Irwin, D. E., & Price, T. (1999). Sexual imprinting, learning and speciation. *Heredity, 82*(4), 347–354.
Jaiswal, T. (2014). *Indian arranged marriages: A social psychological perspective*. Routledge.
Jankowiak, W., & Nelson, A. J. (2021). The state of ethnological research on love: A critical review. In C. H. Mayer & E. Vanderheiden (Eds.), *International handbook of love: Transcultural and transdisciplinary perspectives* (pp. 23–39). Springer.
Karandashev, V. (2017). *Romantic love in cultural contexts*. Springer.
Karandashev, V. (2019). *Cross-cultural perspectives on the experience and expression of love*. Springer.
Karandashev, V. (2021a). *Cultural models of emotions*. Springer.
Karandashev, V. (2021b). Cultural diversity of romantic love experience. In C. Mayer & E. Vanderheiden (Eds.), *International handbook of love* (pp. 59–79). Springer.
Karandashev, V. (in press). Cross-cultural variation in relationship initiation. In J. K. Mogilski & T. K. Shackelford (Eds.), *The Oxford handbook of evolutionary psychology and romantic relationships*. Oxford Publishing.
Karandashev, V., & Evans, N. D. (2019). Quadrangular love theory and scale: Validation and psychometric investigation. *Journal of Methods and Measurement in the Social Sciences, 10*(1), 1–35.
Karandashev, V., Evans, N. D., Neto, F., Zarubko, E., Artemeva, V., Fallah, S., ... & Dincer, D. (2022). Four-dimensional hierarchical structure of love constructs in a cross-cultural perspective. *Measurement Instruments for the Social Sciences, 4*(1), 1–13.
Keller, H. (2013). Attachment and culture. *Journal of Cross-Cultural Psychology, 44*(2), 175–194.
Keller, H. (2018). Universality claim of attachment theory: Children's socioemotional development across cultures. *Proceedings of the National Academy of Sciences, 115*(45), 11414–11419.
Kelly, G. A. (1955). *The psychology of personal constructs* (Vol. 2 vols). Norton.
Kilinc, M., Calderon, D. P., Tabansky, I., Martin, E. M., & Pfaff, D. W. (2016). Elementary central nervous system arousal. In D. Pfaff & N. Volkow (Eds.), *Neuroscience in the 21st Century*. Springer. https://doi.org/10.1007/978-1-4614-6434-1_79-4
Kluge, S. (2000, January). Empirically grounded construction of types and typologies in qualitative social research. *Forum Qualitative Sozialforschung/Forum: Qualitative Social Research, 1*(1). https://doi.org/10.17169/fqs-1.1.1124
Knee, C. R., & Petty, K. N. (2013). Implicit theories of relationships: Destiny and growth beliefs. In J. A. Simpson & L. Campbell (Eds.), *Oxford library of psychology. The Oxford handbook of close relationships* (pp. 183–198). Oxford University Press.
Knee, C. R., Patrick, H., & Lonsbary, C. (2003). Implicit theories of relationships: Orientations toward evaluation and cultivation. *Personality and Social Psychology Review, 7*(1), 41–55.
Kronenfeld, D. (2008). Cultural models. *Intercultural Pragmatics, 5*(1), 67–74.
Lampert, A. (1997). *The evolution of love*. Praeger.
Larsen, R. J., & Ketelaar, T. (1989). Extraversion, neuroticism and susceptibility to positive and negative mood induction procedures. *Personality and Individual Differences, 10*(12), 1221–1228.
Lasswell, T. E., & Lasswell, M. E. (1976). I love you but I'm not in love with you. *Journal of Marital and Family Therapy, 2*(3), 211–224.
Lasswell, M. E., & Lobsenz, N. M. (1980). *Styles of loving: Why you love the way you do*. Doubleday Books.
Le, T. N. (2005). Narcissism and immature love as mediators of vertical individualism and Ludic love style. *Journal of Social and Personal Relationships, 22*, 542–560.

Lee, J. L. (1973). *The colors of love: The exploration of the ways of loving*. New Press.

Lee, J. A. (1975). The romantic heresy. *Canadian Review of Sociology/Revue canadienne de sociologie, 12*(4), 514–528.

Lee, J. A. (1976). *The colors of love*. Prentice-Hall.

Lee, J. A. (1977). A typology of styles of loving. *Personality and Social Psychology Bulletin, 3*(2), 173–182.

Lieberman, D., & Hatfield, E. (2006). Passionate love: Cross–cultural and evolutionary perspectives. In R. J. Sternberg & K. Weis (Eds.), *The new psychology of love* (2nd ed., pp. 274–297). Yale University Press.

Lindholm, C. (1998). Love and structure. *Theory, Culture & Society, 15*(3–4), 243–263.

MacDonald, G., & Jessica, M. (2006). Family approval as a constraint in dependency regulation: Evidence from Australia and Indonesia. *Personal Relationships, 13*(2), 183–194.

MacDonald, G., Marshall, T. C., Gere, J., Shimotomai, A., & Lies, J. (2012). Valuing romantic relationships: The role of family approval across cultures. *Cross-Cultural Research, 46*(4), 366–393.

McKinney, J. C. (1966). *Constructive typology and social theory*. Appleton-Century-Crofts.

McKinney, J. C. (1969). Typification, typologies, and sociological theory. *Social Forces, 48*(1), 1–12.

Meister, R. (1963). *Literary guide to seduction*. Elek Books.

Mikulincer, M., Florian, V., & Hirschberger, G. (2003). The existential function of close relationships: Introducing death into the science of love. *Personality and Social Psychology Review, 7*(1), 20–40.

Mikulincer, M., Florian, V., & Hirschberger, G. (2004). The terror of death and the quest for love: An existential perspective on close relationships. In J. Greenberg, S. L. Koole, & T. Pyszczynski (Eds.), *Handbook of experimental existential psychology* (pp. 287–304). Guilford Press.

Moeller, J., Dietrich, J., Eccles, J. S., & Schneider, B. (2017). Passionate experiences in adolescence: Situational variability and long-term stability. *Journal of Research on Adolescence, 27*(2), 344–361.

Moltz, H. (1960). Imprinting: Empirical basis and theoretical significance. *Psychological Bulletin, 57*(4), 291.

Morgan, L. H. (2013). *Ancient society*. Harvard University Press (Originally published in 1877).

Morris, M. W., Hong, Y., Chiu, C., & Liu, Z. (2015). Normology: Integrating insights about social norms to understand cultural dynamics. *Organizational Behavior and Human Decision Processes, 129*, 1–13. https://doi.org/10.1016/j.obhdp.2015.03.001

Ovid. (1939) *The art of love* (J. J. Perry, Trans.). Harvard University Press.

Park, B., Judd, C. M., & Ryan, C. S. (1991). Social categorization and the representation of variability information. *European Review of Social Psychology, 2*(1), 211–245.

Pfaff, D., & Banavar, J. R. (2007). A theoretical framework for CNS arousal. *Bioessays, 29*(8), 803–810.

Pfaff, D., Westberg, L., & Kow, L. M. (2005). Generalized arousal of mammalian central nervous system. *Journal of Comparative Neurology, 493*(1), 86–91.

Rantala, M. J., & Marcinkowska, U. M. (2011). The role of sexual imprinting and the Westermarck effect in mate choice in humans. *Behavioral Ecology and Sociobiology, 65*(5), 859–873.

Ray, J. J. (1982). Australia's deep north and America's deep south: Effects of climate on conservatism, authoritarianism and attitude to love. *Ableaus, 169*, 4–7.

Ray, J. (1985). Conservatives, permissives and love. *Quadrant, 29*(1–2), 39–40.

Ray, J. J. (1987). Conservatism and attitude to love: An empirical rebuttal of Eisler & Loye. *Personality and Individual Differences, 8*(5), 731–732.

Regan, P. C., Levin, L., Sprecher, S., Christopher, F. S., & Gate, R. (2000). Partner preferences: What characteristics do men and women desire in their short-term sexual and long-term romantic partners? *Journal of Psychology & Human Sexuality, 12*(3), 1–21.

Reiss, I. L. (1960). Toward a sociology of the heterosexual love relationship. *Marriage and Family Living, 22*(2), 139–145.

Reiss, I. L. (1967). *The social context of premarital sexual permissiveness*. Holt, Rinehart, and Winston.
Roland, A. (1988). *In search of self in India and Japan*. Princeton University Press.
Rosch, E. H. (1983). Prototype classification and logical classification: The two systems. In E. Scholnick (Ed.), *New trends in conceptual representation: Challenges to Piagel's theory* (pp. 73–86). Erlbaum.
Rosenblatt, P. C. (1967). Marital residence and the functions of romantic love. *Ethnology, 6*(4), 471–480.
Rosenblatt, P. C., & Cozby, P. C. (1972). Courtship patterns associated with freedom of choice of spouse. *Journal of Marriage and the Family, 34*, 689–695.
Scelza, B. A., Prall, S. P., Blumenfield, T., Crittenden, A. N., Gurven, M., Kline, M., … McElreath, R. (2020). Patterns of paternal investment predict cross-cultural variation in jealous response. *Nature Human Behaviour, 4*(1), 20–26.
Shaver, P. R., & Hazan, C. (1988). A biased overview of the study of love. *Journal of Social and Personal Relationships, 5*, 474–501.
Shaver, P. R., & Mikulincer, M. (2006). Attachment theory, individual psychodynamics, and relationship functioning. In A. L. Vangelisti & D. Perlman (Eds.), *The Cambridge handbook of personal relationships* (pp. 251–272). Cambridge University Press.
Shepher, J. (1971). Mate selection among second generation kibbutz adolescents and adults: Incest avoidance and negative imprinting. *Archives of Sexual Behavior, 1*, 293–307.
Shepher, J. (1983). *Incest: A biosocial view*. Academic.
Simmons, C. H., vom Kolke, A., & Shimizu, H. (1986). Attitudes toward romantic love among American, German, and Japanese students. *Journal of Social Psychology, 126*(3), 327–336.
Singelis, T. M., Triandis, H. C., Bhawuk, D. P., & Gelfand, M. J. (1995). Horizontal and vertical dimensions of individualism and collectivism: A theoretical and measurement refinement. *Cross-Cultural Research, 29*(3), 240–275.
Sinclair, H. C., Hood, K. B., & Wright, B. L. (2014). Revisiting the Romeo and Juliet effect (Driscoll, Davis, & Lipetz, 1972): Reexamining the links between social network opinions and romantic relationship outcomes. *Social Psychology, 45*(3), 170.
Sköld, A. B., & Roald, T. (2020). An existential structure of love. *The Humanistic Psychologist*. https://doi.org/10.1037/hum0000165
Smith, T. W., Berg, C. A., Florsheim, P., Uchino, B. N., Pearce, G., Hawkins, M., Henry, N. J. M., Beveridge, R. M., Skinner, M. A., & Olsen-Cerny, C. (2009). Conflict and collaboration in middle-aged and older couples: I. Age differences in agency and communion during marital interaction. *Psychology and Aging, 24*(2), 259–273. https://doi.org/10.1037/a0015609
Sprecher, S., & Felmlee, D. (1992). The influence of parents and friends on the quality and stability of romantic relationships: A three-wave longitudinal investigation. *Journal of Marriage and the Family, 54*(4), 888–900.
Spaulding, C. B. (1970). The romantic love complex in American culture. *Sociology & Social Research, 55*(1), 82–100.
Sternberg, R. J. (1986). A triangular theory of love. *Psychological Review, 93*(2), 119–135.
Sternberg, R. J. (1995). Love as a story. *Journal of Social and Personal Relationships, 12*(4), 541–546.
Sternberg, R. J. (1996). Love stories. *Personal Relationships, 3*(1), 59–79.
Sternberg, R. J. (1997). Construct validation of a triangular love scale. *European Journal of Social Psychology, 27*(3), 313–335.
Sternberg, R. J. (1999). *Love is a story: A new theory of relationships*. Oxford University Press.
Sternberg, R. J., Hojjat, M., & Barnes, M. L. (2001). Empirical tests of aspects of a theory of love as a story. *European Journal of Personality, 15*(3), 199–218. https://doi.org/10.1002/per.405
Strelau, J. (1994). The concepts of arousal and arousability as used in temperament studies. In J. E. Bates & T. D. Wachs (Eds.), *Temperament: Individual differences at the interface of biology and behavior* (pp. 117–141). American Psychological Association. https://doi.org/10.1037/10149-004

Ten Cate, C., & Vos, D. R. (1999). Sexual imprinting and evolutionary processes. *Advances in the Study of Behavior, 28*, 1–31.

Tran, A. L. (2018). The anxiety of romantic love in Ho Chi Minh City, Vietnam. *Journal of the Royal Anthropological Institute, 24*(3), 512–531.

VanLear, C. A., Koerner, A., & Allen, D. M. (2006). Relationship typologies. In A. L. Vangelisti & D. Perlman (Eds.), *The Cambridge handbook of personal relationships* (pp. 91–110). Cambridge University Press. https://doi.org/10.1017/CBO9780511606632.007

Vicedo, M. (2013). *The nature and nurture of love: From imprinting to attachment in Cold War America*. University of Chicago Press.

Wells, A., & Hakanen, E. A. (1991). The emotional use of popular music by adolescents. *Journalism Quarterly, 68*(3), 445–454.

White, G. L., Fishbein, S., & Rutsein, J. (1981). Passionate love and the misattribution of arousal. *Journal of Personality and Social Psychology, 41*(1), 56–62. https://doi.org/10.1037/0022-3514.41.1.56

Wolf, A. P. (1995). *Sexual attraction and childhood association: A Chinese brief for Edward Westermarck*. Stanford University Press.

Zeki, S. (2007). The neurobiology of love. *FEBS Letters, 581*(14), 2575–2579.

Zuckerman, M. (1987). A critical look at three arousal constructs in personality theories: Optimal levels of arousal, strength of the nervous system, and sensitivities to signals of reward and punishment. In J. Strelau & H. J. Eysenck (Eds.), *Personality dimensions and arousal* (pp. 217–232). Plenum Press.

Chapter 3
Socio-biological Models of Love

3.1 Basics of Evolution

3.1.1 General Theory of Evolution

General Evolutionary Framework

Throughout centuries, biological, social, and cultural evolutionary processes have interacted to determine human behavior and preferences. The evolutionary perspective and framework for data collection and their interpretation have become popular and inspirational in several scientific disciplines, such as biology, psychology, and social science. Several theories have been developed as the *paradigms for interpretation* within this *evolutionary framework*. Their review is beyond the scope of this book.

Scholars shall admit that in many cases these *paradigms* are based on *interpretative schemas*, rather than empirical facts. We shall remember that, as anthropologist de Munck (2019, p. 15) noted, "we know next to nothing about the social organizations of hunters and gatherers (more accurately referred to as foragers from here on)." Therefore, the evolutionary explanation of the role of love in early stages of human evolution is rather a set of interpretative frameworks, without real empirical evidence.

Since evolution occurs on a scale of several generations of species, it is practically challenging to record the *direct longitudinal evidence* of evolutionary variations and causations throughout time. For the human biological evolution, it is difficult to verify whether modern perceptions, emotions, and behaviors resemble those which occurred several thousand years ago, when only biological evolutionary forces worked on humans.

The *evolutionary approach*, as the *scientific framework* of thinking and research, is progressive, productive, and logical for understanding of many phenomena and facts in life, behavior, and society. *General evolutionary theory* proposes that

V. Karandashev, *Cultural Typologies of Love*,
https://doi.org/10.1007/978-3-031-05343-6_3

evolution is the process by which organisms, individuals, societal groups, ideas, cultural phenomena, artifacts, and societal institutions gradually evolve over time. These changes occur as the adjustments to physical, biological, and social environment and help adapt, survive, and thrive. Due to mutations, organisms, species, individuals, and social groups vary in their characteristics creating a diversity of traits. Those which have better-adapted qualities and are well-fit (or fit enough) are more likely to survive, transmit, and be naturally selected to reproduce over time. This is natural selection because it occurs in the natural (not managed) interaction of entities (species, individuals, groups, etc.) and their environment.

Levels of Evolution

Thus, evolutionary processes in humans and societies may occur on various levels and engage different perspectives. First, *evolution* takes place *on the level of individual life*. Evolutionary power of *individual survival* motivates individuals to survive, develop, and thrive. *Individual evolution* interacts with *individual development*. Individuals evolve throughout their life by seeking for security, safety, sex or other personal pleasure, knowledge, wealth, attachment, companionship, etc., depending on what constitute their personhood. This is individual evolution of a person as adaptation to physical, biological, social, and cultural environment. Individuals initiate a relationship, which promises to meet their individual motives. This motivation can change over individual life depending on individual differences and cultural factors.

Second, *evolution* may occur *on the level of species*. This is an evolutionary drive of *genetic survival* which motivates individuals to reproduce themselves and alike in the offspring. It is assumed that people consciously or unconsciously concern about survival of a human species, local community, or family. This motivates individuals to transfer their genes to the offspring of the next generation. They strive to initiate a mating relationship with the best (or good enough) mate. According to the theory of sexual selection, the best genes are heritable and transmitted to physical and behavioral traits of offspring, which are favored over others in particular environment. Even though it is biological evolution, yet cultural evolution appreciates and follows it.

Third, *evolution* also may occur *on the level of local cultural community and social group*, which strive to survive in competition or cooperation with other social groups. Therefore, individuals concern to provide more and better offspring for their tribal community to survive. Personality and individual differences evolve to provide some people an adaptive advantage over others for survival and propagation in specific cultural environment. Social and cultural evolution takes place toward collectivistic society.

Evolutionary Processes of Adaptation

Evolutionary processes involve modification of the phenotype, traits, and behaviors, which facilitate adaptation of humans to physical, biological, and social environment (Gangestad, 2008). In case of biological evolution, natural selection facilitates the transmission of specific genes over others to the next generation of a species. In case of cultural evolution, environment favors some social ideas, artifacts, and cultural norms over others. Such evolution happens because of interaction of a species or community with the environment of local nature and social context. The animal species and humans have the same (or similar) basic needs – in food, water, safety, pleasure, avoiding pain, individual survival, reproduction, and population survival. However, they live in different local biological and social conditions, which provide different affordances to meet these needs. Therefore, they adjust and adapt accordingly. These are the sources of biological and cultural evolution.

3.1.2 Varieties of Evolution

Biological Evolution of Love

The ideas of *biological evolution* are popular in biological sciences and explain how species have been evolving from one generation to another. Evolutionary processes produce the diversity of life and proceed with natural selection of those features, which better fit to increase a chance of a species for survival in current ecological niche. Individuals of the species interact with their environment and continuously adapt to the diversity and variability of their environments. *Asexual and sexual types of reproduction* use different biological mechanisms for evolution.

Sexual selection is among the key mechanisms providing evolution of many species, including humans. This *biological evolutionary perspective* has been extensively and successfully applied to human mating (see for review, e.g., Buss, 1994, 2006; Buss & Barnes, 1986; Buss & Schmitt, 1993; Buss et al., 1990; Fisher, 1998, 2004; Thornhill & Gangestad, 1996) and can explain an *evolutionary model of love attraction* as adaptation and natural selection. Love is considered as the love acts pursuing these purposes (Buss, 1988, 2006). According to this model, human individuals have an evolutionary rooted predisposition to fall in love with the prospective partners to solve the problems of survival and reproduction.

Social Factors in Evolution of Love

In recent many centuries, especially since the early progress of medicine, biological evolution interacted with the technological, social, and cultural forces. Therefore, some evolutionary views and interpretations are rather theoretical beliefs than the scientific theories confirmed by facts. Various interpretations of modern data are possible.

Cultural evolutionary factors of human love and mating determine *social selection* (instead of natural) and *adaptation to social environment* (instead of natural). The processes and mechanisms, however, are substantially similar. The principle of survival still works the same way, but instead of survival of individual and species (as in biological evolution), people value the survival of person (e.g., personality, self-esteem) and cultural community of a certain kind (as in cultural evolution). Instead of genetic mutations, the mutations of cultural artifacts take place. Instead of natural selection – survival of fittest in biological sense, the cultural selection takes place according to the survival of those species which fit sufficiently well in societal sense.

Humans in traditional and modern cultures inherited the biologically valuable strategies of selection and adaptation that their ancestors successfully used. The processes of evolution and sexual selection of individuals in societies follow the same evolutionary principles. However, their mechanisms go beyond biological mechanisms and include additional ecological, social, and cultural criteria for survival and selection. Survival of cultural values, personal identities, moral principles, or ideologies can become more valuable than physical and biological survival. Therefore, individuals implicitly or explicitly take into account a more complex set of criteria when they fall in love.

Societal and Cultural Evolution of Love

Some scholars consider that *social* and *cultural evolution* follows the same evolutionary principles – the social and cultural changes are an evolutionary process (e.g., Boyd, 2010; Henrich & McElreath, 2003; Mead, 1964/2017; Mesoudi, 2016; Mesoudi, Whiten, & Laland, 2006). The *conception of cultural evolution* explains that socially transmitted cultural knowledge, meanings, norms, and practices evolve in the similar ways as biological species – according to the principles of variation, differential fitness, and inheritance. However, not all aspects of genetic evolution (e.g., particulate inheritance and random mutation) are applicable to the cultural evolution (Mesoudi, 2016).

According to the social selection processes, societies acquire and transmit some cultural phenomena more likely than others, transforming and altering those during transmission. The cultural evolution of languages, social organizations, human cooperation and competition, cultural traditions, and norms present such examples (Mace, 2000; Mace & Holden, 2005; Whiten, Hinde, Stringer, & Laland, 2012).

The capability of people for cooperation can characterize the cultural organization of societies in an evolutionary perspective. In several important aspects (Tomasello, 2011), the way of human social life is more cooperative compared to other primates. Consequently, the more cooperative type of people's living can transform the cultural evolution and transmission across generations.

Cultural Evolution of Monogamous Love

Cultural evolution, for example, explains the prevalence of love and monogamous relationships across many societies (Henrich, 2004). Some scholars suggest (e.g., Fisher, 1998; Schmitt, 2008a, 2008b, 2008c) that *biological evolution* predisposes humans to monogamous relations due to evolutionary mechanisms and neurochemistry. However, *cultural evolution* can also contribute to the overall cultural norms of monogamous, rather than promiscuous relationships (Henrich, Boyd, & Richerson, 2012). Cultural communities, countries, and religious organizations have endorsed corresponding beliefs and values. This way, they strengthened motivation and behavior of individuals that promote success for *intergroup competition* and *cultural group selection*.

Nevertheless, monogamy in relationships is not universal across cultures. Anthropological studies (see for review White et al., 1988) have shown that many human societies (roughly 85%) accept polygynous marriage permitting men to marry more than one wife. Probably, later in the history, monogamous marriage spread across most of the developed countries of the world. This shift was rather due to *cultural evolution* when social groups, religions, and societies endorse *monogamous* values, norms, and practices (Henrich, 2004).

3.1.3 Evolution in Traditional and Modern Societies

Interaction of Biological, Ecological, Social, and Cultural Evolution

In the real social world, biological, ecological, social, and cultural evolutions interact in their determination of relationship processes. Therefore, integration of these perspectives as an interpretative framework is useful (e.g., Boyd & Richerson, 1985; Gangestad & Simpson, 2007).

Social norms, psychological experiences, and expressions respect principles of biological evolution, e.g., encouraging extended reproduction of offspring, monogamy, prohibiting incest, etc. It is possible that the regulations of biological evolution have been modified in modern social world. Earlier in human history, men and women wanted to have more children in hope that some of them survive. In modern world, they do not want to have more children, if at all. In early human history, the newborns and infants not well adapted in terms of health died since they did not fit to survival of the fit enough. Nowadays, parents attempt to save even those children with poor physical fit – that is evolutionary worthless, yet culturally acceptable and welcome. According to biological evolution, non-heterosexual partners are useless to produce offspring, yet modern societies are more and more accepting nontraditional sexual orientation in relationship. The latter is already a product of *cultural evolution* of humanity.

The traditional meaning of democracy is the rights of majority to govern situations – majority is usually the fittest in population. The modern meaning of democracy, however, is the respect of the rights of minority – every voice is heard, even though the minority is less fit to a society.

Transitional Evolution from Traditional to Modernized Societies

All these evolutionary tendencies occur in the cultural transition from traditional and modernized societies (Inglehart, 1997, Inglehart & Baker, 2000; Inglehart & Welzel, 2005). In traditional societies, motivations to *survive*, mediated by traditional values of kinship, social hierarchy, and gender inequality, are prevalent. In modernized societies, motivations to *thrive*, mediated by the values of individual autonomy, human rights, and social and gender equality, are prevalent. People in traditional societies are concerned about their basic needs to survive – safety, food, water, etc. *Love relationship* with someone who is valuable to meet the basic needs is worthwhile and appealing. People in modern societies usually do not worry about starvation and physical survival – government or good people can help them to survive. Therefore, they are more concerned *about good life* than *about life itself*. Love relationship with someone who can provide well-being and happiness, the prospect of self-expression, raises a priority in their motivation.

Societal and *cultural evolution* is sensitive to ecological and societal environment and can act along with or counteract biological evolution. Concerning population tendencies, cultural norms of the early historical societies were in accord with biological evolution and encouraged high fertility and extended reproduction of healthy offspring from both male and female evolutionary perspectives. The norms of traditional societies also promote the birth rates and growth of their population (e.g., African countries, India, Indonesia), while modern societies (e.g., European countries, Japan, South Korea) tend to slow in their birth rates (Cilluffo & Ruiz, 2019).

Controversies of Modern Evolution

In many modern societies, cultural evolution of social norms may counteract biological evolution. Due to increasing overpopulation, the modern societies have evolved the cultural norms which discourage extended reproduction of offspring and tolerate unhealthy offspring more than traditional societies. According to these beliefs, humanity, compassion, and survival of everyone, regardless of their health perspective, rather than the number of offspring, are widely acceptable values. Doctors and nurses can help survive even the least survivable newborns – a humanistic cultural norm of modern societies. It is possible that the recent biological and cultural evolution turned to disfavor high fertility producing fewer offspring. According to research (Cilluffo & Ruiz, 2019; Lutz, Sanderson, & Scherbov, 2001), world's population is gradually slowing with projection to nearly stop growing in future.

These new cultural norms decrease motivation to have more children. However, despite this low intention to have children, men and women still fall in love. The health and fertility of a beloved are less crucial for the value of relationship in modern societies, compared to traditional ones (e.g., Inhorn, 2007; Krause, 1999). Due to the progress of medicine – social technological evolution, fertility of partners has less value for love relationships in modern societies. Instead of looking for a young and fertile woman, man may prefer a woman, which he loves, with whom he has affinity, even though she is infertile and older than him.

3.2 The Biology of Love Attraction

3.2.1 Evolution of Neurophysiological Mechanisms of Love

Do Sexually Dimorphic Animals Love Each Other?

The *biological evolutionary* studies have extensively investigated sexual selection, sexual attraction, and mating relationship among sexually dimorphic animals. Their reproductive strategies and mating systems are quite universal in core principles yet vary across species and within population groups. These differences determine variability in mating and courtship behaviors between different sexes. The reproductive and mating strategies develop during evolution depending on the available opportunities for sexual selection. Many animals have discontinuous variation in their morphology and reproductive behavior. Polymorphic phenotypes, as alternative mating strategies, are the most common in the species with separate sexes. Evolution of mating systems favors breadth of mating polymorphisms and diversity of patterns of alternative mating strategies (see for review Shuster, 2010; Shuster & Wade, 2003) and monogamic relationships (see for review Reichard & Boesch, 2003).

Does love motivate courtship and mating relationship between animals? Scholars do not have the self-report data of experience of love emotions and subjective feelings obtained from animals. The facial expressions, on which emotion researchers rely in their studies of people, are limited in many species. However, the presence of love in some mammals, such as dogs, cats, and primates, is evident by various behavioral manifestations: increased energy and focused attention, affectionate and affiliative postures, obsessive following and tendency to proximity, bodily contact, caresses, purrs, and possessive motivation to win and guard a mate. Many species, such as birds and mammals, display mate preferences and focus their energy of courtship on those favorites (see, e.g., Andersson, 1994; Fisher, 1998). H. Fisher provides many behavioral examples of animals engaging in activities that we can anthropomorphically call as romantic love. "They stroke, kiss, nip, nuzzle, pat, tap, lick, tug, or playfully chase this chosen one. Some sing. Some whinny. Some squeak, croak, or bark. Some dance. Some strut. Some preen. Some chase. Most play" (Fisher, 2004, p. 27). Animals also exhibit choosiness and do not mate anyone. They are not promiscuous in sex relationships. They appear to be possessive and guard their mates closely as if they are motivated by jealousy.

Anthropomorphism as the attribution of human-like behaviors, such as love, to nonhuman species can be problematic, as well as beneficial for emotion research (Williams, Brosnan, & Clay, 2020). However, beyond such anthropomorphic imagination, more scientific background is also available.

Neurophysiological Evolution of Love

Theoretical and empirical research (Porges, 1998) shows that evolution of the mammalian autonomic nervous system (ANS) produces a neurophysiological basis for affective processes associated with the experience and expression of love, such as proximity, reproduction, and safety. According to this theoretical model (Porges, 1998), sexual arousal, passionate sexual activities, and the long-term pair bonding develop due to the phylogenetic changes in the ANS. The vagus nerve of the mammalian ANS is anatomically connected to the cranial nerves that control social engagement by vocalization and facial expression. As a result, courting and seduction behavior emerge.

Several brain systems in mammalians exhibit distinct patterns of neural activity associated with affectionate emotions and sexuality. Studies of mate choice among mammals have demonstrated that several brain systems are engaged in mating – the neural systems for sensory perception and cognitive and emotional responses. Dopaminergic reward pathway in the brain is the specific brain mechanism involved in sexual and love attraction (Dixson, 1998, 2009; Fisher, Aron, & Brown, 2006; Panksepp, 1998). Courtship attraction in mammalian species is directly associated with elevated levels of central dopamine and norepinephrine, as well as with decreased levels of central serotonin in reward pathways of the brain (Fisher, 2004; Herbert, 1996).

The studies of human individuals with *functional magnetic resonance imaging* (fMRI) have revealed that passionate attraction to a loved is associated with activity of primitive brain regions (Aron et al., 2005; Bartels & Zeki, 2000, 2004; Fisher et al., 2006; Ortigue, Bianchi-Demicheli, Patel, Frum, & Lewis, 2010). Passionate love involves subcortical reward pathway and motivation systems of the brain to focus on a specific individual. Thus, this basic form of *love emotion* is embedded in basic evolutionary mechanisms. It could appear in early hominid evolution providing individuals the emotional signals for mate selection (Fisher, 2004).

Neurophysiology of Love Types

Many new studies in recent decades (see for review Quintana et al., 2019; Shobitha & Agarwal, 2013) have reported the empirical evidence that passionate love, pair bonding, affiliation, and paternal and maternal love are represented in the different patterns of the physiological mechanisms involved and the brain areas activated. For instance, *oxytocin* is an evolutionarily conserved neuropeptide involved in the functioning of *brain system* associated with development of prosocial behavior and interpersonal bonds, such as attachment love. Neurochemical mechanisms of *dopamine system* are engaged in mating attraction and can be involved in passionate love. Despite their relatively different functional localization, this comprehensive set of neural, endocrinal, and genetic mechanisms, which evolved to help humans survive and thrive, can be an integrated system that helps understand *love* as a *basic human ability*.

3.2.2 *Genetics of Loving Partners*

Genetic Similarity Between Loving Partners

Do we have *genetic predisposition to fall in love* with someone? There is some evolutionary evidence that genetic factors and physical appearance affect sexual and love attraction between individuals. Some scholars talk even about chemistry of love that makes partners compatible to each other.

The principle of optimal genetic similarity plays its important role in evolutionary selection of partners (Lampert, 1997). Human individuals tend to be attracted by a person who is genetically similar, yet they prefer to distance from those who are genetically too much similar to them. Both factors guide them in selection of dating and mating partners with optimal genetic similarity to them.

From a biological evolutionary perspective, the similarity must be important. Intersexual attraction assists humans and other sexually dimorphic animals to select a mate properly because they cannot produce offspring with anyone. It is feasible only with someone with whom the likelihood of mating success is the highest. A human individual can initiate a sexual relationship with goat, dog, cow, or gorilla, and they can be a nice couple. Someone may achieve sexually pleasurable experience, yet evolutionarily such relationships are the waste of energy because they will be childlessness. The partners are genetically too distant. Humans and chimpanzee, however, are more similar, with genetic distance less than 2%. Therefore, in the latter case, a reproductive success is theoretically possible (Lampert, 1997).

The same principle of similarity may be at work among people. An individual tends to fall in love with a person who is genetically similar, to some extent. It is possible that biological evolution has developed a psychological mechanism that unconsciously attracts individuals to similar mates and excludes those significantly different.

Rushton (1988) provided original evidence that such unconscious attraction is possible. He analyzed thousand files describing court cases when genetic testing was used to identify that a man a woman had sex with is the father of her baby. Rushton (1988) examined those cases investigating how men and women, who were at the beginning of their sexual relationship at the time of conceiving a baby, are genetically similar to each other. The results showed that those were more similar than random couples. These findings indicate that it is very likely that potential partners unconsciously recognize their genetic similarity and experience sexual attraction.

The study using genome-wide SNPs is in further support of genetic similarity explanation (Domingue, Fletcher, Conley, & Boardman, 2014). Researchers found that among non-Hispanic American Whites, married partners are genetically more similar to each other, compared with random pairs of individuals. Acknowledging that these findings are descriptively true, Abdellaoui, Verweij, and Zietsch (2014) argue that the genetic similarity between spouses reflects assortment on shared ancestry (i.e., population stratification), rather than genetic assortative mating. Authors argue that genetic similarities in couples can be caused by genetic population stratification due to geographic proximity and social and ethnic homogamy.

In light of these findings, the effect of genetic similarity on interpersonal attraction between close relatives is understandable. Individuals should perceive others who are genetically similar to themselves as more sexually attractive. Thus, the psychoanalytic myths of a boy's unconscious sexual attraction to his mother and girl's attraction to her father may convey a part of truth, due to genetic similarity or due to imprinting.

Genetic Diversity Between Loving Partners

On the other side, evolution makes people to exclude from the pool of possible mates those with extreme genetic similarity because such mating can increase the chance of harmful recessive genes and decrease fitness offspring. Incestual relations increase the poor health quality of offspring, the likelihood of diseases, disabilities, and mortality. Inbreeding has a deleterious biological effect for natural selection.

The more difference between partners in their genetics leads to healthier offspring. Therefore, perhaps natural selection has developed a protective psychological mechanism to reduce the drive for similarity and allow only a suitable measure of variance between partners in sexual relationships. This evolutionary mechanism might be in the origins of the strong incest taboo among many populations of species and human societies (Lampert, 1997, p. 14).

Running against the detrimental effect of incest, cultural norms and incest taboos have been evolved in almost all cultures. Societies in the history and modern time have respected the incest taboo prohibiting sexual relations between those females and males who are in kinship relations. Almost all human societies have cultural norms prohibiting sexual relations among kin (Lampert, 1997; Murdock, 1949; Westermarck, 1891/1921).

3.3 Evolutionary View of Love as Sexual Reproduction

3.3.1 *Love as a Pursuit for Genetic Survival*

Love in the basic functions of *survival mechanisms* strives to reproduce the species and individuals efficiently – for *genetic survival*. We can assume that the human species have a genetic bias for the in-group favorability. Therefore, they prefer to mate with the members of their own species and those in their own "tribal" group for the sake of their *group genetic survival*. To succeed in this pursuit, they need to procreate and protect their offspring.

The pursuit for *individual genetic survival* is also evident in a common motivation to have "own offspring" – to replicate oneself in one or another way. Conscious or unconscious desire to self-replicate is easily recognizable in the way how much many parents care about having "their own children" and interest to recognize their own appearance and trait in their child. The interest for genetic affinity is omnipresent in many other things.

Evolutionary sciences (e.g., Buss, 1988, 1994, 2006; Fisher, 1992, 2000; Trivers, 1972) argue that love appeared early in evolution of a human species and provided an adaptive function for sexual reproduction and pair bonding. Love works as an emotional impetus to procreate and emotional "glue" to connect mating partners together for the time being to feed and nurture children until they are capable to care for themselves.

3.3.2 *Love for Mating and Sexual Reproduction*

Evolutionary scientists (e.g., Buss, 2006; Fisher, 2006; Gangestad & Simpson, 2000; Schmitt, 2005a, 2005b) have stressed the evolutionary function of romantic *love* as *a mating mechanism* which is designed to attract a good mating partner. The *psychological mechanism of love* provides individuals with criteria for sexual selection. The evolutionary mechanism of *intrasexual selection* – as competition between potential mates of the same sex – gives an opportunity to select the best one. It brings the joy of a winner to get a better chance to produce offspring or the despair of a loser that does not transmit to the next generation.

From a traditional evolutionary perspective, *love is a pursuit for reproductive success*; this is a concern about survival of the local population of human species. The reproductive success is appraised in a number or in better quality of offspring. For the humans, as sexually dimorphic species, the selection of a mating partner – sexual selection – is important to secure good genes. Men and women have different contributions to reproduction of offspring and different parental investments (Buss, 1989; Trivers, 1972).

The mating preferences according to the theory of sexual selection admit that individuals have a choice and behave rationally (consciously or unconsciously) striving to select the best mating partner among available. However, ecological and cultural affordances – see in the following sections – often put limitations on the freedom of mating choice. Evolutionary theory may likely intertwine with social and cultural theories (e.g., social theory of market).

3.3.3 Sexual Attraction in Evolutionary Perspective

One cannot ignore that sexual attraction of some kind, which one may call love, is involved in sexual selection and mating as evolutionary processes. It is very likely that the nature developed a biopsychological mechanism of sexual pleasure and selective attraction as motivations encouraging animals and humans to engage in reproductive sexual activity. This attraction is usually accompanied by passionate sexual arousal as a strong motivator that fuels passionate emotions. But passion is usually a short-lived experience and cannot stand for long time to maintain relationship bonds. As for the romantic love, it is more complex emotional experience that requires cultural elaboration. The early *Homo sapiens*, who developed according to evolutionary mechanisms, unlikely had time for this. They were more concerned about their physical survival and instinct of offspring reproduction.

3.3.4 Love Helps Look for a Potential Mate

From an evolutionary approach, *love* is *a psychological mechanism* that promotes sexual selection of mating partners. Those who possess the evolutionary desired qualities have a better chance to be selected, in other words – *be loved*. Such evolutionary perspective maintains that certain qualities make an individual a good mate for sexual selection and, therefore, make her/him attractive for love.

The experience of passionate love motivates men and women to focus their sexual desire exclusively on the loved one for mating and child-rearing. Such exclusive motivation entails jealousy to guard a mate against poaching (Buss, 1994, 2006; Buss & Shackleford, 1997). The couple stayed together as a relatively stable dyad for the time being.

According to the principle of sexual selection, men and women strive to achieve a reproductive success, which is gauged in more offspring and of a good quality, with hope some of them will survive. Sexual dimorphism of their functions in reproduction determines different preferences and strategies in mating.

Multiple valuable qualities of potential partners – in terms of physical appearance, personality, and social and economic benefits – can reinforce motivation to mate, yet they can shine or fade in light of love. People often love not the most beautiful, not the smartest, not the most kind, not the wealthy, but those who they fall in love with. Those who survive in a given generation have a better chance to reproduce. The number of offspring – children – is less important than their quality, which better fit to their current life and survival in it.

3.3.5 The Values of Good Look and Resourcefulness in Love

According to evolutionary perspective of sexual selection, females and males differ in their preferred characteristics of prospective mates because they have different functions in sexual reproduction. The findings, which are most frequently cited in multiple publications (see for review, e.g., Buss, 1988, 1994; Buss & Barnes, 1986; Buss et al., 1990; Buss & Schmitt, 1993; Feingold, 1990), have shown that men rate women's appearance and youth in their preferences for mating partners as more important compared to women in their preferences of men. On the other hand, women rate men's status and earning prospects higher as mating values compared to men's preferences in women. These findings were recently reproduced and replicated once again across a quarter of a century in the cultural contexts of India and Brazil (Kamble, Shackelford, Pham, & Buss, 2014; Souza, Conroy-Beam, & Buss, 2016).

The males prefer to select the females which are young and have a good look because these qualities presumably serve as the signals of health and fertility. These females are more likely to produce the offspring of a good quality. It sounds like a plausible justification. Selection of those who are healthy seems like natural motivation, while a good physical look may serve as a signal of health. However, a good physical look should be a signal of health in mating for both men and women because from a genetic viewpoint, the healthy genes of both males and females contribute to the health and survival of offspring.

We should once again be aware that researchers have limited facts from the historically very early human societies in support of their *evolutionary interpretative schemas*. We do not really know how men and women in those eras of human evolution sexually selected each other. We can just approximate from our knowledge of the societies with recorded history of human life and currently living across the world. The small-scale tribal cultural groups of gatherers and hunters in South America, Africa, and Asia are the examples, which are probably closer to the natural course of human evolution. Ethnographic records have shown that people in many of those societies accept sex equality and love match in mating (de Munck & Korotayev, 1999), with no sex-specific preferences for the good look and earning resources (see for review, e.g., Karandashev, 2017, 2019).

3.3.6 Cultural Variability of the Values of Good Look and Resourcefulness in Love

The evolutionary idea of sex differences in sexual selection, cited above, was more receptive in traditional patriarchal and religious societies, as well as in the societies with cultural models of "man as a breadwinner" and "a trophy wife" – all characterized by gender inequality. The validity of the aforementioned sex differences has been also found in many studies of *love attitudes*, in which men were higher in *eros*, whereas women were higher in *pragma* love attitudes (see for review Karandashev, 2019). A question remains, what are the origins of these sex differences?

It should be noted that even though several studies, cited above, found statistically significant sex differences in these mating preferences, yet practically the differences were of a small size. This can explain why the results of other research were less consistent concerning these sex differences. Many studies revealed that both men and women prefer partners of good physical appearance (e.g., Fletcher, Tither, O'Loughlin, Friesen, & Overall, 2004; Kenrick, Groth, Trost, & Sadalla, 1993; Langlois et al., 2000; Regan & Berscheid, 1997).

3.3.7 Methodological Challenge of Averaging Mate Preference

A possible explanation of inconsistencies of the findings about mate preferences can be in the old methodological tradition to average data across all males and all females in a sample in search for universal findings – "one size fits all" – neglecting diversity of typological variation within each cultural and gender sample. Not all women are the same; not all men are the same. Therefore, it may be not adequate to apply equally the same evolutionary principle in the same way to all of them. *Cluster* and *latent class analysis* can be helpful to better understand *within-gender* and *within-culture variations*.

Research found that preferences in this regard depend on other moderating variables and contexts. Integration of biological evolutionary theory of sexual selection with ecological and cultural perspectives can be more predictive and better explain these mating preferences. For example, the Multiple Fitness model of physical attractiveness (Cunningham & Barbee, 1991; Cunningham, Barbee, & Philhower, 2002) suggested that men and women alter their mating preferences in valuation of good look according to the local ecological context. Several studies have revealed the moderating effect of sex ratio, infant mortality, and other ecological variables (Guttentag & Secord, 1983; Maner & Ackerman, 2020; Moss & Maner, 2016; Stone, Shackelford, & Buss, 2007).

As for the cultural factors, gender role stereotypes and gender inequality in societies also explain sex differences in the mating value of good look and resourcefulness of partners (Buss et al., 1990; Cunningham et al., 2002; De Raad & Doddema-Winsemius, 1992; Fallon, 1990; Kenrick et al., 1993). Thus, the convergence of biological, ecological, and sociocultural evolutionary perspectives can be in a better position to explain mating preferences in the *evolutionary model of love*.

3.3.8 Mate Preferences and Real Mating

Methodological pitfalls also impede the adequate understanding of evolutionary models of mating and love. In large majority of studies investigating characteristics of mates, participants are asked to rate the value of abstract mating qualities, not the qualities of individuals with whom they are in a relationship. As I commented in earlier chapters, these ratings present their *personal models* of desired mates and culturally induced mating preferences, not the actual choices that men and women do. Mating preferences are frequently analyzed as the single qualities, independent from each other like on the shopping shelves, rather than in their complexes. Actually, when individuals mate and date, they make their choices considering several qualities of a prospective partner at once. For instance, a woman will unlikely select a man with *resources*, yet with other unattractive qualities, unless they are tolerable. In the same vein, a man will unlikely select a *good-looking* woman, which has other unattractive traits, unless they are bearable. In real choice, people do not rate the single qualities, but rather weigh their comparative values in a complex image.

The findings from many surveys are limited to show why men and women really mate a person or fall in love (e.g., Eastwick, Eagly, Finkel, & Johnson, 2011; Karandashev & Evans, 2017; Kurzban & Weeden, 2005; Mafra, Fisher, & Lopes, 2021; Malach Pines, 2001). The studies of a real relationship and behavioral evidence of mating and loving partners may provide more realistic results (Eastwick & Finkel, 2008; Kurzban & Weeden, 2005).

People frequently do not weigh – consciously or unconsciously – the preferred and unpreferred qualities of prospective partners when they mate and date. Falling in love can be surprisingly strange and illogical, not rational (Aron et al., 2008; Aron, Dutton, Aron, & Iverson, 1989; Malach-Pines, 2005; Marazziti & Canale, 2004; Riela, Rodriguez, Aron, Xu, & Acevedo, 2010). Laypeople know that girls may often fall in love and mate not the best boys while boys, not the best girls. Love is mysterious and paradoxical.

Here is another methodological point to distinguish *personal models of love* (as mating preferences) and *real love* (as actual feelings and relationship). For example, a man or woman in the old societies of our ancestors might feel preference for a specific mate in their personal model, however, could not afford to choose him/her because of the culturally accepted system of arranged marriages. And phylogenetic findings (Walker, Hill, Flinn, & Ellsworth, 2011) revealed that economic exchange and socially regulated arranged mating were likely practiced in very early human history – during the first modern migrations from Africa.

3.3.9 A Causality Issue in Relations Between Good Look and Love

Sexual selection theory and multiple studies of mating assume that "I love her/him" – *a loved one* – because of their good physical appearance. Evolutionary factors of sexual selection govern men and women, while they seem in a passive dependent position by consciously or unconsciously following evolutionary guide.

However, the opposite causation is likely – "she/he looks physically good, even beautiful to me" because "I love him/her." The subjective nature of the beauty in love is a well-known artifact. *The beauty is in their eyes of beholder*. When a person loves another and selects for sexual reproduction, they may steer the evolution selecting those whom they want to give a chance to survive in the future generation. A person is not passive, but rather active in driving evolution.

There is no doubt that some girls and boys and women and men are so beautiful that they become the objects of loving adoration and romantic attraction for many admirers. It is, for instance, the case of the best girl of a class which has many boys who look at her with a hope for mutual love. Intrasexual competition makes their lives even more tense and risky. However, many other girls and boys and men and women – less physically appealing – find their mating partners who love them and find them beautiful. So, the causal relations between physical appearance and love are bidirectional. Love can be blind in its choice.

3.4 Evolutionary View of Love as the Social Bonding

3.4.1 Evolutionary Value of Community Bonding Model of Love

Community Bonding for Survival

Love as a community bonding is among the important survival mechanisms. Those who live in a community, which can support them, have a better chance to survive. Therefore, the need to belong is deeply rooted in the nature of some animals and humans, while *love as social bonding* has evolutionary and social origins.

There is substantial evidence which documents that some animals and humans in their evolution have developed the psychological mechanisms of cooperation, pro-social behavior, and social bonding which have helped them to survive in natural and social world (e.g., Germonpré, Lázničková-Galetová, Sablin, & Bocherens, 2018; Marshall-Pescini, Virányi, & Range, 2015; Hare, 2017; Fisher, 2004; Rosenblum & Plimpton, 1981). The evolution of oxytocin – the hormone of *love as social bonding* – has occurred along with evolution of human social behavior and capability for social connections (Carter, 1998, 2014; Carter, Williams, Witt, & Insel, 1992; De Boer, Van Buel, & Ter Horst, 2012). The functions of this chemical messenger in the brain have been associated with positive social relations and caring, interpersonal trust, and attachment.

The species, which live in groups, may have different relationship systems (Lukas & Clutton-Brock, 2013; Reichard & Boesch, 2003). Many of those, which are comprised of multiple females and multiple males, are promiscuous. The others are usually the pair-bonded species living in groups, which consist of only one female and one male.

Social Bonding in Dogs

For example, dogs are known for being social and friendly with people. Although dogs are domesticated descendants of the wolves, they differ in sociability from wolves. There are theories and some historical evidence (e.g., Germonpré et al., 2018; Marshall-Pescini et al., 2015; Morell, 1997) that in the ancient times, some variants of the wolves' species began to live near people tribes. But instead of competition for a prey, they gradually preferred to be useful for the people who fed them for their service as a reward. Those friendly *wolves-dogs* had a better chance to survive and reproduce. In this domestication process, those *friendly wolves* were selected for their cooperative tendencies toward humans and finally evolved in domestic dogs. The nature selects those who better fit to the conditions where they need to survive.

Social Bonding in Primates

The chimpanzee groups, as well as other social species, have several varying characteristics, yet they have the common attributes characterizing them as a unique "chimpanzee society." They may have different mating systems (Chapais, 2011).

Some primates may experience such basic forms of *love as bonding*. Infant primates are prewired to cling to their mothers, while a brief separation makes them anxious. They begin searching for their mothers. After returning, they feel joyous and excited. It seems evident that possessing a *desire for union* and *avoidance of separation* are the basic motivations that provide them a better chance to survive (Rosenblum & Plimpton, 1981).

And among other primates, only in human societies multiple reproductive pairs stay together (De Waal & Gavrilets, 2013).

Social Bonding in Human Evolution

It is likely that social skills, prosocial behavior, and social bonding have evolved in human evolutionary history due to natural selection. The theory has proposed (Hare, 2017) that humans in late years of evolution domesticated themselves. When in evolutionary history, natural selection started to favor the *in-group prosociality* more than *aggression*, the human social skills emerged and evolved. As a result of this selective process, a *domestication syndrome* (known in other domestic animals) evolved as a set of human social traits. A review of paleoanthropological, neurobiological, and developmental research has supported this evolutionary theory (Hare, 2017).

There are evident advantages for people to live in cooperative and supportive groups. Individuals living in such social relations with others are safer and feel more secure for physical, social, and psychological survival. Those of human ancestors who lived in tribal communities had a better chance for survival. Due to cooperation, they had a more consistent access to food and higher capability to protect from predators.

Later in evolution, in addition to the need for physical security, the need for psychological security had been added to human motivation. Extended family, kin, and tribal community provided sufficient conditions for social bonding in the tribal subsistence-based and traditional collectivistic societies. In many small-scale low-technology societies, the bonds of tribal community and kinship were the social relations which kept people together.

Varieties of Human Mating Relationship Systems

The human societies are also extremely diverse in the forms of social bonding. However, their social organization and mating systems have evolved differently from other species (Chapais, 2011). Humans as a species have a multi-female, multi-male social organization and the practice of *long-term pair-bonding mating* (Geary & Flinn, 2001; Hill et al., 2011; Rooker & Gavrilets, 2016).

Different from their African ape ancestors (De Waal & Gavrilets, 2013; Flinn, Geary, & Ward, 2005), people in many societies live in nuclear or extended families investing in offspring as parents (Geary & Flinn, 2001). The human long-term pair bonding has evolved and become common practice in societies around the world. The evolutionary pressures have made it beneficial to humans (Rooker & Gavrilets, 2016).

Passionate Love as the Adaptation Mechanism in Social Bonding

Love as biological and psychological mechanism can play a role in evolutionary adaptation and help maintain pair bonding (Buss, 1988, 2006; de Munck, 2019; de Munck, Korotayev, & McGreevey, 2016; Fisher, 2004). From the commitment device theory of love, romantic love makes an individual feel committed to the beloved and signals this commitment (Frank, 1988). This might be true due to *passionate nature of romantic love*. However, romantic is the later cultural creation – see in another chapter.

Some evolutionary scientists (e.g., Fisher, 2004; Fisher et al., 2006) suggested that *passionate love* evolved as an *attachment mechanism*, which keeps a man around a woman for the time being to help the woman in raising their child. This function of love makes sense, and it is in accord with the theory (Fisher et al., 2006) that passionate love is an evolutionary device for pair bonding. It assures that a man would stick around to care for his beloved and their child at least during the period of her pregnancy and early childhood helping the woman to raise their child for 2–3 years. This is a plausible explanation for the short-term duration of passionate love and a good excuse for male promiscuity. This can also explain the practice of frequent pregnancy and childbirth of a woman in early tribal societies – to keep the man attached longer. The lack of effective contraceptives is another reason.

This mechanism is well suited for explanation of a man's passionate love to a woman. On another side, such interpretation does not well fit to justify the passionate love of *women*. Then why do women experience passionate love?

Meanwhile, this evolutionary framework brings rather reasonable justification of why women in many studies show higher scores of the pragmatic love, compared to men. On the hand, men in those studies show higher scores of the passionate love, compared to women.

3.4.2 Ecological and Social Conditions of Evolutionary Adaptive Bonding

Social Conditions of Living and Bonds of Love

The narrative of evolutionary role of passionate love for pair bonding, however, does not always take into account the diversity of ecological and social conditions of living and the social structures and practices of societies. Specific social conditions, rather than biological, psychological, or cultural factors, can play a vital role in societal attitudes toward and values of passionate and romantic love.

Marital residence is also a social factor important for cultural attitudes toward passionate and romantic love. It turns out (Rosenblatt (1967) that the patterns of non-neolocal postmarital residence – where the newlyweds live with bride's or groom's parents, or in proximity to their parental home – are conducive to romantic love. The finding might look surprising.

Structures of Family Relationships and Love

Specific structures of interpersonal relations and conditions of living can be less or more conducive for love and intimacy in a married couple (de Munck, 2019; de Munck et al., 2016). In societies with prevalent norms of living in *joint family* after marriage, or in *extended family*, *romantic* love is of a low value. In such *extended families*, other members of family live together with the married couple, so distribution of relationship functions is less personal than in a nuclear family. The individual roles of spouses are less special in terms of their functions and emotional importance. Other members of family can take care and take over the practical or psychological responsibilities of either wife/mother or husband/father in several respects.

The *neolocal nuclear family* is the key factor of social relations precipitating emotional experience of love and intimacy. The wife and husband do not feel a pressure and influence of their parents. In societies, in which neolocal and nuclear families are the culturally normative ways of postmarital residence, people value romantic love and intimacy higher. Only the wife and husband are the primary adults residing in the household of the nuclear family. Each of spouses plays their important functional, psychological, and emotional roles. Therefore, in case of such social relations, romantic love and intimacy fulfill their important functions by maintaining the family relations and caring for well-being of each other.

The Community Bonding Helps Raise a Child

From evolutionary, sexual selection point of view (Buss, 1988; Fisher, 2004), a passionately attached man could assist a woman providing her the resources for survival of offspring (e.g., protection, food gathering, shelter location).

This interpretation for the function of passionate love of man sounds plausible; however, it is mediated by *neolocal residence* of a *couple* (de Munck, 2019; De Munck et al., 2016). In the *nuclear family*, when the wife and husband after marriage live away from natal or parental households, it is vital for a woman to have secure providers for children and herself because other members of family are likely not nearby and not engaged.

However, other evolutionary interpretations are possible. The tribal societies of the evolutionary past might have less gendered divisions of role than we imagine. Women in tribal societies were frequently engaged in the efforts to sustain themselves, community, and children (e.g., gathering, horticultural work). The tribal community-based societies were cooperative and had strong feelings of mutual responsibility. Women were involved in nursing and parenting of not only their own but also other little children. As an African proverb says, "It takes a village to raise a child." In case of many societies, it is literally true. Therefore, they likely were not so much dependent on men in this regard, as in the "male breadwinner" cultural models in later times.

As for the traditional collectivistic societies of recent past, people typically lived in the communities with social structures of *extended families* (de Munck, 2019; De Munck et al., 2016), which – as we saw above – did not consider romantic love as valuable for their life and survival. The support of family and community was often more important than the support of a man. The importance of passionate love was low. The attachment to a community might be a priority because the extended family provided an opportunity to take care of a pregnant woman and her offspring.

Thus, in many tribal subsistence-based and traditional collectivistic societies, the community of women, or an extended family, rather than a passionate man, take care of each other children. This simple biological evolutionary perspective is plausible in explanation of short-term heterosexual love relations as the fulfillment of their sexual reproduction function. However, it is less convincing to justify long-term love relationships. Other evolutionary mechanisms, like social and pair bonding for individual surviving, can play their role.

3.4.3 Evolutionary Value of the Pair-Bonding Model of Love

Attachment as the Evolutionary Mechanism of Bonding

The *pair bonding* evolved later in human social evolution, in addition to *social bonding*. The extended family structure began to transform into nuclear family structure of human societies, which was more conducive for *pair-bonding attachment*. These were the origins of the *love model as attachment* (see more in the following chapters).

According to the attachment theory (Bowlby, 1969, 1973, 1980), the *attachment behavioral system* of humans gradually evolved in the process of natural selection as a motivational system "designed" to regulate proximity to an attachment figure. Because infants and little children depend on the "older and wiser" adults as the caregivers in care, support, and protection, these individuals become the *attachment figures*. Various forms of *attachment behaviors*, such as searching and crying, have evolved as the adaptive responses of children to a situation of their separation from primary caregivers. Evolutionary, such *attachment behaviors* as maintaining proximity to the attachment figure, provided infants and little children a better opportunity to survive. This psychological mechanism explains the imprinting and development of attachment as the first kind of love, which children feel toward caregivers.

The *feeling of security* activates the *feeling of love* to those who protect us and provide this comfortable emotional state of safety. Experience of *secure attachment*, which a caregiver, an extended family, kin, or community brings, is the feeling of safety due to the bonds with those who have provided it. This *secure attachment* is the subjective evidence of bonding and knowing that you belong to the group and, therefore, you are safe. These feelings of safety and being in *safe haven* are the experience which scholars can call a *basic form* of *love*. This *kind of love* helps *overcome the fear* of unknown or bad. The early studies of attachment were very illustrative in this regard (e.g., Ainsworth, 1989; Ainsworth, Blehar, Waters, & Wall, 1978; Bowlby, 1969, 1973, 1980, 1988/2008; Harlow & Zimmerman, 1959).

Evolutionary Early Forms of Human Mating Relationships

Early anthropologists (as cited in de Munck, 2019, p. 15) noted that love had little evidence in foraging, simple horticultural, and non-industrial societies. Most findings are based on the studies of isolated tribal societies during recent centuries.

As for the archeological data, they substantially limit researchers in the research of early evolution of mating relationships providing hardly conclusive evidence. Genetic investigations of DNA in contemporary hunter-gatherers' societies around the world are useful for these purposes. The comparative phylogenetic analyses using mitochondrial DNA sequences help reconstruct ancestral cultural traits, relationships, and marriage practices.

For instance, the phylogenetic results (Walker et al., 2011) have demonstrated that modern humans in early history – during their first modern migrations from Africa – had low prevalence of polygyny. The marriage was likely arranged as a regulated and even mate exchange. The kin groups negotiated their relationships and agreed on economic exchange. The families of marital partners made such reciprocal exchanges in the forms of bride service and bride price. They further continued their obligations, alliances, and mutual transactions between the families afterward. Reconstruction of love relations in such mating and marriage systems is equivocal, and love has little evidence. The model of *love as a duty* or *filial love* was the most likely in such societal conditions.

Compassion and Caring in Service of Bonding

Compassion and caring are among the basic *evolutionary mechanisms* in human cultural evolution that encourage *in-group social ties* and *cooperation*. Through compassion and caring, people love those who they care about. *Caring* is an *active behavioral love* of helping someone who needs it. In the early times of evolution, primarily motherly caring love was considered as true love. This is the nature of *basic parental love*.

Naturally and evolutionarily, they work in the frame of *in-group versus out-group paradigm*. Through in-group community favoritism, filial and pair-bonding love they help those members of in-group to adapt and survive. In-group "us" versus out-group "them" differentiation, *in-group favoritism*, and *out-group devaluation* are the early evolutionary mechanisms underlying *human love*.

Researchers have suggested convincing reasoning and empirical evidence (Goetz, Keltner, & Simon-Thomas, 2010) that *affective experience of compassion* developed in the history to encourage people's motivation to protect the weak others and those who suffer. It was an important mechanism to support social cooperation. The experience and expression of sympathy, compassion, and altruism fulfill a primary function to support prosocial behavior and cooperation.

The review of multiple studies (Goetz et al., 2010) has demonstrated that *compassion* has its own *antecedents*, *physiology*, *experience*, *expression*, and *behavior* associated with this emotional state. Its distinct *appraisal processes* are adapted to detect undeserved suffering. The physiological response and phenomenological experience of compassion motivate social approach. The distinct signaling behavior associated with compassion has *caregiving patterns* of vocalization, posture, and touch. The empirical data showing this emotional response profile are convincing that compassion is a distinctive emotion (see for review Goetz et al., 2010).

Researchers have documented evidence of compassion and caring among chimpanzees and bonobos – the primates closely related to humans. These animals show the adaptive behavior of caregiving toward vulnerable and wounded members of group (De Waal, Waal, & de Waal, 1996; Warneken & Tomasello, 2006).

The studies of people in various stages of human and social evolution living across different cultures in remote and pre-industrial societies (Eibl-Eibesfeldt, 1989) witness their similar actions of caregiving for kin and non-kin alike, such as specific vocalizations, skin-to-skin contact, and soothing touch. Many of these behaviors resemble the displays of compassion.

References

Abdellaoui, A., Verweij, K. J., & Zietsch, B. P. (2014). No evidence for genetic assortative mating beyond that due to population stratification. *Proceedings of the National Academy of Sciences, 111*(40), E4137–E4137.

Ainsworth, M. D. S. (1989). Attachments beyond infancy. *American Psychologist, 44*, 709–716.

Ainsworth, M. D. S., Blehar, M. C., Waters, E., & Wall, S. (1978). *Patterns of attachment: A psychological study of the strange situation*. Erlbaum.

Andersson, M. (1994). *Sexual selection*. Princeton University Press.

Aron, A., Dutton, D. G., Aron, E. N., & Iverson, A. (1989). Experiences of falling in love. *Journal of Social and Personal Relationships, 6*(3), 243–257.

Aron, A., Fisher, H., Mashek, D. J., Strong, G., Li, H., & Brown, L. L. (2005). Reward, motivation, and emotion systems associated with early-stage intense romantic love. *Journal of Neurophysiology, 94(1)*, 327–337. https://doi.org/10.1152/jn.00838.2004

Aron, A., Fisher, H. E., Strong, G., Acevedo, B., Riela, S., & Tsapelas, I. (2008). Falling in love. In S. Sprecher, A. Wenzel, & J. Harvey (Eds.), *Handbook of relationship initiation* (pp. 315–336). Psychology Press.

Bartels, A., & Zeki, S. (2000). The neural basis of romantic love. *NeuroReport: For Rapid Communication of Neuroscience Research, 11(17)*, 3829–3834. https://doi.org/10.1097/00001756-200011270-00046

Bartels, A., & Zeki, S. (2004). The neural correlates of maternal and romantic love. *NeuroImage, 21*(3), 1155–1166. https://doi.org/10.1016/j.neuroimage.2003.11.003

Bowlby, J. (1969). *Attachment and loss: Vol. 1. Attachment*. Basic Books.

Bowlby, J. (1973). *Attachment and loss: Vol. 2. Separation: Anxiety and anger*. Basic Books.

Bowlby, J. (1980). *Attachment and loss: Vol. 3. Loss*. Basic Books.

Bowlby, J. (1988/2008). *A secure base: Parent-child attachment and healthy human development*. Basic books (Originally published in 1988).

Boyd, B. (2010). *On the origin of stories: Evolution, cognition, and fiction*. Harvard University Press.

Boyd, R., & Richerson, P. J. (1985). *Culture and the evolutionary process*. University of Chicago Press.

Buss, D. M. (1988). Love acts: The evolutionary biology of love. In R. J. Sternberg & M. L. Barnes (Eds.), *The psychology of love* (pp. 100–118). Yale University Press.

Buss, D. M. (1989). Sex differences in human mate preferences: Evolutionary hypotheses tested in 37 cultures. *Behavioral and Brain Sciences, 12*, 1–49.

Buss, D. M. (1994). *The evolution of desire: Strategies of human mating*. Basic Books.

Buss, D. M., & Shackelford, T. K. (1997). Susceptibility to infidelity in the first year of marriage. *Journal of Research in Personality, 31*(2), 193–221.

Buss, D. M. (2006). The evolution of love. In R. Sternberg & K. Weis (Eds.), *The new psychology of love* (pp. 65–86). Yale University Press.

Buss, D. M., & Barnes, M. (1986). Preferences in human mate selection. *Journal of Personality and Social Psychology, 50*(3), 559–570. https://doi.org/10.1037/0022-3514.50.3.559

Buss, D. M., & Schmitt, D. P. (1993). Sexual strategies theory: An evolutionary perspective on human mating. *Psychological Review, 100*, 204–232.

Buss, D. M., et al. (1990). International preferences in selecting mates: A study of 37 cultures. *Journal of Cross-Cultural Psychology, 21*, 5–47.

Carter, C. S. (1998). Neuroendocrine perspectives on social attachment and love. *Psychoneuroendocrinology, 23*(8), 779–818.

Carter, C. S. (2014). Oxytocin pathways and the evolution of human behavior. *Annual Review of Psychology, 65*, 17–39.

Carter, C. S., Williams, J. R., Witt, D. M., & Insel, T. R. (1992). Oxytocin and social bonding. In C. A. Pedersen, G. F. Jirikowski, J. D. Caldwell, & T. R. Insel (Eds.), *Oxytocin in maternal sexual and social behaviors* (Vol. 652, pp. 204–211). Annals of the New York Academy of Science.

Chapais, B. (2011). The deep social structure of humankind. *Science, 331*(6022), 1276–1277.

Cilluffo, A., & Ruiz, N. G. (2019, June 17). *World's population is projected to nearly stop growing by the end of the century*. PEW Research Center. https://www.pewresearch.org/fact-tank/2019/06/17/worlds-population-isprojected-to-nearly-stop-growing-by-the-end-of-the-century/

Cunningham, M. R., & Barbee, A. P. (1991). Differential K-selection versus ecological determinants of race differences in sexual behavior. *Journal of Research in Personality, 25*, 205–217.

Cunningham, M. R., Barbee, A. P., & Philhower, C. L. (2002). Dimensions of facial physical attractiveness: The intersection of biology and culture. In G. Rhodes & L. A. Zebrowitz (Eds.), *Advances in visual cognition, Vol. 1. Facial attractiveness: Evolutionary, cognitive, and social perspectives* (pp. 193–238). Ablex Publishing.

De Boer, A., Van Buel, E. M., & Ter Horst, G. J. (2012). Love is more than just a kiss: A neurobiological perspective on love and affection. *Neuroscience, 201*, 114–124.

De Munck, V. (2019). *Romantic love in America: Cultural models of gay, straight and polyamorous relationship*. Lexington Press.

De Munck, V. C., & Korotayev, A. (1999). Sexual equality and romantic love: A reanalysis of Rosenblatt's study on the function of romantic love. *Cross-Cultural Research, 33*, 265–277.

De Munck, V., Korotayev, A., & McGreevey, J. (2016). Romantic love and family organization: A case for romantic love as a biosocial universal. *Evolutionary Psychology, 14*(4), 1–13. https://doi.org/10.1177/1474704916674211

De Raad, B., & Doddema-Winsemius, M. (1992). Factors in the assortment of human mates: Differential preferences in Germany and the Netherlands. *Personality and Individual Differences, 13*(1), 103–114.

De Waal, F., & Gavrilets, S. (2013). Monogamy with a purpose. *Proceedings of the National Academy of Sciences, 110*(38), 15167–15168.

De Waal, F. B., Waal, F. B., & de Waal, F. (1996). *Good natured: The origins of right and wrong in humans and other animals*. Harvard University Press.

Dixson, A. F. (1998). *Primate sexuality*. Oxford University Press.

Dixson, A. F. (2009). *Sexual selection and the origins of human mating systems*. Oxford University Press.

Domingue, B. W., Fletcher, J., Conley, D., & Boardman, J. D. (2014). Genetic and educational assortative mating among US adults. *Proceedings of the National Academy of Sciences, 111*(22), 7996–8000.

Eastwick, P. W., & Finkel, E. J. (2008). Sex differences in mate preferences revisited: Do people know what they initially desire in a romantic partner? *Journal of Personality and Social Psychology, 94*, 245–264.

Eastwick, P. W., Eagly, A. H., Finkel, E. J., & Johnson, S. E. (2011). Implicit and explicit preferences for physical attractiveness in a romantic partner: A double dissociation in predictive validity. *Journal of Personality and Social Psychology, 101*(5), 993–1011. https://doi.org/10.1037/a0024061

Eibl-Eibesfeldt, I. (1989). *Human ethology*. Aldine de Gruyter.
Fallon, A. (1990). Culture in the mirror: Sociocultural determinants of body image. In T. F. Cash & T. Pruzinsky (Eds.), *Body images: Development, deviance, and change* (pp. 80–109). Guilford Press.
Feingold, A. (1990). Gender differences in effects of physical attractiveness on romantic attraction: A comparison across five research paradigms. *Journal of Personality and Social Psychology, 59*(5), 981–993.
Fisher, H. E. (1992). *Anatomy of love: A natural history of monogamy, adultery, and divorce*. W. W. Norton.
Fisher, H. E. (1998). Lust, attraction, and attachment in mammalian reproduction. *Human Nature, 9*, 23–52.
Fisher, H. E. (2000). Lust, attraction, attachment: Biology and evolution of three primary emotions systems for mating, reproduction, and parenting. *Journal of Sex Education and Therapy, 25*, 96–104.
Fisher, H. E. (2004). *Why we love: The nature and the chemistry of romantic love*. Henry Holt.
Fisher, H. E. (2006). The drive to love: The neural mechanism for mate selection. In R. J. Sternberg & K. Weis (Eds.), *The new psychology of love* (pp. 87–115). Yale University Press.
Fisher, H. E., Aron, A., & Brown, L. L. (2006). Romantic love: A mammalian brain system for mate choice. *Philosophical Transactions of the Royal Society B: Biological Sciences, 361*(1476), 2173–2186.
Fletcher, G. J., Tither, J. M., O'Loughlin, C., Friesen, M., & Overall, N. (2004). Warm and homely or cold and beautiful? Sex differences in trading off traits in mate selection. *Personality and Social Psychology Bulletin, 30*(6), 659–672.
Flinn, M., Geary, D., & Ward, C. (2005). Ecological dominance, social competition, and coalitionary arms races: Why humans evolved extraordinary intelligence. *Evolution and Human Behavior, 26*, 10–46.
Frank, R. H. (1988). *Passions within reason: The strategic role of the emotions*. WW Norton & Co.
Gangestad, S. W. (2008). Biological adaptations and human behavior. In C. Crawford & D. Krebs (Eds.), *Foundations of evolutionary psychology* (pp. 153–172). Taylor & Francis Group/ Lawrence Erlbaum Associates.
Gangestad, S. W., & Simpson, J. A. (2000). The evolution of human mating: Trade-offs and strategic pluralism. *Behavioral and Brain Sciences, 23*(4), 573–587.
Gangestad, S. W., & Simpson, J. A. (2007). An introduction to the evolution of mind: Why we developed this book. In S. W. Gangestad & J. A. Simpson (Eds.), *The evolution of mind: Fundamental questions and controversies* (pp. 1–21). The Guilford Press.
Geary, D., & Flinn, M. (2001). Evolution of human parental behavior and the human family. *Parenting: Science and Practice, 1*(1–2), 5–61.
Germonpré, M., Lázničková-Galetová, M., Sablin, M. V., & Bocherens, H. (2018). Self-domestication or human control? The Upper Palaeolithic domestication of the wolf. In C. Stépanof & J. D. Vigne (Eds.), *Hybrid communities* (pp. 39–64). Routledge.
Goetz, J. L., Keltner, D., & Simon-Thomas, E. (2010). Compassion: An evolutionary analysis and empirical review. *Psychological Bulletin, 136*, 351–374. https://doi.org/10.1037/a0018807
Guttentag, M., & Secord, P. (1983). *Too many women?* Sage.
Hare, B. (2017). Survival of the friendliest: Homo sapiens evolved via selection for prosociality. *Annual Review of Psychology, 68*, 155–186.
Harlow, H., & Zimmerman, R. R. (1959). Affectionate responses in the infant monkey. *Science, 130*, 421–432.
Henrich, J. (2004). Cultural group selection, coevolutionary processes and large-scale cooperation. *Journal of Economic Behavior & Organization, 53*(1), 3–35.
Henrich, J., & McElreath, R. (2003). The evolution of cultural evolution. *Evolutionary Anthropology: Issues, News, and Reviews, 12*(3), 123–135.
Henrich, J., Boyd, R., & Richerson, P. J. (2012). The puzzle of monogamous marriage. *Philosophical Transactions of the Royal Society B: Biological Sciences, 367*(1589), 657–669.

Herbert, J. (1996). Sexuality, stress, and the chemical architecture of the brain. *Annual Review of Sex Research, 7*(1), 1–43.

Hill, K., Walker, R., Bozicevic, M., Eder, J., Headland, T., Hewlett, B., … Wood, B. (2011). Coresidence patterns in hunter-gatherer societies show unique human social structure. *Science, 331*, 1286–1289.

Inglehart, R. (1997). *Modernization and postmodernization: Cultural, economic, and political change in 43 societies*. Princeton University Press.

Inglehart, R., & Baker, W. E. (2000). Modernization, cultural change, and the persistence of traditional values. *American Sociological Review, 65*(1), 19–51. https://doi.org/10.2307/2657288

Inglehart, R., & Welzel, C. (2005). *Modernization, cultural change, and democracy: The human development sequence*. Cambridge University Press.

Inhorn, M. C. (2007). Loving your infertile Muslim spouse. In M. B. Padilla, J. S. Hirsch, M. Munoz-Laboy, R. E. Sember, & R. G. Parker (Eds.), *Love and globalization: Transformations of intimacy in the contemporary world* (pp. 139–160). Vanderbilt University Press.

Kamble, S., Shackelford, T. K., Pham, M. N., & Buss, D. M. (2014). Indian mate preferences: Continuity, sex differences, and cultural changes across a quarter of a century. *Personality and Individual Differences, 70*, 150–155.

Karandashev, V. (2017). *Romantic love in cultural contexts*. Springer.

Karandashev, V. (2019). *Cross-cultural perspectives on the experience and expression of love*. Springer.

Karandashev, V., & Evans, N. D. (2017). *Test of implicit associations in relationship attitudes (TIARA): Manual for a new method*. Springer.

Kenrick, D. T., Groth, G. E., Trost, M. R., & Sadalla, E. K. (1993). Integrating evolutionary and social exchange perspectives on relationships: Effects of gender, self-appraisal, and involvement level on mate selection criteria. *Journal of Personality and Social Psychology, 64*(6), 951–969. https://doi.org/10.1037/0022-3514.64.6.951

Krause, E. L. (1999). *Natalism and nationalism: The political economy of love, labor, and low fertility in central Italy* (Doctoral dissertation, University of Arizona).

Kurzban, R., & Weeden, J. (2005). HurryDate: Mate preferences in action. *Evolution and Human Behavior, 26*(3), 227–244.

Lampert, A. (1997). *The evolution of love*. Praeger.

Langlois, J. H., Kalakanis, L., Rubenstein, A. J., Larson, A., Hallam, M., & Smoot, M. (2000). Maxims or myths of beauty? A meta-analytic and theoretical review. *Psychological Bulletin, 126*(3), 390–423.

Lukas, D., & Clutton-Brock, T. (2013). The evolution of social monogamy in mammals. *Science, 341*(6145), 526–530.

Lutz, W., Sanderson, W., & Scherbov, S. (2001). The end of world population growth. *Nature, 412*(6846), 543–545.

Mace, R. (2000). Evolutionary ecology of human life history. *Animal Behaviour, 59*(1), 1–10.

Mace, R., & Holden, C. J. (2005). A phylogenetic approach to cultural evolution. *Trends in Ecology & Evolution, 20*(3), 116–121.

Mafra, A. L., Fisher, M. L., & Lopes, F. D. A. (2021). Does mate preference represent mate choice? A cross-cultural investigation. *Evolutionary Behavioral Sciences, 15*(1), 64–81. https://doi.org/10.1037/ebs0000221

Malach Pines, A. (2001). The role of gender and culture in romantic attraction. *European Psychologist, 6*(2), 96–102. https://doi.org/10.1027/1016-9040.6.2.96

Malach-Pines, A. (2005). *Falling in love: Why we choose the lovers we choose*. Taylor & Francis.

Maner, J. K., & Ackerman, J. M. (2020). Ecological sex ratios and human mating. *Trends in Cognitive Sciences, 24*(2), 98–100.

Marazziti, D., & Canale, D. (2004). Hormonal changes when falling in love. *Psychoneuroendocrinology, 29*(7), 931–936.

Marshall-Pescini, S., Virányi, Z., & Range, F. (2015). The effect of domestication on inhibitory control: Wolves and dogs compared. *PLoS ONE, 10*(2), e0118469.

Mead, M. (2017). *Continuities in cultural evolution*. Routledge (Originally published in 1964).
Mesoudi, A. (2016). Cultural evolution: A review of theory, findings, and controversies. *Evolutionary Biology, 43*(4), 481–497.
Mesoudi, A., Whiten, A., & Laland, K. N. (2006). Towards a unified science of cultural evolution. *Behavioral and Brain Sciences, 29*(4), 329–347.
Morell, V. (1997). The origin of dogs: Running with the wolves. *Science, 276*(5319), 1647–1648.
Moss, J. H., & Maner, J. K. (2016). Biased sex ratios influence fundamental aspects of human mating. *Personality and Social Psychology Bulletin, 42*(1), 72–80.
Murdock, G. P. (1949). *Social structure*. Macmillan.
Ortigue, S., Bianchi-Demicheli, F., Patel, N., Frum, C., & Lewis, J. W. (2010). Neuroimaging of love: fMRI meta-analysis evidence toward new perspectives in sexual medicine. *The Journal of Sexual Medicine, 7*(11), 3541–3552.
Panksepp, J. (1998). *Affective neuroscience: The foundations of human and animal emotions*. Oxford University Press.
Porges, S. W. (1998). Love: An emergent property of the mammalian autonomic nervous system. *Psychoneuroendocrinology, 23*(8), 837–861.
Quintana, D. S., Rokicki, J., van der Meer, D., Alnæs, D., Kaufmann, T., Córdova-Palomera, A., … Westlye, L. T. (2019). Oxytocin pathway gene networks in the human brain. *Nature Communications, 10*(1), 1–12.
Regan, P. C., & Berscheid, E. (1997). Gender differences in characteristics desired in a potential sexual and marriage partner. *Journal of Psychology & Human Sexuality, 9*(1), 25–37.
Reichard, U. H., & Boesch, C. (Eds.). (2003). *Monogamy: Mating strategies and partnerships in birds, humans and other mammals*. Cambridge University Press.
Riela, S., Rodriguez, G., Aron, A., Xu, X., & Acevedo, B. P. (2010). Experiences of falling in love: Investigating culture, ethnicity, gender, and speed. *Journal of Social and Personal Relationships, 27*(4), 473–493.
Rooker, K., & Gavrilets, S. (2016). Evolution of long-term pair-bonding in humans. In T. K. Shackelford & V. A. Weekes-Shackelford (Eds.), *Encyclopedia of evolutionary psychological science*. Springer. https://doi.org/10.1007/978-3-319-16999-6_99-1
Rosenblatt, P. C. (1967). Marital residence and the functions of romantic love. *Ethnology, 6*(4), 471–480.
Rosenblum, L. A., & Plimpton, L. A. (1981). The infant's effort to cope with separation. In M. Lewis & L. Rosenblum (Eds.), *The uncommon child* (pp. 225–257). Plenum Press.
Rushton, J. P. (1988). Genetic similarity, mate choice, and fecundity in humans. *Ethology and Sociobiology, 9*, 328–335.
Schmitt, D. P. (2005a). Is short-term mating the maladaptive result of insecure attachment? A test of competing evolutionary perspectives. *Personality and Social Psychology Bulletin, 31*(6), 747–768.
Schmitt, D. P. (2005b). Fundamentals of human mating strategies. In D. Buss (Ed.), *The handbook of evolutionary psychology* (pp. 258–291). Wiley.
Schmitt, D. P. (2008a). An evolutionary perspective on mate choice and relationship initiation. In S. Sprecher, A. Wenzel, & J. Harvey (Eds.), *Handbook of relationship initiation* (pp. 55–74). Psychology Press.
Schmitt, D. P. (2008b). Attachment matters: Patterns of romantic attachment across gender, geography, and cultural forms. In J. P. Forgas & J. Fitness (Eds.), *Social relationships: Cognitive, affective, and motivational processes* (pp. 75–100). Psychology Press.
Schmitt, D. P. (2008c). Evolutionary perspectives on romantic attachment and culture: How ecological stressors influence dismissing orientations across genders and geographies. *Cross-Cultural Research, 42*(3), 220–247.
Shobitha, M., & Agarwal, J. L. (2013). Hypothesis formulation for integrated neuroendocrinal mechanisms for pair bonding, romantic love, maternal and paternal love. *International Journal of Physiology, 1*(1), 73–78.

Shuster, S. M. (2010). Alternative mating strategies. In C. Fox & D. F. Westneat (Eds.), *Evolutionary behavioral ecology* (pp. 434–450). Cambridge University Press.
Shuster, S. M., & Wade, M. J. (2003). *Mating systems and strategies*. Princeton University Press.
Souza, A. L., Conroy-Beam, D., & Buss, D. M. (2016). Mate preferences in Brazil: Evolved desires and cultural evolution over three decades. *Personality and Individual Differences, 95*, 45–49.
Stone, E. A., Shackelford, T. K., & Buss, D. M. (2007). Sex ratio and mate preferences: A cross-cultural investigation. *European Journal of Social Psychology, 37*(2), 288–296.
Thornhill, R., & Gangestad, S. W. (1996). The evolution of human sexuality. *Trends in Ecology & Evolution, 11*(2), 98–102.
Tomasello, M. (2011). Human culture in evolutionary perspective. In M. J. Gelfand, C.-y. Chiu, & Y.-y. Hong (Eds.), *Advances in culture and psychology* (pp. 5–51). Oxford University Press.
Trivers, R. (1972). Parental investment and sexual selection. In B. Campbell (Ed.), *Sexual selection and the descent of man: 1871–1971* (pp. 136–179). Aldine.
Walker, R. S., Hill, K. R., Flinn, M. V., & Ellsworth, R. M. (2011). Evolutionary history of hunter-gatherer marriage practices. *PLoS ONE, 6*(4), e19066.
Warneken, F., & Tomasello, M. (2006). Altruistic helping in human infants and young chimpanzees. *Science, 311*(5765), 1301–1303.
Westermarck, E. (1921). *The history of human marriage* (5th ed.). Allerton (Originally work published 1891).
White, D. R., Betzig, L., Mulder, M. B., Chick, G., Hartung, J., Irons, W., … Spencer, P. (1988). Rethinking polygyny: Co-wives, codes, and cultural systems [and comments and reply]. *Current Anthropology, 29*(4), 529–572.
Whiten, A., Hinde, R. A., Stringer, C. B., & Laland, K. N. (Eds.). (2012). *Culture evolves*. Oxford University Press.
Williams, L. A., Brosnan, S. F., & Clay, Z. (2020). Anthropomorphism in comparative affective science: Advocating a mindful approach. *Neuroscience & Biobehavioral Reviews, 115*, 299–307.

Chapter 4
Sexual Models of Love

4.1 The Model of Sexual Love

4.1.1 Sex as Sexual Pleasure

Concepts of Sex and Sexual Love

Once at the conference, the colleagues of mine reported their anthropological study about the songs of love in some African tribal community. However, during their presentation they were talking all the time about sex, sexual dreams, and sexual behaviors. No words were said about love. When asked, the presenters commented that for people in that tribal society love is the same as sex. They do not distinguish these two.

Love and sex are also closely intertwined in the minds of many laypeople and scholars. For instance, love can be considered as rewarding interactions associated with sexual attraction (Centers, 1975). These two concepts are frequently considered in the literature under the same umbrella (e.g., Hatfield & Rapson, 1996, 2005). Conceptualization of how sex and love are related to each other varies across researchers and scientific disciplines. Some scholars suggest that "sex is really love"; others assert that "love is really sex"; still the others consider these two experiences as different yet connected.

Aron and Aron (2014) presented a comprehensive review of these scholarly positions. I believe all these views are valid and exemplify *different types* of *personal models of love*. Being prevalent in certain culture, they become *cultural models of love*. Here, in this chapter, I present some of the sex-related models of love.

Sex and *sexual love*, being behaviorally similar in their forms and manifestations, bear different psychological functions. *Sexual desire* is easily arousable, quickly wading, or terminated. The *desire for sex* can be satisfied by any attractive individual. *Sexual love* is a set of more personal and complex amorous emotions

V. Karandashev, *Cultural Typologies of Love*,
https://doi.org/10.1007/978-3-031-05343-6_4

associated with specific another person. Only a particular individual may satisfy the *desire for sexual love*.

In the ancient Indian Hindu Sanskrit text of *Kamasutra*, the sexuality, erotic love, and emotional fulfillment are clearly recognized. The *Kamasutra* distinguished four types of sex and sexual love (Tannahill, 1992, p. 203).

- First was a simple love of intercourse that resembles a habit or drug.
- Second was like a separate addiction to specific aspects of sex such as kissing, embracing, or oral intercourse.
- Third was the love consisting of mutual attraction between two people, instinctive, spontaneous, and possessive.
- Fourth was the kind of one-sided love that often sprang from the lover's admiration for the beauty of the beloved (Karandashev, 2017, p. 71).

Satisfaction of the first two types of sex depends just on physical proficiency and adherence to the rules and techniques, while the other two – true sexual love – are above and beyond the rules. Lovers just follow their natural feelings of harmony and sensual intuition of love.

Besides explicit culturally evolved connotations, *sex* and *sexual love* can have different implicit meanings, such as in Japanese culture. For the young Japanese men and women in dating relationships *(tsukiau)*, desire for sex *(ecchi wo suru)*, along with passion, is the core experience (Farrer, Tsuchiya, & Bagrowicz, 2008). They expect to begin sex after a *kokuhaku* – formal "confession" symbolizing a *tsukiau* – steady dating relationship. Having sex is the key experience, which distinguishes this kind of relationship from just being a friend or casual acquaintance. Sexual intercourse is a way to increase their feeling of psychological intimacy; communicate their intimacy verbally and physically; express and strengthen their *jou*, passionate feelings; and develop *ai*, the deeper form of love. One can see from these narratives that these young Japanese men and women experience sexual love, not just sex.

Sexual Love

Sexual love is the physical sensations of the body, head, and limbs, which may lead to a climax of sexual excitement or highly intense pleasurable feelings focused on the genitals. Sexual love is usually a copulation, which is performed in the same way, sometimes routinely habitually, to reach an ultimate goal of completion.

Sexual love refers to the sensual experience and action triggering sexual desire and sexual action. Sex brings joy and pleasure for many people. It manifests itself in various sensual experiences: the sense of seeing the most beautiful/handsome person in the world; the sense of hearing the enticing voice; the sense of smelling the pleasant odors of a partner's body and perfume; and the sense of touching, hugging, kissing, penetration, and moving together in synchrony. A variety of sensual (and sexual) experiences triggers *sensual/sexual* love for a particular individual.

Sex can exist without love (Wilson, 1980), and sexual lust and urge for sex are different from the *eros* of love (Lewis, 1960). *Sex* is *a physiological need*; it is the sexual impulse, which an individual needs to fulfill; it is a tension of body, which he/she needs to release. The object, which assists in the release of sexual tension, is not much important – a prostitute or other object can help with this need. Pornography of any kind can fulfill the sexual needs.

Similar, yet different from this, *sexual love* is a *pleasure of sensual experience* with a particular individual– special in some regards and distinctively different from others. A natural drive of body fuels sexual love; it arouses a person, not just a body of lover. Emotions convey the beauty in the sex brightening sexual activities.

Sexual love embraces *sexual fantasies*, *sexual dreams*, and *sexual actions* (Gebhard & Johnson, 1998; Hite, 1976/2004 , 1981/1987; Kinsey, Pomeroy, Martin, & Gebhard, 1948/1998a; Kinsey, Pomeroy, Martin, & Gebhard, 1953/1998b). *Sexual fantasies* and *dreams* about a sexy individual – the object of admiration – fulfill a person's motivation for *sexual love*. They fulfill various sexual needs of men and women (Masters, Johnson, & Kolodny, 1986). As for gender differences, on the *Erotophilic Disposition* subscale of sexual descriptors in the Emotional Investment scale comprised of such adjectives as *lustful* and *kinky*, men on average showed higher scores than women (Schmitt & Buss, 2000).

The *sexual dreams* of *sexual love* are qualitatively different from *pornography* driven by *basic sexual drive*. *Sexual love* also embodies in *sexual dreams* with a specific person – the beloved one. The *pornography fantasies* center on sexual activity itself – can be in a variety of techniques – and the object of sexual fulfillment is of secondary importance. It is activation of a basic sexual drive. Different from this, the *sexual dreams* engage the sexual images and scenes with a *unique beloved person*. *Sexual actions*, or their *imaginations*, such as hugging, kissing, petting, and others fulfill the desires for *sexual love*.

Cross-Cultural Conceptions of Sexual Love

In Western cultures, for example, the Latin *libido* and Greek *epithymia* words convey the meaning of sexual love (Larson, 1983; Tillich, 1954), which includes longing, yearning, and the desire for sensual self-fulfillment. This meaning of love (*epithymia* and *libido)* is about desire for sensual pleasure of body and gratifying release of physical energy, regardless of all other qualities of love.

The word *epithymia* means the *longing for coitus*, the *hungering* and *thirsting* for sexual closeness and union with a partner. These feelings are focused not only on sexual desire and partner's body but also on the whole person encompassing general physical attraction (Lomas, 2018; Tillich, 1954). The *coitus* brings not only physical but also emotional pleasure (Larson, 1983). The broader understanding of coitus (with the root meaning "a coming together") goes beyond physical pleasure. In support of this, it should be noted that for men and women the intimacy of intercourse is more important than the intensity of masturbation (Hite, 1976/2004, pp. 61–78; 1981/1987, pp. 485–502).

The meaning similar to the Greek word *epithymia*, as *sexual love*, is expressed in other cultures as well. The Eastern cultures have their own equivalents of sex and sexual love lexical terms, which might be surprisingly similar. For example, Arabic words for sex and sexual love may have the origins common with English and European languages (Jassem, 2013).

Here are the examples from other parts of the world. The word *kilig* in Tagalog language of the Philippines indicates the subjective experience of *butterflies in the stomach* when a person thinks of or interacts with someone sexually attractive and desired. The word *mamihlapinatapei* in indigenous language Yagán (Chile) stands for the way how persons express in their look *unspoken mutual desire*. Some other American languages have their special words for *sexual love*, which are distinct from the words for *sex*, and other forms of *love* (Brinton, 1886).

Social Origins of Sexual Love

Sex and sexual love are physiological and psychological activities in their sensations, feelings, and emotions. Traditional approach shows the power of biology and how nature of men and women determines the *social models of* their *sexual conduct*. The nature of sex is like a destiny for a man or woman.

However, the social life and media have also a significant impact on human sexuality. Complex psychosocial process of individual development shapes sexual activities (Gagnon & Simon, 1973/2017). Sex and sexuality are learned, implicitly or explicitly. Individuals develop their personal models of behavior and types of *sexual love* based on the social scripts to fit into proper psychosocial framework, certain moments in the life cycle, particular modes of behavior, and cultural context.

4.1.2 Cultural Models of Premarital Sex in Love

Traditional Cultural Models of Premarital Sexual Relations and Chastity

The cultural attitudes to premarital sexual relations are substantially associated with the values of chastity across societies, and the retaliations between them can be *bidirectional*. The fear of out-of-wedlock pregnancy and childbirth could be due to the lack of effective contraceptives. Thus, the risk of unwanted pregnancy precludes a woman from premarital sex which is condemned. These conservative attitudes to premarital sex have developed in the societies where the issues of genetic inheritance and family property are of high priority and determine the future wealth of family. These economic and legal systems have been strongly related to the evolutionary and cultural desire of families in traditional societies to have their own children.

Importance of chastity of a prospective mate substantially varies across traditional and modern societies. In their cross-cultural research, Buss and colleagues (Buss et al., 1990; Buss & Barnes, 1986) found that in such traditional cultures as

India, China, Taiwan, Indonesia, Iran, and the Palestinian Arabs, individuals believe that being "chaste" is very important for their prospective mate. However, in the modern cultures of such countries as the Netherlands, France, West Germany, Sweden, Finland, and Norway, most people view chastity as relatively unimportant for mate choice.

In the USA, the attitudes to the value of chastity vary across ethnic groups and geographical locations. For example, the cross-generational and multisite studies throughout second half of the twentieth century cited above (Buss et al., 2001) indicated that the cultural value of virginity and chastity among university students in California, Massachusetts, Virginia, and Michigan declined over several decades. This tendency, however, was different in Texas. In particular, in 1996, university students from Texas still placed the higher value on chastity than respondents from other samples. The regional difference in this respect even slightly increased by that time. Texas men, and especially women, continued to value chastity in a potential mate more than, for instance, students in Michigan. Buss et al. (2001) attributed this increasing tendency in the value of chastity to increased awareness of AIDS during the late 1980s.

Mormons Models of Premarital Sex in America

Some cultural groups of multicultural America may have their different view, like the *Latter-day Saint culture*, followed by *Mormons* (e.g., Christensen & Christense, 1976; Heaton, 2010; Holman & Harding, 1996; Olson, n.d., Riess, 2015; Smith, 1977). Their cultural values encourage *young men and women* to abstain from premarital sexual activity. Sexual desires shall be fulfilled only in heterosexual marriage. The cultural norms ban premarital and extramarital sexual affairs outside marriage, even petting and necking. They believe that *sex in marriage* carries out the functions of sexual reproduction and having children, as well as the expressions of a couple's unity. Sexual feelings of a mature man and woman are constant and relatively strong.

The Western Sexual Revolution of Love in the 1960s–1970s

Modernization of societies in the late twentieth century promoted the idea of *gender equality* and changed *sexual norms and attitudes*. The role of sex and sexual intimacy in dating relationships also shifted in the 1960s–1980s in Western European and American cultures due to so-called sexual revolution, which transformed their *cultural models of love*.

The discovery of effective oral contraceptives in the middle of the twentieth century also contributed to that sexual revolution. It became one of the great human discoveries with important cultural consequences. Birth control widely spread in modernized nations, gradually expanding to developing countries. Dating partners became less afraid of sexual activity before marriage. Woman felt less fear of unwanted or untimely pregnancy and could enjoy more sexual pleasure. The values surrounding woman chastity underwent cultural evolution and waned its importance in modern countries. Therefore, more lax attitudes to premarital sex became more common in Western modernized societies (see more in Karandashev, 2017).

The *cultural attitudes toward premarital sex* greatly vary across many cultures of the world from being strictly restrictive to the great tolerance, sometimes the obsession with sexual love (see many other cultural models of premarital sex in Karandashev, 2017).

4.1.3 Gender Equality and Premarital Sex

Gender Equality and Sex

The gender stereotypes about premarital sexual relations have been quite rigid in many cultures, and sexual inequality was across many societies (e.g., De Munck & Korotayev, 1999, 2007; Karandashev, 2017).

In the period since the 1970s until recent decades, the practices of heterosexual dating in several American states and European countries have become more egalitarian. The review of extensive research (Eaton & Rose, 2011) has shown that the gender-specific stereotypes of dating behavior have appeared to be durable over time, and the cultural sexual scripts continue to reproduce gender roles. Heterosexual dating of young men and women in the USA has remained highly gender typed. It is evident in cultural scripts, such as beliefs, expectations, and ideals. It is also evident in interpersonal scripts, such as interpersonal emotions, interpersonal communication, and behaviors.

Nevertheless, the dating processes have become less gender typed. Interpersonal scripts became more variable in terms of gender roles. For instance, they revealed the occasions of dating initiated by women. The cases of such scripts, however, were not numerous. The men-initiated dating remained the dominant script. Besides, interpersonal scripts revealed egalitarian model of dating, in which friendship relations played a major role.

The ideology of *gender equality* and *discovery of effective contraceptives* freed many women from the fear of unwanted pregnancy, which had been their typical concern regarding premarital sex for centuries. They could also enjoy sexual pleasure. The ideas of female sexuality as erotic desire and sexual pleasure were increasingly replacing the centuries-long stereotypes of male sexuality as carnal and lustful, while female sexuality as maternal and affectionate. Women equal rights for the free receiving and giving of sensual pleasures were more acceptable by Western cultures. The gender differences in sexual attitudes and behaviors declined. Throughout the 1960s–1980s, many women became less dependent and more self-assertive in sexual love, while many men became less detached and more sexually sensitive (Rubin, 1990). The *new culture of gender equality in sexual relations* encouraged women to experience and express their sexuality and sexual pleasure, not conceal this side of their relations. Men without obsolete gender stereotypes also enjoyed this cultural transformation because this brought them a possibility to have a sexual relationship with women as a free sexual and emotional exchange based on her free choice.

Sexual Freedom and Sexualization of Love

Since the 1960s–1970s, in many European societies and the USA, involvements in sexual contacts and intercourse have become a part of the *modern cultural model of dating love* (e.g., Impett & Peplau, 2002; Regnerus & Uecker, 2011; Roche, 1986; Turner, 2003; Ward, 2015). That time was labeled as *sexual revolution*, with the rights for *sexual freedom* and *gender equality* as the major driving forces of that *cultural revolution* in the *models of love*. Sex and sexuality were considered as a key constituent of the new model of love, encouraging self-exploration and personal transformation. These processes were viewed as important components of personal identity formation and self-awareness (e.g., Comfort, 1972, 1982, 1991, 2003; Hite, 1976/2004, 1978/1987; Masters & Johnson, 1966, 1970).

During that decade, the cultural norms and personal attitudes to premarital sexual intercourse became more liberal for both men and especially for women. The studies in the UK, Denmark, Norway, Sweden, and America showed the change in sexual norms and attitudes over the period in the 1960s–1970s (Comfort, 1972; Christensen & Gregg, 1970; Hite, 1976/2004, 1978/1987; Masters & Johnson, 1966, 1970; Ward, 2015). The attitudes to premarital sexual relations of women became more liberal. The sexual attitudes of men changed much less. Despite this liberal shift in Western cultural beliefs and views, the real premarital sexual behavior changed much less. The quick change in sexual attitudes meant that values and real behavior became less discrepant among men and women.

The modern diversities of sexual orientations in America, which have become recently more available for public and scientific discourse, show even more varieties of cultural models of sex and love. De Munck's (2019) anthropological study presented the detailed accounts of the sex and love in the personal lives of eight straight, five gay, and two polyamorous individuals.

4.1.4 *Relations of Love and Sex in Modern Cultural Models of Relationships*

Premarital Sex and Love Among Modern Americans

In the USA, young adulthood, especially at the age of 18–23, is a time, which is culturally portrayed as a sexually active period of life. Nowadays, *premarital sex* is commonly viewed as acceptable by American public stereotypes in many cultural groups, with some culturally specific exceptions. Sociologists Regnerus and Uecker

(2011) present many personal stories of young men and women, which illuminate their *typical American* personal models of thinking about and behavioral engagement in premarital sex. Young people usually assume that romantic relationship and sexual activity have to go hand in hand. The *normal* attitudes to sex are gender specific. Women and men perceive, appraise, and experience premarital sex in different ways. Common *normative* sexual practices consider women as the gatekeepers deciding *if* and *when* sex occurs. They are more emotionally connected in their sexual expression. They are selective in their choice of a sexual partner. Men are more engaged in the physical aspects of sex. They may have multiple partners (see for review Regnerus & Uecker, 2011).

The cultural norms of dating and premarital sex in modern America encounter a range of challenges, controversies, and new trends (see for review Regnerus & Uecker, 2011; Turner, 2003). Many young adults may experience controversial moral feelings regarding premarital sex. Despite psychological turmoil concerning possible emotional and moral consequences of their premarital sexual engagement, they often consent to take part in sexual intercourse because "everyone else is doing it," and therefore, they "are supposed to." Not many yet realize that making *culturally popular choices* can be less important than *psychologically healthy choices*.

The Modern Japanese Cultural Models of Sex and Love

The shift toward modernization of the sex and love attitudes has also occurred in Japanese society, at least among educated urban population. The meanings and functions of sex in love and dating relationships have changed.

The narratives of Japanese students (Farrer et al., 2008) which are in *tsukiau* ("going steady") dating relationships have revealed the *meaning and functions of sex* in this type of relationships. Along with passion, intimacy, and commitment, many young Japanese women and men perceive the sexual desire *(ecchi wo suru)* and *sexual intercourse as a core experience of love* in *tsukiau* relationship.

Sexual involvement is the key relationship which distinguishes a *tsukiau* relationship from friendship and casual acquaintances. Many believe that sexual intercourse should be reserved only for *tsukiau* partners. A formal "confession" *(kokuhaku)*, establishing a steady relationship, entails eligibility and expectation to have sex that occurs normally *(jutsuu)*, naturally *(shizeri)*, or as a matter of fact *(touzeri)*. Many are sexually engaged with their partner at least once a week.

The first type of the young Japanese men and women are those who believe that *sexual relationships* express many feelings of love *(at)*, romance *(koi)*, and passion *(netsujou)* and develop intimacy between partners. For them, sex is a way of physical and verbal communication.

The second type of young Japanese are those who believe that sex is a hedonic experience pursuing their own desire of sexual pleasure. They believe that having *ecchi* (sex) is a physically sensing desire and passion that express the feelings of love *(koi* and *ai)*. Having sex makes passionate feelings *(jou)* greater leading to the deeper form of Japanese love – *ai*.

Yet, the third type of young Japanese partners in dating relationship believe that they experience *obligation to have sex*. They know that sex is a common practice of dating relationships and avoiding sex can appear insensitive to a partner. This can be viewed as a reasonable cause for dissatisfaction in a relationship and a breakup.

The Role of Sex in Other Types and Models of Love

Sex may play various roles and fulfill several functions in relationships. Not every sexually related activity or intercourse is sexual love. Sex can convey different messages, express different meanings, and, therefore, be a component of several types and models of love.

Among those are the models of passionate love, romantic love, social exchange love, and economic exchange love. The *functions of sex* in these three models are conceptually distinct, yet they may overlap and cross the boundaries between them. For example, a study (Belk & Coon, 1993) found that American students distinguish the *meaning of sex* in three models: *romantic love*, *social exchange*, and *economic exchange*. In these three models, sexual behavior and expressions convey different meanings. While their boundaries can be blurring, and it is sometimes not clear in which model a partner is involved, the conceptual differences between the three models remain clear (Belk & Coon, 1993, p. 407).

In case of *romantic love*, engaging in sexual intercourse, persons (a) express their romanticized tender feelings for partners, (b) strive to please partners with sensitivity to their desires, and (c) experience and symbolize the feeling of sexual unity.

In case of *love as social exchange*, sexual activity can be (a) a cultural normative ritual, (b) a significant sign of social bonding between partners, (c) testing of their compatibility, and (d) a demonstration of their commitment.

In case of *love as economic exchange*, sexual intercourse and other sexual activity of partners are their commodities, which are reciprocated. They are given and exchanged for something rewarding (e.g., social status, material gifts, money) that is beyond sexual pleasure itself.

In real relationships, the differences between these *functions of sex* and *sexual models of love* are not easily distinguishable. Furthermore, some partners may disguise their implicit internal models. In many societies, *sex as an expression of love* is culturally praised, while sex in the role of *social*, and especially *economic exchange*, does not look culturally favorable. Besides, a person, especially a woman, knows that their partner feels more sexually satisfied knowing that their sex is based on a free choice and romantic feelings. Therefore, they may imitate their romantic emotional spirit.

4.2 The Models of Sensual and Erotic Love

4.2.1 The Features of Sensual Love

Hedonic Pleasure of Bodily Sensations

Sensual love involves the senses and physical feelings that are experienced as sexually pleasing and enjoyable. This experience is gratifying itself, being focused on bodily sensations, rather than on ultimate sexual orgasm. *Sensual love* is *centered on bodily sensations*, rather than on orgasm, and engages a wide variety of practices.

In the *sensual model of love*, the primary function of sex is a *hedonic desire of sexual pleasure*; it is a desire for each other as a provider of sensual pleasure. In the UK, the adult individuals with *positive body image* tend to feel more hedonic feelings, such as pleasure and joy, and eudaimonic experiences, such purpose and meaning of life (Swami, Weis, Barron, & Furnham, 2018).

For the Japanese men and women, as I cited above (Farrer et al., 2008), playfully sexual actions (*ecchi*) bring the joy of physically sensing passion. Such experience of love was extensively present in the narratives of Japanese participants in the study of *tsukiau* (dating) relationship.

Indian traditional culture has the elaborated concepts of love distinguishing the experiences of *sexual* and *sensual love*, as well as of other major love experiences. For instance, scholars distinguish the words *rati* and *kama*, related to the love feelings of pleasure arising from sexual union, from other love feelings – *anuraga* (affection) or *bhakti* (devotion). The culture suggests individuals to conquer the senses of their lower self. They should perceive the love for the finite merely temporary and instrumental, with the ultimate goal to achieve the highest infinite pleasure of love (see Gala & Kapadia, 2014, pp. 119–120).

Different from a life-affirming Western view, Indian cultural norms encourage ascetic life and freedom from desire, passion, and attachment. People supposed to enjoy the pleasure of life and love based on self-discipline (Ali, 2002, p. 212).

Kissing in the Model of Sensual Love

Kissing can communicate intimacy or function as an erotic stimulus. It may appear that sexual and romantic kissing is ubiquitous across cultures. It is frequently depicted in a wide range of material culture, such as literature, art, and other media. According to some scholars (Fisher, 1992; Kirshenbaum, 2011; Wlodarski & Dunbar, 2013), in over 90% of cultures mating partners practice romantic and sexual kissing. Romantic-sexual kissing is lip-to-lip contact that may be short or prolonged. Kissing behavior can have an adaptive function in initiation of short-term and long-term mating relationships giving an opportunity to assess physical compatibility between partners. The study among American undergraduate students

(Hughes, Harrison, & Gallup Jr., 2007) showed that after kissing a partner first time 66% of women and 59% of men became less attracted to them.

Scholars from behavioral and social sciences widely believed that romantic-sexual kiss is a typical way of communicating love in many cultures. It is frequently present on the stage of relationship initiation because it allows to assess whether a potential partner is compatible in terms of taste, smell, and other physical features. Romantic kiss induces sexual arousal and receptivity of partners (Hughes et al., 2007; Wlodarski & Dunbar, 2013).

Sexual and Romantic Kiss as a Cultural Phenomenon

Despite the widespread claims about cross-cultural ubiquity of kissing, historical and ethnographic analyses of ancient and modern societies (Crawley, 2005; Danesi, 2013) have shown that the romantic and sexual kisses are not cross-culturally universal and appeared quite late in human history.

Ethnographic analysis of data from a large cross-cultural sample set and a survey (n = 168 cultures) showed (Jankowiak, Volsche, & Garcia, 2015, p. 535) that the romantic-sexual kiss is far from being a near universal. The study documented its presence only in 77 out of 168 cultural samples (46%). The studies of populations in New Guinea, sub-Saharan African, and Amazonian foraging or horticultural societies did not show any evidence of sexual and romantic kisses in those cultures.

A social complexity of societies was a major cultural factor strongly associated with the frequency of the romantic-sexual kiss: "the more socially complex the culture, the higher frequency of romantic–sexual kissing" (Jankowiak, Volsche, & Garcia, 2015, p. 535). The pattern of cultural presence of kissing does not vary by geographical regions and cultural areas. Therefore, authors believe that the emergence of the romantic and sexual kisses might be associated with development of upper-level social classes, the rising of social elite, which started to appreciate and practice self-control of emotional displays. Evolvement of oral hygiene could also play the role.

4.2.2 *Erotic Model of Love*

The Concept of Erotic Love

Physical attractiveness substantially determines their romantic attraction and love. "You are so beautiful!" is a common insight that a lover realizes rapidly falling in love. According to multiple stories, novels, and movies, both women and men seek for the beautiful/handsome.

Love has the intricate or straight psychological connections with erotic feelings. In case of frequent and strong involvement of such feelings, we can call it *erotic model of love*. Love and eroticism of life are tied to each other in many various links (Featherstone, 1998).

In historical origins, the Greek word *eros (érōs)* appeared in the meaning of aesthetic appreciation of and yearning for a beauty (Lomas, 2018). However, in the modern scholarship and public opinion, it has acquired sexual and passionate connotations (see for review Karandashev, 2019).

The concept of *érōs*, being closely related to *epithymia*, as sexual love, stands for different emotional experience. The meaning of the word *érōs* goes beyond basic physical desire; it imbues the broader psychological meanings, such as *appreciation of beauty,* along with *passionate love emotions* triggered by *attractive appearance* of a person (Tillich, 1954). In the same vein, *elation of romantic sex-aesthetic attraction* is different from *sexual arousal of sexual desire*, whereas *non-sexual affection* is different from *sexual love* (Grant, 1976).

Erotic Love Is the Love of Beauty

Erotic love implies that a lover loves a beloved as a *beautiful object*, as an *object of aesthetic admiration. Erotic love* is about aesthetic pleasure, while sexual love is about sensual (sexual) pleasure. However, erotic can easily transfer to sensual in sexually stimulating settings. People frequently experience *erotic love* as closely entangled with sexual love and passionate love. Yet, some tend to perceive a body, face, expressions, and other appearances of a partner as *sexy* while others as *beautiful*. It depends on the lover's dominating motivation currently active in his/her mind.

According to *erotic model of love,* a lover admires *physical characteristics* of a loved one that are perceived via various sensory impressions: visual, auditory, tactile-kinesthetic, olfactory, and gustatory. Interaction between partners and their interpersonal perception are multisensory processes, and these *multiple sensory impressions* are tightly intertwined (see for review Karandashev et al., 2016; Karandashev et al., 2020, b). Men and women not only look at their partners with admiration but also come closer, speak, sing, dance, touch each other, smile, hug, cuddle, kiss, and so on. *Dynamic expressive behavior* frequently talks more about attractiveness than static body and face appearance.

All these perceptions and aesthetic qualities encompass what we call *erotic attraction* – a lover appreciates a partner for his/her attractive erotic impressions. The concept of *erotic love* deserves special scientific attention in the studies of love. Yet, the *erotic love* has not gained its independent scientific status yet – neither conceptually nor operationally.

Erotic Love and Physical Attraction

Erotic love, along with *sexual* and *sensual love*, is a strong emotional experience, which triggers a lover's physical attraction to a loved one. The beloved person attracts the lover by their visual appearances of body and face, sounds of voice and other auditory stimuli, the way how a person moves, the sense of touch of person's skin and cloth, the smell of skin, breath, and other possible olfactory stimuli – all those perceptive and sensory impressions which grow into *erotic physical attraction* (Karandashev et al., 2020, b; Karandashev & Fata, 2014).

Cognitive, affective, and behavioral processes are involved in such attraction, while cognitive aspects of love are frequently suppressed and submerged in the shadow of high emotional arousal. The *affective component* of *erotic physical attraction* is the pleasurable feelings and positive emotions which a lover feels in presence of the loved person. The positive emotional tone of such *physical attraction* is prevalent providing a communicative signal of expected pleasures. *The cognitive component* of *erotic physical attraction* is a lover's perceptions, memories, thoughts, and imaginations of the loved one. These perceptive and cognitive processes provide a cognitive appraisal *signaling the desirable qualities* of the beloved and trigger experience of *erotic emotions*. The percept of the beloved is mostly viewed in a positive glow. This phenomenon explains why passionate love is frequently blind. The *behavioral component* of *erotic physical attraction* is the *action tendencies* of longing to be physically closer to a loved one, yearning for interpersonal vicinity, and craving for the more time spent together. This is a desire for physical and sensual union, cuddling, hugging, and kissing (Karandashev et al., 2020, b; Karandashev & Fata, 2014).

As I noted above, *attractiveness* depends on various dynamic sensory impressions and actions. A lover appreciates not only body shape but also body movement, not only facial features and hair, eyes, and lips but also expressiveness of face and gestures and smile and not only sound of voice but also manners of speaking of the beloved one (Karandashev et al., 2016; Karandashev et al., 2020, b). Certain kinds of hip and breast movement would trigger sexual associations more readily than just appearance of body, face, and hair.

Relations of Erotic Love with Other Models of Love

In their personal life, public view, and modern scholarship, people do not well discern erotic love from sexual love. These two experiences are frequently considered together. Even though practically they are closely intertwined and, sometimes, indivisibly associated, yet conceptually, *erotic love* is different from *sexual* and *sensual love*. As I noted above, *sexual love* is the *physical sensations of body* during copulation causing a *peak of sexual excitement* focused on the *genitals*. *Sensual love* is the pleasurable bodily sensations during variety of sexual interactions and practices, which are centered on enjoyable bodily senses of touch and movement, rather than on reaching an orgasm.

Erotic love, being intricately entangled with both sexual and sensual aspects of love, is conceptually different because it is interpersonal attraction focusing on pleasing and beautiful appearance of another person. *Erotic love* involves a wide variety of practices. Some men and women tend to look at the beloved mainly as a physically beautiful and sexually appealing person. They experience erotic action tendencies and erotic feelings. These are the *lovers of erotic type*. Others tend to experience the *erotic component* only as a part of a more complex picture of their *type of love*.

Erotic feelings are usually highly intensive – *passionate* – in emotional tone. *Erotic model of love*, however, is not equivalent with *passionate* and *romantic models of love*. *Erotic passion* is a cluster of high arousal and strong emotions triggered by the attractiveness of physical appearance of a beloved, while *romantic passion* is a constellation of arousal and emotions prompted by an idealized image of the beloved. "What is beautiful is loved" (Sangrador & Yela, 2000, p. 207); therefore, *erotic passion* is commonly associated with *romantic passion*.

As one can see in the sections above and below, the studies of *erotic attraction* have been mainly focused on the research of physical appearance – youth, hip-to-waist ratio, body and face types, and other features which make a person attractive. An assumption was that a person is loved because she/he is beautiful. However, the opposite assumption is also possible. A person can be beautiful because she/he is loved. As French writer de Saint-Exupéry noted in his novella *The Little Prince*, "The most beautiful things in the world cannot be seen or touched, they are felt with the heart." I believe this is a thought worthwhile to contemplate.

Erotic love is so intertwined with other types of love that it is worthwhile to quote de Saint-Exupéry again:

> You're beautiful, but you're empty...One couldn't die for you. Of course, an ordinary passerby would think my rose looked just like you. But my rose, all on her own, is more important than all of you together, since she's the one I've watered. Since she's the one I put under glass, since she's the one I sheltered behind the screen. Since she's the one for whom I killed the caterpillars (except the two or three butterflies). Since she's the one I listened to when she complained, or when she boasted, or even sometimes when she said nothing at all. Since she's my rose. ("The Little Prince", de Saint-Exupéry)

4.2.3 Erotic Love in Cross-Cultural Perspective

Erotic Art and Erotic Love

The concept of *erotic love* is rooted in the cultural ideas of *erotic art* and *literature* – painting, sculpture, music, songs, dances, theater, fashion design – that convey the aesthetic values of the body shape and movement, the structure and expressiveness of face, and the melody and rhythm of music and singing.

Erotic love – the same way as erotic art – represents the physical beauty of a person and context. A person experiencing erotic love admires the body, being *nude*, not *naked*. The impression of the *nude figure* of a beloved is about presence of his/her good-looking body, while the impression of *naked figure* is about absence of cloths. Both can have different implicit associations.

The history of art across various cultures has witnessed variability of *cultural models of erotic love*. Men and women were the objects of the *Ancient Greek models of erotic love*, which we still enjoy in paintings and sculptures in Greece, as well in the museums of many other countries. In Renaissance era, the painting of the female nude had great popularity with mostly positive connotations. A nude figure became the artistic personification of beauty, graciousness, soul, and love. Many works of poets and artists depicted erotic images. The works of the great creative talents of Renaissance, such as Giorgione, Leonardo, Titian, Michelangelo, and Veronese, celebrated erotic beauty.

For example, the painting of the "Venus of Urbino" presents "a humanly beautiful nude woman whose pose is borrowed from the idealized beauty of the 'Sleeping Venus' by Gorgione" (Grabski, 1999, p. 9), thus creating an allegory of love. This is a *cultural model* of the *victory of love over temptation and time*.

Sanskrit aesthetic philosophy valorized "erotic love" as the emotion of *shringara,* which underlies the emotion of passion (*rati*), yet they are different. The short love lyrics in ancient Sanskrit beautifully depict the *shringara* – erotic love. *Sexual activities* in medical and literary texts of Ancient Indians were still a set of different emotions – *kama,* which were closely related with bodily health, season, and food (Orsini, 2006, p. 10).

Cultural Models of Beauty

Such erotic aesthetics shape the cultural norms and fashions of aesthetic erotic attraction in interpersonal relationships. *Erotic art* and *literature* create the *cultural models of beauty* and *cultural models of erotic love*.

Erotic arts and *literary works* have had enduring cultural ideas and traditions of beauty across times and cultures (e.g., Ahmad, 1994; Feldman & Gordon, 2006; Ishigami & Buckland, 2013; Prettejohn, 2005). The concepts of *erotic love* have been always distinctive from other models of love.

For example, the classical Indian poetry, music, theatre, dance, and sculpture – in accord with *Sanskrit aesthetic tradition* – presented *rati* and *sringara* as the concepts denoting *attraction of beauty* and *erotic love* between women and men. In particular, the Indian love lyrics have beautifully expressed these aesthetical and psychological emotional experiences (Orsini, 2006).

The beauty of human appearance was appreciated in the depictions of erotic as well as pornographic images and scenes (Ahmad, 1994; Ishigami & Buckland, 2013; Prettejohn, 2005). *Erotic art* presented the beautiful images of face, body, cloth, and posture, targeted at *aesthetic appreciation*, while *pornographic arts* and *literature* presented the *images of sexual activity*, targeted at basic sexual drive and sexual fulfillment. However, the distinction of erotic and pornographic was not always apparent.

Cultural Models of Erotic Love Across Cultural History

The world history of art has demonstrated many examples of erotic and pornographic art across centuries and societies, such as *classical ancient Greek culture* (fifth–fourth centuries BC), *ancient Roman culture* (first century of B.C.–the mid-third century of A.D.), the *Chinese culture of the Ming dynasty* (fourteenth–seventeenth centuries), the *Japanese culture of the Edo period of Tokugawa* (seventeenth–nineteenth centuries), *Korean culture of the twentieth century*, early modern Italy, India, and modern Japan (see for review Feldman & Gordon, 2006).

Pre-Christian societies of Greece and Rome were sophisticated in their sexual cultures (Clarke, 1998; Hubbard, 2013; Nussbaum & Sihvola, 2019; Skinner, 2013; Vout, 2013). They had a high value of sexual pleasure and erotic art. The Romans were more sexually liberated than people in Western cultures of the following centuries. The erotic art was displayed in homes and public spaces proudly demonstrating wealth and luxury. Artists sold their erotic works to various consumers, to the elite, as well as to the poor people.

The ancient Greeks and Romans were quite open in their artistic portrayals of sex, sensuality, and erotic. Sculptures and paintings displayed beautiful bodies, phallic images, erotic postures, and sexual scenes of their gods. Scenes of seduction decorated walls, oil lamps, and drinking cups (Vout, 2013). Roman artists depicted various human sexual activities (see for review Clarke, 1998) between men and women, women and women, men and men, threesomes, and foursomes, which illustrate how *ancient models of erotic love and sexual love* were different from the modern cultural models.

In many cultures, *erotic love* was frequently depicted by courtesans – *hetaeras*, *tawaif*-s, *ji*-s – the women who play their "love" with artistic charm, elegant conversation, and sexual favors to excite *erotic love* of men. The courtesans' art represents *erotic love* in beautiful artistic forms. It is different from sexual love that prostitutes provide to fulfill the people's needs of lust. It is different from romantic love since it is not sincere, not personal – it is just a role-played love. It is idealized, but not individual.

Around the world and throughout history, courtesans inspire erotic love for material exchange. The case studies of courtesans' art have shown examples of erotic art and erotic love across centuries and societies (Feldman & Gordon, 2006).

For example, in the late Ming times (sixteenth–seventeenth centuries), women widely participated in *elite Chinese culture*. The courtesans' literary and paining arts played an influential role in forming new beauty ideals, gender roles, and the social and cultural aspirations (Berg, 2009). In the *Edo period of Tokugawa* (seventeenth–nineteenth centuries), *Japanese culture* had widely produced the special erotic arts of "laughing pictures," *shunga*, intended to entertain people with amusing pleasure. The *shunga* art and literature of that time was aesthetical, not pornographic. Nevertheless, in modern Japan, *shunga* is frequently regarded as a taboo (Ishigami & Buckland, 2013).

A Cultural Variety of Erotic Beauty and Attractiveness

Beautiful bodies, faces, adornments, and postures (see for review Brierley, Brooks, Mond, Stevenson, & Stephen, 2016; DeMello, 2007, 2012, 2013; Gilman, 2015; Leist, 2003) excite admiration and erotic appeal. Despite large similarity in erotically attractive attributes (see for review, e.g., Cunningham, Roberts, Barbee, Druen, & Wu, 1995; Fallon, 1990; Karandashev et al., 2016; Karandashev et al., 2020, b; Langlois et al., 2000; Swami & Furnham, 2007), many of those vary across cultures.

Local ecological and cultural conditions have an impact on the perception of what is erotically attractive. Some cultural groups may view women with large nose, large chin, and small eyes as attractive while others as nonattractive. For instance, Marshall (1971) explored the sexual behavior on Mangaia, an island in the South Pacific Ocean, and described one version of Mangaian criteria of attractiveness for girls: "a smiling face, shiny black hair, small eyes 'like those of a pigeon,' with small breasts, large hips and round cheeks; her lips should be neither too everted nor too thin, and she should have skin that is neither black nor white" (Marshall, 1971, p. 124).

Another example is attractiveness preferences for female body characteristics among the UK Caucasian and South African Zulu people. In those cultural contexts, the optimal conditions for survival and reproduction and corresponding social values are different. In the UK, a high body mass is perceived as a sign of low health and low fertility, while in rural South Africa, it is a sign of high health and high fertility (Tovée, Swami, Furnham, & Mangalparsad, 2006).

Erotic Adornment and Attire

Exotic sexually attractive attires can also excite admiration, erotic spectacle, seduction, and sensual love. The idea of *eroticism* has been present in the *fashion history*, being rooted in the cultural myths, traditions, habits, and arts of humans (Chun, 2007; Kim & Yoon, 2005; Oliveira, 2013; Workman, 1996). The attire greatly mediated how erotically attractive men and women look and induced manifestations of sensual love. The modern fashion can be characterized by three dimensions of erotic expressions: *sexy-potency*, *attractiveness*, and *modesty* (Kim & Yoon, 2005). The contents and forms of erotic modes have been used to attain erotic attraction, affection, or passion in several ways (Chun, 2007):

- By primitive and grotesque expressions or natural and direct sexual depictions
- By projecting sex mechanically or symbolically
- By naturally denoting rational beauty or idealization
- By inducing sensual beauty

Erotically designed modes of attire convey a figurative expression of true passion by stimulating the "desire to see" and the "desire to show." The erotic fashion can also be a venue in narcissistic tendencies expressing beauty through magnification or exaggeration (Chun, 2007).

4.2.4 *What Is Erotically Attractive*

What Is Beautiful Is Erotically Attractive

What is beautiful in a person face, body, legs, hands, and cloth is frequently perceived as *sexy*, especially in some *sexually obsessive cultures*. The modern word "*sexy*" metaphorically means erotically attractive and sexually appealing.

Men and women fall in *erotic love* when another person is physically attractive, or at least, they experience a quick and instinctive glimpse of thought about it. This impression of beauty triggers pleasurable emotions, explicitly or implicitly associated with sensual feelings. Erotic feelings may be minor, compared to other emotions, yet they contribute to the whole experience of love, perhaps due to excitation transfer. They are a part of a *complex type of love*, which a man or woman experiences.

The typical norms of beautiful and attractive attributes of physical appearance are significantly similar across cultures (see for review Cunningham et al., 1995; Fallon, 1990; Langlois et al., 2000). For example, neonate qualities, big smile, and raised eyebrows have little cross-cultural variability; appearance of sexual maturity and expressive qualities, intermediate cross-cultural variability; while weight, hairstyle, and other aspects of grooming, high variability across cultures, depending on local ecology and fashion.

Evolutionary Origins of Erotic Attractiveness

The early evolutionary theory of sexual selection, partially supported by data, explained that men rate the value of a good look for a prospective mate higher than women do (see for review, e.g., Buss et al., 1990; Buss, 1994; Buss & Barnes, 1986; Feingold, 1990). Other studies, however, found that both men and women consider an attractive look as equally important for a prospective mate (e.g., Fletcher, Tither, O'Loughlin, Friesen, & Overall, 2004; Kenrick, Groth, Trost, & Sadalla, 1993; Langlois et al., 2000; Regan & Berscheid, 1997). Images of beautiful bodies in terms of shape, size, and proportions of body figure can be also considered from an evolutionary perspective (Swami & Furnham, 2007).

The other studies, however, have demonstrated differential effects of moderating variables, such as local ecological contexts and cultures (e.g., Cunningham et al., 1995; Cunningham & Barbee, 1991; Cunningham, Barbee, & Philhower, 2002; Eastwick, Eagly, Finkel, & Johnson, 2011; Eastwick & Finkel, 2008; Fallon, 1990; Guttentag & Secord, 1983; Langlois et al., 2000; Maner & Ackerman, 2020; Marshall, 1971; Moss & Maner, 2016; Stone, Shackelford, & Buss, 2007). Thus, it is more likely that both cultural and biological evolutions contribute to erotic attractiveness moderating and mediating their effects (e.g., Cunningham et al., 2002; Karandashev, in press; Swami & Furnham, 2007). Besides, the importance of attractiveness varies across cultures (e.g., Anderson, 2019).

Physical appearance in modern societies may have lost its original signaling function. The way of dressing, fashion, and cosmetics can mask their natural attractiveness. Expressive behavior can play more important role than body and face shapes and static features. People can manage and manipulate their physical appearance employing natural artifice and deliberate deception. Because of this, the relation between genotype, phenotype, and social outcomes is confounded (Cunningham et al., 2002).

The inconsistencies in the results on the value of attractiveness in *erotic love model* across cultures and genders might be also due to some methodological issues (see elsewhere). For instance, as I noted in previous chapters, in terms of evolutionary interpretation, theory stresses the good look of females. It is unclear, however, why women should value physical appearance of men less. The healthy genes of males are not less valuable than genes of females. Nevertheless, a common cultural stereotype frequently views health as the most important quality for females.

In recent decades, the values of good looks have undergone a large rising interest in a mate's appearance not only among men but also among women. In recent studies (e.g., Fugère, Madden, & Cousins, 2019), physical attractiveness strongly influenced women's rating of target men as desirable partners. The role of personality profiles interacts with physical attractiveness. Women rated men with desirable personality traits favorably as mating partners only when they perceived them moderately or highly attractive. Women never rated men with desirable personality traits as desirable partners if they perceived them unattractive.

What Is Culturally Erotic Is Beautiful

What qualities are *erotically attractive* in men and women? What can incite *erotic love*? *Physical appearance* is universally valuable across cultures, erotic love is ubiquitous, and the attributes of physical appearance, which are perceived as attractive, are similar (see for review Cunningham et al., 1995; Fallon, 1990; Karandashev et al., 2016; Karandashev et al., 2020, b; Langlois et al., 2000; Marshall, 1971).

Nevertheless, the cultural value of physical appearance and criteria of attractiveness vary across societies. In some cultures (e.g., Ghana in Africa and Korea in Southeast Asia), physical attractiveness is of lower importance in everyday life and mating. People's understanding of attractiveness is also culturally specific (Anderson, 2019; Anderson, Adams, & Plaut, 2008; Wheeler & Kim, 1997).

The importance of physical attractiveness in love and criteria of beauty vary cross-culturally (Anderson, 2019;Anderson et al., 2008 ; Wheeler & Kim, 1997). In the cultures, such as the mainstream America, which are high in the values of *independence*, *autonomy*, and availability of *personal choice*, an erotic appeal of attractiveness is more important than in the cultures, such as Korea and Ghana, which are high in the values of *interdependence*, *connectedness*, *embeddedness*, and *limited relationship affordances*, wherein physical attractiveness is less important in daily life and relationships (Anderson et al., 2008; Wheeler & Kim, 1997).

Some attributes of physical appearance vary in their attractiveness across cultures (Cunningham et al., 2002). According to ecological approach (Cunningham et al., 1995; Cunningham & Barbee, 1991), people adapt and modify their valuation of attractiveness adjusting their values to local ecological and cultural conditions, such as sex ratio and relational mobility (Guttentag & Secord, 1983; Maner & Ackerman, 2020; Moss & Maner, 2016). For example, it was found that across 36 cultures, mate preferences vary with the number of potential mates in a local population (Stone et al., 2007).

The standards of beauty also vary across times and societies (see for review, e.g., DeMello (2007, 2012, 2013)). Ecologically, socially, and culturally appropriate *prototypes* of what kind of *appearance* is *attractive* evolve. Therefore, the fitting to the relevant *cultural prototypes* of what types of body, posture, and adornment are beautiful is a right way for a person to look good (Osborn, 1996).

For example, there are certain cultural patterns of body size ideals. However, the differences in these ideals of body size between cultural groups of different socioeconomic status are larger than between Western and non-Western societies (Swami, 2015). Cultural evolution of ideals of body size in recent decades has been affected by modernization, which coincides with Westernization. Now, due to cultural changes that occurred in many urban populations and among people of middle and high socioeconomic status, a thin ideal is prevalent in urban residency (Swami, 2015). Both Westernization and modernization promote a thin ideal.

Erotic Attraction of Expressive Behavior

Attractiveness is not only in specific *static* and *difficult-to-change physical features of body and facial appearance*, such as *smell*, *skin*, *eyes*, and *lips*, but also in *dynamic* and *flexible expressive behavior*, such as *expressive face and body*, *a manner of speaking*, *smile*, *dancing*, and *dressing*. The preferences for these parameters in a romantic partner vary across cultures (Karandashev et al., 2016; Karandashev et al., 2020, b).

Cross-cultural studies (Karandashev et al., 2020, b) have demonstrated that people in *survival and more conservative cultures* (e.g., Jamaica, Southeast of the USA, Russia, and Georgia), which are less modernized in terms of the lower cultural dimensions of Individualism, lower Indulgence and Emancipative values, and higher Power Distance, are more attracted by a partner's *biological and static physical appearances*, such as *body and facial features*, *lips*, *eyes*, *skin*, *smell*, and others. However, people in *self-expressive and liberal cultures* (e.g., Northeast, Midwest, and Hawaii of the USA), which are more modernized in terms of the lower cultural dimension of Power Distance and higher in the dimensions of Individualism, Indulgence, and Emancipation values, are more attracted by a partner's *social-psychological and dynamic physical appearances,* such as *expressive body, face, and speaking, smiling*, *dancing*, *dressing,* and others.

People in the societies modernized in terms of the lower cultural dimension of Hierarchy and the higher dimension of Egalitarianism, such as France and Portugal, are especially attracted by the voice and eyes since they express a partner's personality. Different from this, people in the societies with the high cultural dimension of Hierarchy and low dimension of Egalitarianism (e.g., Russia and Jamaica) consider voice and eyes as less important qualities in their romantic partner (Karandashev et al., 2020, b). The *expressive voice* can be especially attractive in the regionally culturally specific context. For example, the women from the country of Georgia consider the men's ability to sing songs as an important attractive quality (Karandashev et al., 2016).

Cultural Modernization and Westernization of Erotic Ideals

According to recent studies conducted across 12 countries (Yan & Bissell, 2014), globalization of beauty standards is an overwhelmingly expanding tendency. European and North American magazines keep the dominant position in shaping the beauty standards worldwide. However, the magazines in South Africa and Latin America tend to be assimilated into the Western cultural norms of beauty, while Asian magazines remain relatively independent (Yan & Bissell, 2014).

In the USA, Western standards of beauty are predominant, despite the great racial diversity of population. Many White, Black, Latina, and Asian women in American society tend to follow these White conceptions of mainstream beauty. For people of various races and ethnicities, favoring dominant norms of beauty and denying diversity are quite typical tendencies, yet at the different extent (Poran, 2002).

The Modern Shifts in Erotic Model of Love

The *modern erotic model of love* has become surprisingly similar across cultures, despite the evident diversity in the natural phenotypes of face and body between different racial and ethnic groups. For some men and especially women in many modern societies, their appearance and looking at their best have become an obsession. In many countries of the world, preoccupation with appearance enhancement has become the core cultural values boosted by the beauty and fashion magazines, movies, and TV. *Personal models of love* frequently encourage *face and body modification* using cosmetic surgeries, piercing, tattooing, liposuctions, body implants, and diets for beauty. Such cultural shift is obvious, for instance, in the USA, Mexico, Argentina, Chile, Colombia, Brazil, China, South Korea, and Japan (e.g., Darling-Wolf, 2004; Hua, 2013; Jones, 2017; Peiss, 2011; Sands & Adamson, 2014; Wolf, 1991).

The modern standards of beauty displayed in social media frequently sexualize female figures and encourage the body images, which glorify unrealistic female body types. For instance, in North America the female body weights, as they are portraited in beauty magazines, are substantially lower than the average body weight of women (e.g., Lokken, Worthy, & Trautmann, 2004; Saraceni & Russell-Mayhew, 2007).

The thin ideals of female body have become more culturally restrictive. A *fashion icon of woman* often appears as "fair, tall and willowy, often slightly androgynous; her body flawless due to medical procedures, and most of all thin, well below the recommended weight for her height" (Austin, 2012, p. 1). Many women yearn for the "twiggy" look and waif-like figure.

Men's and Women's Erotic Love

Evolutionary and cultural perspectives explain that men are more interested in physical appearance of women for mating relationship. A common sense and observations tell us that erotic love model is more prevalent in men. This stereotype has set pressure on women who feel cultural necessity to fit the beauty ideals. These are typical norms and practices in men-dominated societies (e.g., Jeffreys, 2005; Wolf, 1991). According to feminist view, beauty standards put women in the status of sexual objects, rather than active actors of sexual relationships.

Commonsense opinions tell us that men are *active erotic spectators*, whereas women are just *passive erotic objects*. However, even historically it is not true. For example, the French and English novels and paintings of the second half of the nineteenth century (Kern, 1996) suggest reconsidering this misconception. The works of Zola and Dickens, Renoir and Rossetti, as well as other writers and painters have recurringly shown a different compositional pattern of "the gaze" eyes of love. Men's and women's eyes of love show that "A man in profile looks at a woman, who looks away from him and in the direction of the viewer." Kern (1996) concludes that "compared with the eyes of men, the eyes of women are more visible, look out into a wider world, consider a more varied range of thoughts, and convey more profound, if not more intense, emotions" (Fraser, 1998, p. 199).

References

Ahmad, A. M. (1994). The erotic and the pornographic in Arab culture. *The British Journal of Aesthetics, 34*(3), 278–285.

Ali, D. (2002). Anxieties of attachment: The dynamics of courtships in medieval India. *Modern Asian Studies, 36*(1), 103–139.

Anderson, S. L. (2019). Chapter 29: The importance of attractiveness across cultures. In K. D. Keith (Ed.), *Cross-cultural psychology: Contemporary themes and perspectives* (2nd ed., pp. 598–613). https://doi.org/10.1002/9781119519348.ch29

Anderson, S. L., Adams, G., & Plaut, V. C. (2008). The cultural grounding of personal relationship: The importance of attractiveness in everyday life. *Journal of Personality and Social Psychology, 95*(2), 352–368. https://doi.org/10.1037/0022-3514.95.2.352

Aron, E. N., & Aron, A. (2014). Love and sexuality. In K. McKinney & S. Sprecher (Eds.), *Sexuality in close relationships* (pp. 41–64). Psychology Press.

Austin, R. (2012). Pencil-like thin icons of feminity in the Indian media. *Global Media Journal, 3*(1), 1–8.

Belk, R. W., & Coon, G. S. (1993). Gift giving as agapic love: An alternative to the exchange paradigm based on dating experiences. *Journal of Consumer Research, 20*(3), 393–417.

Berg, D. (2009). Cultural discourse on Xue Susu, a courtesan in late Ming China. *International Journal of Asian Studies, 6*(2), 171–200.

Brierley, M. E., Brooks, K. R., Mond, J., Stevenson, R. J., & Stephen, I. D. (2016). The body and the beautiful: Health, attractiveness and body composition in men's and women's bodies. *PLoS ONE, 11*(6), e0156722.

Brinton, D. G. (1886). *The conception of love in some American languages*. Press of McCalla and Stavely.

Buss, D. M. (1994). *The evolution of desire: Strategies of human mating*. Basic Books.

Buss, D. M., & Barnes, M. (1986). Preferences in human mate selection. *Journal of Personality and Social Psychology, 50*(3), 559–570. https://doi.org/10.1037/0022-3514.50.3.559

Buss, D. M., et al. (1990). International preferences in selecting mates: A study of 37 cultures. *Journal of Cross-Cultural Psychology, 21*, 5–47.

Buss, D. M., Shackelford, T. K., Kirkpatrick, L. A., & Larsen, R. J. (2001). A half century of mate preferences: The cultural evolution of values. *Journal of Marriage & Family, 63*, 491–503.

Centers, R. (1975). *Sexual attraction and love: An instrumental theory*. Charles. C. Thomas.

Christensen, H. T., & Gregg, C. F. (1970). Changing sex norms in America and Scandinavia. *Journal of Marriage and the Family, 32*(4), 616–627.

Christensen, H. T., & Christense, H. T. (1976). Mormon sexuality in cross-cultural perspective. *Dialogue: A Journal of Mormon Thought, 10*(2), 62–75.

Chun, H. J. (2007). A study on erotic style of fashion. *International Journal of Costume and Fashion, 7*(2), 49–63.

Clarke, J. R. (1998). *Looking at lovemaking: Constructions of sexuality in Roman art, 100 B.C.–A.D. 250*. University of California Press.

Comfort, A. (2003). *The joy of sex*. Simon and Schuster.

Comfort, A., & Dial, L. K. (1991). Sexuality and aging. *An overview. Clinics in Geriatric Medicine, 7*(1), 1–7.

Cunningham, M. R., & Barbee, A. P. (1991). Differential K-selection versus ecological determinants of race differences in sexual behavior. *Journal of Research in Personality, 25*, 205–217.

Cunningham, M. R., Roberts, A. R., Barbee, A. P., Druen, P. B., & Wu, C. H. (1995). "Their ideas of beauty are, on the whole, the same as ours": Consistency and variability in the cross-cultural perception of female physical attractiveness. *Journal of Personality and Social Psychology, 68*(2), 261–279.

Cunningham, M. R., Barbee, A. P., & Philhower, C. L. (2002). Dimensions of facial physical attractiveness: The intersection of biology and culture. In G. Rhodes & L. A. Zebrowitz (Eds.), *Advances in visual cognition, Vol. 1. Facial attractiveness: Evolutionary, cognitive, and social perspectives* (pp. 193–238). Ablex Publishing.

Danesi, M. (2013). *The history of the kiss! The birth of popular culture*. Springer.

Darling-Wolf, F. (2004). Sites of attractiveness: Japanese women and Westernized representations of feminine beauty. *Critical Studies in Media Communication, 21*(4), 325–345.

De Munck, V. (2019). *Romantic love in America: Cultural models of gay, straight and polyamorous relationship*. Lexington Press.

De Munck, V. C., & Korotayev, A. (1999). Sexual equality and romantic love: A reanalysis of Rosenblatt's study on the function of romantic love. *Cross-Cultural Research, 33*, 265–277.

De Munck, V. C., & Korotayev, A. V. (2007). Wife–husband intimacy and female status in cross-cultural perspective. *Cross-Cultural Research, 41*(4), 307–335.

DeMello, M. (2007). *Encyclopedia of body adornment*. ABC-CLIO.

DeMello, M. (2012). *Faces around the world: A cultural encyclopedia of the human face*. ABC-CLIO.

DeMello, M. (2013). *Body studies: An introduction*. Routledge.

Eastwick, P. W., & Finkel, E. J. (2008). Sex differences in mate preferences revisited: Do people know what they initially desire in a romantic partner? *Journal of Personality and Social Psychology, 94*, 245–264.

Eastwick, P. W., Eagly, A. H., Finkel, E. J., & Johnson, S. E. (2011). Implicit and explicit preferences for physical attractiveness in a romantic partner: A double dissociation in predictive validity. *Journal of Personality and Social Psychology, 101*(5), 993–1011. https://doi.org/10.1037/a0024061

Eaton, A. A., & Rose, S. (2011). Has dating become more egalitarian? A 35 year review using sex roles. *Sex Roles, 64*(11–12), 843–862.

Fallon, A. (1990). Culture in the mirror: Sociocultural determinants of body image. In T. F. Cash & T. Pruzinsky (Eds.), *Body images: Development, deviance, and change* (pp. 80–109). Guilford Press.

Farrer, J., Tsuchiya, H., & Bagrowicz, B. (2008). Emotional expression in tsukiau dating relationships in Japan. *Journal of Social and Personal Relationships, 25*(1), 169–188.

Featherstone, M. (1998). Love and eroticism: An introduction. *Theory, Culture & Society, 15*(3–4), 1–18.

Feingold, A. (1990). Gender differences in effects of physical attractiveness on romantic attraction: A comparison across five research paradigms. *Journal of Personality and Social Psychology, 59*(5), 981–993.

Feldman, M., & Gordon, B. (Eds.). (2006). *The courtesan's arts: Cross-cultural perspectives includes CD*. Oxford University Press.

Fisher, H. E. (1992). *Anatomy of love: A natural history of monogamy, adultery, and divorce*. W. W. Norton.

Fletcher, G. J., Tither, J. M., O'Loughlin, C., Friesen, M., & Overall, N. (2004). Warm and homely or cold and beautiful? Sex differences in trading off traits in mate selection. *Personality and Social Psychology Bulletin, 30*(6), 659–672.

Fraser, R. (1998). Reviewed Works: *The vulgarization of art: The Victorians and aesthetic democracy* by Linda Dowling; *Eyes of love: The gaze in English and French paintings and novels 1840–1900* by Stephen Kern. *The Modern Language Review, 93*(1), 199–201. https://doi.org/10.2307/3733670

Fugère, M. A., Madden, S., & Cousins, A. J. (2019). The relative importance of physical attractiveness and personality characteristics to the mate choices of women and their fathers. *Evolutionary Psychological Science, 5*(4), 394–404.

Gagnon, J. H., & Simon, W. (1973/2017). *Sexual conduct: The social sources of human sexuality* (2nd ed.) Routledge.

Gala, J., & Kapadia, S. (2014). Romantic love, commitment and marriage in emerging adulthood in an Indian context: Views of emerging adults and middle adults. *Psychology and Developing Societies, 26*(1), 115–141.

Gebhard, P. H., & Johnson, A. B. (1998). *The Kinsey data: Marginal tabulations of the 1938–1963 interviews conducted by the Institute for Sex Research*. Indiana University Press.

Gilman, S. L. (2015). Posture is beauty. In C. Saunders, J. Macnaughton, & D. Fuller (Eds.), *The recovery of beauty: Arts, culture, medicine* (pp. 72–83). Palgrave Macmillan. https://doi.org/10.1057/9781137426741_5

Grabski, J. (1999). "Victoria Amoris": Titian's "Venus of Urbino." A commemorative allegory of marital love. *Artibus Et Historiae, 20*(40), 9–33. https://doi.org/10.2307/1483663

Grant, V. (1976). *Falling in love*. Springer.

Guttentag, M., & Secord, P. (1983). *Too many women?* Sage.

Hatfield, E., & Rapson, R. L. (1996). *Love and sex: Cross-cultural perspectives*. Allyn & Bacon.

Hatfield, E., & Rapson, R. L. (2005). *Love and sex: Cross-cultural perspectives* (2nd ed.). University Press of America.

Hite, S. (1976/2004). *The Hite report: A nationwide study of female sexuality*. Seven Stories Press (Originally published by Dell Publishing Company in 1976).

Hite, S. (1978/1987). *The Hite report on male sexuality*. Ballantine Books (Originally published by Knopf in 1978).

Holman, T. B., & Harding, J. R. (1996). The teaching of nonmarital sexual abstinence and members' sexual attitudes and behaviors: The case of Latter-Day Saints. *Review of Religious Research*, 51–60.

Hua, W. (2013). *Buying beauty: Cosmetic surgery in China*. Hong Kong University Press.

Hubbard, T. K. (Ed.). (2013). *A companion to Greek and Roman sexualities*. Wiley.

Hughes, S. M., Harrison, M. A., & Gallup, G. G., Jr. (2007). Sex differences in romantic kissing among college students: An evolutionary perspective. *Evolutionary Psychology, 5*(3), 612–631.

Impett, E. A., & Peplau, L. A. (2002). Why some women consent to unwanted sex with a dating partner: Insights from attachment theory. *Psychology of Women Quarterly, 26*(4), 360–370.

Ishigami, A., & Buckland, R. (2013). The reception of "Shunga" in the modern Era: From Meiji to the pre-WWII years. *Japan Review, 26*, 37–55.

Jankowiak, W. R., Volsche, S. L., & Garcia, J. R. (2015). Is the romantic–sexual kiss a near human universal? *American Anthropologist, 117*(3), 535–539.

Jassem, Z. A. (2013). The Arabic origins of "Love and Sexual Terms" in English and European languages: A lexical root theory approach. *International Journal of Language and Linguistics, 1*(4), 97–110. https://doi.org/10.11648/j.ijll.20130104.13

Jeffreys, S. (2005). *Beauty and misogyny: Harmful cultural practises in the West*. Routledge.

Jones, G. (2017). Globalizing Latin American beauty. *ReVista (Cambridge), 16*(3), 10–82.

Karandashev, V. (2017). *Romantic love in cultural contexts*. Springer.

Karandashev, V. (2019). *Cross-cultural perspectives on the experience and expression of love*. Springer.

Karandashev, V. (in press). Cross-cultural variation in relationship initiation. In J. K. Mogilski & T. K. Shackelford (Eds.), *The Oxford handbook of evolutionary psychology and romantic relationships*. Oxford Publishing.

Karandashev, V., & Fata, B. (2014). Change in physical attraction in early romantic relationships. *An International Journal on Personal Relationships, 8*(2), 257–267.

Karandashev, V., Zarubko, E., Artemeva, V., Neto, F., Surmanidze, L., & Feybesse, C. (2016). Sensory values in romantic attraction in four Europeans countries: Gender and cross-cultural comparison. *Cross-Cultural Research, 50*(5), 478–504. https://doi.org/10.1177/1069397116674446

Karandashev, V., Evans, N. D., Zarubko, E., Neto, F., Evans, M., Artemeva, V., … Surmanidze, L. (2020). Physical attraction scale – Short version: Cross-cultural validation. *Journal of Relationships Research, 11*.

Karandashev, V., Zarubko, E., Artemeva, V., Evans, M., Morgan, K. A. D., Neto, F., Feybesse, C., Surmanidze, L., & Purvis, J. (2020). Cross-cultural comparison of sensory preferences in romantic attraction. *Sexuality & Culture, 24*(1), 23–53. https://doi.org/10.1007/s12119-019-09628-0

Kenrick, D. T., Groth, G. E., Trost, M. R., & Sadalla, E. K. (1993). Integrating evolutionary and social exchange perspectives on relationships: Effects of gender, self-appraisal, and involvement level on mate selection criteria. *Journal of Personality and Social Psychology, 64*(6), 951–969. https://doi.org/10.1037/0022-3514.64.6.951

Kern, S. (1996). *Eyes of love: The gaze in English and French paintings and novels, 1840-1900*. Reaktion Books.

Kim, J. S., & Yoon, J. H. (2005). Image perception of modern fashion according to erotic expressions and erotic levels. *Journal of the Korean Society of Clothing and Textiles, 29*(2), 318–327.

Kinsey, A. C., Pomeroy, W. B., Martin, C. E., & Gebhard, P. H. (1998a). *Sexual behavior in the human female*. Indiana University Press (Originally published in 1948 by W. B. Saunders Company).

Kinsey, A. C., Pomeroy, W. B., Martin, C. E., & Gebhard, P. H. (1998b). *Sexual behavior in the human female*. Indiana University Press (Originally published in 1953 by W. B. Saunders Company).

Kirshenbaum, S. (2011). *The science of kissing: What our lips are telling us*. Grand Central Publishing.

Langlois, J. H., Kalakanis, L., Rubenstein, A. J., Larson, A., Hallam, M., & Smoot, M. (2000). Maxims or myths of beauty? A meta-analytic and theoretical review. *Psychological Bulletin, 126*(3), 390–423.

Larson, D. R. (1983). Sexuality and Christian ethics. *A Report from Argentina Second Thoughts on Military Service Inside the Weimar Institute, 15*(1), 10–18.

Leist, A. (2003). What makes bodies beautiful. *The Journal of Medicine and Philosophy, 28*(2), 187–219.

Lewis, C. S. (1960). *The four loves*. Harcourt, Brace and Company.

Lokken, K. L., Worthy, S. L., & Trautmann, J. (2004). Examining the links among magazine preference, levels of awareness and internalization of sociocultural appearance standards, and presence of eating-disordered symptoms in college women. *Family and Consumer Sciences Research Journal, 32*(4), 361–381.

Lomas, T. (2018). The flavours of love: A cross-cultural lexical analysis. *Journal for the Theory of Social Behaviour, 48*, 134–152.

Maner, J. K., & Ackerman, J. M. (2020). Ecological sex ratios and human mating. *Trends in Cognitive Sciences, 24*(2), 98–100.

Marshall, D. S. (1971). Sexual behavior on Mangaia. In D. S. Marshall & R. C. Suggs (Eds.), *Human sexual behavior* (pp. 103–162). Basic Books.

Masters, W. H., & Johnson, V. E. (1966). *Human sexual response*. Little Brown.

Masters, W., & Johnson, V. (1970). *Human sexual inadequacy*. Little Brown.

Masters, W. H., Johnson, V. E., & Kolodny, R. C. (1986). *Masters and Johnson on sex and human loving*. Little, Brown and Company.

Moss, J. H., & Maner, J. K. (2016). Biased sex ratios influence fundamental aspects of human mating. *Personality and Social Psychology Bulletin, 42*(1), 72–80.

Nussbaum, M. C., & Sihvola, J. (Eds.). (2019). *The sleep of reason: Erotic experience and sexual ethics in Ancient Greece and Rome*. University of Chicago Press.

Oliveira, M. M. (2013). Dressing, seducing and signifying: From the symbolic dimension of fashion to the contemporary erotic imagery. *Comunicação e sociedade, 24*, 152–160. https://doi.org/10.17231/comsoc.24(2013).1781

Orsini, F. (Ed.). (2006). *Love in South Asia*. Cambridge University Press.

Osborn, D. R. (1996). Beauty is as beauty does? Makeup and posture effects on physical attractiveness judgments. *Journal of Applied Social Psychology, 26*(1), 31–51.

Peiss, K. (2011). *Hope in a jar: The making of America's beauty culture*. University of Pennsylvania Press.

Poran, M. A. (2002). Denying diversity: Perceptions of beauty and social comparison processes among Latina, Black, and White women. *Sex Roles, 47*(1–2), 65–81.

Prettejohn, E. (2005). *Beauty and art: 1750-2000*. Oxford University Press.

Regan, P. C., & Berscheid, E. (1997). Gender differences in characteristics desired in a potential sexual and marriage partner. *Journal of Psychology & Human Sexuality, 9*(1), 25–37.

Regnerus, M., & Uecker, J. (2011). *Premarital sex in America: How young Americans meet, mate, and think about marrying*. Oxford University Press.

Riess, J. (2015). Mormon popular culture. In T. L. Givens & P. L. Barlow (Eds.), *The Oxford Handbook of Mormonism* (1st ed., pp. 439–453). Oxford University Press.

Roche, J. P. (1986). Premarital sex: Attitudes and behavior by dating stage. *Adolescence, 21*, 107–121.

Rubin, L. B. (1990). *Erotic wars: What happened to the sexual revolution?* Farrar, Straus & Giroux.

Sands, N. B., & Adamson, P. A. (2014). Global facial beauty: Approaching a unified aesthetic ideal. *Facial Plastic Surgery, 30*(02), 093–100.

Sangrador, J. L., & Yela, C. (2000). What is beautiful is loved': Physical attractiveness in love relationships in a representative sample. *Social Behavior and Personality: An International Journal, 28*(3), 207–218. https://doi.org/10.2224/sbp.2000.28.3.207

Saraceni, R., & Russell-Mayhew, S. (2007). Images and ideals: Counselling women and girls in a 'thin-is-in' culture. *Canadian Journal of Counselling, 41*(2), 91–106.

Schmitt, D. P., & Buss, D. M. (2000). Sexual dimensions of person description: Beyond or subsumed by the Big Five? *Journal of Research in Personality, 34*(2), 141–177.

Skinner, M. B. (2013). *Sexuality in Greek and Roman culture*. Wiley.

Stone, E. A., Shackelford, T. K., & Buss, D. M. (2007). Sex ratio and mate preferences: A cross-cultural investigation. *European Journal of Social Psychology, 37*(2), 288–296.

Swami, V. (2015). Cultural influences on body size ideals: Unpacking the impact of westernisation and modernisation. *European Psychologist, 20*, 44–51. https://doi.org/10.1027/1016-9040/a000150

Swami, V., & Furnham, A. (Eds.). (2007). *The body beautiful: Evolutionary and sociocultural perspectives*. Springer.

Swami, V., Weis, L., Barron, D., & Furnham, A. (2018). Positive body image is positively associated with hedonic (emotional) and eudaimonic (psychological and social) well-being in British adults. *The Journal of Social Psychology, 158*(5), 541–552. https://doi.org/10.1080/00224545.2017.1392278

Tannahill, R. (1992). *Sex in history* (2nd ed.). Scarborough House.

Tillich, P. (1954). *Love, power, and justice*. Oxford University Press.

Tovée, M. J., Swami, V., Furnham, A., & Mangalparsad, R. (2006). Changing perceptions of attractiveness as observers are exposed to a different culture. *Evolution and Human Behavior, 27*(6), 443–456.

Vout, C. (2013). *Sex on show: Seeing the erotic in Greece and Rome*. University of California Press.

Wheeler, L., & Kim, Y. (1997). What is beautiful is culturally good: The physical attractiveness stereotype has different content in collectivistic cultures. *Personality and Social Psychology Bulletin, 23*(8), 795–800.

Wilson, J. (1980). *Love, sex, and feminism: A philosophical essay*. Praeger.

Wlodarski, R., & Dunbar, R. I. (2013). Examining the possible functions of kissing in romantic relationships. *Archives of Sexual Behavior, 42*(8), 1415–1423.

Wolf, N. (1991). *The beauty myth: How images of beauty are used against women*. William Morrow and Company.

Ward, J. (2015). *Not gay: Sex between straight white men*. NYU Press.

Workman, N. V. (1996). From Victorian to Victoria's Secret: The foundations of modern erotic wear. *Journal of Popular Culture, 30*(2), 61.

Yan, Y., & Bissell, K. (2014). The globalization of beauty: How is ideal beauty influenced by globally published fashion and beauty magazines? *Journal of Intercultural Communication Research, 43*(3), 194–214.

Chapter 5
Models of Passionate and Affectionate Love

5.1 The Model of Passionate Love

5.1.1 The Attributes of Passionate Love Model

On the Concept of Passion

The term *passion* defines *intensity characteristic of emotions* that people experience in their lives (Solomon, 1995; Vallerand, 2010, 2015; Vallerand et al., 2003). Dualistic model of passion (Vallerand, 2010, 2015) conceptualizes its two distinctive types: harmonious and obsessive passions. The first one represents adaptive emotional experience, while the second one is maladaptive. These two types of passion are assessed with the *Passion Scale* available in English and French (Marsh et al., 2013).

People experiencing passion feel more active, emotionally energetic, devoted, and spend more time doing what they like. In moderation and under control, *passion* inspires human motivation and actions. It is conducive for optimal performance (Vallerand et al., 2003). On another end, individuals with extreme passion can feel as slaves of emotions with the lack of control on their cognitions, actions, and life. This is the case of *obsessional passion*.

Passion characterizes the level of arousal of any emotional process. It is not emotion itself, but rather the attribute of the high intensity of any emotion. In the same vein, passion can characterize highly passionate mood, attitude, or traits. Therefore, it would be worthwhile to use the *word passion* more specifically: the *passion of love*, the *passion of hate*, the *passion for caring*, and others. Some cultures endorse the highly passionate emotional life, while the others discourage experience and expression of passion (see for review, Karandashev, 2021a, 2021b).

The Greek word *pathos* and Latin *pati* ("to suffer," "*be* pathetic") are in the origins of this English *word passion*. Another Greek word *meraki* means an experience of *ardor*, deep fondness, and longing for a particular activity. The term *passion* as

V. Karandashev, *Cultural Typologies of Love*,
https://doi.org/10.1007/978-3-031-05343-6_5

characterizing intense desires, strong emotions, and other affects has the cross-cultural equivalencies, which were identified in other languages and cultures (e.g., Farrer, Tsuchiya, & Bagrowicz, 2008; Lomas, 2018; Solomon, 1995).

Romantics of passionate love tend to equate love with strong and eternal passion as the forever lasting passionate feelings of high intensity (de Roda et al., 1999). The reality of the love course, however, differs from this myth. Sooner or later, two possible scripts evolve: either "the old-time fire is gone," or "the fiery passion died down and gave way to warm affection."

The Passion of Love

Modern theories of love have proposed the concept of *passion* as the most distinctive emotional experience of passionate and romantic love (e.g., Berscheid, 1985, 2010; Berscheid & Walster, 1974, 1969/1978; Hatfield, 1988; Hatfield & Rapson, 1987, 1993; Hatfield & Sprecher, 1986). Across various disciplines, passion is considered as the key feature of *passionate model of love*.

Passion of love is a bundle of strong emotions (such as interest, admiration, excitement, despair, hate, attraction, sexual desire, love) accompanied by several physiological symptoms, such as high body temperature, blushing, and increased heartbeat. Passion makes a person exclusively active, full of high emotional energy and attention. It is a blast of longing and yearning toward a person. Sexual drive is fuel for passion. The explicit or sublimated sexual arousal and sexual drive bring a powerful fuel for the *passionate model of love*.

The intense and strong passion of love can be emotionally burning for a lover (e.g., "I am *burning* with love") that is figuratively expressed in the "fire" and "heat" metaphors, such as "my heart is on fire" (Kövecses, 1990). These conceptual metaphors are present in Western as well as Eastern literary traditions and verbal expressions in many cultures (e.g., Chang & Li, 2006; Lv & Zhang, 2012, see for review, Karandashev, 2019) and languages, such as French, German, Russian, Slovenian, Albanian, Greek, Turkish, Chinese, and Indian.

Passion of love expresses intensity of emotional experience and expression. This is not a single emotion or attitudes, but rather a bunch of strong emotions, which may include joy, happiness, jealousy, anger, and others. *Passion* is the key and the most salient emotion of a person in *passionate love*, yet it is not the only one.

The Model of Passionate Love

A variety of strong and ardent emotions may be involved in passionate love: *longing*, *fear of rejection*, *frustration*, *hatred*, etc. It is usually associated with *sexual desire* and *physical attraction*, like "I felt *hot* all over when I saw her."

Passionate love is a complex experience of intense longing for interpersonal union; it is strong attraction and absorption of lovers, when moods fluctuate between ecstasy and anguish, between joy and pain, between intense pleasure and suffering

(Berscheid & Walster, 1969/1978; Hatfield & Rapson, 1993). Other experiences that are typically associated with this kind of love are the experience of *being-in-love* and *obsession with love*, *infatuation,* and sometimes the symptoms of *lovesickness* (Hatfield & Rapson, 1987, 1993; Sperling & Berman, 1991; Spitzberg & Cupach, 1998; Sternberg, 1986; Tallis, 2004; Tennov, 1979/1998).

Passionate lovers frequently perceive their partner as a special and remarkable individual, uniquely different from others. In this regard, *passionate love* can be *romantic*, but not necessarily—see the *model of romantic love* in the following sections. When love is reciprocated (union with a partner), it is accompanied by the feeling of fulfillment and ecstasy, while being unrequited (separation), it is accompanied by the feelings of emptiness, anxiety, or despair (Hatfield & Rapson, 1993; Karandashev & Clapp, 2016). Passionate lovers implicitly believe that overwhelming intense passionate feelings will last forever.

Passionate cultural models of love, frequently engaging *romantic fantasies,* valorize the dreams and exist in unreal life. For some young men and women, romantic love with its sexually oriented passion is a way to kill their boredom of life. A person, who has fallen passionately in love, tends to think obsessively about his/her lover, relationship, and does not think about anything else. The person weaves his/her own fantasies and dreams and remains lost in the real world. This model of love is a chance to flee from the world of real life and avoid the daily routine. It is a chance to escape from duties and responsibilities.

Functions of Passionate Love

This passionate model of love is representative for the early stage of relationship initiation when a person is falling in love. The young people experience it more frequently than the older do, but not necessarily. Men are more prone to it than women are (Berscheid, 1985, 2010; Berscheid & Walster, 1974, 1969/1978; Hatfield, 1988; Hatfield & Rapson, 1993; Karandashev & Clapp, 2016; Sprecher & Regan, 1998). A variety of experiences and expressions of this type of love is ultimately associated—explicitly or implicitly—with sexual interests and feelings.

Several researchers have proposed that *passionate love* has an evolutionary function (e.g., Buss, 1988; Fisher, 2004; Fletcher, Simpson, Campbell, & Overall, 2015). Passionate attraction and love emotions work as an emotional glue for pair bonding, as a "commitment device" that motivate men and women to stay together to rear a child (Fisher, 2004; Fletcher et al., 2015). Therefore, they were supposed to love passionately for about four years—the period sufficient to conceive and take care of a child until he/she is grown enough to survive. The fading passion after this four-year relationship should be evolutionary natural (Fisher, 2004).

Passionate love can play its cultural function in dating and mating; however, cultural values and norms of emotional life substantially vary in this regard (see more in Karandashev, 2021a, 2021b). Multiple studies (see for review, Lim, 2016) have shown that *Western cultural norms* endorse *high arousal emotions* more than low arousal emotions. Opposite to this, *Eastern cultural norms favor low arousal emotions* more than high arousal emotions. These culturally normative differences can be attributed to individualistic values of Western cultures, compared to collectivistic values of Eastern cultures.

5.2 Ubiquitous Passionate Love Across Cultures

5.2.1 The Model of Passionate Love as a Cultural Idea

Cultural Origins of the Passionate Model of Love

Extensive research has demonstrated that the *model of passionate love,* as a cultural idea, has been ubiquitous across times and cultures. The *love* with *passion* has been a major topic of poetry, music, songs, and dances for centuries and in modern times (see for review, e.g., Cooper, 2021; Karandashev, 2017; Messina, 1903; Washabaugh, 2020; Wolfe-Ralph, 1995). The stories of passionate love have been numerous and widespread in different historical periods and in many societies. The Eastern and Western literatures—dating back hundreds of years—present abundance of real and fictional stories of passion, obsession, violence, and devotion (see for review, Hatfield, 1988; Hatfield & Rapson, 1996, 2005; Karandashev, 2017; Lieberman & Hatfield, 2006).

Passionate model of love, along with romantic ideas, became quite evident in the poetry and music of *courtly love* appeared in the south of France in the twelfth century, borrowed from the cultures of Moslem Spain. *Troubadours*—poets and musicians—created poems and songs which expressed the passionate and ennobling power of love. The strong and burning passion was the key feature of love. However, it was mostly adulterous love of the knights and other aristocracies (Karandashev, 2017).

Although the passionate love has been a cultural reality of educated aristocracy and gentry, the *model of passionate love* as a *cultural idea* has not been widespread and popular among many other people. We also do not know how largely individuals of the upper, middle, and low social class really experienced passionate love in their life. Cultures were not conducive to the *passionate love* in relations. We do not know how much the commoners of that time shared those cultural ideas and rituals of passionate adulterous love and adventures.

Emergence of the Cultural Model of Passionate Love

The Western *cultural model of passionate love* originated and inspired by Lord Byron (1788–1824)—the great English poet of the eighteenth to nineteenth centuries (Solomon, 1995) who was the leading hero of the Romantic movement. *Passionate semantics* of love began to spread in cultural discourse and constituted a symbolic code of communication in several European societies since the second part of the eighteenth century.

Historical research (Luhmann, 1986) has shown that cultural developments of that time lead to the formation of the two *cultural models of love*: *the amour passion* concept of the French and the Puritans' concept of *companionship marriage*. The semantics of *amour passion* was complex and well-elaborated to re-evaluate sexuality that occurred in the eighteenth century. The English, having a preliminary basis for *integration of love and marriage*, evolved into the Victorian model characterized by malformation of sexual morality. The seventeenth- and eighteenth-century novels substantially promoted corresponding *cultural models of love*. The cultural code expressed in those narratives encouraged people to experience appropriate feelings.

The popularity of the *passionate love* as *a cultural model* has been gradually growing since then in Western countries. Romantic novels, poems, art, music. and later cinema have promoted it (see for review, Karandashev, 2017). This tendency continues in modern times.

Nowadays, novels, movies, and songs highly valorize and propagate the *values of passion* in *American cultural model of love*. For instance, the tones of modern songs have high *intensity* and *pitch*, the strong words of *crash* and crazy inspire people to feel the same way—highly passionate. Sometimes, it appears like young people enjoy *being crazy* and *crashed*—the words typically associated with dramatic and frustrated experiences. The same role may play the Spanish songs and the Argentine tango which express high passionate emotions (Washabaugh, 2020; Wolfe-Ralph, 1995).

Cross-cultural Ubiquity of Passionate Love

Passionate love feelings are reflected in many cultural ideas and phenomena, as well as in the real life of many people. The questions remain (1) how much and how often, (2) what the value of passion in different cultures is. The modern comprehensive anthropological studies of 1990s demonstrated that passionate love is present as a cultural concept in 89% of contemporary societies (Jankowiak, 1995; Jankowiak & Fischer, 1992).

This basic *human experience of passion* manifests itself in the lexical forms in many cultural contexts. A conceptual metaphor "my heart is on fire" (Kövecses, 1988, 1990) reflects the *intensity* aspect of *passion*. The word *passion* is present in many languages and frequently associated with human body (see for review, Kovecses, 2000, 2003; Solomon, 1995). The metaphors "heat" and "fire" featuring passionate love are widely present in many languages and various cultures, such as English, Chinese, Portuguese, French, Indian, German, Russian, Greek, Persian, Turkish, Albanian, and others (Chang & Li, 2006; Lv & Zhang, 2012, p. 356, see for review Karandashev, 2019).

5.2.2 Cultural Values and Experiences of Passionate Love

Cultural Values of Passionate Love

Cultural models of love include *culturally specific values, attitudes, and norms* regarding various aspects of individual attitudes, experiences, expressions of love, which people are expected, encouraged, advised, or permitted to have, as well as the relationships, which they can engage in.

Despite its presence as a cultural notion and real personal experience, the *cultural values* of *passionate love* in societies differ. People in many cultural contexts may feel love as a cluster of *passionate emotions* (see for review, Karandashev, 2017, 2019), yet the *cultural value* of passionate experience in love differs.

Western cultures normatively favor a *passionate ideal* of living, strong emotions, and their open expressions (see for review, Karandashev, 2021a, 2021b). Therefore, in Western European and North American cultural contexts, passionate *love* is a desirable ideal for the relationship, emotional experience, and expression.

On the other hand, Eastern cultures favor a *dispassionate ideal* of life when experience and expression of passion are unwelcome and should be moderated. The *emotions of modest intensity* are permissible and acceptable by cultural norms. Therefore, in the East Asian cultural contexts, *passionate love* is less desirable for the emotional experience, expression, and relationship (Dion & Dion, 1988; Solomon, 1995; Toro-Morn & Sprecher, 2003).

Passionate Versus Dispassionate Emotions of Love

Cultures can affect *experience* and *expression* of emotions by regulating their expression or suppression. Some cultural beliefs emphasize *emotional expression*, whereas others emphasize *emotional control*. The Western and Eastern cultural differences in this regard are quite distinctive and originate from Lord Byron—English poet—who inspired a *passionate ideal*, and Buddhist bodhisattvas—enlightened beings—who inspired *dispassionate ideal* of love (Solomon, 1995). Studies explored the cultural norms of experience and expression of emotions in various cultural contexts (see for review, Karandashev, 2021a, 2021b). For example, people in Scandinavian cultures (e.g., Sweden and Finland) tend to be inhibited in their expression of emotion, while people in other European cultures (e.g., Ireland and Italy), are inclined to express their emotion openly. Studies found differences in passionate vs. dispassionate ideals of emotions in Western cultures (e.g., USA) vs. Eastern cultures (e.g., China). The cultural diversity of high, moderate, and low in passion love experience and expression are presented in detail elsewhere (Karandashev, 2021a, 2021b).

The Values and Experience of Passionate Love in Individualistic and Collectivistic Cultures

Experience of passionate love might be associated with the degree of individualism and collectivism as a cultural dimension of societies. In individualistic cultures more than in collectivistic cultures cultural norms cherish passionate love. Passionate love in collectivistic cultures is viewed as disturbing for the tradition of family-approved and arranged marriages (Kim & Hatfield, 2004; Yildirim & Barnett, 2017).

What factors affect the experience of passion in collectivistic cultures? In the societies of this type, *family allocentrism,* as the strength of closeness and devotion between family members, and *parental influence*, as the authority parents have over their children's choices contribute to the love emotions (Bejanyan, Marshall, & Ferenczi, 2015). The contradicting tendencies potentially create an ambivalent experience of love. Due to *family allocentrism,* people in collectivistic social context are under the upward pressure on their experience of passion. On another end, due to high *parental influence,* they are under the concurrent downward pressure on the experience of passion. While the higher family allocentrism increases their passion, the greater acceptance of parental influence on their mate choice affects their decreased passion in love.

The Individual Culturally Specific Preferences in the Experience of Love

Despite expected cross-cultural *similarity* of *passionate love* as a biologically based emotional experience, the *intensity of love emotions* varies across cultures depending on cultural affordances and norms. Cultural values of passionate and dispassionate living affect people's experiences and expressions of love (Karandashev, 2019).

Cultural models of emotions prevalent in cultures considerably reflect on the *experience and expression of passionate love*, mediating the intensity of emotional arousal and passion (Karandashev, 2021a, 2021b). According to multiple studies (see for review, Lim, 2016), people in some Western cultures (e.g., European Americans) prefer to feel emotions of high arousal more frequently than of low arousal. On the other side, people in Eastern-Asian cultures have preference of low arousal emotions more than of high arousal. It is likely that individual experiences of love embody these cultural preferences in general emotional arousal. In Western *passionate cultures* of self-expression, love resembles the *passionate model of love*, while in Eastern *cultures of moderation,* love is more in accord with *affectionate,* or even *dispassionate models of love*.

5.2.3 Experience and Expression of Passionate Love Across Cultures

Cross-cultural Variation in the Experience and Expression of Passionate Love

Psychological experience of passion is grounded in human biology. *Passionate feelings of love* are deeply rooted in the neurophysiological nature of emotions (e.g., Aron et al., 2005; Fisher, 2004; Hatfield & Rapson, 1993, 2009). Therefore, it is reasonable to believe that people experience passion similar across cultures.

The early research suggested that *passionate love* is a cross-culturally universal. Further investigation revealed that people in many cultures experience *passionate love* quite similar (Hatfield, 1988; Hatfield & Rapson, 1987, 1996; Karandashev, 2017; Lieberman & Hatfield, 2006; Reddy, 2012).

The studies using *Passionate Love Scale*, PLS (Hatfield & Sprecher, 1986) demonstrated that the scores on this scale do not differ statistically significantly between respondents in many cultures (e.g., Doherty, Hatfield, Thompson, & Choo, 1994; Hatfield & Rapson, 1996). In some studies, participants in individualistic or collectivistic cultural contexts reported the *same degree of intensity of passionate love,* while in others, researchers found small differences (e.g., Yildirim & Barnett, 2017, see for detailed review, Karandashev, 2019). One study using Triangular Love Scale (Sternberg, 1997) found that the Americans were higher on the *score of passion* than the Chinese (Gao, 2001).

Some scholars believe that Africans and African Americans have more emotional intense experience, greater emotional expressiveness, and therefore, should have higher intensity of passion (Dixon, 1976; White & Parham, 1990). However, empirical evidence of these claims is available so far in cross-cultural studies. Few general differences were found between Blacks and Whites in emotional experience and facial expressiveness depending on the context of interaction (Vrana & Rollock, 2002).

Multiple cross-cultural studies (see for detailed review, Karandashev, 2021a, 2021b) have demonstrated the distinctive and often substantial differences between *passionate, affectionate, and dispassionate cultural models of emotional experience*, between *expressive and nonexpressive cultural models of emotions, between the cultural models of direct and indirect expression of emotions.* These differences are typically between Western and Eastern cultures. Nevertheless, there are significant variations in intensity of passionate emotions and expressivity within each of these cultural groups. Therefore, it is likely that these emotional differences should reflect on the passionate, affectionate, and dispassionate experience of love, as well as on the high or low expressiveness in love. The research of these differences with valid measures and scales are still scarce in empirical studies of individuals.

Cross-cultural Dimensionality of Passionate Love

It should be noted that *Passionate Love Scale* (PLS) measures not only passion of love, but also several other closely associated love feelings. The items of the scale assess a *passionate model of love* in several experiential representations. The use of traditional factor analysis, however, did not allow identifying the constituent components of this type of love. There were two major methodological pitfalls of many cultural studies using *Passionate Love Scale*. First, all item scores were averaged in one total score of passionate love, thus neglecting the possible differences in its components. Second, these total scores of passionate love were used to compute the mean score within each cultural sample, thus neglecting individual and typological variation within each sample.

The later exploration of *Passionate Love Scale*, PLS, showed (Landis & O'Shea III, 2000) that passionate love may have different factor structures in different cultural samples. The data collected in nine samples in North America, Europe, the Middle East, and Pacific Islands and analyzed in three-mode multidimensional scaling with points of view solutions (Tzeng & Landis, 1978, 1979) revealed that *passionate love* is a multifactorial construct and can be defined differently in cultures.

The authors (Landis & O'Shea III, 2000) identified that the variance of the PLS data across cultural samples has a 6-factor group-common structure: Factor 1, Commitment versus Affection; Factor 2, Insecurity versus Security; Factor 3, Other-Centered versus Self-Centered; Factor 4, Instability versus Stability; Factor 5, Affective Longing versus Physical Longing; and Factor 6, Physical Affection versus Cognitive Affection.

Hierarchical clustering with 3M-POV methodology discovered that across nine cultural samples there are six idealized cultures. Further principal component analysis identified different factor structures which are specific for each cultural group, yet they did not reflect the pattern of six group-common factors. The subgroup factors have the group-specific patterns, which are still related to each other. In addition, such factors as Protective Intimacy versus Tender Intimacy, Realistic Closeness versus Idealistic Closeness, and Excitement versus Melancholy are unique.

Thus, the results of those studies (Landis & O'Shea III, 2000) showed that the *structure of passionate love model* may be more complex than the other cultural studies identified. Employing the advanced statistical analyses, such as cluster analysis, latent class analysis, and other new methods of factors analysis, can be advantageous for the construction of more complex structures of *passionate model of love*, within which a comparison of passionate love across cultures brings many interesting new results (see for detailed review, Karandashev, 2019, 2021a, 2021b).

Eros Love Attitudes Across Cultures

Many researchers (see for detailed review, Karandashev, 2019) have employed the *Love Attitude Scale* (LAS, Hendrick & Hendrick, 1986; Hendrick, Hendrick, & Dicke, 1998) to assess love in different cultural samples, interpreting the scores on

Eros subscale as a measure of passion, or passionate love. The data with LAS have been obtained for multicultural (within country), as well as in cross-national comparisons (see for detailed review, Karandashev, 2019).

Some studies revealed no cross-cultural difference in passion measured as *eros love attitude*. Several studies, conducted in the USA (Hawaii, Florida, California), some countries across Europe (France, Portugal, Switzerland), Africa (Angola, Cape Verde, Mozambique), Asia (Macao), and South America (Brazil), showed that *passion* is similar across cultures (Doherty et al., 1994; Hatfield & Rapson, 1996; Hendrick et al., 1998; Hendrick & Hendrick, 1986; Lieberman & Hatfield, 2006; Murstein, Merighi, & Vyse, 1991; Neto et al., 2000), with some exceptions. Another study of Neto and his colleagues (Neto, 2007) also revealed no cross-cultural differences in the *eros* love attitude among British, Portuguese, and Indian participants. Other study collected data in Britain and Turkey (Sanri & Goodwin, 2013) and revealed no significant cultural differences in *eros* love attitudes. Participants in Spanish speaking and Latin-American countries generally demonstrated the high *eros* love attitude, however, no cultural differences were found between Hispanic-, Latino-, and Anglo-Americans in the USA (Contreras, Hendrick, & Hendrick, 1996; Leon, Parra, Cheng, & Flores, 1995; Pérez, Fiol, Guzmán, Palmer, & Buades, 2009; Ubillos et al., 2001). These results support the earlier findings that passion of love might be cross-culturally universal.

As for the cross-cultural differences, these were typically small, but statistically significant. Asian participants in the USA and Canada were lower in their *eros,* compared to White and Black participants (Dion & Dion, 1988; Hendrick & Hendrick, 1986).

In the study of Sprecher and her colleagues (Sprecher et al., 1994), administered in Japan, Russia, and the USA, *eros* love attitude was considerably lower among Japanese, compared to Americans and Russians. The authors explained these differences by high influence of European romantic ideology on Russian and American culture, compared to Eastern Buddhist ideology, which influenced Japanese culture. Despite these cultural differences, the Japanese are not dispassionate in love. The study of the narratives of informants involved in dating (*tsukiau*) relationships revealed passion (*netsujou*) as the key experience of love (Farrer et al., 2008).

Another study (Goodwin & Findlay, 1997) showed that Chinese participants were less passionate in their *eros* love attitude, compared to British. Gao (2001) investigated passion with corresponding subscale of Triangular Love Scale and found that passion is substantially higher among Americans, compared to Chinese.

In the study of Neto and his colleagues that was mentioned above (Neto et al., 2000), the researchers revealed few relatively small cross-cultural differences among several European and African countries. However, they found the significant difference between Macao (as Chinese culture), where participants were lower in their *eros* love attitude, and Portuguese (as European culture). This finding coincides with other data that demonstrated the lower passion among Asians compared to Europeans.

Although the studies cited above revealed high *eros* love attitude in Spanish speaking and Latin-American countries (Pérez et al., 2009; Ubillos et al., 2001), yet participants in Mexico (Leon et al., 1995) showed low rating of *eros* love attitude, while in the USA, the Hispanic-, Latino-, and Anglo-Americans showed no differences in this attitude (Contreras et al., 1996).

Commonality and Variation in the Cultural Models of Passionate Love

The studies of *passion* throughout recent several decades have demonstrated that it is a key *experience of passionate love* in Western as well as in Eastern cultures. Such experience of passion is high in many cultures with relatively minor differences from culture to culture. When the differences were found, they were quite small, sometimes statistically significant, sometimes not. These inconsistencies might be due to several methodology issues, which are discussed in the following section, and the lack of comprehensive cross-cultural studies.

Eastern-Western differences are the most pronounced across cultures. People in Eastern cultures (such as Japan, China, and India) had the lower scores on *passion*, compared to European (France, Portugal, Britain, Switzerland, Spain) and North American (the USA and Canada). Participants in Spanish-speaking and Latin-American countries were high on passion, with low scores in Mexico, yet it is difficult to compare with other cultures because there were no studies with direct comparison. It is worth noting (see for detailed review, Karandashev, 2019) that the cross-cultural studies of passionate love have been quite sporadic, patchy, and piecemeal. Their results provide limited knowledge for the construction of *comprehensive cultural passionate love models*.

Thus, the data on cross-cultural similarities and differences in passionate love are quite inconsistent. Many researchers conclude that the *model of passionate love* is universal across cultures. This might be true due to strong neurophysiological roots of passion. However, other scholars have shown reasonable expectation and evidence of a cultural diversity of passionate love (see for review, Karandashev, 2017, 2019, 2021a, 2021b). The solution of this seeming controversy can lie in the current methodology available for assessment.

5.3 Affectionate Models of Love

5.3.1 On the Concept of Affection

Since the Ancient scholarship and across cultures, *affection* was a distinct emotional experience of love. The Greek word *chōros,* which is distinct from *meraki* as *ardor*, stands for *affection*—moderately passionate emotion—as being spiritually rooted in a specific place. The emotional experience of *chōros* combines *meraki* as *ardor* with *érōs* as sensual love, aroused by physical appearance (Lomas, 2018). Thus, the *chōros* word may express the rooted connections of moderate arousal, which is related to various things.

The scholars and laypeople of the eighteenth to nineteenth centuries and early twentieth century commonly used the word *affection* in their lexicon of love, while in recent decades, the word *passion* became more widespread in the Western English-speaking literature.

Affection is a kind of *passion*, yet of a moderate degree. It is a calmer and less emotionally aroused experience of a lesser intensity. While the *passion* is an intense emotional experience of love, the *affection* encompasses less intense and calmer affectionate sentiments toward partner. The feelings of *affection* are closely associated with tenderness, admiration, respect, appreciation, being considerate, gentle, and subtle in compliments (Karandashev & Evans, 2019). The lovers experience immense affection, and feel a high physical and personality attraction to their loved ones. In affectionate companionate love, love can be expressed in "She feels *warm* all over when her husband comes home from work." Experiences of *affection* are the quietly glowing, fond, tender, warm, and deeply personal feelings.

The modern English commonly refers to *affection* as the core experience and expression of love. For instance, the dictionaries (e.g., *American Heritage Dictionary, Merriam-Webster Dictionary,* and *The Random House College Dictionary*) include in their *definitions of love* a strong *feeling of affection* and concern for another person, a profoundly *tender, passionate affection* for a person, *affection* and *tenderness* felt by lovers (e.g., Love, n.d. https://www.ahdictionary.com/word/search.html?q=love). This affectionate and tender feelings of love can arise in kinship, close friendship, sexual, romantic, and other love relationships. Therefore, they can characterize the qualities of romantic, companionate, parental, and other models of love (e.g., Floyd, 2001, 2006; Gerhardt, 2014; Gulledge, Gulledge, & Stahmannn, 2003; Horan & Booth-Butterfield, 2010; Karandashev & Evans, 2019; Lawton, Silverstein, & Bengtson, 1994; Li, 1999).

The construct of affection can characterize the affectionate emotions and attitudes, as well as affectionate expressions and communication in love relationships. Researchers have explored several love attitudes of affection (Karandashev & Evans, 2019) and communication of affection (Floyd, 2002; Floyd et al., 2005; Floyd & Morman, 1998), along with development of appropriate measurement instruments.

Cross-cultural studies have identified *affection* among the most prototypical terms of emotional lexicon belonging to the love category in the American English, in the Bahasa Indonesian (an Austronesian language), in the Chinese language, and in the Basque language lexicons, which are culturally and linguistically different (Alonso-Arbiol et al., 2006; Shaver, Murdaya, & Fraley, 2001; Shaver, Schwartz, Kirson, & O'Connor, 1987; Shaver, Wu, & Schwartz, 1992).

5.3.2 *Affectionate Versus Passionate Models of Love*

American scholars frequently contrast the *companionate model* of love with *passionate model of love* (Hatfield, 1982, 1988; Lieberman & Hatfield, 2006; Sprecher & Regan, 1998).

The concepts of affection, passion, and other associated emotions associated with these models have been evolving throughout centuries and in different cultural contexts (Dixon, 2003).

Cultural conceptions of affectionate and passionate love, however, differ in their attitudes to affection, as the less intense, and passion as the more intense experience and expression of love emotions. Generally, the values of East-Asian cultures suggest that a person shall moderate the experience of emotions and reserve their expression, while the values of Western cultures suggest that a person has a right to experience and express emotion naturally and openly (e.g., Pennebaker & Graybeal, 2001).

The distinction between *affectionate and passionate cultural models of love* began to form since the eighteenth century (Luhmann, 1986). The French (and similar Italian) concept of *amour passion* and the English concept of *companionship marriage* were in the origins of those two types of love. The Roman Catholics of France and Italy embraced the *passionate sensual model*, while the Protestant Christians of England and Germany preferred the Puritans' *affectionate companionate model of love*. The English Puritan version evolved into the Victorian *marital model of love* in the nineteenth century. It was also quite common among early American settlers as the *puritan model of love*. *Both types* of love looked *romantic*, yet in different ways.

Other origins of affectional model of love came from Eastern cultures. For instance, Indian traditional conceptions of love distinguish *anuraga,* as affectionate emotions, *bhakti,* as devotional feelings from *rati* and *kama,* as passionate emotions derived from sexual love. According to cultural teachings, the appropriate enjoyment of life and love shall rely on self-disciplined emotions. The Indian beliefs encourage to master desire, passion, and attachment, the values considerably different from the values of Western cultures affirming passionate love (Ali, 2002; Gala & Kapadia, 2014).

These differences between passionate and affectionate models of love are also recognized in the lexicon of many languages in other cultures. For example, the English metaphors tend to reflect the *culturally normative* European American *culture of open expression of emotions,* the *culture of passionate love* in the expression of *love as a fire,* as the *brilliant and shining sun*. On the other hand, Chinese metaphors reflect the Chinese *normative culture of moderation* of emotions and a relatively *dispassionate model of love* in the expression of *love* as a *silk, as the moon light*—indirect and gentle (Karandashev, 2021a, 2021b; Lv & Zhang, 2012). These examples of metaphors reflect "the more introverted character of speakers of Chinese, while the love-as-fire metaphor reflects the extroverted characteristic of

English speakers. …Westerners talked about love with great passion and bravery, Chinese talked about love indirectly and tactfully" (Lv & Zhang, 2012, p. 356).

The case of Indonesian lexicon is another example. The word *asmara* conveys the meaning of *sexually passionate love* (sexual/desire/arousal), while the word *cint* has the meaning of affectionate love (affection/liking/fondness) (Shaver et al., 2001).

5.3.3 Chinese and Japanese Traditions of Muted Expression of Affectionate Love

The Chinese cultural norms discourage talking about passionate and romantic love openly and expressing love in emotional words. The culture of moderation and restrain has been traditionally highly valued since the time of Confucius. Love is the private emotions and shall be deeply inward (Potter, 1988).

Japanese culture has been highly influenced by *Zen Buddhism*. Therefore, silence and stillness, rather than words, are respected. Many things remain unspoken. Talking about love between partners in Japan is deemed as exaggerating and overplaying. In the study of 1977 (cited in Morsbach, 1988), researchers found the importance of stillness and silence in communication of love. The minimal wording were the key cultural features of love in Japanese couples. Few partners occasionally walked arm in arm (4%) or whispered, "I love you" (6%). In the ideal marriage "the husband and wife understand each other without speaking" (Morsbach, 1988, p. 210).

Chinese believe the parental love to a child shall be also muted. The close relationships between parents and their children assume the hidden nature of feelings (Potter, 1988). A cultural tradition recommends parents to keep the proper social and physical distance with children, thus communicating their parental love in a limited manner. According to the Chinese proverb, "The son does not know the mother's heart; the mother does not know the son's heart" (Potter, 1988, p. 201). In the same vein, a loving father should not express openly his affectionate feelings to a son. The cultural belief is that parents can undermine the potency of the proper relationship with child if openly express their love. Fostering the children's obedience and respect shall be the goal of parental love.

The increasing westernization in Chinese and Japanese societies throughout recent decades has changed the normative and real love relations between partners. The Confucian influence is diminished in China now, while the *Zen Buddhism* is rare in modern Japan. The silent communication is rather an idealized myth. The silence is still the ideal, however, real communication practices are different. The modern young Chinese and Japanese men and women became more verbal and open in their expression of love (Jankowiak et al., 2015, 2015).

References

Ali, D. (2002). Anxieties of attachment: The dynamics of courtships in medieval India. *Modern Asian Studies, 36*(1), 103–139.

Alonso-Arbiol, I., Shaver, P. R., Fraley, R. C., Oronoz, B., Unzurrunzaga, E., & Urizar, R. (2006). Structure of the Basque emotion lexicon. *Cognition and Emotion, 20*(6), 836–865.

Aron, A., Fisher, H., Mashek, D. J., Strong, G., Li, H., & Brown, L. L. (2005). Reward, motivation, and emotion systems associated with early-stage intense romantic love. *Journal of Neurophysiology, 94(1)*, 327–337. https://doi.org/10.1152/jn.00838.2004

Bejanyan, K., Marshall, T. C., & Ferenczi, N. (2015). Associations of collectivism with relationship commitment, passion, and mate preferences: Opposing roles of parental influence and family allocentrism. *PLoS ONE, 10*(2), e0117374.

Berscheid, E. (1985). Interpersonal attraction. In G. Lindzey & E. Aronson (Eds.), *The handbook of social psychology* (3rd ed., pp. 413–484). Random House.

Berscheid, E. (2010). Love in the fourth dimension. *Annual Review of Psychology, 61*(1), 1–25. https://doi.org/10.1146/annurev.psych.093008.100318

Berscheid, E., & Walster, E. (1974). A little bit about love. In T. L. Huston (Ed.), *Foundations of interpersonal attraction* (pp. 355–381). Academic.

Berscheid, E., & Walster, E. (1978). *Interpersonal attraction* (2nd ed.). Addison-Wesley (Originally work published 1969).

Buss, D. M. (1988). Love acts: The evolutionary biology of love. In R. J. Sternberg & M. L. Barnes (Eds.), *The psychology of love* (pp. 100–118). Yale University Press.

Chang, D., & Li, Y. (2006). *Visual representations of Kövecses's conceptual metaphor "Love is Fire" in the Chinese comic old master Q'*. Bayreuth, Germany. Retrieved from http://citeseerx.ist.psu.edu/viewdoc/download?doi=10.1.1.507.7887&rep=rep1&type=pdf

Contreras, R., Hendrick, S. S., & Hendrick, C. (1996). Perspectives on marital love and satisfaction in Mexican American and Anglo-American couples. *Journal of Counseling & Development, 74*(4), 408–415.

Cooper, B. L. (2021). Valentine's Day: 29 tributes to love and passion. *Rock Music Studies*, 1–3. https://doi.org/10.1080/19401159.2021.1914930

de Roda, A. B. L., Martínez-Iñigo, D., De Paul, P., & Yela, C. (1999). Romantic beliefs and myths in Spain. *The Spanish Journal of Psychology, 2*, 64–73.

Dion, K. L., & Dion, K. K. (1988). Romantic love: Individual and cultural perspectives. In R. J. Sternberg & M. L. Barnes (Eds.), *The psychology of love* (pp. 264–289). Yale University Press.

Dixon, V. J. (1976). World views and research methodology. In L. M. King, V. J. Dixon, & W. W. Nobles (Eds.), *African philosophy: Assumptions and paradigms for research on Black persons* (pp. 51–100). Fanon Center Press.

Dixon, T. (2003). *From passions to emotions: The creation of a secular psychological category*. Cambridge University Press.

Doherty, R. W., Hatfield, E., Thompson, K., & Choo, P. (1994). Cultural and ethnic influences on love and attachment. *Personal Relationships, 1*, 391–398.

Farrer, J., Tsuchiya, H., & Bagrowicz, B. (2008). Emotional expression in tsukiau dating relationships in Japan. *Journal of Social and Personal Relationships, 25*(1), 169–188.

Fisher, H. E. (2004). *Why we love: The nature and the chemistry of romantic love*. Henry Holt.

Fletcher, G. J., Simpson, J. A., Campbell, L., & Overall, N. C. (2015). Pair-bonding, romantic love, and evolution: The curious case of Homo sapiens. *Perspectives on Psychological Science, 10*(1), 20–36.

Floyd, K. (2001). Human affection exchange: I. Reproductive probability as a predictor of men's affection with their sons. *The Journal of Men's Studies, 10*(1), 39–50.

Floyd, K. (2002). Human affection exchange: V. Attributes of the highly affectionate. *Communication Quarterly, 50*(2), 135–152.

Floyd, K. (2006). *Communicating affection: Interpersonal behavior and social context*. Cambridge University Press.
Floyd, K., & Morman, M. T. (1998). The measurement of affectionate communication. *Communication Quarterly, 46*(2), 144–162.
Floyd, K., Hess, J. A., Miczo, L. A., Halone, K. K., Mikkelson, A. C., & Tusing, K. J. (2005). Human affection exchange: VIII. Further evidence of the benefits of expressed affection. *Communication Quarterly, 53*(3), 285–303.
Gala, J., & Kapadia, S. (2014). Romantic love, commitment and marriage in emerging adulthood in an Indian context: Views of emerging adults and middle adults. *Psychology and Developing Societies, 26*(1), 115–141.
Gao, G. (2001). Intimacy, passion, and commitment in Chinese and US American romantic relationships. *International Journal of Intercultural Relations, 25*(3), 329–342.
Gerhardt, S. (2014). *Why love matters: How affection shapes a baby's brain*. Routledge.
Goodwin, R., & Findlay, C. (1997). "We were just fated together." Chinese love and the concept of yuan in England and Hong Kong. *Personal Relationships, 4(1)*, 85–92.
Gulledge, A. K., Gulledge, M. H., & Stahmannn, R. F. (2003). Romantic physical affection types and relationship satisfaction. *The American Journal of Family Therapy, 31*(4), 233–242.
Hatfield, E. (1982). Passionate love, companionate love, and intimacy. In M. Fischer & G. Stricker (Eds.), *Intimacy*. Springer. https://doi.org/10.1007/978-1-4684-4160-4_17
Hatfield, E. (1988). Passionate and companionate love. In R. J. Sternberg & M. L. Barnes (Eds.), *The psychology of love* (pp. 191–217). Yale University Press.
Hatfield, E., & Rapson, R. L. (1987). Passionate love: New directions in research. In W. H. Jones & D. Perlman (Eds.), *Advances in personal relationships* (Vol. 1). JAI.
Hatfield, E., & Rapson, R. L. (1993). *Love, sex, and intimacy: Their psychology, biology, and history*. HarperCollins.
Hatfield, E., & Rapson, R. L. (1996). *Love and sex: Cross-cultural perspectives*. Allyn & Bacon.
Hatfield, E., & Rapson, R. L. (2005). *Love and sex: Cross-cultural perspectives* (2nd ed.). University Press of America.
Hatfield, E., & Rapson, R. L. (2009). The neuropsychology of passionate love and sexual desire. In E. Cuyler & M. Ackhart (Eds.), *Psychology of social relationships*. Hauppauge, NY.
Hatfield, E., & Sprecher, S. (1986). Measuring passionate love in intimate relationships. *Journal of Adolescence, 9*, 383–410.
Hendrick, C., & Hendrick, S. S. (1986). A theory and method of love. *Journal of Personality and Social Psychology, 50*, 392–402.
Hendrick, C., Hendrick, S. S., & Dicke, A. (1998). The love attitudes scale: Short form. *Journal of Social and Personal Relationships, 15*(2), 147–159.
Horan, S. M., & Booth-Butterfield, M. (2010). Investing in affection: An investigation of affection exchange theory and relational qualities. *Communication Quarterly, 58*(4), 394–413.
Jankowiak, W. (Ed.). (1995). *Romantic passion: A universal experience?* Columbia University Press.
Jankowiak, W., & Fischer, E. (1992). A cross-cultural perspective on romantic love. *Ethnology, 31*(2), 149–155.
Jankowiak, W., Shen, Y., Yao, S., Wang, C., & Volsche, S. (2015). Investigating love's universal attributes: A research report from China. *Cross-Cultural Research, 49*(4), 422–436.
Jankowiak, W. R., Volsche, S. L., & Garcia, J. R. (2015). Is the romantic–sexual kiss a near human universal? *American Anthropologist, 117*(3), 535–539.
Karandashev, V. (2017). *Romantic love in cultural contexts*. Springer.
Karandashev, V. (2019). *Cross-cultural perspectives on the experience and expression of love*. Springer.
Karandashev, V. (2021a). *Cultural models of emotions*. Springer.
Karandashev, V. (2021b). Cultural diversity of romantic love experience. In C. Mayer & E. Vanderheiden (Eds.), *International handbook of love* (pp. 59–79). Springer.
Karandashev, V., & Clapp, S. (2016). Psychometric properties and structures of passionate and companionate love. *Interpersonal: An International Journal on Personal Relationships, 10*(1), 56–76. https://doi.org/10.5964/ijpr.v10i1.210

Karandashev, V., & Evans, N. D. (2019). Quadrangular love theory and scale: Validation and psychometric investigation. *Journal of Methods and Measurement in the Social Sciences, 10*(1), 1–35.

Kim, J., & Hatfield, E. (2004). Love types and subjective well-being: A cross-cultural study. *Social Behavior and Personality: An International Journal, 32*(2), 173–182.

Kövecses, Z. (1988). *The language of love: The semantics of passion in conversational English.* Bucknell University Press.

Kövecses, Z. (1990). *Emotion concepts*. Springer.

Kovecses, Z. (2000). *Metaphor and emotion: Language, culture, and body in human feeling*. Cambridge University Press.

Kövecses, Z. (2003). *Metaphor and emotion: Language, culture, and body in human feeling*. Cambridge University Press.

Landis, D., & O'Shea, W. A., III. (2000). Cross-cultural aspects of passionate love: An individual differences analysis. *Journal of Cross-Cultural Psychology, 31*(6), 752–777.

Lawton, L., Silverstein, M., & Bengtson, V. (1994). Affection, social contact, and geographic distance between adult children and their parents. *Journal of Marriage and the Family, 56*, 57–68.

Leon, J. J., Parra, F., Cheng, T., & Flores, R. E. (1995). Love-styles among Latino community college students in Los Angeles. *Psychological Reports, 77*(2), 527–530.

Li, T. S. (1999). The content and measurement of marital intimate affection. *Chinese Journal of Mental Health, 12*(4), 197–216. (In Chinese).

Lieberman, D., & Hatfield, E. (2006). Passionate love: Cross–cultural and evolutionary perspectives. In R. J. Sternberg & K. Weis (Eds.), *The new psychology of love* (2nd ed., pp. 274–297). Yale University Press.

Lim, N. (2016). Cultural differences in emotion: Differences in emotional arousal level between the East and the West. *Integrative Medicine Research, 5*(2), 105–109.

Lomas, T. (2018). The flavours of love: A cross-cultural lexical analysis. *Journal for the Theory of Social Behaviour, 48*, 134–152.

Luhmann, N. (1986). *Love as passion: The codification of intimacy*. Harvard University Press.

Lv, Z., & Zhang, Y. (2012). Universality and variation of conceptual metaphor of love in Chinese and English. *Theory and Practice in Language Studies, 2*(2), 355–359.

Marsh, H. W., Vallerand, R. J., Lafrenière, M.-A. K., Parker, P., Morin, A. J. S., Carbonneau, N., Jowett, S., Bureau, J. S., Fernet, C., Guay, F., Salah Abduljabbar, A., & Paquet, Y. (2013). Passion: Does one scale fit all? Construct validity of two-factor passion scale and psychometric invariance over different activities and languages. *Psychological Assessment, 25*(3), 796–809. https://doi.org/10.1037/a0032573

Messina, J. (1903). *Love and passion: (Pensèe pathetique)*. Joe Morris Music.

Morsbach, H. (1988). The importance of silence and stillness in Japanese nonverbal communication: A cross-cultural approach. In F. Poyatos (Ed.), *Cross-cultural perspectives in nonverbal communication* (pp. 201–215). Hogrefe.

Murstein, B. I., Merighi, J. R., & Vyse, S. A. (1991). Love styles in the United States and France: A cross-cultural comparison. *Journal of Social and Clinical Psychology, 10*(1), 37–46.

Neto, F. (2007). Love styles: A cross-cultural study of British, Indian, and Portuguese college students. *Journal of Comparative Family Studies, 38*(2), 239–254.

Neto, F., Mullet, E., Deschamps, J. C., Barros, J., Benvindo, R., Camino, L., et al. (2000). Cross-cultural variations in attitudes toward love. *Journal of Cross-Cultural Psychology, 31*(5), 626–635.

Pennebaker, J. W., & Graybeal, A. (2001). Patterns of natural language use: Disclosure, personality, and social integration. *Current Directions in Psychological Science, 10(3)*, 90–93.

Pérez, V. A. F., Fiol, E. B., Guzmán, C. N., Palmer, C. R., & Buades, E. G. (2009). The concept of love in Spain. *Psychology in Spain, 13*(1), 40–47.

Potter, S. H. (1988). The cultural construction of emotion in rural Chinese social life. *Ethos, 16*(2), 181–208.

Reddy, W. M. (2012). *The making of romantic love: Longing and sexuality in Europe, South Asia, and Japan, 900-1200 CE*. The University of Chicago Press.
Sanri, Ç., & Goodwin, R. (2013). Values and love styles in Turkey and Great Britain: An intercultural and intracultural comparison. *International Journal of Psychology, 48*(5), 837–845.
Shaver, P. R., Schwartz, J., Kirson, D., & O'Connor, C. (1987). Emotion knowledge: Further explorations of a prototype approach. *Journal of Personality and Social Psychology, 52*, 1061–1086.
Shaver, P. R., Wu, S., & Schwartz, J. C. (1992). Cross-cultural similarities and differences in emotion and its representation: A prototype approach. In M. S. Clark (Ed.), *Review of personality and social psychology* (pp. 175–212). Sage.
Shaver, P. R., Murdaya, U., & Fraley, R. C. (2001). Structure of the Indonesian emotion lexicon. *Asian Journal of Social Psychology, 4*, 201–224.
Solomon, R. C. (1995). The cross-cultural comparison of emotion. In J. Marks & R. T. Ames (Eds.), *Emotions in Asian thought* (pp. 253–294). State University of New York Press.
Sperling, M. B., & Berman, W. H. (1991). An attachment classification of desperate love. *Journal of Personality Assessment, 56*(1), 45–55.
Spitzberg, B. H., & Cupach, W. R. (1998). *The dark side of close relationships*. Routledge.
Sprecher, S., & Regan, P. (1998). Passionate and companionate love in courting and young married couples. *Sociological Inquiry, 68*(2), 163–185.
Sprecher, S., Aron, A., Hatfield, E., Cortese, A., Potapova, E., & Levitskaya, A. (1994). Love: American style, Russian style, and Japanese style. *Personal Relationships, 1*, 349–369.
Sternberg, R. J. (1986). A triangular theory of love. *Psychological Review, 93*(2), 119–135.
Sternberg, R. J. (1997). Construct validation of a triangular love scale. *European Journal of Social Psychology, 27*(3), 313–335.
Tallis, F. (2004). *Lovesick: Love as a mental illness*. Thunder's Mouth Press.
Tennov, D. (1979/1998). *Love and limerence: The experience of being in love*. Scarborough House.
Toro-Morn, M., & Sprecher, S. (2003). A cross-cultural comparison of mate preferences among university students: The United States vs. The People's Republic of China (PRC). *Journal of Comparative Family Studies, 34*(2), 151–170.
Tzeng, O. C. S., & Landis, D. (1978). Three-mode multidimensional scaling with points of view solutions. *Multivariate Behavioral Research, 13*, 181–213.
Tzeng, O. C. S., & Landis, D. (1979). A multidimensional scaling methodology for cross-cultural research in communications. In M. K. Asante, E. Newmark, & C. A. Blake (Eds.), *Handbook of intercultural communication* (pp. 283–318). Sage.
Ubillos, S., Zubieta, E., Paez, D., Deschamps, J.C., Ezeiza, A., & Vera, A. (2001). Amor, cultura y sexo. *Revista Electronica de Motivacion y Emocion (REME), 4*(8–9). Available at: http://reme.uji.es/articulos/aubils9251701102/texto.html
Vallerand, R. J. (2010). On passion for life activities: The dualistic model of passion. In M. P. Zanna (Ed.), *Advances in experimental social psychology* (Vol. 42, pp. 97–193). Academic.
Vallerand, R. J. (2015). *The psychology of passion: A dualistic model*. Oxford University Press.
Vallerand, R. J., Blanchard, C., Mageau, G. A., Koestner, R., Ratelle, C., Léonard, M., … Marsolais, J. (2003). Les passions de l'ame: on obsessive and harmonious passion. *Journal of Personality and Social Psychology, 85*(4), 756.
Vrana, S. R., & Rollock, D. (2002). The role of ethnicity, gender, emotional content, and contextual differences in physiological, expressive, and self-reported emotional responses to imagery. *Cognition and Emotion, 16*, 165–192.
Washabaugh, W. (Ed.). (2020). *The passion of music and dance: Body, gender and sexuality*. Routledge.
White, J. L., & Parham, T. A. (1990). *The psychology of Blacks: An African American perspective* (2nd ed.). Prentice Hall.
Wolfe-Ralph, C. A. (1995). *The passion of Spain: The music of twentieth-century Spanish composers with special emphasis on the music of Enrique Granados* (Doctoral dissertation, University of Maryland, College Park).
Yildirim, F., & Barnett, R. V. (2017). Comparing the effects of specific variables on passionate love among young people: A cross-cultural study. In N. R. Silton (Ed.), *Family dynamics and romantic relationships a changing society* (pp. 62–83). IGI Global.

Chapter 6
Models of Romantic Love

6.1 The Conception of Romantic Love Model

6.1.1 Cultural and Psychological Complexity of Romantic Love

What Is Romantic in the Romantic Love Model

For recent decades, many scholars and laypeople have widely used the words *romantic love* and *romantic relationship* in quite loose and vague meaning, often interchangeably with the words passionate love and dating relationship. This way, the terms *romantic love* and *romantic relationship* have been losing their original and true meaning. Their erosion has been transforming them into the very general labels, without appropriate scholarly conceptualization.

Romantic love and *romantic relationship* are the subjective beliefs, emotions, attitudes, and behaviors. And people are free to consider any of those things as *romantic* if they *perceive* and believe they are *romantic*. In this regard, the word *romantic* is just a label, which people may attach to anything. If they believe that physical or other violence in a romantic relationship is still compatible with calling the *relationship romantic*, it is okay. *Romantic* is anything what people *call romantic*.

Love researchers, however, shall be more accurate in their scholarly lexicon. I would encourage them to be more specific in their scientific terminology. It is important to treat the love constructs always defining them and respecting scholarly traditions and the knowledge in the field, which have been accomplished.

The *concept of romantic love* can characterize *love* as a *cultural ideals, beliefs, emotional states, attitudes, behaviors,* or *relationships*. It is important to *distinguish* these aspects of romantic love, *define* those, and *specify* what kinds of romantic love are the subject of scholarly exploration.

V. Karandashev, *Cultural Typologies of Love*,
https://doi.org/10.1007/978-3-031-05343-6_6

The Major Distinctions of Romantic Love Model

The romantic love, as an *ideal and unrealistic model of love*, has been primarily contrasted with *real and realistic models of love*, such as rational, practical, and pragmatic ones. The *romantic beliefs* have been opposed to *realistic and pragmatic beliefs. Romantic lovers* wanted to live in the idealized world of fantasies and dreams, which poets, novelists, playwrights, artists, musicians, and film directors created in their works. These imaginative ideals and visions of social and personal relationships inspired to favor the personal choice over practical and social affordances. They brought individuals away from their boring or unpleasant reality of life to another plane of existence.

This model of love has been in oppositions to pragmatic beliefs. The romantic love was considered as idealistic, whereas pragmatic love was realistic. The romantic love was viewed as irrational, whereas pragmatic love was rational. The romantic love assumed that the perfect partners should be destined and compatible, whereas pragmatic love recognized the need of building a loving relationship. In *romantic love model*, partners express their love in emotions and attitudes, whereas in *pragmatic love model,* they express their love in actions (Karandashev, 2021b).

Subjective Notion of the Romantic Love and Romantic Relationships?

Throughout centuries, and especially in the twentieth century, scholars of various disciplines have achieved a lot (see for review, Karandashev, 2017, 2019). Explorations of *romantic love* have been popular for centuries in the history, philosophy, and literature and still play their pivotal role. In the twentieth century, researchers in anthropology, sociology, linguistics, psychology, and communication studies have advanced our knowledge of romantic love. They have explored *romantic love* in different, yet intertwined perspectives, complementing each other with their knowledge and methods.

What is romantic in love is primarily determined by cultural and personal beliefs. They vary across times and cultures, as well as across different individual types of people. The most common consensus, which the love researchers have achieved so far, is that *romantic love model* is characterized by a certain set of romantic beliefs and "idealization of a lover's unique qualities and considering a relationship with him/her as exceptionally perfect" (Karandashev, 2021b, p. 63).

Such *romantic idealization* may reflect on the love experience as emotions, moods, or attitudes. In *romantic love,* the key features of this experience are "viewing the partner at a given moment in a highly positive way, probably but not necessarily with desire or passion, and the seeking of and yearning for sexual intimacy, which may have already been attained" (Lazarus, 1991, p. 276).

Briefly, the "*romantic*" means *something idealized and beautiful*. "*Romantic love* is a combination of beliefs, ideals, attitudes, and expectations, which coexist in our conscious and unconscious minds." (Karandashev, 2017, p. 30). Various romantic beliefs and facets of this concept are summarized in the following sections.

Multifaceted Conception of Romantic Love

The concept of *romantic love* has evolved historically bearing various interpretations in cultures across time and world and loading diverse meanings in different scholarly disciplines. *Romantic love experience* involves certain patterns of emotions, cognitive processes, and behaviors. A comprehensive review of scholarly literature and research demonstrated its complex nature and phenomenology. Being closely intertwined with other types of love, romantic love is characterized by a specific set of features. Among the most typical experiences and expressions of people being in romantic love are (see Karandashev, 2017, 2019 for detailed reviews)

1. *Idealization of the beloved and a relationship* (e.g., Dion & Dion, 1996; Kephart, 1966, 1967; Lindholm, 1988; Murstein, 1988; Sprecher & Metts, 1989; Romantic, n.d., 2016a, 2016b; Rosenblatt, 1967). A romantic lover accentuates the positive qualities and overlooks or rationalizes the negative traits of the beloved one. A lover is remarkable in his/her capacity to highlight what is admirable in the beloved and ability to convert the negative quality into a positive one. As Rubin (1970) noted, romantic love is the idealization of the other within an erotic context.
2. *Sexual attraction to the beloved one* (e.g., Berscheid & Walster, 1974/1978; Dion & Dion, 1996; Dueñas-Vargas, 2015; Kephart, 1966, 1967; Lewis, 1960; Lindholm, 1988; Paris, 1883; Sangrador & Yela, 2000). Scholars traditionally and overwhelmingly in agreement that erotic, physical, and sexual attractions are the essential experiences of a romantic lover. Longing and yearning for reciprocity of these feelings are natural, along with a desire to be an exclusive sexual partner with a beloved one. Otherwise, sexual jealousy is a dramatic experience.
3. *Passionate and affectionate emotions associated with the beloved one*. The *passion* (e.g., Berscheid & Walster, 1974/1978; Dueñas-Vargas, 2015; Lindholm, 1988; Paris, 1883) or *affection* (e.g., Floyd, 2006; Floyd & Morman, 1998; Floyd et al., 2005; Romantic, n.d., 2016a, 2016b) are treated in scholarly literature as distinctive features of romantic love and core characteristics of many romantic beliefs. The word *passionate love* is frequently used in scholarly literature as a synonym of *romantic love*, what is not quite adequate.
4. *Cognitive and emotional preoccupation with the beloved one and relationship* (e.g., Dion & Dion, 1996; Romantic, n.d., 2016a, 2016b). This includes intrusive thinking about a beloved one and being together. When love unrequited, vivid imagination helps to imagine the desired reciprocation. A lover is very sensitive to any behavior that might be interpreted favorably. He/she is especially capable to perceive "hidden" passion in seeming neutral behavior of a partner.

5. *Intense desire for physical, mental, and emotional union with the beloved one*, with a desire to be in physical proximity, psychological congruency, and emotional intimacy (Berscheid & Walster, 1974/1978, Hatfield & Rapson, 1993, Fisher, 2004; Karandashev, 2017; Kövecses, 1988, 2005; Lomas, 2018; Reddy, 2012).
6. *Exclusive attraction to the beloved and commitment to relationship* (Lindholm, 1988; Rosenblatt, 1967; Sprecher & Metts, 1989; Sternberg, 1986), along with hope for *endurance of love* Commitment naturally assumes *a desire for exclusiveness of a relationship* and *experience of jealousy* in case of possible break-up of commitment (Rubin, 1970; Rosenblatt, 1967). A romantic lover pays unique emotional, cognitive, and motivational attention to one special person who is *exceptionally different* in his/her real or idealized qualities, which distinguish him or her from all other people. Experience of true romantic love admits no capability to love more than one person at a time. In addition to this, a romantic lover is longing for reciprocation of his/her love. In case of unrequited love—deep suffering.
7. *Affiliation, emotional attachment*, and *dependency* (Hazan & Shaver, 1987; Kephart, 1966, 1967; Rosenblatt, 1967; Rubin, 1970). Development of these strong feelings, emotions, and attitudes goes along with caring and concern for the beloved. A romantic love wants to do (almost) anything to satisfy his/her needs.
8. *Happiness, fulfillment, the transformational power of love* (Rosenblatt, 1967; Paris, 1883). A romantic lover reorders his/her life priorities and hierarchies of values. The care for a relationship becomes a central point of attention, frequently at the expense of other interests and responsibilities. The pursuit for union and happiness together with a beloved is so strong that any adversity intensifies passionate feelings (Fisher, 2004). Romantic love grows especially strong in the conditions of adversity.

These qualities of love beliefs, feelings, emotions, moods, attitudes, expressions, behaviors, and relationships can be present in the higher or lower degree in *different models of romantic love*. Varieties of their combinations, values, and experiences create the *diversity of romantic love models across individuals and cultures*. These characteristics of love experience, expression, and relationship can be also present in the models of love different from the romantic one. In such cases, the *features of romantic love* overlap with *other models of love*. The different models of love are not exclusive from each other.

6.1.2 Romantic Love Model Across Times and Cultures

The Early Cultural Evolution of Romantic Love Model

The Ancient Greeks, Romans, Egyptians, and Chinese probably did not acknowledge the *notion of romantic love*, at least they did not have the special words designated for it. They had several words for different kinds of love, yet surprisingly not for this one. The *elements and ideals of romantic love* might be on their minds, yet the conceptions of romantic love were elaborated throughout later centuries (Karandashev, 2017).

Oral folk traditions of storytelling and written novels have been on the front line generating and disseminating such love ideals and fantasies among educated gentry (see for review, Karandashev, 2017). The narratives of medieval *courtly love* arising around the twelfth century in Provence, in south France, were quite prominent in the evolution of romantic love model.

According to the nineteenth-century literary critic G. Paris (1883), *amour courtois* (*courtly love*) was a precedent of romantic love denoting specific emotions, attitudes, and patterns of behavior. The plots, poems, and songs of *troubadours* and *trobairitz*—poet-musicians—expressed the romantic dreams of noble and knightly life, partially reflecting the reality of their life. These romantic poetries and melodies might have the roots in the cultures of Moslem Spain where romantic literary traditions were established earlier.

Courtly love was the chivalry romances of a passionate lover (e.g., knight) and his admired noble lady. The elegant manners, rituals, and feats of the lover were to concur the heart of the lady. The focus on the *course of loving* was more important than the beloved lady herself. The culture of *courtly love* with its *worship* and *idealization* was like a religion of devotional love (Lewis, 1936/2013).

These ideals of *courtly love* were just the artistic explorations of possibilities. The feudal life of that time had quite limited mobility. According to the cultural traditions of that time, noble individuals conformed to the domestic way of life, which often could be bored. The possibility of new extramarital adventures was quite intriguing and exciting for some among the bored nobility. So, what courtly love as a literary invention invented were the plots of extramarital affairs. These themes have been proliferated and elaborated in literature and art since then.

Evolvement of Truly Romantic Love

The romantic cultural ideals of courtly love further developed in England, Italy, Germany, and some other European countries in the following centuries (Karandashev, 2017). English poet Chaucer (1340s–1400) and playwright and poet Shakespeare (1564–1616) were the prominent literary figures who contributed to the evolution of romantic love ideals in poems, plays, and novels.

In the seventeenth and eighteenth centuries, the concept of romantic love shifted in its meaning to the ideals of authentic feelings, emotions, and expressions and self-validation. In the second part of the eighteenth century, that transformation embodied in romantic literature, music, art, and philosophy. The *cultural model of romantic love* progressed foremost as a literary tradition (Landgraf, 2004).

> The Romantic Movement in novel, poetry, and drama changed Western culture and people's relationships. Romanticism regarded an individual as an agent of free choice in life and personal values. As for love, men and women in their relationships were presumably motivated by their personal decisions and chosen values. Romantics convinced people to follow

> their passion and portrayed love stories in romantic novels, plays, and poems. They understood love as the desire for union between two individual souls; therefore, the choosing of the appropriate person was highly important for them. Women appeared as equal to men in intellect and in passion, though that view of women was not the prevailing one. (Karandashev, 2017, p. 2015).

The romantics of the seventeenth to nineteenth centuries have further developed and elaborated the various possibilities, which romantic love may have. This was the development of a *cultural idea of the romantic love model.* The real life of people in some cultural and social circles often evolved accordingly being inspired by these romantic ideals, yet the reality of love for many people lagged due to limited affordances of their social life.

The History of Relations Between Cultural Ideals of Romantic Love and Reality

Historians have documented largely the history, life, and love of kings, queens, emperors, sheiks, duke, duchesses, princes, princesses, noble, and other famous persons. The literary stories have also documented largely the life of these elites, rather than the middle and lower social classes. Only later, they documented the life of other educated people. They were primarily affected by such romantic cultural models of love.

Romantic love was possible among such nobility and educated middle class. They have wealth and spare time to entertain in romantic dreams and adventures. They produce the stories and poems about romantic love.

The history of the commoners and their emotions have been known little, until recent times. It is likely that these models of love affected commoners, especially illiterate, to a lesser extent. More likely, they learned from the oral folklore tales, which were transmitted from one cultural generation to another throughout the centuries. Many of these folk stories had their versions of love, which resembled the model of romantic love.

Sexual and pragmatic love were more common realities of their life among ordinary people. They were busy with their hard daily work, bread earning, and therefore did not have much time to engage in romantic games. They might want and dream, but they could not afford such entertainment due to various hardships and other obstacles.

Nerveless, for many commoners, servants, and factory workers, it was a dream to engage and experience in romantic love, like nobility did. Such a dream is even expressed in linguistic metaphors. Many girls still dream to become princesses and find their prince. Boys imagine themselves as knights, not only for military dreams… Man expressing his love calls his beloved "you are my queen." Woman expressing her love call her beloved "you are my king" (or prince).

Thus, historical spreading and dissemination of the *cultural model of romantic love* have been slow and gradual.

How Romantic Love Model Conquered Premarital Relationships in Modernized Societies

The first part of the twentieth century was the time when *romantic love model* became popular in public opinion and became more real in the relationship of people in many modern societies (Karandashev, 2017). The major transformation of love ideology and marriage occurred in England, as well as in several other European countries and American states (e.g., Coontz, 2005; Szreter & Fisher, 2010). The young people approaching marriage in many Western cultures did so with romantic ideals of love, sex, and intimacy. Cultural norms shifted to gender equality acknowledging that women have the abilities for sexual pleasure more equal with men. Many young women, however, avoided premarital sex (Coontz, 2005). *Falling in love* was viewed as a legitimate basis for a relationship, while marriage focused on love and passion (Karandashev, 2017).

Although romantic love model was widely circulated in the English culture, yet the real romantic practices were fragmented, sparse, and scattered. They significantly varied between different classes and generations (Gillis, 1985). The social norms of working-class young adults were still against romantic love and emotional intimacy. The oral testimonies showed a lighthearted anti-romanticism in their themes. The retrospective stories downplayed the role of passion and romance. The social, economic themes, and pragmatic reasons were evident and typical when young people considered the paths toward marriage (Szreter & Fisher, 2010).

Many girls had premarital passionate relations in their young years. As for marriage, they often preferred to choose the marital relations with material security, rather than with their romantic partners. Working-class young women sought respect and stability more than emotional excitement and sexual fulfillment. Nevertheless, many young women had minimal criteria of suitability—not an alcoholic, or not a gambler, and limited expectations of the relationship hoping that their husband would not be violent. They wanted a breadwinner who could secure their decent marital life and resources for family. Men, on another side, wanted a good housekeeper and a mother for their children.

The disagreement with parents about romantic beliefs and pragmatic choices for marriages was manageable. The young men and women did not oppose the opinions of family and community. They sought to balance romanticism and realism acknowledging the importance of love and intimacy. The romantic passion was more essential in the marital choice in middle-class courtship subcultures, rather than in working-class ones.

The romantic love faced difficulties when women became wives and mothers, even though marital relationships became more acceptable to the ideals of companionate and close relationship (Szreter & Fisher, 2010). To establish stable and companionate marriages, they needed education and skills on how to manage a good relationship. The book *Married Love* (M. Stopes, 1918) precipitated this new relationship ideology (cited in Szreter & Fisher, 2010). Not all subcultures and partners were receptive to the companionate model of marriage. It was especially true in the cultural contexts of working-class (Giles, 2004). Thus, the *romantic love model* as *a cultural idea* and as a *personal model of premarital relationships* did not preclude pragmatic or companionate marital relationship.

Only by the 1960s, love in American and West-European societies conquered marriage (Coontz, 2006). However, marriage started to lose its institutional popularity (see more Karandashev, 2017).

Other cultures of the world have had their evolutionary histories of their versions of romantic love (see more in Karandashev, 2017; Murstein, 1974; Singer, 1984a, 1984b, 1987). Their models of love and romanticism may look less romantic by Western European standards. They might not always call it as "romantic," yet many elements of the *romantic love model* outlined in this chapter were present in their *experiences, expressions, and relationships of love*.

The Cultural Model of Romantic Love Across Cultures

Although many studies in the twentieth century, which identified these *characteristics of romantic love*, were conducted in Western cultures, the recent cross-cultural research has revealed that these experiences and expressions are also present in other cultures. Characteristics of those *eight features of romantic love*, which are summarized above, can be a good guide for the review following in the next sections, as well for the further studies. The more extensive and detailed set of these characteristics is presented elsewhere (Karandashev, 2017).

The idea of romantic love seems almost cross-culturally universal. Anthropologists identified indicators of love across 164 societies (Jankowiak & Fischer, 1992). The importance of romantic love for mating and marriage, however, can vary across cultures because of socio-cultural suppression and different organization of social life (de Munck, 2019; Jankowiak & Fischer, 1992).

The importance of romantic love and its motivational power significantly varies across societies. Its energy is not comparable to the motives of hunger or sex, while even cultural attitudes to these strong drives vary considerably across cultures (de Munck, 2019; De Munck, Korotayev, & McGreevey, 2016).

Although *romantic love can be present* in the *majority of societies*, it *is not culturally normative* in many of them (de Munck, 2019; de Munck et al., 2016). It can be likely that some individuals in each society occasionally or during a longer time experience romantic love, yet the number of such individuals may vary substantially across societies. Besides, laypeople and scholars may construe some experiences, expressions, and behaviors as reflective of romantic love, while others may not. These are some pitfalls for the claims of the cross-cultural universality of romantic love.

Experience of Romantic Love Across Cultures

Scholars have strived to explore whether love is universal across cultures or not. Many found support in favor of its universality. The question, however, remains what is universal: the idea of love or reality of love? Historical, literary, lexical, and anthropological studies have shown that the concept of love is present in many cultural artifacts—fairy tales, stories, songs, poems, lexicon, fine arts, and movies—across the majority of cultures (see for review, Karandashev, 2017). Does it mean that people have actually experienced love as depicted? Not necessarily. Some noble individuals of the twelfth century in south France—kings and knights—who were free from the struggle for survival, might experience courtly love as it is reflected in troubadours' songs. However, many laypeople did not have time (or ability) to entertain the courtly love rituals being occupied by everyday concerns for survival, or not having a right partner. The dream of romantic love is attractive, yet not always and not easily achievable. The romantic novels and movies can help with that. They depict beautiful love stories in beautiful settings with beautiful actors, thus elevating the routine life of many individuals on another plane of existence. This allows them to experience romantic love at least in their dreams. This is the power of art!

Some people in some societies have more opportunities and are lucky to find romantic love in their real life. Others may have limited possibilities in terms of social affordances, available pool of candidates for love, or skills to entertain romantic ideals.

Throughout cultural evolution, which coincided with socio-economic evolution from subsistence-based to traditional, and further to modern types of society, more people had more free time for leisure and entertainment of love. Priority of needs for survival shifted to the needs for self-expression—the needs to love and be loved were among those.

The question whether real experience of love by people is cross-culturally universal is important, yet it should again be clarified and framed in more specific questions. Do we inquire about the universality of *individuals' capability to experience love*, or the universality of *actual experiencing love in their life* in different cultures? Are people in some cultures more capable to experience love than in others? Do people in some cultures experience love more often than in others?

If people in all cultures can love and experience love, does it mean that every individual in a society can love and really experience love? Does cross-cultural universality mean cross-individual universality of love within a culture? Additional questions may be about frequency and length of experiencing love.

6.2 Sex in Romantic Love Model

6.2.1 Romantic Love and Sexual Feelings

The Role of Sex in Romantic Love

The love scholars commonly consider sexual desire and sexual attraction as essential experiences in the *model of romantic love.* They view yearning, longings for sexual union, and associated erotic fantasies as natural concomitants of romantic love. However, as Lindholm (1998) argued, it is inadequate to consider sexual attraction as the key characteristic of romantic love. Traditional scholarship and research (Karandashev, 2017, 2019) has considered idealization and romantic beliefs as the defining features of romantic love. Of course, beautiful sex often boosts romantic emotions and idealization of life.

For example, *romantic love* has been considered as a blend of *sexual desire, affection, and tenderness* (Ellis (1897–1910/2014)), as a *sublimated expression of sexual desire* (Hutcheon, 1995; Freud, 1947), as a fusion of *sexual attraction* with *affection* and *tenderness,* (Hutcheon, 1995; Singer, 1987), and as a *merger of sex into love* (de Munck, 2019).

Many other scholars have been also in an overwhelming agreement that *physical, sexual, and erotic attractions* are the essential experiences of romantic love (Berscheid & Walster, 1978; Dion & Dion, 1996; Dueñas-Vargas, 2015; Kephart, 1966, 1967; Lewis, 1960; Lindholm, 1988; Paris, 1883; Sangrador & Yela, 2000). *Longing and yearning,* the strong *desire* for reciprocity of these feelings, are natural, along with a *craving* to be an exclusive sexual partner with a beloved one. Otherwise, sexual jealousy is a dramatic experience.

How Sex Evolves into Romantic Love

The psychoanalytic theory interpreted *romantic love* as the sublimation of sexual desire, as the sublimated expression of sexual impulses (Freud, 1947). In the Freud's view *romantic love is a regressive pursuit* for physical gratification and protective union. *Romanticism* is a *frustration of sexual longing* resulting in an *over idealization* (Hutcheon, 1995).

Freud *was* partially *right* stating that *romantic love is a sublimation of human sexual desire*. However, he *was wrong* degrading romantic love to basic sexual forces. Instead, I believe that *romantic love enriches* and *elevates* sexual desires, sexual feelings,and emotions *upgrading* (rather than degrading) and making them beautiful.

Other scholars contended that sex and sexual love are different from romantic love and affection. Sexual urge and lust are the experiences different from the *eros* of love and can exist separately from each other. They claimed that romantic love is a desire for the beautiful, which is different from the particularities of the physical body (C.S. Lewis, 1960; Singer, 1984a, 1984b, 1987; Wilson, 1980). Several conceptions of *romantic love* closely relate this type of love with sex. For instance, a blend of *sexual desire, affection,* and *tenderness* (Ellis (1897–1910/2014)) and a fusion of *sexual attraction* with *affection* and *tenderness* (Hutcheon, 1995; Singer, 1987) were considered as the core components of romantic love.

Based on his research, De Munck (2019) suggested a *merger of sex into love*, rather than love into sex. Positive emotional charge of sex binds it with perception of other partner's attributes and relationship (non-sexual) and create *psychological complex of romantic love*.

According to the theory of *excitation transfer* (e.g., Cummins, 2017; Meston & Frohlich, 2003) and *psychophysiological principle of dominant* (e.g., Pavlova, 2017; Rusinov, 1973; Ukhtomsky, 1966), it is reasonable to state that *"Arousal transfer is probably the best psychological mechanism to explain this shift of pleasure from sex to romantic images and love"* (Karandashev, 2017, p. 270).

Relative Independence of Romantic Love from Sex

Romantic love is closely intertwined with *erotic love* as admiration of beauty. People tend to fall in romantic love with those who have physically attractive appearances. It is worthwhile to note, however, that sexual desire does not necessarily entail romantic love, and sexual desire is not a prerequisite for romantic love (Diamond, 2003, 2004; Wilson, 1980).

Research in developmental psychology has revealed that children before their pubertal hormonal changes, which are responsible for sexual motivation, are capable to experience romantic infatuations (Hatfield, Schmitz, Cornelius, & Rapson, 1988). In addition, later in adulthood, men and women are able to experience romantic love without sexual desire (Tennov, 1979/1998).

Sex, love, and romantic love are relatively independent concepts in people's minds. According to studies, people have independent prototypes for these constructs (de Munck, 2019). *Sex*, as a unique concept, has the highest frequency of unique terms, which are different from *love and romantic love*. This means that *sex* is not a subset of either of the other two categories.

An experimental observational study (Gonzaga, Turner, Keltner, Campos, & Altemus, 2006) has demonstrated the distinctive functions, which *romantic love* and *sex* play in close relationships. A brief *experience of romantic love* during a 3-min interaction was associated for partners with the emotional states, nonverbal displays, and relationship outcomes *related to commitment*. Under another experimental condition, a brief *experience of sexual desire* during a 3-min interaction was associated for partners with the emotional states, nonverbal displays, and relationship outcomes *related to reproduction*. Thus, the study again confirms a relative functional independence of sex from romantic love.

6.2.2 *Sex and Romantic Love Across Times and Cultures*

Christiaan and Buddhist Cultures About Relations Between Sex and Love

In the view of many people in modern societies, romantic emotions are closely linked to sexual feelings. The extensive cross-cultural review of evidence that came from different historical and modern cultures (Karandashev, 2017) has demonstrated the support for this assertion.

However, in the history of human cultures, religious teachings and beliefs have played pivotal roles in the cultural conceptualization of relations between sex and love.

For centuries, Western cultures of many Christian societies divided them into two different and opposite realms of human existence: "*bodily*" and "*spiritual.*" Their scriptures advised the higher priority of spirituality in life, keeping bodily desires under control. On the other hand, Eastern cultures of many Buddhist cultures did not consider sex and love as dualistic and oppositional spheres of life. They advised people that physical sexual experiences are closely connected with spiritual, caring, and devotional love (Reddy, 2012).

Influence of Social Conditions on Sex and Romantic Love

Several publications of de Munck and Korotayev (1999, 2007, 2016) have demonstrated that social conditions can have a priority over cultural influence on the importance of romantic love. Culture and psychology adapt to social, biological, and physical environments. In particular, the female status allowing gender equality, intimate social relations, including the time spent together while eating, sleeping, and having leisure, are related positively with the presence of romantic love in a culture. The authors argue that the cultural norms of romantic love and sex develop in response to the complex of social conditions, including the forms of marriage, female status, etc. Sex plays its role in reproduction and love plays its role in bonding and investment in children. However, romantic love is a special type of love; it is "an emergent property of the two biopsychological universals of love and sex," which evolves as a cultural norm only in certain social conditions (p. 11). On the other hand, some social conditions do not favor romantic love suppressing and rejecting romantic love as a cultural value.

Nonetheless, within any culture of any time, some people (e.g., in elite groups or among educated individuals) experience romantic dispositions.

Cultural Effect of Sexual Inequality and Equality on Romantic Love

Anthropological data (de Munck & Korotayev, 1999) have demonstrated a detrimental effect of *sexual inequality* on the cultural value of romantic love. In the societies, in which cultural norms allow premarital and adulterous sexual relations *only for men*, cultural values *do not* respect *romantic love* and cultural customs *do not* see it as an important prerequisite for marriage. In comparison, in the societies, where cultural norms prohibit premarital and adulterous sexual relations *for both men and women*, the cultural acceptance of romantic love is higher and cultural customs regard it as an important prerequisite for marriage. Thus, sex, romantic love, and marriage are compatible with each largely in the societies where *sexual equality* exist. In such cultures, both men and women are free to give or not give love. A society acknowledges their *sexual equality and non-marital sexual freedom*. These cultural conditions are favorable for close association between sex, romantic love, and marriage.

Modernization of societies in many countries makes a gradual, but steady cultural shift toward more recognition of gender and sexual equality. Recent sexual surveys (Burger, 2012) and ethnographic studies (Jankowiak, 2013) have demonstrated, for example, that the new generation of young Chinese is more accepting sexual equality and mutual sexual attraction for long-term relationships and marriages.

6.3 Idealization in Romantic Love Model

6.3.1 Passionate and Affectionate Romantic Love Models

Passionate Romantic Love Model

Many scholars perceive *passion* (Berscheid & Walster, 1969/1978; Dueñas-Vargas, 2015; Lindholm, 1988; Paris, 1883) and *affection* (Floyd & Morman, 1998; Floyd et al., 2005; Romantic, n.d., 2016a, 2016b) as the defining qualities of *romantic love*. This is in accord with the long-standing scholarly traditions.

The *passionate emotions*—from the elated joys to desperate frustrations—are viewed as the most salient cultural features of *romantic love* in Western scholarship. This is perhaps why many American scholars equate *passionate love* with the *romantic love* (e.g., Fisher, 2004; Hatfield & Rapson, 1996; Jankowiak & Fischer, 1992; Regan, Kocan, & Whitlock, 1998). That makes some sense because the concepts of *passionate love* and *romantic love* have a lot in common. They both are substantially sexually motivated. They both are passionate—the highly passionate emotions, fuelled by high sexual arousals, are strong and frequent.

Romantic Myth of Passion

The myths on passion are also the strong beliefs of romantic lovers. They think that their love is in strong passion (De Roda, Martínez-Iñigo, De Paul, & Yela, 1999). Equating romantic myths with love, they are convinced that their passionate emotions will be forever. Therefore, experiencing fading passion, they are disappointed assuming their love for the partner is gone.

The romantic lover in the fire of their *passion* is "blind" and unable to perceive adequately the reality of life. Therefore, lovers tend to idealize and romanticize the loved one and relationship. This is a core feature of *romantic love model* (see for details, Karandashev, 2019).

Passionate Love Is Not Necessarily Romantic Love

However, the *passion of love* itself is not the only feature of romantic love. The *passionate model of love* represents a *narrower* constellation of emotions than the *romantic love*. Thus, due to many similarities, *romantic love* and *passionate love* are the largely overlapping models of love, yet they are different in several other attributes. The *romantic love model* is substantially mediated by culture, while *passionate model of love* is more biologically based (see for details, Karandashev, 2017). As Jankowiak (1995) commented, "Romantic passion is a complex multifaceted emotional phenomenon that is a byproduct of an interplay between biology, self, and society" (p. 4).

Affectionate Romantic Love Model

While overwhelmingly powerful passion is considered as a distinctive feature of romantic love, the less strong emotional experience of affection has been in the shadow of love research so far. I reviewed the affectionate model of love and its variations across cultures in the earlier chapter. Here, I wish to highlight once again the idea that different models of love are not dichotomous categories, they do not exclude one from another. They often overlap with each other due to their shared attributes and features. In particular, people can experience *affection of love* not only in the affectionate model, but also in the romantic model of love.

Scholars and educated public in the eighteenth to nineteenth centuries, and even the first part of the twentieth century, frequently used the term *affection* in reference to romantic love. However, in the second part of the twentieth century, the term *passion* replaced the word *affection* as the most characteristic feature of romantic love. This might happen due to the societal shift in the cultural ideals of the Western world of that time.

Affection has been postulated as a core component in several conceptions of *romantic love* (e.g., Ellis (1897–1910/2014); Hutcheon, 1995; Singer, 1987). As many empirical studies have demonstrated, experience and expression of affection in various forms are involved as the maintenance strategies in romantic and marital relationships (e.g., Dainton, Stafford, & Canary, 1994; De Boer, Van Buel, & Ter Horst, 2012; Dillow, Goodboy, & Bolkan, 2014; Gulledge, Stahmann, & Wilson, 2004; Gulledge, Hill, Lister, & Sallion, 2007; Hill, 2009; Luerssen, Jhita, & Ayduk, 2017; Sprecher, 1987).

6.3.2 How Idealization Works in Relationships

The Concept of Idealization

Idealization, embellishment, and beautification of reality are the key features of romanticism in art and life. Idealization of a partner and a relationship is the main characteristic of romantic love. Romantic lovers tend to accentuate the positive qualities, while overlooking or rationalizing the negative traits of the beloved one (Dion & Dion, 1996; Kephart, 1967; Lindholm, 1988, Lindholm, 1998; Murstein, 1988; Sprecher & Metts, 1989; Romantic, n.d., 2016a, 2016b; Rosenblatt, 1967). They are remarkable in their capacity to highlight the admirable qualities of the beloved and convert the negative qualities into a positive one. As Rubin (1970) noted, romantic love is the idealization of the other within an erotic context.

Passion of Love Triggers Idealization

Passion—due to high arousal—makes the perception of a beloved and relationship with him or her subjective: their merits appear brighter that they objectively are, while perception of demerits fades. Therefore, a passionate lover tends to be more romantic and idealistic looking at the world, beloved, and relationship through rosy filters. Then, it is not surprising that participants in the studies frequently rate passion as a prototypical feature of romantic love (Regan et al., 1998).

Are Romantic Love Attitudes and Emotions the Symptoms of Immaturity?

Some people believe that only youngsters and immature adults tend to fall in romantic love and experience idealization. They believe that romantic love is an illusionary, childish, and an immature set of attitudes and emotions that drives youth dating, mating, and sexual relationships. For example, Brickman (1987) claimed that romantic idealization and infatuation is a dangerous malady, which characterizes the early stage of dating and mating relationship. Giddens (1992) maintained that destructive romantic fantasies and delusions about relationships distract young men and women from serious exploration of personal identity, freedom, and sexual diversity.

The research obtained so far (Dean, 1964; Medora et al., 2002) does not allow concluding that romantic love is really a sign of immaturity. Two findings are in support of this. First, the correlation of romantic scores is minimal among American students (even though statistically significant), but absent among Indian and Turkish students. The university samples used in that study do not allow extrapolation to the older adults (Medora et al., 2002). Second, the scores of romanticization do not correlate with emotional adjustment (Dean, 1964).

6.3.3 Constructive and Destructive Roles of Romantic Idealization

Perceptual Romantic Illusions in Love

The *romantic love model* is characterized by the idealized perception of the beloved as a unique person and a relationship with this person as uniquely exceptional and perfect. Such *idealization* may have both positive and negative consequences for a relationship (Karandashev, 2019). The tendency of *idealization* in the romantic love model makes the feelings of a lover and *romantic* relationships inspirational, hopeful, uplifting, and fulfilling.

Romantic idealization sometimes resembles a perceptual illusion, with its positive and negative aspects. It can bring positive consequences for relationship satisfaction and longevity. *Idealistic beliefs* work as a psychological buffer: it protects individuals from paying attention to displeasing qualities of their partner (Murray & Holmes, 1997). A lover perceives the positive qualities of a beloved as brilliant and outstanding, yet interprets frailties and faults as merits or, at least, cute features. Research showed that men and women involved in stable relationships are capable to use compensatory "Yes, buts . . ." psychological mechanism integrating a partner's virtues and faults in a holistic image. It seems better for maintaining relationship than "leaving pockets of doubt" in mind (Murray, Holmes, & Griffin, 1996b, p. 1179). These processes of idealization reduce doubt in making and maintaining commitment to a partner and romantic relationship.

The Unique Person to Love and Exceptional Relationship

In the *romantic model of love*, a lover perceives a beloved as an unusual, unique, distinctive, and extraordinary person, who is the best and uniquely different from others and exceptional in many regards (De Munck, Korotayev, de Munck, & Khaltourina, 2011; Giddens, 1992; Fisher, 2004; Knee, 1998; Sprecher et al., 1994). The English conceptual metaphor "You are the most wonderful person in the world" characterizes such a romantic belief (Kövecses, 1988; Kövecses, 2005). The lover focuses on merits and fails to notice the demerits of the beloved.

A lover views the relationship with this partner as the best of its kind, perfect, exclusive, unique, and irreplaceable. He/she believes that passion of romantic love will find its way and last forever. The beliefs of romantic love assume (a) one unique romantic match in love, (b) appearance of love at first sight, (c) encouragement to follow heart rather than mind in choice of a partner, and (d) belief that love alters and conquers all (Knee, 1998).

The Benefits of Romantic Love Ideals

Positive illusions can lead to higher relationship satisfaction. Studies showed (Murray, Holmes, & Griffin, 1996a; Murray et al., 1996b; Taylor et al., 1989) that moderate idealization is conducive to satisfaction and happiness in dating relationships, especially in the case of mutual idealization. Such romantic idealization also helps in maintaining marital relationship (Baucom et al., 1996a; Knee, 1998; Sharp & Ganong, 2000).

Romantic love, like a beautiful dream, brings joy. Romantic lover attributes his or her lovely fantasy to the reality of relationship available. The corresponding idealistic romantic attitudes function as a motivational resource for goodwill, generosity, and optimism. Perception of a partner in a good light, seeing the best in one another, helps to overcome relationship difficulties and prevents the complications of everyday problems (Murray et al., 1996a). This positive approach to each other may be self-fulfilling: the partners idealizing one another may be not blind, but rather *prescient* (Murray et al., 1996b).

Romantic idealization is pleasant as a good dream. It is typical for an ideal model of love, which inspires lovers to look for relationship self-fulfillment. It encourages young men and women to search for a true love, which is presumably best for dating and marriage (Swidler, 2001). Pragmatic model of love, however, can work better for mating purposes.

The Adverse Effects of Idealization in Romantic Love Model

Idealization, however, can have long-term *adverse costs* for relationship development. Life and love are multifaceted; they are not white or black. Therefore, its excessive idealization can have various negative consequences.

According to several studies (Baucom et al., 1996b; Epstein et al., 1993; Glenn, 1991), the excessively high standards and expectations of a relationship, unrealistic romantic beliefs may lead to the further disillusionment, discontent, marital conflict, and divorce.

The romantics often love the idealized image, which they construct, not a real partner. Therefore, there is another possible path of how the idealized perception of a beloved can affect the relationship. The lack of awareness and recognition of a partner's frailties may cause fading illusions and dampening satisfaction later in the relationship. Self-deception and elusive hope for everlasting happiness can leave lovers susceptible to possible disappointments.

The evolving closer relationship with a partner can reveal that he or she does not fully meet the lover's ideals and high expectations. Once the lover continues to idealize his/her beloved one in the face of negative evidence, this tendency can make him/her vulnerable to disenchantment and impede successful adjustment. The adequate understanding of a real partner's virtues and faults is vital for enduring satisfaction (Murray et al., 1996a).

Critics of Romantic Love Model

There were several skeptics in social science in 1950–1970s, who, admitting the reality of romantic love complex in American culture, still believed that it is inadequate motivation for marriage. Waller and Hill (1951), for instance, commented that

> Love is blind, but only for a season, and passionate kindness does not last forever. . .
>
> It is possibly very unfortunate that people must make one of their most important decisions on the basis of certain delusive emotions of adolescence. . . and persons who have the power to excite this madness in others are by no means always the persons with whom it is possible to live happily after the knot it tied. (pp. 127–128)

S. Putney and G. Putney (1964/1972) claimed that culturally typical forms of American love are the projections of frustrated personal aspirations onto a prospective mate.

The Romantic Love Complex as a Cultural Ideal

The *romantic love* has been a desirable basis for satisfactory marriage in several European and North American cultures for many years. It is important, however, to distinguish the *romantic love model* and *romantic love complex*. The idea of *romantic love* in Europe, Australia, the United States, and Canada have gained popularity in the twentieth century. This romantic attitude meets the needs of young men and women in these highly differentiated societies and serves an inspirational role for marriage.

However, *the romantic love complex,* as a cultural idea, is not identical with *the true romantic love*. Its glamour pattern typifies the extreme romanticism as a derivative, which developed in a culturally specific artifact. *Romantic love* must be accepted in its true form, not in its unrealistic misrepresentations.

Effects of Cultural Values on the Romantic Idealistic Beliefs

It is reasonable to expect that culturally approved beliefs about love should influence the expectations, attitudes, experiences, and behaviors which young men and women in particular culture have (Kelley, 1983). Some scholars suggested that romantic idealization is related to *individuation of the self* and, therefore, this phenomenon may be more prevalent in modern individualistic cultures and less prevalent in traditional collectivistic cultures (e.g., Averill, 1985; Goode, 1959, 1963).

For example, American culture and social media elevate the romantic tendency to perceive the beloved one and the relationship in idealized ways. Cultural propaganda encourages men and women to believe that there should be one unique and ideal person who is a perfect match for them (Sastry, 1999). The widespread stereotype portrayed Americans as the greatest proponents of romantic love. However, according to the studies, cited in previous sections, Americans are moderate in their romantic beliefs and lower than many Europeans.

The effects of individualism on emotions and romantic beliefs in love marriage are multifaceted (Karandashev, 2019, 2021a). For example, a multinational study conducted by Levine et al. (1995) showed that people with high individualism tend to view the lack of romantic love as a barrier to marriage. Americans had the highest endorsement of the belief that lack of romantic love is a reason not to marry. As for the belief that lack of romantic love is a good reason to dissolve a marriage, Americans were only on the ninth rank out of 11 nations.

On the other side, Averill (1985) claimed that in the collectivistic Asian societies, where personal identity is not well distinguished from the group, a person is less likely to experience romantic idealization and less like considering romantic love as a prerequisite for marriage. According to the studies, cited in previous sections, Indians, Chinese, Japanese, Turkish, and Africans had the lower romantic beliefs in the ideals of romantic love, compared to many Americans and Europeans.

The anthropological story of A. Richards from the African tribe Bemba, which was recorded in the 1930s, is quite illustrative in this regard. She told the Bemba people a romantic folktale of how a young prince did numerous feats to gain the favor of his beloved maiden. The Bemba listeners were evidently bewildered. The old chief of the tribe expressed their confusion in a simple question: "Why not take another girl?" (cited in Karandashev, 2019, p. 125). The people apparently did not grasp the romantic ideal of exclusivity in love and marriage.

6.4 The Romantic Beliefs that Make Love Romantic

6.4.1 What the Romantic Beliefs Are?

The Origins of Romantic Beliefs

It is commonly believed that *romanticism* as a literary, artistic, musical, and intellectual ideology appeared in the cultures of European countries (Germany, France, Italy, Russia, and Britain) in the eighteenth and nineteenth centuries. However, the origins and elements of the romantic cultural beliefs are evident in many other cultural contexts of the Western and Eastern worlds. The ideals of romantic love have been especially popular in cultural literary and philosophical traditions throughout recent three hundred years (Karandashev, 2017).

In general, romanticism focused on the interests of individuals explored their potential for personal growth. It contrasted the intuitive and emotional over the rational. Romantics tended to idealize reality and followed raw intuition instead of knowledge. They explored human extreme psychological and intense emotional states. Romanticism highlighted intense emotion as a genuine source of aesthetic experience. Romantic poets, artists, and musicians reflected personal experiences, which represented universal themes (see for review, Barzun, 1961/1975; Karandashev, 2017; Lucas, 1936/2013; Prettejohn, 2005); Prickett, (1981/2016, Ed.). The word *romantic* in relation to emotional life and feeling of love meant *beautiful*, *sensible*, *sentimental, tender*, *gentle*, *melancholic*, and *sad*.

Romantic Views of Life and Love

Romantics had the complex psychological and emotional views of life. They portrayed people and depicted their emotional interaction with nature. The focal points of romanticism are emphasis (1) on freedom, individualism, and self-expression, (2) on emotion and love of nature, (3) the beliefs in importance of imagination idealizing the real world and nature and devotion to beauty, rather than of reasoning and knowledge, and (4) the beliefs in myths and mysticism.

These romantic ideals were popular among intellectuals; however, in the second half of the nineteenth century, the popularity of *romanticism* declined, and *realism* came to the stage of artistic and literary life as an opposite. However, the romantic beliefs continued to play their role in the dreams and life of educated peoples in many societies for a long time forward (see for review, Karandashev, 2017).

The romantic cultural ideology of the twentieth century has been precipitated by multiple bitter-sweet romantic novels, French and Italian cinema, Hollywood and Bollywood movies. In modern cultures and public opinions, the term *romantic* has come in many various connotations and meanings. It can imply many things according to scholarly and personal needs. There have been plenty of its definitions (see for review, Barzun, 1961/1975; Lucas, 1936/2013; Prettejohn, 2005; Prickett, 1981/2016, ed.).

The Modern Scholarly View of Romantic Love Model

Romantic love, characterized by idealization of partner and relationship, is an individual experience and expression involved in the initiation of many romantic relationships. The greater idealization and admiration lead to the higher romantic attraction and desire to see a person nearby. The tendency to fall in romantic love is widely attributed to the people of middle and high socioeconomic classes in Western cultures (see for review Karandashev, 2017).

Generalization of multiple romantic love studies (e.g., de Munck et al., 2011; Giddens, 1992; Gross, 1944; Fisher, 2004; Hinkle & Sporakowski, 1975; Kephart, 1967; Knee, 1998; Knox & Sporakowski, 1968; Munro & Adams, 1978; Sprecher & Metts, 1989; De Roda et al., 1999) lead to the following specific list of features characterizing romantic love model:

1. believing that a beloved is an ideal romantic match,
2. thinking that the beloved is the best and unique individual,
3. paying attention to the positive qualities of the beloved,
4. overlooking his/her negative qualities,
5. trusting to follow your heart,
6. believing that love conquers all (see for review, Karandashev, 2021b, p. 63).

Throughout years, researchers have operationalized romantic beliefs in love and romantic idealization with several psychometric scales. Among those, which have been used in multiple empirical studies, were the *Belief pattern scale of attitudes toward romanticism* (Gross, 1944), which assessed the *romantic culture pattern and realist culture pattern*, the *Knox-Sporakowski Attitudes Toward Love Scale* (Hinkle & Sporakowski, 1975), which was unidimensional, the *Munro-Adams Love-Attitude Scale* (Munro & Adams, 1978), which measured the beliefs in *romantic idealism, conjugal love, romantic power,* and the *Romantic Beliefs Scale* (Sprecher & Metts, 1989) with four beliefs measured in the scale: *love finds a way*, *one and only*, *idealization*, and *love at first sight*.

Later in the 1990s, the survey of *Romantic Myths* (De Roda et al., 1999) elaborated *romantic beliefs* in more detail, opposing them to pragmatic beliefs. Among those *romantic beliefs* are (1) the equivalence myth, (2) the "better-half" myth, (3) the exclusiveness (of being love) myth, (4) the eternal passion myth, (5) the omnipotence (love conquers all) myth, (6) the fidelity myth, (7) the marriage myth, and (8) the couple myth (p. 65).

These romantic love beliefs and attitudes may have their positive and negative effects in different interpersonal situations and cultural contexts (see for review, Karandashev, 2019).

6.4.2 *Romantic Beliefs Across Cultures*

Cross-Cultural Studies of Romantic Beliefs

The beliefs in romantic love have been popular across many cultures and across times. They were reflected in the genres and themes of literature, music, and art in various cultural contexts. Philosophers and other culturally influential scholars contemplated about romantic love (Karandashev, 2017). In different societies and real life of people, however, there were diverse attitudes to such romantic ideals. The romantic beliefs became a subject of empirical scientific research only in the middle of the twentieth century.

Cross-cultural *empirical studies of romantic beliefs* in many countries across the world, which have been completed since 1960–1980s until 2000s, allow to estimate the general cultural geography of romantic beliefs. We need to keep in mind that those studies have been administered in a limited number of cultural samples, which were selected sporadically, and had relatively moderate or small sample sizes. Besides, the cultures of many countries might change during these decades (see for their detailed review and multiple references, Karandashev, 2019, 2021b). Therefore, their comparison may have limited validity and reliability.

Cross-Cultural Variations of Romantic Beliefs

The results of multiple cross-cultural studies (see for review and references, Karandashev, 2019, 2021b) have shown that many respondents from the US samples had the romantic beliefs of a moderate degree, much lower that the American cultural myths represent. They express rather companionate and friendship-oriented love beliefs, probably due to the long-standing puritan and practical values, which the settlers of the early generations lived with (see more in other sections). Women had more pragmatic attitudes than did men.

The results have revealed that German, French, Spanish, and Russian respondents had the higher romantic beliefs compared to Americans, probably due to the strong European romantic cultural traditions. Despite these relative differences, the North American and European respondents were more romantic in comparison with those in Japanese, Chinese, Turkish, and Indian samples.

The results of the studies (see for review, Karandashev, 2019, 2021b) have revealed that the respondents from several African samples had lower romantic beliefs, compared to European and American samples, probably due to the lower exposure of the European and American cultural romantic ideals. The cultural understanding of love in African cultures balanced a mixture of the Western ideals of romantic love and traditional indigenous conceptions of love, which fused together in the people's minds. The respondents from the Caribbean region, such as West Indies, had the romantic beliefs comparable to Americans, yet higher than in

African samples. The Caribbean respondents probably had the greater exposure to American romantic ideals through various cultural media and touristic exchange.

The Role of Culture, Gender, and Age in Romantic Beliefs

The summary of cross-cultural variations in romantic beliefs, presented above, has shown that British, German, French, and Russian cultural traditions substantially shaped the romantic views of people in several European countries. The North American cultures have been less romantic, despite cultural stereotypes, but moderately romantic due to the values of freedom and independence. The East Asian Japanese and Chinese, the Middle East Turkish, South-Asian Indian, Latin American Caribbean, and African cultures were much less romantic in their cultural models and beliefs. These differences partially can be explained by cultural literary and artistic traditions, and by the degree of modernization in societies (modern cultures versus traditional cultures).

Even though no recent studies of romantic beliefs have been conducted so far, one may speculate that the romantic beliefs in The North American and European societies are on decline, while in many other societies mentioned above are on rise.

The results of cross-cultural studies are controversial about gender differences in romantic beliefs, while age was not related to romanticism. Even though the early studies in the United States showed that men were more romantic than women, the studies in other cultures showed the opposite—women were more romantic in their love beliefs. For example, women in Spain, Turkey, America, West Indies, and several other cultural samples, were more romantic than men. Some studies (e.g., De Munck, Korotayev, & Khaltourina, 2009) showed that culture matters more than gender—the differences in romantic beliefs are larger between cultural samples than between respondents of different gender.

6.4.3 Romantic Love Is Irrational

Unknown Causes and Nature of Love

Some scholars think that the secrets of romantic love are beyond our rational understanding and reasoning. They even acknowledge irrationality of one or another kind in their conceptions of love. The modern "scientific" reference to the *chemistry of love* may look more scientifically than the *magic of love*. Nevertheless, the essence of both notions admits unexplainable irrationality of romantic love. The *scientific nature* of the *chemistry* of love still looks beyond our rational understanding.

The attitudes to irrationality in romantic love may vary across cultures. For example, French students tend to believe in the irrational nature of love more than do Americans (Murstein, Merighi, & Vyse, 1991).

The concepts of the fate, human destiny, the destiny of God, or the destiny of our nature are of the same kind describing our understanding of irrational nature of romantic love. A cross-cultural perspective can be illuminating and will be reviewed in the following section.

Irrationality frequently goes along with strong passion characterizing *romantic love model.* Being passionate, romantic love is experienced as an uncontrollable emotion, as an external force that dominates one's life (Heimer & Stinchcombe 1980). A romantic lover seems irrational and inaccessible to rational endeavor, as in the state of any other mystical experience. In this sense, Weber (1958) compared romantic love with religious experience. Rationality is opposite to the sphere of romantic love the same way as rationality is opposite to the sphere of religion. In this regard, romantic love is akin to religion. A lover becomes freed from "the cold skeleton hands of rational orders, just as completely as from the banality of everyday routine" (p. 347).

Romantic love is not an intentional decision for a person. Being irrational, a romantic lover "falls in love not by design and conscious choice, but according to some accident of fate over which the victim has no control" (Greenfield, 1965, p. 363). According to this belief, love can strike at any time and in any place making a lover a helpless victim who behaves irrationally and loses control over his/her actions and reasons. As a magical transcendence, romantic love is experienced an "aching of the heart" and an "infection of the brain" (Tennov, 1998).

The Mystics of Love

The mystic ideals of love have been popular among people for centuries. A major reason of these enduring beliefs is inability of scholars and researchers scientifically and rationally explain why people fall in love. Multiple anecdotal evidence and stories of love show that people do not really know why they love one person, but not another. They usually do not choose a beloved and do not fall in love based on rational reasons.

Romantic love is not realistic, but rather idealistic. It is not rational, but rather irrational. Some scholars believe that individuals do not love for reasons, and they cannot rationally be aware of why they fall in love (see for review, Carlsson, 2018).

The appraisals of the qualities of other person and love attitudes cause love. Romantic love has *causes*, but not *reasons:* people usually cannot think of what has caused their love to a particular loved one. Carlsson (2018) believes the following factors determine these challenges:

(a) The lover may be attracted to a quality without appraising that quality reflectively.

(b) Personal qualities are not perceived in isolation; rather, our assessment of one quality will affect how we perceive another. In fact, we tend to posit essences in persons, and these guide our interpretation of their other qualities.

(c) We do not see persons as bundles of qualities but as unique wholes. This is due to our capacity to fetishize particulars, and it dispels the problem of fungibility.
(d) We have a tendency to see meaning in things retrospectively—philosophers have mistaken this sense of meaning for rationality.

A folk metaphysics that is deeply built into our psyches resists scholars' attempts to rationally explain love (Carlsson, 2018).

Chemistry of Love

The Western-educated and scientific conceptions of love strive to be rational, reasonable, and evidence-based in their scholarly approach to love. Therefore, the attempts to refer to something mistic and unexplainable are usually condemned. The references to the stars, which come together for a couple, or destiny sound pseudoscientific. The Amour's, or Cupid's, arrow in a heart looks nice symbolically, yet the myth is too naïve to believe in the modern time.

Nevertheless, the unexplainable and irrational causes of love seem to exist. So, the notion of *chemistry of love* came in light in scholarship and research. The term sounds scientifically respectable, even though it is irrational in its content (e.g., Fisher, 2004; Hendrick & Hendrick, 1986).

Love at first sight is among the core feature of *classical romantic love model*. The *love at first sight* phenomenon is embodied in the mythological image of the Cupid's "love arrows." The myth in other incarnation is popular in romantic novels and movies. The prototypical script of romantic love is "falling in love," very likely at the first sight, as many romantic movies teach us this lesson (Hefner & Wilson, 2013). The "choosing to love" is a rare romantic script.

This notion connotates with the idea that it is impossible to explain the *love at first sight* rationally. The biochemistry of love or destiny in love is well fit for the irrational explanation (see more in the next section).

The phenomenon can be interpreted as a biased idealized perception of another person due to infatuation in love. This is the "love is blind" bias. The scientific studies of the *love at first sight* are on the rise in recent years (e.g., Barelds & Barelds-Dijkstra, 2007; Grant-Jacob, 2016; Hefner & Wilson, 2013; Zsok, Haucke, De Wit, & Barelds, 2017). The detailed review of their results goes beyond the scope of this book.

6.4.4 Romantic Love as a Destiny

Cultural Models of Love as a Fate or Choice

A *belief in fate* and *destiny* means that only one predestined true love with a unique partner is possible, that potential partners are either meant for each other or not. Individuals in romantic love rely on this intuitive feeling of destiny and succumb to what is destined for them. They do not select a beloved one rationally; they fall in love being driven by the internal impulse of natural attraction as their fate (Aronson, 2015).

Rational love, which is based on the principle of choice, selects the best option possible, while romantic love does not select relying on an intuitive feeling of destiny (Aronson, 2015). *Rational love* strives to maximize rewards and happiness, while romantic love succumbs to what is destined accommodating happiness and affliction all together.

Love, according to romantic ideals, on the other hand, is an unpredictable force and unknown reality, which is psychologically risky and can make us vulnerable. Romantic lovers accept such existential vulnerability, being ready to accept positive and negative emotions—joy and pain of love. They accept the right to pain and dare to agonize about love. As Brown articulated this, "our capacity for whole-heartedness can never be greater than our willingness to be broken-hearted" (Brown, 2012).

Romantic lovers believe that there is one unique partner who matches them—with all strengths and weaknesses, and he/she is their true love. In the choice of a partner, it is more important to follow your heart, rather than mind. The true love will conquer all, find its way, and last forever.

A longitudinal study of romantic relationships conducted in the United States (Knee, 1998) demonstrated that those partners who believed in romantic destiny experienced higher initial satisfaction and have longer relationship (Knee, 1998).

Cross-Cultural Presence of the Love Destiny Concept

The idea of love and a spouse for life as a fate and destiny has been widespread across times and cultures. This is a classical ideal of European literature and scholarship about romantic love. The modern studies show the presence of this cultural belief in several African and Asian cultures.

These cultural ideals are reflected in the words representing love as *destiny and fate* assuming the existence of ultimate agency guiding a person to the perfect love and predetermined relationships. A person's willpower cannot control the romantic love—true love is an inevitable fate. The examples are the *anánkē* (star-crossed love)—the classical Greek word for a binding and unshakable destiny, *yuán fèn*—the Chinese word for a force impelling a relationship destiny, *koi no yokan*—the Japanese word for the feeling that love with this person is inevitable, *sarang*—the Korean word for the lifelong unshakable love (Lomas, 2018). Thus, the analogous idea of predestined love has evolved in various cultural contexts.

Love as a Destiny in Burmese Culture

Located in Southeast Asia, the *Myanmar* country (formerly known as *Burma*) is highly shaped by Buddhist culture. According to the tradition of Burmese folklore, love is the *destiny*. The Hindu god Brahma writes the one's love "destiny on the forehead," shortly after one's birth. The Burmese society has no customs of arranged marriage and dowries. Weddings are sacred rites in Burmese culture. People can organize the religious and well-elaborated ceremonies, yet they may keep these wedding practices secular and simply beautiful.

Love is largely present in the marital relationship (de Munck, 2019. The sentimental affection and love emotions are involved in emotional experiences. In the Burmese language, there are many words designated for these emotions. These words express romantic love, sexual attractions, affection, sympathy, and attachment bonds. However, the Bamar people do not frequently use these words to show their feelings of psychological intimacy and emotions. They are reserved, like in other East Asian societies, in emotional expressiveness. Thus, romantic love, despite being valuable in the marital life of men and women, is expressed in moderation (Spiro, 1977).

Love as a Destiny in Chinese Culture

Chinese relational fatalism is embodied in *yuan* (predestined relational affinity)—the beliefs in a predestined relational affinity (Goodwin & Findlay, 1997; Yang, 2006). People think that affinity predetermines the occurrence, duration, type, and the outcome of an interpersonal relationship. Different types of relationships are attributed to different kinds of *yuan* as external and stable causal factors. This external attribution to *yuan* has an important ego-defensive and social-defensive function and keeps interpersonal and family relationships stable and harmonious (Yang, 2006).

When a relationship is established, Chinese people especially value relational harmony. They pursue harmony for the sake of harmony and have a strong fear of disharmony (Yang, 2006).

6.4.5 Romantic Beliefs and the Real Life

The Issue of Universality of Romantic Love Model

Some argued that *romantic love* has been cross-culturally universal across cultures and times (see for review, Karandashev, 2017). Discussing this issue, scholars should distinguish what they are talking about. The question should be considered depending on the planes of love existence. Whether romantic love is a universal cultural idea, a universal real experience of all people across cultures, or a universal capability of people to experience romantic love.

There are at least two planes on which scholars consider romantic love:

- *romantic love people fantasize by*—romantic love as a *cultural idea* of desired and undesired,
- *romantic love people live by*—romantic love as a short-term or long-term *personal experience.*

Romantic love, as a set of cultural ideals, concepts, scripts, descriptions, and images, can be an *ideal cultural model* or a *real model (type) of relationships and actions (emotional experience).* Throughout centuries, poets, playwrights, novelists, philosophers, musical composers, artists, and scholars have been elaborating the *model of romantic love* as a *cultural idea*, as the *ideal cultural model,* in their creative works. The *ideal cultural model* does not mean the best and most desirable in a society. The *ideal* means—*existing* in the works of art and writing, in the cultural objects and artifacts, and subsequently, in the minds of readers and spectators. These *ideal cultural models* have been depicting the *world of possibilities*, rather than realities, which life and love can have. The *real-life stories* of love, presented in romantic novels and movies, have been also perceived by people as the possibilities, along with their good and bad things, experiences, and consequences. Sometimes, they worked as the positive or negative role models in a broad sense.

Propaganda of Romantic Love Model

The social media in many societies and cultures, in certain periods of history, have propagated the *ideals of romantic love*. These ideals are interesting, entertaining, exciting, and inspirational for those who are capable to appreciate them. This is a reason why romantic love has been a proliferating topic of writings, paintings, and movies for years. The question remains, whether people, at least some of them, have actually lived and loved this or similar way?

Various social and public media in many modern countries continue to entertain and propagate their variants of romantic love via romantic tales and cinema, beautiful pictures, scenes, and consumerism in the new settings designed by authors, scriptwriters, and artistic directors. These media, like novels and movies, must be entertaining to excite and arouse emotions and not be routine or boring—otherwise, no one will watch them. This is the reason that their popular genres and plots are comedy, drama, melodrama, crime and mystery fiction, thriller, or tragedy. Only romantic and extramarital stories of love can fit to this entertaining function of romantic love. In this regard, they surpass any other models of love.

The *ideal romantic model of love* largely influences the relationships and emotions of early adults and those who are in premarital relations (Hefner & Wilson, 2013), probably because these are the typical plots of romantic stories. Marital relationships have been rarely in romantic scripts unless they involve extramarital affairs.

Many *models of romantic love* are rather *cultural models*, which can be accepted as *personal models* or not, which can become the *reality of relationship* or not. As I commented elsewhere, *romantic love model* can play two roles: (1) *inspirational function* for the young chronologically or psychologically men and women, or (2) *escapist function* for those who are tired of the frustrating routine of real relationship. Reading and watching, they live through their dreams, which bring emotional relief and entertainment.

There is also the *third role of romantic love model*, which are similar to the first one. It is *inspirational modeling,* which is *like fashion arts*. People usually don't wear the dresses, which are designed for fashion shows—they are two extravagant. Designers appreciate them as the pieces of art, which demonstrate new fashion ideals. However, some of those ideals are used then in the production of real clothes. The same way, the *inspirational modeling* function of romantic love admits that individuals may use *some elements of this model* in their real emotional life and relationship.

Compatibility of the Romantic Model of Love with Other Models of Love in American Society

In the same vein, the American culture of the late twentieth century entertained romantic love as an ideal model aspiring young men and women to follow their hearts. The romantic novels and Hollywood movies shaped the cultural models for such aspirations. The practices of relationship initiation and dating frequently followed such romantic scripts (Karandashev, in press).

Sociological interviews (Swidler, 2001) demonstrated that for many people in California, USA, the two cultural models of love still existed, as a century ago: *romantic* and *realistic*. The *romantic love myth* is still a *typical ideal model*, which encouraged men and women to look for one right person, the true love that conquers all and last for a whole life. Many Americans followed the romantic love myth when they initiated the relationship and decided whom to marry and whether it is worthwhile to stay in a marriage.

However, the American informants (Swidler, 2001) rejected the romantic myth of love for their real life-long relationship. They chose another model of love—realistic, practical, and routine, which frequently resembles the *companionate,* sometimes *pragmatic one*. This model needs the relationship building, managing the daily chores, occasional complications, compromises, and sometimes sacrifices.

The studies of Swidler (2001) and De Munck et al. (2009, 2010) have shown that many Americans use both models of love in their relationships, integrating them relatively well. Different from these views, Lithuanians and Russians conceptualize these models of love as distinctively different, which are difficult to combine. For them, romantic love is a temporary fairy-like tale of passion, an entertainment and adventure, while for real life, which is totally different—the pragmatic and practical love, less likely the companionate one (De Munck et al., 2009, 2010, see more in other section).

The historians, scholars, journalists, and sociologists of recent times have documented their observations of how *romantic model of love* became the reality of relationships for many people in various societies. However, romantic love has become the reality for only premarital relationship, while marital relationship turned to real models of love, such as pragmatic, practical, and companionate ones.

It is worth noting that in modernized Western societies, many men and women shy away from romantic lexicon, romantic experience, and expression of love. They strive to be simple in their relationships in many regards. They may be *romantic in a different sense* –the *cultural model of romantic love may have transformed* in recent decades.

6.4.6 Romantic and Other Models of Love in Modern World

Romantic Model Versus Other Models of Love

The Western scholarly and public discussions about opposition between romantic love and realistic love models have been active since the middle of the twentieth century (see for review, Karandashev, 2017). Many middle-class educated Americans embraced the ideal of romantic love as a prerequisite for marriage. It looked like the love had concurred marriage (Coontz, 2006; Murstein, 1974). The scholarly exploration and scientific investigation enthusiastically engaged in the topic of love. However, some scholars advised against the value of romantic love (e.g., Giddens, 1992; Murstein, 1974; Singer, 1984a, 1984b, see for review, Karandashev, 2017, 2019). They contrasted *romantic love as disapproved* and *realistic love as preferred* model of love. This distinction, however, can be not necessarily sharp, dichotomous, and binary.

In the modern Chinese society, romantic love is also considered as the model of love distinguishable from pragmatic love. Young urban people conceptualize the feelings, words, and expressions of love in the two major groups of qualities of being in love: (1) idealized, both positive and negative, and (2) pragmatic (Jankowiak et al., 2015, 2015).

Romantic Love Versus Pragmatic Love

The model of romantic love, as opposed to the model of pragmatic (realistic) love, declares that *love* and *money* are incomparable. When the *economic exchange model* supersedes the *romantic love model*, it is insincere love. As Singer noted (1984), romantic love is an idealistic conception, and in this regard it is contrasting with the realistic conception of the exchange paradigm of love.

Romantic love refers generally to the temporary or life-long exclusive bonds—with some exemptions. Other types of love can also be romantic in terms of idealization, physical, emotional, behavioral beauty, and sexual engagement (Karandashev, 2017). As Lomas (2018) commented, several categories of love are closely related to what might be called *romantic love*. This type of love can also involve *storgē* and *philia*.

Romantic Love and Companionship

Romantic love is frequently considered as a model of love different from companionate love. It should be noted, however, that companionate love is not just habitual living of partners together with fading passion and idealization. Companionate love is a love in which new important feelings evolve. Gently taking care of each other, expressing tenderness, and sharing intimate thoughts and feelings with each other is quite romantic. This companionate love is willing to share everyday life and chores, to find the meaning in simple tasks and appreciate the relatedness, value, and beauty in the ordinary things (Karandashev, 2017).

For example, in the American cultural model, romantic love is well compatible with companionate love. Passionate feelings of moderate energy accompany the romantic love emotions during relationship initiation, yet they easily transform into the companionate emotions of *comfort, security, friendship*, and other *mutual compatible virtues*. Individuals rarely mention such terms as *crazy, temporary, delusional, like fairytale,* and *dream-like state that is not real*, which people in some other cultures (e.g., Lithuania, Russia) frequently use to characterize romantic love (De Munck et al., 2009, 2010). The romantic love being merged into companionate love create the positive realm of low energy.

The years of love and relationship do not necessarily kill romantic emotions. The studies (Acevedo & Aron, 2009) convincingly demonstrated that romantic love can exist and last in a long-term relationship. Obsessional feelings, quite characteristic to passionate love, may be absent in the later years. Yet, companionate love does not necessarily lack romantic attraction and sexual desire. Partners in the later stages of their relationship can be romantic and experience such romantic qualities as sexual liveliness, intensity, and engagement.

In other cultures, laypeople conceptualization of romantic love and its relations with companionate love can be different. Lithuania and Russia are the two examples of a different kind, which may be typical for Eastern European countries (De Munck et al., 2009, 2010). People say about romantic love as a *preliminary stage of relationship*, in which lovers go *a little crazy* and *delusional*. It is a *temporary fairytale, dream-like state that is not real, not pragmatic,* that is quite different from the companionate model of love.

In both Lithuanian and Russian cultures, friendship is not a salient quality of romantic love. People rarely mention such terms as *secure, content, comfortable,* and *commitment* (De Munck et al., 2009, 2010). Friendship for them is associated with those who they know for a long time.

6.5 Admiration Models of Romantic Love

6.5.1 The Human's Need for Admiration and Adoration

The Need to Admire

The *need for admiration* is among the key social motivations in interpersonal relationships, especially for some people. There are two positions of social communication, which involve admiration: the *position of admirer* and *position of admired*—in each of these positions a person satisfies their specific needs. In both cases, admiration satisfies important personal functions in social interaction.

On the one hand, many individuals generally need the standards and ideals, which aspire them to become better in one or another regard, achieve some goals, or fulfill their plans. *Significant others* in our *social* or *parasocial relations* may represent our personal models of excellence inspiring us to learn from them and become a better person. The admiring individuals attempt to emulate the behaviors and attributes of admired models (Sarapin, Christy, Lareau, Krakow, & Jensen, 2015). Having in mind another, who is better than ourselves, elevates our self-esteem due to personal identification with that person. Psychologically, it works like self-expansion (Aron & Aron, 1986, 1996, 2016). This kind of admiration needs is a source of *admiration models of love*. However, such admiration may also humiliate if individuals have narcissistic tendencies and value themselves more than anyone else.

The Need to Be Admired

On the other hand, many individuals want to be praised, respected, and admired by others because such tokens of appreciation enhance their self-esteem. So, when they see or imagine others' admiration, this is pleasing. This kind of admiration needs is a source of *self-love models of love*. Knowing this, excellent communicators take any opportunity to compliment, praise, or congratulate others, even at the expense of flattering. For individuals with *perfectionist and narcissistic personality*, this kind of admiration from others is especially vital for their well-being (e.g., Cramer, 2011; Hill & Yousey, 1998; Rice & Preusser, 2002).

Thus, in interpersonal relations, admiration for each other is gratifying. It creates social bonds and leads to a better interpersonal contact and psychologically beneficial communication (Onu, Kessler, & Smith, 2016).

The Concepts of Admiration and Adoration

There are several concepts, which describe how people can experience and express this bundle of related love emotions and attitudes. These are what have variously been labeled as admiration, adoration, reverence, worship, awe, and respect. They are similar in some respects, yet they differ in the patterns of appraisal and action tendencies (Onu et al., 2016; Schindler, Zink, Windrich, & Menninghaus, 2013). They all play their important roles in the *admiration model of love*.

Attitudes and emotions of admiration inspire an individual to *approach, internalize, and emulate the ideals*, which another person as a successful and outstanding *role model* embodies (Onu et al., 2016; Schindler et al., 2013). Admiration works to enhance the agency of individuals in their striving for ideals. Admiration promotes *social learning* and change at the individual level of interpersonal relations and *transmission of cultural models* at the societal level (Onu et al., 2016; Schindler, 2014). Admiration also functions to regulate and maintain social hierarchy in groups. People tend to feel admiration for powerful and competent others (Sweetman, Spears, Livingstone, & Manstead, 2013).

Emotional experience of adoration is sparked by perceiving someone so outstanding that others cannot completely understand and attain such excellent quality. The adoring adherent perceives the other—loved one—as superb, ideal, and sacred, which is forever out of reach for the ordinary person. Others cannot achieve such excellence, but they may wish to benefit and share. They can do this by uniting with this adorable loved one. Therefore, the main *action tendency of adoration* is to connect and relate with the adorable role model—even though in phantasy. The values, ideals, and other things associated with this adorable individual become a part of personal identity of an adoring adherent.

While in admiration, another is a role model, the adorable other is a meaning maker and benefactor who unites him/her with an adherent lover. Thus, creating and maintaining social cohesion is the central function of adoration. Adoration binds individuals and relationships together (Schindler, 2014; Schindler et al., 2013).

Anyway, both *admiration* and *adoration* bind people to their ideal role models. Some of them can move closer to their ideals, while others cannot. Therefore, these emotional experiences can be the potential sources of either personal satisfaction, or frustration (Schindler, 2014).

The Admiration and Adoration Scales (ADMADOS) was developed to measure *dispositional admiration and adoration*, with six items reflecting admiration and seven items reflecting adoration. The item statistics and exploratory factor analyses lead to a revised version of the scale with a set of eight items (Schindler, 2014).

The positive correlation of admiration and adoration with several other variables of emotional experience showed that love, fascination, gratitude, awe, and inspiration are important constituents of this model of love (Schindler, 2014).

6.5.2 *Admiration of Celebrities and Parasocial Romantic Model of Love*

Cultural Valorization of Celebrities

It is worthwhile to note that American and British cultures cherish the idea that celebrities are worthy of special attention and valorization (Giles, 2002; McCutcheon et al., 2002). Among celebrities, some may be more appealing for *loving admiration* than others. The favorite celebrity of the same age and the opposite gender has more chance to be loved. The celebrity usually belongs to glamorous profession. The typical celebrity are the well-known figures in acting, singing, or being a TV talk-show host. Musicians, actors, or athletes are the most favorite celebrities (about 75%) for admiration worship (Green, Griffith, Aruguete, Edman, & McCutcheon, 2014). The adoration of entertainers, pop singers, and athletes in the popular magazines and other social media is very high. The *cultural model of idolizing celebrities* precipitates this *parasocial personal model of admiration love.*

In addition, many modern American and British young men and women (of 18-to 25-year-olds) not only admire fame, but eagerly desire to become celebrity themselves or, at least, become a personal assistant of a celebrity. Just being close to a celebrity is viewed by many as the more desirable purpose than being a successful businessperson or a public servant. The important goals and "the very best things in the world" of their generation are "becoming famous," "being a celebrity," "good looks," and "being rich," while "God" and "becoming more spiritual" came in last (Twenge & Campbell, 2009). Such motivation paves down the pathway to the *narcissistic model of love.*

Cultural Model of Idolizing Celebrities

Admiration of celebrities can be also considered as *love*. This is the *parasocial love* in which people love with admiration—*bottom-up*—the admirable individuals, with whom they do not have real contact relationships. This love is in an admirers' phantasies only. The worship of celebrity may sometimes be benign.

The genres of television series, sitcoms, and soap operas have become popular across many societies (see for review, Allen & Allen, 1995) and shape the new *culturally universal model of love* and relationship. The United States has dominated the international television marketplace of this kind. American television programs have been exported in other countries in the forms of cultural imperialism, usually on the "one-way flow," and have had substantial impact on national cultures (Bielby & Harrington, 2005; Giles, 2002).

A celebrity's fan may have hundreds of replications of her/his idol in their possession——posters, pictures, and photographs, regularly spending a lot of money on magazines and clothes from their celebrity' shop. The fans can make pilgrimages, move to be near their hero. They can even renounce their former friends: "We all moved away from our school friends and things like that… This is more like the entry into a religious cult than a passing 'teen phase'" (Giles, 2002, p. 133–134). They meet new friends through attending the concerts, which a pop idol plays at, and coming to fan clubs.

The admirers with the *ludus style* fantasize to include their favorite celebrity in their imaginary romance. They experience a temptation to act and behave compulsively with the attitude, like "I often feel compelled to learn the personal habits of my favorite celebrity." Sometimes, the admiring lovers feel ready to do something illegally, like in the attitudes, "If…my favorite celebrity asked me to do something illegal as a favor, I would probably do it" (McCutcheon, 2002, p. 92).

The Parasocial Model of Love, which Substitutes External Social Relationships

The modern world is the world of new reality, which is overflooded with photo magazines, performance stages, broadcast communication, TV, mass media, and dynamic screens. In some regards, for some people, this new social media world has replaced the directly experienced world. People frequently completely immerse themselves in the dramatic experience, avoiding the experience of reality.

Actors of this social media world frequently appear in people's life becoming their regular companions, heroes, and the objects of love and admiration. The relationships with the characters in this *mediated world* and the celebrities are characterized by *parasocial interaction.*

The concept of *parasocial interaction* characterizes psychological phenomenon that appeared with the advent of the new mass media, such as radio, the movie, and television. At a distance, these media give the impression of *personal face-to-face relationship* with the actor, show person, and performer. This relationship can be very intimate (Horton & Wohl, 1956). This *parasocial relationship* develops from social/task *attraction* to the television character, then to *parasocial interaction,* and further to the appearance of a *sense of relationship importance*. The essential difference in the experience of such a relationship is the lack of active reciprocity. The interaction is one-sided, yet the bonds of intimacy can develop (e.g., Giles, 2002; Horton & Wohl, 1956; Rubin & McHugh, 1987).

Some individuals, who are socially inactive, lonely, and isolated, may spend many days and substantial time during the day in front of the TV, Internet, and IT social media. Their life is experientially deprived from external social and interpersonal relations. Over time, their regular technology-mediated contacts with other people may evolve in "*parasocial relationships.*" The personalities of characters, TV show hosts, pop stars, which they see, become the reality of their social life. Television series, sitcoms, and soap operas create parallel realities (Slade & Beckenham, 2005), which are especially important for socially isolated individuals who satisfy their needs for actual relationships. Such parasocial relationships have real emotional significance for them draining and defusing emotional energy.

The relationships with those personalities may substitute other possible interpersonal relations, in some sense, according to the same psychological mechanism as *pornography and parasocial sexual interaction* can *substitute real sexual relationships*. Such shy, withdrawn, or otherwise socially awkward individuals can live their vicarious virtual lives through these social media scripts and plots, which work for them as the alternative substituting real relationships (Giles, 2002). This *imitation style of relationship and emotion* brings the opportunity to avoid the challenges of difficult, uncomfortable, and embarrassing relationship initiation with others of the opposite or same sex. For them, it is easier to live and meet their needs through these *fulfilling relationships* than encounter the risks and complexities of forming a *real relationship*.

Many scales of love are not suitable to measure this type of love because they generally assess the attitudes *toward a real partner*. So, to investigate this *admiration of celebrity love*, researchers have developed the *Celebrity Attitude Scale* (CAS) that measures the favorability of attitudes toward one's favorite celebrity (Maltby et al., 2002; McCutcheon, 2002).

Parasocial Versus Contact Romantic Model of Love

In these *parasocial relationships* (Giles, 2002), people can lose touch with real world of relationships not clearly distinguishing between fiction and reality. The distinction between soap characters and real-life celebrities is substantially blurred. The people can treat soap characters as though "in character."

A *parasocial relationship* is under personal control because there is no real interpersonal interaction. A *parasocial partner* can be the ideal partner having all desired attributes and fulfilling any fantasies (Giles, 2002). The favorite celebrity represents a person of fantasized romantic *parasocial feelings* and *relationship*. This type of love has a better chance to be reciprocated since it is *experienced and enacted in the admirer's phantasy*. Then, a risk of *unrequited love is minimal.*

Such *parasocial love* can be a stepping stone toward real love and fuller relationship. Such relationship may be good for the teenagers who still explore their motivations for relationship in the real world. The *parasocial relationships* are *less deep* than *real relationships*. Nevertheless, they can be the good substitutes for many lonely people.

The *parasocial model of love* is still missing many tangible qualities, compared with the relationship in the *contact model of love* as the two-way interaction. The behaviors and actions in real relationship involve *closeness, warmth, tactility, smell*—all things that a person can *feel* in contact intimacy—feeling sensitive touch, embracing another body, sleeping in bed together.

Such interactive qualities as shared living space, reciprocity, personal recognition, obligations, and domestic arrangements are not available *parasocial relationship,* yet they can be vital for personal well-being.

Personalities Predisposed to the Parasocial Model of Love

Several parameters predict this *type of admiration love*. As for personality traits, dependent lovers are especially prone to this kind of *parasocial love*. They are frequently unconfident in the love of their real partner and are afraid of a possible breakup of real relationship. Due to this low self-confidence, their *anxious need for love* transfers to celebrities and embraces passion to their own passionate phantasy. Thus, a strong romantic attachment to a celebrity works as a back-up phantasy providing an imaginary blanket of security (McCutcheon, 2002). The shy and lonely individuals are much less likely and less prone to the strong parasocial love to celebrities (Ashe & McCutcheon, 2001).

The *absorption-addiction model* (McCutcheon, 2002) explains psychological factors of individual predisposition to *celebrity worship*. A *weak identity* of a person facilitates psychological absorption with a celebrity to strengthen the identity and personal fulfillment. When an addictive predisposition blends with the absorption, such psychological mixture leads to the more extreme behavior that sustains the personal satisfaction with one's favorite celebrity. *Fantasy proneness, obsessive-compulsive tendencies, celebrity worship,* and *preoccupied attachment style* are among the key dispositions of such *celebrity stalking experience and behavior* that may resemble *obsessive love* and *fanatic models of love* (McCutcheon, Aruguete, McCarley, & Jenkins, 2016; Roberts, 2007).

Individuals of ludus love style, with playful and sociable character, interested in multiple relationships also have tendency to experience parasocial love to celebrity. They experience romantic admiration to a celebrity as a fantasized external projection of their personal model of love to the real social relationships. They view the attractive celebrity as a person to conquer, even though this conquest is illusory (McCutcheon, 2002; Woll, 1989). The lovers of ludus style also show evidence of mild pathology perceiving the celebrity as a romantic object.

The studies have shown (see for review, Deci & Flaste, 1996) that striving to become famous, beautiful, and rich may likely lead to anxiety, depression, and low well-being. These things bring many psychological problems, yet they may not bring stable feelings of personal happiness.

Fanatic Model of Love

This fans' *love of celebrity* resembles *fanatic love*, which seems also evident in many cults, religious, political, or media-cultural social groups. This is a *love for authority*, whichever the source of the authority is. The sharing love for the same authority makes individuals closer to each other, more contagious and conformist. The ties with other fans become like a "new family" bonds. They share obsession and a common language, which distinguish them from the outside world. The normal fan behavior sometimes resembles psycho-pathological behavior. It is worth noting that the term *fan* is related to the word *fanatic,* which is derived from the Latin word *fanaticus*, with literal meaning of "belonging to the temple." The fans' views of the idol and relationship are often characterized by quasi-religious attributes. The fanatical fans strive to model themselves on their idol.

Sometimes, fans involve into the *stalking* of the star. They may want to get to know their idols closer entering into a tangible relationship. They may act on their hope and become annoying to the star in their behavior, especially when they attempt to project their own hang ups onto the star (Giles, 2002; Hoffmann, 2006; Hoffmann & Sheridan, 2008). The wish of fans to meet and know their idol closer is the expression of their love and desire for human communication and relationship. However, it is unlikely and maybe impossible to fulfill such love in an ordinary way.

6.5.3 Narcissistic Romantic Model of Self-Love

The Concept of Self-Love

A positive view of self seems natural for the social nature, probably due to the human evolutionary basic need of personal survival. Everyone would like to love him- or herself, although individuals may occasionally or frequently experience controversial and negative feelings for themselves. The Ancient Greeks denoted even a special term *philautia* for this type of *self-love*.

However, it is important to have the *right self-love,*—that has been the theme of public and scholarly discourse for the centuries (e.g., Annas, 1989; Lippitt, 2013; O'donovan, 2006; Van der Stockt, 1999; Weaver, 2002). This type of love remains the topic of scholarly and research interests (e.g., Campbell et al., 2002; Fromm, 1939; Gebauer, Göritz, Hofmann, & Sedikides, 2012; Xue, Huang, Wu, & Yue, 2021). The right *self-love* is sometimes considered as a prerequisite for the love for others (Bransen, 2006; Gallagher, 1999). *Avoiding the warped self-perception* and *inadequate self-love* in the wider contexts of environment has been the major point.

Love of Narcissistic Person

Individuals with narcissistic personality, however, have *malignant self-love* (Vaknin, 2001). They are self-centered and overconfident admiring themselves immensely. They have an overinflated view of their own personality and abilities. They like to look grandiose and pretentious, snobbery, and arrogant.

People in individualistic societies, especially with narcissistic culture, know they have the *freedom of choice*. However, they do not learn to compromise. Young men and women believe they are entitled for a relationship that is always easy, beautiful, and fun. They anticipate the relationships and love to be the way how they want—on their own preferences, conditions, and terms. The *attitudes to receive* and *expectations to have* in relationships prevail over the *attitudes to give* and *expectations to accommodate*. "What have you done for me?" is a more valuable question than "What have I done for you?"

The cultural mainstream of movies, TV, and pop magazines promote the messages "all-or-nothing": the best partner or none, love or not love. In the same vein, some advice books (Schefft, 2009) discourage men and women to stick for a relationship with someone just because they are afraid that they will not do any better. The advisers guide assertive individuals that they are too good to settle for less with a partner with flaws. As Twenge and Campbell (2009) commented, no one is flawless, and if some individuals expect a partner to be perfect, they are either narcissistic or delusional.

Due to these culturally typical ideals, a narcissistic person is overly selective and wants to get the *best partner* for their love and marriage relationship to be fully content. They exhibit *all-or-nothing behavior*—when they see the small faults in their partner, they prefer to withdraw from the relationship. Sometimes, they may not really know what they are looking for in a partner. According to the self-reports of narcissistic persons, as well to their partners in current and past relationships (Campbell et al., 2002), they tend to engage in the *game playing type of love* (see in the following chapters).

Perfectionistic style of a narcissistic individual advises him/her to look for a perfect partner that is often turn out to the "never settling" search. The narcissists lack the feeling of gratitude for what they have, for what others do for them. The low motivation of appreciation is among the major obstacles in their relationships.

Evolution of Narcissistic Love in the United States

American culture has historically valued individualism, persistence, achievements, self-reliance, and personal responsibility. The individualism was understood as hard work, effort, and responsibility. Young people were encouraged to work hard rather than show off (Emerson, 1987, cited in Twenge & Campbell, 2009).

Many scholars have commented the appearance of *narcissistic culture* in the United States in the 1970s (e.g., Battan, 1983; Lasch, 1979; Twenge & Campbell, 2009; Wolfe, 1976). The changes were noticeable different since the 1950s. The topic provoked the important questions and discussions, whether *narcissism* is a *new cultural phenomenon* evolved in the United States in the 1970s. What were its *cultural underpinnings*?

There is some evidence (see for review, Campbell, Miller, & Buffardi, 2010; Twenge & Campbell, 2009) that narcissism has been increasing in the United States throughout recent decades. An American culture has become a "culture of self-worth" with inflated self-related constructs such as self-esteem, self-focus, and self-importance.

The American cultural values of recent decades, however, have made a surprising twist focusing more on admiring oneself than on the efforts. Cultural obsession with the values of individual independence, autonomy, achievements, and impression management has headed many Americans to the *passion of entitlement* and *preoccupation with self-admiration*. The concept of *self-love* has become amazingly popular in recent decades among laypeople and scholars of social sciences. The *narcissism epidemic* (Campbell et al., 2010; Twenge & Campbell, 2009) has become an increasing cultural trend. The grandiose fantasies have distorted the adequate perception of reality and adequacy. Many things are showy and pretentious, excessively bright and colorful, flamboyant, and exuberant.

The evolution of American society has been manifested in many cultural products—books, television shows, and song lyrics. Their content and lexicon have changed over time. The texts of American books since 1960s have become progressively more focused on the self and uniqueness. Individualistic words, such as "self," "unique," "personalize," and phrases, such as "I'm the best," "I am special," and "all about me" became much more frequently used throughout 1960–2008s, compared to the changes in the use of communal words and phrases (Twenge, Campbell, & Gentile, 2012b).

People strive for individualism and uniqueness in everything, even in the first names of American babies. For example, from 1880 to 2007, parents have increasingly given their children less common names (Twenge, Abebe, & Campbell, 2010).

The evolution of the US society has been placed the increasing emphasis on self-esteem and self-worth. The meta-analyses of studies have shown the increase in self-esteem of American middle school, high school, and college students throughout generations from 1988 to 2008 (Gentile, Twenge, & Campbell, 2010). The generation of modern American university students believe that their personal leadership ability, the drive to achieve, self-confidence, academic abilities, as well as the abilities for public speaking and writing are above average (Twenge, Campbell, & Gentile, 2012a).

Modern American Narcissistic Culture

As we saw, since the 1970s, scholars have noted that American society is characterized as *the culture of narcissism* (e.g., Lasch, 1979; Twenge & Campbell, 2009; Wolfe, 1976). The topic has been very popular and highlighted this remarkable feature of American societies, especially among celebrities.

The survey studies have shown (Campbell et al., 2010; Miller et al., 2015) that Americans see the *America's national character* as *highly narcissistic*. However, they rate their *own narcissism and the narcissism of their acquaintances* much lower than in general American social life. Thus, one can see a difference—Americans perceive themselves and those who they know well as less narcissistic compared to the broader American culture. People of the Basque Country, Turkey, England, and China have shown the same tendency of lower rating of themselves and their acquaintances, compared to the national character (my smaller size effect).

The studies of personality traits and externalizing behaviors (Campbell et al., 2010; Miller et al., 2015), which are associated with narcissism, have revealed that Americans are viewed as extraverted, disagreeable, and antisocial. In terms of demographics of the US population, young people, men, and the Americans working in the occupations of high status and high visibility are perceived as more narcissistic.

Americans are also viewed as highly narcissistic by other nationals. For example, the respondents from the Basque Country, Turkey, England, and China rated Americans as more narcissistic, extraverted, and antagonistic than people in their own societies.

Ethnic, Gender, and Age Variation of Narcissism in the United States

In terms of ethnicities, Asians generally show lower narcissism and self-esteem scores than people of other ethnic groups. Hispanics show in some samples the relatively low narcissism and self-esteem, while in others high, compared to Whites. The Blacks show consistently the highest narcissism and self-esteem (Foster, Campbell, & Twenge, 2003). The results on the ethnic effects, however, are not always consistent across samples.

Men show somewhat higher narcissism than women, and the young people are more narcissistic than those in older age. Men are higher than women in the attitudes of *superiority, authority, entitlement, self-sufficiency,* and *exploitativeness*, however do not differ significantly in the attitudes of *vanity* and *exhibitionism* (Foster et al., 2003).

Twenge and Campbell (2009) highlighted the five major causes of such growing narcissism in American culture. These are (1) a focus on self-admiration, (2) child-centered parenting, (3) celebrity glorification and media encouragement, (4) the attention seeking promoted on the Internet, and (5) easy credit.

Narcissistic Love Across Cultures

An important question is also whether the *narcissistic culture* is only the American or Western social phenomenon. What about Eastern societies?

One of the most well-studied cultural differences between societies is the value of social *interdependence* and *independence*. Scholars commonly referred this distinction to the East and the West as the two culturally contracting regions. However, the pictures of the world cultures are more complex. So, due to the typical samples of the studies, it is more adequate to call these two broad categories of the world regions as *East Asian culture*—interdependent and collectivistic, and *European–American culture*—independent and individualistic (see for review, Karandashev, 2021a, 2021b). They differ in the way how individuals in those societies tend to experience their *self.* People in *collectivistic interdependent* cultures (e.g., China, Japan) tend to have *interdependent model of self,* while in *individualistic interdependent* cultures (e.g., the United States)—*independent model of self* (Markus & Kitayama, 1991; Mesquita & Leu, 2007; Tsai & Clobert, 2019).

Accordingly, the East Asian conception of individuality emphasizes the interdependence of a *person* with *others*. This *interdependent model* has the *self-construal,* which construes the *self* as the *self-in-relationship-with-others* with the close ties between the *personal self* and the *selves of others.* The *personal self* is *inseparable* from *and interdependent* with *others,* not much focused on *the unique self, self-esteem, and self-worth. Standing-in* relationships is more important than *standing-out* (Morling, Kitayama, & Miyamoto, 2002; Tsai & Clobert, 2019; Weisz, Rothbaum, & Blackburn, 1984). Such *self-construal* is a widespread psychological phenomenon in East Asian cultures (e.g., Markus & Kitayama, 1991; Uchida, Norasakkunkit, & Kitayama, 2004).

This model of *self* with *self-in-relationship-with-others* motivations and emotions in focus seems less conducive to the *narcissistic model of love* and reflects on the quality and features of relationship. Individuals feel the need to consider the interests of others when they enter a new relationship or leave. They tend to adjust in the relationship, rather than to make a choice to quit. They prefer to accommodate another person's differences, rather than influence him/her or look for someone else. Their value of freedom is strongly imbedded in responsibilities and social connections.

Some scholars, however, believe that narcissism in Asian cultures may be just different from American culture. The narcissism of collectivistic cultures can be manifested in the inflated view on *communal traits*, rather than *agentic traits* as in individualistic cultures (see Campbell & Foster, 2007; Sedikides, Gaertner, & Toguchi, 2003).

The European American conception of individuality emphasizes the independence of a *personal self* from *others*. This *independent model* has the *self-construal,* which construes the *self* as *distinctive, separate, and independent from others, expressing the unique self,* and focused on *personal self-esteem and self-worth*. The *standing-out* is more important than *standing-in* relationships (Morling et al., 2002; Weisz et al., 1984).

This model of *self* with *individual* motivations and emotions in focus seems more conducive to the *narcissistic model of love* and reflects on the quality and features of relationship, which a person is free to enter and free to leave. Personal self-expression and satisfaction are the priorities. Individuals consider their individual interests and rights as priorities. They appreciate their freedom to make a choice to *stay* or *go,* rather than adjust in the relationship. They prefer to influence their partner or look for someone else, rather than accommodate their differences. Their value of freedom is strongly imbedded in their individual rights, rather than relationship responsibilities.

The studies have found (see for review, Twenge & Campbell, 2009) that cross-cultural differences in narcissism are in accord with the *cultural models of interdependence and self,* as outlined above. People in the East show lower narcissistic attitudes compared to the West. That coincide with corresponding cultural differences in self-esteem and values of independence (Heine, Lehman, Markus, & Kitayama, 1999). The cultures emphasizing the values of independence, individualism, and "standing out from the crowd" are more conducive to the growth of narcissism.

Looking generally across the world regions, studies (Foster et al., 2003) have shown in a large sample of participants (n = 3445), yet mostly from the United States, that people in the United States have the highest narcissism ($M = 15.3$), with relatively lower scores in Europe (15.0), Canada (14.8), Asia (14.3), and the Middle East (13.9). Americans of the early 2000s were statistically higher in narcissism only compared with Asia and Middle East respondents. The respondents from *individualistic societies* showed the higher narcissistic attitudes of *superiority, authority, and self-sufficiency*, compared to those from collectivistic societies. However, no cultural differences were found in narcissistic attitudes of entitlement, vanity exhibitionism, and exploitativeness.

References

Acevedo, B. P., & Aron, A. (2009). Does a long-term relationship kill romantic love? *Review of General Psychology, 13*(1), 59–65.

Allen, R. A., & Allen, R. C. (Eds.). (1995). *To be continued: Soap operas around the world.* Psychology Press.

Annas, J. (1989). Self-love in Aristotle. *The Southern Journal of Philosophy, 27*(Supplement), 1–18.

Aron, A., & Aron, E. N. (1986). *Love and the expansion of self: Understanding attraction and satisfaction.* Hemisphere Publishing Corp/Harper & Row Publishers.

Aron, E. N., & Aron, A. (1996). Love and the expansion of the self: The state of the model. *Personal Relationships, 3*(1), 45–58. https://doi.org/10.1111/j.1475-6811.1996.tb00103.x

Aron, A., & Aron, E. N. (2016). An inspiration for expanding the self-expansion model of love. *Emotion Review, 8*(2), 112–113.

Aronson, P. (2015, October). *Romantic regimes.* Aeon, Retrieved on December 1, 2018 from https://aeon.co/essays/russia-against-the-western-way-of-love

Ashe, D. D., & McCutcheon, L. E. (2001). Shyness, loneliness, and attitude toward celebrities. *Current Research in Social Psychology, 6*(9), 124–133.

Averill, J. R. (1985). The social construction of emotion: With special reference to love. In K. J. Gergen & K. E. Davis (Eds.), *The social construction of the person* (pp. 89–109). Springer.

Barelds, D. P., & Barelds-Dijkstra, P. (2007). Love at first sight or friends first? Ties among partner personality trait similarity, relationship onset, relationship quality, and love. *Journal of Social and Personal Relationships, 24*(4), 479–496.

Battan, J. F. (1983). The "New Narcissism" in 20th-century America: The shadow and substance of social change. *Journal of Social History, 17*(2), 199–220.

Baucom, D. H., Epstein, N., Rankin, L. A., & Burnett, C. K. (1996a). Assessing relationship standards: The Inventory of Specific Relationship Standards. *Journal of Family Psychology, 10*(1), 72–88. https://doi.org/10.1037/0893-3200.10.1.72

Baucom, D. H., Epstein, N., Daiuto, A. D., Carels, R. A., Rankin, L. A., & Burnett, C. K. (1996b). Cognitions in marriage: The relationship between standards and attributions. *Journal of Family Psychology, 10*(2), 209–222.

Berscheid, E., & Walster, E. (1974). A little bit about love. In T. L. Huston (Ed.), *Foundations of interpersonal attraction* (pp. 355–381). Academic.

Berscheid, E., & Walster, E. (1978). *Interpersonal attraction* (2nd ed.). Addison-Wesley (Originally work published 1969).

Bielby, D. D., & Harrington, C. L. (2005). Opening America? The telenovela-ization of US soap operas. *Television & New Media, 6*(4), 383–399.
Bransen, J. (2006). Selfless self-love. *Ethical Theory and Moral Practice, 9*(1), 3–25.
Brickman, P. (1987). *Commitment, conflict, and caring*. Prentice Hall.
Brown, B. (2012). *Daring greatly: How the courage to be vulnerable transforms the way we live, love, parent, and lead*. Gotham Books.
Burger, R. (2012). *Behind the red door: Sex in China*. Earnshaw.
Campbell, K. W., & Foster, J. D. (2007). The narcissistic self: Background, an extended agency model, and ongoing controversies. In C. Sedikides & S. J. Spencer (Eds.), *The self: Frontiers of social psychology* (pp. 115–138). Psychology Press.
Campbell, W. K., Foster, C. A., & Finkel, E. J. (2002). Does self-love lead to love for others? A story of narcissistic game playing. *Journal of Personality and Social Psychology, 83*(2), 340–354. https://doi.org/10.1037/0022-3514.83.2.340
Campbell, W. K., Rudich, E. A., & Sedikides, C. (2002). Narcissism, self-esteem, and the positivity of self-views: Two portraits of self-love. *Personality and Social Psychology Bulletin, 28*(3), 358–368.
Campbell, K. W., Miller, J. D., & Buffardi, L. E. (2010). The United States and the "Culture of Narcissism" an examination of perceptions of national character. *Social Psychological and Personality Science, 1*(3), 222–229.
Carlsson, U. (2018). The folk metaphysics of love. *European Journal of Philosophy, 26*(4), 1398–1409.
Coontz, S. (2005). *Marriage, a history: From obedience to intimacy, or how love conquered marriage*. Viking.
Coontz, S. (2006). *Marriage, a history: How love conquered marriage*. Penguin.
Cramer, P. (2011). Young adult narcissism: A 20 year longitudinal study of the contribution of parenting styles, preschool precursors of narcissism, and denial. *Journal of Research in Personality, 45*(1), 19–28.
Cummins, R. G. (2017). Excitation transfer theory. *The International Encyclopedia of Media Effects*.https://doi.org/10.1002/9781118783764.wbieme0080
Dainton, M., Stafford, L., & Canary, D. J. (1994). Maintenance strategies and physical affection as predictors of love, liking, and satisfaction in marriage. *Communication Reports, 7*(2), 88–98.
De Boer, A., Van Buel, E. M., & Ter Horst, G. J. (2012). Love is more than just a kiss: A neurobiological perspective on love and affection. *Neuroscience, 201*, 114–124.
De Munck, V. (2019). *Romantic love in America: Cultural models of gay, straight and polyamorous relationship*. Lexington Press.
De Munck, V. C., & Korotayev, A. (1999). Sexual equality and romantic love: A reanalysis of Rosenblatt's study on the function of romantic love. *Cross-Cultural Research, 33*, 265–277.
De Munck, V. C., & Korotayev, A. V. (2007). Wife–husband intimacy and female status in cross-cultural perspective. *Cross-Cultural Research, 41*(4), 307–335.
De Munck, V., Korotayev, A., & Khaltourina, D. (2009). A comparative study of the structure of love in the US and Russia: Finding a common core of characteristics and national and gender differences. *Ethnology: An International Journal of Cultural and Social Anthropology, 48*(4), 337–357.
De Munck, V. C., Korotayev, A., de Munck, J., & Khaltourina, D. (2011). Cross-cultural analysis of models of romantic love among US residents, Russians, and Lithuanians. *Cross-Cultural Research, 45*(2), 128–154.
De Munck, V., Korotayev, A., & McGreevey, J. (2016). Romantic love and family organization: A case for romantic love as a biosocial universal. *Evolutionary Psychology, 14*(4), 1–13. https://doi.org/10.1177/1474704916674211
De Roda, A. B. L., Martínez-Iñigo, D., De Paul, P., & Yela, C. (1999). Romantic beliefs and myths in Spain. *The Spanish Journal of Psychology, 2*, 64–73.
Dean, D. G. (1964). Romanticism and emotional maturity: A further exploration. *Social Forces, 42*(3), 298–303.

Deci, E. L., & Flaste, R. (1996). *Why we do what we do: Understanding self-motivation*. Penguin books.
Diamond, L. M. (2003). What does sexual orientation orient? A biobehavioral model distinguishing romantic love and sexual desire. *Psychological Review, 110*, 173–192.
Diamond, L. M. (2004). Emerging perspectives on distinctions between romantic love and sexual desire. *Current Directions in Psychological Science, 13*(3), 116–119.
Dillow, M. R., Goodboy, A. K., & Bolkan, S. (2014). Attachment and the expression of affection in romantic relationships: The mediating role of romantic love. *Communication Reports, 27*(2), 102–115.
Dion, K. K., & Dion, K. L. (1996). Cultural perspectives on romantic love. *Personal Relationships, 3*(1), 5–17.
Dueñas-Vargas, G. (2015). *Of love and other passions: Elites, politics, and family in Bogota, Colombia, 1778–1870*. The University of New Mexico Press.
Emerson, R. W. (1987). Self-Reliance (1841). In J. Porte (Ed.), *Essays and Lectures* (p. 261). Library of America, 1983.
Epstein, N., Baucom, D. H., & Rankin, L. A. (1993). Treatment of marital conflict: A cognitive-behavioral approach. *Clinical Psychology Review, 13*(1), 45–57.
Fisher, H. E. (2004). *Why we love: The nature and the chemistry of romantic love*. Henry Holt.
Floyd, K. (2006). *Communicating affection: Interpersonal behavior and social context*. Cambridge University Press.
Floyd, K., & Morman, M. T. (1998). The measurement of affectionate communication. *Communication Quarterly, 46*(2), 144–162.
Floyd, K., Hess, J. A., Miczo, L. A., Halone, K. K., Mikkelson, A. C., & Tusing, K. J. (2005). Human affection exchange: VIII. Further evidence of the benefits of expressed affection. *Communication Quarterly, 53*(3), 285–303.
Foster, J. D., Campbell, W. K., & Twenge, J. M. (2003). Individual differences in narcissism: Inflated self-views across the lifespan and around the world. *Journal of Research in Personality, 37*, 469–486.
Freud, S. (1947). *Freud: On war, sex and neurosis*. Arts and Science Press.
Fromm, E. (1939). Selfishness and self-love. *Psychiatry, 2*(4), 507–523.
Gallagher, D. M. (1999). Thomas Aquinas on self-love as the basis for love of others. *Acta Philosophica, 8*(1), 23–44.
Gebauer, J. E., Göritz, A. S., Hofmann, W., & Sedikides, C. (2012). Self-love or other-love? Explicit other-preference but implicit self-preference. *PLoS ONE, 7*(7), e41789.
Gentile, B., Twenge, J. M., & Campbell, W. K. (2010). Birth cohort differences in self-esteem, 1988–2008: A cross-temporal meta-analysis. *Review of General Psychology, 14*(3), 261–268.
Giddens, A. (1992). *The transformation of intimacy: Sexuality, love, and eroticism in modern societies*. Polity.
Giles, D. C. (2002). Parasocial interaction: A review of the literature and a model for future research. *Media psychology, 4*(3), 279–305.
Gillis, J. R. (1985). *For better, for worse: British marriages, 1600 to the present*. Oxford University Press.
Giles, J. (2004). *The parlour and the suburb: Domestic identities, class, femininity, and modernity*. Berg.
Glenn, N. D. (1991). The recent trend in marital success in the United States. *Journal of Marriage and the Family, 53*(2), 261–270.
Gonzaga, G. C., Turner, R. A., Keltner, D., Campos, B., & Altemus, M. (2006). Romantic love and sexual desire in close relationships. *Emotion, 6*(2), 163–179. https://doi.org/10.1037/1528-3542.6.2.163
Goode, W. J. (1959). The theoretical importance of love. *American Sociological Review, 24*, 38–47.
Goode, W. J. (1963). *World revolution and family patterns*. The Free Press of Glencoe.
Goodwin, R., & Findlay, C. (1997). "We were just fated together." Chinese love and the concept of yuan in England and Hong Kong. *Personal Relationships, 4(1)*, 85–92.

Grant-Jacob, J. A. (2016). Love at first sight. *Frontiers in Psychology, 7*, 1113.
Green, T., Griffith, J., Aruguete, M. S., Edman, J., & McCutcheon, L. E. (2014). Materialism and the tendency to worship celebrities. *North American Journal of Psychology, 16*, 33–42.
Gross, L. (1944). A belief pattern scale for measuring attitudes toward romanticism. *American Sociological Review, 9*(5), 463–472.
Greenfield, S. M. (1965). Love and marriage in modern America: A functional analysis. *The Sociological Quarterly, 6*(4), 361–377.
Gulledge, A. K., Stahmann, R. F., & Wilson, C. M. (2004). Seven types of nonsexual romantic physical affection among Brigham Young University students. *Psychological Reports, 95*(2), 609–614.
Gulledge, A. K., Hill, M., Lister, Z., & Sallion, C. (2007). Non-erotic physical affection: It's good for you. In L. L'Abate (Ed.), *Low-cost approaches to promote physical and mental health* (pp. 371–384). Springer.
Hatfield, E., & Rapson, R. L. (1993). *Love, sex, and intimacy: Their psychology, biology, and history*. HarperCollins.
Hatfield, E., & Rapson, R. L. (1996). *Love and sex: Cross-cultural perspectives*. Allyn & Bacon.
Hatfield, E., Schmitz, E., Cornelius, J., & Rapson, R. L. (1988). Passionate love: How early does it begin? *Journal of Psychology and Human Sexuality, 1*, 35–52.
Hazan, C., & Shaver, P. (1987). Romantic love conceptualized as an attachment process. *Journal of Personality and Social Psychology, 52*(3), 511–524. https://doi.org/10.1037/0022-3514.52.3.511
Hefner, V., & Wilson, B. J. (2013). From love at first sight to soul mate: The influence of romantic ideals in popular films on young people's beliefs about relationships. *Communication Monographs, 80*(2), 150–175.
Heimer, C. A., & Stinchcombe, A. L. (1980). Love and irrationality: It's got to be rational to love you because it makes me so happy. *Social Science Information, 19*(4–5), 697–754.
Heine, S. J., Lehman, D. R., Markus, H. R., & Kitayama, S. (1999). Is there a universal need for positive self-regard? *Psychological Review, 106*, 766–794.
Hendrick, C., & Hendrick, S. S. (1986). A theory and method of love. *Journal of Personality and Social Psychology, 50*, 392–402.
Hill, M. T. (2009). *Intimacy, passion, commitment, physical affection and relationship stage as related to romantic relationship satisfaction* (Doctoral dissertation, Oklahoma State University).
Hill, R. W., & Yousey, G. P. (1998). Adaptive and maladaptive narcissism among university faculty, clergy, politicians, and librarians. *Current Psychology, 17*(2–3), 163–169.
Hinkle, D. E., & Sporakowski, M. J. (1975). Attitudes toward love: A reexamination. *Journal of Marriage and the Family, 37*(4), 764–767.
Hoffmann, J. (2006). *Stalking*. Springer.
Hoffmann, J., & Sheridan, L. (2008). Celebrities as victims of stalking. In J. R. Meloy, L. Sheridan, & J. Hoffmann (Eds.), *Stalking, threatening, and attacking public figures: A psychological and behavioral analysis* (pp. 195–213). Oxford University Press.
Hutcheon, P. D. (1995). Through a glass darkly: Freud's concept of love. In D. Goicoechea (Ed.), *The nature and pursuit of love: The philosophy of Irving Singer* (pp. 183–195). Amherst.
Jankowiak, W. (Ed.). (1995). *Romantic passion: A universal experience?* Columbia University Press.
Jankowiak, W. (2013). From courtship to dating culture: China's emergent youth. In P. Link, R. Madsen, & P. Pickowitz (Eds.), *China at risk* (pp. 191–214). McGraw-Hill.
Jankowiak, W., & Fischer, E. (1992). A cross-cultural perspective on romantic love. *Ethnology, 31*(2), 149–155.
Jankowiak, W., Shen, Y., Yao, S., Wang, C., & Volsche, S. (2015). Investigating love's universal attributes: A research report from China. *Cross-Cultural Research, 49*(4), 422–436.
Jankowiak, W. R., Volsche, S. L., & Garcia, J. R. (2015). Is the romantic–sexual kiss a near human universal? *American Anthropologist, 117*(3), 535–539.
Karandashev, V. (2017). *Romantic love in cultural contexts*. Springer.

Karandashev, V. (2019). *Cross-cultural perspectives on the experience and expression of love*. Springer.

Karandashev, V. (2021a). *Cultural models of emotions*. Springer.

Karandashev, V. (2021b). Cultural diversity of romantic love experience. In C. Mayer & E. Vanderheiden (Eds.), *International handbook of love* (pp. 59–79). Springer.

Karandashev, V. (in press). Cross-cultural variation in relationship initiation. In J. K. Mogilski & T. K. Shackelford (Eds.), *The Oxford handbook of evolutionary psychology and romantic relationships*. Oxford Publishing.

Kelly, H. H. (1983). Love and commitment. In I. H. H. Kelley et al. (Eds.), *Close relationships* (pp. 265–314). Freeman & Company.

Kephart, W. M. (1966). *The family, society, and the individual*. Houghton Mifflin.

Kephart, W. M. (1967). Some correlates of romantic love. *Journal of Marriage and the Family, 29*(3), 470–474.

Knee, R. (1998). Implicit theories of relationships: assessment and prediction of romantic relationship initiation, coping, and longevity. *Journal of Personality and Social Psychology, 74*, 360–370.

Knox, D. H., & Sporakowski, M. J. (1968). Attitudes of college students toward love. *Journal of Marriage and the Family, 30*(4), 638–642.

Kövecses, Z. (1988). *The language of love: The semantics of passion in conversational English*. Bucknell University Press.

Kövecses, Z. (2005). *Metaphor in culture: Universality and variation*. Cambridge University Press.

Landgraf, E. (2004). Romantic love and the Enlightenment: From gallantry and seduction to authenticity and self-validation. *German Quarterly, 77*(1), 29–46.

Lasch, C. (1979). *The culture of narcissism: American life in an age of diminishing expectations*. Norton.

Lazarus, R. S. (1991). *Emotion and adaptation*. Oxford University Press.

Lewis, C. S. (1960). *The four loves*. Harcourt, Brace and Company.

Lewis, C. S. (2013). *The allegory of love: A study in medieval tradition*. Cambridge University Press (Originally work published 1936).

Levine, R., Sato, S., Hashimoto, T., & Verma, J. (1995). Love and marriage in eleven cultures. *Journal of Cross-Cultural Psychology, 26*, 554–571.

Lindholm, C. (1988). Lovers and leaders: A comparison of social and psychological models of romance and charisma. *Social Science Information, 27*(1), 3–45.

Lindholm, C. (1998). Love and structure. *Theory, Culture & Society, 15*(3–4), 243–263.

Lippitt, J. (2013). *Kierkegaard and the problem of self-love*. Cambridge University Press.

Lomas, T. (2018). The flavours of love: A cross-cultural lexical analysis. *Journal for the Theory of Social Behaviour, 48*, 134–152.

Luerssen, A., Jhita, G. J., & Ayduk, O. (2017). Putting yourself on the line: Self-esteem and expressing affection in romantic relationships. *Personality and Social Psychology Bulletin, 43*(7), 940–956.

Markus, H. R., & Kitayama, S. (1991). Culture and the self: Implications for cognition, emotion, and motivation. *Psychological Review, 98*, 224–253.

Maltby, J., Houran, J., Lange, R., Ashe, D., & McCutcheon, L. E. (2002). Thou shalt worship no other gods—unless they are celebrities: the relationship between celebrity worship and religious orientation. *Personality and Individual Differences, 32*(7), 1157–1172.

McCutcheon, L. E., Lange, R., & Houran, J. (2002). Conceptualization and measurement of celebrity worship. *British Journal of Psychology, 93*(1), 67–87.

McCutcheon, L. E., Aruguete, M., McCarley, N. G., & Jenkins, W. J. (2016). Further validation of an indirect measure of celebrity stalking. *Journal of Studies in Social Sciences, 14*(1), 75–91.

Medora, N. P., Larson, J. H., Hortaçsu, N., & Dave, P. (2002). Perceived attitudes towards romanticism: A cross-cultural study of American, Asian-Indian, and Turkish young adults. *Journal of Comparative Family Studies, 33*, 155–179.

Mesquita, B., & Leu, J. (2007). The cultural psychology of emotion. In S. Kitayama & D. Cohen (Eds.), *Handbook of cultural psychology* (pp. 734–759). Guilford Press.

Meston, C. M., & Frohlich, P. F. (2003). Love at first fright: Partner salience moderates roller-coaster-induced excitation transfer. *Archives of Sexual Behavior, 32*(6), 537–544.

Miller, J. D., Maples, J. L., Buffardi, L., Cai, H., Gentile, B., Kisbu-Sakarya, Y., … Campbell, W. K. (2015). Narcissism and United States' culture: The view from home and around the world. *Journal of Personality and Social Psychology, 109*, 1068–1089.

Morling, B., Kitayama, S., & Miyamoto, Y. (2002). Cultural practices emphasize influence in the United States and adjustment in Japan. *Personality and Social Psychology Bulletin, 28*(3), 311–323.

Munro, B., & Adams, G. (1978). Correlates of romantic love revisited. *Journal of Psychology, 98*, 211–214.

Murray, S. L., Holmes, J. G., & Griffin, D. W. (1996a). The benefits of positive illusions: Idealization and the construction of satisfaction in close relationships. *Journal of Personality and Social Psychology, 70*(1), 79–98.

Murray, S. L., Holmes, J. G., & Griffin, D. W. (1996b). The self-fulfilling nature of positive illusions in romantic relationships: Love is not blind, but prescient. *Journal of Personality and Social Psychology, 71*(6), 1155–1181.

Murray, S. L., & Holmes, J. G. (1997). A leap of faith? Positive illusions in romantic relationships. *Personality and Social Psychology Bulletin, 23*(6), 586–604.

Murstein, B. I. (1974). *Love, sex, and marriage through the ages*. Springer.

Murstein, B. I., Merighi, J. R., & Vyse, S. A. (1991). Love styles in the United States and France: A cross-cultural comparison. *Journal of Social and Clinical Psychology, 10*(1), 37–46.

Murstein, B. I. (1988). A taxonomy of love. In R. J. Sternberg & M. L. Barnes (Eds.), *The psychology of love* (pp. 13–37). Yale University Press.

O'donovan, O. (2006). *The problem of self-love in St. Augustine*. Wipf and Stock Publishers.

Onu, D., Kessler, T., & Smith, J. R. (2016). Admiration: A conceptual review. *Emotion Review, 8*(3), 218–230.

Paris, G. (1883). Études sur les romans de la Table Ronde: Lancelot du Lac. II: Le conte de la charrette. *Romania, 12*, 459–534.

Pavlova, L. P. (2017). *Dominants of the working brain: A systemic psychophysiological approach to EEG analysis*. Inform-Navigator.

Prettejohn, E. (2005). *Beauty and art: 1750-2000*. Oxford University Press.

Reddy, W. M. (2012). *The making of romantic love: Longing and sexuality in Europe, South Asia, and Japan, 900-1200 CE*. The University of Chicago Press.

Regan, P. C., Kocan, E. R., & Whitlock, T. (1998). Ain't love grand! A prototype analysis of the concept of romantic love. *Journal of Social and Personal Relationships, 15*(3), 411–420.

Rice, K. G., & Preusser, K. J. (2002). The adaptive/maladaptive perfectionism scale. *Measurement and Evaluation in Counseling and Development, 34*(4), 210–222.

Roberts, K. A. (2007). Relationship attachment and the behaviour of fans towards celebrities. *Applied Psychology in Criminal Justice, 3*(1), 54–74.

Romantic. (2016a). *Oxford dictionaries*. Oxford University Press. Retrieved from http://www.oxforddictionaries.com/us/definition/american_english/romantic

Romantic. (2016b). *Your dictionary*. LoveToKnow Corp. Retrieved from http://www.yourdictionary.com/romantic

Romantic. (n.d.). *Dictionary.com unabridged*. Retrieved from http://dictionary.reference.com/browse/romantic

Rosenblatt, P. C. (1967). Marital residence and the functions of romantic love. *Ethnology, 6*(4), 471–480.

Rubin, Z. (1970). Measurement of romantic love. *Journal of Personality and Social Psychology, 16*, 265–273.

Rubin, R. B., & McHugh, M. P. (1987). Development of parasocial interaction relationships. *Journal of Broadcasting and Electronic Media, 31*, 279–292.

Rusinov, V. S. (1973). *The dominant focus: electrophysiological investigations*. Springer.
Sangrador, J. L., & Yela, C. (2000). What is beautiful is loved': Physical attractiveness in love relationships in a representative sample. *Social Behavior and Personality: An International Journal, 28*(3), 207–218. https://doi.org/10.2224/sbp.2000.28.3.207
Sarapin, S. H., Christy, K., Lareau, L., Krakow, M., & Jensen, J. D. (2015). Identifying admired models to increase emulation: Development of a multidimensional admiration scale. *Measurement and Evaluation in Counseling and Development, 48*(2), 95–108.
Sastry, J. (1999). Household structure, satisfaction and distress in India and The United States: A comparative cultural examination. *Journal of Comparative Family Studies, 30*(1), 135–152.
Schefft, J. (2009). *Better single than sorry: A no-regrets guide to loving yourself and never settling*. Harper Collins.
Schindler, I. (2014). Relations of admiration and adoration with other emotions and well-being. *Psychology of Well-being, 4*(1), 1–23.
Schindler, I., Zink, V., Windrich, J., & Menninghaus, W. (2013). Admiration and adoration: Their different ways of showing and shaping who we are. *Cognition & Emotion, 27*(1), 85–118.
Sedikides, C., Gaertner, L., & Toguchi, Y. (2003). Pancultural self-enhancement. *Journal of Personality and Social Psychology, 84*, 60–79.
Sharp, E. A., & Ganong, L. H. (2000). Raising awareness about marital expectations: Are unrealistic beliefs changed by integrative teaching? *Family Relations, 49*(1), 71–76.
Singer, I. (1984a). *The nature of love: Courtly and romantic* (Vol. 2, 2nd ed.). University of Chicago Press.
Singer, I. (1984b). *The nature of love: Plato to Luther* (Vol. 1, 2nd ed.). University of Chicago Press.
Singer, I. (1987). *The nature of love: The modern world* (Vol. 3, 2nd ed.). University of Chicago Press.
Slade, C., & Beckenham, A. (2005). Introduction: Telenovelas and soap operas: Negotiating reality. *Television & New Media, 6*(4), 337–341. https://doi.org/10.1177/1527476405279860
Spiro, M. E. (1977). *Kinship and marriage in Burma: A cultural and psychodynamic analysis*. University of California Press.
Sprecher, S. (1987). The effects of self-disclosure given and received on affection for an intimate partner and stability of the relationship. *Journal of Social and Personal Relationships, 4*(2), 115–127.
Sprecher, S., & Metts, S. (1989). Development of the romantic beliefs scale and examination of the effects of gender and gender-role orientation. *Journal of Social and Personal Relationships, 6*, 387–411.
Sprecher, S., Aron, A., Hatfield, E., Cortese, A., Potapova, E., & Levitskaya, A. (1994). Love: American style, Russian style, and Japanese style. *Personal Relationships, 1*, 349–369.
Sternberg, R. J. (1986). A triangular theory of love. *Psychological Review, 93*(2), 119–135.
Stopes, M. C. (1918). *Married Love*. Fifield and Co..
Sweetman, J., Spears, R., Livingstone, A. G., & Manstead, A. S. (2013). Admiration regulates social hierarchy: Antecedents, dispositions, and effects on intergroup behavior. *Journal of Experimental Social Psychology, 49*(3), 534–542.
Swidler, A. (2001). *Talk of love: How culture matters*. University of Chicago Press.
Szreter, S., & Fisher, K. (2010). *Sex before the sexual revolution: Intimate life in England 1918–1963*. Cambridge University Press.
Taylor, S. E., Collins, R. L., Skokan, L. A., & Aspinwall, L. G. (1989). Maintaining positive illusions in the face of negative information: Getting the facts without letting them get to you. *Journal of Social and Clinical Psychology, 8*, 114–129.
Tennov, D. (1979/1998). *Love and limerence: The experience of being in love*. Scarborough House.
Tsai, J. L., & Clobert, M. (2019). Cultural influences on emotion: Empirical patterns and emerging trends. In S. Kitayama & D. Cohen (Eds.), *Handbook of cultural psychology* (2nd ed., pp. 292–318). Guilford Press.
Twenge, J. M., & Campbell, W. K. (2009). *The narcissism epidemic: Living in the age of entitlement*. Simon and Schuster.

Twenge, J. M., Abebe, E. M., & Campbell, W. K. (2010). Fitting in or standing out: Trends in American parents' choices for children's names, 1880–2007. *Social Psychological and Personality Science, 1*(1), 19–25.
Twenge, J. M., Campbell, W. K., & Gentile, B. (2012a). Generational increases in agentic self-evaluations among American college students, 1966–2009. *Self and Identity, 11*(4), 409–427.
Twenge, J. M., Campbell, W. K., & Gentile, B. (2012b). Increases in individualistic words and phrases in American books, 1960–2008. *PLoS ONE, 7*(7), e40181.
Uchida, Y., Norasakkunkit, V., & Kitayama, S. (2004). Cultural constructions of happiness: Theory and empirical evidence. *Journal of Happiness Studies, 5*(3), 223–239.
Ukhtomsky, A. A. (1966). *The dominant.* Leningrad State University. (In Russian).
Vaknin, S. (2001). *Malignant self love: Narcissism revisited.* Narcissus Publishing.
Van der Stockt, L. (1999). A Plutarchan hypomnema on self-love. *The American Journal of Philology, 120*(4), 575–599.
Waller, W., & Hill, R. (1951). *The family: A dynamic interpretation.* Dryden Press.
Weaver, D. F. (2002). *Self love and Christian ethics.* Cambridge University Press.
Weber, M. (1958). *From Max Weber: Essays in Sociology* (H. H. Gerth, & C. W. Mills, Eds. and Trans.). Galaxy.
Weisz, J. R., Rothbaum, F. M., & Blackburn, T. C. (1984). Standing out and standing in: The psychology of control in America and Japan. *American Psychologist, 39*(9), 955–969.
Wilson, J. (1980). *Love, sex, and feminism: A philosophical essay.* Praeger.
Wolfe, T. (1976). The me decade and the third great awakening. *New York Magazine, 23*(8), 26–40.
Woll, S. B. (1989). Personality and relationship correlates of loving styles. *Journal of Research in Personality, 23*, 480–505.
Xue, L. M., Huang, X. T., Wu, N., & Yue, T. (2021). A qualitative exploration of Chinese self-love. *Frontiers in Psychology, 12*.
Yang, K. S. (2006). Indigenous personality research: The Chinese case. In U. Kim, K.-S. Yang, & K.-K. Hwang (Eds.), *Indigenous and cultural psychology: Understanding people in context* (pp. 285–314). Springer. https://doi.org/10.1007/0-387-28662-4_13
Zsok, F., Haucke, M., De Wit, C. Y., & Barelds, D. P. (2017). What kind of love is love at first sight? An empirical investigation. *Personal Relationships, 24*(4), 869–885.

Chapter 7
Models of Love as Social Connections

7.1 The Community-bonding and Pair-bonding as the Cultural Models of Love

7.1.1 Community and Kinship Love

The Individual Interdependence in Community and Kinship

The positive social connections are the core conditions of human life. Individuals need others—the close or distant ones—to survive and thrive. They need their service and support from others. People are dependent on each other in many regards. So, the distinction between interdependent and independent cultures does not perfectly adequately reflect the reality. Individuals in those cultures are just more or less dependent or independent. The supremacy of independence is rather the *myth of independence*, which is irrational. People serve each other in many daily things—big and small. They live for the sake of each other, for many others with who they are connected and bonded by service, support, and kindness, especially for those who belong to their community, family, and close relationship.

Evolutionary and culturally saying, *community bonding* was the *earliest form of love*. This type of love was from basic survival needs, ecological, economic, and social conditions, in which societies lived. The tribal community-based societies were collaborative, united, and supportive, with necessary mutual responsibility—all what can be called *love for each other*. The *love within a group—community love*—was an important survival mechanism, which later became a source of *in-group favorable bias*. Of course, in many cases, this love was a duty, yet the dutiful love is also an *important model of love* in interdependent living conditions. The *community responsibility* was a form of collective love. Many were involved in servicing, supporting, and helping each other, including the raising of offspring. The nursing and parenting of children were not only a woman care, but rather a

V. Karandashev, *Cultural Typologies of Love*,
https://doi.org/10.1007/978-3-031-05343-6_7

community care. The *extended family* or other women took care of children. It really took a village to raise children.

Later in cultural evolution, some religious beliefs have continued supporting the humane ideology of the *love for all and everyone*. The Christian and Buddhist traditions have been providing the inspiring examples of this type of love for a very long time. The recent admirable model of the Roman Catholic missionary Mother Teresa (1910–1997) perfectly illustrates this idea and value of *a universal love* as *kindness, empathy, compassion, caring*, and *bringing out the best in people* (Allegri, 2011; Greene, 2004; Scott, 2009).

The Kinship Love in Traditional Societies

The *love* for *kinship and extended family* have been important for physical and social survival. This *form of love* provided *food supply, protected housing, safe haven, other accommodations and resources*. Therefore, *filial love* and *social attachment* were valuable for this evolutionary goal functioning as psychological mechanisms, which supported such social bonding. Kinship love has been a complex model of love providing several other functions as well. These aspects of kinship love are presented elsewhere in this book.

In many traditional collectivistic societies, people have lived in the communities of *extended families* (De Munck, 2019; De Munck, Korotayev, & McGreevey, 2016). The support of family was the *kinship love*. The bonding and attachment to kins and the extended family was a priority because they provided security, wealth, and care resources.

The Confucian Chinese philosophy valorizes *kinship love* as the high priority. Confucianism teaches that the *kinship love for one's relatives* is a basic type of love and *consanguineous affection* is the *supreme principle* (Liu, 2007, p. 5). It is higher in primacy compared to the *humane love for other people in general.* Therefore, if the social situation and context occur when they conflict with each other, then the *kinship love* shall override the *humane love* (Liu, 2007). So, the favoritism for the *in-group kinship* over *out-group others* seems understandable.

The cultural practice of *within-kinship favoritism* has been widespread and is still preferred in many traditional collectivistic and conservative cultures. According to some estimates, *kinship favoritism* is deeply rooted in one-fifth of the world population, largely in West Asian, and North African, and Middle Eastern societies, especially in Muslim countries (Hamamy, 2012). This *in-group positive bias* also extends to their cultural preferences for *consanguineous marriage.* A common practice of matchmaking favors *personal kinship connections* and *consanguine marriage*, in which "individuals are closely related as first cousins, first cousins once removed, second cousins, third cousins, or more distantly related persons." Generally speaking, "when a potential partner is a descent from the same ancestor as another person and belongs to the same kinship" (Karandashev, in press). It is worth noting that these conservative cultural practices continue to endure among emigrants from those societies in North American, European counties, and Australia (El-Hazmi et al., 1995; Hamamy, 2012).

Familial Model of Love

Throughout centuries, many cultures valued *familial love* very high, among other models of love. The Ancient Greek philosophers believed that *familial love* is primal and natural affection that includes the love of parents toward their children, as well as the love of children toward their parents. They called it *storge*. Another Greek word *philia* also describes some aspects of the familial love, yet more often refer to comradery friendship.

One specific type of *familial love* is the *filial model of love*. This term commonly refers to the love that children experience toward their parents. It seems natural to love mother and father because they fulfill all kid's basic needs. So, the survival value of an infant's love is essential—it is reviewed elsewhere in this book. Besides, the attachment processes evolve early in the childhood—it is discussed in the following sections.

As children grow, enculturalization processes further support these filial emotions and attitudes toward parents. The Confucian moral values of *filial piety*, emphasizing the duties to kin and family, are high in many East Asian countries, as well as among Americans of Asian descent (Liu, 2007; Sarkissian, 2010). Confucianism "places filial piety absolutely above everything else" (Liu, 2007, p. 5).

These cultural norms teach the child to love mother and father—that doesn't matter whether or not the parents are lovable. In Confucian teaching, *filial piety* is a high priority for the *filial love of children for their parents*. The *love of filial piety* can be expressed in *respect* and *obedience to parents and elders*. *Obedience to parents* is among the core cultural attitude of the *filial love*. The studies among Americans (Dixon, Graber, & Brooks-Gunn, 2008) have demonstrated that Asian Americans, African Americans, and Latina girls show more respect for parental authority compared to European Americans.

The Confucian ethics also teach children to respect and care for their aging parents. The *filial obligations* of children are commonly viewed as their payments back *for parental sacrifices*. However, the *traditional notions of filial piety* have been gradually changing due to social and economic transformation of environment. The modern Asian families vary in their filial beliefs and adjust to modernization of societies (Canda, 2013; Kim, Cheng, Zarit, & Fingerman, 2015; Sung, 2001). This *dutiful model of love* is discussed in more detail in the following sections.

An alternative *model of filial love as friendship* is also possible (Dixon, 1995). Although some scholars believe that feelings of friendship toward parents are flimsy for filial duties, nevertheless, children can enjoy friendship with their parents. The *friendship model* of *filial love* considers the filial duties as voluntary and loving relationships.

7.1.2 Models of Love as Pair-bonding

Emergence of Pair-bonding Love

As I noted above, many traditional collectivistic societies had *extended family structure* (De Munck, 2019; De Munck et al., 2016). In a *joint family*, other relatives lived together with the married couple. In such relationship conditions, men and women frequently had little interest in *romantic* love. The marriage was frequently arranged by kin. The distribution of functions in family relations was communal, rather than personal. The individual roles of wife and husband were less emotional and more practical. In several matters, other members of family could take charge of the practical and psychological duties of husband and wife, father and mother.

Later in cultural evolution, societal structures evolved into the *neolocal residences* of *couples* (De Munck, 2019; De Munck et al., 2016). The *nuclear families* emerged as the forms of relationship organization with more personal responsibilities of spouses and parents in a couple. Then, the *need for pair-bonding* in practical and emotional sense became more important. The social conditions conducive for pair-bonding love emerged.

Diversity of Pair-bonding Relationships

Human pair-bonding is the long-term social and emotional connections between two individuals who live together in a committed relationship. Following the evolutionary tradition, pair-bonding frequently refers to a *lasting reproductive relationship* (Rooker & Gavrilets, 2016). The *pair-bonding* characterizes the *long-term relationships* between certain males and females: between two individuals—in *monogamous relations*—or more than two individuals—*polyandrous* and *polygynous relations* (polygamy). In case of *polygyny*, one male has the long-lasting reproductive relations with several females, thus, several distinct pair-bonds occur simultaneously (Chapais, 2008; Reichard & Boesch, 2003).

According to some estimates (Reichard & Boesch, 2003), people in about 17 % of human societies throughout the world practice social monogamy, while in many others (more than 80%) they may practice polygyny. Among the polygynous societies, a small number of men are in fact polygynous since they often have a lack sufficient resources to support several female mates.

Sexual Monogamy

The term monogamy has been used in several meanings. *Sexual monogamy* refers to the sexual relations, in which one male and one female have sexual intercourse exclusively with one another. In case of *genetic monogamy*, the offspring produced by one female or male in the pair have that same father and mother, thus producing the similar genetic makeup of all offspring. *Social monogamy* implies exclusive mating relations between one female and one male. They share a common territory, sleep and copulate with each other, spend their time together, live together for more than one breeding season, and have the common genetics of their offspring (Lukas & Clutton-Brock, 2013; Reichard & Boesch, 2003). This type of social monogamy is commonly called *pair-bonding*.

Cultural Monogamy

The special social type of mating relationships, such as marriage, is called *cultural monogamy* (Reichard & Boesch, 2003). In socially monogamous societies, extra-pair mating and sexual promiscuity are widespread as the forms of mating system. Monogamy can be of different duration. In *long-term monogamy,* a pair of one female and one male remains together for many years (a few breeding seasons). In *life-long monogamy,* the relationship lasts for the partners' whole life. In *short-term monogamy*, the relationship lasts for about a year (one breeding season): the partners are monogamous to each other within a limited time. S*erial monogamy* is the short-term monogamy in which an individual lives in different short-term relationships throughout their lives—in each new case of short-term monogamy with a different partner (Reichard & Boesch, 2003).

7.2 Models of Love as Attachment

7.2.1 Need to Belong and Attachment Love

The Need to Belong Is a Basic Human Need

The *need to belong* is among the basic human motives that guides individuals in social life. People are *social* animals. The *need in social bonding* drives an individual *need to belong* to a group and the *need to be accepted* by the group: family, kinship, tribe, parent, or mating partner. Evolutionary origins of bonding and the need to belong were extensively reviewed in Chap. 3.

The *social bonding* is the foundation of *love relations* as *positive social connections*, which has evolutionary and social origins (see more in the early chapter about *evolutionary models of love*). Social groups provide a better chance for an individual to survive in terms of physical conditions, such as sustenance and security. People living in tribal communities feel safer in social relations than living solitary life. Social cooperation gives everyone a more consistent access to food and provides better capability to defend from predators.

Later in evolution, the need for psychological security added to the basic human motives. And social relations helped not only with physical, but also with psychological survival.

Need to Belong and Love

Generally, all people have "the love needs" as the needs for belongingness (Baumeister & Leary, 1995; Maslow, 1943). In the same vein, love is defined as the *physiological and emotional bond*, which an individual experiences toward others (Pinkus, 2020). These needs to belong and affiliative love fulfilled in different types of in-group relationship, including close relationships. People who have a strong *need to belong* should have a higher value of affiliative love and union in love, compared to other kinds of love.

In-group Bonding and Pair-bonding as the Types of Attachment

Human attachment evolved as a *psychological mechanism* supporting *social bonding* of an individual with extended family and tribal community. *In-group bonding* and *attachment* were common in the societies with such family and community social structures and collectivistic cultures. *Attachment* of a child developed as *imprinting* and could be not less strong to kin than to mother. Later in the history, *pair-bonding and attachment* evolved in the societies with nuclear family structure and individualistic cultures. The *pair-bong attachment* of a child developed as the *love to mother*, or another caregiver.

7.2.2 Attachment Models of Love

The Love of Child as Attachment

Harlow and Zimmerman (1959), Bowlby (1969, 1973, 1980, 1988/2008), Ainsworth (1989), and colleagues (Ainsworth, Blehar, Waters, & Wall, 1978) were among the early researchers who showed evidence that *love as attachment* is important for wellbeing and development of infant and child. *Attachment to a caregiver* is the first type of love which humans experience in their life.

Thus, the *model of love as attachment* was conceptualized as the *bonding love of a child to mother*, along with associated emotions of attachment, separation, and loss. The *typology of love* is characterized by the patterns of attachment behavior that children exhibit in safe and frightening contexts (Ainsworth, 1989; Ainsworth et al., 1978; Belsky & Fearon, 2008; Belsky, Campbell, Cohn, & Moore, 1996; Cassidy & Shaver, 1999; Shaver & Mikulincer, 2006b).

The distinct *types of their love attachment* are characterized by *anxiety* and *avoidance* displayed in their emotions and motivations. Sometimes, they can be *ambivalent*.

Children develop the *model of love* characterized by *securely attachment* if their parents are *responsive to their needs*, *affectionate,* and *independent* in the relations with their children. Children become upset when the situations separate them from parents and actively communicate with parents when they are back and comfort them.

Children develop the *model of love* characterized by *anxious-resistant attachment* if their parents are *insensitive to their needs,* providing *inconsistent* care, and *rejecting* their requests. Then, children learn to be fearful, dependent, and clingy, when they have anxious and ambivalent relations with their caregivers. Children feel embarrassed and distressed when the situations separate them from parents and demonstrate ambivalent and conflicting behaviors when parents are back. It is challenging sooth them since they are cranky and fickle.

Children develop the *model of love* characterized by *anxious-avoidant attachment* if they feel emotionally abandoned in early years. They often demonstrate anxious emotions and avoidant behaviors. These avoidant children do not look like they are distressed when the situations separate them from parents and avoid contact with them, look disengaged, showing more attention to the toys, when parents are back.

This attachment model of children's love, however, does not reflect variations in cultural socialization strategies and childrearing philosophies. The typology is based on the individualistic middle-class *concept of psychological autonomy* as a cultural value.

The new *culture-sensitive framework* of attachment model (Keller, 2013, 2018) includes cultural foundations of attachment in non-Western and rural cultures, including the ethnically specific socialization and multiple caregiving practices. This *model of children' love as attachment* incorporates culturally different models of attachment (Keller, 2003, 2007).

The Love of Adult as Attachment

Shaver and colleagues (Fraley & Shaver, 2000; Hazan & Shaver, 1987; Shaver & Hazan, 1988; Shaver, Hazan, & Bradshaw, 1988; Shaver & Mikulincer, 2006a) found several similarities between *infant attachment to caregiver* and *adult romantic attachment* to a partner. Therefore, they conceptualized *love* as a process of adult attachment, in which people exhibit their typological differences. The types of attachment have been described in terms of *categories*—as attachment patterns and attachment styles, or later, in terms of dimensions—as typical combinations of *anxiety* and *avoidance* dimensions (see more details in the earlier chapters). These types were initially classified as *secure*, *avoidant*, and *anxious-resistant*. The later studies suggested four types of attachment: *secure, preoccupied, fearful-avoidant*, and *dismissing-avoidant*.

As one can see, the typologies and patterns of adult attachment are analogous in many respects with children's attachment. Researchers proposed that the *childhood attachment types* may influence their *adult attachments*. However, the findings have shown small and moderate correlations between *secure attachment* of individuals *with their mothers* and their *secure attachment with their romantic partners* (e.g., Feeney & Noller, 1990; Fraley, 2002; Fraley & Shaver, 2000; Hazan & Shaver, 1987).

The persons, who had secure attachment with their parent in childhood, are more likely to experience *love as secure attachment* to a mating partner in their adult relationships. They feel comfortable to trust and depend on the partner, they are easy-going with psychological intimacy and caring.

The persons, who acquired *anxious and ambivalent attachment* with their parent in childhood, are more likely to be dependent, clingy, and fearful in their adult love relationships. They fall in love easily crossing personal boundaries and seeking excessive closeness, yet they feel afraid to be abandoned by a partner. Due to these problems in emotional experience, their love relationships are prone to be short-term affairs.

The persons, who formed the *avoidant attachment* with their parent in childhood, are more likely to feel *avoidant emotional attachment* in their *adult relationship*. The difficulty in trusting and depending on a partner, the fear of being emotionally neglected, and being uncomfortable in getting close in relations create emotional problems in their love and relationships.

Adult Attachment Model of Love Across Cultures

The cross-cultural studies of *adult attachment model of love* have shown that people in many countries rate the *secure romantic attachment* very high as a cultural ideal and it is quite typical as a *personal model of love* (Schmitt, 2005a, 2005b, 2008a, 2008b, 2008c, 2010). However, its prevalence in several societies is significantly lower than any of the other three insecure attachment models—*fearful, dismissing*, or *preoccupied romantic attachment*. Across many countries (Schmitt, 2008b, 2008c) the three types of insecure attachment combined are more prevalent than the secure attachment type.

The low ecological stress is conducive to *secure romantic attachment*, while the high-stress ecological conditions precipitate *insecure attachment* to a partner. It is likely that the early childhood experience of secure or insecure environment determines the relationship strategies of men and women. In the social context of lower stress and ample resources, men and women prefer long-term mating and monogamous relationships. Due to their *secure romantic attachment,* they tend to substantially invest in fewer children.

However, men and women, which grew in the social context of highly stressful, harsh physical, economic conditions, had the parents who were insensitive to their needs being preoccupied with daily hassles, are more likely to acquire the *personal models of insecure attachment*, such as *fearful* and *dismissing*, and prefer short-term mating relationships (Belsky, 1997; Schmitt, 2008b, 2008c, 2010; Schmitt et al., 2004). This kind of living conditions with high stress and scarce resources,—for example, in several African countries,—predispose men and women to experience *insecure* types of *romantic attachment* (Schmitt, 2005a, 2005b, 2008a, 2008b, 2008c) and engage in *promiscuous sexual behavior* focusing on the benefits of short-term relationships (Chisholm, 1996, 1999).

Another major cultural parameter affecting the people's *cultural and personal models of romantic attachment* is the *collectivistic interdependent orientation* of their personality and interpersonal relations (Markus & Kitayama, 1991; Sprecher et al., 1994). For instance, in the East Asian collectivistic societies, individuals commonly appraise their self in terms of interdependent relationships with others. The high values of interconnectedness and what they do for others shape their *collective attachment* to family and kinship, rather than their individual attachment to another person. Their psychological romantic validation greatly depends upon the opinion of others that make East Asian men and women (e.g., in Japan and Taiwan) prone to *preoccupied romantic attachment* (Schmitt, 2005a, 2005b; Schmitt et al., 2004).

The studies in Western cultures have revealed that, despite the large within-sex variation in *dismissing romantic attachment,* the *men's personal models of romantic love* on average show more *dismissing type of attachment* than women's (Bartholomew, 1990; Brennan et al., 1998; Kirkpatrick, 1998). Men tend to avoid emotional closeness in their relationships. They prefer *relational independence* and are *uncomfortable with emotional disclosure* and *seeking emotional support.* They generally are less trusting, and nurturing. They are less inclined to get along with a partner and express emotions of social bonding and affiliation. These all are the typical characteristics of the *dismissing romantic attachment* type, which women find in men less fulfilling for their relationships (see for review Schmitt, 2008a, 2008b, 2008c). The studies in non-Western societies (Schmitt, 2005a, 2005b, 2010; Schmitt et al., 2003, 2004) have demonstrated that *dismissing romantic attachments* among men vary across cultures. Men in East Asian, Southern European, and South American countries show *lower dismissing attachment* in their *personal models of love.* On the other hand, men in South and Southeast Asian societies, in Oceanian and African countries show *higher dismissing romantic attachment,* compared to other cultural regions of the world.

Love as Attachment in Relations with Other Models of Love

Several theoretical perspectives have placed *love attachment* in the context of other models of love. *Evolutionary model* explained that the *attachment love* evolved in very early human history to support the *group bonding* and *pair bonding.*

For Fisher (2000), *attachment*, along with *attraction* and *sex drive*, are the three basic emotional systems, which fulfill evolutionary functions of mating, reproduction, and parenting. The *attraction* is described as "increased energy and focused attention on one or more potential mates, accompanied in humans by exhilaration, intrusive thinking, and craving for emotional union." From psychophysiological view, attraction is characterized by increased *dopamine* and *norepinephrine* and decreased *serotonin* in the brain. The system of *sex drive, or lust*, is described as "the craving for sexual gratification." The system of *attachment* is described as "close social contact and feelings of calm, comfort, and emotional union" (Fisher, 2000, p. 96).

For Shaver and Mikulincer (2006a, 2006b), the *attachment-theoretical perspective on love* considers the *attachment love*, along with *sex love* and *caregiving love,* as the *three* innate *behavioral systems*. These distinct *behavioral systems* play their own evolutionary functions. Affecting each other in various ways, the systems create individual differences in patterns of love.

7.3 Models of Love as Commitment

7.3.1 The Dutiful Model of Love

The Concept of Love as a Duty

In the *model of love as a duty*, an *individual* is *committed to love* another, due to family bonds, responsibilities imposed by circumstances, by given obligations, and other reasons. A *sense of duty* compels the individual to *feel love*, *display love*, and *act out of love*, despite the qualities of another.

For instance, one must love his/her mother and father. One loves them just because they are parents, not because of their good look or personality. This model of love is called *filial love*. When a parent has good character, loving personality, and does good things for a son or daughter, it is a plus. However, *love as a duty* is prompted by the *duty to love,* by *obligation to do good things to the parent.*

The same way, an individual may experience a pledge to love a spouse or a child. Once again, such a *required love* is due to social or cultural ties, not the virtues of another. The individual *loves* because he/she *must love*. This duty of love can be imposed (a) by social expectations, cultural norms, family obligations, and other *external social motivation*, which are internalized by an individual, or (b) an individual may impose the obligation on him/herself *voluntarily* due to the moral feeling of duty, and other *internal social motivation.*

Varieties of Love as a Duty

Thus, in the case of *externally imposed motivation*, love is due to *social obligation*, while in the case of *internally imposed motivation*, love is due to *moral commitment*.

External social motivation to love, being adopted by an individual, is common in collectivistic cultures with strong social ties in kin relations and imposed family responsibilities. *Internal social motivation* to love, being accepted by an individual, may occur in individualistic cultures when the individual feels responsible to do something good to another person because that person did something good to the individual in the past. This is a *duty to love* due to the *moral norm of reciprocity*. In other cases, an individual loves another person because of unhappy or pitiful circumstances, which occurs in his/her life. This is a *duty to love* due to the *moral norm of compassion*.

The *ideas of love as a duty* and *moral obligation* have been elaborated in social philosophy (Driver, 2014; Frankfurt, 1998; Liao, 2006; Solheim, 1999), however, have not received attention of scholars in empirical disciplines.

Emphasis on Love as a Duty in Traditional Collectivistic Societies

In traditional collectivistic cultures people put special emphasis on their duties since their fulfillment is essential for the normal functioning of a society. To avoid a cognitive and emotional dissonance, their emotions normally conform to those duties and vice versa. "A father fulfils his duties because he loves his son, and he loves his son because he is the father." Filial piety (*xiao dao*) defines the parent-child as the primary relationship. "Parents demand love, reverence, obedience, and respect from their children. Children expect love, wisdom, and benevolence from their parents" (Kim & Park, 2006, p. 39). Emotions in romantic relationships supposed to subordinate to these foundational kinship relationships: youngsters tend to subordinate their mating feelings, while spouses know how to subordinate theirs.

Appreciation in the Duty Model of Love

In the *model of love as a duty*, an individual must love, express love, and do good things to others as the acts of love because they are expected or required to do so. On the other hand, a person, who is loved and cared for by a loving individual, is expected to *express their gratitude and appreciation*. Not meeting such an expectation is impolite, morally not right, and not appreciative. *Gratitude and appreciation* are conducive for the mutually gratifying emotional experience of partners. They are important in companionate love, as well as in the love as a duty relationship.

Instead of the feeling that you are entitled, that others are due to you, being sincerely grateful and not shy to express this, are the important provisions of reciprocally satisfying relationships. Instead of thinking about what you deserve to have, but have not get, please, pay attention and appreciate what you have. Be grateful for what another one did for you, do not expect more. The studies (see for review, Twenge & Campbell, 2009) have demonstrated that those people, who think regularly about everything they are grateful for, experience more frequent and greater feelings of well-being and health. They are more psychologically supportive to others.

For instance, the indigenous Chinese concept of *enqing* is grateful love (Chen & Li, 2007). This kind of love includes the feelings of responsibilities and obligations associated with a spouse's feelings of appreciation, gratitude, and indebtedness for what the partner has done in the marriage. Marital *enqing* is rooted in traditional Confucian value of duty in marriage and Chinese relationship orientation.

7.3.2 *Externally and Internally Imposed Commitment of Love*

Typology of Commitment

According to the tripartite theory of commitment (Johnson, Caughlin, & Huston, 1999), partners may stay in a relationship due to *personal commitment*, when they feel attracted to the partner, to the relationship, or they experience strong feeling of couple identity. They may also experience *structural commitment* when they see perceive the barriers and constraints in the possibility to leave the relationship. And they may feel *moral commitment*, when they experience a sense of ethical obligation to continue the relationship.

I propose the *model of commitment* including *externally and internally imposed types*, as drafted below. They are not dichotomous, but present rather the spectrum of their mixture and can explain the cultural models of love, which permit different degrees of freedom in the love choice.

Love as Externally Imposed Commitment

Life and love of humans since early times have given people the limited freedom for choices. They needed to adjust to ecological and social affordances available in isolated tribal societies, as well as in traditional collectivistic societies. Individuals were embedded in social structures and family relations, which required them to fulfill their functions and duties. They accepted and internalized these socially imposed responsibilities because their violation would be disruptive for a society. Therefore, social institutions penalized such violation of social norms. So, socialization of individuals taught them to accept, internalize, and follow those norms. They were free to do anything they wanted within these norms. They were free to love anyone they wanted within socially and culturally available options.

A Dutch philosopher Spinoza (1632–1677) reasoned in his *Ethics* (1677) that *freedom* and *necessity* are inter-related. According to his thesis, *freedom is the knowledge of necessity*, or in other words, *freedom lies in the recognition of necessity.*

One could also say that *freedom is learning to like what it is rational to like*. *Love as commitment* can stem from the *duty* and *responsibility* imposed by a society, kin relations, and family obligations. Once a person willingly accepts them, they become his/her commitment to a community, family, or other person. For instance, in collectivistic cultures, such *external social commitment* to cooperate with others and love another is common among individuals.

As we saw in the early sections, humans as social animals survived and thrived through cooperation. However, people in traditional societies were frequently compelled to cooperate and had no choice in some regards.

Such reasoning of *freedom* and *necessity* brings a corresponding perspective on arranged marriages, see elsewhere (Karandashev, in press, and in other sections of this book).

Love as Internally Imposed Commitment

In case of this *type of love as commitment*, Spinoza's reasoning about *freedom* and *necessity* can also be suitable. *Freedom is just a certain kind of necessity,* even in individualistic societies with high value of autonomy and freedom.

Responsibility shall come along with *freedom. Freedom of choices* shall come along with awareness and acceptance that individuals take their responsibilities for the consequences of their choices. The *freedom of choice* shall also respect and protect the freedom of another. A problem arises when someone behaves inconsiderately not respecting such responsibility. Freedom without mutual responsibility can lead to injustice in relationships.

Different from external compulsion, an individual with *internally imposed commitment* is free to cooperate and make choices. Freedom and necessity, however, can mean different things to different people. Necessity can be *forceful*—external necessity, and *free*—internal necessity. Thus, the freedom of choice can be viewed as the *free necessity* to do something fulfilling obligations.

In modern individualistic cultures, the individuals shall be aware of themselves as responsible for doing something good to another person due to the cultural *norms of reciprocity, care, or compassion*. As de Saint-Exupéry noted in *The Little Prince,* "It is only with the heart that one can see rightly: what is essential is invisible to the eye." A *loving person* in this case internally imposes *moral commitment* for the love, relationship, and beloved. As de Saint-Exupéry also noted, "You become responsible for what you have tamed. You're responsible for your rose." Unfortunately, "People have forgotten this truth," the fox said.

The Role of Individualistic and Collectivistic Values in Experience of Love as Commitment

The cultural attitudes to the *experience of commitment in love* differ in Eastern societies, associated with *collectivistic values,* and Western societies, associated with *individualistic values.* Several studies have revealed cultural differences; however, the data are not sufficiently representative across cultures to make conclusions about their *models of love as commitment.*

Some studies (Agnew & Lee, 1997; Kemmelmeier, Sanchez-Burks, Cytron, & Coon, 1998), for example, have shown that *higher individualism* among European Americans correlates with their lower relationship commitment.

The studies conducted in India, the UK, and the USA (Bejanyan, Marshall, & Ferenczi, 2015) suggested that *parental influence* and *family allocentrism,* which are frequently present in collectivistic societies, may affect people's experience of commitment. The results showed that people in those societies have ambivalent love experiences of commitment: (1) those individuals high in collectivism undergo upward pressure on their feeling of commitment due to their family allocentrism (stronger family ties), and (2) they undergo concurrent downward pressure on the feeling of commitment due to high parental influence. Thus, stronger family ties (family allocentrism) of collectivistic societies increase their experience of love commitment up, while greater acceptance of parental influence over mate choice decreases their experience of commitment down.

7.4 Models of Companionate Love

7.4.1 Companionate Love in Marital and Family Relationships

Concept of Companionate Love

The concept of *companionate love* characterizes the experiences, expressions, and actions of those partners who live together for a number of years, being married or just living together. Sometimes, this is called a *conjugal love* (Berscheid & Walster, 1974; Waller & Hill, 1951). The feelings between a man and a woman affectionate, yet less passionate than in *passionate model of love*. Partners feel and express love as less intense, but more spiritual, respectful, and content; they enjoy each other's company. They are willing to share everyday life and chores, to find the meaning in simple tasks, appreciate the relatedness and union with another. They find the meaning and beauty in doing ordinary things (Karandashev, 2017).

Companionate love is commonly defined as a model of love different from *romantic, passionate,* and *sexual* love. It is frequently viewed as an opposite type of relationship, along with corresponding emotional experiences, expressions, and actions. However, that is not quite adequate judgment. Companionate love is not just the habitual living of partners together with fading passion and idealization. Gently taking care of each other, expressing tenderness, and sharing intimate thoughts and feelings with each other are quite romantic love experiences, expressions, and actions. The years of companionate love do not necessarily kill passionate and romantic feelings, partners can still be sexually active. These emotional experiences and expressions just transform and evolve into the new love sentiments and attitudes that bring partners relationship satisfaction, high self-esteem, and psychological well-being (Acevedo & Aron, 2009. Passionate feelings decline over the years of living together. However, for some individuals and couples, these changes are relatively small in absolute terms—passionate love remains on a moderate level (Acevedo, Aron, Fisher, & Brown, 2012; Tucker & Aron, 1993).

Love for Marriage

Throughout centuries, love and marriage have been quite different fields of relationships with different functions. For centuries, marriage was a social institution with traditional functions to provide a person the legal security, access to social status, property, finances, and a legitimate opportunity to raise children. Love was not a prerequisite for marriage, even though it was allowed when did not contradict with social aspects of marriage. The latter was of a primary importance. Arranged marriages were widespread and in many cases could not allow love to interfere with social affordances.

The religious doctrines teach that marriage is a sacred relationship. And love can make men and women happy only in marriage. In some cultural and religious traditions, love is not completely fulfilled without marriage. And the white wedding as a beautiful tradition brings a lot of sense to many.

Love is widely compatible with the modern culture of marriage (Abbott, 2010). Many men and women are able to pursue both love and marriage. Happy relationship and social benefits of marriage merge. Modern romantic stories presented in novels, movies, and real life demonstrate that it is possible to marry a person whom an individual loves and who have a good social and financial status.

Acceptance of love and equality of relationship are becoming more typical for marriage relationship. Yet, gender stereotypes are persistent. Initiation of marriage is commonly a man's role. And romantic movies and novels reproduce these stereotypes. Love entails marriage. "Would you marry me?" is a typical image of romance, with waiting a response from a woman. It seems weird to see that a woman would say a beloved man "Would you marry me?"

Some individuals in modern societies may be practical in some respects. The stories in novels, movies, and real life show how men and women may imitate their affection, pretend that they love their beloved, and manipulate for the sake of social benefits.

In modern societies, men and women may move in and live together as partners without marriage. They are independent in many social, financial, and legal aspects of life. They think that love relationships are valuables in their own rights, even without official marriage. They may live in cohabitation for years (https://www.livescience.com/28420-cohabiting-marriage-cdc-report.html). Love as partnership, which assumes an equality in relationship, becomes more popular type of long-term committed relationship.

The Cultural Model of Marital and Family Love

This cultural model of love is an alternative for the passionate model of love. It highlights the importance of love which takes place in marriage and family. Sometimes, it is opposed to the transient love relationship, such as passionate and romantic. This cultural model emphasizes that *marital love* is an everlasting relationship that brings personal satisfaction in life. This is a more reliable source of enjoyment than unrealistic romantic relationship and fleeting passionate feelings of love which is based on infatuation and lust.

People cannot live in the world of *passionate romance* forever. The reality of life requires to bear responsibilities and solve daily tasks. The *marital and family* love provides more realistic basis for personal life and gives a more valid and reliable source to enjoy life with stability and satisfaction.

Thus, one can see that essentially, this *cultural model of love* is a tribute of *companionate love*. It engages the emotions of affection, companionship, personal attachment to each another, and helps in daily challenges of life. This type of relationship becomes more rewarding in the long run for life compared to passionate romantic love.

The *marital and family model of love* has been cultivated, valorized, and promoted in many cultural works of poetry, novels, and art. For example, this kind of love is largely present in many novels of Indian poet and novelist Vikram Seth, such as his verse novel *The Golden Gate* (1986) and his epic novel *A Suitable Boy* (1993), where love is portrayed as a sacred social relationship (Sharma, 2016).

The *marital models of love* have some cross-culturally common qualities and values, however, may differ across societies. Cultural traditions and societal norms can place emphasis on different aspects of family life depending on cultural values, traditions, and modernization of a society. For example, according to the opinions of informants from Beijing, Hong Kong, and the UK (Wong & Goodwin, 2009), the *cultural models of marital love* include the stable relationship, partnership with the spouse, spousal support, and stable family finances as important factors for marital satisfaction. As for the cultural differences, for British informants, the companionship relations were more important, while for Hong Kong informants, the harmonious marital relations were more important.

7.4.2 Western Cultural Models of Companionate Love

Western Scholarly Model of Companionate Love

Western scholarly tradition, such as American, contrasts *companionate love* with *passionate love*. The *passionate love* is more characteristic for the early stage of romantic relations during initiation of relationships and dating, while *companionate love* emerges in an enduring relationship of partners. These two types of love are viewed in the successive transition as the stages of love (Berscheid, 1985, 2010; Berscheid & Walster, 1974, 1969/1978; Hatfield, 1988; Hatfield & Rapson, 1993; Sprecher & Regan, 1998). Such representation of love progression can be considered as an *ideal American cultural model of love*, which can be frequently observed in real life of European Americans.

In *companionate love* people experience a strong affection, lasting attachment, intimacy, and devotion with a partner with whom the life is deeply entwined. The relationship is more fulfilling, committed, and characterized by friendship, understanding, and concern. Long-term peaceful and comfortable affiliation, the continuing investment builds these feelings over time (Hatfield, 1988; Hatfield & Rapson, 1993). Companionate love is selfless, forgiving, caring for, and accepting their partner with gratitude. The identity of "*we*" is formed, so the partners see each other as their own extension and seek to serve each other. Irrationality, obsession, and possessiveness are less common among partners; their unity and harmony appear rationally. The sexual desire is expressed in respectful ways through affection and fondness. Lovers consider care, service, and equality as more important than their feelings of suitability to the partner. The attachment to a partner is generally secure. Sharing and connectedness between partners are especially important, yet they may still live relatively independently and maintain their autonomy. Companionate love is preferred by many females (Karandashev & Clapp, 2016).

How the American Model of Companionate Love Evolved

The model of companionate love has been quite popular in American societies and typical among partners, yet in different ways. This *cultural model of love* has likely had its cultural origins in the puritan way of life and relationships, which have been widespread since the early American settlements from Europe. Protestant Christians were a large cultural group among early American pioneers and presumably determined such puritan traditions (see in another chapter).

The role of *companionate model of love* in American society was growing in the nineteenth century, along with the increasing urbanization of social life (Karandashev, 2017). Husbands and wives in urban populations became less socially and economically dependent on each other in marital relations. Their marriages did not function anymore as social and economic institutions, as in the rural settings of the farming households where they were practically and economically dependent on each other in survival.

The rigid traditional gender roles in the nineteenth century faded. The free choice for both genders became a norm of marriage in America. American women had more freedom and more natural relations with men. The relationships between men and women were more like friendship. The role of physical passion in marital choice was condemned. Being a good Christian, industrious, kind, caring, and thrifty were the virtues which should be acceptable traits desirable for marriage. An ideal American marriage in the nineteenth century was viewed as a compatible union. A symbol of sentimental marital life is embodied in the image of the "two birds within a nest." Some men and women promoted their rights to satisfy personal needs in marriage. Individualistic values among American men and women of the middle class encourage them to experience and express romantic and companionate love more openly love (Lystra, 1989).

The Modern American Model of Companionate Love

Since approximately 1850s and until 1960s, American marriage gradually embraced the *companionate model of love* (Finkel, 2018). Men, and in later decades women, increasingly worked outside of their home to earn money for their family. They occupied different social and economic spheres. With the growing wealth of their families, American men and women started to be interested in the marriage which could meet their personal and companionship needs. They looked at their marital relationships for the fulfillment of their desire to love, be loved, experience emotional intimacy and joy of sexual life.

In the twentieth century, a Hollywood movies tradition of romanticizing love substantially affected American ideals and fairy dreams. Nevertheless, in accord with their long-standing puritan cultural tradition, many Americans still preferred the *companionate love* based on companionship and friendship for their real marital relationships (Karandashev, 2017).

Americans seem *uncomfortable* with *romantic love* in their real life. Even though their pursuit for positive and happy emotions is inspiring and enduring, passionate, *romantic love* is too turbulent and saturated with high emotional energy. Therefore, they prefer to turn down the high arousal and intensity of initial love feelings (De Munck, Korotayev, & Khaltourina, 2009, 2010; De Munck & Kronenfeld, 2016). For many Americans, *romantic love, passionate love,* and *sexual love* are non-prototypical for their cognitive representations of love. These types of love are rather marginal. The *friendship love* and *familial kinds of love* are deemed as more prototypical for them (Fehr, 1988, 1994; Fehr & Russell, 1991).

Instead, Americans foster companionship, friendship, the feelings of security and comfort (De Munck et al., 2009, 2010; De Munck & Kronenfeld, 2016). The "mutual compatible virtues," the feelings of being "secure" and "comfortable" are the most frequent terms mentioned by American informants regarding the concept of love. The features of being *secure*, *comfortable*, *committed,* and *content* show the general importance of filling in positive low energy emotional experience.

Family Union, Comfort, and Friendship Are the Core Features of American Companionate Love

Exploring *American cultural model of love*, researchers (e.g., D'Andrade & Strauss, 1992; De Munck, 2019; Fehr, 1988, 1994; Fehr & Russell, 1991), identified *being together* and *friendship* as the most salient features of the motivation and the state of being in love, indicative for *companionate model of love*. In a cross-cultural perspective, a survey of the two small cultural samples of college students has shown that compared to Malays, Americans were the stronger advocates of companionate love attitudes.

The processes of deinstitutionalization, which have occurred in the United States during the twentieth century (Burgess & Locke, 1945; Cherlin, 2004), have weakened the social, gender roles, and the norms of behavior in a relationship. The value of a *partners' union*, which is formed on a free personal choice, has substantially increased. The freedom of choice available in many regards has increased the diversity and complexity of *relationship unions*. For example, individuals of any gender have received the possibilities to marry or cohabit, freely initiate, suspend, or stop a relationship, to choose a partner of another or the same sex.

Thus, the decreasing role of institutional and economic limitations, social and gender roles in American society have increased the role of *personal choice*, *self-expression*, *self-development*, and *companionate love* in the partners' relationships. Nevertheless, marriages have retained their symbolic significance, status, and prestige. The cherished attitudes and detailed elaboration, which are involved in the planning of white weddings in America, provide a convincing evidence of it. They fulfill the sacred dreams of many.

I acknowledge, however, that a diversity of American population in terms of ethnicity, religious beliefs, social classes shall remind us to avoid the excessive generalization of these *companionate tendencies in love*. Many Asian American, African American, Latino American cultural communities can have different views on love and marriage. For example, in the Mexican and Islam communities in the United States, people still may follow their traditional models of love relationship (e.g., Badahdah & Tiemann, 2005; Hirsch, 2007; Hirsch & Wardlow, 2006).

The degrees of changes also depend on the social classes and education of people. The great differences between social classes in this regard are still persistent over the past decades. In many cases, the behaviors of partners within marriage have changed toward more *companionate model of love*. Education also plays its role. However, deinstitutionalization of marriage in the United States occurs on a slower pace than scholars earlier believed (Cherlin, 2020).

7.4.3 Eastern Cultural Models of Companionate Love

Cultural Universality of Companionate Love Model

Although the concept of companionate love was proposed by Western scholars (Berscheid, 1985, 2010; Berscheid & Walster, 1974, 1969/1978; Hatfield, 1988; Hatfield & Rapson, 1993; Sprecher & Regan, 1998), it is quite characteristic to other societies. The Eastern cultures, for example, place especial emphasis on this type of emotional experience, expression, and actions as a cultural model of love.

Doherty et al. (1994) in their study with Japanese American, Chinese Americans, Filipino American, Pacific Islanders, and European American samples from the University of Hawaii, cited above, found that participants of different ethno-cultural background—individualist or collectivist—had the scores on Companionate Love scale on the same level, not significantly different from each other.

Lomas (2018) in his study of love lexicon in various languages, identified *connection*, *care*, and *appreciation* among the core characteristics of companionate love across many cultures, but especially valuable in Eastern cultural conception of love.

Chinese Companionate Love

The Chinese culture and people in their daily functioning have been frequently described by anthropologists, sociologists, and psychologists as relation-based or relation-centered (e.g., Ho, 1991; Hwang, 2000; Yang, 1995). Such attitudes as interpersonal harmony, relational determinism, *yuan* (predestined relational affinity), *xiaodao* (filial piety), and marital *enqing* (grateful love or affection) are among the core characteristics of this culturally specific Chinese relationship orientation (Yang, 1995, 2006). All these and relational-oriented propensities and feelings are especially applicable to close relationship and family life.

Having strong relationship orientation in their thought and behavior (Yang, 1995), Chinese perceive norms and regulations as the abstract principles that should be modified to apply to specific cases. Exceptions are always possible and necessary in the context of specific relationships. People are willing to give a favor, bypass or relax rules and principles for a person with whom they are in an intimate or other harmonious special relationship. Relationship with a person *determines* what kind of exceptional favor can be given to him or her.

Among the most important relational feelings in family-life are *filial piety* and *enqing* (marital grateful love or affection). Filial piety is a specific mental disposition, which includes an intention and behavior of being good to one's parents.

The Chinese Concept of Enqing—Grateful Love and Affection

As for the relationship between romantic partners, husband and wife in family, *enqing*—grateful love and affection—describe culturally important Chinese feelings of love (Li, 1999). The marital *enqing* is experienced as "affection and sentiment between husband and wife that is mainly based upon one party's feeling of indebtedness, gratitude, and appreciation for the other's kindness, consideration, favor, and tolerance during the history of the marital relationship" (Yang, 2006. p. 301).

The Chinese concept of *enqing*—grateful love or affection—represents the type of love that is rooted in Chinese relationship orientation (Chen & Li, 2007; Yang, 2006) and might be considered as indigenous. *Enqing* is a focal component of Chinese marital affection. Even though, intimacy has been identified as a component of Chinese marital affection, this particular form of affection in marriage cannot be fully explained by the concept of intimacy. For Chinese people *enqing* is higher than intimacy in the hierarchy of marital affection. It is a grateful love and includes benevolence, forgiveness, forbearance, and unconditional care. Passion, erotic love, and sexual desire are de-emphasized by couples in marital relationship. This non-erotic nature of Chinese affection is different from American passion, which carries more erotic sentiments. *Enqing* represents the particular form of affection which highlights a moral dimension of love rather than just the emotional and cognitive dimensions. This moral aspect of Chinese marital affection stems from the traditional Confucian ethics assuming certain roles of husbands and wives in marriage.

7.5 Models of Love as Union

7.5.1 Compatibility of Partners in Companionate Model of Love

Love as a Union

Concepts of unity and union are the widely recognized cultural beliefs and perceptions of love with other related connotations (see for review, Karandashev, 2019). They are commonly accepted in folklore myth, public views, and scholarly literature. The *unity metaphor* has been an enduring *cultural model of love* for centuries and across many languages (Kövecses, 1988, 2005). The modern social attitudes and scholarly philosophies consider inspiration to *be together, unite, affiliate, and merge in unity* with another as the leading motivation of love. These others can be parents, kins, friends, a beloved man or woman, romantic partner, spouse, and children. These others can also be the loved toys, characters of novels and movies, pop stars, celebrities, and others who are worthy to admire. For devoted and practicing believers, *uniting with God* is the *ultimate experience of love*.

The *allegory of union and unity*, however, is more commonly applied to the romantic and companionate love and relationship (see for review, Karandashev, 2019). The typical scholarly definitions characterize love as a state of intense desire and longing for union with another, a total absorption of lovers (e.g., Berscheid & Walster, 1969/1978; Fisher, 2004; Hatfield & Rapson, 1993; Reddy, 2012). Many empirical studies have demonstrated that people in several societies (e.g., North America, Lithuania, Russia, Japan, China) experience love this way. These cultural ideas are in their personal models of love (e.g., De Munck, Korotayev, de Munck, & Khaltourina, 2011; Farrer, Tsuchiya, & Bagrowicz, 2008).

Love is a subjective experience that the *two is one*—yet it is the extended and expanded ONE. In various linguistic and cultural lexicon, love is expressed as a *unity of two complementary parts* (Chang & Li, 2006; Karandashev, 2017, 2019; Kövecses, 1988, 2005). This *cultural model of love* as a union is romantically portrayed in *Romeo and Juliet* (Sánchez, 1995). The metaphorical connotations of union are common in English (e.g., *doves, lovey-dovey*), Chinese (e.g., *mandarin ducks, flying twin swallows*), and other languages (Lv & Zhang, 2012).

Love as the *longing for affiliation* implies an interpersonal fusion of partners uniting with each other in emotional, spiritual, and mental sense—that is feeling each other and together. Yet, love is not only sighing on a bench and walking in the moonlight, but also something more. Love is the union in a practical sense. It is the doing together and serving each other as a well-coordinated team—protecting, producing, shopping, cooking, doing laundry, raising kids, etc. This idea of love as a union in a broad sense is suitable in various cultures, yet its specific meaning can vary.

Compatibility and Coordination Between Partners

The compatible partners in a close companionate relationship may be compatible in several respects from the early romantic onset of their relationship. The mating and sexual compatibility of individuals is a commonly known occurrence, which is expressed in the notions of "you've clicked with someone," biochemistry, or destiny. Such compatibility can be biologically based at the first place.

The *inter-individual coordination* of partners underlies relationship initiation and maintenance, as well as *bi-parental care*. The evidence suggests (see for review, Roth, Samara, Tan, Prochazkova, & Kret, 2021) that such coordination at physiological and behavioral levels characterizes the potential for relationships to be long-lasting.

This biological predisposition can be a common evolutionary path for several monogamous species, including birds and humans. Some non-human species also show such ability for *inter-individual coordination* at behavioral, as well as at physiological level (see for review, Roth et al., 2021).

Interdependence and Synchrony of Partners in Companionate Love

Partners in companionate love are interdependent from each other in many regards, especially in emotional life. Their emotional interdependence includes frequent interactions, exchanges, influences, and responses to one another's emotions. Over time, their physiological linkage and synchrony may increase, emotions can converge and become closely aligned (e.g., Anderson, Keltner, & John, 2003; Freihart & Meston, 2019; Helm, Sbarra, & Ferrer, 2012; Liu, Rovine, Cousino Klein, & Almeida, 2013; Reed, Randall, Post, & Butler, 2013; Schoebi, 2008; Timmons, Margolin, & Saxbe, 2015; Wilson et al., 2018). The emotional interdependence of partners may also arise. According to a recent study (Sels et al., 2020), on average, the general level of interdependence in couples is higher compared to non-couples. However, the extent of such interdependence substantially varies across couples, types of emotions (negative vs. positive vs. emotional extremity), and situational contexts (supportive vs. conflictual).

Love as Interpersonal Complementarity and Self-expansion

The two is more than one. The two is better than one. There are plenty of sayings which express this simple wisdom. The social benefit of cooperation is that two can do many things better together than alone. Each partner expands the knowledge, skills, and strength of each other. The love relationship also expands psychological experience and self-awareness.

The metaphor "*the better half*" beautifully expresses this idea of complementarity in *love as a union*. Since a married couple is a union of the two halves as a whole, then the woman is the better half. Seriously, it is a romantic compliment, even though some feminists may perceive it ironically. The metaphor goes beyond gender equality elevating the status of woman. In the same vein, the Chinese cultural idea of *yin* and *yang* expresses complementarity of woman and man in in a relationship—*better together*. They are better when they are together because they expand themselves in another.

Model of Love as Self-expansion

The *model of love as self-expansion* is the possible *personal model of love*, which an individual may follow. Some culture can be more favorable to this type of love than others.

The *self-expansion model* of love explains that an individual *desire for love relationship* with a particular other is a desire to include that other person in the individual self, thus expanding the self through association with him/her (Aron & Aron, 1986, 1996, 2016). The partners' interactions can change the *self* of one, another, or both. While they become closer, they may experience some psychological "overlapping" between their self-concepts. They acquire characteristics of the close other subsuming those into their expanded self-concept. They tend to perceive the beliefs, qualities, and available resources of their close other as their own, at least partially, and act accordingly (Aron, Aron, Tudor, & Nelson, 1991). They sometimes confuse their self with the self of close other, incorporating the features of the loved one into their own self (Aron, Paris, & Aron, 1995; Mashek, Aron, & Boncimino, 2003).

According to interpersonal social-cognitive theory, the *self is the relational self.* This means that *mental representation of the self* relates to *mental representations of significant others*. And these links embody *self-other relationships* (Andersen & Chen, 2002). The *self,* as an individual mental model *of loving person,* encompasses the *relational schemas* of the *loved one* along with his/her emotional states and behaviors during interaction with partner, as well as the *scripts of their patterns of interaction* (Baldwin, 1992; Hinkley & Andersen, 1996; Ogilvie & Ashmore, 1991).

According to cultural theories (see in Karandashev, 2021a, 2021b), for people in collectivistic cultures with interdependent self, their interpersonal relationships are a *part of their self.* The mental representations of their close others are stored in their memory in conjunction with representation of themselves. These theoretical assumptions, however, have not had the empirical finding to support. The *model of love as self-expansion* is still waiting comprehensive cross-cultural investigation.

Self-transcendence in Love as Self-expansion

For some people, *social connections in love* and *cultural model of love union* can be the ways to *self-transcendence*. The concept of *self-transcendence* characterizes the *individual experience* of *expanding personal boundaries* and focusing on the interests, purposes, and perspectives beyond their self, while still appreciating the present context of life and the self (Reed, 2015). As the trait, self-transcendence is the person's ability to go *beyond self-centered consciousness*, to *perceive* the *things* with *clear and unconditional awareness*

The *expansion of self-boundaries* in *self-transcendence* can be attained and assessed in various means and ways (Coward, 1996; Reed, 1986, 2018). Some scholars consider *self-transcendence* as the core experience of *existential self-expansion model of love* (e.g., Aron & Aron, 1986, 1996, 2016; Fromm, 1956, 1976; Levenson, Jennings, Aldwin, & Shiraishi, 2005; Lindholm, 1995, 1998; Maslow, 1968, 1970).

The *self-transcendent love emotions,* such as *awe, gratitude, and compassion*, foster individuals to transcend their own desires and needs while focusing on those of another person—their loved one. *Love as self-transcendence* makes personal love attitudes and actions mature and wise (Levenson et al., 2005). The men and women experiencing *mature and wise love* can overcome their narcissism (Fromm, 1956, 1976).

In terms of *self-actualization model of personality* (Maslow, 1968, 1970), self-actualizers appreciate *ego transcendence*, *detachment*, and *individuality*. They are capable to maintain balance between *individuality* and *ego-transcendence,* between autonomy and unity with others. They *regard love as the ultimate pursuit* for personal and interpersonal growth. They love others without clinging attachment and feel greater satisfaction in their love relationships.

Certain cultures may promote or hinder productive, wise, and mature forms of love (Fromm, 1956). Some spiritual cultural traditions, such as Sufism (Karamustafa, 2007; Lings, 1975) and Mahayana Buddhism (Keown, 2016; Keown & Prebish, 2013; Williams, 2008), teach that *love is the transcendental compassion* that leads to the wisdom of life and relationship. In Asian collectivistic societies, with their culturally fostered *relational focus of self*, the *transcendental experience* of love has been culturally natural for centuries.

On the other side, as Fromm (1956) argued that capitalistic Western cultures (e.g., American one) hinder mature and wise forms of love. In American and some Western European cultures, with their *individualistic values* and *self-focused self*, people may have difficulties in attaining *experience of self-transcendence*. The results of cross-cultural studies (Le & Levenson, 2005) with different cultural samples in the United States have shown that such cultural syndrome as *vertical individualism* is related to *immature love* and *low disposition to self-transcendence*.

The comparative study across the United States, Lithuania, and Russia (De Munck et al., 2011)—presumably culturally different countries—has demonstrated that in all three cultural samples, informants consider *transcendence* as the core characteristic of romantic love. They believe that the l*ove union of two lovers transforms them into something more meaningful* than just the two parts of a couple. The two other essential attributes of romantic love, which informants frequently highlighted, are (a) *the person's love boosts the beloved's psychological well-being* and (b) *altruism,* or *agape* love and—both also expressing the idea of transcendence. The latter love attitude—*agape* as altruistic, selfless, all-giving love, is also a *type of love* in the typologies of love styles (Lee, 1973, 1976, 1977) and love attitudes

(Hendrick & Hendrick, 1986, 1989). The *agape type of love* is characterized by benevolent emotional and spiritual identification of a loving person with the loved one. The person experiencing the *true agape love* overcomes their self-focused motives caring more about the needs of the beloved one—their interests are the priorities.

The Model of Love as the Relationship Building

The importance of similarity, like-mindedness, and compatibility for the successful loving relations between partners is commonly understood in many societies, especially in individualistic cultures. Therefore, people look for a perfect match, or at least for a prospective partner who is matching good enough. The right "chemistry of love"—whatever this means—is expected, along with a good look, personality, resourcefulness, and other decent qualities.

Predetermination of love by these and other preexisting conditions is a typical feature of several individualistic models of love. Another possible model of love is the relationship-building model. It is not necessarily an alternative to *predetermination model of love*. Instead, they can be a nice addition to each other.

This quote from *The Little Prince* by Saint-Exupéry wisely and beautifully conveys the idea of this model of love,

- "I am looking for friends. What does that mean—tame?"
- "It is an act too often neglected," said the fox. "It means to establish ties."
- "To establish ties?"
- "Just that," said the fox. "To me, you are still nothing more than a little boy who is just like a hundred thousand other little boys. And I have no need of you. And you, on your part, have no need of me. To you I am nothing more than a fox like a hundred thousand other foxes. But if you tame me, then we shall need each other. To me, you will be unique in all the world. To you, I shall be unique in all the world…." —Antoine de Saint-Exupéry, *The Little Prince*

And another idea, quoted elsewhere in the book, perfectly complements this one. The fox said, "You become responsible for what you have tamed." The idea of commitment in a relationship union is discussed in the following sections.

The companionate *model* of *love as a relationship union* can be successful and satisfying for the loving partners, but only if they are emotionally involved and participate in each other and relations. They shall invest their positive motivation, psychological energy, and personal time to let the relationship grow. Then, their union will survive and thrive, while partners attain personal satisfaction and a good quality of relations (Finkel, 2018).

Love as a union of people is goal-directed and action-oriented relationship. Similarities of values, goals, and mutual understanding are among the key features of this model of love. As French writer Antoine de Saint-Exupéry noted in his *Airman's Odyssey,* "Love does not consist of gazing at each other, but in looking outward together in the same direction." It is a worthy wisdom of love and life.

7.5.2 *Typologies of Relationship Dependency in Love*

Interdependence in Love and Close Relationship

Partners in close relationships are interdependent from each other in many regards, especially in emotional life. Their emotional interdependence includes frequent interactions, exchanges, influences, and responses to one another's emotions. Over time, their physiological linkage and synchrony may increase, emotions can converge and become closely aligned (e.g., Anderson et al., 2003; Freihart & Meston, 2019; Helm et al., 2012; Liu et al., 2013; Reed et al., 2013; Schoebi, 2008; Timmons et al., 2015; Wilson et al., 2018). The emotional interdependence of partners may also arise. According to a recent study (Sels et al., 2020), on average, the general level of interdependence in couples is higher compared to non-couples. However, the extent of such interdependence substantially varies across couples, types of emotions (negative vs. positive vs. emotional extremity), and situational contexts (supportive vs. conflictual).

A certain degree of dependence is normal in close relationship. Meanwhile, the *interdependence* theory suggests that the high *dependence in a relationship* may not lead to *satisfaction with the relationship*. A person in the *state of dependence* may subjectively experience *commitment to a relationship*. Nonetheless, the stronger commitment evolves due to higher satisfaction with interaction in relationship, greater degree of personal investment in relationship, and awareness that no better alternatives are available (Rusbult, Drigotas, & Verette, 1994).

Individual Types of Relationship Dependency

Following the Davidson's (1991) suggestions, I propose the three types of love, which distinguish the love relationship with different *degree of interdependence* between individuals.

The first type is the *independent (parallel) type of relationship*. Partners tend to live their separate lives, which are relatively independent and parallel to one another. They spend time with each other on rare occasions. Spending time together, they mostly focus on the fulfillment of their duties, rather than on disclosing and sharing intimacies. Ending of such relationship does not cause emotional suffering.

The second type is the *interdependent type of relationship*. Partners are relatively interdependent from each other. They feel strong emotional connections, but not constant dependencies. Each of partners has self-respect and self-love. Self-confidence strengthens their selves and enriches the relationship. They love each other without losing a sense of self. Therefore, should the relationship end, they are able to cope with such situation without devastating sense of suffering. The partners are saddened and hurt, yet they are still able to stand alone. A strong sense of self-love supports the ability to adapt to expected or unexpected changes.

The third type is the *codependent type of relationship*. Partners tend to strongly lean and rely on each other being highly dependent on the partner for their psychological survival. The desperate need for love, along with low self-confidence in own personality and the future of their love relationships, makes them to experience anxious and conflicting feelings about love. Partners experience difficulties in adjustment to any changes in a partner's emotions, attitudes, behaviors, and relationships. Such events and circumstances put them at risk of "falling over." Should changes occur, this makes them vulnerable, while a breakup can be devastating.

The Cultural Value of Interdependence and Independence

The relative values of interdependence and independence in relationships substantially distinguish traditional collectivistic cultures and modern individualistic cultures. People in individualistic countries cherish their independence, self-reliance, autonomy, individuality, personal identity, self-esteem, and their individual rights. *Narcissism* is just a *deviation of individualism*, which inflated the self-worth and devalued the worth of others.

All individuals, however,—whether they live in individualistic or collectivistic societies, whether they are narcissists or not—shall pay attention to the multiple social connections that they have in the world. They shall be aware of manifold interdependent relations, which they live in. People cannot exist without service and support from others. The others also need their support and service. Independence in the nature and society is a myth. We relate to numerous ties and links, which we frequently do not notice, or do not pay attention. So, it is irrational and irresponsible to talk about supremacy of independence. This is a myth. In daily life, we are here for the sake of each other. Our happiness depends on the bonds of sympathy, smiles, well-being, and fate of others. We owe each other a lot. We ought to give and receive.

The Cultures of Interdependency and Independency in Love Relationships

The variation of interdependence in love and close relationship can be expected between interdependent and independent cultures in terms of quality and degree of interdependence (see for review, Karandashev, 2021a, 2021b). Collectivistic societies are typically interdependent cultures, in which people are limited in their choices due to restricted social affordances and high value of embeddedness. So, individuals in a couple are interdependent from each other, yet this interdependence is due to external forces.

On the other hand, individualistic societies are usually independent cultures, in which people generally have many opportunities and choices due to freedom of social and individual rights and high value of autonomy. So, partners in a relationship are frequently interdependent in many respects. They become interdependent from each other throughout the time of their relationships. They become interdependent voluntary, on their own choice, not by external forces, and mostly psychologically and emotionally, rather than by necessity.

Cultural Attitudes Toward Dependency in Love

Individualistic and collectivistic cultures hold different views on *interpersonal dependency* (see for review, Karandashev, 2019). For example, unlike Western individualistic focus on *autonomy*, Japanese culture highly values *mutual dependency* in intimate relationships. The concept of *dependency* in Western cultures (e.g., the United States) frequently has negative (or, at least, ambivalent) connotations. It is due to the high cultural value of individuality and autonomy. Partners in love still prefer to keep independence. Different from this, the Japanese concept of *amae* admits a positive attitude toward dependency upon others. It has positive connotation, and people use it when they describe sentimental feelings in close relationships: between parent and son/daughter, romantic partners, husband, and wife. It is a pleasant feeling when a person depends on the other who provides considerate affection and indulgent gratification. Dependency in love can be pleasurable.

Love as Relational Adjustment and Accommodation

Love in its *companionate model* is the *relational interdependence*. Partners shall act considering not only their own interest and well-being, but also the interests and well-being of another.

Partners in *interdependent love relationship* may have different options to behave during interaction. They can choose a partner, change the partner, or they can adjust their attitude to him/her accommodating his/her needs. Some may consider these dichotomies as a dilemma "either…, or…"

The first strategy is more typical for *modern individualistic cultures of choice*, while the second one is more typical for *arranged marriages in traditional collectivistic cultures*. Nevertheless, both tactic approaches can work together and flexibly optimizing a relationship.

The relationship management requires to adjust their behavior and accommodate the needs of each other. People in collectivistic and individualistic cultures may differ in these dispositions. Eastern-Asian collectivistic cultural values emphasize the need to belong and connect in relationships. People from collectivistic societies tend to conform their personal identities to the preferences and expectations of their partner. The self-identities of collectivist East Asians seem to be rather situation-specific. They have lesser cross-situational stability than Westerners when they describe themselves (Kanagawa, Cross, & Markus, 2001; Suh, 2002). Their cross-situational consistency is relatively weakly related to the *sense of self*, and it is less valued compared to Westerners (Kashima et al., 2004).

Cultural Variations in the Attitudes to be Assertive or Accommodating to the Partner

Cultures differ in their normative values and tendencies to *conquer, lead, and be self-assertive* versus *adjust, conform, and stepping back*. These attitudes are related to different conceptualization of personal self-construal and identity—in individual or relational terms. They affect initial course of interaction with a dating partner and subsequent relationship management.

The worldviews and mentalities of Western and East-Asian cultures differ in the attitudes, which people have in interactions (Lim, 2016). In Western societies, culturally normative attitudes of individuals are to conquer a situation influencing others. Their high arousal emotions serve well to achieve this goal (Karandashev, 2021a, 2021b; Lim, 2016). Western individualistic cultural values encourage the stability and consistency of personal identities across time and social settings. People from individualistic societies have relatively high identity stability and consistency (e.g., Conley, 1985; Costa Jr. & McCrae, 1988; English & Chen, 2007).

In Eastern societies, normative attitudes are to accommodate a situation conforming and adjusting to other people and their preferences of low arousal emotions well suit to achieve this aim (Lim, 2016). For instance, results of a cross-cultural study (the mainland of the USA, Hawaii, and South Korea) showed that the dating partners from collectivistic and individualistic culture tend to approach accommodative dilemmas differently. While people in collectivistic societies are in *favor of accommodation strategy* expressed in loyalty and voice, the partners from individualistic cultures prefer *non-accommodation strategy* expressed in neglect and exit (Yum, 2004). It is worthwhile to note that individuals with bicultural self-construal consistently endorse accommodation. We can call these two strategies as characterizing *accommodative adaptable* and *non-accommodative assertive models of love interaction*.

Self-change in Love

The positive perception and ability of *self-change* in love are important for success and quality of a relationship. It is reasonable to expect that couples in collectivistic culture—with relational orientation, would have the higher endorsement of self-change in relationships than couples in individualistic culture—with strong self-affirmation orientation. Such cultural differences in the role of self-change in relationships have been found between Chinese and European Americans. The studies (Joo et al., 2021) have shown that the Chinese couple considers *self-change* in relationships more favorably and they are more predisposed for such self-change compared to the European Americans. They strongly endorse *dutiful adjustment beliefs* and think that their self-change will lead to the better quality of their relationships.

7.5.3 Cultural Typologies of Psychological Intimacy in Love

Intimacy as Closeness and Its Cultural Value

Western scholarship and studies consider *intimacy* as the core construct characterizing love experiences and relationships. The *construct of intimacy* is widely conceptualized as the degree of closeness between two persons. For example, factor analysis of love scales (Hendrick & Hendrick, 1989) identified *closeness* as one of the five major factors of love among American students.

Intimacy as *closeness* includes physical (bodily or sexual), cognitive, and emotional aspects. Such behavioral manifestations, as partners' sleeping privacy and proximity, organization of their eating, spending leisure time together, can signify intimacy (De Munck & Korotayev, 2007). In addition, intimacy as closeness can embrace such subjective psychological experience, as openness to self-disclosure, the sharing of intimate thoughts and emotions, feelings of interdependence, and experience of emotional warmth (Clark & Reis, 1988; Perlman & Fehr, 1987; Reis & Shaver, 1988; Rosenbluth & Steil, 1995).

The *value of closeness* varies across cultures. Intimacy in close relationships is a much cherished experience in modern Western cultures. However, the traditional Eastern cultures hold the lower normative value of intimacy between romantic and marital partners. Research revealed that East Asians experience less intimacy in marital relationships than do Westerners (DeVos, 1985; Dion & Dion, 1993; Ting-Toomey, 1991) and in Eastern societies, the intimacy in heterosexual love has been traditionally less important (e.g., Dion & Dion, 1993; Gao, 2001; Roland, 1988).

Cultural Diversity of Intimacy

In Western scholarship, the *construct of intimacy* is widely present in the models and emotional experiences of love. Attribution of its meaning can vary from its equating with the general concept of love to the very specific connotation with sexual intimacy as sexual intercourse. However, most researchers consider intimacy as psychological closeness and disclosure, as we discussed in previous sections. Studies have also shown a diversity of cultural interpretation of intimacy and its value. Western and Eastern cultures differ in their conceptualizations and expressions of intimacy. Some cultures encourage intimacy between romantic partners, between wives and husbands, while others do not (Castaneda, 1993; Hsu, 1981; Kumar, 1991; Seki, Matsumoto, & Imahori, 2002).

A cultural perspective helps explore the diversity of intimacy. Cultural patterns of intimacy are grounded in specific social contexts and reveal complex differences and diverse cultural understanding of intimacy (Adams, Anderson, & Adonu, 2004; Seki et al., 2002). Examples from the studies in the West African and the North American societies illuminate how people's experience and expression of intimacy reflect certain constructions of social reality and self.

Intimacy in love relationships may have both positive and negative sides. Intimacy produces the pleasurable feeling of comfortable attachment and trust. Yet, it can bring the feeling of vulnerability in the cases of deception and dishonesty. Behaviors of those, with who we feel close and intimate, hurt us the most.

Intimacy as Self-disclosure and Its Cultural Variation

Western scholarship frequently conceptualizes *intimacy* as *self-disclosure*, which involves the revealing of personal thoughts, feelings, and experiences to another person. Such experience is considered as important for relationship satisfaction (Altman & Taylor, 1973; Jourard, 1971; Sprecher & Hendrick, 2004).

Generally, Americans reveal a tendency to *higher degrees of self-disclosure* than the Japanese (Barnlund, 1975; Gudykunst & Nishida, 1983; Ting-Toomey, 1991). In Western cultural view, *self-disclosure* is a prototypical way to express intimacy (Jamieson, 1998, 1999). The verbal and non-verbal expressions of empathy, support, and affection to a beloved are valued in Western societies (Davis & Perkowitz, 1979; Miller, Berg, & Archer, 1983; Prager, 1995).

On the other hand, in East Asian cultural traditions, *self-disclosure* is less important (Chen, 1995; Goodwin & Lee, 1994). In other cultures, the *concept of intimacy* can engage various practices of communication, such as practically caring for a beloved one, giving to, sharing with, and spending time with. The practical responsiveness to the needs of the loved one expresses affection, empathy, and support to a partner is highly significant for relationships in East Asian cultures (Heine, 2001; Lebra, 1976; Markus & Kitayama, 1991).

Japanese and American Cultural Models of Expressing Intimacy

People in various cultures express intimacy differently. For instance, Americans are much more expressive than Japanese in both verbal and non-verbal behaviors and prefer communicating intimacy in more various ways (see for review, Seki et al., 2002). Americans tend to understand intimacy in concrete actions and behaviors, rather than in abstract and subjective experiences.

The Japanese intimacy is inexpressive. In intimate relationships, people prefer high-contextual interaction (Barnlund, 1975; Seki et al., 2002; Ting-Toomey, 1991). The Japanese conceptualize intimacy as less concrete than Americans. Their construal of intimacy embraces intangible and feelings, including "a greater number of emotions, feelings, and role understandings and appreciations rather than tangible behavioral manifestations" (Seki et al., 2002, p. 305).

The results concerning cultural differences in expressions of intimacy in Japanese and American cultures are complex and inconsistent. Even though some findings have demonstrated that Japanese are less expressive than Americans, yet in some respects, the young Japanese individuals evaluate higher than Americans their preferences for direct verbalization, and lower preferences for indirect verbalization of "how you feel about each other" (p. 317). Authors attempt to explain these presumably controversial findings by the methodological interpretation that "the ratings for expression mode preferences ... are not necessarily indicative of the frequency, intensity, or duration of each of the categories' usage..." It is possible that Americans may rate some categories lower than do Japanese, yet Americans "may actually use the categories more frequently, more forcefully, or for greater durations than Japanese..." (Seki et al., 2002, p. 317).

In my opinion, the *rating of preferences* for expression of intimacy reveals *cultural models* of Japanese and American cultures, as reflected in the personal models of individuals in corresponding cultural context. On the other hand, the actual use of direct and indirect expressions may show their *actual behavioral types* of expressions of intimacy. Thus, the *cultural* and *personal models* may not coincide with *real typology of expressiveness*.

Sharing and Communication in the Hispanic Cultural Model of Love

Sharing with the loved one and communication in practical ways are especially important expressions of intimacy for people in Hispanic cultures. Communication and sharing are the means to know and become closer to a partner. Such communication leads to relational intimacy. For example, among Mexican Americans in northern California, these characteristics are of high importance (Castaneda, 1993). Communication in love allows one to be one's true self, without fear of rejection or judgment. In love, such unconditional acceptance is possible and expected. In their mutual communication, individuals feel that they can express their true selves. Such communication assumes honesty. According to Castaneda (1993), these culturally specific expectations are typical in collectivistic cultures because people tend to account for the needs of another person. They also highly value sharing responsibilities, avoidance of conflict, respect, and cooperation.

Intimacy in Latin American Cultures

According to several studies of 1980s–2000s, men and women in Latin American, African societies, and the Caribbean culture of West Indies have low intimacy in their companionate relationships. However, a small number of cultural samples and their sporadic collection (see for the detailed review, Karandashev, 2019, 2021b) should admit the limited validity and reliability.

Africans, West Indians, and other Latin Americans were not much involved in marital intimacy. Women had moderate-to-small interest in intimate emotional relationship with men, because for them, community relationship and kinship were more important. Besides, many men with the cultural model of macho masculine role considered sexual relationship with women as important for a macho man, yet they did not view the maintaining of an emotionally intimate relationship with women as worthwhile.

Emotional intimacy in marital relationships is also affected by the "double standards" which cultural stereotypes impose on sexual behavior of men and women in the Caribbean and some other Latin American countries (e.g., Jamaica, Nicaragua). Sexual infidelity and extramarital affairs of men are frequently viewed in those societies as acceptable, and they are quite widespread. However, infidelity of women is considered as unacceptable, e.g., Berglund, Liljestrand, Marín, Salgado, & Zelaya, 1997; Eggleston, Jackson, & Hardee, 1999; Garcia, Pereira, & Bucher-Maluschke, 2018; Payne & Vandewiele, 1987; Rani, Figueroa, & Ainsle, 2003).

Effect of Individualism and Collectivism on the Cultural Value of Intimacy

In many Western individualistic societies (i.e., Australia, New Zealand, Western European countries, Canada, and the USA) emotional intimacy with romantic partner and spouse are culturally expected. Experience of intimacy in a romantic relationship predicts better physical and psychological well-being of individuals, and relational satisfaction (Dion & Dion, 1993; Hassebrauck & Fehr, 2002; Kiecolt-Glaser et al., 1988; Laurenceau, Feldman Barrett, & Pietromonaco, 1998).

On the other hand, Eastern cultures have the lower expectations of emotional intimacy in marriage, therefore, many people experience lower intimacy (Ting-Toomey, 1991). Compared to married partners in individualistic societies, such as Canada and the United States, the *psychological intimacies* of spouses in collectivistic societies, such as Japan, China, and India, are moderately associated with relationship satisfaction and personal well-being (Dion & Dion, 1993).

However, the effect of *individualism* and *collectivism,* as cultural dimensions, in these differences is much lower than the gender-role ideology in the societies. People with extreme individualism may perceive intimacy and commitment as the threat to their independence (Dion & Dion, 1991). The study of intimacy in two cultural groups in Canada (Marshall, 2008) was also in accord with such interpretation. The results have shown that compared to the Chinese Canadians, the European Canadians are *not* substantially more individualistic. In addition, *individualism* in the European Canadian sample correlated negatively with intimacy, not *positively,* as previous studies reported (e.g., Gao, 2001; Hsu, 1981; Ting-Toomey, 1991).

Thus, the studies of how cultural parameters affect intimacy in emotional experiences and relationships of people across cultures shall include several cultural and societal parameters in their complex effect on intimacies. Such analysis would be more productive and less controversial.

7.6 Friendship Models of Love

7.6.1 Lovers as Friends

The Terminology Standing for the Friendship-Based Love

The two Ancient Greek terms are associated with friendship type of love: *philia* and *storge*. The Aristotelian word *philia* means *friendly and brotherly love*, while the word *storgē* is rather *kinship, familial love*, and *familiarity love*. Their meanings, however, are more diverse (Soble, 1989). For example, Aristotle distinguished *four types of filia*: (1) the friendship between teenage boys of the same age, (2) the love of parents to children, (3) the love of elder men to boys, as well as (4) the friendship between free adult citizens (Porubjak, 2008). In modern literature, these words are sometimes used with the mixing meaning without clear connotational borders.

Therefore, I believe that labeling the types of love with the words of ancient civilizations might be problematic due to their *polysemy*. The etymologies of Greek terms related to friendship are still debated (Konstan, 1997) and, therefore, can be an unreliable basis for modern scholarly discourse. Selection of such terms shall be made with assumption of contingency and possible misunderstandings. For example, in the Lee's typology (Lee, 1973, 1976, 1977), the *friendship-based style of love* is labeled as the *storge* love. As one can see from the review above, this word does not perfectly convey the meaning of friendship, as it is understood in the modern scholarship. This is a reason that I preferred in this book the term *friendship model of love*, or *friendship-based model of love*. This concept captures better the salient feature of this type.

Friendship-Based Love

The archetypical concepts of friendship and romantic love have several essential features in common (Davis & Todd, 1982). For example, in both types of relationships, being supportive in emotional and practical ways and being able to count on each other are the essential attributes. The qualities of support, which most appropriately characterize it, are "giving the utmost" and "being a champion or advocate" of another. The major conceptual distinctions of *friendship* from *love relationships* lie in the contrast between *mild passion of friendship* and *strong passion of love*. So, due to these substantial similarities of friendship and romantic love, the *friendship-based love* appears as *a variety of* the same species—*love*.

The descriptive self-report accounts generating features and types of love also found that *friendship love*, along with *passionate love*, are two most salient representations of *romantic love*, at least in the North American samples (Fehr, 1988, 1994; Fehr & Russell, 1992; Hendrick & Hendrick, 1993).

This type of love gradually develops from a friendship relationship or can evolve over time from the initially passionate and romantic love. It is the love based on shared interests and trust. Partners in the *friendship-based love* experience their love as engaged companionship and friendship relations. They feel emotionally engaged, psychologically intimate, affectionate, comfortable, understanding, and fully trust each other in their relationship. Like friends, they enjoy their mutual interests, common activities, and shared laughter with partner. Researchers (Grote & Frieze, 1994) have developed a measurement scale to assess the theoretical construct of *friendship-based love* in terms of general and specific characteristics. They showed that the love relationships characterized by this model are related to the partners' relationship satisfaction and well-being.

Pseudo Opposition of Love and Friendship

Romantic love is frequently opposed to friendship relations. Many men and women prefer love, rather than friendship. The controversial emotions of unreciprocated love are familiar for many and experienced as a bummer. It is tough when a man has opened his loving heart to the beloved—"I love you"—and hear in response "let's be just friends." His romantic heart is broken, the feelings are down. Women are also well familiar with such frustrated situations. They want more than just friendship; they want real love.

However, everything may be not so bad. The circumstances can look less dramatic and disappointing, but rather promising. The love may come along the way if the friendship persists. The patient perseverance may be rewarded. Love can begin from friendship.

The *friendship model of love* can have different paths. One possibility is that partners begin their relationship as friends. Then, their friendship can gradually—sooner or later—evolves into love and sexual relationships. Certain circumstances and personal factors can precipitate such development and spark romantic feelings. The love excitement and sexual attraction can grow.

The studies have shown (see meta-analysis in Stinson, Cameron, & Hoplock, 2021) that the *friends-first model* of love is quite typical among students and other adults. The two-thirds of 1,897 respondents reported that they had *friends-first initiation* of their relationships. Many considered this path as a preferred way of romantic relationship initiation. Thus, this model of love appears as widely prevalent and preferred.

Another possibility is that love may grow on a companionate path from the start—without initial romantic crush and crazy emotions, without excessive idealizations and expectations. Sex and passion can be pleasurable even in moderation, without being high. The calm and friendly pleasure of being and doing together, understanding each other without romantic biases, real psychological intimacy can be valuable love experience. This friendship model of love is experienced and expressed with a substantial friendship component.

7.6.2 *Friendship Model of Love in Cultural Contexts*

American Model of Love as Friendship

Romantic model of love is highly representative in American social media and the minds of many Americans when they refer to the courtship. *Romantic relationship* is a popular word to communicate about dating relationships. It is likely, however, that this prototype conveys their *ideal model of love* (De Munck et al., 2009, 2010; Swidler, 2001). Ideally, Americans may dream about romantic love—being inspired, for instance, by romantic novels and Hollywood movies, yet they place higher value on familial and friendship love for real life.

The descriptive methodologies of free-list tasks (Fehr, 1988, 1994; Fehr & Russell, 1992) and free-form accounts (Hendrick & Hendrick, 1993) identified friendship as the most prototypical type of romantic love in American and Canadian cultural samples.

As I commented elsewhere, for many Americans, the *romantic model is compatible with friendship model of love*. They easily transition from romantic to friendship feelings in their relationships (De Munck et al., 2009, 2010; Swidler, 2001). Even their descriptions of romantic love include—in addition to the romantic and passionate features—the qualities of friendship. American informants characterize *romantic love* as "high and low energy associated with good feelings (e.g., excited, passion, comfortable, content), a mental ledger indexing mutuality (in commitment, altruism, trust), and personal virtues (e.g., honest, intelligent, humor)." (De Munck & Kronenfeld, 2016, p. 14).

Nevertheless, for Americans (Cancian, 1987; De Munck et al., 2009, 2010; Swidler, 2001), *friendship* appears to be a *core feature of love*. The general importance of such positive components of the *low energy love experience* as "secure," "commitment," "comfortable," "content," and "mutual compatible virtues" are evident in the American model of love. Americans do not feel comfortable with the high-energy emotions. The dominant metaphor of the lovers for American married couples is a "team" that conveys this *meaning of friendship*. They perceive love as *real and permanent, not temporary, or dream-like*. This *American cultural model of love* is quite different from several East European models of love, such as Lithuanian and Russian.

De Munck (2019) summarizes the *American cultural model of romantic love* as follows:

> It begins with initial attraction that leads to a desire to be together, and when they are together, the couple feel happy. They both feel passion for each other as well as do things that show care and trust for one another. Interactions are quite carefully shaped to be non-threatening, tender, and to frame sexual attraction as passion that is contained by expressions of friendship, care, and concern for the other. Sex is passionate, but it must also be mutual and expressed in a secure and caring way. The particular features of the high energy field—passion, excitement, giddy—are counterbalanced by or perhaps even embedded in the normative features in the low energy field—comfort and security as well as those features nestled along the border of these two fields—mutuality, commitment, and various personal virtues. (p. 32)

Friendship and comfort love are listed as the essential characteristics in the American conceptualization of romantic love, while nonexistent in romantic love concepts of Lithuanians and Russians (De Munck et al., 2011).

Friendship-based Love Across Cultural Groups in North America and Nearby

The cross-cultural studies of *friendship-type love* have been widely used the *Love Attitude Scale* (Hendrick & Hendrick, 1986; Hendrick, Hendrick, & Dicke, 1998), in which the self-ratings on the *storge* subscale operationalize *friendship love attitudes*. Some studies explored the ethnic groups in the United States and Canada, while others compared the storge love attitudes across countries.

Many of these cross-cultural studies were administered in 1980–1990s, so the results are a little outdated. Despite the small subcultural samples, statistically significant, yet very small differences were found. The Chinese, other Asian, and Black students in the United States and Canada were on average slightly higher in their self-ratings of the *storge love attitudes* compared to those of European origins and other Whites (Dion & Dion, 1993; Hendrick & Hendrick, 1986). The Hispanic-oriented Mexican American, the bicultural Mexican American, and the Anglo-American married couples showed high endorsement of the storge love attitudes, with no cross-cultural differences (Contreras, Hendrick, & Hendrick, 1996). The Hispanic and Latino students living in the United States and outside of the country showed high endorsement of the storge love attitudes (Leon, Parra, Cheng, & Flores, 1995; Leon, Philbrick, Parra, Escobedo, & Malcesini, 1994), with similar average scores as the samples noted above. It is worthwhile to note that the *storge* love attitudes, being similar in self-ratings with *pragma* and *agape* attitudes, valued substantially higher than the *eros, ludus,* and *mania* love attitudes. Thus, the relatively small sample size data have shown that the *storge love attitudes* (friendship-based love) are valued high, along with *pragma* and *agape*, and higher than *eros love attitude* (presumably passionate love) in all North American, Latino, and Mexican cultural samples. The only cultural group, which is higher than these, are the Asian Americans. The low self-rating of the *ludus and mania* attitudes are easily understandable because of their negative cultural connotations.

Friendship-based Love Across Countries

The studies with cultural samples in other countries have demonstrated relatively larger differences in average of scores on the *storge love attitudes*. These attitudes are higher among American students compared to the French, Russians, and Japanese (Murstein, Merighi, & Vyse, 1991; Sprecher et al., 1994).

The *storge* love attitudes are only on the fourth place (after *eros, agape, and pragma*) in Spanish-speaking and Latin-American cultures (Pérez, Fiol, Guzmán,

Palmer, & Buades, 2009; Ubillos et al., 2001). The *storge* love attitudes are higher in Turkish samples compared to the British ones (Sanri & Goodwin, 2013).

Swiss and French students showed the lower storge love attitudes compared to those in the African countries of Mozambicans, Angolans, and Cape Verdeans. The average scores of the Portuguese and Macanese (East Asian ethnic group) were in between those two groups. Indian students showed higher *storge* love attitudes compared to British and Portuguese (Neto, 2007; Neto et al., 2000).

This brief synopsis of the research reviewed elsewhere (Karandashev, 2019) summarizes the cross-cultural studies conducted mostly in the 1990–2000s, so can be a little outdated. Nevertheless, one can roughly see that the *friendship-based model of love* is of a higher value in traditional collectivistic Asian, East-Asian, and African cultures, or subcultures of these origins in other countries, as well as in the north American countries (with their cultural traditions of Puritan love). The lower rating of the *friendship model of love* are in many European countries, in which the romantic British, French, German, and Russian literary traditions have had a strong influence. The Iberian cultures of Spain and Portugal seem to have slightly different values of the friendship love. I shall note that many of these studies were occasional, sporadic, piecemeal, and administered with convenience samples of different size—all these decrease the validity and reliability of the whole picture.

7.7 Altruistic and Benevolent Models of Love

7.7.1 Altruism and Benevolence in Love

The Construct of Altruism

Altruism is *a multilayered construct*, which includes *altruistic values, traits, attitudes, moods, emotions, they expressions,* and *actions*. Altruism is the motivation, action tendency, and action undertaken for others' own sake, for their own good, promoting their welfare. Benevolence is a major motivation of altruism. *Love* in its ultimate sense is probably *benevolence*. It is a desire to *do something good* for another person—the beloved, the loved one, and anyone else who is worthy of our benevolence.

The construct of altruism means the disinterested concern and care for another's welfare. Altruistic behaviors are the intentional and voluntary actions, which are motivated by benevolent and attitudes to help and benefit another. The altruistic actions are selfless, without expectations of external rewards. They pursue only the interests of another.

We shall acknowledge, however, that altruism and benevolence are likely not purely selfless actions. People are rewarded for these behaviors psychologically through *hedonistic motivation* of *internal and intrinsic motives*. A study showed (Cialdini & Kenrick, 1976) the validity of the *hedonistic view of altruism*. Adult benevolence is *rewarding* and *self-gratifying* to some individuals—the motivation that derives from their experience of socialization.

Disciplinary Explorations and Cross-cultural Research of Altruism

Throughout history, the topic has received the extensive scholarly discussions and research by philosophers, theologians, sociologists, psychologists, and biologists. The studies have been conducted from social, religious, cultural, evolutionary, psychological, developmental, and neurological perspectives (see for review, Post, 2002; Post, Underwood, Schloss, & Hurlbut, 2002).

Some scholars of philosophy, science, and theology believe that humans are the altruistic species by nature. However, they suggest distinguishing the concepts of benevolence and altruism, as well as their diversity (Jencks, 1990; Nunney, 2000), and show that these human experiences evolve in specific societal contexts (e.g., Flescher & Worthen, 2007; Jellal & Wolff, 2002; Nunney, 2000; Sober & Wilson, 1998). The results of historical and cultural investigations are generally in accord with such assertion, despite the adversity, selfishness, and aggression which people experienced and exhibited in the former times (see for review, Karandashev, 2017, 2019).

The anthropological and linguistic studies have shown that cultures may differ substantially in their understanding and lexicon of love (see for review, Karandashev, 2017, 2019). Some societies do not have the *word love* in their vocabulary because it is too abstract. Nevertheless, the societies have other words which express specific experiences, expressions, and actions of love in particular cultural contexts.

Cross-cultural studies of love can encounter such cross-linguistic challenges of equivalency. Despite this linguistic diversity of love, all cultures and languages are able to communicate the ultimate meaning of love expressed in the basic semantic constituent "person X do good things for person Y." (Wierzbicka, 1999). Thus, it appears that the experience and expression of benevolent giving and doing something good for another one is the key cross-culturally universal attitude of love.

The Benefits of Altruism and Prosocial Behavior

The studies have shown that *altruistic attitudes, prosocial behavior, benevolence,* and *providing support* to others are advantageous for those who give support. They experience higher relationship satisfaction and have better health (e.g., Brown, Nesse, Vinokur, & Smith, 2003; Soosai-Nathan, Negri, & Delle Fave, 2013). The longitudinal study in American sample of married couples in Michigan has shown that *giving a support* is more beneficial than *receiving support*. The persons providing *emotional and practical support* to their spouses, relatives, friends, and neighbors feel better, healthier, and live longer.

Another study qualitatively explored altruism in Italy and India (Soosai-Nathan et al., 2013). showed that Italians and Indians understand *altruism* as the social and human values emphasizing the psychological and relational features of pro-social behavior. The findings of the study have documented being altruistic is beneficial for relationship satisfaction and health.

Cross-cultural Universality of Benevolent Love

The *benevolent love* has been an enduring cultural idea through centuries. The Ancient Greeks had many words for love. The word *agápē* was designated for the love motivated by benevolence and selfless goodwill extended to all people, including family members, and strangers. The comparable Latin word of Ancient Romans for this kind of benevolent love for all was *caritas*. The Ancient Chinese word *ren* meant benevolent love to one another in various social and interpersonal contexts.

The cultural idea of *benevolent love for all and everyone* is cross-cultural and present not only in Western and Eastern cultures, but also in Christian and Confucian religious traditions. The lexicon of this kind of love appears in many languages (Lomas, 2018). The attitude of *metta—loving-kindness*—is a traditional Buddhist cultural concept. Other examples depicting the loving kindness are the Yiddish concept of *gemilut hasadim*, the Sanskrit one *maitrī*, the Inuit one *pittiarniq*, the Nguni Bantu one *ubuntu*, and the Pashto one *melmastia.*

7.7.2 *Love as Caring and Giving*

Love as Caring

Many people believe that love is a wholehearted pursuit for caring about other(s).

This kind of love is the key to a person's fulfilled life. As Frankfurt asserts (2009), *love* is the most authoritative *form of caring*, while the purest form of love is self-love. Through *caring love,* people infuse their life with meanings, interests, concerns, aims, and ambitions.

Benefits of Caring

The authors (Clark & Mills, 1979) maintained that implicitly a person in his/her interaction with a partner is capable to distinguish communal relationship from exchange relationships, even if they are not always explicitly aware how such attitude affects their interactions with a partner.

The authors found the support for their hypothesis that "the receipt of a benefit after the person has been benefited leads to greater attraction when an exchange relationship is preferred and decreases attraction when a communal relationship is desired" (Clark & Mills, 1979, p. 12).

> As expected from the hypothesis that a request for a benefit after the person is aided by the other leads to greater attraction when an exchange relationship is expected, it was found that liking for the other was higher in the exchange-aid-request condition than in the exchange-aid-no-request condition. As predicted from the hypothesis that a request for a benefit after the person is aided decreases attraction when a communal relationship is expected, liking was lower in the communal-aid-request condition than in the communal-aid-no-request condition. In line with the hypothesis that a request for a benefit in the absence of aid from the other decreases attraction when an exchange relationship is expected, liking for the other was lower in the exchange-no-aid-request condition than in the exchange-no-aid-no-request condition. (Clark & Mills, 1979, p. 21)

As the authors comment these results in terms of possible consequences to intimate relationships. The assumption that exchanges of benefits may be the basis for successful intimate relationships can impair such relationships: treatment of a communal relationship in terms of exchange can compromise the relationship.

A communal relationship can be strained by dickering about what each of the partners does for the other.

> Of course, if one of the partners in a communal relationship is convinced that he or she is being exploited by the other because that person is concerned about the other's welfare while the other is not concerned about his or her welfare, the communal relationship has disintegrated. If this happens in a marriage, there may be attempts to preserve the marriage by changing it into an exchange relationship through dickering. (Clark & Mills, 1979, p. 23)

Love as Giving

The giving love, and giving everything that love entails, is perhaps among the core features of altruistic love. Such a giving does not assume the exchange of the giving, or expectation of something in return. This is the true essence of (altruistic) love.

The concept of love in this *giving* sense, for example, is presented in the theory of *communal love* (Clark & Mills, 1979). The authors differentiate this kind of love attitude (based on altruistic motives) from exchange love attitude (exchange relationship based on interpersonal economics). A person with such a *giving love attitude* considers a relationship as *communal*—"the giving of a benefit in response to a need for the benefit is viewed appropriate." Opposite to this, a person with *exchange love attitude* considers a relationship as *exchange*—"the giving of a benefit in response to the receipt of a benefit is appropriate" (p. 12).

Communal Relationship in Love

Clark and Mills (2013) believe that while relationships between strangers, acquaintances, and businesspersons are characterized as *exchange relationship*, the romantic and family relationships usually assume *communal relationship*. In such a communal relationship, the benefits given and received are frequently not viewed as an exchange. The receipt of a benefit is not supposed to create a feeling of specific debt or obligation to return a comparable benefit. The general obligation that partners have to each other is to aid the partner when she or he needs it, not contingent on the receipt of a specific benefit.

Giving Everything and Anything

Individuals in a *true* (*benevolent*) *love* are willing to give many things, even their life to the beloved—if necessary. Plenty of real stories, novels, and fables have been told about this ability of true lovers throughout human cultural history.

Are they ready to *take the loved one's life* as an act of love to him/her? Is really it an act of love? This can be an acute personal dilemma of love, besides the continuous ethical, theological, medical, and legal debates on the battleground of the *right-to-life*. One example is the case of Nancy Cruzan, 32, who had been in a coma for seven years (Gibbs & Painton, 1990). Her parents requested the court permission to remove her feeding tube and "let her go." Was that the parental love for Nancy? In cases like this, the decisions can be guided by the feeling and the acts of parental love.

Sometimes, in some situations, facilitating death can also be the *acts of love* in relations between the beloved partners. The unhappy and intolerable living circumstances can occur at any stage of love relationships. Such a drama occasionally happens in the life of elderly couples (e.g., Drake & Drake, 2014; Haneke, Trintignant, Huppert, & Riva, 2012).

7.7.3 Love as Agape

The Concept of Agape

The term *agape* expresses a very general meaning—*love for everyone*. This is a love what an individual gives as benevolence, compassion, kindness, and caring to all and everyone. These are any people—strangers, acquaintances, kin, and family. This is a universal and unconditional *loving kindness*.

The word *agape* stems from the Ancient Greek philosophy. The Latin word *caritas* is comparable to the Greek *agape*. Since then, the words have been used in various social contexts with slightly different connotations. The core meaning of *agape* is the *other-centered love*, *selfless love,* and *selfless giving* of anything that may convey the love feelings, emotions, attitudes, and values.

The extent of the *agape love* can be gauged by the measure of how many and how important things are, which an individual is ready to sacrifice for the sake of another as an act of love. The *ultimate form of agape love* is the feeling that an individual is willing to die—sacrifice even life as the most precious thing for a person.

The highlight of the *agape love* is that nothing is expected in return—the reciprocity is not projected. I believe the last point is the very challenging to hear for many lovers. This is true. Most people, when they are doing something good for their beloved, implicitly hope to be rewarded. It is understandable. This is a reason why the *true agape love is rare*.

It shall be noted that the *agape cultural model of love* may also include *experience of love as a duty*. This aspect of *agape love* is reviewed in the next section of this book. A mixture of *duty* and *benevolence in agape love* makes the *dutiful benevolence model of love*.

Altruistic Love in Christian Culture

Throughout centuries, Christian faith and theology has substantially influenced many cultures of Europe and America, as well as the other world regions. *Christian cultures* elevated the ideals of *altruistic values* and *agape love* (Post, 1990, 2002). The *agape* love is a God's unconditional compassionate and caring love for humankind valorized as a pre-eminent theological virtue. This is the *love of God for humans*, as well as the *human's reciprocal love for God*. These kinds of love also serve as the role models for the love of humans to each other—through God.

Altruistic love is in the core of the Jesus Christ's teachings. The Gospel of Luke highlights the Jesus' love that goes beyond all boundaries (Meisinger, 2000). A perfect example of *altruistic love* is presented in the parable of the Good Samaritan (Luke 10:25-37). The story teaches us that human benevolence and kindness must be given to all people. The summary of the Jesus commandment:

> Love [agapao] the Lord your God with all your heart and with all your soul and with all your mind. This is the first and greatest commandment. And the second is like it: "Love [agapao] your neighbor as yourself." All the Law and the Prophets hang on these two commandments. (Matthew 22:36-39, NRSV)

In Christian teachings, love is the responsibility of caring for others. Practically, this means the importance of loving people around oneself—the members of the immediate family, as well as foreigners. The range of altruism in Christianity implies *loving everyone*. Unconditional love is the highest form of love. The golden rule of love means "In everything do to others as you would have them do to you; for this is the law and the prophets" (Matt 7:12 NRSV).

Altruism of agape love in Christian culture means universal love. The *agape* is the highest form of Christian love—the "gift love" (Lewis, 1960; Post, 2003; Templeton, 1999).

Altruistic Love in the Confucian Culture

The three Chinese religious philosophies—Confucianism, Buddhism, and Taoism—have tremendously influenced the Chinese culture and its conceptualization of altruistic love. The Confucian religious and philosophical teachings have been the pillars of the ethics and social and moral philosophy of Chinese values.

Altruism is the central topic in *Confucian ethical teaching.* The *benevolent love* was in the center of Confucian ethical teaching. One of his famously quoted teachings says: "Do not do to others what you would not like yourself." One can see how similar this Chinese love concept to the Christian teaching of agape love, cited above. However, this concept stands for the *love structurally graded,* not universal love as in Christian teachings. In Christianity, altruism is more equal in nature—the *love for all others,* and not hierarchically structures.

The basic concept and virtue in the Confucian moral ethics is "*ren*" that is frequently translated as *kindness, altruism, compassion, benevolence, and benevolent love,* the virtue highly ranked also in Buddhist and Taoist cultures (Chan, 1955; Dubs, 1951). Confucius explained the word *ren* with the common Chinese word *ai*—love. The Chinese character for ren consists of two parts: *human* and *two.* Then, the Confucius definition of *ren* meant that it is an essential human quality of life, in which two humans express *benevolent love to one another.*

However, the Confucian conception of *ren* was different from Christian ideal of agape love and reflected the hierarchical social structure of Chinese society. The hierarchy of group relationships distinguished the five areas ("wu-lun"). These five cardinals of *wu-lun* in the Chinese culture in descending order are (1) Emperor-Ministers (state level), (2) Father-son (family level), (3) Husband-wife (family level), (4) Older-younger brothers (family level), (5) Friends (individual level). These *wu-lun* establish the relationship web in Chinese culture.

Confucius considered *ren* mostly as a *love attitude of a bountiful lord,* in which the *superior manifests a benevolence and kindness to his inferiors.* The Confucian ethics did not expect that inferiors show benevolent love to the superior since this would be presumption. The appropriate love attitudes expected from the inferior to the superior are loyalty and obedience (Chan, 1955; Dubs, 1951).

Confucius commented that people show more natural love to parents, relatives, and other close people. *Altruistic love* within people in this close web of relationship is expected to be stronger than with those outside this relationship network.

Confucius and his descendants considered equal love for all unnatural (Chan, 1955; Dubs, 1951). For centuries, the roots of this *graded love* have been prevailing in several Asian societies (Ma, 2009). Consequently, this hierarchical model of love is still widely adopted the Chinese society and in other Confucius-dominated cultures.

Cultural Religious Models of Altruistic Love

The idea of *agape* also appears in many other religious traditions. Worldwide, *altruistic and unconditional agape* loves are the main human virtues of such religions as Judaism, Christianity, Islam, Hinduism, Buddhism, Taoism, Confucianism, and Native American Spirituality (see for review, Templeton, 1999). For instance, Theravāda Buddhism extols the idea of *mettā*—"universal loving kindness." The *altruistic love* encourages the spiritual person to "love without thought of return." This love flows out to other people as the kindness, tenderness, compassion, and charitable giving. For Buddhists, following a pathway of compassion and caring for others is the major motivating force of their lives (Templeton, 1999).

The Agape Love in Non-religious Contexts

The term *agape* has been also extended in its use for non-religious contexts—see elsewhere in this book.

In recent times, the decline of agape love has been noticeable in many countries (Zaki, 2011). In the United States, as will see more in the following sections, throughout 1979–2009s, the emotions and attitudes of empathy among young Americans have substantially declined, and the most drastically this decline occurred in 2000s (Konrath, O'Brien, & Hsing, 2011). It looks like the capacity to concern about others has decreased. The results showed that about 75% of university students rated themselves as *less empathic* compared to the average scores of students 30 years ago. The decrease in the experience of empathy coincided with the increase in social isolation among young people.

According to some other studies (e.g., Lin & Huddleston-Casas, 2005), people who have more education show *lower agape love* attitudes, compared to less educated people. And women show *lower agape attitudes* than do men.

The Western Agape Attitudes in Relationships

The Christian ideals of Western cultures emphasized the high value of *agape* love rather than *eros* love. While the experience of *eros love* predisposes a person to be acquisitive, possessive, and egocentric, the experience of *agape love* predisposes a person to give freely and act benevolently, be unselfish and ready to sacrifice (Nygren, 1989). Such cultural values have been encouraging for many romantic lovers throughout the centuries.

These cultural ideas may also look inspiring for some modern lovers, even beyond religious traditions. Individuals with the prevalent *agape love* in a heterosexual relationship perceive the beloved idealistically, as a unique person. Their *passion* is the *passion* to make the beloved happy. Their love is capable to overcome selfishness in a relationship focusing on the happiness of a beloved.

They place the concerns of the beloved as the highest priority and can sacrifice many things in their life for the sake of their loved one. They are willing to experience inconvenience, discomfort, suffering, pain and—if it is needed—even die for the life of a beloved and relationship. Such *agape model of love* is very *romantic* and can be not less romantic than passionate love (e.g., Ben-Ze'ev & Goussinsky, 2008).

Their altruistic attitude puts the beloved first, goes beyond a lover's ego. They do not expect anything in return. Reciprocation is not important—they are willing to give the beloved rather than receive from him/her. *Giving* for them is a *joy of love*. They spontaneously give their self and everything they can without thinking of the cost. As E. Fromm (1956) beautifully noted,

> "Giving is the highest expression of potency. In the very act of giving, I experience my strength, my wealth, my power. This experience of heightened vitality and potency fills me with joy. I experience myself as overflowing, spending, alive, hence as joyous. Giving is more joyous than receiving, not because it is a deprivation, but because in the act of giving lies the expression of my aliveness." (Fromm, 1956/2006, p. 21)

The Chinese Agape Attitudes in Relationships

Selfless giving is among the key feelings and behaviors of the *agape model of love* that follows the classical Christian idea of love as altruistic and undemanding (Chen & Li, 2007).

In the Confucian cultural ideology, commitment of an individual in marital affection also implies *sacrifices*. Chinese people commonly are capable and disposed to subordinate their personal interests, goals, and welfare for the sake of harmony, solidarity, and prosperity in their families.

Wang (1999) considered *self-sacrifice,* along with *devotion,* as a main component of family commitment and provided evidence supporting the value of sacrifice in Taiwanese marriage. Thus, even in contemporary society, sacrifice in marriage is expected. Spouses are generally willing to give up something in the interest of enhancing their relationship or their partner's well-being.

A culture can influence the willingness to sacrifice that a spouse feels in a marriage, depending on its individualistic and collectivistic values. In Chinese society with collectivist tendencies, societal beliefs can interfere with individual rights of a spouse, e.g., a woman's right for equality. That is what people in another culture—with the emphases on individualism—often view as not acceptable: their societal beliefs about individual rights may interfere with a possible need to self-sacrifice that a marriage may require. Thus, the struggle to achieve a balance between personal and family needs may present a dilemma.

References

Abbott, E. (2010). *A history of marriage*. Seven Stories Press.

Acevedo, B. P., & Aron, A. (2009). Does a long-term relationship kill romantic love? *Review of General Psychology, 13*(1), 59–65.

Acevedo, B. P., Aron, A., Fisher, H. E., & Brown, L. L. (2012). Neural correlates of long-term intense romantic love. *Social Cognitive and Affective Neuroscience, 7*(2), 145–159. https://doi.org/10.1093/scan/nsq092

Adams, G., Anderson, S. L., & Adonu, J. K. (2004). The cultural grounding of closeness and intimacy. In D. J. Mashek & A. P. Aron (Eds.), *Handbook of closeness and intimacy* (pp. 321–339). Lawrence Erlbaum Associates Publishers.

Agnew, C. R., & Lee, B. (1997, May). *Individualism in romantic relationships: Associations with commitment, satisfaction, and self-other inclusion.* Paper presented at the annual meeting of the American Psychological Society, Washington, DC.

Ainsworth, M. D. S. (1989). Attachments beyond infancy. *American Psychologist, 44*, 709–716.

Ainsworth, M. D. S., Blehar, M. C., Waters, E., & Wall, S. (1978). *Patterns of attachment: A psychological study of the strange situation*. Erlbaum.

Allegri, R. (2011). *Conversations with Mother Teresa: A personal portrait of the saint, her mission, and her great love for God*. The Word Among Us Press.

Altman, I., & Taylor, D. A. (1973). *Social penetration: The development of interpersonal relationships*. Holt, Rinehart & Winston.

Andersen, S. M., & Chen, S. (2002). The relational self: An interpersonal social-cognitive theory. *Psychological Review, 109*, 619–645.

Anderson, C., Keltner, D., & John, O. P. (2003). Emotional convergence between people over time. *Journal of Personality and Social Psychology, 84*(5), 1054–1068. https://doi.org/10.1037/0022-3514.84.5.1054

Aron, A., & Aron, E. N. (1986). *Love and the expansion of self: Understanding attraction and satisfaction*. Hemisphere Publishing Corp/Harper & Row Publishers.

Aron, E. N., & Aron, A. (1996). Love and the expansion of the self: The state of the model. *Personal Relationships, 3*(1), 45–58. https://doi.org/10.1111/j.1475-6811.1996.tb00103.x

Aron, A., & Aron, E. N. (2016). An inspiration for expanding the self-expansion model of love. *Emotion Review, 8*(2), 112–113.

Aron, A., Aron, E. N., Tudor, M., & Nelson, G. (1991). Close relationships as including other in the self. *Journal of Personality and Social Psychology, 60*, 241–253.

Aron, A., Paris, M., & Aron, E. N. (1995). Falling in love: Prospective studies of self – Concept change. *Journal of Personality and Social Psychology, 69*, 1102–1112.

Badahdah, A. M., & Tiemann, K. A. (2005). Mate selection criteria among Muslims living in America. *Evolution and Human Behavior, 26*, 432–440.

Baldwin, M. (1992). Relational schemas and the processing of social information. *Psychological Bulletin, 112*(3), 461–484. https://doi.org/10.1037/0033-2909.112.3.461

Barnlund, D. C. (1975). *Public and private self in Japan and the United States: Communicative styles of two cultures*. Simul.

Bartholomew, K. (1990). Avoidance of intimacy: An attachment perspective. *Journal of Social and Personal Relationships, 7*, 147–178.

Baumeister, R. F., & Leary, M. R. (1995). The need to belong: Desire for interpersonal attachments as a fundamental human motivation. *Psychological Bulletin, 117*, 497–529. https://doi.org/10.1037/0033-2909.117.3.497

Bejanyan, K., Marshall, T. C., & Ferenczi, N. (2015). Associations of collectivism with relationship commitment, passion, and mate preferences: Opposing roles of parental influence and family allocentrism. *PLoS ONE, 10*(2), e0117374.

Belsky, J. (1997). Attachment, mating, and parenting: An evolutionary interpretation. *Human Nature, 8*, 361–381.

Belsky, J., Campbell, S. B., Cohn, J. F., & Moore, G. (1996). Instability of infant–parent attachment security. *Developmental Psychology, 32*(5), 921–924.

Belsky, J., & Fearon, R. M. P. (2008). Precursors of attachment security. In J. Cassidy & P. R. Shaver (Eds.), *Handbook of attachment: Theory, research, and clinical applications* (pp. 295–316). The Guilford Press.

Ben-Ze'ev, A., & Goussinsky, R. (2008). *In the name of love: Romantic ideology and its victims*. Oxford University Press.

Berglund, S., Liljestrand, J., Marín, F. D. M., Salgado, N., & Zelaya, E. (1997). The background of adolescent pregnancies in Nicaragua: A qualitative approach. *Social Science & Medicine, 44*(1), 1–12.
Berscheid, E. (1985). Interpersonal attraction. In G. Lindzey & E. Aronson (Eds.), *The handbook of social psychology* (3rd ed., pp. 413–484). Random House.
Berscheid, E. (2010). Love in the fourth dimension. *Annual Review of Psychology, 61*(1), 1–25. https://doi.org/10.1146/annurev.psych.093008.100318
Berscheid, E., & Walster, E. (1974). A little bit about love. In T. L. Huston (Ed.), *Foundations of interpersonal attraction* (pp. 355–381). Academic.
Berscheid, E., & Walster, E. (1978). *Interpersonal attraction* (2nd ed.). Addison-Wesley (Originally work published 1969).
Bowlby, J. (1969). *Attachment and loss: Vol. 1. Attachment*. Basic Books.
Bowlby, J. (1973). *Attachment and loss: Vol. 2. Separation: Anxiety and anger*. Basic Books.
Bowlby, J. (1980). *Attachment and loss: Vol. 3. Loss*. Basic Books.
Brennan, K. A., Clark, C. L., & Shaver, P. R. (1998). Self-report measurement of adult attachment: An integrative overview. In J. A. Simpson & W. S. Rholes (Eds.), *Attachment theory and close relationships* (pp. 46–76). Guilford.
Brown, S. L., Nesse, R. M., Vinokur, A. D., & Smith, D. M. (2003). Providing social support may be more beneficial than receiving it: Results from a prospective study of mortality. *Psychological Science, 14*(4), 320–327.
Burgess, E. W., & Locke, H. J. (1945). *The family: From institution to companionship*. American Book.
Cancian, F. (1987). *Love in America: Gender and self-development*. Cambridge University Press.
Canda, E. R. (2013). Filial piety and care for elders: A contested Confucian virtue reexamined. *Journal of Ethnic and Cultural Diversity in Social Work, 22*(3–4), 213–234.
Cassidy, J., & Shaver, P. R. (Eds.). (1999). *Handbook of attachment: Theory, research, and clinical applications*. Rough Guides.
Castaneda, D. M. (1993). The meaning of romantic love among Mexican-Americans. *Journal of Social Behavior and Personality, 8*(2), 257.
Chan, W. T. (1955). The evolution of the Confucian concept jên. *Philosophy East and West, 4*, 295–319.
Chang, D., & Li, Y. (2006). *Visual representations of Kövecses's conceptual metaphor "Love is Fire" in the Chinese comic old master Q'*. Bayreuth, Germany. Retrieved from http://citeseerx.ist.psu.edu/viewdoc/download?doi=10.1.1.507.7887&rep=rep1&type=pdf
Chapais, B. (2008). *Primeval kinship*. Harvard University Press.
Chen, G. (1995). Differences in self-disclosure patterns among Americans versus Chinese: A comparative study. *Journal of Cross-Cultural Psychology, 26*, 84–91.
Chen, F. M., & Li, T. S. (2007). Marital *enqing*: An examination of its relationship to spousal contributions, sacrifices, and family stress in Chinese marriages. *The Journal of Social Psychology, 147*(4), 393–412.
Cherlin, A. J. (2004). The deinstitutionalization of American marriage. *Journal of Marriage and Family, 66*(4), 848–861.
Cherlin, A. J. (2020). Degrees of change: An assessment of the deinstitutionalization of marriage thesis. *Journal of Marriage and Family, 82*(1), 62–80.
Chisholm, J. S. (1996). The evolutionary ecology of attachment organization. *Human Nature, 7*, 1–38.
Chisholm, J. S. (1999). Steps to an evolutionary ecology of the mind. In A. L. Hinton (Ed.), *Biocultural approaches to the emotions* (pp. 117–149). Cambridge University Press.
Cialdini, R. B., & Kenrick, D. T. (1976). Altruism as hedonism: A social development perspective on the relationship of negative mood state and helping. *Journal of Personality and Social Psychology, 34*(5), 907–914. https://doi.org/10.1037/0022-3514.34.5.907
Clark, M. S., & Mills, J. S. (1979). Interpersonal attraction in exchange and communal relationships. *Journal of Personality and Social Psychology, 37*, 12–24.

Clark, M. S., & Mills, J. S. (2013). Communal and exchange relationships: Controversies and research. In R. Erber & R. Gilmour (Eds.), *Theoretical frameworks for personal relationships* (pp. 41–54). Psychology Press.

Clark, M. S., & Reis, H. T. (1988). Interpersonal processes in close relationships. *Annual Review of Psychology, 39*, 609–672.

Conley, J. J. (1985). Longitudinal stability of personality traits: A multi-trait–multimethod–multi-occasion analysis. *Journal of Personality and Social Psychology, 49*, 1266–1282.

Contreras, R., Hendrick, S. S., & Hendrick, C. (1996). Perspectives on marital love and satisfaction in Mexican American and Anglo-American couples. *Journal of Counseling & Development, 74*(4), 408–415.

Costa, P. T., Jr., & McCrae, R. R. (1988). Personality in adulthood: A six – Year longitudinal study of self – Reports and spouse ratings on the NEO Personality Inventory. *Journal of Personality and Social Psychology, 54*, 853–863.

Coward, D. D. (1996). Correlates of self-transcendence in a healthy population. *Nursing Research, 45*(2), 116–121.

D'Andrade, R. G., & Strauss, C. (Eds.). (1992). *Human motives and cultural models*. Cambridge University Press.

Davidson, D. (1991). Three varieties of knowledge. *Royal Institute of Philosophy Supplement, 30*, 153–166.

Davis, D., & Perkowitz, W. T. (1979). Consequences of responsiveness in dyadic interactions: Effects of probability of response and proportion of content related responses. *Journal of Personality and Social Psychology, 37*, 534–550.

Davis, K. E., & Todd, M. J. (1982). Friendship and love relationships. In K. E. Davis & T. D. Mitchell (Eds.), *Advances in descriptive psychology* (Vol. 2, pp. 79–122). JAI Press.

De Munck, V. (2019). *Romantic love in America: Cultural models of gay, straight and polyamorous relationship*. Lexington Press.

De Munck, V. C., & Korotayev, A. V. (2007). Wife–husband intimacy and female status in cross-cultural perspective. *Cross-Cultural Research, 41*(4), 307–335.

De Munck, V. C., & Kronenfeld, D. B. (2016). Romantic love in the United States: Applying cultural models theory and methods. *Sage Open, 6*(1). https://doi.org/10.1177/2158244015622797

De Munck, V., Korotayev, A., & Khaltourina, D. (2009). A comparative study of the structure of love in the US and Russia: Finding a common core of characteristics and national and gender differences. *Ethnology: An International Journal of Cultural and Social Anthropology, 48*(4), 337–357.

De Munck, V. C., Korotayev, A., de Munck, J., & Khaltourina, D. (2011). Cross-cultural analysis of models of romantic love among US residents, Russians, and Lithuanians. *Cross-Cultural Research, 45*(2), 128–154.

De Munck, V., Korotayev, A., & McGreevey, J. (2016). Romantic love and family organization: A case for romantic love as a biosocial universal. *Evolutionary Psychology, 14*(4), 1–13. https://doi.org/10.1177/1474704916674211

DeVos, G. (1985). Dimensions of the self in Japanese culture. In A. J. Marsella, G. DeVos, & F. L. K. Hsu (Eds.), *Culture and self: Asian and Western perspectives* (pp. 141–184). Tavistock.

Dion, K. K., & Dion, K. L. (1991). Psychological individualism and romantic love. *Journal of Social Behavior and Personality, 6*(1), 17–33.

Dion, K. K., & Dion, K. L. (1993). Individualistic and collectivistic perspectives on gender and the cultural context of love and intimacy. *Journal of Social Issues, 49*(3), 53–69. https://doi.org/10.1111/j.1540-4560.1993.tb01168.x

Dixon, N. (1995). The friendship model of filial obligations. *Journal of Applied Philosophy, 12*(1), 77–87.

Dixon, S. V., Graber, J. A., & Brooks-Gunn, J. (2008). The roles of respect for parental authority and parenting practices in parent-child conflict among African American, Latino, and European American families. *Journal of Family Psychology, 22*(1), 1–10. https://doi.org/10.1037/0893-3200.22.1.1

Doherty, R. W., Hatfield, E., Thompson, K., & Choo, P. (1994). Cultural and ethnic influences on love and attachment. *Personal Relationships, 1*, 391–398.
Drake, V. C., & Drake, W. (2014). Written and directed by Michael Haneke. *Psychological Perspectives, 57*(1), 118–121.
Driver, J. (2014). Love and duty. *Philosophic Exchange, 44*(1), 1.
Dubs, H. H. (1951). The development of altruism in Confucianism. *Philosophy East and West, 1*(1), 48–55.
Eggleston, E., Jackson, J., & Hardee, K. (1999). Sexual attitudes and behavior among young adolescents in Jamaica. *International Family Planning Perspectives, 25*(2), 78–91.
El-Hazmi, M. A., Al-Swailem, A. R., Warsy, A. S., Al-Swailem, A. M., Sulaimani, R., & Al-Meshari, A. A. (1995). Consanguinity among the Saudi Arabian population. *Journal of Medical Genetics, 32*(8), 623–626.
English, T., & Chen, S. (2007). Culture and self-concept stability: Consistency across and within contexts among Asian Americans and European Americans. *Journal of Personality and Social Psychology, 93*, 478–490.
Farrer, J., Tsuchiya, H., & Bagrowicz, B. (2008). Emotional expression in tsukiau dating relationships in Japan. *Journal of Social and Personal Relationships, 25*(1), 169–188.
Feeney, J. A., & Noller, P. (1990). Attachment style as a predictor of adult romantic relationships. *Journal of Personality and Social Psychology, 58*(2), 281.
Fehr, B. (1988). Prototype analysis of the concepts of love and commitment. *Journal of Personality and Social Psychology, 55*, 557–579.
Fehr, B. (1994). Prototype-based assessment of Laypeople's views of love. *Personal Relationships, 1*(4), 309–331.
Fehr, B., & Russell, J. A. (1991). The concept of love viewed from a prototype perspective. *Journal of Personality and Social Psychology, 60*(3), 425–438. https://doi.org/10.1037/0022-3514.60.3.425
Finkel, E. J. (2018). *The all-or-nothing marriage: How the best marriages work*. Dutton.
Fisher, H. E. (2000). Lust, attraction, attachment: Biology and evolution of three primary emotions systems for mating, reproduction, and parenting. *Journal of Sex Education and Therapy, 25*, 96–104.
Fisher, H. E. (2004). *Why we love: The nature and the chemistry of romantic love*. Henry Holt.
Flescher, A. M., & Worthen, D. L. (2007). *The altruistic species: Scientific, philosophical, and religious perspectives of human benevolence*. Templeton Foundation Press.
Fraley, R. C. (2002). Attachment stability from infancy to adulthood: Meta-analysis and dynamic modeling of developmental mechanisms. *Personality and Social Psychology Review, 6*, 123–151.
Fraley, R. C., & Shaver, P. R. (2000). Adult romantic attachment: Theoretical developments, emerging controversies, and unanswered questions. *Review of General Psychology, 4*(2), 132–154.
Frankfurt, H. G. (1998). Duty and love. *Philosophical Explorations, 1*(1), 4–9.
Freihart, B. K., & Meston, C. M. (2019). Preliminary evidence for a relationship between physiological synchrony and sexual satisfaction in opposite-sex couples. *The Journal of Sexual Medicine, 16*(12), 2000–2010.
Fromm, E. (1956). Love and its disintegration. *Pastoral Psychology, 7(68)*, 37–44.
Fromm, E. (1976). *To have or to be*. Continuum.
Gao, G. (2001). Intimacy, passion, and commitment in Chinese and US American romantic relationships. *International Journal of Intercultural Relations, 25*(3), 329–342.
Garcia, A., Pereira, F. N., & Bucher-Maluschke, J. S. (2018). Close relationships and happiness in South America. In M. Demir & N. Sümer (Eds.), *Close relationships and happiness across cultures* (pp. 69–85). Springer.
Gibbs, N., & Painton, P. (1990). Love and let die. *Time, 135*(12), 62–70.
Goodwin, R., & Lee, I. (1994). Taboo topics among Chinese and English friends. *Journal of Cross-Cultural Psychology, 25*, 325–328.
Greene, M. (2004). *Mother Teresa: A biography*. Greenwood Press.
Grote, N. K., & Frieze, I. H. (1994). The measurement of Friendship-based Love in intimate relationships. *Personal Relationships, 1*(3), 275–300.

Gudykunst, W. B., & Nishida, T. (1983). Social penetration in Japanese and American close friendships. In R. Bostrom (Ed.), *Communication Yearbook 7* (pp. 592–610). Sage.

Hamamy, H. (2012). Consanguineous marriages. *Journal of Community Genetics, 3*(3), 185–192.

Haneke, M., Trintignant, J. L., Huppert, I., & Riva, R. (2012). *Amour*. Actes Sud.

Harlow, H., & Zimmerman, R. R. (1959). Affectionate responses in the infant monkey. *Science, 130*, 421–432.

Hassebrauck, M., & Fehr, B. (2002). Dimensions of relationship quality. *Personal Relationships, 9*(3), 253–270.

Hatfield, E. (1988). Passionate and companionate love. In R. J. Sternberg & M. L. Barnes (Eds.), *The psychology of love* (pp. 191–217). Yale University Press.

Hatfield, E., & Rapson, R. L. (1993). *Love, sex, and intimacy: Their psychology, biology, and history*. HarperCollins.

Hazan, C., & Shaver, P. (1987). Romantic love conceptualized as an attachment process. *Journal of Personality and Social Psychology, 52*(3), 511–524. https://doi.org/10.1037/0022-3514.52.3.511

Heine, S. J. (2001). Self as cultural product: An examination of East Asian and North American selves. *Journal of Personality, 69*, 881–906.

Helm, J. L., Sbarra, D., & Ferrer, E. (2012). Assessing cross-partner associations in physiological responses via coupled oscillator models. *Emotion, 12*(4), 748–762. https://doi.org/10.1037/a0025036

Hendrick, C., & Hendrick, S. S. (1986). A theory and method of love. *Journal of Personality and Social Psychology, 50*, 392–402.

Hendrick, C., & Hendrick, S. S. (1989). Research on love: Does it measure up? *Journal of Personality and Social Psychology, 56*(5), 784–794. https://doi.org/10.1037/0022-3514.56.5.784

Hendrick, S. S., & Hendrick, C. (1993). Lovers as friends. *Journal of Social and Personal Relationships, 10*(3), 459–466.

Hendrick, C., Hendrick, S. S., & Dicke, A. (1998). The love attitudes scale: Short form. *Journal of Social and Personal Relationships, 15*(2), 147–159.

Ho, D. Y. F. (1991). Relational orientation and methodological relationalism. *Bulletin of the Hong Kong Psychological Society, 26/27*, 81–95.

Hinkley, K., & Andersen, S. M. (1996). The working self-concept in transference: Significant – Other activation and self – Change. *Journal of Personality and Social Psychology, 71*, 1279–1295.

Hirsch, J. S. (2007). "Love makes a family": Globalization, companionate marriage, and the modernization of gender inequality. In M. Padilla, J. S. Hirsch, M. Munoz-Laboy, R. E. Sember, & R. G. Parker (Eds.), *Love and globalization: Transformations of intimacy in the contemporary world* (pp. 93–106). Vanderbilt University Press.

Hirsch, J. S., & Wardlow, H. (Eds.). (2006). *Modern loves: The anthropology of romantic love and companionate marriage*. University of Michigan Press.

Hsu, F. L. K. (1981). *Americans and Chinese: Passage to differences* (3rd ed.). The University Press of Hawaii.

Hwang, K. K. (2000). Chinese relationalism: Theoretical construction and methodological considerations. *Journal for the Theory of Social Behavior, 30*, 155–178.

Jamieson, L. (1998). *Intimacy: Personal relationships in modern societies*. Polity Press.

Jamieson, L. (1999). Intimacy transformed? A critical Look at the 'pure relationship'. *Sociology, 33*, 477–494.

Jellal, M., & Wolff, F. C. (2002). Cultural evolutionary altruism: Theory and evidence. *European Journal of Political Economy, 18*(2), 241–262.

Jencks, C. (1990). Varieties of altruism. In J. Mansbridge (Ed.), *Beyond self-interest* (pp. 53–67). The University of Chicago Press.

Johnson, M. P., Caughlin, J. P., & Huston, T. L. (1999). The tripartite nature of marital commitment: Personal, moral, and structural reasons to stay married. *Journal of Marriage and the Family, 61*, 160–177.

Joo, M., Lam, B. C., Cross, S. E., Chen, S. X., Lau, V. C., Ng, H. K., & Günsoy, C. (2021). Cross-cultural perspectives on self-change in close relationships: Evidence from Hong Kong

Chinese and European Americans. *Personality and Social Psychology Bulletin*. https://doi.org/10.1177/01461672211026129

Jourard, S. M. (1971). *Self-disclosure: An experimental analysis of the transparent self*. Wiley.

Kanagawa, C., Cross, S., & Markus, H. (2001). "Who am I?" The cultural psychology of the conceptual self. *Personality and Social Psychology Bulletin, 27*, 90–103.

Karamustafa, A. T. (2007). *Sufism*. Edinburgh University Press.

Karandashev, V. (2017). *Romantic love in cultural contexts*. Springer.

Karandashev, V. (2019). *Cross-cultural perspectives on the experience and expression of love*. Springer.

Karandashev, V. (2021a). *Cultural models of emotions*. Springer.

Karandashev, V. (2021b). Cultural diversity of romantic love experience. In C. Mayer & E. Vanderheiden (Eds.), *International handbook of love* (pp. 59–79). Springer.

Karandashev, V. (in press). Cross-cultural variation in relationship initiation. In J. K. Mogilski & T. K. Shackelford (Eds.), *The Oxford handbook of evolutionary psychology and romantic relationships*. Oxford Publishing.

Karandashev, V., & Clapp, S. (2016). Psychometric properties and structures of passionate and companionate love. *Interpersonal: An International Journal on Personal Relationships, 10*(1), 56–76. https://doi.org/10.5964/ijpr.v10i1.210

Kashima, Y., Kashima, E., Farsides, T., Kim, U., Strack, F., Wert, L., & Yuki, M. (2004). Culture and context-specific self: The amount and meaning of context-sensitivity of phenomenal self differ across cultures. *Self and Identity, 3*, 125–141.

Keller, H. (2013). Attachment and culture. *Journal of Cross-Cultural Psychology, 44*(2), 175–194.

Keller, H. (2018). Universality claim of attachment theory: Children's socioemotional development across cultures. *Proceedings of the National Academy of Sciences, 115*(45), 11414–11419.

Kemmelmeier, M., Sanchez-Burks, J., Cytron, A., & Coon, H. M. (1998, August). *Individualism and romantic love: A comparison of two hypotheses*. Poster presented at the 106th Annual Convention of the American Psychological Association, San Francisco, CA.

Keown, D. (2016). *The nature of Buddhist ethics*. Springer.

Keown, D., & Prebish, C. S. (Eds.). (2013). *Encyclopedia of Buddhism*. Routledge.

Kiecolt-Glaser, J. K., Fisher, B. S., Ogrocki, P., Stout, J. C., Speicher, C. E., & Glaser, R. (1988). Marital discord and immunity in males. *Psychosomatic Medicine, 50*, 213–229.

Kim, U., & Park, Y.-S. (2006). The scientific foundation of indigenous and cultural psychology: The transactional approach. In U. Kim, K.-S. Yang, & K.-K. Hwang (Eds.), *Indigenous and cultural psychology: Understanding people in context* (pp. 27–48). Springer.

Kim, K., Cheng, Y. P., Zarit, S. H., & Fingerman, K. L. (2015). Relationships between adults and parents in Asia. In S. T. Cheng, I. Chi, H. Fung, L. Li, & J. Woo (Eds.), *Successful aging* (pp. 101–122). Springer. https://doi.org/10.1007/978-94-017-9331-5_7

Kirkpatrick, L. A. (1998). Evolution, pair-bonding, and reproductive strategies: A reconceptualization of adult attachment. In J. A. Simpson & W. S. Rholes (Eds.), *Attachment theory and close relationships* (pp. 353–393). Guilford.

Konrath, S. H., O'Brien, E. H., & Hsing, C. (2011). Changes in dispositional empathy in American college students over time: A meta-analysis. *Personality and Social Psychology Review, 15*(2), 180–198.

Konstan, D. (1997). *Friendship in the classical world*. Cambridge University Press.

Kövecses, Z. (1988). *The language of love: The semantics of passion in conversational English*. Bucknell University Press.

Kövecses, Z. (2005). *Metaphor in culture: Universality and variation*. Cambridge University Press.

Kumar, U. (1991). Life stages in the development of the Hindu woman in India. In L. L. Adler (Ed.), *Women in cross-cultural perspective* (pp. 142–158). Praeger.

Laurenceau, J.-P., Feldman Barrett, L., & Pietromonaco, P. R. (1998). Intimacy as an interpersonal process: The importance of self-disclosure, partner disclosure, and perceived partner responsiveness in interpersonal exchanges. *Journal of Personality and Social Psychology, 74*, 1238–1251.

Le, T. N., & Levenson, M. R. (2005). Wisdom as self-transcendence: What's love (& individualism) got to do with it? *Journal of Research in Personality, 39*(4), 443–457.

Lebra, T. S. (1976). *Japanese patterns of behavior*. University of Hawaii Press.
Lee, J. L. (1973). *The colors of love: The exploration of the ways of loving*. New Press.
Lee, J. A. (1976). *The colors of love*. Prentice-Hall.
Lee, J. A. (1977). A typology of styles of loving. *Personality and Social Psychology Bulletin, 3*(2), 173–182.
Leon, J., Philbrick, J. L., Parra, E., Escobedo, E., & Malcesini, F. (1994). Love-styles among university students in Mexico. *Psychological Reports, 74*, 307–310.
Leon, J. J., Parra, F., Cheng, T., & Flores, R. E. (1995). Love-styles among Latino community college students in Los Angeles. *Psychological Reports, 77*(2), 527–530.
Levenson, M. R., Jennings, P. A., Aldwin, C. M., & Shiraishi, R. W. (2005). Self-transcendence: Conceptualization and measurement. *The International Journal of Aging and Human Development, 60*(2), 127–143.
Lewis, C. S. (1960). *The four loves*. Harcourt, Brace and Company.
Li, T. S. (1999). The content and measurement of marital intimate affection. *Chinese Journal of Mental Health, 12*(4), 197–216. (In Chinese).
Liao, S. M. (2006). The idea of a duty to love. *The Journal of Value Inquiry, 40*(1), 1–22.
Lim, N. (2016). Cultural differences in emotion: Differences in emotional arousal level between the East and the West. *Integrative Medicine Research, 5*(2), 105–109.
Lin, L. W., & Huddleston-Casas, C. A. (2005). Agape love in couple relationships. *Marriage & Family Review, 37*(4), 29–48.
Lindholm, C. (1995). Love as an experience of transcendence. In W. Jankowiak (Ed.), *Romantic passion: A universal experience?* (pp. 57–71). Columbia University Press.
Lindholm, C. (1998). Love and structure. *Theory, Culture & Society, 15*(3–4), 243–263.
Lings, M. (1975). *What is sufism?* University of California Press.
Liu, Q. (2007). Confucianism and corruption: An analysis of Shun's two actions described by Mencius. *Dao: A Journal of Comparative Philosophy, 6*(1), 1–19.
Liu, S., Rovine, M. J., Cousino Klein, L., & Almeida, D. M. (2013). Synchrony of diurnal cortisol pattern in couples. *Journal of Family Psychology, 27*(4), 579–588. https://doi.org/10.1037/a0033735
Lomas, T. (2018). The flavours of love: A cross-cultural lexical analysis. *Journal for the Theory of Social Behaviour, 48*, 134–152.
Lukas, D., & Clutton-Brock, T. (2013). The evolution of social monogamy in mammals. *Science, 341*(6145), 526–530.
Lv, Z., & Zhang, Y. (2012). Universality and variation of conceptual metaphor of love in Chinese and English. *Theory and Practice in Language Studies, 2*(2), 355–359.
Lystra, K. (1989). *Searching the heart: Women, men, and romantic love in nineteenth-century America*. Oxford University Press.
Ma, A. (2009). Comparison of the origins of altruism as leadership value between Chinese and Christian cultures. *Leadership Advance Online, 15*, 1–9.
Markus, H. R., & Kitayama, S. (1991). Culture and the self: Implications for cognition, emotion, and motivation. *Psychological Review, 98*, 224–253.
Marshall, T. C. (2008). Cultural differences in intimacy: The influence of gender-role ideology and individualism – Collectivism. *Journal of Social and Personal Relationships, 25*(1), 143–168.
Mashek, D. J., Aron, A., & Boncimino, M. (2003). Confusions of self with close others. *Personality and Social Psychology Bulletin, 29*, 382–392.
Maslow, A. H. (1943). A theory of human motivation. *Psychological Review, 50*, 370–396. https://doi.org/10.1037/h0054346
Maslow, A. H. (1968). *Toward a psychology of being*. Van Nostrand.
Maslow, A. H. (1970). *Motivation and personality* (2nd ed.). Harper.
Meisinger, H. (2000). Christian love and biological altruism. *Zygon, 35*(4), 745–782.
Miller, L. C., Berg, J. H., & Archer, R. L. (1983). Openers: Individuals who elicit intimate self-disclosure. *Journal of Personality and Social Psychology, 44*, 1234–1244.
Murstein, B. I., Merighi, J. R., & Vyse, S. A. (1991). Love styles in the United States and France: A cross-cultural comparison. *Journal of Social and Clinical Psychology, 10*(1), 37–46.

Neto, F. (2007). Love styles: A cross-cultural study of British, Indian, and Portuguese college students. *Journal of Comparative Family Studies, 38*(2), 239–254.
Neto, F., Mullet, E., Deschamps, J. C., Barros, J., Benvindo, R., Camino, L., et al. (2000). Cross-cultural variations in attitudes toward love. *Journal of Cross-Cultural Psychology, 31*(5), 626–635.
Nunney, L. (2000). Altruism, benevolence and culture. *Journal of Consciousness Studies, 7*(1–2), 231–236.
Nygren, A. (1989). Agape and Eros. In A. Soble (Ed.), *Eros, agape, and philia: Readings in the philosophy of love* (pp. 85–95). Paragon House.
Ogilvie, D. M., & Ashmore, R. D. (1991). Self-with-other representation as a unit of analysis in self-concept research. In R. C. Curtis (Ed.), *The relational self: Theoretical convergences in psychoanalysis and social psychology* (pp. 282–314). Guilford.
Payne, M., & Vandewiele, M. (1987). Attitudes toward love in the Caribbean. *Psychological Reports, 60*(3), 715–721.
Pérez, V. A. F., Fiol, E. B., Guzmán, C. N., Palmer, C. R., & Buades, E. G. (2009). The concept of love in Spain. *Psychology in Spain, 13*(1), 40–47.
Perlman, D., & Fehr, B. (1987). The development of intimate relationships. In D. Perlman & S. Duck (Eds.), *Intimate relationships: Development, dynamics, and deterioration* (pp. 13–42). Sage.
Pinkus, R. T. (2020). Love and belongingness needs. In V. Zeigler-Hill & T. K. Shackelford (Eds.), *Encyclopedia of personality and individual differences*. Springer. https://doi.org/10.1007/978-3-319-24612-3_1487
Porubjak, M. (2008). Priatel'stvo ako cnosť súkromná i verejná. *Ostium, 4*(1).
Post, S. G. (1990). *A theory of agape: On the meaning of Christian love*. Bucknell University Press.
Post, S. G. (2002). The tradition of agape. In S. G. Post, L. G. Underwood, J. P. Schloss, & W. B. Hurlbut (Eds.), *Altruism & altruistic love: Science, philosophy, & religion in dialogue* (pp. 51–66). Oxford University Press.
Post, S. G. (2003). *Unlimited love*. Templeton Foundation Press.
Post, S. G., Underwood, L. G., Schloss, J. P., & Hurlbut, W. B. (2002). *Altruism and altruistic love: Science, philosophy, and religion in dialogue*. Oxford University Press.
Prager, K. J. (1995). *The psychology of intimacy*. Guilford.
Rani, M., Figueroa, M. E., & Ainsle, R. (2003). The psychosocial context of young adult sexual behavior in Nicaragua: Looking through the gender lens. *International Family Planning Perspectives, 29*(4), 174–181.
Reddy, W. M. (2012). *The making of romantic love: Longing and sexuality in Europe, South Asia, and Japan, 900-1200 CE*. The University of Chicago Press.
Reed, P. G. (1986). Developmental resources and depression in the elderly. *Nursing Research, 35*, 368–374.
Reed, P. G. (2015). Pamela reed's theory of self-transcendence. In M. C. Smith & M. E. Parker (Eds.), *Nursing theories & nursing practice* (4th ed., pp. 411–420). F.A. Davis.
Reed, P.G. (2018). Self-transcendence: Scale and theory. *STS-2018*. https://nursologycom.files.wordpress.com/2018/10/sts-2018.pdf
Reed, R. G., Randall, A. K., Post, J. H., & Butler, E. A. (2013). Partner influence and in-phase versus anti-phase physiological linkage in romantic couples. *International Journal of Psychophysiology, 88*(3), 309–316.
Reichard, U. H., & Boesch, C. (Eds.). (2003). *Monogamy: Mating strategies and partnerships in birds, humans and other mammals*. Cambridge University Press.
Reis, H. T., & Shaver, P. (1988). Intimacy as an interpersonal process. In S. W. Duck (Ed.), *Handbook of personal relationships* (pp. 367–389). Wiley.
Roland, A. (1988). *In search of self in India and Japan*. Princeton University Press.
Rooker, K., & Gavrilets, S. (2016). Evolution of long-term pair-bonding in humans. In T. K. Shackelford & V. A. Weekes-Shackelford (Eds.), *Encyclopedia of evolutionary psychological science*. Springer. https://doi.org/10.1007/978-3-319-16999-6_99-1
Rosenbluth, S. C., & Steil, J. M. (1995). Predictors of intimacy for women in heterosexual and homosexual couples. *Journal of Social & Personal Relationships, 12*, 163–175.

Roth, T. S., Samara, I., Tan, J., Prochazkova, E., & Kret, M. E. (2021). A comparative framework of inter-individual coordination and pair-bonding. *Current Opinion in Behavioral Sciences, 39*, 98–105.

Rusbult, C. E., Drigotas, S. M., & Verette, J. (1994). The investment model: An interdependence analysis of commitment processes and relationship maintenance phenomena. In D. J. Canary & L. Stafford (Eds.), *Communication and relational maintenance* (pp. 115–139). Academic.

Sánchez, A. B. (1995). Metaphorical models of romantic love in Romeo and Juliet. *Journal of Pragmatics, 24*(6), 667–688.

Sanri, Ç., & Goodwin, R. (2013). Values and love styles in Turkey and Great Britain: An intercultural and intracultural comparison. *International Journal of Psychology, 48*(5), 837–845.

Sarkissian, H. (2010). Recent approaches to Confucian filial morality. *Philosophy Compass, 5*(9), 725–734.

Schmitt, D. P. (2005a). Is short-term mating the maladaptive result of insecure attachment? A test of competing evolutionary perspectives. *Personality and Social Psychology Bulletin, 31*(6), 747–768.

Schmitt, D. P. (2005b). Fundamentals of human mating strategies. In D. Buss (Ed.), *The handbook of evolutionary psychology* (pp. 258–291). Wiley.

Schmitt, D. P. (2008a). An evolutionary perspective on mate choice and relationship initiation. In S. Sprecher, A. Wenzel, & J. Harvey (Eds.), *Handbook of relationship initiation* (pp. 55–74). Psychology Press.

Schmitt, D. P. (2008b). Attachment matters: Patterns of romantic attachment across gender, geography, and cultural forms. In J. P. Forgas & J. Fitness (Eds.), *Social relationships: Cognitive, affective, and motivational processes* (pp. 75–100). Psychology Press.

Schmitt, D. P. (2008c). Evolutionary perspectives on romantic attachment and culture: How ecological stressors influence dismissing orientations across genders and geographies. *Cross-Cultural Research, 42*(3), 220–247.

Schmitt, D. P. (2010). Romantic attachment from Argentina to Zimbabwe: Patterns of adaptive variation across contexts, cultures, and local ecologies. In K. Ng & P. Erdman (Eds.), *Cross-cultural attachment across the life-span* (pp. 211–226). Routledge.

Schmitt, D. P., Alcalay, L., Allensworth, M., Allik, J., Ault, L., Austers, I., et al. (2003). Are men universally more dismissing than women? Gender differences in romantic attachment across 62 cultural regions. *Personal Relationships, 10*, 307–333.

Schmitt, D. P., Alcalay, L., Allensworth, M., et al. (2004). Patterns and universals of adult romantic attachment across 62 cultural regions: Are models of self and of other pancultural constructs. *Journal of Cross-Cultural Psychology, 35*, 367–402.

Schoebi, D. (2008). The coregulation of daily affect in marital relationships. *Journal of Family Psychology, 22*(4), 595–604. https://doi.org/10.1037/0893-3200.22.3.595

Scott, D. (2009). *A revolution of love: The meaning of Mother Teresa*. Loyola Press.

Seki, K., Matsumoto, D., & Imahori, T. T. (2002). The conceptualization and expression of intimacy in Japan and the United States. *Journal of Cross-Cultural Psychology, 33*(3), 303–319.

Sels, L., Cabrieto, J., Butler, E., Reis, H., Ceulemans, E., & Kuppens, P. (2020). The occurrence and correlates of emotional interdependence in romantic relationships. *Journal of Personality and Social Psychology, 119*(1), 136–158.

Sharma, K. (2016). Victory of marriage and family over romance, love, and passion in the fiction of Vikram Seth. *An International Refereed e-Journal of Literary Exploration, 4*, 54–60.

Shaver, P. R., & Hazan, C. (1988). A biased overview of the study of love. *Journal of Social and Personal Relationships, 5*, 474–501.

Shaver, P. R., & Mikulincer, M. (2006a). A behavioral system approach to romantic love relationships: Attachment, caregiving, and sex. In R. J. Sternberg & K. Weis (Eds.), *The new psychology of love* (pp. 35–64). Yale University Press.

Shaver, P. R., & Mikulincer, M. (2006b). Attachment theory, individual psychodynamics, and relationship functioning. In A. L. Vangelisti & D. Perlman (Eds.), *The Cambridge handbook of personal relationships* (pp. 251–272). Cambridge University Press.

Shaver, P. R., Hazan, C., & Bradshaw, D. (1988). Love as attachment. In R. J. Sternberg & M. L. Barnes (Eds.), *The psychology of love* (pp. 68–99). Yale University Press.
Sober, E., & Wilson, D. S. (1998). *Unto others: The evolution and psychology of unselfish behavior*. Harvard University Press.
Soble, A. (Ed.). (1989). *Eros, Agape, and Philia: Readings in the philosophy of love*. Paragon House.
Solheim, B. P. (1999). The possibility of a duty to love. *Journal of Social Philosophy, 30*(1), 1–17.
Soosai-Nathan, L., Negri, L., & Delle Fave, A. (2013). Beyond pro-social behaviour: An exploration of altruism in two cultures. *Psychological Studies, 58*(2), 103–114.
Sprecher, S., & Hendrick, S. S. (2004). Self-disclosure in intimate relationships: Associations with individual and relationship characteristics over time. *Journal of Social & Clinical Psychology, 23*, 857–877.
Sprecher, S., & Regan, P. (1998). Passionate and companionate love in courting and young married couples. *Sociological Inquiry, 68*(2), 163–185.
Sprecher, S., Aron, A., Hatfield, E., Cortese, A., Potapova, E., & Levitskaya, A. (1994). Love: American style, Russian style, and Japanese style. *Personal Relationships, 1*, 349–369.
Stinson, D. A., Cameron, J. J., & Hoplock, L. B. (2021). The friends-to-lovers pathway to romance: Prevalent, preferred, and overlooked by science. *Social Psychological and Personality Science*. https://doi.org/10.1177/19485506211026992
Suh, E. M. (2002). Culture, identity consistency, and subjective well-being. *Journal of Personality and Social Psychology, 83*, 1378–1391.
Sung, K. T. (2001). Elder respect: Exploration of ideals and forms in East Asia. *Journal of Aging Studies, 15*(1), 13–26.
Swidler, A. (2001). *Talk of love: How culture matters*. University of Chicago Press.
Templeton, J. (1999). *Agape love: Tradition in eight world religions*. Templeton Foundation Press.
Timmons, A. C., Margolin, G., & Saxbe, D. E. (2015). Physiological linkage in couples and its implications for individual and interpersonal functioning: A literature review. *Journal of Family Psychology, 29*(5), 720–731. https://doi.org/10.1037/fam0000115
Ting-Toomey, S. (1991). Intimacy expressions in three cultures: France, Japan, and the United States. *International Journal of Intercultural Relations, 15*(1), 29–46.
Tucker, P., & Aron, A. (1993). Passionate love and marital satisfaction at key transition points in the family life cycle. *Journal of Social and Clinical Psychology, 12*(2), 135–147.
Twenge, J. M., & Campbell, W. K. (2009). *The narcissism epidemic: Living in the age of entitlement*. Simon and Schuster.
Ubillos, S., Zubieta, E., Paez, D., Deschamps, J.C., Ezeiza, A., & Vera, A. (2001). Amor, cultura y sexo. *Revista Electronica de Motivacion y Emocion (REME), 4*(8–9). Available at: http://reme.uji.es/articulos/aubils9251701102/texto.html
Waller, W., & Hill, R. (1951). *The family: A dynamic interpretation*. Dryden Press.
Wang, C.-K. (1999). The relations between gender-role beliefs, family commitment, work commitment and work value. *Indigenous Psychological Research in Chinese Societies, 11*, 59–89. (In Chinese).
Wierzbicka, A. (1999). *Emotions across languages and cultures: Diversity and universals*. Cambridge University Press.
Williams, P. (2008). *Mahayana Buddhism: The doctrinal foundations*. Routledge.
Wilson, S. J., Bailey, B. E., Jaremka, L. M., Fagundes, C. P., Andridge, R., Malarkey, W. B., … Kiecolt-Glaser, J. K. (2018). When couples' hearts beat together: Synchrony in heart rate variability during conflict predicts heightened inflammation throughout the day. *Psychoneuroendocrinology, 93*, 107–116.
Wong, S., & Goodwin, R. (2009). Experiencing marital satisfaction across three cultures: A qualitative study. *Journal of Social and Personal Relationships, 26*(8), 1011–1028.
Yang, K. S. (1995). Chinese social orientation: An integrative analysis. In W. S. Tseng, T. Y. Lin, & Y. K. Yeh (Eds.), *Chinese societies and mental health* (pp. 19–39). Oxford University Press.
Yum, Y. O. (2004). Culture and self-construal as predictors of responses to accommodative dilemmas in dating relationships. *Journal of Social and Personal Relationships, 21*(6), 817–835.
Zaki, J. (2011, January 19). What, me care? Young are less empathetic. *Scientific American Mind*. Retrieved from http://www.scientificamerican.com/article.cfm?id¼what-me-care.

Chapter 8
Models of Rational Love

8.1 Realistic and Pragmatic Models of Love

8.1.1 Real Love Versus Ideal Romantic Love

Positive Biases and Unrealistic Expectations of Romantic Love

As we saw in the previous chapters, the key features of the *romantic model of love* are idealized perceptions of a beloved and relationship, adoration, and positively biased appraisals, which entail other associated qualities of romantic love. The opposite type of love is the *realistic model of love,* which is characterized by realistic perceptions of the loved one and relationships, respect, and relatively adequate appraisals.

Dating partners and newlyweds frequently have strong positive emotions and passions toward each other. These feelings precipitate idealization and romantic love, associated with positively biased perceptions and expectations. Such inadequate prospects and excessive anticipations turn to disappointments in many marriages.

The Value of Realistic Perception and Choice in Love

Different from the cultural beliefs in *a destiny* in *romantic love model*, the belief in the power of the rational choice of a partner is a feature of the *rational model*. Love in this model is a rational matter to marry, or to stay married. Love is the rational choice of one right person whom one will or could marry. Many cases of love-to-marry in North America are typical examples of this kind.

Some scholars of love suggest that the more realistic beliefs and accurate perceptions of the partner's specific qualities, instead of global adoration, can be more conducive for the long-term relationship satisfaction. Longitudinal studies (Neff &

V. Karandashev, *Cultural Typologies of Love*,
https://doi.org/10.1007/978-3-031-05343-6_8

Karney, 2005) have shown that while many newlyweds have enhanced global perceptions of their partners, they may perceive some qualities of the partner more accurately than others. The results of the studies have demonstrated that love with more accurate and specific perception tends to be stronger than love with lack of such accuracy. It is especially true for women. The wives with more specific and accurate perceptions are characterized by more supportive behaviors, feelings of control in the marriage, and ability to maintain satisfying relationships. The husbands frequently rely more on global adoration than on accuracy of perception. And their knowing of partner does not reflect substantially on their marital relationships. These results are in accordance with other data (cited in this and previous chapters) that men tend to follow *romantic model of love*, whereas women—*rational* or *pragmatic models of love*.

While romantic ideals of relationship inspire our expectations of "falling in love," realistic ideals motivate the expectations of "choosing to love." Individuals weigh pros and cons in their decisions to love and marry.

8.1.2 Love in Practical Ways

Love Through Doing

Different from other conceptions of love, this model of love focuses on human actions and fulfillment of the daily needs of people. Individuals following the practical model of love may not introspect too much about how they feel, what attitudes they have toward another, may not express love facially and vocally. They just do something for each other.

Would you prefer that your loving partner talk about his/her love to you? Would you prefer that they talk about how beautiful/handsome you all the time? Or would you prefer that they cook, dishwash, and help with other household chores? All these things can be called *love*, yet in different ways.

People have individual differences and preferences in their conceptualization of love, both in terms of expression and in terms of perception. *Love as an action of service* is one of them (Chapman, 2015). In these cases, actions speak louder than words.

Historically, this practical model of love has been perhaps evolutionary and culturally the primary model of love for centuries. Being busy with daily work for the survival and subsistence of themselves, their closed ones, and community, people might not have time to think and talk about love. Therefore, they rather showed their love in doing something good for them. On the other hand, the acts and actions of love might also be more valuable for the loved ones than the love words, smiles, and kisses.

Such *practical models of love* have been present in many societies in history. In modern times, these models continue to exist in the intertwined relations with other models of love, such as pragmatic, caring, and so on. For example, *practical* and *pragmatic models of love* are sometimes indistinguishable. The high value of practical and pragmatic aspects of love should not be necessarily deemed as contradicting to other aspects of love. Some practical models of love are the *caring models* because people frequently service others out of their caring love.

Across cultures, women are especially good with this ability. Many of the studies cited in the following sections reported sex differences in *pragma* love style: women place the higher value on this love attitude than men do.

The Puritan Model of Love in the Early American History

The *Puritan model of love* as a *rational* and *practical* type of *love* was quite common in American history from the times of the first colonies until the middle of the nineteenth century. The Puritan ideology and ethics of early settlers advocated that love should bring survival benefits, be productive, and conducive to development.

It was naturally integrated in the institute of marital life (Cherlin, 2010; Coontz, 2006; Finkel, 2018). Americans lived prevalently in individual rural households, where the main concerns of wife and husband were about survival—house routines, farming work, food resources, providing security and protection.

Gender inequality was common in the Puritan American, as well as in European cultures of the sixteenth to eighteenth centuries, with a social belief of women's mental and physical inferiority. Despite being intellectually not equal to men, women should be educated to be good companions of their husbands and treated with kindness. The highly valued qualities of a good wife were purity, piety, domesticity, and submissiveness. In the farming households, being industrious and vigorous were also important female features (Karandashev, 2017; Murstein, 1974).

The experience of love as psychological affinity between spouses was a good quality of marital life, yet such emotional relations were not the central point of their marriage. The day-to-day and seasonal life of husband and wife revolved around multiple practical concerns of farming, family life, and children. The ability for hard work, commitment, stamina, and caring for family were more important qualities of marital partners than their physical appearance and personality traits. Practical aspects of daily living—what partners did for each other, for family survival and prosperity—were the essential features of their model of love.

The individualistic American culture of European origins was open for the freedom of love. Many religious confessions and ethnic groups of immigrants had relatively liberal views on marriage. Generally, men and women could marry following their interpersonal likings and preferences. *Passionate love* was not important in their marital choice. They tried to consider *practical affordances* and needs of their real, not ideal life (Karandashev, 2017).

Anti-Romantic Puritan Model of Love

The *Puritan culture* substantially determined the *anti-romantic model of love* which relied on the *God's will* and *commonsense, rather than passion and emotional intimacy.* Traditionally, the American men and women were apparently cold and expressed little ardor in their relations. These emotional aspects of American marital life could be due to the historical influences of the Puritan and Anglican cultural heritage.

It was assumed that the experience and expression of passion, intimacy, and sexual yearning should not let them forget about God. The *Puritan values* taught that having rational attitudes, being industrious, keeping oneself busy daily are the basic human virtues that help master overwhelming passions. People tried to control leisure activities. They frowned men and women endlessly kissing and dallying and encouraged them to be prudent in sex life.

In the *Puritan courtship*, a young man should receive the consent of the young woman's parents to woo her. It was important to marry a person inside the Church and with approximately the same financial means. Equality of age and social status, as well as religious homogamy, were important for a good marriage. However, most parents did not force their sons and daughters to wed against their wants. The wooing in the eighteenth century of America became a more ceremonial courtship than in the early Puritan days. The ritualized interactions between a suitor and a woman were expected to show his honest intention (Karandashev, 2017; Murstein, 1974).

Although social norms endorsed the initial *liking of a man and a woman*, yet physical attraction and love were not necessary for a good marriage. Love was rather an intentional and rational process. A man and a woman liking each other tried to justify their feelings on a rational basis. They thought they could be a good Christian couple helping each other to find God and be pious, industrious, and thrifty in their family life. A relationship in a decent Puritan couple presumably should lead them to love, despite any personal differences or shortcomings. If the spouses would have a lack of love in their family, they should tacitly acknowledge that they failed to be the good Christians. That would be a challenging awareness for them (Murstein, 1974).

It shall be acknowledged, however, the diverse populations of early Americans—in different colonies and religions, in the New England, mid-Atlantic, and Southern states—had their cultural attitudes and customs, which they brought along from their countries of origins. They pursued their cultural beliefs and practices also in the following centuries. American Indians still maintained their traditional cultural marital mores. We review other *American models of love* elsewhere—in other chapters.

Mexican Practical Love

In Mexico, for a very long time, relationships in marriage have connected husband and wife by the bonds of obligation. They have lived together being hold by the values of respect, gendered responsibilities, and the mutual service and care provided to each other and their children. A man fulfilled his responsibility as a breadwinner by earning, constructing, repairing, and taking care of children, while a woman fulfilled her responsibility as a housekeeper by cooking, maintaining a house clean, washing, and ironing the clothes, and raising children.

Love was a matter of living well together and doing something useful for each other and family. It was neither a prerequisite for marriage, nor expectation of marital life. The love should supposedly grow out of mutually respectful and committed everyday relationship of spouses. Yet, it was not the focal point of their marital life. Marriage served the practical purposes of social functioning and reproduction. The personal self-expression and love satisfaction were not priorities (Hirsch, 2007).

The 1950s–1960s years in Mexico have witnessed the slightly increased value of companionate love. The further progress in popularity of the *companionate love model* has been slow since then. Transformation of marital relationships among urban population was faster than in rural areas of the country (Hirsch, 2003, 2007).

Practical Love in China and Africa

Many Chinese women believe that companionate, caring, and practical love in relationship do not contradict each other, but rather can, and should, go together. One 20-year-old woman clearly articulated this motivation, "I want a man who loves me, cares for me, and also understands me as I understand him. We can work together for our future" (Jankowiak et al., 2015, 2015, p. 8–9).

Aka people (a group of African pygmies living in the Central African Republic and Congo) and Hadza people (an indigenous ethnic group in north-central Tanzania) have similar love and mate preferences. It is possible that in all foraging cultures women "de-emphasize physical attraction in favor of male behavior that demonstrates a *love* manifested as a *willingness to work* (i.e., do things) *for the family*" (Crittenden and Hewlett, email correspondence, September, 2014, quoted in Jankowiak et al., 2015, 2015, p. 9).

8.2 Exchange Models of Love

8.2.1 The Love Models of Economic and Social Exchange

What are the Exchange Models of Love?

The exchange models of love assume that in a love relationship partners give something that is beneficial to a partner and receive something that is beneficial to him/her. These expectations can be explicit or implicit, communicated or assumed, consciously calculated or unconsciously appraised. Many theories use the terms *rewards* and *costs* describing love relationships. The rewards and costs can be of different kind: material, economic, social, emotional, and others.

Anyway, partners in love relationships openly or tacitly, directly or indirectly assume that they give and receive something in a relationship. The statements like this definitely show such motivation: "I just wasn't getting anything out of that relationship." "He wasn't worth the effort." "She was too high maintenance." (Stafford, 2008, p. 377).

Such statements indicate partners' actions and decisions based on their perceptions of rewards (what we are getting out of a relationship) versus costs (what we are putting into a relationship). This exchange idea of interpersonal interaction in love is basic to all theories of exchange. Interdependence Theory, Resource Theory, and Equity Theory are the examples of such theories (see for review, Stafford, 2008). These and other exchange theories and research are reviewed here.

Mating and Dating as Exchange

The *love is an economic exchange* model was typical for many people in generations of old traditional cultures, for which pragmatic qualities of partners for the survival and growth of a family household were very important. Young boys, girls, and their families were interested in economic survival and wealth of offspring after they have left the home of their parents. Economic and social benefits of the extended families, from which sons and daughters came, were important priorities in mating and courtship.

In early modern cultures (sixteenth to nineteenth centuries), some people became less concerned about their household survival and did have more spare time to cultivate the idea of *love as a spiritual and emotional unity.* This new model of love inspired the wealthy and educated youth for a very long time. Nevertheless, economic and status relations as exchange continued to play an important role in mating and courtship.

The consumeristic cultures of the twentieth century, however, reverted to the model of *love as an economic exchange*, yet in a new sense: they embraced not only pragmatic qualities, as before, but a broader spectrum of motivations, including sexual. New sexual and consumerist culture emphasized "the rewards an individual should get from a relationship rather than the higher unity of the relationship itself" (Stearns, 1994, p.173). Economic-exchange-based models of dating associated with expenditures and gifts became common in America (Bailey, 1988; Modell, 1983; Whyte, 1990).

The gift-giving has been quite common in mating and dating for a long time across many societies. These relationship practices can be interpreted in different ways: as a concomitant of courtship to conquer the favor of a beloved or her relatives, as an altruistic action of benevolence towards the loved one, or as a cultural tradition of economic gift exchange commonly practiced in some societies (Belk & Coon, 1993).

The later form of gift exchange is suitable for interpretation here. In this case, a gift is given with expectation that something *was/is/will be* given in return of something in the *past/present/future*. Reciprocity is expected without formal obligations. The economic gift exchange must be beneficial for both sides, according to the *quid pro quo principle* (see more in Karandashev, 2019).

According to the *economic exchange model of love*, the exchange is based on the market value of gifts in terms of their monetary price, scarcity, and availability of alternative supply sources. In the *social exchange model*, however, such exchange is based on a giver's and recipient's subjective values of gifts (Belk & Coon, 1993; Otnes & Beltramini, 1996). These two models of gift exchange in love are difficult to clearly distinguish in practice of a relationship. Both are widely used, for example, in American, European, and Japanese societies, along with some cultural differences (Areni, Kiecker, & Palan, 1998; Belk, 1996; Belk & Coon, 1993; Minowa & Gould, 1999).

Economic Exchange Model of Love

In the twentieth century, social scientists in America widely adopted the *economic model of exchange* in their interpretation of heterosexual dating relationships. Becker (1991) was among those scholars who suggested the pragmatic reasoning to the choices which people make in the matters of marriage and family. This idea was also present in public opinion and became especially popular in the United States. This model of love assumes that individuals receive the economic rewards in love relationship, while spending their personal resources. These resources and rewards can be of very different kinds yet related to economic relations. According to Kövecses (2005), the *exchange metaphor of love* represents a prevalent model of love in American culture. Due to the cultural influence of American materialistic values, this conceptual metaphor of love became in recent decades popular in modern Chinese (Lv & Zhang, 2012). Nevertheless, the *unity metaphor of love* is still widespread as a preferred cultural ideal in many other societies.

In the *traditional economic exchange framework*, dating partners are engaged in a bargaining relationship: a woman tries to place a high price on her sexual favors while a man strives to attain them at the lowest possible price. Looking for a marital partner, a man exchanges his commitment of marriage for beauty and sexual gratification, or for something else. Men and women are "consumers." Men perceive their money, wealth, properties as valuable assets and women regard their charms as "assets." And they can exchange those on "auction." In marriage, the mutually dependent relationship can develop due to relationship satisfaction, the lack of better alternatives, and the cumulative resources invested in the relationship.

Generally saying, anything that a person can choose to give to another person and that can be useful to the person receiving it can be a benefit. Rusbult (1980, 1983) explained *balanced economic exchange* in dating as several consecutive investments. According to this conceptualization, a long-term relationship develops when a person's rewards continuously exceed costs, when he/she has a lack of better alternative partners, and when a high cumulative investment in the relationship occurs.

So, one can say that love grows along with economic and social benefits, which a person receives in relationships.

Upward Mobility Model of Love

The *upward mobility model—hypergamy—*describes *a relationship* between a man and a woman from unequal socio-economic and educational levels who have interest in each other to begin a relationship. A person from low socio-economic group is interested in dating because this relationship increases their position in a society. A potential partner from the upper social group, on the other hand, perceives the person of low social group highly positive, regardless of social inequity.

The concept of *hypergamy* exemplifies the reality of the economic exchange model in traditional cultures, such as India (Van Den Berghe, 1960). *Hypergamy* is a mating case of "marrying up," when a person marries a spouse of a higher social stratum, compared to the status of the person. In this type of mating relationship, women tend to marry men of a slightly higher social class than their own. The opposite, when men marry women of higher status, is a less frequent case. At any rate, this kind of relationship will advance their status in social relations.

Men and women of different economic, social, and educational strata fall in love with each other and may decide to marry. Nevertheless, their differences in social class and status will inevitably play a role as the relationship progresses. This case of *hypergamy* mating can be called the *status model of love*, which is characterized as *upward mobility model of love* for a person.

The opposite perspective—*hypogamy*—is a case when a person marries a partner of lower social status. This is the case of *marrying down,* which may entail *downward mobility model*, or not. The real progression of love and relationship in such cases of *status models of love* are mediated by other social and psychological factors. A man or woman from the upper class can perceive the individual of low social status as being attractive and having good qualities worthwhile to love. Then, his/her merits can overshadow their social inequity.

Social and gender equality, population distributions of educational and social attainments of men and women in a society predict the prevalence of various models of love and relationship associated with social status (Blossfeld & Timm, 2003). In modern societies with greater economic independence of women and changing gender roles, the equality in mating relationship has a better chance and the cases of hypergamy in marriages are on decline.

Nowadays, in modern egalitarian societies, both men and women may have better access to such resources as the financial, social, and educational status than before. In many countries, college education became more prevalent among women than among men (Esteve, García-Román, & Permanyer, 2012). All these societal factors reflect on the formation of corresponding love and relationship (see for review, Karandashev, in press).

Status Exchange Model of Love in Intercultural Relationships

The *status-caste exchange theory* of interracial and interethnic love relationships (Merton, 1941; Sassler & Joyner, 2011; Schoen & Wooldredge, 1989) implies that individuals of lower socioeconomic status in one area are more likely to seek out relationships with others of a higher status to make up for their low status (Rosenfeld, 2005).

The fairy tales across cultures commonly depict the girls dreaming to encounter a charming prince to love and marry. The girls are typically kind and beautiful, but poor, while the prince is brave, handsome, and rich. The first two qualities of both definitely predispose them to fall in love with each other—*romantic model of love*, yet the third qualities of both predispose the *status-caste exchange* model of love. Such mixed *cultural model of love* in fairy tales inspired many girls in the past and continue to inspire in modern Hollywood movies. The reality of love, however, does not frequently work this way.

The research and interpretations of the divergent findings with minority groups in the United States (i.e., Blacks, Hispanics, and Asians) are inconsistent. For instance, the alternative explanations of the Black-White intermarriage are possible. Black-White *inequality* and *gender differences* among young couples can be the confounding variables, which obscure the role of the actual social status. These analyses make doubt on status-caste exchange theory (Rosenfeld, 2005).

However, other scholars provide their evidence in support that the *status-caste exchange model* works in many instances of intermarriages—more frequently in Black-White relationships than in other combinations of races and ethnicities, such as Asians, Latinos, and others (e.g., Gullickson & Fu, 2010; Kalmijn, 2010). Due to the important role of homogamy in love attraction—see other sections of the book—the *status-caste exchange* model resembles a *pragmatic model of love,* unless *romantic idealization of passion* wipes any differences in the eyes of the beholder. The latter is possible—for initial stage of relationships.

The *status-exchange model* might have been luckily working for some individual cases in the societies with high *social inequality*. However, the preferences for endogamous marriages have been common across many cultures. The modern increase in social and economic equality, in educational levels of young men and women in many societies, has decreased the value of *status-exchange.*

8.2.2 Investment Models of Love

The Structure of Psychological Investment in Love

The *investment model of developing relationships* explains that *attraction to a partner* and *satisfaction with a relationship* depend on how a man/woman appraises the *value of relationship outcome* (as a balance of rewards and costs) in comparison with his/her expectations—*satisfaction level*, and *comparison level of alternatives* (Rusbult, 1980, 1983). The magnitude of his/her personal investment in the relationship and the quality of other candidates available for an alternative relationship are the two more parameters in the investment model.

1. Commitment level—degree one intends to persist in the relationship.
2. Relationship satisfaction—degree that the relationship fulfilled needs for intimacy, sex, companionship, security, and emotional involvement.
3. Quality of alternatives—degree that one believes the satisfaction needs (above) could be fulfilled in another relationship.
4. Investment size—measures perceptions of time invested, interconnected identity, memories, and shared experiences.

Generally, the higher extrinsic and intrinsic investment of personal resources increases the costs of ending the relationship, which in turn increases commitment to current relationship. In conclusion, the higher extent of investment, the higher value of relationship, and the lower value of alternative possibilities increase the commitment to a current relationship. Experimental and survey studies have supported this theory in all predictions; however, the cost value of relationship had the weak effects. Thus, investment size, satisfaction level, and comparison with alternatives are the three major contributing factors to commitment in relationships.

Investment Constructs

The later conceptual operationalization of *investment construct* with the *Investment Model Scale* (Rusbult, Martz, & Agnew, 1998) identified four aspects of *love as investment*. The two constructs—*level of commitment* and *satisfaction level*—looks rather as the resulting variables, while the other two—*investment size* and *quality of alternatives*—are really the investment constructs. The Rusbult's Investment Model became the *model of commitment* assessing how *investments in a relationship* and *available alternatives* contribute to the *feeling of commitment* within one and the same scale. The authors treat *satisfaction with relationship* as independent variable *predicting commitment*—the prediction that is valid. Nevertheless, one may think that since the measurement instrument is an *investment model scale*, it would be more adequate to treat satisfaction with relationship as a resulting dependent variable, along with commitment, rather than independent variable (e.g., Rusbult, Johnson, & Morrow, 1986). The confusion, however, resolves when an attentive reader understands that *satisfaction with relationship* is really the *comparison of rewards with costs* of staying in a relationship, as in the earlier version of the model. Therefore, the *balance of rewards and costs* sounds more like an independent variable of the relationship. I believe the latter term would be more adequate in this case because satisfaction with relationship results from these and other factors.

Personal Investment and Commitment

Further studies (e.g., Rusbult & Buunk, 1993; Rusbult et al., 1986; Rusbult et al., 1998; Pistole, Clark, & Tubbs, 1995) of adult romantic and marital relationships showed the generalizability of the investment model. Results found that commitment of partners to a relationship increases when they invest resources in the relationship, the poor quality of available alternative partners, and the greater feeling of reward, which the relationship brings, while low cost much less powerfully and less consistently contributed to commitment to maintain relationship. Contribution of these investment factors worked in addition to their greater relationship satisfaction. In the same vein, when partners believe that their relationship bring them high rewards and incur low costs, they are more satisfied with the relationship.

The *Investment Model of relationships* has shown the importance of *interdependence in the partners' relationships* for the commitment to stay in the relationship (Rusbult & Buunk, 1993). Their commitment can increase not only due to increasing relationship satisfaction, but also due to the increasing feeling of dependence that evolves because many valuable resources have been invested in a relationship and the available alternatives are apparently poor.

Investments in a partner and relationship importantly contribute to the development of commitment in the relationship (Lund, 1985). This means the more a partner invests his/her energy, thinking, emotions, efforts, actions, labor, time, and other personal resources into a partner and relationship, the more he/she feels committed to love this partner and appreciate their relationship, despite any adverse effects. For example, the study of married couples (Impett, Beals, & Peplau, 2001) has demonstrated that greater investments in a relationship and limited quality of alternatives for the current relationship in small, yet statistically significant degree contribute to their commitment and stability of marital relationship. However, their roles were lower than the impact of relationship satisfaction.

Cross-Cultural Validity of Investment Model of Love

Multiple other studies (see for meta-analysis of 52 studies, Le & Agnew, 2003) have been in support of the findings that *greater investment in a relationship* and *limited quality of alternatives* substantially contribute in the commitment to romantic and marital partnerships in both individualistic (e.g., the USA) and collectivistic (e.g., Taiwan) cultures, thus validating the *Investment Model* across different cultural contexts. Despite this assertion, the *investment model of love relationship* appears as quite Americanistic and reflects the individualistic, materialistic, calculated, and rational aspects of European American culture. There are no doubts that the investment model works in many societies; however, cultural specifics can be expected, for example, due to specific self-construals. The more research of how this model works in other cultures would be interesting to explore its cross-cultural variability.

Types of Personal Investment Models

The individuals' *personal investment models of love* can be qualitatively different depending on their type of *attachment model of love*. Those, who feel securely attached to a partner, think that they *invest substantially*, have *fewer costs, stronger commitment, and greater satisfaction* in their relationships. Different from this experience, individuals with *insecure attachments* feel disbalance and dissatisfaction with their investment experience in relationships. Those with *avoidant attachment model of love* believe they invest insufficiently, while with *anxious-ambivalent attachment model* think they have high costs in a relationship (Pistole et al., 1995).

Emotional investment is a specific component of *personality investment*—literally, it is investment of emotions into another and relationship. The concept of *emotional investment* defines such features of love as emotional engagement, being high or low emotionally involved, and relationship depth.

These types of emotional experience characterize individual *emotional investment* in the parental, as well as adult love relations.

Model of Love as Parental Emotional Investment

From an evolutionary perspective, *emotional investment* can be viewed as a part of *parental investment* (Belsky, Steinberg, & Draper, 1991; Kaplan, 1996; Trivers, 1972) in raising children and caring about them. The *construct of emotional investment* defines how much mother, father, kin, and family are emotionally engaged in the life of a growing child. *Parental emotional investment* involves empathy, concern, care, and love for a child, which over time evolve into *parental attachment*. When their child loses his/her life, or departs other way, the parents may feel themselves dramatically sad, unhappy, and desperate for a long time since this lose breaks their *important attachment ties*. Because of this, parents in the early stages of societal evolution, characterized by stressful and risky life with high infant mortality, may not invest too much in their feelings and energy. They knew the high risk and low value of life. The chance of survival was low. Unconsciously, mothers tend avoid the likely experience of emotionally broken heart. And therefore, they invest rather in the high birth rates compensating the survival loss of offspring.

The validity of this assumption has been supported in the studies of relations between risk-factors of childhood life and parental investment. High levels of environmental risk, associated with unpredictable and unreliable availability of food, pathogen stress and high prevalence of infectious diseases, high frequency of warfare and severity of intragroup violence affect the population tendency toward lower parental investment (e.g., Nettle, 2010; Quinlan, 2007). Maternal care is lower during times of famine and warfare (Quinlan, 2007). Co-residence of fathers in families is less common (Nettle, 2010), thus reducing parental investment even more. On the positive side, however, the evidence that *modernization* of societies associated with lower environmental risk and higher safety of living conditions shapes parental investment strategies leading to higher investment in children (e.g., Gibson & Lawson, 2011; Kaplan, 1996).

Model of Love as the Adult Emotional Investment in Relationship

The *circumplex model of interpersonal behavior* (Wiggins, 1979) identified *Emotional Investment* as an important factor affecting interpersonal relationships. The essence of this construct is in the individual predisposition toward *interpersonal nurturance in a relationship* (Wiggins & Trapnell, 1997).

The high or low *personal tendencies in emotional investment* can be related to individual preferences of long- or short-term, committed or uncommitted relationships. The dimension of *sociosexual orientation* (Simpson & Gangestad, 1991) can define these individual, gender, and cultural differences in the *models of love*.

Those men and women who are high in *sociosexual orientation* (Simpson & Gangestad, 1991, 1992) prefer the less deep emotional relationship. They tend to invest little in their relationship, thus, protecting their personal self from being interdependent. The short-term sexual encounters can fulfill these relationship preferences well. Love for them is a short-term adventure, an enjoyable episode, a temporary state of mind and emotion. Due to their low emotional investment in a relationship, they experience few emotional ties with partner, feel relatively independent, less committed, and can leave the relationship when their exciting, joyful, and possibly passionate emotions fade. On the other end of spectrum, men and women who are low in *sociosexual orientation* prefer to build a long-term relationship investing their emotional energy and deep personal self. They tend to develop a long and lasting emotional and sexual relationship. They are willing to admit personal commitment and invest in their long-term monogamous relationship.

Emotional Investment as a Personality Trait

Schmitt and Buss (2000) proposed to define *emotional investment* as a *sexuality-related personality trait* consisting of the self-descriptive words *Loving, Lovable, Romantic, Affectionate, Cuddlesome, Compassionate*, and *Passionate* taken from the list of 67 sexually connotative adjectives. This *Emotional Investment scale* apparently deviates from specific meaning of the concept and shows poor face and content validity, despite otherwise excellent psychometrics. Researchers actually admit this fact, stating that the scale is a broad-based dimensional indicator of "love." Thus, one can see that the construct stands for the overall love, more precisely, for the self-rating of a respondent's overall ability to love. Unfortunately, there is *no beloved one* and *no specifically emotional investment* measure in the scale.

Researchers found (Schmitt et al., 2009) that in the majority of cultural samples, women rated higher their *self-descriptive personality trait—ability to love* ("emotional investment") compared to men. Across fifty-six nations, higher national levels of ecological stress—as indicated in Childhood Malnutrition rates, the Pathogen Stress of local environments, and Infant Mortality rates,—predict lower levels of *self-descriptive personality trait—ability to love* ("emotional investment"). And versus versa, the higher national scores of HDI and GDP were associated with higher *self-descriptive personality trait—ability to love* ("emotional investment"). Although these results look plausible and make sense, however, one shall keep in mind the content definition of the construct "emotional investment," as described above.

8.2.3 Communal and Equitable Models of Love

Communal Relationship Versus Exchange Relationship

The *love attitude of exchange* is highlighted in the theory of *communal relationship vs. exchange relationship* (Clark & Mills, 1979, 2013), briefly mentioned in other sections. A person with an *exchange love attitude* understands a relationship as *exchange*—the giving of a benefit in response to the receipt of a benefit seems natural. Exchange relationships are based on interpersonal economics, not necessarily monetary.

The concept of *exchange relationship* in this theory expands beyond *economic exchange* and considers a benefit as anything (not only with monetary value) that a person can choose to give to another person that is of use to the person receiving it. The authors in their theory also distinguish benefits from rewards as the satisfactions, pleasures, or gratifications. Even though the receipt of a benefit generally is a reward, yet rewards can occur for reasons other than the receipt of a benefit. The rewards that a lover receives from a partner may not be a benefit when the partner gives a reward without intentional choice. For example, looking at the beautiful or handsome partner is rewarding, but it is generally a benefit that a partner intentionally gives to a lover.

Partners in an *exchange relationship* assume that "benefits are given with the expectation of receiving a benefit in return" (Clark & Mills, 1979, p. 12). Once a person has received a benefit, it incurs his or her obligation or debt to give back a comparable benefit. For a person with such an *exchange attitude,* it is important how much she or he receives in exchange for giving the partner, and how much she or he owes to the partner for the benefits received.

The Mix of Communal and Exchange Models of Love in Close Relationships

The model of *communal relationship,* rather than *exchange model*, frequently works in cases of friendship, romantic, dating, and family relationships (Belk & Coon, 1993; Cherlin, 2000; Clark & Mills, 2013; Karandashev, 2019). Many people are capable for self-less benevolence, caring, and doing something good for others without expectations to receive something in return. They often do their deeds not by calculated and rational choices, but rather by love. They often give gifts expressing their *agapic love*, not expecting anything in return (Belk & Coon, 1993). They can be, and they are *communal* in their social nature and capable for the true love. In close interpersonal relationships, they can live according to the *model of communal relationship*, rather than the exchange model.

Nevertheless, the truth is that even though most people in the modern types of societies tend to marry for love, they still do not marry only for love (Cherlin, 2000). Many also make obvious or intuitive rational calculations about the benefits and costs of marrying the person they love. Without deliberate reckoning, an individual in his/her interaction with a partner still implicitly understand this kind of exchange relationship, even though may not be explicitly aware of this attitude and it affects the relationship with a partner (Clark & Mills, 1979).

The *exchange relationship attitudes* still take place in marital and other close relationships; they are viable and can be useful for life. For instance, the expectations of the equal distribution of household chores (each partner with their own obligations and contribution) seem natural in many relationships.

Partners want a relationship where they work together and equal for the good of their family in everything. They both work, do household chores, cook, and take care of their children, even though in some areas one may do a little more than a partner, while the partner may do a little more in other areas. Their roles within the household might be fluid, with an assumption that each honestly strives to contribute, not loafing and leaving the partner with burden of excessive chores.

The Equity Theory of Love

The *equity theory* considers justice and equity principles as the key variables of interpersonal relationships (Hatfield, Traupmann, Sprecher, Utne, & Hay, 1985). The *equity theory* proposes that a relationship is equitable, when the person evaluating the relationship concludes that all participants receive *equal relative gains* from the relationship. In love relationships, each of the two partners estimates how well they do (how much they get)—relatively to the partner—in several areas of their relationships. As a result of such estimates, they may feel *over-benefited*—if they gain relatively more than their partners, *under-benefitted*—if they gain relatively smaller of their partners, or *equitably treated* in their relations—if they gain relatively equal to their partners. The equal balance of such estimates, when both partners view themselves and another as *equitably treated,* is considered as conducive for fair and satisfied love relationships. Partners feel psychologically more comfortable when they give and get in their relationship what they deserve—no more and no less, when they perceive their relationships are profitable for both (Hatfield et al., 2011a, b).

How Equitable Relationships Work

The *equity theory* of intimate relationships has been extensively investigated in the studies (e.g., Hatfield & Traupmann, 1981; Hatfield et al., 2011, 2011; Lloyd, Cate, & Henton, 1982; Lujansky & Mikula, 1983; Van Yperen & Buunk, 1990). According to this theory and some studies (e.g., Hatfield & Traupmann, 1981; Hatfield et al., 2011, 2011), the relationships when a person of a lower status has a high-status mate frequently do not work out very well. These are the cases when the partners are from different social class, socio-economic status, and unequal ethnic backgrounds.

Although across times and many societies, *equity, fairness,* and *social justice* have been important principles, yet cultures have viewed them from different perspectives. Here are some examples of these views: "Winners take all"; "The more time and energy you invest, the more you're entitled to."; From each according to his ability, to each according to his needs"; "All men are created equal."

Cultural Variability in Perception of Equity

Due to culturally normative ideas, people differ in their views of how important they consider *the equity* in *relationship,* how *equitable* they perceive *their relationship,* and how the *feelings of equity* affect their *relationship satisfaction.*

Cross-cultural researchers commonly believe that the cultural norms of many cultures in Western and Northern Europe, North America, Australia, and New Zealand highly regard the equity in interpersonal relationships, whereas the cultural norms of many cultures in Africa, Asia, and Latin America are less concerned about fairness in relationship. For instance, in the United States, many couples believe that *equity and fairness* are very important for many aspects of their relationship (see for review, Aumer-Ryan, Hatfield, & Frey, 2007; Hatfield et al., 2011, 2011). These moral principles have become essential features of the *American cultural model of love* to determine.

In this regard, comparison of Hawaiians, as an American and egalitarian society, and Jamaicans, as a Latino and affluent society is interesting (Aumer-Ryan et al., 2007). People in both countries consider *equity to be important* in their romantic relationships. However, compared to the men and women in Jamaica, people in Hawai'i view their relationships a little more equitable, however, much more satisfying. The Hawaiians are more satisfied in their romantic relationships when the relationships are equitable. On another hand, Jamaicans are more satisfied when they are over-benefited from their relationships. *Equity* seems to be of less importance for them as a factor of relationship satisfaction. This might be due to the emphasis they place on their roles and familial kin support. As for intercultural love, in Jamaica, where equity is generally valued relatively low, the rates of intermarriages are far lower than in Hawaii', where equity is highly valued (Aumer-Ryan et al., 2007).

8.3 Performing Models of Love

8.3.1 Psychologically Disengaged Love

Performing Play and Game of Love

The core emotional experiences of people following these models of love are being psychologically disengaged, internally estranged, and feeling detached from a partner and relationship. However, this type of love is externally expressive, actional, and performative. Lovers tend to perform love, rather than experience it. They can perform very stylishly, elegantly, beautifully, and seductively. Therefore, they can be very attractive to fall in love with.

However, the individuals following these models of love are insincere, psychologically distant, focusing on the external aspects of love, rather than on internal experience. They try to avoid the wholehearted experience of passion, understanding its irresistible power, even though they can imitate its expression to look passionate. They try to avoid the sincere experience of psychological intimacy, understanding its potential risk, even though they can demonstrate that they are intimate with partner. They demonstrate romantic emotions, expressions, and behaviors, understanding their value, even though they prefer not to fall sincerely in romantic illusions. Thus, they prefer to *play and perform love*, like actors, gamers, or sport players, rather than to *live through love*.

The lovers of this type are skillful and artful in entertainment and seduction of the loved one. These models of love have been evolving throughout centuries, at least since Ancient Greeks (*paixnidi*) and Romans (ludus), along with the art of seduction (Meister, 1963; Ovid, 1939).

These models of love are especially challenging to categorize in one or another group. They do not neatly fit in any categories among those presented in the chapters of this book. Many of them are not passionate, not romantic, not committed, not intimate, not companionate, not pragmatic, and not caring. Yet, they may have the features and elements of different models.

These types of love may appear as rational models in some respects because they are usually consciously chosen by individuals. However, these individuals are typically unaware of these causes and reasons why they select these models. Therefore, I shall admit that these models are in this chapter just—conventionally, contingently, and conveniently—due to some of their features. Such categorization is still not perfect.

Gaming and Playful Aspects of Love Relationships

Gaming and playing elements can be present in *any model of love*. They do the love more entertaining and enjoyable. The love relationships and feelings, which involve the games and play, are more pleasurable and thrilling for partners. They help avoid the boredom of relationship routine and bring something new and exciting.

The problem, however, may arise when some individuals fully and permanently engage in these types of gaming and playing, not taking anything seriously. The game is good as an overture to something else, or as occasional entertainment. However, it can be challenging to live and love through it all time.

8.3.2 Love as the Role Play

Why Love Is a Play

The terms play and game are closely related to each other, yet they convey slightly different meanings. These differences may be important in the context of love. The play is the activity that has imitating purpose, rather than practical pursuit of a goal. The *children play* is an excellent example. They play with objects—toys, which for them imitate real objects. One object is used in place of another. They play interacting with other kids performing their actions and interactions, which imitate real behavior of people. The *role playing* is the core of the *children play*. They perform and act under other names imitating real life. They pretend that… Why? Because they find this fun and enjoyable.

Sexually playful behaviors are common among lower and higher mammals, as well as humans (Foote, 1954).

The Imitation Game of Love

Learning to love is a part of socialization and enculturation in childhood and teenage. It is a role play. Children can play love with each other. Do they really love? Or do they play love?

Sexual plays fulfill the children's curiosity about genitalia and sex. These plays may involve looking or limited touching, drawing of genitalia and simulated engagement in sexual intercourse or other sexually related activities (e.g., Davies, Glaser, & Kossoff, 2000).

Seeing how their peers are engaged in romantic relationships, they feel they must engage in love too. The following of their role models and the imitation of the common "how this must be" are very important things at the teenage. So, many of them just pretend that they love—they play love learning what it is.

Adolescents and emerging adults also *love to play love*. It is well-known that some teenagers *play love* with their peers just to *learn what love is*. They imitate the adult love scripts pretending that they love in a relationship (Moore, 1995).

Falling in love with celebrities, *parasocial models of love*, and *pornography love* are the ways to fulfill this *play function of teenage love* (see more in another chapter of this book).

Flirting Is Also a Game of Mating

Flirting is the verbal, nonverbal communication, and expressive actions indicating sexual attraction and signaling interest in a potential partner. This is a *playful way* to entice someone for entertaining, rather than for a serious relationship. Generally, flirtatious behaviors engage playful indirect techniques, subtle facial expressions, and gestures.

Researchers have identified the *five flirting styles* characterizing individual differences in nonverbal and verbal behaviors associated with flirting: traditional, polite, sincere, physical, and playful (Hall, Carter, Cody, & Albright, 2010). During recent years, the field of flirting has been actively investigated in interpersonal communication of romantic interest (e.g., Apostolou & Christoforou, 2020; Cunningham & Barbee, 2008; Hall, 2013; Hall & Xing, 2015; Henningsen, 2004).

Occasional studies and scholarly observations have suggested that flirting in the Western cultures is culturally acceptable (e.g., Givens, 1978; Hanna, 2010; Moore, 1985), while in the Middle Eastern cultures, it is viewed as culturally controversial (e.g., Al-Dawood, Abokhodair, & Yarosh, 2017). However, no systematic and comprehensive cross-cultural studies have been conducted so far.

Flirting is a more commonly used tactic by women due to traditional gender stereotypes that men in a relationship shall be active, while women—reactive. Since in many cultures, the direct initiation of relationship is culturally frown, women have developed the ways of flirting to attract and encourage a man.

Learning to flirt starts still in childhood and teenage. A study has shown (Moore, 1995) that girls employ many flirting signals, which grown up women commonly exhibit. In the girls' flirting, however, many signals are exaggerated compared to adult women. Girls more frequently utilize teasing behavior and play.

Playful Model of Love

Playful love is a type of love, which is frequent between children or casual lovers when they display playful affection pretending that they are in love. This style of love looks the child-like: it is very flirtatious and fun.

Dancing at the party with a stranger can be viewed as a play of temporary love, which may be considered as a playful proxy for sex itself. This is why rivals can be jealous when they see their loved dancing with someone else.

Some individuals prefer this playful style or elements of playful love in their relationships. A *benevolent "playfulness"* is nice and romantic. The playful expressions of love are amusing and entertaining. These can be playful gestures or hiding the longing and sexual interest for someone to incite his/her greater attraction. These can be teasing, flirting, joking, laughing, and being plain silly. Such a playful love brings spice and excitement in the early stages of a relationship.

The modern youth generation seems like the playful love even more than in the former times. Nowadays, one can see this type of love a lot. However, some cultural and social norms may frown on this adult frivolity. For example, in Vietnam as a traditional country people can rarely see the public displays of affection, such as kissing and hugging.

Cross-Cultural Universality of Playful Forms of Love

Is the playful love a cross-cultural phenomenon? Scholars do not have sufficient comprehensive findings so far. However, occasionally available data from psycholinguistics provide a glimpse of knowledge that it can be the culturally universal occurrence in love relationships. Several examples are below.

The Hindu notion of *lila* (*divine play*) is essential in Hindu philosophy. The concept expresses the idea of "divine sport, play, or dalliance" (Kinsley, 1974, p. 108). In the mythology of major Hindu deities, the various scriptures explicitly or implicitly teach that play is vital for divine activity in different contexts.

The Indian indigenous dialect Boro distinguishes the verb *onsay*—"to pretend to love," as playful love, from the *onguboy*—"to love from the heart" (Lomas, 2018).

According to the study of lexicon (Lomas, 2018), people in several cultures play the love game *cheeky displays of affection*. For example, the Tagalog word *gigil* denotes the irresistible urge to pinch or squeeze a cherished partner.

Playboys and Playgirls

Playboys and *playgirls* are especially good in the love play. A *playboy* can make a girl feel beautiful, extraordinary, and special, like the only one in his life, while really, she is just one among others. A playboy is amazing in appearance, gestures, and manners. Love for him is a pursuit of pleasure of any kind, especially sexual pleasure. He is generous and careless in spending money to enjoy himself and entertain a partner. He looks irresponsible and seems not caring about any long-term perspectives and consequences. He does not want to get psychologically attached to a partner. Such behaviors are charming, attractive, and difficult to resist. Love for him is a moment, an episode, a story, and not a long-term standpoint.

A *playgirl* is the female equivalent of *playboy*. She has the same psychological and behavioral attributes, along with some gender-specific variations. Otherwise, she performs the same *playful model of love*.

8.3.3 Love as a Game

Why Love Is Game

Game is a form of play which is competitive in the nature. Individuals compete with each other, or with some external force, in the pursuit of a *goal to win* according *to certain rules*. Sport games, table games, and video games are the examples with evident goal to win. What about love? How the love can be a game.

Love can be a competitive game which entails winners and losers. Winning and gaining something are the goals of love games. If no one loses in play—both are winners—then, it is a *play of love*, rather than a *game of love*.

Love games can be insincere and hidden manipulations that individuals employ to deceive partner with a purpose to gain benefits, for example, sex or money. A person may ask their partner to do something as a condition to engage in sex. Many criminal love dramas involve manipulations with love for the sake of gaining money as the inheritance after the death of a partner.

Love games can also be playful imitations without attempts to deceive another. Partners just play the roles to get more enjoyment from their relations. They are aware of the honest intentions. What they do and how they act is just an entertaining game and role play. For example, the classical interactive scene of love in many romantic movies is when he is chasing her, while she is running away—playfully. This looks like an evolutionary or cultural game "chase and run away." The "rule" of the game—catching and kissing with breathtaking excitement. He and she pretend knowing that they are playing this exciting game which enhances the joy of their dating. You may recall the *excitement transfer effect* (e.g., Dutton & Aron, 1974).

Mating Games

The *goal of mating game* is to win a prize whatever it is. It can be a good mating partner with qualities that are conducing to mating. Many evolutionary principles of mating, which were described in the earlier chapters, are at work in case of mating game. The specific goals of this game can be (a) attracting a desirable mate, (b) making this mate committed to a relationship, (c) making the other potential mates to lose, or excluding them from availability, and (d) protecting the mate from poachers.

The *theory of love acts* (Buss, 1988, 2006), cited in earlier chapters, has presented many examples of how behaviors of humans pursue the goals of mate attraction, selection, reproduction, and other evolutionary important *love acts*. Men and women interested in mating can employ some of these acts as the *love devices* in their mating game.

Evolutionary competition is real in human life. According to the *principle of survival* (see elsewhere in the earlier sections)—biological, psychological, or social,—the course of mating is the competition for surviving. It is a game that resembles the *competitive model of love*. Who is better than another? The period of teenage, and beyond, has plenty of examples of this kind. This might be the status competition. This might be a pleasure of a winner getting the best or better mating partner than others. Who wins the mating game, who lost it?

The word "mating game" is frequently used metaphorically and in a general sense. Nevertheless, the abundance of references to the term *mating game* in relationship literature (e.g., Dillon, Adair, Geher, Wang, & Strouts, 2016; Hill & Reeve, 2004; Regan, 2003/2008) is not accidental, I guess. It is rather meaningful and suggestive that the *relationship games* in many cases are really the *game-like mating*.

Playing Sexual Games

Sexual games can be of different kinds including sexually implicit or explicit activities, such as frolicking, flirting, dancing, prostitution, and pornography. The goals of sexual plays and games are to make partners sexually aroused and, therefore, maximize sexual pleasure. Sexual games are the intertwining of playful and gamification principles. In these games, one or both participants pretend that they love, rather than sincerely engage in sex. They do not allow themselves to attach emotionally to each other. They are intimate in some regards, yet distant in other aspects of intimacy. They do not admit another one close in their internal personal sphere, only in the pretending sexual intimate arena.

Dancing and singing are the common sexual or romantic plays and games during mating, dating, and sometimes beyond this period of love. In these games, the partners who initiate relationships or are already in real relationship play sexually arousing or, sometimes, provocative games.

The courtship dance is commonly present as individual activity and gives an opportunity to estimate the physical appearance of potential mating partners, as well as bodily compatibility of (e.g., Hugill, Fink, & Neave, 2010; Freedman, 1991; Grammer, Kruck, & Magnusson, 1998; Guéguen, Jacob, & Lamy, 2010; Neave et al., 2011; Suire, Raymond, & Barkat-Defradas, 2018). A human body of dancing person demonstrates health, strength, coordination, and nonverbally attracts a mating partner (Miller, 2000; Pitcairn & Schleidt, 1976). The way how people dance can signal their mating ability and make them attractive to the opposite sex (Brown et al., 2005; Grammer et al., 1998; Hugill, Fink, Neave, & Seydel, 2009; Neave et al., 2011).

According to the studies in anthropology, communication, journalism, psychology, sociology, and other disciplines (see for review, Hanna, 2010), across many cultures, dancing is obviously linked to sexual experience and expression. The dances of symbolic erotic expression, fertility, and reproduction are also performed by people in indigenous and traditional cultures in Northern India, Near Eastern, Caribbean, Java, Polynesia, and Africa (e.g., Asare, 2014; Hansen, 1967; Gerstin, 2004; Lysloff, 2001; Yagi, 2008). In Western cultures, going to night dance parties with following sexual relations is quite common. Sexuality as flirtation, courtship, and seduction is certainly involved (Givens, 1978; Hanna, 2010; Moore, 1985).

Explicit Sexual Games

Body movements in several dances (e.g., can-can, striptease, burlesque, lap dance) are obviously erotic, exciting, and resemble sexual actions (Brown, 2007; Jarrett, 1997; Kultermann, 2006; Ross, 2009; Shteir, 2004).

> Dance is a rhythmic repetition of body movements, including the pelvis. There is only one similar activity that involves a rhythmic repetition of body movements and the pelvis—sexual intercourse. In this way, the courtship dancer mirrors a very similar activity. (Garfinkel, 2018, p. 5).

Striptease is an illustrative example of the *explicit sexual game*. It is a playful form of the sexually and emotionally manipulative acts of stripping. It is an *erotic dancing* of a performer with gradual undressing in a seductive style (Wortley, 1976). A stripper interacts with a customer intricately *manipulating emotions*. The carefully designed symbolical interaction resembles a *confidence game* communicating with emotional reactions of the customer. Specifically, the stripper "(1) forge feelings of intimacy and emotional connectedness; and/or (2) fulfill customer fantasies by assuming the sex- object role." (Pasko, 2002, p.49). Psychologically, these manipulative stripping actions lead to relational and psychological estrangement and stigmatization for the performing dancer.

Pornography is another means to play a *sexual game*. Pornography is imitation of reality to gain sexual pleasure (Orel, 2020; Rea, 2001; Schaschek, 2013). It is a relatively safe place to play with no commitment and no risk of being dumped. Pornography is only *pretending of sexual intimacy*. Otherwise, everything is in a power of a spectator.

Pornography was a cultural invention of the sixteenth to nineteenth centuries. As a cultural phenomenon, it has evolved in the modern cultures, proliferating and burgeoning in some societies (Ashton, McDonald, & Kirkman, 2019; Huer, 1987; Hunt, 1993).

Relationship Games

When partners are in relationship, one or both may also play their games. The goals of those games are to gain some benefits and advantages in relationship. Some *games of love* can be fun when they are played sincerely and honestly, without attempts to cheat and deceive a partner. These are just the verbal and nonverbal interactions in relationships, which have certain stereotypical scripts. For example, this one looks like a traditional evolutionary game of love—"*men chase, women choose*" (Maslar, 2016).

However, some individuals play manipulative *love games,* which are negative in their consequences. One can see many of these dramatic relationship deception plots in the movies and TV serials.

The most illustrative examples of relationship games are presented in the Berne's transactional analysis (Berne, 1964/1968, 2011). The theoretical conceptualization of the Berne's counseling practice provides the in-depth understanding of how interpersonal interactions can be interpreted as *relationship games,* in which partners play their implicit roles of the *Child*, the *Parent*, or the *Adult*. These roles are the *ego states*, according to which they are currently involved in interaction and relationship. These games can differ in *how seriously* partners are playing. They relationship games are the typical patterns of interaction pursuing some goals. The *marital games* and *sexual games* are very suitable in the context of *love topic*.

8.3.4 The Model of Ludus Love

The Ludus Type Is a Manipulator

The *ludus model of love* represents a *type of love*, in which individuals primarily *engage in both playful and gaming ways of love*. They play their role as the actors on a stage performing typical romantic scripts, words, facial expressions, gestures, and postures. All these acts, however, are insincere. They do not admit this behavior close to their heart. They perform love, rather than experience it. At the same time, this *playful love* is *game-like* and can be mischievous.

The *ludus love type* as a manipulator, who plays their own game in intimate relationships, has several traits which disposes him/her to sexual coercion and sexual aggression (Sarwer, Kalichman, Johnson, Early, & Ali, 1993).

The *ludus lovers* have dispositions to scheming, deception, cynicism, and manipulation. They are *ambivalent toward love* that is evident in their cynic remarks, joking, yet they can be sentimental. These traits can make them very attractive. They have cynic attitudes in love because they are afraid to become the victims of illusions, which—they believe—entrap others and themselves. They wish to believe in trust, but do not trust anyone. Their joking is a symptom of conflicting emotions concerning status relationships. Their sentimentality is to lavishly counterfeit genuine emotions in particular social situations when the genuine emotions shall be appropriate but are not experienced naturally. I believe the Freudian conceptualization of love as an ambivalent disposition in which the fear and hate are associated with love is suitable in this case for understanding the ludus love type. Such interpretation, however, still needs to be refined.

The Ludus Type Is a Conqueror

A game is a competition, or conquest, in which there are a winner and a loser. The *ludus lovers* use their playful methods to win a game of love. A goal of this game is to sexually seduce another or gain their power otherwise. They enjoy sexual pleasure during playful seduction, saturated by emotional anticipation of sex, as well as sexual entertainment during sexual intercourse. Yet, even more, they enjoy their achievement in seduction—one more is conquered—in this playful game. They enjoy the feeling of a winner as any gambler. They may brag that they can seduce anyone. As gamblers, they need another and new game of love.

Several sexual games of E. Berne are illustrative for the behavior of the *ludus lover*. One game, for example, is sometimes played at the parties, where people mingle together. A person flirts with someone until he/she expresses a romantic or sexual interest in return. Then the person frowns and moves on to mingling with other guests. That someone being left behind feels like a bit of a fool. A person initiated the game is paid off—satisfaction by reassurance that he/she has sexual power and the feeling that he/she embarrassed and fooled someone—the feeling of winner. Basically, it is a harmless game. We can easily recognize in this situation the *ludus playful type*, with obvious game-like emotions.

Individuals of *ludus type* are uncommitted to a long-term relationship. They keep their emotions closed and locked in an anxiety to be hurt by others. They experience a lack of trust in others, and want to avoid the risk of pain. They protect their emotional heart.

Ludul Model of Love Across Cultures

Throughout historical and across modern cultures, many individuals follow this ludus model of love. Corresponding lexicon is present in many languages. The Latin *ludus* love is the same as the Greek *paixnidi* love *(playful and game-playing love)*. This conceptual idea of *ludus love* is also present in the lexicon of several other languages (Karandashev, 2019; Lomas, 2018).

Some cultural factors can predispose people to the ludus model of love. For example, as it was cited in the earlier chapters (Le, 2005), the *individualism* considering men and women as autonomous individuals, when they perceive inequality as acceptable, predisposes them to narcissistic traits and *ludus love*. The results obtained in cross-cultural studies with *Love Attitude Scale* (Hendrick & Hendrick, 1986; Hendrick, Hendrick, & Dicke, 1998) are inconclusive, sometimes controversial so far (see for detailed review, Karandashev, 2019).

References

Al-Dawood, A., Abokhodair, N., & Yarosh, S. (2017). *"Against marrying a stranger": Marital matchmaking technologies in Saudi Arabia*. Paper presented at the Proceedings of the 2017 conference on designing interactive systems (pp. 1013–1024).

Apostolou, M., & Christoforou, C. (2020). The art of flirting: What are the traits that make it effective? *Personality and Individual Differences, 158*, 109866.

Areni, C. S., Kiecker, P., & Palan, K. M. (1998). Is it better to give than to receive? Exploring gender differences in the meaning of memorable gifts. *Psychology & Marketing, 15*(1), 81–109.

Asare, S. (2014). Erotic expressions in Adowa dance of the Asante: The stimulating gestures, costuming and dynamic drumming. *Journal of Music and Dance, 4*(1), 1–9.

Ashton, S., McDonald, K., & Kirkman, M. (2019). What does 'pornography' mean in the digital age? Revisiting a definition for social science researchers. *Porn Studies, 6*(2), 144–168.

Aumer-Ryan, K., Hatfield, E. C., & Frey, R. (2007). Examining equity theory across cultures. *Interpersonal: An International Journal on Personal Relationships, 1*(1), 61–75.

Bailey, B. L. (1988). *From front porch to back seat: Courtship in twentieth century America*. John Hopkins University Press.

Becker, G. (1991). *A Treatise on the Family*. Harvard University Press.

Belk, R. W. (1996). The perfect gift. In C. Otnes & R. F. Beltramini (Eds.), *Gift giving: A research anthology* (pp. 59–84). Bowling Green State University Popular Press.

Belk, R. W., & Coon, G. S. (1993). Gift giving as agapic love: An alternative to the exchange paradigm based on dating experiences. *Journal of Consumer Research, 20*(3), 393–417.

Belsky, J., Steinberg, L., & Draper, P. (1991). Childhood experience, interpersonal development, and reproductive strategy: An evolutionary theory of socialization. *Child Development, 62*, 647–670.

Berne, E. (1964). *Games people play: The psychology of human relationships*. Grove Press.

Blossfeld, H. P., & Timm, A. (Eds.). (2003). *Who marries whom? Educational systems as marriage markets in modern societies*. Springer.

Brown, L. (2007). Performance, status and hybridity in a Pakistani red-light district: The cultural production of the courtesan. *Sexualities, 10*(4), 409–423.

Brown, W. M., Cronk, L., Grochow, K., Jacobson, A., Liu, C. K., Popović, Z., & Trivers, R. (2005). Dance reveals symmetry especially in young men. *Nature, 438*(7071), 1148–1150.

Buss, D. M. (1988). Love acts: The evolutionary biology of love. In R. J. Sternberg & M. L. Barnes (Eds.), *The psychology of love* (pp. 100–118). Yale University Press.

Buss, D. M. (2006). The evolution of love. In R. Sternberg & K. Weis (Eds.), *The new psychology of love* (pp. 65–86). Yale University Press.

Chapman, G. D. (2015). *The five love languages: The secret to love that lasts*. Northfield Publishing (Originally published by Northfield Pub., 1992).

Cherlin, A. J. (2000). Toward a new home socioeconomics of union formation. In L. Waite, C. Bachrach, M. Hindin, E. Thomson, & A. Thornton (Eds.), *Ties that bind: Perspectives on marriage and cohabitation* (pp. 126–144). Aldine de Gruyter.

Cherlin, A. J. (2010). *The marriage-go-round: The state of marriage and the family in America today*. Vintage.
Clark, M. S., & Mills, J. S. (1979). Interpersonal attraction in exchange and communal relationships. *Journal of Personality and Social Psychology, 37*, 12–24.
Clark, M. S., & Mills, J. S. (2013). Communal and exchange relationships: Controversies and research. In R. Erber & R. Gilmour (Eds.), *Theoretical frameworks for personal relationships* (pp. 41–54). Psychology Press.
Coontz, S. (2006). *Marriage, a history: How love conquered marriage*. Penguin.
Cunningham, M. R., & Barbee, A. P. (2008). Prelude to a kiss: Nonverbal flirting, opening gambits, and other communication dynamics in the initiation of romantic relationships. In S. Sprecher, A. Wenzel, & J. Harvey (Eds.), *Handbook of relationship initiation* (pp. 97–120). Psychology Press.
Davies, S. L., Glaser, D., & Kossoff, R. (2000). Children's sexual play and behavior in pre-school settings: Staff's perceptions, reports, and responses. *Child Abuse & Neglect, 24*(10), 1329–1343.
Dillon, H. M., Adair, L. E., Geher, G., Wang, Z., & Strouts, P. H. (2016). Playing smart: The mating game and mating intelligence. *Current Psychology, 35*(3), 414–420.
Dutton, D. G., & Aron, A. P. (1974). Some evidence for heightened sexual attraction under conditions of high anxiety. *Journal of Personality and Social Psychology, 30*(4), 510–517. https://doi.org/10.1037/h0037031
Esteve, A., García-Román, J., & Permanyer, I. (2012). The gender-gap reversal in education and its effect on union formation: The end of hypergamy? *Population and Development Review, 38*(3), 535–546.
Finkel, E. J. (2018). *The all-or-nothing marriage: How the best marriages work*. Dutton.
Foote, N. N. (1954). Sex as play. *Social Problems, 1*(4), 159–163.
Freedman, D. C. (1991). Gender signs: An effort/shape analysis of Romanian couple dances. *Studia Musicologica Academiae Scientiarum Hungaricae, 33*(Fasc. 1/4), 335–345.
Garfinkel, Y. (2018). The evolution of human dance: Courtship, rites of passage, trance, calendrical ceremonies and the professional dancer. *Cambridge Archaeological Journal, 28*(2), 283.
Gerstin, J. (2004). Tangled roots: Kalenda and other neo-African dances in the circum-Caribbean. *New West Indian Guide/Nieuwe West-Indische Gids, 78*(1-2), 5–41.
Gibson, M. A., & Lawson, D. W. (2011). "Modernization" increases parental investment and sibling resource competition: Evidence from a rural development initiative in Ethiopia. *Evolution and Human Behavior, 32*(2), 97–105.
Givens, D. B. (1978). The non-verbal basis of attraction: Flirtation, courtship, and seduction. *Psychiatry, 41*, 346–351.
Grammer, K., Kruck, K. B., & Magnusson, M. S. (1998). The courtship dance: Patterns of nonverbal synchronization in opposite-sex encounters. *Journal of Nonverbal Behavior, 22*(1), 3–29.
Guéguen, N., Jacob, C., & Lamy, L. (2010). 'Love is in the air': Effects of songs with romantic lyrics on compliance with a courtship request. *Psychology of Music, 38*(3), 303–307.
Gullickson, A., & Fu, V. K. (2010). Comment: An endorsement of exchange theory in mate selection. *American Journal of Sociology, 115*(4), 1243–1251.
Hall, J. A. (2013). *The five flirting styles: Use the science of flirting to attract the love you really want*. Harlequin Nonfiction.
Hall, J. A., & Xing, C. (2015). The verbal and nonverbal correlates of the five flirting styles. *Journal of Nonverbal Behavior, 39*(1), 41–68.
Hall, J. A., Carter, S., Cody, M. J., & Albright, J. M. (2010). Individual differences in the communication of romantic interest: Development of the flirting styles inventory. *Communication Quarterly, 58*, 365–393.
Hanna, J. L. (2010). Dance and sexuality: Many moves. *Journal of Sex Research, 47*(2-3), 212–241.
Hansen, C. (1967). Jenny's toe: Negro shaking dances in America. *American Quarterly, 19*(3), 554–563.

Hatfield, E., & Traupmann, J. (1981). Intimate relationships: A perspective from equity theory. *Personal Relationships, 1*, 165–178.

Hatfield, E., Traupmann, J., Sprecher, S., Utne, M., & Hay, J. (1985). Equity and intimate relations: Recent research. In W. Ickes (Ed.), *Compatible and incompatible relationships* (pp. 91–117). Springer. https://doi.org/10.1007/978-1-4612-5044-9_5

Hatfield, E., Rapson, R. L., & Bensman, L. (2011a). Equity theory. In D. J. Christie (Ed.), *The encyclopedia of peace psychology*. Wiley Blackwell.

Hatfield, E., Salmon, M., & Rapson, R. L. (2011b). Equity theory and social justice. *Journal of Management, Spirituality & Religion, 8*(2), 101–121.

Hendrick, C., & Hendrick, S. S. (1986). A theory and method of love. *Journal of Personality and Social Psychology, 50*, 392–402.

Hendrick, C., Hendrick, S. S., & Dicke, A. (1998). The love attitudes scale: Short form. *Journal of Social and Personal Relationships, 15*(2), 147–159.

Henningsen, D. D. (2004). Flirting with meaning: An examination of miscommunication in flirting interactions. *Sex Roles, 50*(7), 481–489.

Hill, S. E., & Reeve, H. K. (2004). Mating games: The evolution of human mating transactions. *Behavioral Ecology, 15*(5), 748–756.

Hirsch, J. S. (2003). *A courtship after marriage: Sexuality and love in Mexican transnational families*. University of California Press.

Hirsch, J. S. (2007). "Love makes a family": Globalization, companionate marriage, and the modernization of gender inequality. In M. Padilla, J. S. Hirsch, M. Munoz-Laboy, R. E. Sember, & R. G. Parker (Eds.), *Love and globalization: Transformations of intimacy in the contemporary world* (pp. 93–106). Vanderbilt University Press.

Huer, J. (1987). *Art, beauty, and pornography: A journey through American culture*. Prometheus.

Hugill, N., Fink, B., Neave, N., & Seydel, H. (2009). Men's physical strength is associated with women's perceptions of their dancing ability. *Personality and Individual Differences, 47*(5), 527–530.

Hugill, N., Fink, B., & Neave, N. (2010). The role of human body movements in mate selection. *Evolutionary Psychology, 8*(1). https://doi.org/10.1177/147470491000800107

Hunt, L. (Ed.). (1993). *The invention of pornography, 1500–1800: Obscenity and the origins of modernity*. MIT Press.

Impett, E. A., Beals, K. P., & Peplau, L. A. (2001). Testing the investment model of relationship commitment and stability in a longitudinal study of married couples. *Current Psychology, 20*(4), 312–326.

Jankowiak, W., Shen, Y., Yao, S., Wang, C., & Volsche, S. (2015). Investigating love's universal attributes: A research report from China. *Cross-Cultural Research, 49*(4), 422–436.

Jankowiak, W. R., Volsche, S. L., & Garcia, J. R. (2015). Is the romantic–sexual kiss a near human universal? *American Anthropologist, 117*(3), 535–539.

Jarrett, L. (1997). *Stripping in time: A history of erotic dancing*. Rivers Oram Press.

Kalmijn, M. (2010). Educational inequality, homogamy, and status exchange in black-white intermarriage: A comment on Rosenfeld. *American Journal of Sociology, 115*(4), 1252–1263.

Kaplan, H. (1996). A theory of fertility and parental investment in traditional and modern human societies. *Yearbook of Physical Anthropology, 39*, 91–135.

Karandashev, V. (2017). *Romantic love in cultural contexts*. Springer.

Karandashev, V. (2019). *Cross-cultural perspectives on the experience and expression of love*. Springer.

Karandashev, V. (in press). Cross-cultural variation in relationship initiation. In J. K. Mogilski & T. K. Shackelford (Eds.), *The Oxford handbook of evolutionary psychology and romantic relationships*. Oxford Publishing.

Kinsley, D. R. (1974). Creation as play in Hindu spirituality. *Studies in Religion/Sciences Religieuses, 4*(2), 108–119.

Kövecses, Z. (2005). *Metaphor in culture: Universality and variation*. Cambridge University Press.

Kultermann, U. (2006). The "Dance of the Seven Veils." Salome and erotic culture around 1900. *Artibus et Historiae, 27*, 187–215.
Le, T. N. (2005). Narcissism and immature love as mediators of vertical individualism and Ludic love style. *Journal of Social and Personal Relationships, 22*, 542–560.
Le, B., & Agnew, C. R. (2003). Commitment and its theorized determinants: A meta–analysis of the Investment Model. *Personal Relationships, 10*(1), 37–57.
Lloyd, S., Cate, R. M., & Henton, J. (1982). Equity and rewards as predictors of satisfaction in casual and intimate relationships. *Journal of Psychology, 110*, 43–48.
Lomas, T. (2018). The flavours of love: A cross-cultural lexical analysis. *Journal for the Theory of Social Behaviour, 48*, 134–152.
Lujansky, H., & Mikula, G. (1983). Can equity explain the quality and stability of romantic relationships? *British Journal of Social Psychology, 22*, 101–112.
Lund, M. (1985). The development of investment and commitment scales for predicting continuity of personal relationships. *Journal of Social and Personal Relationships, 2*(1), 3–23.
Lv, Z., & Zhang, Y. (2012). Universality and variation of conceptual metaphor of love in Chinese and English. *Theory and Practice in Language Studies, 2*(2), 355–359.
Lysloff, R. T. (2001). Rural Javanese "tradition" and erotic subversion: Female dance performance in Banyumas (Central Java). *Asian Music, 33*(1), 1–24.
Maslar, D. (2016). *Men chase, women choose: The neuroscience of meeting, dating, losing your mind, and finding true love*. Health Communications, Inc.
Meister, R. (1963). *Literary guide to seduction*. Elek Books.
Merton, R. K. (1941). Intermarriage and the social structure. *Psychiatry, 4*(3), 361–374. https://doi.org/10.1080/00332747.1941.11022354
Miller, G. (2000). Evolution of human music through sexual selection. In N. L. Wallin, B. Merker, & S. Brown (Eds.), *The origins of music* (pp. 329–360). MIT Press.
Minowa, Y., & Gould, S. J. (1999). Love my gift, love me or is it love me, love my gift: A study of the cultural construction of romantic gift giving among Japanese couples. *Advances in Consumer Research, 26*, 119–124.
Modell, J. (1983). Dating becomes the way of American youth. In L. P. Moch & G. D. Stark (Eds.), *Essays on the family and historical change* (pp. 91–126). Texas A&M University Press.
Moore, M. M. (1985). Nonverbal courtship patterns in women: Context and consequences. *Ethology and Sociobiology, 6*(4), 237–247.
Moore, M. M. (1995). Courtship signaling and adolescents: "Girls just wanna have fun"? *Journal of Sex Research, 32*(4), 319–328.
Murstein, B. I. (1974). *Love, sex, and marriage through the ages*. Springer.
Neave, N., McCarty, K., Freynik, J., Caplan, N., Hönekopp, J., & Fink, B. (2011). Male dance moves that catch a woman's eye. *Biology Letters, 7*(2), 221–224.
Neff, L. A., & Karney, B. R. (2005). To know you is to love you: The implications of global adoration and specific accuracy for marital relationships. *Journal of Personality and Social Psychology, 88*(3), 480–497. https://doi.org/10.1037/0022-3514.88.3.480
Nettle, D. (2010). Dying young and living fast: Variation in life history across English neighbourhoods. *Behavioral Ecology, 21*, 387–395.
Orel, M. (2020). Escaping reality and touring for pleasure: The future of virtual reality pornography. *Porn Studies, 7*(4), 449–453.
Otnes, C., Lowrey, T. M., & Kim, Y. C. (1993). Gift selection for easy and difficult recipients: A social roles interpretation. *Journal of Consumer Research, 20*(2), 229–244.
Otnes, C., & Beltramini, R. F. (1996). Gift giving and gift giving: An overview. In I. C. Otnes & R. F. Beltramini (Eds.), *Gift giving: A research anthology* (pp. 3–15). Bowling Green State University Popular Press.
Ovid. (1939) *The art of love* (J. J. Perry, Trans.). Harvard University Press.
Pasko, L. (2002). Naked power: The practice of stripping as a confidence game. *Sexualities, 5*(1), 49–66.

Pistole, M. C., Clark, E. M., & Tubbs, A. L. (1995). Love relationships: Attachment style and the investment model. *Journal of Mental Health Counseling, 17*(2), 199–209.

Pitcairn, T. K., & Schleidt, M. (1976). Dance and decision an analysis of a courtship dance of the Medlpa, New Guinea. *Behaviour, 58*(3–4), 298–315.

Quinlan, R. J. (2007). Human parental effort and environmental risk. *Proceedings of the Royal Society B: Biological Sciences, 247*, 121–125.

Rea, M. C. (2001). What is pornography? *Noûs, 35*(1), 118–145.

Regan, P. (2003/2008). *The mating game: A primer on love, sex, and marriage*. Sage.

Rosenfeld, M. J. (2005). A critique of exchange theory in mate selection. *American Journal of Sociology, 110*(5), 1284–1325. https://doi.org/10.1086/428441

Ross, B. (2009). *Burlesque west: Showgirls, sex, and sin in postwar Vancouver*. University of Toronto Press.

Rusbult, C. E. (1980). Commitment and satisfaction in romantic associations: A test of the investment model. *Journal of Experimental Social Psychology, 16*, 172–186.

Rusbult, C. E. (1983). A longitudinal test of the investment model: The development (and deterioration) of satisfaction and commitment in heterosexual involvements. *Journal of Personality and Social Psychology, 45*(1), 101–117. https://doi.org/10.1037/0022-3514.45.1.101

Rusbult, C. E., & Buunk, B. P. (1993). Commitment processes in close relationships: An interdependence analysis. *Journal of Social and Personal Relationships, 10*, 175–204. https://doi.org/10.1177/026540759301000202

Rusbult, C. E., Johnson, D. J., & Morrow, G. D. (1986). Predicting satisfaction and commitment in adult romantic involvements. *Social Psychology Quarterly, 39(1)*, 81–89.

Rusbult, C. E., Martz, J. M., & Agnew, C. R. (1998). The investment model scale: Measuring commitment level, satisfaction level, quality of alternatives, and investment size. *Personal Relationships, 5*, 357–391. https://doi.org/10.1111/j.1475-6811.1998.tb00177.x

Sarwer, D. B., Kalichman, S. C., Johnson, J. R., Early, J., & Ali, S. A. (1993). Sexual aggression and love styles: An exploratory study. *Archives of Sexual Behavior, 22*(3), 265–275.

Sassler, S., & Joyner, K. (2011). Social exchange and the progression of sexual relationships in emerging adulthood. *Social Forces, 90*(1), 223–245. https://doi.org/10.1093/sf/90.1.223

Schaschek, S. (2013). *Pornography and seriality: The culture of producing pleasure*. Springer.

Schmitt, D. P., & Buss, D. M. (2000). Sexual dimensions of person description: Beyond or subsumed by the Big Five? *Journal of Research in Personality, 34*(2), 141–177.

Schmitt, D. P., Youn, G., Bond, B., Brooks, S., Frye, H., Johnson, S., … Stoka, C. (2009). When will I feel love? The effects of culture, personality, and gender on the psychological tendency to love. *Journal of Research in Personality, 43*(5), 830–846.

Schoen, R., & Wooldredge, J. (1989). Marriage choices in North Carolina and Virginia, 1969-71 and 1979-81. *Journal of Marriage and Family, 51*(2), 465–481. Retrieved from http://www.jstor.org/stable/352508

Shteir, R. (2004). *Striptease: The untold history of the girlie show*. Oxford University Press.

Simpson, J. A., & Gangestad, S. W. (1991). Individual differences in sociosexuality: Evidence for convergent and discriminant validity. *Journal of Personality and Social Psychology, 60*(6), 870–883. https://doi.org/10.1037/0022-3514.60.6.870

Simpson, J. A., & Gangestad, S. W. (1992). Sociosexuality and romantic partner choice. *Journal of Personality, 60*, 31–51.

Stafford, L. (2008). Social exchange theories. In L. A. Baxter & D. O. Braithwaite (Eds.), *Engaging theories in interpersonal communication: Multiple perspectives* (pp. 377–389). Sage.

Stearns, P. (1994). *American cool*. New York University Press.

Suire, A., Raymond, M., & Barkat-Defradas, M. (2018). Human vocal behavior within competitive and courtship contexts and its relation to mating success. *Evolution and Human Behavior, 39*(6), 684–691.

Trivers, R. (1972). Parental investment and sexual selection. In B. Campbell (Ed.), *Sexual selection and the descent of man: 1871–1971* (pp. 136–179). Aldine.

Van Den Berghe, P. L. (1960). Hypergamy, hypergenation, and miscegenation. *Human Relations, 13*(1), 83–91.

Van Yperen, N. W., & Buunk, B. P. (1990). A longitudinal study of equity and satisfaction in intimate relationships. *European Journal of Social Psychology, 20*(4), 287–309.

Whyte, M. K. (1990). *Dating, mating, and marriage*. Aldine de Gruyter.

Wiggins, J. S. (1979). A psychological taxonomy of trait-descriptive terms: The interpersonal domain. *Journal of Personality and Social Psychology, 37*(3), 395–412. https://doi.org/10.1037/0022-3514.37.3.395

Wiggins, J. S., & Trapnell, P. D. (1997). Chapter 28: Personality structure: The return of the Big Five. In R. Hogan, J. Johnson, & S. Briggs (Eds.), *Handbook of personality psychology* (pp. 737–765). Academic.

Wortley, R. (1976). *A pictorial history of striptease: 100 years of undressing to music*. Octopus Books.

Yagi, Y. (2008). Women, abuse songs and erotic dances: Marriage ceremonies in Northern India. *Senri Ethnological Studies, 71*, 35–47.

Conclusions

Toward a Comprehensive Science of Love

Throughout centuries, love studies have paved a broad path of thoughts and discoveries about what love is, what love is supposed to be, and what love can be. After many centuries of philosophical contemplations, historical observations, and literary explorations, in the twentieth century, love scholarship has been grounded on the empirically based research. Philosophers, theologists, sociologists, and literary scholars continued their abstract, analytical, contemplative exploration of what love can be based on their general expert observations of life. Yet, in the middle of twentieth century many researchers of anthropology, sociology, communication, and psychology were gradually turning to favor empirical data.

During the twentieth century and in the early twenty-first century, love researchers have collected an abundance of data, interesting results, and discovered new concepts of love. Empirical research on love has made tremendous progress in the recent century. Now, the scholarship of love is enormously large, multi-faceted, and multi-perspective, yet it is fragmented.

The general scholarly picture of love is still piecemeal, patchy, and not sufficiently comprehensive. Scholars of various disciplines have elaborated their conceptions, in agreement with some of their colleagues and in argument with others. They usually work within their traditional schools of thought, with little interest in other schools of thought and disciplines. Different concepts and conceptions, which researchers have proposed so far, are not connected to each other. The theories of love are rather independent from each other. The research groups worship on their theoretical conceptions, paradigms and work hard planting, precipitating, and harvesting their own gardens. No many researchers attempt to connect and coordinate these different theories, concepts, scientific models, and findings in a more comprehensive understanding of love.

Empirical investigations of love are *theory-driven, school-of-thought-oriented,* and *task-focused*. Researchers strive to run the studies (1) supporting one or another

V. Karandashev, *Cultural Typologies of Love*,
https://doi.org/10.1007/978-3-031-05343-6

theory, (2) associated with one or another school of thought and research paradigm, and (3) solving the tasks to discover or confirm various relations of their love construct with others. Relationship satisfaction and well-being are among the favorites. These approaches make the *science of love sporadic, piecemeal,* and *patchy*, characterized by largely limited validity and reliability (see for review, Karandashev, 2019).

So, the puzzle of love is still far from being complete or nearing its completion. The more work shall be done with the purpose of understanding. The studies in support of the theories, in search of multiple predictive, mediating, and moderating factors are not sufficient to reach this goal.

The *modern science of love* shall be more integrative and interconnected in terms of both theories and findings. It shall present a *comprehensive scientific picture of knowledge*, rather than isolated theories and findings. This book is a modest attempt to put together all various pieces of love puzzle in a general system and highlight the perspectives available and useful for future love research.

The Lexicon of Love Research

We have seen in the book that the *scholarly lexicon of love* has been frequently used in vague, loose, and ambiguous meanings. This tendency reflects the multifaceted nature of the love concepts, as well as the tendency of scholars to follow the laypeople's vocabulary of love. The words *love, intimacy, passion, romantic love,* and *romantic relationship* are eye-catching, yet not well defined, if at all.

The word *love* has been used in multiple senses as a synonym of such concepts as *attraction, sex, attachment, intimacy, passion*, and so on. The word *intimacy* has been often used as a synonym of love. Even in more specific meaning, *intimacy* can imply *sexual intimacy, emotional intimacy,* and *psychological intimacy*. The word *passion* has more general meaning, so it is *not a good substitute* for the *love concept*.

For example, the words *romantic love* and *romantic relationship*, as you saw in the romantic chapter of this book, have more specific meanings in the scholarship of love. They stand for more specific categories of scholarship of love. The *term romantic love* has been used too loosely for a scientific concept and sometimes employed not quite adequate operational definitions. The concept *romantic love* has frequently interchanged with sexual love and passionate love. That is not quite adequate because, as one could see in the book, these categories of love are based on different criteria. Such indicators as passion and sexual attraction are not suitable to identify romantic love. They may be concomitant, yet not defining for the love to be romantic. It is confusing that *love researchers* continue calling any mating and dating relationships as *romantic*. This *word* can be quite far from reality. There have been long and good conceptual traditions in scholarly research of romantic love and romantic relationship, which love researchers shall be aware of. We shall respect, not neglect, this rich scholarly background.

Conceptual and Operational Definitions of Love

I believe that scholarly lexicon of love shall be more scientific and follow the traditions of scientific definitions, with their appropriate attributes. The studies of love shall be specific in the conceptual and operation definitions of the love phenomena, which they explore. It is important for scientific research since love and romantic relationship are still very loosely used terms with vague meanings. It is not a good practice for scientists to use loosely and vaguely defined concepts, such as romantic relationships. For example, it is important to know what the word "*romantic*" means in a particular context.

Conceptual clarification and refinement of love constructs, categories, and their structures are needed for love research. Using the love concepts as the free-floating labels of any love experience, expression, and relationship does not help better understanding the *love things*. The *science of love* needs more specific conceptual and operational definitions to be a scientific discipline. Researchers shall be clearer in writing whether they are talking about love as emotions, attitudes, moods, traits, personal models, or cultural models, whether they are talking about realities of love or the possibilities of what love can be, whether the realities they are talking about represent certain cultural views and experiences, as well as certain social categories of people.

Multiplicity of the Things We Call Love

As we saw in the book, various concepts of love and other related concepts can mean *many things*: sensations associated with love, emotions, moods, attitudes, traits, values, relationships, personal or cultural models of love, what people think about love, and how they really experience love, ideal and real models of love.

Researchers shall be aware and distinctively define conceptually what kind of *love things* they study:

1. Individual love experiences, expressions, and actions, or love relationships as dyadic relations and interactions
2. Personal models of love, or real experiences, expressions, and actions of love
3. Personal models of love, or cultural models of love

Appeal for the Multifaceted, Descriptive, and Complex Models of Love

As we saw in the book, the love studies have commonly been operating on the descriptive and dimensional level. The qualitative descriptions of the things, which we call love, are important. The valid and reliable measurements of the constructs, which are worthwhile to measure, are important. ANOVA, correlation and regression analyses, as well as identification of mediating and moderating parameters/variables, are important.

Descriptive findings are very valuable for typological research. Unfortunately, the theory-based and inferential research often overshadows the descriptive nature of our scientific knowledge. Researchers sometimes are more concerned about hypotheses, associated with their theory, and verification of whether these hypotheses are confirmed or not, rather than about description of knowledge which they gain. They are frequently more concerned about the statistical significance of differences and correlations, rather than about their meaning. Technical details of their reports sometimes overshadow the descriptive knowledge. So, I believe the descriptive nature of science shall not be sacrificed for the sake of scientific technicality.

Majority of love studies so far have been focused on the comparison of means for love measures using different variation statistics (e.g., *t*-test, ANOVA, and other derivative statistics), or on correlational comparison of variations (e.g., *r*, regression, and other derivatives). A recent comparative multi-variable and multi-cultural study of intimate relationships across many countries (Hill, 2019) represents an exemplary research project of this kind, using various well-established methods of analysis. The results have brought many interesting findings.

I believe the cross-cultural studies of love, which are more multifaceted in terms of emotional things included in their scientific models, can help us understand more complex, systemic, and comprehensive pictures of love models and typologies, rather than the sets of variations and correlations between variables of love and culture. Multilevel studies can include not just the abstract personal attitudes of passion, affection, compassion, commitment, intimacy, and other, but also how these attitudes are emotionally experienced and expressed in certain situations of the lovers' everyday life, or specific events of a relationship.

I suggest *researchers of love* to move beyond the methodologies, which are well established and worthy in many respects, yet limited in their capacities to capture the complex and holistic conceptions of love, such as cultural models and typologies. I encourage to entertain typological approaches in their studies of love. Typological methods are valuable because they allow multidimensional, complex, and comprehensive systems of scientific knowledge.

Typologies of Love Things and Typologies of Cultures

Most typologies, which have been developed in love research so far, are one- or two-dimensional. The typological approach based on *distinctive features* and *salient dimensions* are common in typological research of love and cultures. The individual and cultural models, and individual and cultural typologies of love presented in this book are of these sorts. As we saw in many chapters, these models and typologies advance our scientific knowledge and scholarly understanding of love and related concepts. I have enjoyed compiling, classifying, and reviewing these models and typologies to present in this book.

However, the more complex analysis of love typologies, which include several love variables and several cultural variables are on demand. They need different methodologies, such as *exploratory factor analysis, confirmatory factor analysis, bi-factor analysis, cluster analysis, latent class analysis*, and others. The typologies of love can *categorize emotions associated with love, appraisals, love action tendencies, love dispositions, or they complex relations* with each other.

The typologies of cultures can categorize societies based on the complex of their cultural dimensions, not just single dimensions. Even though classification of cultures as individualistic or collectivistic is still viable for love research, however such categorization hides and obscures the effect of many other cultural factors, which correlate with individualism-collectivism distinction (e.g., Power distance), or mediate and moderate their affects. The old categorization of societies as Western and Eastern cultures shall be abandoned as outdated and obsolete. Such classification does not reflect multifaceted systems of cultures. More specific cultural characteristics, as well as the diversity of individualism and collectivism (Karandashev, 2021a, 2021b) shall be considered for the future typologies of cultures. *Cluster analysis and latent class analysis* will be useful in this regard.

Basic Approaches to the Construction of Cultural Models and Typologies of Love

The two major approaches to the construction of cultural models of love as an emotional phenomenon are useful: the *top-down* and *bottom-up methods* (Karandashev, 2021a, 2021b). In the *top-down method*, researchers begin the construction of a typology from the definition of a cultural parameter as an independent variable—the *top of typology*, and then move down to explore the cultural patterns of love variables—the *foundation of typology*, which are then interpreted in terms of the "top" cultural variable. In the opposite *bottom-up method*, researchers begin construction of a typology from the *bottom*—exploration of the patterns of love variables, and them move *up* to the cultural parameters—the *top*, to explain these patterns of love variables. Both approaches call for suitable statistical analyses. Several examples of applying these methodologies based on the patterns of *domains, components, and variables* of *emotional experience and expression* are presented in the *Cultural Models of Emotions* (Karandashev, 2021a, 2021b).

The Diversity in Cultural Typology of Love

This book pursued the two perspectives: methodological and exemplary. The first two chapters played their methodological roles. They presented the multi-faceted, multi-level, and multi-functional concepts of love. The major appeals of these chapters are to demonstrate and elaborate the diverse conceptual nature of love. The metaphor of "the elephant in the dark room" is very suitable in this case. I hope that love researchers will be interested to look beyond their theories and paradigms in attempt to create a more comprehensive and holistic picture of love. I believe more complex and hierarchical typologies and models of love will come on arena of research. Love concepts will look like the constellations of *love things* of different kinds and levels, outlined in Chap. 1. Cultural variables will add more complexity to their constructions. Chapter 2, along with methodological chapter of my other book (Karandashev, 2021a), will serve as the methodological introduction and guide to the construction of cultural typologies of love. It presented the framework and instruction for this purpose.

The remaining chapters presented an attempt to classify varieties of models and typologies of love into six groups. This classification is certainly conventional. It is based on some shared characteristics and features of the models, which are included in those groups. The classification is open for criticism. The presented models can be classified differently if other criteria are considered. The classification is not dichotomous, it is rather topological with various overlapping. The diversity of possible models and typologies of love is also enormous.

I was eager to present and explain in this book as many models and typologies of love as possible. However, limitations in the volume capacity have not allowed me to accomplish this unrealistic goal. The complexity of others did not allow to include others. Several models and typologies are evidently not covered in the book. Among those are parental love, motherly and fatherly love, the love of God and love for God. They are only tangentially coved in the context of some other umbrella models and typologies in cases when and wherever they were suitable.

In their diversity of functions and forms, these models are too complex to fit to the categories presented in this book. They have elements of different models and deserve special attention in the future. Some other models, such as the compassionate model of love, are only briefly commented due to volume limitations.

References

Hill, C. T. (2019). *Intimate relationships across cultures: A comparative study*. Cambridge University Press.

Karandashev, V. (2019). *Cross-cultural perspectives on the experience and expression of love*. Springer.

Karandashev, V. (2021a). *Cultural models of emotions*. Springer.

Karandashev, V. (2021b). Cultural diversity of romantic love experience. In C. Mayer & E. Vanderheiden (Eds.), *International handbook of love* (pp. 59–79). Springer.

Index

V. Karandashev, *The Cultural Typologies of Love*,
https://doi.org/10.1007/978-3-031-05343-6_1

MIX
Papier aus verantwortungsvollen Quellen
Paper from responsible sources
FSC® C105338

Printed by Books on Demand, Germany